Royal Descents of
500 Immigrants

Edward III, King of England (1312–1377, reigned 1327–1377), a central figure of this work (see pages 107–93), from a rubbing of the Hastings Brass in Elsing Church, Norfolk, as published in Joseph Foster, *Some Feudal Coats of Arms* (James Parker and Co., Oxford and London, 1902), p. 78. Note that the king's tunic features his coat-of-arms, post 1340, as depicted also on the front cover.

THE

ROYAL DESCENTS

OF

500 IMMIGRANTS

to the American Colonies
or the United States

Who Were Themselves Notable
or Left Descendants
Notable in American History

2nd Printing, with a
Bibliographical Supplement, 1993–2000

Gary Boyd Roberts

Baltimore, 2001

A full second edition of this work, with an updated title, is scheduled for publication in 2002.

Stamping on front cover: Shield of Edward III, King of England (died 1377), post 1340, with the arms of England (three lions) in the second and third quarters, and those of France (fleurs-de-lis) in the first and fourth quarters, as drawn from the king's tomb at Westminster Abbey and published in C. W. Scott-Giles, *Looking at Heraldry* (rev. ed., Phoenix House, London, 1967), p. 77.

Acknowledgments

This book cites hundreds of sources, and to their authors, especially the 150 twentieth-century scholars listed in the introduction that follows, I owe both this book and the enormous pleasure I have derived from tracing American notables of royal descent. Beyond its sources this book has two additional, mostly "silent," sponsors -- Ralph J. Crandall, Director of the New England Historic Genealogical Society in Boston and Michael Tepper, Managing Editor of Genealogical Publishing Company in Baltimore. Both have believed in me for almost twenty years and acted accordingly. They are my two best friends, each has massively reinvigorated the institution he directs, each is thus owed much by the genealogical community overall, and I am delighted that our partnership in producing 15 volumes of excerpts from *The New England Historical and Genealogical Register,* plus *American Ancestors and Cousins of The Princess of Wales* and several other books, continues with *The Royal Descents of 500 Immigrants.*

A third partner in this endeavor has been Alicia Crane Williams, editor since 1985 of *The* (newly revived) *Mayflower Descendant,* who, as Williams Word Processing, 18 Martin's Cove Road, Hingham, Mass. 02043 (to whom I have probably sent, and received, over 100 envelopes or packages of various drafts and parts of this book) read, keyboarded, indexed, and prepared camera-ready copy for this volume. Alicia also typed or word processed almost all of my genealogical articles through early 1989. Only she, Michael J. Wood of London (who indexed the American section of *The Mowbray Connection*) and Julie Helen Otto of the *NEHGS NEXUS* can readily read my handprinting, and without Alicia and the resources of Williams Word Processing, this volume, and much of my scholarly life's work, would have come to fruition only with considerably more difficulty. In addition to Alicia, Eileen Perkins, GPC Production Manager, and Joseph Garonzik, GPC Marketing

Director, have, as always, been helpful and encouraging. They are among the best professionals in the field.

I also wish to thank, profusely, the eight scholars who twice examined the 472 pages of charts, made various suggestions regarding additional immigrants or "better" lines, and detected numerous "gremlins" or typographical errors. These eight were John Hutchinson Cook, who suggested the line of biographer Ted Morgan (Sanche de Gramont), and whose magnificent gift to NEHGS of several thousand books on British and Continental genealogy I also used extensively; H.M. West Winter, author of *The Descendants of Charlemagne (800-1400)*, 10 vols., covering 16 generations, who added many diacritical marks and contributed both the line of George Mosle of N.Y., his maternal grandfather, and a much improved royal descent for Peter Paul Rubens, the painter, and H.J. Stier of Maryland; William Addams Reitwiesner of the Library of Congress, my colleague on *American Ancestors and Cousins of The Princess of Wales*, who contributed the line of (F.G.E.) Louis (W.) Viereck and extracted from Bartrum's *Welsh Genealogies* almost all of the Welsh lines herein (often unraveling the best or better descents for various Welsh immigrants, most notably Mrs. Mary Jones Lloyd, and considerably improving that section of the book); former NEHGS trustee Brice McAdoo Clagett, who allowed me to use all his research for the forthcoming *Seven Centuries: Ancestors for Twenty Generations of John Brice de Treville Clagett and Ann Calvert Brooke Clagett*, including unpublished material on John Cra(y)croft and the Lowes of Maryland, Anthony Savage of Virginia, and Gibbses of South Carolina; Douglas Richardson, prolific article writer and contributor to *Ancestral Roots* and *Magna Charta Sureties*, who added, among other items, his identification of the mothers of Joan (Plantagenet), Princess of North Wales, and William Longspee, Earl of Salisbury, illegitimate children of, respectively, Kings John and Henry II of England; Henry Bainbridge Hoff, editor of *The New York Genealogical and Biographical Record*, Gignilliat, Nelson and Lloyd-Yale-Eaton scholar, who also brought to my attention the de Grasse and Rudyard descents; Michael J. Wood, mentioned above, who undertook Henshaw and Ligon/Lygon research and contributed to the descent of Mrs. Thomasine Ward Thompson Buffum; and David Faris, recent co-editor of *Ancestral Roots* and *Magna Charta*

The Royal Descents of 500 Immigrants

Sureties, responsible especially, in the seventh edition of the former, for the Holand-Swinnerton and Marmion notes at the end of lines 32 and 246A. Jerome E. Anderson of the NEHGS library staff, a contributing editor of *The American Genealogist* and consulting editor for *The New England Historical and Genealogical Register,* also read the entire last draft and offered useful suggestions, and Marshall Kirk of the NEHGS library staff carefully reviewed the introduction. Other readers of the introduction were Michael Tepper and W.A. Reitwiesner.

Finally, I wish to acknowledge my own royally descended immigrant ancestors, Col. Thomas Ligon/Lygon of Virginia and Act. Gov. Jeremiah Clarke of Rhode Island. My descent from the former inspired *The Mowbray Connection,* discussed in the introduction that follows. Learning in the late 1960s of my descent from the latter considerably reinforced my interest in western royal genealogy generally. My two Ligon/Lygon lines and my Clarke descent, largely but not quite fully outlined in Margaret Hardwick Miller, *Ligons and Their Kin of Graves County, Kentucky* (1978), *passim* (I appear on p. 117), are derived through my maternal grandfather, George Wesley Boyd (1880-1952) of Navarro County, Texas, and three of his four grandparents. These lines may be outlined as follows, in the format used in my "Notable Kin" columns in the *NEHGS NEXUS.* Following my name and birth year are the names of my parents, a set of grandparents, great-grandparents, etc., backwards in time to the underlined immigrants of royal descent (RD), with semi-colons separating generations and commas separating couples of the same generation in my "ahnentafel."

> **Gary Boyd Roberts** b. 1943; Jack Carl Roberts and Mary Elizabeth Boyd; George Wesley Boyd and Fannie Kate Root; Hugh Blair Boyd and Mary Elizabeth Bressie; John Boyd and Mary S. Puryear, Joseph Addison Bressie and Martha Ann Edens; William Puryear and Mary Ligon, John Bressie and Elizabeth Ligon, Ezekiel Edens and Mary Gammill; Joseph Ligon and Mary Church (parents of Mary and Elizabeth), James Edens and Fereby Averitt; Thomas Ligon and

Ann ----, Benjamin Averitt and Amy Spooner; Matthew Ligon and Elizabeth Anderson, John Spooner and Hannah Stanton; Richard Ligon and Mary Worsham, Henry Stanton and Mary Hull; *Col. Thomas Ligon/Lygon* of Va. (RD, see pp. 204, 206) and Mary Harris, Robert Stanton and Mary Clarke; *Jeremiah Clarke,* Acting Governor of R.I. (RD, see pp. 248-49) and Mrs. Frances Latham Dungan.

Table of Contents

The Royal Descents of 500 Immigrants

Introduction

I

Royal descent is the "gateway" ancestry that links modern America to the ancient and feudal world. The pertinent western genealogical evolution can be summarized as follows. Barbaric tribes invade and finally conquer the Roman Empire, and victors and vanquished -- imperial or senatorial families, plus, later, possible descendants of Egyptian, Persian, Syrian, Parthian, Armenian, Byzantine, Exilarch, Judean, Biblical Jewish or Muslim rulers -- undoubtedly intermarry. During the "dark" and early "middle" ages, warrior chiefs of barbaric tribes become kings, feudalism begins, and territory and people begin to solidify into nations. Especially after 1200 or so kings of England, Scotland, France, Aragon and Castile (later Spain), Denmark, and Sweden, plus Russian czars and finally Italian Renaissance princes, try to consolidate their possessions geographically and tame noble kinsmen into courtiers -- processes still continuing as the New World is settled in the sixteenth and seventeenth centuries. From almost the beginning of each kingdom younger sons and non-reigning sons-in-law of kings become noblemen, as do most kinsmen of conquerors. This nobility, which early assumes surnames, often rivals, in the aggregate, the power of its royal head (whom it often tries to choose). Its nemesis, often royal allies, consists in large part of its own younger sons and sons-in-law and their descendants, who form, or head, the European "gentry" -- knights, manorial lords, gentlemen with coats-of-arms and "settled" estates, and finally baronets in England; lairds in Scotland; seigneurs in France; and counts, barons, lords or knights in Germany. In England, Scotland or Wales younger sons and sons-in-law of this gentry become leading merchants, lords mayor or aldermen; clergymen, Anglican bishops, or early Puritan leaders; university fellows, lawyers (via Inns of Court) or bureaucrats under

The Royal Descents of 500 Immigrants

Tudors and Stuarts; and professional soldiers (i.e., officers, sometimes under foreign kings). Younger sons and sons-in-law of these last groups -- plus some gentlemen (especially among the "lesser gentry"), a few peers who often become governors, several continental nobles (mostly later immigrants) and a handful of European "bourgeois," mostly French Huguenots of mercantile and "robe" background -- form the royally descended elite that settled the American colonies and is the subject of this book. The evolution that generates royal and "ancient" ancestry for millions of Americans -- most, probably, with New England Yankee, Pennsylvania Quaker, or Tidewater planter forebears -- is thus (1) *barbaric* chieftains solidifying into (2) *feudal kings,* whose own younger offspring become (3) *last-name national nobilities*, whose younger offspring form a (4) *landed gentry,* whose younger offspring in turn become (5) *merchants, ministers, intellectuals, bureaucrats and soldiers.* Offspring of these last, together with some members of (3) and (4) and many ambitious or discontented leaders of (5), help found the American colonies. Ministers, merchants and gentlemen go everywhere, but Puritans go to New England, Quakers (often Welsh) largely to Pennsylvania, Scots largely to mid-Atlantic states (some to Virginia), and Anglican "cavaliers" to Tidewater Maryland, Virginia, and South Carolina.

This volume outlines the "best" royal descents -- from the most recent king -- of 500 immigrants to the American colonies or the United States (but not Canada, Mexico, or South America), from the seventeenth century to the present, who were notable themselves or left descendants notable in American history. My standard for notability is inclusion usually in the *Dictionary of American Biography (DAB),* but sometimes only *Who's Who in America* or the *National Cyclopaedia of American Biography* (in one or two cases even lesser compendia). Included are all colonial governors for whom I could find royal descent, even if they returned to England or Scotland and left only British descendants, plus their wives if these wives were descended from a later king than their husbands or if the wives were very nearly related (to about second cousins, perhaps once or twice removed) to others of the 500. Included also were various town, settlement, or colony founders, officials other than governors, and British military officers of the French and Indian wars (but not the Revolution, at least past Lexington), and/or their wives, again if treated in the *DAB*; several clergymen or missionaries (and/or their wives) and engineers, if in the *DAB*; and a half-dozen or so European nobles -- LaFayette and Noailles (brothers-in-law, plus their wives), Rochambeau, de Grasse, Steuben and von Fersen -- who played a significant role (on our side) in the American Revolution. Many of these last groups also returned to England, Scotland, or the Continent. Treated as immigrants too, even though they never came here, are Sir Ferdinando Gorges, founder and Lord Proprietor of Maine, and his four wives; Lady Juliana Fermor, wife of Pennsylvania proprietor Thomas Penn; and Cecil Calvert, 2nd Baron Baltimore, proprietor of Maryland, and his wife (Hon. Anne Arundell) and granddaughter-in-law (Lady Charlotte Lee), both baronesses Baltimore. Given this liberal counting of "immigrants," plus the probability, discussed below, that the royal descents of ten percent or more of these immigrants may be disproved or significantly altered in the next decade or generation, I have extended their number beyond 500, to 570. In future editions of this compendium, this final count may likewise vary.

These 500 (or 570) immigrants fall into three categories. The first consists of the above-named colonial notables -- governors and other officials, founders and proprietors, soldiers, clergymen and engineers -- who often returned to their pre-American homes. The second consists of noted nineteenth- or twentieth-century figures, or their wives, parents or grandparents. Included herein are Irish patriot Thomas Addis Emmet, Texas pioneer Prince Carl of Solms-Braunfels, theosophist Madame Blavatsky and spouses of explorer Sir Henry Morton Stanley, *Monitor* builder John Ericsson and spiritualist Victoria Claflin Woodhull among nineteenth-century figures; Christopher Isherwood, Jessica Mitford, Peter Lawford, Olivia de Havilland and Joan Fontaine (sisters), Rachel Ward and Catherine Oxenberg among California or Hollywood writers and actors; Dag Hammarskjöld and wives of Averill Harriman and David K.E. Bruce among diplomats; journalist Arnaud de Borchgrave, biographer Ted Morgan, and wives of poet Robert Lowell and novelist Norman Mailer; wives of James Cox Brady, Marshall Field III and Edgar Bronfman among tycoons; rocket scientist Wernher von Braun and his wife; Mother Alexandra (Ileana of Roumania) of the Orthodox Monastery of the Transfiguration in

The Royal Descents of 500 Immigrants

Ellwood City, Pennsylvania; fathers of "Tammany" boss Richard Croker, cabinet officer Charles Joseph Bonaparte, Wyoming Senator Malcolm Wallop, and actress Gloria Grahame; fathers-in-law of Czech president Tomas Garrigue Mazaryk and novelist J.D. Salinger; the mother of Sheraton Hotel founder Ernest Henderson; both maternal grandparents of Mrs. Dean Acheson, wife of the Secretary of State; and paternal grandmothers of writer H.P. Lovecraft and model Brooke Shields. These colonial "notables in their own right" and nineteenth- and twentieth-century figures, their parents and grandparents I traced largely in the course of checking available printed sources for the known ancestry of all 15,000 figures in the *DAB*, a project I undertook at the Newberry Library in Chicago, 1966-74 (much amplified by research, 1974-93, at the New England Historic Genealogical Society in Boston, and elsewhere). Included herein are *all* my findings regarding the royal descents of these 15,000 or their traceable immigrant ancestors.

The remainder of these 500 (570), almost 350, are very largely colonial immigrants who have left sizable, often huge, progenies. Over 225 are ancestors of five or more figures in the *DAB* and over 165 are ancestors of at least ten. Probably over 100 are ancestors of five or more *major* figures in American history (the 500 or so who receive quarter-page or longer coverage in the *Concise DAB*). And over a dozen, including governor Thomas Dudley, Samuel and Judith (Everard) Appleton, Rev. Peter Bulkeley and Dr. Richard Palgrave of Massachusetts, Mrs. Anne Marbury Hutchinson of Rhode Island, Mrs. Margaret Wyatt Allyn, Mrs. Anne Lloyd Yale Eaton, Mrs. Agnes Harris Spencer Edwards, Mrs. Alice Freeman Thompson Parke, and Thomas Trowbridge of Connecticut, Robert Livingston the elder of New York, and Henry Isham and William Randolph of Virginia -- are ancestors of probably over 100 *DAB* notables. Immigrants with almost as many noted descendants as these last 14, perhaps 75 in the *DAB*, include Robert Abell, Griffith and Margaret (Fleming) Bowen, Mrs. Jane Allen Bulkeley (who died in England, first wife of Rev. Peter), Mrs. Mary Gye Maverick and Constant Southworth of Massachusetts; Mrs. Mabel Harlakenden Haynes (Eaton) and Governor William Leete of Connecticut; John Underhill of New York; and Mrs. Sarah Ludlow Carter, Henry and Alice (Eltonhead) Corbin, Col. George Reade, Anthony Savage and Mrs. Mary Towneley

The Royal Descents of 500 Immigrants

Warner of Virginia (for comments or doubts about the descents of Southworth, Leete, Underhill and Savage see their respective charts). Many of these 350 mostly colonial immigrants are treated in the five major, but still flawed, modern compendia of such lines -- the 1992 seventh edition of *Ancestral Roots of Certain American Colonists Who Came to America Before 1700* (formerly *of Sixty Colonists Who Came to New England Between 1623 and 1650*) and the 1991 fourth edition of *The Magna Charta Sureties, 1215,* by F.L. Weis, W.L. Sheppard, Jr., and David Faris; the five volumes of *Living Descendants of Blood Royal* (1959-73), by H.H. d'Angerville; the three volumes of *Pedigrees of Some of the Emperor Charlemagne's Descendants* (1941, 1974, 1978), by M.D.A.R. von Redlich, A.L. Langston, J.O. Buck and T.F. Beard; and *Lineage Book, Descendants of the Illegitimate Sons and Daughters of the Kings of Britain* (my copy covers 237 lines, through members joining in 1987). Most, but not all, of the New England immigrants herein were listed in my own royal descent bibliographies of such colonists in *The Connecticut Nutmegger* 10 (1977-78):187-98, 400, and *The New England Historical and Genealogical Register (NEHGR)* 141 (1987): 92-109.[1] Still, over 125 of these 350 have appeared in no such compendium or listing but have been culled from journal articles, genealogies, visitations, and other printed sources acknowledged on the charts.

It is important to remember that this book covers only immigrants notable in their own right or ancestors of notable

---

[1]The sole immigrant listed in this last but not mentioned on the charts herein is Mrs. Dorothy May Bradford, a *Mayflower* passenger who drowned off the tip of Cape Cod before the landing in Plymouth, the first wife of Governor William Bradford, and the mother of only one child who himself died without issue. Dorothy's parentage is disputed -- see E.A. Stratton, *Plymouth Colony, Its History and People, 1620-1691* (1986), pp. 324-26 -- and Cordelia Bowes, her alleged mother, was descended only from Hugh Lupus, Earl of Chester, d. 1101, thought to be a kinsman of William the Conqueror but probably not a half-nephew (see *The Complete Peerage*, vol. 12, part I [1953], appendix K, pp. 30-34).

Americans. Such limits include almost all royally descended *colonial* immigrants, for most Great Migration New Englanders who left children and grandchildren now have probably a million or more living descendants, and early New York or New Jersey settlers of royal descent (mostly English or Scots rather than Dutch), early Pennsylvanians of such descent (mostly Welsh or English Quakers, with some Scots) and Maryland, Virginia and South Carolina planters so descended (mostly English with some Scots, often Catholic in early Maryland, Anglican elsewhere) have thousands, often hundreds of thousands of such descendants. Thus every colonial immigrant who left issue that left issue in turn almost certainly has at least a few notable descendants. The genealogical literature on the progeny of royally descended members of these colonial populations is also usually good enough that we can trace such descendants *from printed sources.* Finally, these 350 are a large enough group so that living Americans with 50-100 immigrant ancestors in New England (or Long Island), in Quaker (but not German or Scots-Irish) Pennsylvania, or in the Tidewater South (but often *not* the Piedmont, Shenandoah Valley, or mountainous "backcountry") can *expect* to find a royally descended forebear herein.

But many nineteenth- and twentieth-century immigrants have left only a few, a few dozen, a few hundred, or a few thousand descendants -- not enough for at least one to be almost certainly notable, not enough for living Americans to expect to find any of a small group of such immigrants in their ancestry, and not yet enough to have generated a sizable body of published genealogy. Yet undoubtedly, because of their sheer quantity, many post-colonial immigrants have royal descents and my selection of them, discussed briefly above and despite much perusal of sources, is *very* partial. Mr. Joseph L. Druse of East Lansing, Michigan, has combed various modern Burke's works, especially the *Peerage* and *Landed Gentry,* plus Arthur Addington's *Royal House of Stuart,* Ruvigny's *Plantagenet Roll of the Blood Royal,* and other sources, and found numerous nineteenth- or twentieth-century immigrants to America none of whose descendants yet seem to be covered in the *DAB.* Much similar combing could be undertaken in *Burke's Irish Family Records,* F.A. Crisp's modern *Visitation of England and Wales* (and *Notes*) and *Visitation of Ireland* series, *Genealogisches Handbuch des*

Adels, and sources for the *Rolls of Arms* of the NEHGS Committee on Heraldry, all of which I have checked for immigrants of royal descent *and notable progeny.* Many recent "gentry" immigrants from Great Britain, or royal, noble or royally descended immigrants from the Continent simply have not *yet* had notable progeny -- they almost certainly eventually will. Some who may have had such descendants already, but are also not treated herein, are nineteenth century Germans and Scandinavians, no doubt often of royal descent, who have sometimes been studied by Duderstadt scholar C. Frederick Kaufholz (see *National Genealogical Society Quarterly* 49 [1961]: 201-4, 63 [1975]:268-71, and *The American Genealogist* 51 [1975]: 225-29, 59 [1983]:150-56), Norwegian-American scholar Gerhard Brandt Naeseth (see his *Naeseth-Fehn Family History* [1956] for midwestern kinsmen of Queen Sonja [Haraldsen] of Norway, p. 146, plus Erling Arnold Smedal, *The Smedal Family History and Genealogy* [1966] and *Supplement* [1973-77], and *Pedigrees of Some of the Emperor Charlemagne's Descendants,* vol. 3, pp. 240, 255-60), W.L. Sheppard, Jr. (see *NEHGR* 111 [1957]:99-103, reprinted in *English Origins of New England Families From NEHGR,* 1st ser. [1984], 3:255-59) and others. I have, I think, combed the printed literature on *colonial immigrants* fairly thoroughly, and have looked at many sources for nineteenth- and twentieth-century immigrants of royal descent as well. Concerning non-noble mid-nineteenth-century Germans, Scandinavians, Dutch and others, however, I am ignorant of the primary sources in Europe often necessary to trace their ancestry, and without the oral history or local documentation needed to know their progeny.

II

Having discussed royal descent generally, the scope of this book, and the types of royally descended immigrants it covers, I now wish to say something about the history of this project, and of the massive scholarship it summarizes. In 1965-66, as a first-year graduate student at the University of Chicago (and after extensive earlier research at Yale and the New York Public Library), I began the almost encyclopedic genealogical study that has become my life's work -- *The Mowbray Connection,* subtitled *An Analysis of the*

The Royal Descents of 500 Immigrants

Genealogical Evolution of British, American, and Continental Nobilities, Gentries, and Upper Classes Since the End of the Middle Ages. Twenty-three volumes -- six of British charts, three of introductory text to the American section, ten of American charts, two of Continental charts, one of bibliography, and one (by Michael J. Wood of London) of index to the American charts -- are now at the New England Historic Genealogical Society (NEHGS) in Boston, the New York Public Library, and the Society of Genealogists in London, and I wrote of *The Mowbray Connection* in *The Connecticut Nutmegger* 10 (1977-78):3-12, 187-98, 393-400, *The Detroit Society for Genealogical Research Magazine* 41 (1977-78): 142, 42 (1978-79):191, and *Genealogical Journal* 12 (1983-84):70, 13 (1984-85):66. As I suggested in these last, my aim was twofold. Since British and American genealogy are most frequently connected through the Tudor-Stuart gentry, and British and continental genealogy through the common descent of most European nobilities from a common core of high medieval kings (mostly Plantagenets, Capets and Hohenstaufens), and since, as noted above, nobilities sire gentries from whom later intellectual and professional elites, twentieth-century "establishments" and even America's contemporary suburban middle class often derive -- given these facts, I wanted to produce a single, stem study that by assimilating enough data would allow me to examine much of the genealogical history of the Western world. A secondary aim was to organize much of the best modern scholarship in our field, both Anglo-American and Continental. In so doing I hoped to examine further some of the suggestions in Sir Anthony Richard Wagner's *English Genealogy,* to develop hypotheses that genealogy could now offer demography, local, national, and world history, sociology and anthropology, and to document from *good* printed sources the sizable number of American immigrants of royal descent. In 1965, and to some extent still, the magnificent ongoing literature on this last topic was marred by association with poor earlier compendia.

The focus of *The Mowbray Connection* is Thomas Mowbray, 1st Duke of Norfolk (d. 1399; his widow, Lady Elizabeth FitzAlan, who also left children by a later husband, Sir Robert Goushill, survived until 1425), great-great-grandson of Edward I, King of England, d. 1307; heir to the English crown after the descendants of

Edward III; a minor character in Shakespeare's *Richard II*; and ancestor of Lady Jane Grey, Queen Elizabeth I, and many Tudor-Stuart peers, including Dudleys and Howards. Mowbray is a forebear too of almost all major clans of the eighteenth-century Whig oligarchy (including the great ducal progeny of the 1st Earl Gower), many nineteenth and twentieth-century intellectual figures (including Byron, Shelley, E.B. Browning, Tennyson, Swinburne, Jane Austen, Charles Reade, Lewis Carroll, Darwin, Bertrand Russell, Ralph Vaughan Williams, T.E. Lawrence and the Mitfords, Sitwells, and Trevelyans, plus, among genealogists, John and Sir J.B. Burke, J.H. Round, G.E. Cokayne and Vicary Gibbs) and most members of this century's "British establishment." Mowbray and/or his above-named wife (also a great-great grandchild of Edward I) were also ancestors, or siblings or first cousins of ancestors, of slightly over half of the 500/570 American immigrants treated herein. Mowbray's own American colonial progeny included the Delaware West-Pelham-Bellingham and Ligon/Lygon-Gorges-Berkeley-Dudley-Dale clusters of governors (pp. 115-18, 204-6 herein), Saltonstalls of Massachusetts and Randolphs of Virginia. Elizabeth FitzAlan's, in addition, included Abells, Bulkeleys, Pynchons, (probably) Southworths, Tyngs, and Willards (these last via Mrs. Mary Launce Sherman) of Massachusetts; Mainwarings of Connecticut; Lloyds (via John Nelson) of Long Island; Abbotts, Fenwicks and Rudyards of New Jersey; Claypooles and Biddles (via Rebecca Owen) of Philadelphia; the Lowe-Sewall-Calvert clan of Maryland; probably Thorntons (via Anthony Savage) and Carringtons of Virginia; Alstons and Fenwicks of South Carolina; and J.E. Oglethorpe of Georgia. Near kinsmen of Mowbray or his wife with many American descendants include Mowbray's sister Eleanor, wife of John de Welles, 5th Baron Welles (see pp. 207-9, 213-21, 246-47, 270, 272-73); Elizabeth's sister, Alice FitzAlan, wife of John Cherleton, 4th Baron Cherleton of Powis and mistress of Henry Beaufort, Cardinal Beaufort (see pp. 134-35, 165-66); two double first cousins of Elizabeth FitzAlan -- Mary Bohun, queen of Henry IV of England (see pp. 80-85) and Eleanor Bohun, wife of Thomas Plantagenet of Woodstock, 1st Duke of Gloucester (son of Edward III) (see pp. 132-33, 146-47, 163, 182); and Elizabeth FitzAlan's aunt, another Alice FitzAlan, wife of Thomas Holand, 2nd Earl of Kent (half-brother of Richard II) and mother of Edmund Holand, 4th Earl of Kent (see pp. 157-58, 167-68, 179, 181, 192-93), of Eleanor Holand, wife secondly of Edward Cherleton, 4th Baron Cherleton of Powis (see pp. 243, 280), and of Margaret Holand, wife of John Beaufort, Marquess of Somerset and Dorset (see pp. 115-18, 155-56) and mother in turn of Queen Joan Beaufort (Stewart) of Scotland (see pp. 71-78, 107-14, plus the progeny of James II, James IV and James V of Scotland, James I of England, etc.).

Furthermore, one-fourth of the ancestry of Mowbray and his wife -- that derived through Edward I, both his queens (Eleanor of Castile and Margaret of France), his brother (Edmund Plantagenet, 1st Earl of Lancaster) and his brother's wife (Blanche of Artois) -- was Continental and largely royal, sovereign, or comital. This quadrant of the Mowbray-FitzAlan ancestry was fairly widespread, I found, among several Continental nobilities, especially those of France, Spain, Rhineland Germany, and Austria. Among figures herein this quadrant, or most of it, is shared by (among others) Dag Hammarskjöld, Steuben, LaFayette, Zinzendorf and his wife, Rochambeau, and R.P. Garrigue and the Masaryks. Focused, then, on Mowbray, his wife and their near Continental cousins, my life's work outlines the best Mowbray-connected royal descent of over 500 major figures in European history, of 1000 British figures of note, and of roughly 25 percent of the almost 15,000 notable Americans who died before 1941 and are treated in the *DAB*. When no major portion of the Mowbray-FitzAlan ancestry is shared by a royally descended figure the best "single strand" of royal descent is presented -- often, for British or American figures, a line from King John, Henry II, Henry I or Ethelred II of England, William I (the Lion) or David I of Scotland, or Henry I, Hugh Capet or Louis IV of France.

The Royal Descents of 500 Immigrants (*RD500*) is, in effect, the first volume of *The Mowbray Connection* to be published. For this book, however, I undertook extensive research into immigrants not yet included in *The Mowbray Connection* -- and deleted lines disproved since the late 1960s -- so for awhile *RD500* will partly supersede its parent. For this book also I have tried to outline not the closest Mowbray connection of any immigrant, but the *best* (i.e. from the eldest child, sons preferred to daughters) descent from the most *recent* king. This last effort involved tracing various new descents from Edward III and later kings, and probably a few more will be uncovered by various genealogical colleagues. All such "improved" lines will be welcome and future editions of this book may thus be considerably rearranged.

III

As suggested above, this book rests upon, and is a distillation of, a massive quantity of scholarship -- much of the best work of the Jacobus generation, and of contemporary American genealogists, plus many monographs in English journals; the great (New) *Complete Peerage, Scots Peerage* (by Sir J.B. Paul), and *Welsh Genealogies, 300-1400 AD* and *1400-1500* (by P.C. Bartrum); various Burke's works and earlier peerage compendia by Collins, Douglas, and Lodge; the sometimes erroneous but invaluable visitations, especially those published by the Harleian Society; the great seventeenth- through twentieth-century English county histories, Dugdale through the (New) *History of Northumberland* and the ongoing *Victoria County History* series; and the various great Continental sets -- Anselme, Courcelles, Saint Allais, *Dictionnaire de la Noblesse* and *Grand Armorial de France* for France, *Europäische Stammtafeln, Genealogisches Handbuch des Adels*, the *Almanach de Gotha* and *Deutsche Geschichte in Ahnentafeln* for Germany, Elgenstierna for Sweden, Ikonnikov for Russia, etc. I also readily acknowledge my great debt to the above-cited *Ancestral Roots* and *Magna Charta Sureties, 1215* volumes (the last two editions of both of which include various additions and changes I submitted to Mssrs. Sheppard and Faris) and liberal use of *Living Descendants of Blood Royal, Pedigrees of Some of the Emperor Charlemagne's Descendants*, and the *Lineage Book, Descendants of the Illegitimate Sons and Daughters of the Kings of Britain*. I readily concede too that except for one of my own ancestors, Col. Thomas Ligon (Lygon) of Virginia, I have not undertaken or commissioned work in English *primary* sources -- parish registers, wills, inquisitions post mortem, chancery or manorial records, etc. Instead I have -- as exhaustively, I think, as time and my bibliographical knowledge allow -- combed *printed* genealogical sources for royally descended immigrants who were notable themselves or left noted American progeny. I have undertaken this more than 25 years of research mostly at the Newberry Library in Chicago and, most importantly, NEHGS in Boston, where I have been reference librarian or director of research, special projects or publications 1974-77 and 1981 to the present. I have looked at most printed genealogies, examined most major periodicals issue-by-issue, used dozens of compendia (and I think exhausted the bad older compilations of Charles Henry Browning, John Sparhawk Wurts, and Frederick Adams Virkus, which may *sometimes* be used for clues but should *never* be cited), talked about their contributions to this subject with most living authors named below, and for virtually all British families or New England immigrants herein sought the *best* source listed by George H. Marshall, J.B. Whitmore, Geoffrey B. Barrow (England, Wales, and Ireland), Margaret Stuart (Scotland) or Clarence Almon Torrey (New England).

Most of the Continental sets I used for this book were well described by John Insley Coddington in "Royal and Noble Genealogy," *Genealogical Research: Methods and Sources,* Milton Rubincam, ed. (1st ed., 1960), pp. 299-319. The history of British genealogical literature was well covered by Sir A.R. Wagner in *English Genealogy* (3rd ed., 1983), pp. 351-407. I wrote on the Jacobus generation in *The Connecticut Nutmegger* 12 (1979-80):372, on George Andrews Moriarty, Jr., and various other scholars of royal descents in my introductions to *English Origins of New England Families* (1st and 2nd series, 1984-85), and on post-1960 scholarship concerning royally descended New Englanders in *NEHGR* 141 (1987):92-109. To these discussions I think I can most usefully add simply the following list of twentieth-century scholars, many still living, and the immigrants on whom they have worked -- sometimes establishing not the entire descent outlined in this book but nonetheless a significant part of it. The 150 such scholars are as follows:

1. Arthur Adams -- George Elkington (superseded by Col. C.M. Hansen, below), Mrs. Margaret Halsnode Denne (with additions by C.M. Hansen and M.A. Nicholson below), *MCS* and *LDBR* 1 (although his contribution to both of these last may have been slight)

2. Arthur C. Addington (*The Royal House of Stuart*) --
   descendants herein, in legitimate lines, of James I,
   King of England (Mother Alexandra; Catherine
   Oxenberg; Mrs. Avery Brundage; Egon, Prince zu
   Fürstenberg; Felix, Prince of Salm-Salm)

3. Mrs. Sarah Cantey Whitaker Allen -- Whitakers (3)

4. Robert Charles Anderson -- Thomas Bradbury
   (rejection of FitzWilliam and Poyntz lines), Lady Anne
   Bell Gorges, forthcoming Great Migration compendium

5. David A. Avant, Jr. -- Lawrence Smith

6. Augustine H. Ayers -- Joseph Bolles

7. Joseph Gardner Bartlett -- Peter Talbot (note that the
   line he developed for Thomas Newberry of Mass.,
   included in the *Ancestral Roots* series and, as a
   possibility, in my 1989 *Ancestors of American
   Presidents,* is excluded herein, following Sir A.R.
   Wagner's doubts about it in *English Genealogy*)

8. Peter C. Bartrum (*Welsh Genealogies*) -- Griffith and
   Margaret (Fleming) Bowen (with General Herman
   Nickerson, Jr., below); all Welsh lines herein through
   1500 (as extracted by W.A. Reitwiesner and checked
   by me)

9. Timothy Field Beard -- Robert Drake, Mrs. Anne
   Lloyd Yale Eaton (with H.B. Hoff, below), T.L.
   Stuart-Menteth, Richard Wright, *PSECD* 2&3 plus
   corrections for Col. Walter Aston and Mrs. Muriel
   Gurdon Saltonstall

10. Joseph M. Beatty Jr. -- Mrs. Christiana Clinton Beatty,
    Charles Clinton

11. Henry Lyman Parsons Beckwith, Jr. -- Mrs. Mary
    Fulford Lovecraft, comments on various immigrants as
    compiler of the 8th-10th rolls of arms of the NEHGS
    Committee on Heraldry

12. Robert Behra -- Mrs. Mary Mainwaring Gill, Oliver
    Mainwaring

13. Eversley M.G. Belfield -- Henry Edward Bellew (6th Viscount Exmouth)

14. Col. John C. Bell -- Joseph Bickley

15. John Bennett Boddie II (*VHG, SVF, HSF*, not always reliable) -- Col. Walter Aston, Lancelot Bathurst, two Battes and Roger Mallory, William Boddie, Thomas Boteler and Mrs. Elizabeth Boteler Claiborne, Act. Gov. Edmund Jennings, Richard Kempe, Col. Thomas Ligon/Lygon (corrected by G.B. Roberts, below), Col. George Reade, William Strother, Thomas Warren, three Washingtons

16. Ross Boothe, Jr. -- Mrs. Amy Wyllys Pynchon

17. Richard LeBaron Bowen -- Marburys (Mrs. Hutchinson, Mrs. Scott, Wentworth, Lawson)

18. Homer Worthington Brainerd -- Henry Isham, two Randolphs

19. James C. Brandow -- George Carrington, Mrs. Elizabeth Hannah Carrington Willing

20. John Anderson Brayton -- John Fisher

21. Chester Horton Brent -- Brents (4)

22. Bennet B. Browne -- Act. Gov. Robert Brooke

23. Howard M. Buck -- Oliver Mainwaring

24. Henry DeSaussure Bull -- Stephen Bull

25. Dr. Joseph Gaston Baillie Bulloch -- Col. Kenneth Baillie, James Cuthbert, John Irvine

26. Arthur Edwin Bye -- Thomas and Margaret (Davis) Bye, Joseph Kirkbride

27. Arnaud Chauffanjon -- LaFayette, Noailles, and their wives

28. Brice McAdoo Clagett -- Act. Gov. Robert Brooke, Dr. Charles Carroll, Wiseman Clagett, John Cra(y)croft, Gibbses of S.C. (3), Mrs. Mary Mainwaring Gill and James Neale, Lowes (3), Alexander Magruder (and Dr. Charles D. Kurz, below), Anthony Savage (with N.D. Thompson, below)

29. John Insley Coddington -- John Alston, Rev. John Davenport (with G.B. Roberts, below), two Eddoweses, John Fenwick of N.J., Edward FitzRandolph, Lady Christian Stuart Griffin, Mrs. Elizabeth Coytmore Tyng

30. Peter Wilson Coldham -- Thomas Weston, *Complete Book of Emigrants* and *Emigrants in Bondage* series, *American Wills and Administrations in the Prerogative Court of Canterbury*, "Genealogical Gleanings in England" series in *NGSQ*

31. Meredith Bright Colket -- Marburys (4), Ludlows (3), Delaware West-Pelham cluster

32. Francis Northrop Craig -- Gov. Thomas Dudley, Marburys (4)

33. J. Robert T. Craine -- Matthew Clarkson

34. Leander Howard Crall -- William Asfordby

35. G.Rodney Crowther -- Lowes (3)

36. Robert Joseph Curfman -- Thomas Dongan, 2nd Earl of Limerick; Yales (3)

37. Noel Currer-Briggs -- Thomas Warren (as reported in *PSECD* 3)

38. John F. Curwen -- George Curwen

39. Walter Goodwin Davis, Jr. -- two Appletons, two Batts, Thomas Bressie, two Lewises of Me.

40. John Ross Delafield -- John Underhill

41. Rev. Henry Lyttelton Lyster Denny -- Rev. William Narcissus Lyster

42. Katharine Dickson (Brown) -- John Stockman

43. John Frederick Dorman (plus Virginia M. Meyer, Prentiss Price, Annie Lash Jester and Martha Woodruff Hiden - *AP&P*) -- Col. William Bernard, Christopher Branch, Calverts of Md., Mrs. Elizabeth Boteler Claiborne, Francis Dade, Gov. Edward Digges, William Farrar, John Fisher, Henry Fleete, Col. Gerard Fowke, Mrs. Anne Lovelace Gorsuch, Col. Thomas Ligon/Lygon, Nathaniel Littleton, Gov. Francis

Lovelace, Henry Lowe, Col. George Reade, Mrs. Alicia Arnold Ross, St. Legers (Codd, Horsmanden and Mrs. Colepepper/Culpeper), Stracheys (3), Delaware Wests, Henry Woodhouse, Rev. Hawte Wyatt

44. Hervé Douxchamps -- Henri Joseph Stier

45. William M. Ellicott -- Mrs. Mary Fox Ellicott

46. Ludlow Elliman -- John Underhill

47. Mrs. George F. Elmendorf -- Gov. Thomas Dudley

48. Lucy L. Erwin -- William Clopton, Mrs. Thomasine Clopton Winthrop

49. Charles Frederick Holt Evans -- John Bevan, two Robert Livingstons, Gov. Thomas and Mary (Jones) Lloyd (with I.H. Leet, below), Margaret of Teschen (for Mrs. Margaret Tyndal Winthrop)

50. Margaret Dickson Falley -- George (Holmes) Pomeroy

51. David Faris -- much editing of *AR6,7* and *MCS4*

52. Claude W. Faulkner -- Thomas Gerard, Mrs. Amy Wyllys Pynchon

53. Charles Fitch-Northen -- Thomas Trowbridge

54. David M. Foley -- various Scottish and other lines in *MCS3,4*, notably Home (41E), Spotswood (43A), Griffin (43B), Mercer (91B), Houstoun (92A), and probably Lunsford (88A), Coke (94A), Gorsuch (113A), and Dudley (149B)

55. Thomas Allen Glenn (*WFP* 1,2, *Merion*) -- most Welsh immigrants herein, as confirmed by Bartrum

56. Glenn H. Goodman -- Oliver Mainwaring

57. Raymond Gorges -- Sir Ferdinando Gorges and his four wives, two Nortons

58. David L. Greene -- Nathaniel Browne (addition to D.L. Jacobus, below), Nathaniel Burrough (with G.I. Nelson and G.E. Russell, below), Lawrences (5), Mrs. Alice Freeman Thompson Parke

59. Jane E. Grunwell -- James Cudworth

60. W.J.T. Gun -- John Henry and noted kin, Dryden-Swift-Walpole kin of Marbury sisters

61. George Hamilton (*A History of the House of Hamilton*) -- two Alexander Hamiltons

62. Col. Charles M. Hansen -- Samuel Appleton, James Claypoole, Mrs. Margaret Halsnode Denne, George Elkington, and William Rodney, plus, with N.D. Thompson, below, "The Ancestry of Charles II" and Margaret de Kerdeston and Woodville studies

63. Fairfax Harrison -- Colepeppers/Culpepers (3)

64. Robert Jesse Harry -- Daniel and Hugh Harry

65. James William Hawes -- Edmond Hawes

66. Ernest Flagg Henderson III -- Mrs. Berta von Bunsen Henderson

67. John Goodwin Herndon -- two Wingfields, Mrs. Mary (prob.) Waller Herndon and Col. John Waller

68. Mrs. Napier Higgins -- Bernards, especially Sir Francis, 1st Bt. and Amelia (Offley)

69. Henry Bainbridge Hoff -- Mrs. Anne Lloyd Yale Eaton (with T.F. Beard, above), Jean Francois Gignilliat, Nelsons (J. Alston, J. Nelson, Mrs. M.N. Teackle)

70. William J. Hoffman -- Mrs. Sophia van Lodensteyn de Beauvois or Debevoise

71. Harry Hollingsworth -- Mrs. Diana Skipwith Dale, Sir Grey Skipwith, 3rd Bt.

72. (Mrs.) Winifred Lovering Holman (Dodge) -- Deighton sisters (3) (with chart in *TG* 6 by N.D. Thompson, below)

73. Alvahn Holmes -- William Farrar

74. Edgar Erskine Hume -- George Home

75. John Griffiths Hunt -- Bulkeleys, plus Jane Allen (7), two Carletons (with G.A. Moriarty, Jr., and W.L. Sheppard, Jr., below), Mrs. Mary Gye Maverick, Robert Throckmorton, George Yate

76. Donald Lines Jacobus -- Nathaniel Browne, Obadiah Bruen, Bulkeleys (including Rev. Thomas James, Jane Allen and Grace Chetwode) (8), Mrs. Mary Launce Sherman, Thomas Trowbridge, Mrs. Anne Rich Willis

77. Edward Miller Jefferys -- Sir Herbert Jeffreys

78. William Perry Johnson -- Gov. Peter and Gov. Philip de Carteret

79. Christopher Johnston -- William Bladen, Blakistons (4), Act. Gov. Robert Brooke, Christopher Lowndes, James Neale, Richard Tilghman

80. Edith Duncan Johnston -- Sir Patrick Houston, 5th Bt.

81. Alfred Rudolph Justice -- Act. Gov. Jeremiah Clarke

82. David Humiston Kelley -- various additions, including line 223 (Mrs. Olive Welby Farwell) to the *Ancestral Roots* series

83. Charles Kidd -- Reginald Michael Bloxam Hallward

84. George Harrison Sanford King -- Sir Marmaduke Beckwith, 3rd Bt., Rev. John Munro

85. Dr. Charles G. Kurz -- Alexander Magruder

86. Francis Leeson -- Christopher Tilghman, as reported in *LDBR 5*

87. Irene Haines Leet -- Gov. Thomas and Mary (Jones) Lloyd (with C.F.H. Evans, above)

88. Asselia Strobhar Lichliter -- Essex Beville

89. William Daniel Ligon -- Ligon/Lygon cluster (especially Col. Thomas Ligon/Lygon, corrected by G.B. Roberts, below; Gorges; Berkeley; Foliot; Deighton sisters; and Savage, corrected by B. McA. Clagett, above, and N.D. Thompson, below), Henry Corbin

90. E.L. Lomax -- Sir Thomas Lunsford

91. Charles M. Lord -- James Veatch

92. Daniel MacGregor -- Mrs. Marina Torlonia Shields Slater

93. Charles R. Maduell, Jr. -- Carondelet
94. George Englert McCracken -- William Rodney
95. Mary Burton Derrickson McCurdy -- Towneleys (L. Smith, L. Towneley, and Mrs. M.T. Warner)
96. Gerhard Meyer -- Zinzendorf(s) and Schweinitz(es)
97. Patrick W. Montague-Smith -- Mrs. Mary Wolseley Brooke, Mrs. Anne Wolseley Calvert, Mrs. Alicia Arnold Ross
98. George Andrews Moriarty, Jr. -- two Carletons, Dr. Richard Palgrave, Rev. William Sargent (and Mrs. Alice Freeman Thompson Parke), John Throckmorton (and George Yate)
99. R.W. Munro -- Rev. John Munro
100. Glade Ian Nelson -- Nathaniel Burrough (with D.L. Greene and G.E. Russell, above and below), Ralph Hilton/Hylton
101. Mary Ann Nicholson -- Mrs. Margaret Halsnode Denne
102. General Herman Nickerson, Jr. -- Griffith and Margaret (Fleming) Bowen, with P.C. Bartrum, above
103. J.B. Calvert Nicklin -- Calverts (barons Baltimore and wives, Hon. Leonard and Mrs. Anne Wolseley Calvert), Francis Dade, William Strother
104. Rev. V.F. O'Daniel -- Cuthbert Fenwick
105. J.Hall Pleasants -- Richard Curzon
106. F.H. Pollard -- Mrs. Sarah Blair Watkinson
107. F.W. Pyne -- John Pyne of S.C.
108. M. Taylor Pyne -- Thomas Pyne of N.Y.
109. James A. Rasmussen -- Edward Raynsford
110. Harmon Pumpelly Read -- Rev. George Ross
111. Franz V. Recum -- Warren-Johnson-Shedden cluster (4)
112. Paul C. Reed -- Mrs. Elizabeth Harleston Ball and John Harleston
113. William Addams Reitwiesner -- Lady Charlotte Lee Calvert, Baroness Baltimore (in *MCS3,4*), Louis Nicola,

extraction from *Bartrum 1,2* (and general review) of all Welsh lines herein

114. Douglas Richardson -- Mrs. Margaret Wyatt Allyn, John Baynard, Thomas Colepepper (Culpeper), Anthony Collamore, Mrs. Agnes Harris Spencer Edwards, various additions to *AR6,7* and *MCS4*

115. Hannah Benner Roach -- Peter Penn-Gaskell

116. Clarence Vernon Roberts -- Edward Foulke, John Williams

117. Gary Boyd Roberts -- Thomas Bressie, Rev. John Davenport (with J.I. Coddington, above), Edmond Hawes, Col. Thomas Ligon/Lygon (with M.S. Wood, below); Mackintoshes (McIntoshes), J.E. Oglethorpe, Robert Traill and others in *NEXUS*; bibliographies in *The Connecticut Nutmegger* and *NEHGR*; various additions to *AR6,7* and *MCS3,4*; *The Mowbray Connection*; *RD500*

118. Christine Rose -- Rev. Robert Rose

119. Mrs. Dunbar Rowland -- William Dunbar

120. Milton Rubincam -- Lady Charlotte Lee Calvert, Baroness Baltimore, James Claypoole, Thomas Gordon, Sancha de Ayala and some of her American progeny, comments on many lines in *NGSQ* book reviews

121. Daniel Wood Rudgers -- Dep. Gov. Thomas Rudyard

122. George Ely Russell -- Nathaniel Burrough (with D.L. Greene and G.I. Nelson, above)

123. William Kenneth and Anna Clay (Zimmerman) Rutherford -- James Burd, Archibald Russell, Walter Rutherford

124. Marquis of Ruvigny and Raineval (*The Plantagenet Roll of the Blood Royal*) -- most descendants herein, in legitimate lines, of Henry VII, King of England; George Plantagenet, Duke of Clarence; Anne St. Leger Manners, Baroness Ros; Walter Devereux, 1st Viscount Hereford; and Henry Percy, 4th Earl of Northumberland)

125. Charles Richard Sanders -- Stracheys (3)

126. Dr. David A. Sandmire -- John Stratton, Mrs. Elizabeth Stratton Thorndike

127. Helen Jefferson Sanford -- two Mahons

128. Mrs. Elizabeth Wellborn Schieffelin -- Col. Gerard Fowke

129. Edwin Jaquett Sellers -- John Fenwick of N.J., Thomas Fenwick, Mrs. Maria de Carpentier Jaquet

130. Herbert Furman Seversmith -- three Ludlows, two Nortons

131. Mrs. Henrietta Dawson Ayres Sheppard -- Robert Drake

132. Walter Lee Sheppard, Jr. -- Joseph Bolles, two Carletons (with G.A. Moriarty, Jr., and J.G. Hunt, above), James Claypoole, "Royal Bye-Blows" list in *NEHGR*, *Ancestral Roots* and *Magna Charta Sureties, 1215* since 1952 (recent editions with David Faris), *Feudal Genealogy,* founder of Descendants of the Illegitimate Sons and Daughters of the Kings of Britain

133. Mrs. Patricia Wright Strati --Rudolph Pierre Garrigue

134. Eugene Aubrey Stratton -- Gov. William Leete, William Wentworth, de Braose ancestry of Bressie, N. Browne, Davenport and Hawes

135. Alistair and Henrietta Tayler (*The House of Forbes*) -- John Forbes of Pa., Rev. John Forbes of Fla. and Forbes line of Hans Axel, Count von Fersen

136. Neil D. Thompson -- Robert Abell, Anthony Savage (with B. McA. Clagett, above), much editing and additions to royal descent articles in *TG* (on Eve of Leinster, Llywelyn and Joan of Wales, 3 Nelsons, Mrs. A.F.T. Parke, Wolseleys and Mrs. A.A. Ross, de Braose ancestors of Bressie, Browne, Davenport and Hawes, the Deighton sisters [especially Mrs. Negus], George Elkington, William Wentworth, Bressie and Hawes, Thomas Trowbridge, H.J. Stier, two Harlestons, and forthcoming Lawrence and Gibbes articles, plus, with

C.M. Hansen, above, "The Ancestry of Charles II" and Margaret de Kerdeston and Woodville studies)

137. John Brooks Threlfall -- Thomas Bradbury

138. Clayton Torrence -- Mrs. Anne Lovelace Gorsuch, Gov. Francis Lovelace

139. Clarence Almon Torrey -- Rev. Thomas James (with D.L. Jacobus, above), Mrs. Alice Freeman Thompson Parke

140. Peter G. Van der Poel -- Gov. John Cranston (as noted in *MCS3,4*), Yales (3)

141. Sir Anthony Richard Wagner -- Mrs. Mabel Harlakenden Haynes (Eaton), Richard More, comments on others (especially Mrs. Anne Bainton Batt, Mark Catesby and Edward FitzRandolph) in *English Genealogy* or *Pedigree and Progress*

142. Peter Walne -- Christopher Branch, Col. John and Lawrence Washington (father)

143. George Sydney Horace Lee Washington -- Charles Calvert alias Lazenby alias Butler (perhaps untenable), three Washingtons (and H.E. Pellew)

144. Walter Kendall Watkins -- Alexander Cochrane, Robert Gibbs

145. Frederick Lewis Weis -- two Southworths, first editions of *Ancestral Roots* and *Magna Charta Sureties, 1215*

146. Wayne Howard Miller Wilcox -- Mrs. Catherine Hamby Hutchinson

147. York Lowry Wilson -- Thomas Chamberlayne, Mrs. Dorothy Chamberlayne Daniell, John Hinton, Col. George Reade

148. Henry Mosle (H.M.) West Winter -- George Mosle, *The Descendants of Charlemagne* (covering 16 generations)

149. Michael J. Wood -- Mrs. Thomasine Ward Thompson Buffum, Col. Thomas Ligon/Lygon (with G.B. Roberts, above), plus commissioned research on Joshua Henshaw

150. Henry James Young -- Edmond Hawes, Rev. Thomas
James, and Mrs. Alice Freeman Thompson Parke
(ancestor tables for all three)

Note: In almost all cases the specific works of these scholars,
on each immigrant listed, are cited on the chart(s) outlining that
immigrant's royal descent. Virginia scholars William Stanard Glover
and Lyon Gardiner Tyler, editors between them of all three of the
major Virginia genealogical journals of the early twentieth century,
are omitted from this list because most of their work, although widely
used, has been superseded by later contributions from various of the
above.

The above list, which could be expanded even further,
emphasizes *living* scholars, contributors to the major *current* American genealogical journals (*NEHGR, TAG, NYGBR, TG, NGSQ* and
TVG) or to the *Ancestral Roots* and *Magna Charta Sureties* series,
and English, Welsh or Scottish genealogists with much interest in
American families (Addington, Bartrum, Coldham, Currer-Briggs,
Evans, Gun, Hamilton, Kidd, Montague-Smith, Ruvigny, Sanders,
Wagner, Walne and Wood). A sizable number of scholars now work
in this field, or at least trace gentry and noble connections of their
own forebears. Numerous clues still remain to be pursued, including
many discovered by a dozen or more "gleanings" abstractors -- Henry
FitzGilbert Waters (*Genealogical Gleanings in England*), Lothrop
Withington (*Virginia Gleanings in England*), J. Henry Lea, J.R.
Hutchinson and William Gilbert (*English Origins of American
Colonists From NYGBR*), George Sherwood (*American Colonists in
English Records*), Charles Edward Banks (*Topographical Dictionary
of 2885 Emigrants to New England, 1620-1650*, with many mistakes),
Donald Whyte (*A Dictionary of Scottish Emigrants to the U.S.A.*),
David Dobson (various books on Scottish immigrants), Harry Wright
Newman (*To Maryland from Overseas*), William Armstrong Crozier
(*Virginia Heraldica*) and the above Peter Wilson Coldham (note also
the older *Aspinwall Notarial Records* and *Note-Book Kept by Thomas
Lechford*, plus the various lists that compose appendices A-C of
English Origins of New England Families from NEHGR, 1st ser.,
vol. 1). In addition, moreover, to a major flowering of scholars and

a plethora of clues, English source records at the county level are now being published in profusion (the complete Bedfordshire parish register series and the Elizabethan *Essex Wills* prepared by F.G. Emmison are particularly notable recent examples), parish registers continue to be copied, filmed, or published, *The Index Library* and other works list all PCC (and many local) wills and administrations through 1700, publication of Tudor inquisitions post mortem has begun, and the Mormon International Genealogical Index (IGI) is now in its 4th (1992) edition. This last contains 187 million birth, baptism or marriage entries from around the world, roughly early sixteenth to mid-nineteenth centuries, includes perhaps 30 percent of all English parish registers, and is widely available on microfiche and CD-ROM.

Thus many more English origins and royal descent discoveries are likely in the near future. Judging from my experience in trying to update *The Mowbray Connection* more or less continuously, and in following the periodical literature, I should estimate that the immediate origin or royal descent of as many as 10-15 percent (50-75) of these immigrants could be altered -- and as "old" lines or immigrants are dropped, probably even more will be added -- in the next decade or two. Thus this book will require various future editions. Many possible changes, or at least problems to explore, are in fact suggested on the charts herein. For I have both noted near kinsmen of many (especially Welsh Quaker Pennsylvania) immigrants who also came here but for whom I can find no notable descendants, and indicated any areas of doubt in the outlined royal descents. Such ancestry for almost all immigrants herein will stand, I think, but some lines may well be "improved" (i.e., superseded by another descent from a later king) or changed. On various charts I noted that a thorough monograph on a certain family or person would be welcome. On others I note that a particular identification (as of an immigrant or an immigrant's parent) would benefit from further confirmation. Some lines herein, including a few I discovered, are "virtually proved" -- seemingly validated by a series of reliable printed sources -- but not yet the subject of a separate monograph that brings together printed and all record or documentary sources. A main purpose of this book is to generate and encourage articles on these "problem" families, persons, and identifications, and suggest detailed studies on immigrants whose "virtually proved" lines appear herein for perhaps the first time.

I shall conclude this section with a list, in page-number order, of immigrants some aspect of whose royal descents, as noted on their charts, merits further study.

1. Charles Calvert alias Lazenby alias Butler of Md. (p. 13)

2. Robert Sinclair of N.Y. (29)

3. Mrs. Dorothy Chamberlayne Daniell of S.C. (44)

4. Robert Langton Douglas of N.Y. (57)

5. Mrs. Margaret Stirling Forbes (Alexander) of Va. (59)

6-7. Hugh Mercer of Va. and Mrs. Euphan Scott Johnstone of N.J. (97)

8. Col. Kenneth Baillie of Ga. (114)

9. John Hinton of N.C. (134)

10. Mrs. Margaret Davis Bye of Pa. (163)

11. Joshua Henshaw of Mass. (177)

12. William Strother of Va. (184)

13. John Cra(y)croft of Md. (224)

14. John Washington of Surry Co., Va. (243)

15-16. Constant and Thomas Southworth of Mass. (245)

17. Gov. Thomas Dudley of Mass. (250) (alternate descent outlined)

18. Anthony Savage of Va. (253)

19. Mrs. Mary Mainwaring Gill (of Md.) (255) (whether she immigrated or died in England)

20-21. George Carrington of Va. and Mrs. Elizabeth Hannah Carrington Willing of Pa. (257)

22. John Snelling of Mass. (268)

23. James Cudworth of Mass. (270)

24. Mrs. Elizabeth Alsop Baldwin (Fowler) of Conn. (272)

25. Mrs. Mary Fox Ellicott of Pa. (279)

26. Mrs. Mary Gye Maverick of Mass. (295) (alternate descent noted and referenced but not outlined)

27-28. Rev. Hugh Peter(s) of Mass. (319) and Mrs. Arabella Maria Smith Dallas of Pa. (320)

29. John Roberts of (Pencoyd) Pa. (323)

30. John Williams of Pa. (324)

31. Robert Lloyd of Pa. (326)

32. Lawrence Smith of Va. (331)

33. Mrs. Mary (prob.) Waller Herndon of Va. (332)

34. Gov. William Leete of Conn. (336)

35. John Goode of Va. (337)

36-39. Mrs. Martha Eltonhead Conway (348), Mrs. Alice Eltonhead (Burnham) Corbin (Creek) and (Lady) Agatha Eltonhead (Kellaway) Wormeley Chichele of Va. and Mrs. Jane Eltonhead (Moryson) Fenwick of Md. (alternate descent outlined)

40-42. Richard More of Mass. (a *Mayflower* passenger) (350), William Wentworth of N.H. (351), and Christopher Lawson of Mass. (351)

43-44. Edward Whalley, regicide, of Mass. and Conn. and John Lovelace, 4th Baron Lovelace, governor of N.Y. (353)

45. Cuthbert Fenwick of Md. (354)

46. Mrs. Thomasine Ward Thompson Buffum of Mass. (355)

47. Dr. Thomas Wynne of Pa. (357)

48. Col. Gerard Fowke of Va. (363)

49. Benjamin Heron of N.C. (367)

50. John Gibbes of Goose Creek, S.C. (377)

51. Thomas Weston of Mass. (378)

52-54. Act. Gov. Robert Brooke of Md., Richard Towneley of N.J. and Mrs. Margaret Frances Towneley of Md. (385-86) (alternate descent noted for Towneley and Mrs. Chase)

55-56. Robert Jones and Mrs. Sidney Rees Roberts of Pa. (392)

57. John Underhill of N.Y. (398)

58-59. Mark Catesby, traveler to the South, and Mrs. Elizabeth Catesby Cocke of Va. (417)

60-61. Walter Norton of Mass. and Henry Norton of Me. (420)

62-63. John Stratton (425) and Mrs. Elizabeth Stratton Thorndike of Mass. (426)

64-68. Robert Gibbs of Mass. (431); John Josselyn, traveler to New England (432); William Strachey, 1st Secretary of the Va. Colony (432); William Strachey of Va. (432); Thomas Colepepper (Culpeper) of Va. (432); and Thomas Colepepper (Culpeper), 2nd Baron Colepepper (Culpeper), governor of Va. (433)

69. Edward Raynsford of Mass. (439)

70. Anthony Collamore of Mass. (444)

71. William Boddie of Va. (460)

72. Thomas Bradbury of Mass. (461)

IV

Having completed my discussion of the genealogical scholarship that lies behind this work, with listings that both evoke the contribution of my colleagues and suggest problems for further study, I now proceed to a further examination of the 350 or so royally descended colonial immigrants who left notable American progeny. The exact number of such immigrants treated herein, I believe, is 348, of whom 103 (30 percent) settled in New England (68, or 20 percent, in Massachusetts; 21, or 6 percent, in Connecticut; 7, or 2 percent, in Rhode Island; 3 in New Hampshire; and 4 in Maine); 128 (37 percent) in the Middle Atlantic states (19, or 5 percent, in New York; 12, or 4 percent, in New Jersey; 60, or 17 percent, in Pennsylvania; 5 in Delaware; and 32, or 9 percent, in Maryland); and 117 (34 percent) in the South (92, or 26 percent, in Virginia; 5 in North Carolina; 15, or 4 percent, in South Carolina; 4 in Georgia; and 1 in Florida). Almost 200 of these 348 -- 195, or 56 percent -- were descendants of the above-discussed Thomas Mowbray, 1st Duke of Norfolk, and Elizabeth FitzAlan, his wife; of Elizabeth FitzAlan and her third husband, Sir Robert Goushill; of Mowbray's or his wife's sisters, double first cousins or aunt, also named above; or of various other cousins of Mowbray and his wife who bore over half their combined ancestry. These 195, of whom 55 settled in New England (38 in Massachusetts, 7 in Connecticut, 7 in Rhode Island, 1 in New Hampshire, and 2 in Maine), 66 in the Middle Atlantic states (11 in New York, 6 in New Jersey, 23 in Pennsylvania, 3 in Delaware, and 23 in Maryland) and 74 in the South (55 in Virginia, 4 in North Carolina, 11 in South Carolina, and 4 in Georgia), shared a sizable quantity of medieval baronial ancestry; sprang, in general, from the center, rather than the periphery, of the English, Scottish or Welsh gentry; and were usually descendants of Edward I (d. 1307), Edward III (d. 1377) or later English or Scottish kings. Over 55 percent, then, of these 348 -- although often Puritans, Quakers, younger sons or cadets (sons or grandsons, etc., of younger sons), clergymen, merchants, or ambitious office holders -- were usually descended from late medieval earls and often nearly related to peers and baronets (a few were such themselves). Descendants of Beauforts, St. Johns, Woodvilles, Nevilles, Sir Henry "Hotspur" Percy or Howards were often 5th (or closer) cousins of Tudor sovereigns, and the colonial descendants of these 195 were frequently 5th to 7th cousins of the ruling Whig families (the "ducal oligarchy") of post-Restoration and eighteenth-century Great Britain. The remaining 153 of these 348, descendants of earlier kings, often shared only a few "strands" of baronial ancestry and sometimes belonged to the middling or lesser gentry -- families who owned only one or a few manors, were mostly non-knighted, did not produce many Tudor peers or perhaps even Stuart baronets, were perhaps "declining" by the time of the English civil war (1640s), and did not often figure in the ancestry of the Augustan ducal oligarchies. Note that three major Tidewater plantation colonies -- Maryland, Virginia, and South Carolina -- claimed 139 (39 percent) of the 348, but fully 89 (45 percent) of the 195.

Of the 348 royally descended colonial immigrants who left notable American progeny, at least 230 -- as I have found to date -- are ancestors of five or more figures treated in the *DAB* (or sometimes *NCAB* or *Who's Who*). Of these 230 -- that 40 percent of the 570 who are, of course, the likeliest forebears of contemporary Americans and thus the subjects herein of keenest interest -- 81 (35 percent) settled in New England (58, or 25 percent, in Massachusetts; 14, or

6 percent, in Connecticut; 5, or 2 percent, in Rhode Island; 3 in New Hampshire; and 1 in Maine); 75 (33 percent) in the Middle Atlantic states (15, or 7 percent, in New York; 6, or 3 percent, in New Jersey; 31, or 13 percent, in Pennsylvania; 4 in Delaware; and 19, or 8 percent, in Maryland); 74 (32 percent) in the South (56, or 24 percent, in Virginia; 3 in North Carolina; 11, or 5 percent, in South Carolina; 3 in Georgia; and 1 in Florida); and (rearranged) 86 (37 percent) in the three major Tidewater colonies. One hundred twenty-five of these 230 were descendants of Mowbray, his wife, their siblings or kinsmen sharing over half their ancestry. Of these 125, 43 settled in New England (33 in Massachusetts, 3 in Connecticut, 5 in Rhode Island, 1 in New Hampshire, and 1 in Maine), 36 in the Middle Atlantic states (8 in New York, 3 in New Jersey, 10 in Pennsylvania, 2 in Delaware, and 13 in Maryland), 46 in the South (33 in Virginia, 3 in North Carolina, 7 in South Carolina, and 3 in Georgia) and (rearranged) 53 in the three major Tidewater colonies. These figures reflect several trends that become even more pronounced as smaller groups of royally descended immigrants with even more notable progeny are considered. New Englanders with royal ancestry left far more notable descendants than such immigrants to the Middle Atlantic states or the South, as one might expect from the prominence of New England in the nineteenth century elites listed below. Since the New York Dutch community included almost no royally-descended immigrants yet traced (the sole exception is Mrs. Sophia van Lodensteyn de Beauvois or Debevoise), the Middle Atlantic group herein is dominated by Pennsylvania Quakers, both English and Welsh. These last, however, and especially the Welsh, leave -- relative to Puritan New Englanders, Tidewater planters, and New York Livingstons -- comparatively few descendants, and the Welsh Quakers herein are mostly descendants of illegitimate children of either David, Prince of Wales, or William FitzRobert, 2nd Earl of Gloucester (themselves grandsons respectively, through other illegitimacies, of Kings John and Henry I of England). Virginia massively dominates the South, but if the three major Tidewater colonies -- Maryland, Virginia, and South Carolina -- are combined, such a region surpasses even New England as a settlement area for immigrants with five or more notable descendants. Virginia also

surpasses New England, but only barely, as a settlement area for immigrants with considerable rather than meager baronial ancestry.

At the next division of immigrants leaving a larger notable progeny, however, New England's dominance emerges clearly. Of the 63 immigrants for whom, after considerable tracing, I can find only 5,6,7,8 or 9 notable descendants, only 8 were New Englanders, but 26 Middle Atlantic colonists, 29 southerners, and 31 immigrants to Maryland, Virginia, or South Carolina. Of the 167 royally descended immigrants who left 10 or more notable descendants, 73 (44 percent) settled in New England (52, or 31 percent, in Massachusetts; 14, or 8 percent, in Connecticut; 5, or 3 percent, in Rhode Island; 1 in New Hampshire; and 1 in Maine); 49 (29 percent) in the Middle Atlantic states (11, or 7 percent, in New York; 4, or 2 percent, in New Jersey; 19, or 11 percent, in Pennsylvania; 2 in Delaware; and 13, or 8 percent, in Maryland); 45 (27 percent) in the South (39, or 23 percent, in Virginia; 1 in North Carolina; 3 in South Carolina; and 2 in Georgia); and (rearranged) 55 in the three major Tidewater colonies. Ninety-two of these 167 were descendants of Mowbray, his wife, their siblings or kinsmen sharing over half their ancestry. Of the 92, 39 settled in New England (30 in Massachusetts, 3 in Connecticut, 5 in Rhode Island, and 1 in Maine), 23 in the Middle Atlantic states (5 in New York, 2 in New Jersey, 6 in Pennsylvania, 1 in Delaware, and 9 in Maryland), 30 in the South (25 in Virginia, 1 in North Carolina, 2 in South Carolina, and 2 in Georgia) and (rearranged) 36 in the three major Tidewater colonies. I might note that Mrs. Barbara Bennet Murray of North Carolina, the sole royally descended immigrant to that state among these 167, only died there; her also royally descended husband, James Murray, moved to Massachusetts and their notable progeny is totally northern.

These 167, the royally descended immigrants to the thirteen colonies who left 10 or more notable descendants -- only 29 percent of the 570 but ancestors of millions of Americans -- can be listed as follows, alphabetically, by colony:

Massachusetts:

    1. Robert Abell

    2-3. Samuel and Judith (Everard) Appleton

4-5. Christopher and Anne (Bainton) Batt

6-7. Griffith and Margaret (Fleming) Bowen

8. Thomas Bradbury

9. Edward Bromfield

10. Mrs. Thomasine Ward Thompson Buffum

11-13. Rev. Peter, Jane (Allen), and Grace (Chetwode) Bulkeley

14. Mrs. Mary Lawrence Burnham

15-16. Edward and Ellen (Newton) Carleton

17. Rev. Charles Chauncey

18. George Curwen

19-20. Gov. Thomas and Katherine (Deighton Hackburne, later Allyn) Dudley

21. Mrs. Olive Welby Farwell

22. Mrs. Jane Lawrence Giddings

23. William Goddard

24. Mrs. Elizabeth Bulkeley Whittingham Haugh

25. Edmond Hawes

26. Mrs. Catherine Hamby Hutchinson

27. Simon Lynde

28. Mrs. Mary Gye Maverick

29. Mrs. Martha Bulkeley Mellowes

30. James Murray (husband of #162)

31. Mrs. Jane Deighton Lugg Negus

32. John Nelson

33. Rev. John Oxenbridge

34. Dr. Richard Palgrave

35. Mrs. Anne Humphrey Palmes (Myles)

36-37. Herbert and Jemima (Waldegrave) Pelham

38. William Poole

39. Mrs. Amy Wyllys Pynchon

40. Edward Raynsford
41-42. Richard and Muriel (Gurdon) Saltonstall
43. Rev. William Sargent
44. Mrs. Mary Launce Sherman
45. Gov. William Shirley (some of whose notable progeny is British)
46-47. Constant and Thomas Southworth
48. Peter Talbot
49. Mrs. Elizabeth Stratton Thorndike
50. Mrs. Jane Haviland Torrey
51. Mrs. Frances Deighton Williams
52. Mrs. Margaret Tyndal Winthrop (some of whose notable progeny is British)

plus Maine (part of Massachusetts until 1820)

53. Joseph Bolles

Connecticut

54. Mrs. Margaret Wyatt Allyn
55. Mrs. Elizabeth Alsop Baldwin (Fowler)
56. Thomas Bressie
57. Obadiah Bruen
58. Rev. John Davenport
59. Mrs. Anne Lloyd Yale Eaton
60. Mrs. Agnes Harris Spencer Edwards
61. Mrs. Mabel Harlakenden Haynes (Eaton)
62. Gov. William Leete
63. Dep. Gov. (of Mass.) Roger Ludlow
64. Oliver Mainwaring
65. Mrs. Alice Freeman Thompson Parke
66. Thomas Trowbridge
67. Thomas Yale

The Royal Descents of 500 Immigrants

Rhode Island

    68. Act. Gov. Jeremiah Clarke

    69. Gov. John Cranston

    70. Mrs. Anne Marbury Hutchinson

    71. Mrs. Katherine Marbury Scott

    72. John Throckmorton

New Hampshire

    73. William Wentworth

New York

    74. Matthew Clarkson

    75. Alexander Hamilton

    76. John Lawrence

    77. Thomas Lawrence

    78. William Lawrence

    79. Robert Livingston the elder

    80. Robert Livingston the younger

    81. Gabriel Ludlow

    82. Walter Rutherford

    83. Robert Sinclair

    84. John Underhill

New Jersey

    85. Edward FitzRandolph

    86. Mrs. Euphan Scott Johnstone

    87-88. William and Isabel (Burnett) Montgomery

Pennsylvania

    89-90. Thomas and Margaret (Davis) Bye

    91. John Cadwalader

    92. James Claypoole

    93. Mrs. Arabella Smith Dallas (who immigrated in 1783)

    94. Mrs. Mary Fox Ellicott

95. Robert Jones
96. Joseph Kirkbride
97-98. Gov. Thomas and Mary (Jones) Lloyd
99. James Logan
100-101. Robert and Rebecca (Owen) Owen
102-103. Hugh and Jane (Owen) Roberts
104-105. John and Gainor (Roberts) Roberts
106. Mrs. Sidney Rees Roberts (daughter-in-law of 104-5) (some of the notable progeny of 104-6 is British)
107. Dr. Thomas Wynne

Delaware

108. Mrs. Margery Maude Fisher
109. Rev. George Ross

Maryland

110. Hon. Anne Arundell Calvert, Baroness Baltimore
111. Cecil Calvert, 2nd Baron Baltimore (husband of 110)
112. Lady Charlotte Lee Calvert, Baroness Baltimore
113. Jane Lowe Sewall Calvert, Baroness Baltimore (some of the notable progeny of 110-13 is British)
114. William Bladen
115. Thomas Boteler (Butler)
116. Act. Gov. Robert Brooke
117. Thomas Gerard
118. Mrs. Mary Mainwaring Gill
119. Mrs. Anne Lovelace Gorsuch
120. Alexander Magruder
121. James Neale
122. Richard Tilghman

Virginia

123. Col. Walter Aston

157. Col. John Waller

158. Mrs. Mary Towneley Warner

159. John Washington of Surry Co.

160. John Washington of Westmoreland Co.

161. Gov. Hon. John West

North Carolina

162. Mrs. Barbara Bennet Murray (wife of #30)

South Carolina

163. John Alston

164. Stephen Bull

165. Gov. Robert Gibbes

Georgia

166. Col. Kenneth Baillie

167. John Irvine

V

      Almost as fascinating as the geographical distribution of the 348 royally descended immigrants who left notable progeny, and as the identification of those who left increasingly greater numbers of such descendants, are the numerous and complex kinships among these 570, and the connections forged in the colonies by intermarriage among their children, grandchildren, and great- or great-great-grandchildren. The charts that form the body of this book delineate at least 85 clusters of near kinsmen -- siblings, uncles/aunts and nieces/nephews, first or second cousins, and for a few immigrants who returned to the "Old World," grandparents or great- or great-great-grandparents and grandchildren or great- or great-great-grandchildren. Over 250 of the 570 belonged to one of these 85 clusters. Three groups -- the Delaware/de la Warr West (pp. 115-7), Ligon/Lygon (pp. 204-6) and Evan Robert Lewis (pp. 305-7) progenies -- included 8 or 9 immigrants. Clusters with 5 or 6 immigrants are Rutherford-Bennet-Murray (pp. 66-67), Wyatt (p. 123), Oxenbridge-Coke-Blennerhasset-Emmet (pp. 125-26),

Tucker (pp. 208-9), Bulkeley (pp. 210-12), Edwards-Roberts (pp. 309-10), Marbury (pp. 350-51, 233) and Lawrence (pp. 455-57).

Furthermore, several dozen fourteenth- or fifteenth-century English, Welsh or Scottish peers, knights or gentlemen were ancestors of between 15 and 50 of these 570. In addition to the myriad Mowbray and FitzAlan descendants mentioned above, among the progeny herein of Edward III, King of England (d. 1377), I have charted 39 immigrant descendants of Elizabeth Mortimer (d. ca. 1417/18) and Sir Henry "Hotspur" Percy and 54 immigrant descendants (including the 21 covered on pp. 35-44) of Joan Beaufort (d. 1440) and Ralph Neville, 1st Earl of Westmoreland. Once in the colonies, moreover, of the 348 royally descended immigrants who left notable progeny, and in only those lines that produced it, 70 percent or more had a child, grandchild, great-grandchild, or great-great-grandchild who married a child, grandchild, great- grandchild, or great-great-grandchild of another of the 348. The early progeny of most of these 70 percent, moreover, made two or more such connections, so even by the time of the American Revolution, major historical figures sometimes had three or more royally descended immigrant ancestors. Beginning with the late nineteenth century, some figures had 10 or more such ancestors. The children of Confederate General Robert Edward Lee and Mary Anne Randolph Custis were descended from Henry and Alice (Eltonhead) Corbin (twice), William Randolph and Henry Isham (twice), Act. Gov. Edmund Jennings, Lawrence Towneley, Mrs. Mary Towneley Warner, Mrs. Sarah Ludlow Carter (twice), Mrs. Anne Lovelace Gorsuch, Col. William Bernard, Gov. Alexander Spotswood, Cecil Calvert, 2nd Baron Baltimore, Hon. Anne Arundell Calvert, Baroness Baltimore, Jane Lowe Sewall Calvert, Baroness Baltimore, Lady Charlotte Lee Calvert, Baroness Baltimore, Charles Calvert alias Lazenby alias Butler, Thomas Gerard, Robert Peyton, and Col. Walter Aston, all of Virginia or Maryland. The children of President Franklin Delano Roosevelt and his cousin (Anna) Eleanor Roosevelt are descendants of Thomas Lawrence, Mrs. Elizabeth Coytmore Tyng, John Nelson, Thomas Southworth, Dr. Richard Palgrave, Mrs. Anne Marbury Hutchinson, Mrs. Catherine Hamby Hutchinson, James Murray, Mrs. Barbara Bennet Murray of N.C., John Irvine of Ga., Col. Kenneth Baillie of Ga., Gabriel Ludlow, Robert Sinclair, and both Robert Livingstons, all except the designated southerners of Massachusetts, Rhode Island, or New York. The Lee offspring had 19 royally descended immigrant ancestors (or, in the case of the Baltimores, figures treated herein as immigrants); the Roosevelts, 15.

The colonial English, Scottish, Welsh and (small) Anglo-Irish contingent of these 570 compose, I wish to suggest, a significant section of the first British colonial gentry. Derived largely from the genealogical center, not the periphery, of their parent gentry, in numerous ways and complexly related when they arrived, often in clusters or following other kinsmen, the royally descended colonial immigrants and their immediate progeny intermarried here just as they would have in England, Scotland, Wales or Ireland. Consisting largely of colony or settlement founders, proprietors, acting or deputy governors, other appointed or elected officials, noted clergymen, large landowners or wealthy merchants, this gentry also divides into four regional elites -- the Puritans of New England; the Hudson Valley and Long Island manorial aristocracy (the least represented of these four elites among the 167 immigrants listed above, but including the Livingstons); the Philadelphia and Main Line Quakers; and the plantation aristocracy of Tidewater Virginia (plus Maryland and to a much lesser extent South Carolina). The first of these elites was clerical and political, later mercantile, and the third was America's first urban oligarchy. A mercantile section of the second elite developed colonial New York City, and the fourth, somewhat urbanized in Baltimore and Charleston, both owned and governed much of the South. From these four colonial elites and this first colonial British gentry are also genealogically derived the bulk of the nineteenth- and twentieth-century groups that dominate much of American history, ie.:

1. The Salem-Boston mercantile "Brahmins" (Peabody-Endicott-Crowninshield-Higginson-Cabot-Lowell), dominant from 1800, or earlier, to 1830.

2. The intellectual aristocracy centered at Harvard (dominant 1830-60), which led the Unitarian, abolitionist, feminist, and other reform movements and produced the literary "flowering of New England"; and at Yale (dominant 1865-1900), which produced many

business leaders (and "Wall Street") and developed social Darwinism and intercollegiate sports. The Harvard elite was often derived from #1, the Yale elite from locally notable families in Connecticut, the Connecticut Valley, and Connecticut-derived upstate New York or the Midwest.

3. The post-Civil War robber-baron industrial oligarchy.

4. The turn-of-the-century eastern inter-city "society" (Astors, Vanderbilts, and Whitneys), centered in New York City and Newport, to some extent a second-generation "gentrification" of #3 above.

5. The early twentieth-century "Social Register," a consolidation of numbers 1-4.

6. The post-World War II suburban upper-middle-class corporation executives, descendants of nineteenth-century "pioneers" and largely associated with new provincial cities and the "Sunbelt" (Miami, Houston and Dallas, Phoenix, Denver, and Los Angeles).

The first and second of these groups are derived almost solely from New England, a region that contributed heavily to the third, fourth, and fifth groups (and somewhat, as the colonial origin of many "pioneers," to the sixth group as well). For the royal descent of various major intellectual, literary reform leaders, and of various tycoons see, in addition to *The Mowbray Connection,* my *NEXUS* "Notable Kin" articles on these topics (4 [1987]:69-73, 159-62, 192-5, 240-44, 6 [1989]:108-12, 202-6, 7 [1990]:26-30, 154-59, 208-13, 8 [1991]:66-70).

VI

Having completed my introduction to royal descent generally, to this book's scope and the types of royally descended immigrants it covers, to the history of this project and the scholarship on which it rests, and to the immigrants themselves, their geographical distribution, numbers of noted descendants, kinships to each other and participation in American history overall -- having covered these major substantive topics, I now move to the more mundane subject of format. The body of this book consists of charts outlining, with numbered generations, the "best" royal descent -- or sometimes two or more nearly equal descents -- of the 570 immigrants discussed above and listed in the "immigrant subject index." The order of the charts is determined by the death year of the king who heads it, most recent first (the few exceptions are noted below). Except for birth and death years of immigrants notable in their own right and treated in the *DAB*, no other dates are used. Places are likewise omitted, except for Scottish lairds or gentlemen, but following each chart is a full list of sources documenting the descent. Over 150 of these sources are abbreviated (an abbreviations list immediately follows the text). In most cases sources for the immigrant's immediate origin are listed first, and then those for each generation and family between immigrant and king, *in backward order from the immigrant.*

Clusters of very near kinsmen, and many immigrants sharing over seven or so generations of ancestors are treated together. Charts for such groups precede those for only one immigrant in the sequence under each king, and groups themselves are arranged by number of immigrants (charts treating six precede those treating five, which precede those treating four, etc.). Both groups and singles among each king's immigrant progeny are arranged geographically -- New England colonists first, then Middle Atlantic settlers, and finally southerners, in the same order for colonies or states as the above list of 167 colonial immigrants who left 10 or more notable descendants. In the list of sources for groups of immigrants, the first immigrant on the chart is the first whose line is documented. The shared ancestry is usually referenced with the first immigrant, or immediately thereafter, and for each additional immigrant, cited sources cover only his or her descent from the shared "stem," *occasionally in forward order* from the ancestry already documented. Groupings were organized for convenience of presentation only, and will probably change somewhat in future editions. For ease of presentation also I chose in a few cases to treat immigrants who shared six or more outlined generations with other immigrants (but were not "very near" kinsmen) as "singles" and simply repeated the mutual lines.

The Royal Descents of 500 Immigrants

As regards "best" royal descents -- those from the most recent king -- within the progeny of the same king (especially that of Edward III or Edward I), elder sons were preferred to younger sons (Lionel of Antwerp to John of Gaunt, John of Gaunt to Edmund of Langley, and Edmund of Langley to Thomas of Woodstock), younger sons to daughters (Thomas of Brotherton or Edmund of Woodstock to their half-sisters Joan and Elizabeth), and the sons of daughters to the daughters of daughters (William de Bohun, 1st Earl of Northampton, to any of his female de Clare first cousins). Legitimate children were preferred to illegitimate children but illegitimate children of later kings were preferred to legitimate children of earlier kings. As it happens, however, all descents herein from Edward III or Edward I (and Henry III) are through *legitimate* children, whereas all lines charted herein from Kings Edward IV, John, Henry II, and Henry I of England, and James V, James IV, and William the Lion, Kings of Scotland, are from illegitimate children (of these kings or of John's son, Richard Plantagenet, King of the Romans).

There are three exceptions to the king-by-death-year order. Descendants of Henry VII, King of England, via his daughter Mary Tudor are treated before descendants of James V, King of Scotland, as the immediate royal-heir kinsmen of Queen Elizabeth I (d. 1603). Descendants of James V of Scotland, all through illegitimate sons, follow as next-of-kin of Mary, Queen of Scots (d. 1587). Descendants of Edward IV, of his brother George Plantagenet, 1st Duke of Clarence, of their sister Anne Plantagenet and Sir Thomas St. Leger, and of their aunt Isabel Plantagenet and Henry Bourchier, Count of Eu and 1st Earl of Essex, precede those of James IV of Scotland as the royal kinsmen of Henry VIII (d. 1547). In addition, descendants of Joan Beaufort, Dowager Queen of Scotland (d. 1445) and her second husband, Sir James Stewart, the "Black Knight of Lorne," are treated before other descendants of Edward III. Two near connections of immigrants to later kings or princes are also charted in the main body of this work -- the line from LaFayette to Queen Paola of the Belgians and her children and the descent from Oglethorpe's sister to the kings of Italy. The line from Mrs. Alice Freeman Thompson Parke to Susan May Williams, wife of Jerome Napoleon Bonaparte, son of the King of Westphalia, is covered as well. An appendix treats the descents of H.M. the Queen and H.M. Queen

The Royal Descents of 500 Immigrants

Elizabeth The Queen Mother from Richard and Anna (Cordray) Bernard, Mrs. Mary Towneley Warner and Col. George Reade, all of Virginia; of H.R.H. The Princess of Wales from Mrs. Alice Freeman Thompson Parke; of princes of Monaco (Louis II and Rainier III) from Rev. John Oxenbridge of Mass.; and of Queen Geraldine of the Albanians and her son from Thomas Trowbridge of Conn. Only one immigrant herein -- Thomas Lewis of Maine, the last -- is *not* descended from an English, Scots or Continental king, but only from early Welsh rulers; Lewis's wife, however, was Mrs. Elizabeth Marshall Lewis of Maine, another of the 570 and a descendant of Edward I.

Whenever I mention doubts about any particular connection, and an alternate lesser descent is fully proved, or in a few cases just to cross-reference some obvious secondary descents (especially for lines from illegitimate children of kings), I have noted that a spouse on one chart is a child, grandchild, etc., of someone on a following chart. Sources for these secondary lines are included among the cited references that follow each chart. Many more secondary descents are often outlined in the *Ancestral Roots* and *Magna Charta Sureties, 1215* series. About a few matters, too, I have been a bit arbitrary. *SETH* (see elsewhere in this volume) replaces the more standard "*q.v.*" I sometimes use the article "de" for persons living after 1400 (who probably did *not* use it themselves) but omit it before a few surnames (Badlesmere, Baliol, Chaworth, Courtenay, Ferrers of Groby, Grey [of Codnor, Powis, Rotherfield, and Wilton], Hastings, Holand, Mortimer, Mowbray, Stafford and possibly others) whose pre-1400 family members probably used it. I also refer to seventeenth-century immigrants with modern terms of address (Mrs. Anne Mauleverer Abbott, etc.) and modern titles (Hon. Anne Arundell Calvert, Baroness Baltimore, Hon. Leonard Calvert, etc.). Catherine is *usually* spelled with a "C," I consistently use Westmoreland instead of Westmorland, and I have omitted the cedilla under the "c" for Francois and Francoise. Other idiosyncracies may be noted by readers and changed, if deemed harmful, in future editions.

I shall conclude this section on format with yet another list -- of the kings from whom descent to these 570 is outlined herein. In order, with death years and the pages on which immigrant progeny appear, and a few notes on their kinship to each other, these are:

lii

The Royal Descents of 500 Immigrants

1. Ferdinand I, King of Roumania, d. 1927 (p. 1)
2. George I, King of Greece, d. 1913 (p. 2)
3. Frederick William III, King of Prussia, d. 1840 (p. 3), great-grandson of
4. Frederick William I, King of Prussia, d. 1740 (p. 4)
5. Victor Amadeus II, King of Sardinia, d. 1730 (pp. 5-6)
6. Joseph I, Holy Roman Emperor, d. 1711 (p. 7)
7. Charles II, King of England, d. 1685 (pp. 8-12), brother of
8. James II, King of England (reigned 1685-88), d. 1701 (pp. 8,13)

   (all descents charted herein of 7 and 8 are through illegitimate children)
9. James I, King of England (and VI, King of Scotland, d. 1625) (p. 14), father of 7 and 8, son-in-law of
10. Frederick II, King of Denmark, d. 1588 (pp. 15-16)
11. Eric XIV, King of Sweden, d. 1577 (p. 17)
12. Henry VII, King of England, d. 1509 (pp. 18-27; pp. 18-21 also cover descendants of William the Silent, Prince of Orange, 1st Stadholder of the Netherlands, d. 1584, and pp. 22-26 cover descendants of Edward Seymour, Baron Beauchamp, heir to the English throne in 1603 according to the will of Henry VIII)
13. James V, King of Scotland, d. 1542 (pp. 28-31), grandfather of 9, grandson of 12
14. Edward IV, King of England, d. 1483 (pp. 32-34), father-in-law of 12

    (all descents charted herein of 13 and 14 are through illegitimate children)
15. George Plantagenet, 1st Duke of Clarence (pp. 35-39); Anne Plantagenet, wife of Sir Thomas St. Leger (pp. 40-44); and Isabel Plantagenet, wife of Henry Bourchier, Count of Eu, 1st Earl of Essex (pp. 45-47) --

brother, sister, and aunt of Kings Edward IV, #14, and Richard III, d. 1485

16. James IV, King of Scotland, d. 1513 (pp. 48-60), son-in-law of 12, father of 13

(all descents charted herein through illegitimate children)

17. John I, King of Denmark, d. 1513 (pp. 61-62), great-uncle of 10

18. Casimir IV, King of Poland, d. 1492 (p. 63)

19. Charles VII, King of France, d. 1461 (pp. 64-65)

20. James II, King of Scotland, d. 1460 (pp. 66-70), grandfather of 16, son of

21. James I, King of Scotland, d. 1437 (pp. 71-78)

22. Charles VI, King of France, d. 1422 (p. 79), father of 19, great-grandfather of 12

23. Henry IV, King of England, d. 1413 (pp. 80-85)

(all through an illegitimate daughter of his son, Humphrey Plantagenet, Duke of Gloucester)

24. Robert III, King of Scotland, d. 1406 (pp. 86-91), father of 21, son of

25. Robert II, King of Scotland, d. 1390 (pp. 92-102)

26. Charles II, King of Navarre, d. 1387 (pp. 103-6)

27. Edward III, King of England, d. 1377 (pp. 107-93, 107-14 through Joan Beaufort, Dowager Queen of Scotland, 115-8 through William Cary and Mary Boleyn, aunt of Queen Elizabeth I), grandfather of 23

28. John II, King of France, d. 1364 (pp. 194-200, 194-98 via Reuss-Ebersdorf and Zinzendorf cousins of Victoria, Queen of Great Britain, d. 1901), grandfather of 22

29. Philip III, King of Navarre, d. 1343 (pp. 201-2), father of 26

30. Robert I, King of Scotland, d. 1329 (p. 203), grandfather of 25

31. Edward I, King of England, d. 1307 (pp. 204-92, 291-92 via John de Foix, 1st Earl of Kendal, and Margaret de Kerdeston, grandparents of Anne de Foix, wife of Ladislaus V, King of Bohemia and Hungary, d. 1516), grandfather of 27

32. Przemysl Ottokar II, King of Bohemia, d. 1278 (pp. 293-94)

33. Henry III, King of England, d. 1272 (pp. 295-96), father of 31

34. St. Louis IX, King of France, d. 1270 (pp. 297-300) (33 and 34 were brothers-in-law, married to sisters), grandfather-in-law of 31

35. Ferdinand III, King of Castile, d. 1252 (pp. 301-2), first father-in-law of 31

36. Alphonso IX, King of Leon, d. 1230 (pp. 303-4), father of 35

37. John "Lackland," King of England, d. 1216 (pp. 305-29, 317-18 via Richard Plantagenet, King of the Romans, his son, and 305-312, 321-24, 326-29 via illegitimate children of David, Prince of North Wales, his grandson), father of 33

38. William the Lion, King of Scotland, d. 1214 (pp. 330-42)

39. Frederick I Barbarossa, Holy Roman Emperor, d. 1190 (pp. 343-44)

40. Henry II, King of England, d. 1189 (pp. 345-64), father of 37

41. Louis VII, King of France, d. 1180 (pp. 365-66) (40 and 41 both married the famed Eleanor of Aquitaine), great-grandfather of 34

42. David I, King of Scotland, d. 1153 (pp. 367-77, 367-70 via sisters of Robert I, King of Scotland, 371-72 via a sister of John Baliol, King of Scotland, d. 1313), grandfather of 38

43. Louis VI, King of France, d. 1137 (pp. 378-81), father of 41

44. Henry I, King of England, d. 1135 (pp. 382-410), grandfather of 40

45. Wladislaw I, King of Poland, d. 1102 (pp. 411-14, 411-13 via an aunt of Michael III, Czar of Russia, d. 1645, 413-14 via a great-aunt of Ivan III, 1st Czar of Russia, d. 1505)

46. Donald III Bane, King of Scotland, d. 1099 (p. 415), uncle of

47. Duncan II, King of Scotland, d. 1094 (p. 416)

48. William I, the Conqueror, King of England, d. 1087 (pp. 417-18), father of 44

49. Henry I, King of France, d. 1060 (pp. 419-30), grandfather of 43

50. Robert II, King of France, d. 1031 (pp. 431-34), father of 49

51. Ethelred II the Unready, King of England, d. 1016 (pp. 435-43, with Mrs. Jerome Napoleon Bonaparte, daughter-in-law of Jerome Bonaparte King of Westphalia, on page 436)

52. Hugh Capet, King of France, d. 996 (pp. 444-54), father of 50

53. Louis IV, King of France, d. 954 (pp. 455-64, with 455-60 and 463-64 possibly descended instead from 52 and a sister of 48)

54. Angharad II, Queen of Powys (whose son Rhywallon, Prince of Powys, d. 1070) (pp. 465-66 -- only Thomas Lewis of Maine, whose wife was descended from 31)

VII

The Royal Descents of 500 Immigrants both stands on its own as the most comprehensive compendium of such American lines to date and is the third of a projected tetralogy of books based in part on the American section of *The Mowbray Connection*. The first of

The Royal Descents of 500 Immigrants

these books, co-authored with William Addams Reitwiesner of the Library of Congress, was *American Ancestors and Cousins of The Princess of Wales* (GPC, 1984). It considered the British royal family as the genealogical centerpiece of the Anglo-American world and examined New England and mid-Atlantic connections of The Princess of Wales and her sons, plus the Virginia ancestors and cousins of H.M. Queen Elizabeth The Queen Mother, as key contemporary reinforcements of a "special kinship" centered on seventeenth-century immigration here but much strengthened since. My second book, *Ancestors of American Presidents* (Carl Boyer 3rd, publisher, 1989), considered the ancestry of our first 40 presidents as a summary of much of the genealogical evolution of the United States (an ancestor table of 41st President William Jefferson Clinton appeared in *NEXUS* 9 [1992]:204-9 and will be abstracted in future editions of my *Presidents* volume). Nineteen presidents were found to be of royal descent, or very likely so, plus the wives or "First Ladies" of eight others. Note, however, that the very tentative line of James Buchanan, Sr., of Pennsylvania, father of the 15th president, is omitted from this compendium -- more research on the Buchanans of Ramelton is required. Also omitted is the proposed descent, doubted by Sir A.R. Wagner, for Hayes and Ford ancestor Thomas Newberry of Massachusetts, also a forebear of Mrs. Ellen Wilson, Mrs. Truman and Mrs. Reagan. The lines of 18 presidents (these 19, less Buchanan) and of Mrs. John Adams, Mrs. W.H. Harrison, Mrs. Grant, Mrs. Garfield, Mrs. Arthur, both Mrs. Wilsons, Mrs. Truman, Mrs. Eisenhower, and Mrs. Reagan from 49 immigrants herein are repeated from that volume. As also appears herein, Mrs. Arthur's Digges descent now seems invalid, but a line from Mrs. Mary (prob.) Waller Herndon is substituted. Royal descents for "First Ladies" Jane Pierce, Edith and Eleanor Roosevelt, Helen Taft and Barbara Bush, plus Martha Jefferson and Alice Roosevelt, Theodore's first wife, all of whose husbands also shared such ancestry, are outlined in *NEXUS* 10 (1993):70-74. Much of the usefulness of *The Royal Descents of 500 Immigrants* to the genealogical public overall, and much of its centrality to American genealogical evolution, is suggested by noting that 26 of our 41 presidents to date, or their wives, provably or probably have royal forebears. This compendium pinpoints the genealogical "connecting tissue" that links the modern

The Royal Descents of 500 Immigrants

U.S. and early medieval Europe. Having earlier examined the current British royal family and American presidents for their central roles I have now covered (herein) a major strand of Anglo-American kinship -- easily the most documented and most nearly allied to Continental Europe, and some think among the most intrinsically interesting as well.

My fourth, forthcoming book, to be published by Carl Boyer 3rd of Santa Clarita, California, will be an edited -- but not condensed or merely selective -- anthology of my "Notable Kin" columns in the NEHGS *NEXUS*. Begun in 1986, with some additions to the Princess of Wales volume published in 1985, this column has been my "genealogical voice" on many subjects. In it I and a few guest contributors -- Michael J. Wood, Richard E. Brenneman, John Anderson Brayton, and David Curtis Dearborn -- have considered the ancestry of well over 100 major figures in American history, plus a few Canadian, British, and Continental figures as well. This anthology will cover notable descendants of many of the immigrants herein, especially the 167 whose progeny includes at least 10 subjects of biographies in the *DAB* or *Who's Who*. Together these four books will offer not only a preview of many descents in *The Mowbray Connection* but also a distillation of much of my life's work to date.

Additions and corrections to this book are, of course, welcome and eagerly anticipated. Most -- but undoubtedly not all -- royal descents of colonial immigrants that have already appeared in printed sources, but are not included herein, have been seen and rejected. I shall be delighted to hear from scholars developing new or "better" lines from either printed or record sources (preferably both). In addition, however, to forwarding such lines to me (for much appreciated inclusion in future editions of this compendium), I also wish to recommend monographic publication -- both because I can then simply cite the book or article, and because the process of composing a monograph often suggests new lines of inquiry or argument. The major American genealogical journals, especially the *Register, TAG*, and *The Genealogist,* are always pleased to publish well-documented, newly-proved royal descents. And I personally stand ready to assist a bit (in person preferably, or via telephone) with finding printed collaboration.

Gary Boyd Roberts

570 Immigrants of Royal Descent:
A Subject Index and Guide

G

H

M

O

P

S

U

V

W

Y

Z

The Royal Descents of 500 Immigrants

1. Ferdinand I, King of Roumania, d. 1927 = Marie of Edinburgh, daughter of Alfred of Great Britain, Duke of Edinburgh (and Marie of Russia), son of Albert, Prince of Saxe-Coburg and Gotha and Victoria, Queen of Great Britain

2. **Ileana of Roumania** (1909-1991), Mother Abbess (known as **Mother Alexandra**) of the Monastery of the Transfiguration, Ellwood City, Pa. = (1) Anton Maria Franz Leopold Blanka Karl Joseph Ignaz Raphael Michael Margareta Nicetas, Archduke of Austria, Prince of Tuscany; (2) Stefan Virgil Issarescu. Her eldest son, Stefan, Archduke of Austria and Prince of Tuscany, is an American citizen as Stefan Habsburg-Lothringen of Farmington, Mich. (= Mary Jerrine Soper).

Sources: Marlene A. Eilers, *Queen Victoria's Descendants* (1987), pp. 102, 189, 192-94, 203; *BRFW* 1:457-58, 344-45.

The Royal Descents of 500 Immigrants

1. George I, King of Greece, d. 1913 = Olga of Russia (paternal grandparents of Philip of Greece and Denmark, Duke of Edinburgh, consort of Elizabeth II, Queen of Great Britain)

2. Nicholas, Prince of Greece and Denmark = Helen of Russia

3. Olga of Greece = Paul (Karadjordjevic), Prince Regent of Yugoslavia, 1st cousin of Alexander I, King of Yugoslavia

4. Elizabeth (Karadjordjevic) of Yugoslavia = Howard Oxenberg of N.Y.

5. **Catherine Oxenberg** (b. 1961) of N.Y., actress, unm.

Sources: *BRFW* 1:543-44, 325-26; *RHS* 2:392-93.

The Royal Descents of 500 Immigrants

1. Frederick William III, King of Prussia, d. 1840 = (1) Louise of Mecklenburg-Strelitz; (2) Augusta von Harrach

2. (by 1) Albert, Prince of Prussia = Marianne of the Netherlands, daughter of William I, King of the Netherlands (and Wilhelmine of Prussia, sister of King Frederick William III), son of William V of Orange, Stadholder of the Netherlands (and Wilhelmine of Prussia, sister of Frederick William II, King of Prussia, and aunt of Frederick William III), son of William IV of Orange, Stadholder of the Netherlands, and Anna of Great Britain, daughter of George II, King of Great Britain, d. 1760, and Caroline of Brandenburg-Anspach

3. Alexandrine of Prussia = William, Duke of Mecklenburg (uncle of Henry, Duke of Mecklenburg, husband of Wilhelmina, Queen of The Netherlands, and son of Paul Frederick, Grand Duke of Mecklenburg-Schwerin, and Alexandrine of Prussia, daughter of Frederick William III, King of Prussia, and Louise of Mecklenburg-Strelitz, above

4. Charlotte of Mecklenburg-Schwerin = Henry XVIII, Prince Reuss-Köstritz

5. Henry XXXVII, Prince Reuss-Köstritz = Anna Christa Stefanie Clemm von Hohenberg

6. **Marianne Charlotte Katharina Stefanie, Princess Reuss-Köstritz** = Avery **Brundage** (1887-1975), president of the U.S. Olympic Association, 1929-53, and of the International Olympic Committee, 1952-72.

Sources: *BRFW* 1:256 and *passim*; *RHS* 2:240-41 and *passim*.

The Royal Descents of 500 Immigrants

1. Frederick William I, King of Prussia, d. 1740 = Sophie Dorothea of Great Britain

2. Ferdinand, Prince of Prussia = 3. Louise of Brandenburg-Schwedt, his niece, daughter of Frederick William, Margrave of Brandenburg-Schwedt and 2. Sophie of Prussia, elder sister of Ferdinand and daughter of Frederick William I, King of Prussia, and Sophie Dorothea of Great Britain, above

3,4. August, Prince of Prussia, d. unm.

4,5. (illegitimate by Auguste Arend, enobled as "von Prillwitz") (Friedrich Wilhelm August) Ludwig von Prillwitz = Georgine Marie Elizabeth Eugenie, Countess von Moltke

5,6. (illegitimate by Edwina Viereck, actress) (**Franz Georg Edwin**) **Louis** (**Withold**) **Viereck** of N.Y. = Laura Viereck, a first cousin (parents of George Sylvester Viereck, 1884-1962, writer and pro-German propagandist, who married Margaret Edith Hein).

Sources: *DAB* (G.S. Viereck), G.S. Viereck, *My Flesh and Blood: A Lyric Autobiography with Indiscreet Annotations* (1931), pp. 236-38; *Gothaisches Genealogisches Taschenbuch der Briefadeligen Häuser* (1915), pp. 739-40 (von Prillwitz); *ES*, charts for Prussia and Brandenburg-Schwedt.

The Royal Descents of 500 Immigrants

1. Victor Amadeus II, King of Sardinia, d. 1730 = (1) Anne Marie of Orleans; (2) Anna Teresa Canali, Marchesa di Spigno

2. (illegitimate by Jeanne Baptiste d'Albret) Victoria Francesca of Savoy, Madamigella di Susa = Victor Amadeus I of Savoy, Prince of Carignan, a cousin, son of Emanuel Philibert, Prince of Carignan (and Angelina Caterina d'Este of Modena), son of Thomas, Prince of Carignan (and Marie of Bourbon-Soissons), son of Charles Emanuel I, Duke of Savoy, and Catherine of Spain, daughter of Philip II, King of Spain, d. 1598, and Elizabeth of France

3. Louis Victor of Savoy, Prince of Carignan = Christine Henrietta of Hesse-Rheinfels-Rotenberg

4. Leopolda of Savoy-Carignan (great-aunt of Charles Albert, King of Sardinia, and great-great aunt of this latter's son, Victor Emanuel II, King of Italy) = Giovanni Andrea, Prince Doria-Pamfili-Landi (Andrew IV Doria-Pamphili-Landi, 2nd Prince of Torriglia)

5. Luigi Doria-Pamfili-Landi, Prince of Valmontore (John Andrew V Doria-Pamphili-Landi, 3rd Prince of Torriglia) = Teresa Orsini of Gravina

6. Leopoldina Doria-Pamfili-Landi = Sigismundo, Prince Chigi-Albani (Sigismund V Chigi-Albani, 6th Prince of Farnese)

7. Teresa Chigi-Albani = Guilio Torlonia, 2nd Duke of Poli and Guadagnolo

8. Marino Torlonia, 4th Prince of Civitella-Cesi = Mary Elsie Moore of N.Y.

9. **Marina Torlonia** of N.Y. = (1) Francis Xavier **Shields**; (2) Edward W. **Slater**. Marina's son, Francis Alexander Shields, married Teri Schmon and is the father of (Christa) Brooke (Camille) Shields (b. 1965), model and actress.

Sources: Daniel MacGregor, *Brooke's Book: Ancestry of Brooke Shields* (privately distributed, 1988); *BRFW* 1:360, 362-63 (generations 1-4); Christoph Weber, *Kardinäle und Prälaten in den Letzten Jahrzehnten des Kirchenstaates* (1978), tafel 34 (Doria-Pamphili) and tafel 3 (Albani/Chigi); *GHdesA*, Fürstliche Häuser, Band IV (1956), pp. 530, 532, and newspaper accounts (*N.Y. Times*, etc.) of the marriage of Marina Torlonia and Francis Xavier Shields.

The Royal Descents of 500 Immigrants

1. Joseph I, Holy Roman Emperor, d. 1711 = Wilhelmine Amalie of Brunswick-Lüneburg

2. Maria Josepha of Austria = Frederick Augustus II, Elector of Saxony, (elected) King of Poland, d. 1763

3. Francis Xavier of Saxony = Clara Spinucci, Countess von der Lausitz

4. Maria Christina Sabina of Saxony, Countess von der Lausitz = Camillo (VIII) Massimiliano Massimo, Prince of Arsoli

5. Camillo Vittorio Emanuele Massimo, Prince of Arsoli = Giacinta della Porta Rodiani

6. Maria Francesca Massimo = Ranieri Bourbon del Monte, Prince of San Faustino

7. Carlo Bourbon del Monte, Prince of San Faustino = Jane Allen Campbell of Montclair, N.J.

8. Virginia Bourbon del Monte = Edoardo Agnelli

9. Clara Agnelli (sister of Giovanni Agnelli, the Italian industrialist and head of Fiat) = Tassilo, Prince zu Fürstenberg, nephew of Maximilian Egon II, Prince zu Fürstenberg, the "Beer Baron," adviser and friend of William II, German Emperor, and half-nephew of Louis II, Prince of Monaco

10. **(Eduard) Egon (Peter Paul Giovanni), Prince zu Fürstenberg** (b. 1946) of N.Y., fashion designer = Diane Halfin, known as Diane von Fürstenberg (b. 1946), fashion designer.

Sources: *RHS* 2:8-9, 13, 62, 66, 71-72; *Who's Who in America,* recent editions (Egon Edvard Furstenberg).

The Royal Descents of 500 Immigrants

1. Charles II, King of England, d. 1685 = Catherine of Braganza

1. James II, King of England, reigned 1685-88, d. 1701 = (1) Anne Hyde; (2) Mary of Modena

2. (illegitimate by Barbara Villiers, Duchess of Cleveland) Charlotte Fitzroy = Edward Henry Lee, 1st Earl of Lichfield

2. (illegitimate by Catherine Sidley, Countess of Dorchester) Catherine Darnley = James Annesley, 3rd Earl of Anglesey

3. George Henry Lee, 2nd Earl of Lichfield = Frances Hales

3. Catherine Annesley = William Phipps

4. Charlotte Lee = Henry Dillon, 11th Viscount Dillon

4. Constantine Phipps, 1st Baron Mulgrave = Lepell Hervey

5. Charles Dillon-Lee, 12th Viscount Dillon =

5. Henrietta Maria Phipps

6. Henry Augustus Dillon-Lee, 13th Viscount Dillon = Henrietta Browne

7. Henrietta Maria Dillon-Lee = Edward John Stanley, 2nd Baron Stanley of Alderley

8. Henrietta Blanche Stanley = David Graham Drummond Ogilvy, 7th Earl of Airlie

9. Clementina Gertrude Helen Ogilvy = Algernon Bertram Freeman-Mitford, 1st Baron Redesdale

10. David Bertram Ogilvy Freeman-Mitford, 2nd Baron Redesdale = Sydney Bowles

11. **Hon. Jessica Lucy Mitford**, known as Jessica Mitford (b. 1917) of Calif., writer = (1) Esmond Marcus David **Romilly**; (2) Robert Edward **Treuhaft.**

Sources: *CP* (Lichfield, Dillon, Anglesey, Mulgrave, Stanley of Alderley, Airlie, Redesdale); *BP* (Redesdale); *Who's Who in America,* recent editions (Jessica Mitford).

The Royal Descents of 500 Immigrants

1. Charles II, King of England, d. 1685 = Catherine of Braganza

2. (illegitimate by Barbara Villiers, Duchess of Cleveland) Charlotte Fitzroy = Edward Henry Lee, 1st Earl of Lichfield

3. **Lady Charlotte Lee** = (1) Benedict Leonard **Calvert**, 4th Baron Baltimore, proprietor of Maryland, ARD, SETH; (2) Christopher **Crewe**

4. (by 1) Charles Calvert, 5th Baron Baltimore, colonial governor of Md. = Mary Janssen

5. Hon. Caroline Calvert = Sir Robert Eden, 1st Bt. (1741-1784), colonial governor of Md., ARD, SETH.

5. (illegitimate by ----) Benedict "Swingate" Calvert (of Md.) = Elizabeth Calvert, daughter of Charles Calvert alias Lazenby alias Butler, colonial governor of Md., ARD, SETH, and Rebecca Gerard. Among the children of Benedict and Elizabeth, Eleanor Calvert married firstly John Parke Custis, step-son of George Washington, 1st U.S. President, SETH, and son of Daniel Parke Custis and Martha Dandridge. According to G.H.S.L. Washington (*NEHGR* 104[1950]:175, reprinted in *EO* 2:3:413) the mother of Benedict "Swingate" Calvert was Melusina de Schulenberg, Countess of Walsingham and wife of Philip Dormer Stanhope, 4th Earl of Chesterfield, the man of letters, illegitimate daughter of George I, King of Great Britain, d. 1727, and Ermengarde Melusina de Schulenberg, Duchess of Kendal.

Sources: *MCS4*, line 17C and *GVFVM* 2:621-27; *MG* 1:140-41, 159-61; *CB & BP* (Eden of Maryland, later also of West Auckland, baronets).

1. Charles II, King of England, d. 1685 = Catherine of Braganza

2. (illegitimate by Mary Davies) Mary Tudor = Edward Radcliffe, 2nd Earl of Derwentwater

3. James Radcliffe, 3rd Earl of Derwentwater = Anna Maria Webb

4. Anna Maria Barbara Radcliffe = Robert James Petre, 8th Baron Petre

5. Catherine Petre = George Fieschi Heneage

6. George Robert Heneage = Frances Anne Ainslie

7. George Fieschi Heneage = Frances Tasburgh

8. **Charles Heneage = Agnes Elizabeth Winona Leclerq Joy** of Vt., known as **Princess (Agnes Elizabeth Winona Leclerq Joy** of) **Salm-Salm** (1840-1912), adventuress who attempted the rescue of the Emperor Maximilian of Mexico (her 2nd husband; she = (1) Felix Constantin Alexander Johann Nepomuk, Prince of Salm-Salm, ARD, SETH).

Sources: *BP* (Heneage) and *CP* (Heneage, Petre, Derwentwater); *Clarence,* pp. 384-85 (where Charles Heneage is unfortunately omitted), 425; *BLG,* 8th ed. (1894), p. 935 and *DAB* (A.E.W.L. Joy, Princess Salm-Salm).

The Royal Descents of 500 Immigrants

1. Charles II, King of England, d. 1685 = Catherine of Braganza

2. (illegitimate by Louise Renée de Penancoët de Kéroualle, Duchess of Portsmouth) Charles Lennox, 1st Duke of Richmond and Lennox = Anne Brudenell

3. Charles Lennox, 2nd Duke of Richmond and Lennox = Sarah Cadogan

4. Lord George Henry Lennox = Louisa Kerr

5. Charles Lennox, 4th Duke of Richmond and Lennox = Charlotte Gordon, daughter of Alexander Gordon, 4th Duke of Gordon (and Jane Maxwell), son of Cosmo George Gordon, 3rd Duke of Gordon, and Catherine Gordon, daughter of William Gordon, 2nd Earl of Aberdeen, and Susan Murray, daughter of John Murray, 1st Duke of Atholl, and Catherine Hamilton, SETH

6. Lord Arthur Lennox = Adelaide Constance Campbell

7. Constance Charlotte Elisa Lennox = Sir George Russell, 4th Bt.

8. Marie Clotilde Russell = Hon. Arthur Ernest Guinness

9. Maureen Constance Guinness = Basil Sheridan Hamilton-Temple-Blackwood, 4th Marquess of Dufferin and Ava

10. **Lady Caroline Maureen Hamilton-Temple-Blackwood,** known as Caroline Blackwood (b. 1931), sometime of N.Y., writer = (1) Lucian Michael **Freud** (b. 1922), painter, grandson of Sigmund Freud, the founder of psychoanalysis; (2) Israel **Citkowitz** (1909-1974), composer; (3) Robert (Traill Spence) **Lowell** (IV) (1917-1977), the American poet.

Sources: *CP* (Dufferin and Ava, Richmond, Gordon, Aberdeen, Atholl), *BP* (Dufferin and Ava, Iveagh, Russell of Swallowfield, baronets, and Richmond) and *BP*, recent editions (Dufferin and Ava). See also *BRB*, tables I, LXXXII, CIV, CVIII, CIX, pp. 1, 48, 64-67, 467.

The Royal Descents of 500 Immigrants

1. Charles II, King of England, d. 1685 = Catherine of Braganza

2. (illegitimate by Barbara Villiers, Duchess of Cleveland) Henry Fitzroy, 1st Duke of Grafton = Isabella Bennet

2. (illegitimate by Eleanor "Nell" Gwynn) Charles Beauclerk, 1st Duke of St. Albans = Diana de Vere

3. Charles Fitzroy, 2nd Duke of Grafton = Henrietta Somerset

3. Lord Sidney Beauclerk = Mary Norris

4. Lord Augustus Fitzroy = Elizabeth Cosby, dau. of William Cosby, colonial governor of N.Y. and N.J., ARD, SETH, and Grace Montagu

4. Topham Beauclerk = Diana Spencer, great-granddaughter of John Churchill, 1st Duke of Marlborough, the victor at Blenheim

5. Augustus Henry Fitzroy, 3rd Duke of Grafton, British "prime minister" = Elizabeth Wrottesley

5. Charles George Beauclerk = Emily Charlotte Ogilvie

6. Lord Henry Fitzroy = Caroline Pigot

7. Henry Fitzroy   =   6.   Jane Elizabeth Beauclerk

7,8. Blanche Adeliza Fitzroy = Robert Francis St. Clair-Erskine, 4th Earl of Rosslyn

8,9. Millicent Fanny St. Clair-Erskine = Cromartie Leveson-Gower, 4th Duke of Sutherland

9,10. Rosemary Millicent Leveson-Gower = William Humble Eric Ward, 3rd Earl of Dudley

10,11. Hon. Peter Alistair Ward = Claire Leonora Baring

11,12. **Rachel (Claire) Ward** (b. 1957) of Calif., actress = Bryan Brown (b. 1947), actor.

Sources: *BP* (Dudley, Sutherland, Rosslyn, Grafton, St. Albans).

The Royal Descents of 500 Immigrants

1. James II, King of England, reigned 1685-88, d. 1701 = (1) Anne Hyde; (2) Mary of Modena

2. (illegitimate by Arabella Churchill, sister of John Churchill, 1st Duke of Marlborough, the soldier and hero of Blenheim) Henrietta Fitz James = Piers Butler, 3rd Viscount Galmoye

3. (illegitimate, born before the marriage of his parents -- an hypothesis, perhaps untenable, of G.H.S.L. Washington) **Charles Calvert alias Lazenby alias Butler,** colonial governor of Md. = Rebecca Gerard, daughter of John Gerard (and Elizabeth ----), son of Thomas Gerard of Md., ARD, SETH and Susannah Snow.

Sources: *NEHGR* 104(1950):175 (reprinted in *EO*2:3:413); *CP* (Galmoye); E.W. Beitzell, *The Cheseldine Family: Historical* (1949), pp. 8, 10. Except for the above hypothesis of G.H.S.L. Washington, Governor Charles Calvert is usually thought to be an illegitimate son of Charles Calvert, 3rd Baron Baltimore, governor of Maryland, ARD, SETH (husband of Mrs. Jane Lowe Sewall); see *TG* 9 (1988):69-70.

The Royal Descents of 500 Immigrants

1. James I, King of England (and VI, King of Scotland), d. 1625 = Anne of Denmark

2. Elizabeth of England = Frederick V of the Palatinate, Elector Palatine of the Rhine, (elected) King of Bohemia, d. 1632

3. Edward of the Palatinate = Anna Gonzaga of Nevers and Mantua

4. Louise Marie of the Palatinate = Charles Theodore, Prince of Salm-Neufville

5. Louis Otto, Prince of Salm-Neufville = Albertine Johannette of Nassau-Hadamar.

6. Dorothea of Salm-Neufville = Nicholas Leopold, Prince of Salm-Salm

6. Christina of Salm-Neufville = Joseph, Landgrave of Hesse-Rheinfels-Rotenburg

7. Maximilian, Prince of Salm-Salm, Duke of Hoogstraeten = 7. Louise of Hesse-Rheinfels-Rotenburg

8. Constantin, Prince of Salm-Salm = Victoria Felicitas of Löwenstein-Wertheim-Rochefort

9. Florentin, Prince of Salm-Salm = Flamina Rossi

10. Felix Constantin Alexander Johann Nepomuk, Prince of **Salm-Salm = Agnes Elizabeth Winona Leclerq Joy** of Vt., known as Princess (Agnes Elizabeth Winona Leclerq Joy of) Salm-Salm (1840-1912), adventuress who attempted the rescue of the Emperor Maximilian of Mexico (her 1st husband; she = 2) Charles Heneage, ARD, SETH).

Sources: *RHS* 1:3, 7, 151-53, 162.

The Royal Descents of 500 Immigrants

1. Frederick II, King of Denmark, d. 1588 = Sophie of Mecklenburg-Güstrow (parents of Anne of Denmark, wife of James I, King of England)

2. Augusta of Denmark = John Adolf, Duke of Holstein-Gottorp

2. Elizabeth of Denmark = Henry Julius, Duke of Brunswick-Wolfenbüttel

3. Frederick III, Duke of Holstein-Gottorp = Marie Elizabeth of Saxony

3. Elizabeth of Brunswick-Wolfenbüttel = John Philip, Duke of Saxe-Altenburg

4. Magdalene Sybil of Holstein-Gottorp = Gustav Adolf, Duke of Mecklenburg-Güstrow

4. Elizabeth Sophie of Saxe-Altenburg = Ernest I, Duke of Saxe-Gotha

5. Christine of Mecklenburg-Güstrow = Louis Christian I, Count of Stolberg-Gedern

5. Elizabeth Dorothea of Saxe-Gotha = Louis VI, Landgrave of Hesse-Darmstadt

6. Frederica Charlotte of Stolberg-Gedern = Frederick Ernest, Count of Solms-Laubach

6. Ernest Louis, Landgrave of Hesse-Darmstadt = Dorothea Charlotte of Brandenburg-Anspach

7. Christian August, Count of Solms-Laubach = Elizabeth Amalie of Isenburg

7. Louis VIII, Landgrave of Hesse-Darmstadt = Charlotte of Hanau-Lichtenberg

8. Sophie Christine Wilhelmine of Solms-Laubach = Frederick William Ernest, Prince of Solms-Braunfels

8. George William, Landgrave of Hesse-Darmstadt = Louise of Leiningen-Heidesheim

9. Frederica of Hesse-
Darmstadt = Charles II,
Grand Duke of
Mecklenburg-Strelitz,
brother of (Sophie)
Charlotte of
Mecklenburg-Strelitz,
wife of George III,
King of Great Britain
(Frederica and Charles II
were parents of Louise of
Mecklenburg-Strelitz,
wife of Frederick
William III, King of
Prussia)

9. Frederick, Prince of   = 10. Frederica of
   Solms-Braunfels   Mecklenburg-Strelitz.
                               She m. (3) Ernest
                               Augustus, King of
                               Hanover

10,11. (Frederick William) **Charles** (Louis George Alfred
Alexander), **Prince of Solms-Braunfels**, known as **Prince
Carl of Solms-Braunfels** (1812-1875), founder of New
Braunfels and German colonization in Texas, where he
resided 1 July 1844-15 May 1845 = (Marie Josephine)
Sophie, Princess of Löwenstein-Wertheim-Rosenberg.
Note that Prince Carl was a 1st cousin of William I,
German Emperor, and a 2nd cousin of Victoria, Queen
of Great Britain.

Sources: C.W. and E.H. Geue, *A New Land Beckoned, German
Immigration to Texas, 1844-1847* (rev. ed., 1972), p. 20 esp.; *ES*,
charts for Solms-Braunfels, Solms-Laubach, Stolberg-Gedern,
Mecklenburg, Holstein, Hesse-Darmstadt, Saxe-Gotha, Saxe-
Altenburg, Brunswick, and Denmark, plus any *Almanach de Gotha*,
1812-75, for Prince Carl himself.

The Royal Descents of 500 Immigrants

1. Eric XIV, King of Sweden, d. 1577, son of Gustav I (Vasa), King of Sweden and Katherine of Saxe-Lauenburg = Katherine Månsdotter
2. (illegitimate by Agda Persdotter) Constantia Eriksdotter = Henrik Frankelin
3. Maria Catharina Frankelin = Agders Koskull
4. Erik Koskull = Anna Maria Gyllensÿärd
5. Anders, Baron Koskull = Anna Catharina Stromberg
6. Eleonora, Baroness Koskull = Claes Didrik Breitholtz
7. Catharina Mariana Breitholtz = Carl Gustaf Hammarskjöld
8. Carl Ake Hammarskjöld = Charlotta Eleonora Rääf i Smaland
9. Knut Vilhelm Hammarskjöld = Maria Louisa Cecilia Vilhelmina Cöster
10. (Knut) Hjalmar (Leonard) Hammarskjöld, prime minister of Sweden (1914-17), diplomat = Agnes Maria Caroline Almquist
11. **Dag (Hjalmar Agne Carl) Hammarskjöld** (1905-1961), Swedish economist and statesman, second Secretary-General of the United Nations (and resident of New York City), 1953-61, d. unm.

Sources: *Elgenstierna,* vol. 3, pp. 470-73, vol. 1, p. 606, vol. 4, pp. 241-44, vol. 2, p. 817 (Hammarskjöld, Breitholtz, Koskull, Frankelin); *ES* (Sweden).

The Royal Descents of 500 Immigrants

1. Henry VII, King of England, d. 1509 = Elizabeth Plantagenet

2. Princess Mary Tudor = Charles Brandon, 1st Duke of Suffolk

3. Eleanor Brandon = Henry Clifford, 2nd Earl of Cumberland

4. Margaret Clifford = Henry Stanley, 4th Earl of Derby

5. William Stanley, 6th Earl of Derby = Elizabeth Vere

6. James Stanley, 7th Earl of Derby = Charlotte de la Trémoille, daughter of Claude de la Trémoille, Duc de Thouars, and Charlotte of Nassau-Dillenburg, daughter of William the Silent, Prince of Orange, 1st Stadholder of the Netherlands (d. 1584), and Charlotte of Bourbon-Montpensier, a second cousin once removed of Henry IV, King of France

7. Amelia Sophia Stanley = John Murray, 1st Marquess of Atholl

8. Charles Murray, 1st   8. William Murray, 2nd
   Earl of Dunmore   Baron Nairne =
   = Catherine Watts   Margaret Nairne

9. William Murray, 3rd   =   9. Catherine Murray
   Earl of Dunmore

10. **John Murray, 4th Earl of Dunmore** (1730-1809), colonial governor of N.Y. and Va. = Lady Charlotte Stewart, see below.

9. Anne Murray (sister of the 3rd Earl of Dunmore) = John Cochrane, 4th Earl of Dundonald

10. Catherine Cochrane = Alexander Stewart, 6th Earl of Galloway

11. **Lady Charlotte Stewart** = John **Murray**, 4th Earl of Dunmore (1730-1809), colonial governor of N.Y. and Va., see above.

11. John Stewart, 7th Earl of Galloway = Anne Dashwood

12. George Stewart, 8th   12. Susan Stewart = George
    Earl of Galloway   Spencer-Churchill,
    = Jane Paget   5th Duke of Marlborough

13. Jane Stewart   =   13. George Spencer-
                                   Churchill, 6th Duke of
                                   Marlborough

14. John Winston Spencer-Churchill, 7th Duke of
    Marlborough = Frances Anne Emily Vane-Stewart

15. Cornelia Henrietta Maria Spencer-Churchill = Ivor
    Bertie Guest, 1st Baron Wimborne

16. Hon. Frederick Edward Guest = Amy Phipps of
    Pittsburgh

17. **Winston Frederick Churchill Guest** (1906-1982) of N.Y.,
    sportsman = (1) Helena Woolworth McCann,
    granddaughter of department store magnate Frank
    Winfield Woolworth and first cousin of Barbara Hutton;
    (2) Lucy Douglas Cochrane.

17. **Raymond Richard Guest** (1907-1992) of Va., U.S.
    diplomat = (1) Elizabeth Sturges Polk; (2) Mrs. Ellen
    Tuck French Astor; (3) Princess Caroline Cécile
    Alexandrine Jeanne Murat, daughter of Prince
    Alexandre Michel Eugène Joachim Napoléon Murat (and
    Yvonne Noële Marie Gillois), son of Joachim Napoléon,
    5th Prince Murat (and Marie Cécile Michelle Ney), son
    of Joachim Joseph Napoléon, 4th Prince Murat (and
    Maley Louise Caroline Frédérique Berthier), son of
    Lucien Charles Joseph Napoléon, 3rd Prince Murat (and
    Caroline Georgina Fraser of Bordentown, N.J.), son of
    Joachim Murat, 1st Prince Murat, and Marie Annonciade
    Caroline Bonaparte, Princess of France, sister of
    Napoleon I, Emperor of the French.

8. John Murray, 1st Duke of Atholl (brother of the 1st Earl of Dunmore and Lord Nairne) = Catherine Hamilton

9. John Murray, 3rd Duke of Atholl = Jean Frederick   9. Lord George Murray = Emilia Murray

10. Charlotte Murray, Baroness Strange, Lady of the Isle of Man   =   10. John Murray, 4th Duke of Atholl

11. Lord George Murray = Anne Charlotte Grant

12. Caroline Leonora Murray = Henry Stephen Fox-Strangways, 3rd Earl of Ilchester

13. Theresa Anne Maria Fox-Strangways = Edward St. Vincent Digby, 9th Baron Digby

14. Edward Henry Trafalgar Digby, 10th Baron Digby = Emily Beryl Sissy Hood

15. Edward Kenelm Digby, 11th Baron Digby = Constance Pamela Alice Bruce

16. **Hon. Pamela Beryl Digby, known as Mrs. Pamela Beryl Digby Spencer-Churchill Hayward Harriman** (b. 1920), diplomat, of N.Y. and Washington, D.C. = (1) Randolph Frederick Edward Spencer-Churchill (1911-1968), British M.P., author, biographer of his father, Sir Winston Leonard Spencer-Churchill, the statesman; (2) Leland Hayward (1902-1971), theatrical producer; (3) (William) Averell Harriman (1891-1986), governor of N.Y., U.S. Secretary of Commerce, diplomat.

8. Amelia Murray (sister of the 1st Duke of Atholl, the 1st Earl of Dunmore, and Lord Nairne) = Hugh Fraser, 9th Baron Lovat

9. Catherine Fraser = Sir William Murray, 3rd Bt.

10. Catherine Murray = Sir Thomas Moncreiffe, 3rd Bt.

11. Sir William Moncreiffe, 4th Bt. = Clara Guthrie

12. Sir Thomas Moncreiffe, 5th Bt. = Elizabeth Ramsay

13. Sir David Moncreiffe, 6th Bt. = Helen Mackay

14. Sir Thomas Moncreiffe, 7th Bt. = Louisa Hay
15. Helen Moncreiffe = Sir Charles John Forbes, 4th Bt.
16. Evelyn Elizabeth Forbes = William Dodge James
17. **Audrey Evelyn James,** sometime of N.Y. = (1) Muir Dudley **Coats;** (2) Marshall **Field** III (1893-1956), Chicago newspaper publisher and grandson of department store magnate Marshall Field I; (3) Peter **Pleydell-Bouverie.**

Sources: *BRB,* tables I, LXXXII, CIV, CXIII-CXV, CXXIII, pp. 1, 48, 64-65, 69-71, 75 (Dunmore and his wife); CXV, CXVIII, pp. 71-72, 498-99, *BP* (Wimborne, Marlborough) and *BRFW* 1:121, 123-24 (the Guest brothers); CIV, CV, pp. 64-66, 453-54 and *BP* (Digby) (Mrs. Harriman); CIV, CXXVII, CXXXI, CXXXII, pp. 64, 77, 79, 555-56, *BP* (Moncreiffe and Forbes of Newe, baronets) and *BLG* (James of West Dean Park).

The Royal Descents of 500 Immigrants

1. Henry VII, King of England, d. 1509 = Elizabeth Plantagenet

2. Princess Mary Tudor = Charles Brandon, 1st Duke of Suffolk

3. Frances Brandon = Henry Grey, 1st Duke of Suffolk

4. Katherine Grey (sister of Lady Jane Grey, aspirant to the English crown) = Edward Seymour, 1st Earl of Hertford

5. Edward Seymour, Baron Beauchamp (whose progeny were heirs to the English throne after the descendants of James I) = Honora Rogers

6. William Seymour, 2nd Duke of Somerset = Frances Devereux

7. Mary Seymour = Heneage Finch, 3rd Earl of Winchilsea

8. Frances Finch = Thomas Thynne, 1st Viscount Weymouth

9. Frances Thynne = Sir Robert Worsley, 4th Bt.

10. Frances Worsley = John Carteret, 1st Earl of Granville, British Prime Minister

11. Georgiana Caroline Carteret = Hon. John Spencer

12. John Spencer, 1st Earl Spencer = Margaret Georgiana Poyntz

13. Georgiana Spencer = William Cavendish, 5th Duke of Devonshire

14. Georgiana Dorothy Cavendish = George Howard, 6th Earl of Carlisle, see below

15. Harriet Elizabeth Georgiana Howard = George Granville Sutherland-Leveson-Gower, 2nd Duke of Sutherland, see below

16. Elizabeth Georgiana Sutherland-Leveson-Gower = George Douglas Campbell, 8th Duke of Argyll

17. Lord Walter Campbell = Olivia Rowlandson Milns

18. Douglas Walter Campbell = Aimee Marie Suzanne Lawrence

19. Ian Douglas Campbell, 11th Duke of Argyll = Janet Gladys Aitken

20. **Lady Jeanne Louise Campbell** of N.Y. and S.C. = (1) Norman **Mailer** (b. 1923), the American novelist (his 3rd wife); (2) John Sergeant **Cram.**

3. Eleanor Brandon (sister of Frances) = Henry Clifford, 2nd Earl of Cumberland

4. Margaret Clifford = Henry Stanley, 4th Earl of Derby

5. Ferdinando Stanley, 5th Earl of Derby = Alice Spencer

6. Frances Stanley = John Egerton, 1st Earl of Bridgwater

7. John Egerton, 2nd Earl of Bridgwater = Elizabeth Cavendish

8. John Egerton, 3rd Earl of Bridgwater = Jane Powlett

9. Scroope Egerton, 1st Duke of Bridgwater = Rachel Russell

10. Louisa Egerton = Granville Leveson-Gower, 1st Marquess of Stafford

11. Margaret Caroline Leveson-Gower = Frederick Howard, 5th Earl of Carlisle

12. George Howard, 6th Earl of Carlisle = Georgiana Dorothy Cavendish, see above

11. George Granville Leveson-Gower, 1st Duke of Sutherland (brother of the Countess of Carlisle) = Elizabeth Gordon, Countess of Sutherland

12. George Granville Sutherland-Leveson-Gower, 2nd Duke of Sutherland = Harriet Elizabeth Georgiana Howard, his cousin, see above

12. Charlotte Sophia Sutherland-Leveson-Gower (sister of the 2nd Duke of Sutherland) = Henry Charles Fitzalan-Howard, 13th Duke of Norfolk

13. Edward George Fitzalan-Howard, 1st Baron Howard of Glossop = Augusta Talbot

14. Angela Mary Charlotte Fitzalan-Howard = Marmaduke Francis Constable-Maxwell, 11th Baron Herries

15. Angela Mary Constable-Maxwell = James Eric Drummond, 16th Earl of Perth, known earlier as Sir Eric Drummond, Secretary-General of the League of Nations

16. **Lady Margaret Gwendolen Mary Drummond** of Washington, D.C. = John **Walker** (b. 1906), director of the National Gallery of Art, 1956-1969.

Sources: *BRB*, tables I, XIV, XXIV, XXXII, XXXVII, XXXVIII, LXXXII, LXXXIII, LXXXV, pp. 1, 13, 18, 22, 24-25, 48-50, 230, 371, 276 and *BP* (Argyll) (Lady J.L.C.M. Cram); table LXXXIII, pp. 49, 371-72 and *BP* (Norfolk, Howard of Glossop, Herries, Perth) (Lady M.G.M.D. Walker).

The Royal Descents of 500 Immigrants

1. Henry VII, King of England, d. 1509 = Elizabeth Plantagenet

2. Princess Mary Tudor = Charles Brandon, 1st Duke of Suffolk

3. Frances Brandon = Henry Grey, 1st Duke of Suffolk

4. Katherine Grey (sister of Lady Jane Grey, aspirant to the English crown) = Edward Seymour, 1st Earl of Hertford

5. Edward Seymour, Baron Beauchamp (whose progeny were heirs to the English throne after the descendants of James I) = Honora Rogers

6. Francis Seymour, 1st Baron Seymour of Trowbridge = Frances Prynne

7. Charles Seymour, 2nd Baron Seymour of Trowbridge = Elizabeth Alington

8. Charles Seymour, 6th Duke of Somerset = Elizabeth Percy

9. Catherine Seymour = Sir William Wyndham, 3rd Bt.

10. Charles Wyndham, 1st Earl of Egremont = Alicia Maria Carpenter

11. Elizabeth Alicia Maria Wyndham = Henry Herbert, 1st Earl of Carnarvon

12. Hon. William Herbert = Letitia Dorothea Allen

13. **Henry William Herbert** (1807-1858) of N.Y., field sports writer under the pseudonym "Frank Forrester" = (1) Sarah Barker; (2) Adela R. Budlong.

12. Henry George Herbert, 2nd Earl of Carnarvon (brother of Hon. William Herbert) = Elizabeth Acland

13. Henry John George Herbert, 3rd Earl of Carnarvon = Henrietta Anna Howard

14. Eveline Alicia Juliana Herbert = Isaac Newton Wallop, 5th Earl of Portsmouth, see below

15. Oliver Henry Wallop, 8th Earl of Portsmouth = Marguerite Walker

16. **Hon. Oliver Malcolm Wallop** of Wyo. = Jean Moore [parents of Malcolm Wallop, b. 1933, U.S. Senator from Wyoming, who married (1) Josephine Vail Stebbins; (2) Judith Warren; (3) Mrs. French Addison Gamble Goodwin].

10. Elizabeth Wyndham (sister of the 1st Earl of Egremont) = Hon. George Grenville, Prime Minister, Chancellor of the Exchequer

11. Hester Grenville = Hugh Fortescue, 1st Earl Fortescue

12. Catherine Fortescue = Newton Fellowes Wallop, 4th Earl of Portsmouth

13. Isaac Newton Wallop, 5th Earl of Portsmouth = Eveline Alicia Juliana Herbert, see above

Sources: *BRB*, tables I, XIV, L, LI, pp. 1, 13, 31-32, 265 and *BP* (Carnarvon) (H.W. Herbert); and tables L, LI, LIII, LV, pp. 31-34, 264, 284 and *BP* (Portsmouth). See also V.J. Watney, *The Wallop Family and Their Ancestry*, 4 vols. (1928), passim.

The Royal Descents of 500 Immigrants

1. Henry VII, King of England, d. 1509 = Elizabeth Plantagenet

2. Princess Mary Tudor = Charles Brandon, 1st Duke of Suffolk

3. Eleanor Brandon = Henry Clifford, 2nd Earl of Cumberland

4. Margaret Clifford = Henry Stanley, 4th Earl of Derby

5. Ferdinando Stanley, 5th Earl of Derby = Alice Spencer

6. Elizabeth Stanley = Henry Hastings, 5th Earl of Huntingdon

7. Ferdinando Hastings, 6th Earl of Huntingdon = Lucy Davies

8. Theophilus Hastings, 7th Earl of Huntingdon = Frances Leveson Fowler

9. Catherine Maria Hastings = Granville Wheeler

10. Catherine Maria Wheeler = James Stuart-Menteth

11. Sir Charles Granville Stuart-Menteth, 1st Bt. = Ludivina Loughnan

12. **Thomas Loughnan Stuart-Menteth** of Canandaigua, N.Y. = Isabella Maria Tobin.

Sources: *BRB*, tables I, LXXXII, CII, CIII, pp. 1, 48, 63, 441 and *BP* (Stuart-Menteth, baronets). Note also *PSECD* 2:268-75 (including the line from T.L. Stuart-Menteth to contemporary genealogist Timothy Field Beard, b. 1930).

The Royal Descents of 500 Immigrants

1. James V, King of Scotland, d. 1542 = (1) Madeleine of France; (2) Mary of Guise

2. (illegitimate by Eupheme Elphinstone) Robert Stewart, 1st Earl of Orkney = Janet Kennedy

3. Jean Stewart = Patrick Leslie, 1st Baron Lindores

4. David Leslie, 1st Baron Newark, parliamentary general in the English Civil War = Joan Yorke

5. Mary Leslie = Sir Francis Kinloch, 2nd Bt.

6. **James Kinloch** of S.C. = (1) Mrs. Susannah (----) Strode; (2) Marie Esther Page.

4. Elizabeth Leslie (sister of the 1st Baron Newark) = Sir James Sinclair, 1st Bt.

5. Anne Sinclair = George Mackenzie, 1st Earl of Cromarty

6. John Mackenzie, 2nd Earl of Cromarty = Mary Murray

7. George Mackenzie, 3rd Earl of Cromarty = Isabel Gordon

8. **Lady Mary Mackenzie** of S.C. = (1) Robert **Clarke**; (2) Thomas **Drayton**; (3) John **Ainslie**; (4) Henry **Middleton** (1717-1784), planter, South Carolina legislator, president of the Continental Congress. Lady Anne Mackenzie, a sister of Lady Mary, also immigrated to S.C. and married (1) Edmund Atkins, president of His Majesty's Council for S.C. and first Superintendent of Indian Affairs for the Southern District of the American Colonies; (2) John Murray, asst. and act. sec. of the Province of S.C. Both husbands, however, are omitted from the *DAB* and *NCAB*.

3. (illegitimate by Janet Robertson) James Stewart of Graemsay = ---- ----

4. Margaret Stewart = Francis Moodie of Breckness

5. Barbara Moodie = Patrick Balfour of Pharay

6. George Balfour of Pharay = Marjorie Baikie

7. Barbara Balfour = William Traill of Westness

8. William Traill of Kirkwall = Isabell Fea

9. **Robert Traill** of N.H. = Mary Whipple, sister of William Whipple, Jr., signer of the Declaration of Independence. Several kinsmen of Robert Traill may also have immigrated to New England. An uncle, John Traill (son of William and Barbara and husband of Mary Gale), was of Boston, Mass., but left no NDTPS.

3. (illegitimate by ----) Mary Stewart, said to = John Sinclair

4. William Sinclair = Joanna Gordon of Clairston

5. James Sinclair of Kirkwall = Anna Sinclair

6. **Robert Sinclair** of N.Y. = Maria Duyckinck.

Sources: *CP* or *SP* (Orkney, Lindores, Newark), *CB* and *BP* (Kinloch of Gilmerton, baronets) and *SCG* 3:58-59 (James Kinloch); *CB* (Sinclair of Mey, baronets), *CP* or *SP* (Cromarty/ie) and *NGSQ* 52 (1964):25 (Lady M.M.C.D.A. Middleton); *NEXUS* 6(1989):205-6, H.L. Norton Smith, *A Collection of Armorials of the County of Orkney* (1902), pp. 13-14, 138 esp. (Stewart of Graemsay, Moodie, Balfour), William Traill of Woodwick, *A Genealogical Account of the Traills of Orkney* (1883), pp. 73-76 esp. and *The New Hampshire Genealogical Record* 4(1907):1-6 (Traill, Spence) (Robert Traill); *NYGBR* 50(1919):46-47 (Robert Sinclair). For the identification of Mary, natural daughter of Robert Stewart, 1st Earl of Orkney, said in the *Record* to be the wife of a John Sinclair and paternal grandmother of James Sinclair of Ricena and Kirkwall, the immigrant's father, I would like to see further evidence. According to *SP* 6:575, this Mary Stewart is "said to have married Lawrence Sinclair of Goat in Shetland."

1. James V, King of Scotland, d. 1542 = (1) Madeleine of France; (2) Mary of Guise

2. (illegitimate by Elizabeth Carmichael) John Stewart, prior of Coldingham = Jean Hepburn

3. Francis Stewart, 1st Earl of Bothwell = Margaret Douglas

4. John Stewart of Coldingham = Margaret Home

5. Margaret Stewart = Sir John Home of Renton

6. Sir Patrick Home, 1st Bt. = Jean Dalmahoy

7. Margaret Home = Sir George Home, 3rd Bt.

8. **George Home** of Va. = Elizabeth Proctor.

Sources: *MCS4*, lines 41E and 92B; *CB* (Home of Lumsden and Home of Wedderburn, baronets), *SP* and *CP* (Bothwell). See also *BLG* (Home-Robertson of Wedderburn and Paxton) and E.E. Hume, *A Colonial Scottish Jacobite Family: The Establishment in Virginia of a Branch of the Humes of Wedderburn* (1931) and *Memorial to George Hume, Esquire, Crown Surveyor of Virginia and Washington's Teacher of Surveying* (1939, originally published in *TM* and reprinted in *GVFT* 2:263-377).

The Royal Descents of 500 Immigrants

1. James V, King of Scotland, d. 1542 = (1) Madeleine of France; (2) Mary of Guise
2. (illegitimate by Margaret Erskine) James Stewart, 1st Earl of Moray, Regent of Scotland = Agnes Keith
3. Elizabeth Stewart = James Stewart, 2nd Earl of Moray, a cousin
4. James Stewart, 3rd Earl of Moray = Anne Gordon
5. James Stewart, 4th Earl of Moray = Margaret Home
6. Mary Stewart = Archibald Campbell, 9th Earl of Argyll
7. Hon. John Campbell = Elizabeth Elphinstone
8. John Campbell, 4th Duke of Argyll = Mary Bellenden
9. **Lord William Campbell** (d. 1778), colonial governor of S.C. = Sarah Izard.

Sources: *SP, CP* and *BP* (Argyll, Moray).

The Royal Descents of 500 Immigrants

1. Edward IV, King of England, d. 1483 = Elizabeth Woodville
2. (illegitimate by Elizabeth Lucy) Elizabeth Plantagenet = Thomas Lumley
3. Roger Lumley = ----
4. Agnes Lumley = John Lambton
5. Robert Lambton = Frances Eure
6. John Lambton = Katherine Kirby
7. John Lambton = Margaret Hall
8. Margaret Lambton = Sir Robert Eden, 1st Bt.
9. Sir John Eden, 2nd Bt. = Catherine Shafto
10. Sir Robert Eden, 3rd Bt. = Mary Davison
11. **Sir Robert Eden, 1st Bt.** (1741-1784), colonial governor of Md. = Hon. Caroline Calvert, ARD, SETH.

6. Ralph Lambton (brother of John) = Eleanor Tempest
7. William Lambton = Catherine Widdrington
8. Sir Thomas Lambton = Margaret Freville
9. Freville Lambton = Thomasine Milwood
10. Thomas Lambton = Dorothy Bewicke
11. Dorothy Lambton = Robert Surtees
12. Jane Surtees = Crosier Surtees, a cousin
13. Robert Surtees = Elizabeth Cookson
14. Charles Freville Surtees = Bertha Chauncey
15. Sir Herbert Conyers Surtees = Madeleine Augusta Crabbe
16. Bertha Etelka Surtees = Edward Bell
17. **Evangeline Bell** of Va. = David Kirkpatrick Este **Bruce** (1898-1977), diplomat, whose first wife was Mrs. Ailsa Mellon Bruce, philanthropist and art patron.

Sources: *Surtees* 2:163 (Lumley), 174-75, 3:36 (Lambton); *CB* and *BP* (Eden of Auckland and Eden of Md., baronets); *BLG* (Surtees of Redworth and Surtees of Mainsforth Hall) and various Harvard class books for the class of 1904 (Edward Bell).

The Royal Descents of 500 Immigrants

1. Edward IV, King of England, d. 1483 = Elizabeth Woodville

2. (illegitimate by Elizabeth Lucy) Elizabeth Plantagenet = Thomas Lumley

3. Richard Lumley, 5th Baron Lumley = Anne Conyers

4. Hon. Anthony Lumley = ---- Gray

5. Roger Lumley = Anne Kurtwich

6. Richard Lumley, 1st Viscount Lumley = Frances Shelley

7. Hon. John Lumley = Mary Compton

8. Richard Lumley, 1st Earl of Scarbrough = Frances Jones

9. Mary Lumley = George Montagu, 1st Earl of Halifax, son of Edward Montagu and Elizabeth Pelham, SETH

10. **Lady Mary Montagu** = Sir Danvers **Osborne**, 3rd Bt., colonial governor of N.Y., ARD, SETH.

Sources: *CB* (Osborne of Chicksands, baronets); *CP* (Halifax, Scarbrough, Lumley); *Surtees* 2:163-64 (Lumley).

The Royal Descents of 500 Immigrants

1. Edward IV, King of England, d. 1483 = Elizabeth Woodville

2. (illegitimate by Elizabeth Lucy) Elizabeth Plantagenet = Thomas Lumley

3. Sibyl Lumley = Sir William Hilton

4. William Hilton = Margaret Metcalfe

5. Sir William Hilton = Anne Yorke

6. Henry Hilton = ---- Brandling

7. Henry Hilton = Elizabeth Kitchen

8. Robert Hilton = Isabel Selby

9. Henry Hilton = Sarah Clarke

10. John Hilton = Mrs. Hannah ---- Moore

11. **Ralph Hilton** (Hylton) of N.Y. = Mehitabel Lawrence.

Sources: *TAG* 50(1974):81-86 and sources cited therein.

The Royal Descents of 500 Immigrants

1. Edward III, King of England, d. 1377 = Philippa of Hainault

2. Lionel of Antwerp, Duke of Clarence = Elizabeth de Burgh

3. Philippa Plantagenet = Edmund Mortimer, 3rd Earl of March

4. Roger Mortimer, 4th Earl of March = Eleanor Holand

5. Anne Mortimer = Richard Plantagenet, Earl of Cambridge, son of Edmund of Langley, 1st Duke of York (and Isabel of Castile), son of Edward III, King of England, and Philippa of Hainault, above

6. Richard Plantagenet, 3rd Duke of York = Cecily Neville, daughter of Ralph Neville, 1st Earl of Westmoreland, and Joan Beaufort, SETH

7. George Plantagenet, 1st Duke of Clarence, brother of Kings Edward IV (d. 1483) and Richard III (d. 1485) = Isabel Neville

8. Margaret Plantagenet, Countess of Salisbury = Sir Richard Pole

9. Henry Pole, 1st Baron Montagu = Joan Neville

10. Katherine Pole = Francis Hastings, 2nd Earl of Huntingdon

11. George Hastings, 4th Earl of Huntingdon = Dorothy Port

12. Francis Hastings, Lord Hastings = Sarah Harington

13. Sir George Hastings = Seymour Prynne

14. Catherine Hastings = Bridges Nanfan

15. **Catherine Nanfan** = Richard **Coote**, 1st Earl of Bellomont (1636-1701), colonial governor of N.Y., Mass. and N.H., ARD, SETH.

11. Katherine Hastings (sister of the 4th Earl of Huntingdon) = Henry Clinton, 2nd Earl of Lincoln

12. Sir Edward Clinton = Mary Deighton

13. Francis Clinton = Priscilla Hill

14. Francis Clinton, 6th Earl of Lincoln = Susan Penniston
15. **Hon. George Clinton** (c. 1686-1761), colonial governor of N.Y. = Anne Carle.

11. Frances Hastings (sister of the 4th Earl of Huntingdon and the Countess of Lincoln) = Henry Compton, 1st Baron Compton
12. William Compton, 1st Earl of Northampton = Elizabeth Spencer
13. Spencer Compton, 2nd Earl of Northampton = Mary Beaumont
14. James Compton, 3rd Earl of Northampton = Mary Noel
15. George Compton, 4th Earl of Northampton = Jane Fox
16. James Compton, 5th Earl of Northampton = Elizabeth Shirley, Baroness Ferrers of Chartley
17. Charlotte Compton, Baroness Ferrers of Chartley = George Townshend, 1st Marquess Townshend
18. Lord John Townshend = Georgiana Anne Poyntz
19. John Townshend, 4th Marquess Townshend = Elizabeth Jane Stuart
20. John Villiers Stuart Townshend, 5th Marquess Townshend = Anne Elizabeth Clementina Duff
21. John James Dudley Stuart Townshend, 6th Marquess Townshend = Gladys Ethel Gwendolen Eugenie Sutherst
22. George John Patrick Dominic Townshend, 7th Marquess Townshend = Elizabeth Pamela Audrey Luby
23. **Lady Carolyn Elizabeth Ann Townshend** of N.Y. = (1) Patrizio Genovese Antonio **Capellini**; (2) (=Dec. 1973, annulled Dec. 1974) Edgar Miles **Bronfman** (b. 1929), chairman and chief executive officer of Seagram Co., Ltd., distillers.

19. Lord George Osborne Townshend (brother of the 4th Marquess Townshend) = Jessie Victoria MacKellar

20. Charles Thornton Townshend = Louise Graham

21. Sir Charles Vere Ferrers Townshend, British World War I commander = Alice Cahen d'Anvers

22. Audrey Dorothy Louise Townshend = Baudouin, Count Borchgrave d'Altena

23. **Arnaud, Count Borchgrave d'Altena**, known as Arnaud de Borchgrave (b. 1926) of N.Y., editor and correspondent (associated with *Newsweek* magazine) = (1) Dorothy Solon; (2) Eileen Ritschel; (3) Alexandra D. Villard.

10. Winifred Pole (sister of Katherine) = Sir Thomas Barrington

11. Sir Francis Barrington, 1st Bt. = Joan Cromwell, aunt of Oliver Cromwell, the Lord Protector

12. Joan Barrington = Sir Richard Everard, 1st Bt.

13. Sir Richard Everard, 2nd Bt. = Elizabeth Gibbs

14. Sir Hugh Everard, 3rd Bt. = Mary Brown

15. **Sir Richard Everard,** 4th Bt., colonial governor of N.C. = Susan Kidder.

9. Ursula Pole (sister of the 1st Baron Montagu) = Henry Stafford, Baron Stafford

10. Dorothy Stafford = Sir William Stafford

11. Elizabeth Stafford = Sir William Drury

12. Frances Drury = (1) Sir Nicholas Clifford; (2) Sir William Wray

13. (by 1) Frances Clifford = Sir Edward Ayscough

14. Anne Ayscough = Edward King

15. Edward King = Bridget Neville

16. Neville King = Mary Middlemore

17. Anne King = Richard Welby

18. **Marianne Welby** of Md. = Samuel **De Butts.**

13. (by 2) Frances Wray = Sir Anthony Irby
14. Elizabeth Irby = George Montagu
15. Edward Montagu = Elizabeth Pelham
16. **Grace Montagu** = William **Cosby** (c. 1690-1735/6), colonial governor of N.Y. and N.J., ARD, SETH.

13. (by 2) Sir Christopher Wray (brother of Frances) = Albinia Cecil
14. **Frances Wray** = Sir Henry **Vane** (1613-1662), Puritan statesman, colonial governor of Mass., ARD, SETH

14. Sir Drury Wray, 6th Bt. (brother of Frances) = Anne Casey
15. Diana Wray = William Twigge, Archdeacon of Limerick
16. Jane Twigge = Stackpole Pery
17. William Cecil Pery, 1st Baron Glentworth = Jane Walcot
18. Edmund Henry Pery, 1st Earl of Limerick = Mary Alice Ormsby
19. Henry Hartstonge Pery, Viscount Glentworth = Annabella Edwards
20. William Henry Tennison Pery, 2nd Earl of Limerick = Susannah Sheaffe   20. Emilie Caroline Pery = Henry Gray
21. William Hale John Charles Pery, 3rd Earl of Limerick   =   21. Caroline Maria Gray
22. William Henry Edmond de Vere Sheaffe Pery, 4th Earl of Limerick = May Imelda Josephine Irwin
23. **Lady Victoria May Pery** of N.Y. = James Cox **Brady** (1882-1927), businessman, founder of Maxwell Motor Co., later absorbed into Chrysler Corp.

Sources: *Clarence*, tables I, II, V, pp. 1-2, 5 (Lady Bellomont); tables II, XVII, XVIII, pp. 2, 13-14 (Clinton); tables II, XX, pp. 2, 16-17,

194 and *BP* and *DP* (Townshend) (Lady C.E.A.T.C. Bronfman); table XX, pp. 16-17, 195, *BP* (Townshend) and *Who's Who in America* (Arnaud de Borchgrave); tables II, LVII, LXIII, pp. 2, 46, 53 and *CB* (Everard of Much Waltham, baronets); tables LXVII, LXVIII, LXX, LXXV, pp. 56-57, 59, 64, Rev. A.R. Maddison, ed., *Lincolnshire Pedigrees* (*HSPVS*, vols., 50-52, 55), vol. 1 (1902), pp. 65-66 (Ayscough), vol. 2 (1903), p. 566 (King), *BLG* (Reeve-King of Ashby de la Launde), and *GVFWM* 1:586 (De Butts); tables LXX, LXXVI, pp. 59, 65 (G.M. Cosby); tables LXX, LXXIII, pp. 59, 62 (Lady Vane); tables LXX, LXXI, pp. 59-60, 558-60 and *BP* (Limerick) (Lady V.M.P. Brady).

The Royal Descents of 500 Immigrants

1. Edward III, King of England, d. 1377 = Philippa of Hainault

2. Lionel of Antwerp, Duke of Clarence = Elizabeth de Burgh

3. Philippa Plantagenet = Edmund Mortimer, 3rd Earl of March

4. Roger Mortimer, 4th Earl of March = Eleanor Holand

5. Anne Mortimer = Richard Plantagenet, Earl of Cambridge, son of Edmund of Langley, 1st Duke of York (and Isabel of Castille), son of Edward III, King of England, and Philippa of Hainault, above

6. Richard Plantagenet, 3rd Duke of York = Cecily Neville, daughter of Ralph Neville, 1st Earl of Westmoreland and Joan Beaufort, SETH

7. Anne Plantagenet, sister of Kings Edward IV (d. 1483) and Richard III (d. 1485) = Sir Thomas St. Leger

8. Anne St. Leger = George Manners, Baron Ros

9. Thomas Manners, 1st Earl of Rutland = Eleanor Paston

10. Sir John Manners = Dorothy Vernon

11. Sir George Manners = Grace Pierpont

12. John Manners, 8th Earl of Rutland = Frances Montagu

13. John Manners, 1st Duke of Rutland = Catherine Noel

14. John Manners, 2nd Duke of Rutland = Catherine Russell

15. Elizabeth Manners = John Monckton, 1st Viscount Galway

16. **Hon. Robert Monckton** (1726-1782), colonial governor of N.Y., British commander in America during the French and Indian wars, d. unm.

15. John Manners, 3rd Duke of Rutland (brother of Viscountess Galway) = Bridget Sutton

16. John Manners, Marquess of Granby = Frances Seymour

16. Lord George Manners-Sutton = Diana Chaplin

17. (illegitimate by ----) = 17. John Manners-Sutton
    Anne Manners

18. Mary Georgiana Manners-Sutton = Robert Nassau Sutton

19. Mary Isabella Sutton = Sir George Baker, 3rd Bt.

20. Sir George Barrington Baker Wilbraham, 5th Bt. =
    Katherine Frances Wilbraham

21. Sir Philip Wilbraham Baker Wilbraham, 6th Bt. = Joyce
    Christabel Kennaway

22. **Mary Frances Baker Wilbraham** of Mass. = Elliot
    Perkins (1901-1985), educator, master of Lowell House
    at Harvard.

10. Katherine Manners (sister of Sir John) = Sir Henry Capell

11. Sir Arthur Capell = Margaret Grey

12. Sir Henry Capell = Theodosia Montagu

13. Arthur Capell, 1st Baron Capell = Elizabeth Morrison

14. Theodosia Capell = Henry Hyde, 2nd Earl of Clarendon,
    brother of Anne Hyde, wife of James II, King of
    England, and uncle of Mary II and Anne, Queens of
    England

15. **Edward Hyde, 3rd Earl of Clarendon** (1661-1723),
    colonial governor of N.Y. and N.J. = Catherine O'Brien,
    Baroness Clifton, see below.

10. Elizabeth Manners (sister of Sir John and Katherine) =
    Sir John Savage

11. Margaret Savage = William Brereton, 1st Baron Brereton

12. Mary Brereton = Henry O'Brien, 4th Earl of Thomond

13. Anne O'Brien = Henry O'Brien, 6th Earl of Thomond, a
    cousin

14. Henry O'Brien, Lord Ibrackan = Catherine Stuart,
    Baroness Clifton

15. **Catherine O'Brien, Baroness Clifton** = Edward Hyde, 3rd Earl of Clarendon (1661–1723), colonial governor of N.Y. and N.J., see above.

10. Frances Manners (sister of Sir John, Katherine, and Elizabeth) = Henry Neville, 6th Baron Abergavenny

11. Mary Neville, Baroness le Despencer = Sir Thomas Fane

12. Francis Fane, 1st Earl of Westmoreland = Mary Mildmay

13. Elizabeth Fane = William Cope

14. Elizabeth Cope = Thomas Geers

15. Elizabeth Geers = William Gregory

16. Elizabeth Gregory = John Nourse

17. **James Nourse** of Pa. = Sarah Faunce.

9. Katherine Manners (sister of the 1st Earl of Rutland) = Sir Robert Constable

10. Sir Marmaduke Constable = Jane Conyers

11. Katherine Constable = Sir Robert Stapleton

12. Jane Stapleton = Christopher Wyvill

13. Sir Marmaduke Wyvill, 2nd Bt. = Isabel Gascoigne

14. Mary Wyvill = Arthur Beckwith

15. Sir Roger Beckwith, 1st Bt. = Elizabeth Jennings, daughter of Sir Edmund Jennings and Margaret Barkham, and sister of Act. Gov. Edmund Jennings of Va., ARD, SETH

16. **Sir Marmaduke Beckwith, 3rd Bt.,** of Va. = Mrs. Elizabeth Brockenbrough Dickenson.

10. Barbara Constable (sister of Sir Marmaduke) = Sir William Babthorpe

11. Margaret Babthorpe = Sir Henry Cholmley

12. Mary Cholmley = Hon. Henry Fairfax

13. Henry Fairfax, 4th Baron Fairfax = Frances Barwick

14. Thomas Fairfax, 5th Baron Fairfax = Catherine Colepepper (Culpeper), daughter of Thomas Colepepper (Culpeper), 2nd Baron Colepepper (Culpeper), colonial governor of Va., ARD, SETH, and Margaret van Hesse

15. **Thomas Fairfax, 6th Baron Fairfax (1692-1781) of Va.,** proprietor of the Northern Neck of Virginia, d. unm.

14. Hon. Henry Fairfax (brother of the 5th Baron Fairfax) = Anne Harrison

15. **William Fairfax of Va.,** governor of the Bahamas, president of the Colonial Council of Va. = (1) Sarah Walker; (2) Mrs. Deborah Clarke Gedney.

12. Barbara Cholmley (sister of Mary) = Thomas Belasyse, 1st Viscount Fauconberg

13. Hon. Henry Belasyse = Grace Barton

14. Arabella Belasyse = Sir William Frankland, 1st Bt.

15. Sir Thomas Frankland, 2nd Bt. = Elizabeth Russell, granddaughter of Oliver Cromwell, the Lord Protector

16. Henry Frankland, Governor of Bengal = Mary Cross

17. Sir Charles Henry Frankland, 4th Bt., British consular officer = **Agnes Surriage, known as Lady Agnes Surriage Frankland** (1726-1783), Boston, Mass., social leader.

17. Sir Thomas Frankland, 5th Bt., admiral (brother of Sir C.H.) = Sarah Rhett of S.C.

18. Charlotte Frankland = Robert Nicholas

19. Harriet Nicholas = Henry Theodosius Browne Collier, admiral

20. Gertrude Barbara Rich Collier = Charles Tennant

21. **Dorothy Tennant** = (1) Sir Henry Morton **Stanley** (1841-1904), the journalist and African explorer, long an American resident; (2) Henry **Curtis.**

9. Margaret Manners (sister of the 1st Earl of Rutland and of Katherine) = Sir Henry Strangways

10. Sir Giles Strangways = Joan Wadham

11. John Strangways = Dorothy Thynne

12. Grace Strangways = Edmund Chamberlayne

13. Edmund Chamberlayne = Eleanor Colles

14. **Thomas Chamberlayne** of Va. = (1) Mary Wood; (2) Elizabeth Stratton.

14. **Dorothy Chamberlayne** of S.C. = Robert **Daniell**, colonial governor of S.C.

Sources: *Exeter*, tables I, II, VII, pp. 1–2, 9 and *BP* (Galway) (Monckton); table VII, pp. 9, 159–62 and *BP* (Baker Wilbraham, baronets, for Mrs. Perkins); tables II, XXVII, XXXV, XLII, pp. 2, 30–31, 39, 46 and *CP* (Clarendon) (Clarendon and his wife); tables II, XXIV, pp. 2, 27, *MGH*, 3rd ser., 4(1902):219–20 (Cope), *Duncumb* 4:30 (Geers), 3:233 (Gregory) and Maria Catharine Nourse Lyle, *James Nourse and His Descendants* (1897), pp. 2–23 (Nourse); tables II, XLVII, XLIX, LII, pp. 2, 52, 54, 56, 554, *CB* (Beckwith of Aldborough, Wyvill of Constable Buxton), *LDBR* 2:532–33 and G.H.S. King, *Marriages of Richmond County, Virginia, 1668–1853* (1964), pp. 13–14 (Beckwith); tables XLVII, LIV, LVIII, LXIII, pp. 52, 58, 63, 68, and *CP* and *BP* (Fairfax) (two Fairfaxes); tables LVIII, LX, pp. 63, 65, *CB* and *BP* (Frankland, baronets) and *DAB* (Lady A.S. Frankland); table LX, pp. 65, 635–36, *SCG* 4:3–4, 9 (Rhett, Frankland, Nicholas, Collier), *MGH*, new ser., 3 (1878–80):129 (Collier, Tennant) and *BLG* (Coombe Tennant of Cadoxton) (Lady H.M. Stanley); tables II, LXIX, pp. 2, 74, J.P. Rylands, ed., *Visitation of Dorset, 1623* (*HSPVS*, vol. 25, 1885), pp. 86–87 (Strangways), T.F. Fenwick and W.C. Metcalfe, eds., *Visitation of the County of Gloucester, 1682–1683* (1884), pp. 37–38 (where, however, Dorothy Chamberlayne is said to have married "Edward Ridley, Steward to the Duke of Somerset"), and *Wilson*, pp. 4–5, 8–25 (esp. chart opp. p. 20) (Chamberlayne and Mrs. Daniell).

The Royal Descents of 500 Immigrants

1. Edward III, King of England, d. 1377 = Philippa of Hainault

2. Lionel of Antwerp, Duke of Clarence = Elizabeth de Burgh

3. Philippa Plantagenet = Edmund Mortimer, 3rd Earl of March

4. Roger Mortimer, 4th Earl of March = Eleanor Holand

5. Anne Mortimer = Richard Plantagenet, Earl of Cambridge, son of Edmund of Langley, 1st Duke of York (and Isabel of Castile), son of Edward III, King of England, and Philippa of Hainault, above

6. Isabel Plantagenet = Henry Bourchier, Count of Eu, 1st Earl of Essex, son of William Bourchier, Count of Eu, and Anne Plantagenet, SETH

7. William Bourchier, Viscount Bourchier = Anne Woodville, sister of Elizabeth Woodville, Queen of Edward IV

8. Cecily Bourchier = John Devereux, Baron Ferrers of Chartley

9. Walter Devereux, 1st Viscount Hereford = Mary Grey

10. Sir Richard Devereux = Dorothy Hastings

11. Walter Devereux, 1st Earl of Essex = Lettice Knollys

12. Robert Devereux, 2nd Earl of Essex, favorite of Elizabeth I, leader of "Essex's Rebellion" = Frances Walsingham

13. Dorothy Devereux = Sir Henry Shirley, 2nd Bt.

14. Sir Robert Shirley, 4th Bt. = Catherine Okeover

15. Robert Shirley, 1st Earl Ferrers = Selina Finch

16. Mary Shirley = Charles Tryon

17. **William Tryon** (1729-1788), colonial governor of N.C. and N.Y. = Margaret Wake.

12. Penelope Devereux (sister of the 2nd Earl of Essex) = Robert Rich, 1st Earl of Warwick

The Royal Descents of 500 Immigrants

13. Robert Rich, 2nd Earl of Warwick = Frances Hatton

14. Anne Rich = Edward Montagu, 2nd Earl of Manchester

15. Robert Montagu, 3rd Earl of Manchester = Anne Yelverton

16. Charles Montagu, 1st Duke of Manchester = Doddington Greville

17. Robert Montagu, 3rd Duke of Manchester = Harriet Dunch

18. **Lord Charles Greville Montagu**, colonial governor of S.C. = Elizabeth Bulmer.

12. Dorothy Devereux (sister of the 2nd Earl of Essex and the Countess of Warwick) = Sir Thomas Perrott, son of Sir John Perrott (and Anne Cheyney, a 1st wife), SETH, possibly an illegitimate son, by Mary Berkeley (wife of Sir Thomas Perrott), of Henry VIII, King of England, d. 1547

13. Penelope Perrott = Sir William Lower

14. Dorothy Lower = Sir Maurice Drummond

15. Henrietta Maria Drummond = Robert Middlemore

16. Mary Middlemore = Sir John Gage, 4th Bt.

17. Mary Gage = Sir John Shelley, 3rd Bt.

18. Richard Shelley = Mary Fleetwood

19. Frances Shelley = James Best

20. George Best = Caroline Scott

21. Dorothy Best = Joseph George Brett

22. William Baliol Brett, 1st Viscount Esher = Eugénie Mayer

23. Reginald Baliol Brett, 2nd Viscount Esher, army reformer and diplomat, friend of Edward VII, King of Great Britain = Eleanor Frances Weston Van de Weyer

24. **Hon. Dorothy Eugénie Brett** (1883-1977) of Taos, N.M., artist, patroness, friend of the novelist D.H. Lawrence, d. unm.

24. Hon. Sylvia Leonora Brett, known as H.H. The Ranee of Sarawak = H.H. Sir Charles Vyner Brooke, last Rajah of Sarawak

25. **Elizabeth Brooke** of Fla. = (1) Harry **Roy** (1904-1971), bandleader; (2) Richard **Vidmer**.

10. Sir William Devereux (brother of Sir Richard) = Jane Scudamore

11. Margaret Devereux = Sir Edward Littleton

12. Margaret Littleton = Richard Skinner

13. Margaret Skinner = Thomas Joliffe

14. Benjamin Joliffe = Mary Joliffe, a cousin

15. Anne Joliffe = Robert Biddulph

16. Michael Biddulph = Penelope Dandridge

17. John Biddulph = Augusta Roberts

18. Mary Anne Biddulph = Robert Martin

19. John Biddulph Martin = **Mrs. Victoria Claflin Woodhull Blood, known as Mrs. Victoria Claflin Woodhull** (1838-1927) of N.Y., spiritualist, suffragette, American presidential candidate of the Equal Rights Party in 1892 [she = (1) Canning Woodhull and (2) James H. Blood].

Sources: *Essex,* tables I-III, pp. 1-4, *DNB* and *DAB* (William Tryon); tables II, VIII, pp. 2, 9, 103 and *BP* (Manchester, for Lord C.G. Montagu); table II, p. 2, *DNB* (Sir John Perrott and Sir Robert Naunton), *VC,* p. 300 (Lower, Drummond), W.P.W. Phillimore and W.F. Carter, *Some Account of the Family of Middlemore of Warwickshire and Worcestershire* (1901), pp. 68-69, *BP* (Gage, Shelley [baronets] and Esher), *BLG,* 18th ed., vol. 3 (1972), pp. 120-21 (Brooke of Sarawak), *BLG* 1937, pp. 149-50 (Best, now Best-Davison of Park House) and *RLNGF* 1:74 (Shelley, Best) (Hon. D.E. Brett, Mrs. Roy); tables II, XVII, XXVIII, pp. 2, 19, 30, 342, 345, and *BLG* 1937, p. 1541 (Martin late of Ledbury) (J.B. Martin).

The Royal Descents of 500 Immigrants

1. James IV, King of Scotland, d. 1513 = Margaret Tudor of England

2. (illegitimate by Margaret Drummond) Margaret Stewart = John Gordon, Lord Gordon

3. Alexander Gordon, Bishop of the Isles and of Galloway

4. (illegitimate by Barbara Logie) John Gordon = Geneviève Petau

5. Louisa (Lucy) Gordon = Sir Robert Gordon, 1st Bt., son of Alexander Gordon, 12th Earl of Sutherland (and Jean Gordon), son of John Gordon, 11th Earl of Sutherland and Helen Stewart, daughter of John Stewart, 3rd Earl of Lennox (and Elizabeth Stewart), son of Matthew Stewart, 2nd Earl of Lennox and Elizabeth Hamilton, daughter of James Hamilton, 1st Baron Hamilton, and Princess Mary Stewart, daughter of James II, King of Scotland, d. 1460, and Mary of Guelders

6. Katherine Gordon = David Barclay of Urie

7. Robert Barclay, Quaker apologist and nominal governor of East N.J. (East Jersey) = Christian Mollison (parents of John Barclay of N.J., who = Katherine [Rescarrick?] but left no NDTPS)

8. David Barclay = Priscilla Freame

9. John Barclay = Susanna Willet

10. Robert Barclay = Ann Ford

11. Elizabeth Lucy Barclay = Henry Birkbeck

12. Emma Birkbeck = Georg Friedrich von Bunsen

13. **Berta von Bunsen** of Mass. = Ernest Flagg **Henderson**. Among their children was Ernest Flagg Henderson, Jr. (1897-1967), founder of the Sheraton hotel chain, who married Mary Gill Caldwell Stephens and Faryl Finn.

8. Jean Barclay (sister of David) = Alexander Forbes of Aquorthies and London

9. Christian Forbes = William Penn (III), son of William Penn, Jr. (and Mary Jones), son of William Penn, the founder of Pennsylvania, and Gulielma Maria Springett

10. Christiana Gulielma Penn = Peter Gaskell

11. **Peter Penn-Gaskell** of Pa. = Elizabeth Edwards.

Sources: *MP*, pp. 470-71 (for Mrs. Henderson); *BLG*, Birkbeck of Westacre, Barclay of Leyden, and Barclay of Bury Hill (formerly of Mathers and Urie); *AR7*, line 252 (John Barclay of N.J.); *SP* and *CP* (Sutherland, Lennox, and Hamilton -- under Arran); *GPFPGM* 2: 574-75, 579-83 and R. Burnham Moffatt, *The Barclays of New York* (1904), pp. 74-77, 222-23 (for Peter Penn-Gaskell). The full known ancestry of Mrs. E.F. Henderson, for many generations, will be treated in a multi-volume study of his children's forebears by Ernest Flagg Henderson III of Wellesley, Mass., grandson of the above, and son of Ernest Flagg Henderson, Jr. and Mary Gill Caldwell Stephens.

The Royal Descents of 500 Immigrants

1. James IV, King of Scotland, d. 1513 = Margaret Tudor of England
2. (illegitimate by Agnes Stewart, Countess of Bothwell) Joan Stewart = Malcolm Fleming, 3rd Baron Fleming
3. Joan Fleming = David Crawford of Kerse
4. Marion Crawford = James Boswell of Auchinleck
5. David Boswell of Auchinleck = Isabel Wallace
6. Margaret Boswell = David Blair of Adamton
7. Margaret Blair = William Blair of Giffordland
8. David Blair of Giffordland = Mrs. Sarah --- Lawson
9. **Sarah Blair** of Conn. = Samuel **Watkinson**.

5. James Boswell (younger brother of David of Auchinleck) = Margaret Cunningham
6. David Boswell of Auchinleck = Anne Hamilton
7. James Boswell of Auchinleck = Elizabeth Bruce (their son, Alexander Boswell, senator of the College of Justice as Lord Auchinleck, married Euphemia Erskine and was the father of James Boswell of Auchinleck, the man of letters, traveler, and biographer of Samuel Johnson)
8. John Boswell, president of the Royal College of Physicians (Edinburgh) = Anne Cramond
9. Robert Boswell of St. Boswells = Sibella Sandeman
10. Sibella Boswell = William Egerton
11. Philip Henry Egerton = Mary Marjoribanks
12. **Graham Egerton** of Washington, D.C. = Julia Easley (their son, William Graham Egerton, married Rebecca Crenshaw White and was the father of John Walden Egerton, b. 1935, author of *The Americanization of Dixie,* etc., who married Ann Elizabeth Bleidt).

Sources: *TAG* 47 (1971):65-69, 48(1972):79-80 (Mrs. Watkinson); *BLG,* 18th ed., vol. 3 (1972):80 (Boswell of Auchinleck), *BP* (Grey Egerton, baronets), and *Who's Who in America* (J.W. Egerton) (for Graham Egerton).

The Royal Descents of 500 Immigrants

1. James IV, King of Scotland, d. 1513 = Margaret Tudor of England
2. (illegitimate by Margaret Drummond) Margaret Stewart = Sir John Drummond of Innerpeffry
2. (illegitimate by Agnes Stewart, Countess of Bothwell) Joan Stewart = Malcolm Fleming, 3rd Baron Fleming
3. Agnes Drummond = Hugh Montgomery, 3rd Earl of Eglinton
3. Agnes Fleming = William Livingston, 6th Baron Livingston
4. Margaret Montgomery = Robert Seton, 1st Earl of Winton
4. Alexander Livingston, 1st Earl of Linlithgow = Eleanor Hay
5. Alexander Montgomery, 6th Earl of Eglinton (heir of his maternal grandfather) =
5. Anne Livingston
6. Hugh Montgomery, 7th Earl of Eglinton = Mary Leslie
7. Margaret Montgomery = James Campbell, 2nd Earl of Loudoun
8. Hugh Campbell, 3rd Earl of Loudoun = Margaret Dalrymple
9. **John Campbell, 4th Earl of Loudoun** (1705-1782), British commander in America during the French and Indian War, d. unm.

7. Alexander Montgomery, 8th Earl of Eglinton (brother of the Countess of Loudoun) = Elizabeth Crichton
8. Alexander Montgomery, 9th Earl of Eglinton = Margaret Cochrane
9. Euphemia Montgomery = George Lockhart of Carnwath
10. George Lockhart of Carnwath = Fergusia Wishart
11. Sir James Lockhart-Wishart (1st Count of Lockhart in the Holy Roman Empire) = Annabella Crawford
12. Mariana Matilda Lockhart-Wishart = Anthony Aufrere

13. **Louisa Anna (or Louise Ann) Matilda Aufrere** of N.Y. =
George **Barclay**.

Sources: *SP* and *CP* (Loudoun, Eglinton, Winton, Linlithgow, Livingston, Fleming) (4th Earl of Loudoun); *MP*, table XI, pp. 12, 185, *BP* 1898, pp. 914–15, and *NEXUS* 8(1991):150 (Mrs. Barclay).

The Royal Descents of 500 Immigrants

1. James IV, King of Scotland, d. 1513 = Margaret Tudor of England

2. (illegitimate by Margaret Boyd) Catherine Stewart = James Douglas, 3rd Earl of Morton

2. (illegitimate by Margaret Drummond) Margaret Stewart = John Gordon, Lord Gordon

3. Margaret Douglas = James Hamilton, 2nd Earl of Arran, Duke of Châtellerault, regent of Scotland, son of James Hamilton, 1st Earl of Arran (and Janet Beaton), son of James Hamilton, 1st Baron Hamilton, and Princess Mary Stewart, daughter of James II, King of Scotland, d. 1460, and Mary of Guelders

3. George Gordon, 4th Earl of Huntly = Elizabeth Keith

4. Anne Hamilton   =   4. George Gordon, 5th Earl of Huntly

5. George Gordon, 1st Marquess of Huntly = Henrietta Stewart

6. Mary Gordon = William Douglas, 1st Marquess of Douglas

7. Lucy Douglas = Robert Maxwell, 4th Earl of Nithsdale

8. Mary Maxwell = Charles Stuart, 4th Earl of Traquair

9. John Stuart, 6th Earl of Traquair = Christian Anstruther

10. **Lady Christian Stuart** of Va. = Cyrus **Griffin** (1748-1810), jurist, last president of the Continental Congress.

4. Claude Hamilton, 1st Baron Paisley (brother of the Countess of Huntly) = Margaret Seton

5. Margaret Hamilton = William Douglas, 1st Marquess of Douglas

6. Jean Douglas = John Hamilton, 1st Baron Bargeny

7. Anne Hamilton = Sir Patrick Houston, 1st Bt.

8. Patrick Houston = Isabel Johnstone

9. **Sir Patrick Houston, 5th Bt.**, president of the colonial council of Ga. = Priscilla Dunbar.

Sources: *NGSQ* 52(1964):25-36 (Lady Griffin, generations 4-10), *SP* and *CP* (Huntly, Morton, Arran, Douglas, Nithsdale, Traquair); *MCS4*, line 92A and Edith Duncan Johnston, *The Houstouns of Georgia* (1950).

The Royal Descents of 500 Immigrants

1. James IV, King of Scotland, d. 1513 = Margaret Tudor of England
2. (illegitimate by Margaret Drummond) Margaret Stewart = Sir John Drummond of Innerpeffry
2. (illegitimate by Agnes Stewart, Countess of Bothwell) Joan Stewart = Malcolm Fleming, 3rd Baron Fleming
3. Margaret Drummond = Robert Elphinstone, 3rd Baron Elphinstone
3. Agnes Fleming = William Livingston, 6th Baron Livingston
4. Alexander Elphinstone = 4. Jean Livingston 4th Baron Elphinstone
5. Helen Elphinstone = Sir William Cockburn, 1st Bt.
6. Sir William Cockburn, 2nd Bt. = Margaret Acheson
7. Sir Alexander Cockburn, 4th Bt. = Marion Sinclair, daughter of John Sinclair of Stevenson and Isabel Boyd, daughter of Robert Boyd, 7th Baron Boyd, and Christian Hamilton, SETH
8. Helen Cockburn = Sir Robert Steuart, 1st Bt.
9. Helen Steuart = Sir Gilbert Elliot, 2nd Bt.
10. Eleanor Elliot = John Rutherford of Edgerston (and N.Y.), ARD, SETH
11. Jane Rutherford = William Oliver of Dinlabrye
12. Eleanor Oliver = James Russell
13. **Archibald Russell** of N.Y. = Helen Rutherford Watts, daughter of John Watts and Anne Rutherford, daughter of John Rutherford (and Magdalen Morris), son of Walter Rutherford of N.Y., ARD, SETH (brother of John Rutherford of Edgerston and N.Y., above) and Catherine Alexander.

Sources: Livingston Rutherfurd, *Family Records and Events* [Rutherfurd family] (1894), chapters 2-3 (pp. 85-256), esp. 255-56; *DNB* (James Russell, 1754-1836); *Rutherford*, vol. 1, pp. 70-71, 73-74, 98-99, and rev. ed., vol. 2, p. 802, 815; Hon. George F.S. Elliot, *The*

Border Elliots and *The Family of Minto* (1897), pp. 308-24; *CB* (Steuart of Allanbank); Thomas H. Cockburn-Hood, *The House of Cockburn of That Ilk and the Cadets Thereof* (1888), pp. 83-95; *SP* and *CP* (Boyd, under Kilmarnock in *SP*; Elphinstone; and Livingston, under Linlithgow in *SP*).

The Royal Descents of 500 Immigrants

1. James IV, King of Scotland, d. 1513 = Margaret Tudor of England
2. (illegitimate by Agnes Stewart, Countess of Bothwell) Joan Stewart = Malcolm Fleming, 3rd Baron Fleming
3. John Fleming, 5th Baron Fleming = Elizabeth Ross
4. Mary Fleming = Sir James Douglas
5. William Douglas, 1st Earl of Queensberry = Isabel Ker
6. Sir Archibald Douglas of Dornock = Eleanor Davis
7. James Douglas of Jamaica = ----
8. Thomas Douglas of Jamaica = ---- Watson
9. Samuel Douglas of Jamaica = ---- James
10. Samuel Douglas of Jamaica = Isabella Moncreiffe
11. Robert Douglas = ----
12. Samuel Douglas = ----
13. Robert Douglas = Annie Johnson
14. **Robert Langton Douglas**, sometime of N.Y. = (1) Margaret Jane Cannon (parents of William Sholto Douglas, 1st Baron Douglas of Kirtleside, British Air Marshal); (2) Mary Henchman; (3) Jean Stewart (parents of Claire Alison Douglas, wife of Jerome David [J.D.] Salinger, b. 1919, the American novelist, author of *Catcher in the Rye*).

Sources: *BP* (Baron Douglas of Kirtleside), *SP* and *CP* (Queensberry, Fleming -- in *SP* under Wigton). Further documentation of generations 7-12 would be desirable.

The Royal Descents of 500 Immigrants

1. James IV, King of Scotland, d. 1513 = Margaret Tudor of England

2. (illegitimate by Margaret Drummond) Margaret Stewart = Sir John Drummond of Innerpeffry

3. Agnes Drummond = Hugh Montgomery, 3rd Earl of Eglinton, son of Hugh Montgomery, 2nd Earl of Eglinton, and Mariot Seton, daughter of George Seton, 3rd Baron Seton, and Janet Hepburn, daughter of Patrick Hepburn, 1st Earl of Bothwell, and Janet Douglas, daughter of James Douglas, 1st Earl of Morton and Princess Joan Stewart, daughter of James I, King of Scotland, d. 1437, and Joan Beaufort

4. Agnes Montgomery = Robert Semphill, 4th Baron Semphill

5. Barbara Semphill = Sir Colin Lamont of Ineryne

6. Anne Lamont = William Crauford of Auchenames

7. Barbara Crauford = Alexander Orr

8. Alexander Orr of Hazelside = Agnes Dalrymple

9. **John Orr** of Va. = Susannah Monroe Grayson.

Sources: *GVFT* 2:783-86; *SP* and *CP* (Semphill, Eglinton, Seton, Bothwell, Morton).

The Royal Descents of 500 Immigrants

1. James IV, King of Scotland, d. 1513 = Margaret Tudor of England

2. (illegitimate by Margaret Drummond) Margaret Stewart = Sir John Drummond of Innerpeffry

3. Isabel Drummond = Sir Matthew Campbell of Loudoun

4. Margaret Campbell = Thomas Boyd, 6th Baron Boyd

5. Hon. Robert Boyd = Jean Ker

6. Robert Boyd, 7th Baron Boyd = Christian Hamilton

7. Marion Boyd = Sir James Dundas of Arniston

8. Christian Dundas = Sir Charles Erskine, 1st Bt., son of Sir Charles Erskine (and Mary Hope), SETH, a descendant of James II, King of Scotland, d. 1460, and Mary of Guelders

9. Mary Erskine = Sir William Stirling, 2nd Bt.

10. Christian Stirling = John Stirling of Herbertshire

11. George Stirling of Herbertshire = ----

12. **Margaret Stirling** of Va. = (1) David **Forbes**; (2) ---- **Alexander**.

Sources: A.M. Sterling, *The Sterling Genealogy* (1909), 1:120, 178, 2:1209; *CB* (Stirling of Ardoch, Erskine of Alva); *Douglas*, p. 180 (Dundas of Arniston); *SP* and *CP* (Boyd -- under Kilmarnock in *SP*; Loudoun). I should like to see further documentation for generations 11 and 12, especially since I cannot find David Forbes (the immigrant's first husband), or his alleged (by A.M. Sterling) parents, "Sir William Forbes of Pitsligo and his wife Jean Erskine" in *Forbes*.

The Royal Descents of 500 Immigrants

1. James IV, King of Scotland, d. 1513 = Margaret Tudor of England

2. (illegitimate by Margaret Drummond) Margaret Stewart = John Gordon, Lord Gordon, son of Alexander Gordon, 3rd Earl of Huntly (and Janet Stewart), son of George Gordon, 2nd Earl of Huntly, and (prob.) Princess Annabella Stewart, daughter of James I, King of Scotland, d. 1437, and Joan Beaufort

3. George Gordon, 4th Earl of Huntly = Elizabeth Keith

4. Elizabeth Gordon = John Stewart, 4th Earl of Atholl

5. Elizabeth Stewart = Hugh Fraser, 5th Baron Lovat

6. Simon Fraser, 6th Baron Lovat = Jean Stewart

7. Sir James Fraser of Brae = Beatrix Wemyss

8. Magdalen Fraser = George Cuthbert of Castle Hill

9. John Cuthbert of Castle Hill = Jean Hay

10. **James Cuthbert** of S.C. = (1) Mrs. Patience Stobo Hamilton; (2) Mrs. Mary Hazzard Wigg.

Sources: J.G.B. Bulloch, *The Cuthberts, Barons of Castle Hill, and Their Descendants in South Carolina and Georgia* (1908), pp. 8-14, 35-37; *SP* and *CP* (Lovat, Atholl, Huntly).

The Royal Descents of 500 Immigrants

1. John I, King of Denmark, d. 1513 = Christine of Sweden

2. Elizabeth of Denmark = Joachim I, Elector of Brandenburg

3. Margaret of Brandenburg = John II, Prince of Anhalt-Zerbst

4. Joachim Ernest, Prince of Anhalt-Zerbst = Agnes of Barby

5. Sybil of Anhalt-Zerbst = Frederick, Duke of Württemberg-Mömpelgard

6. Louis Frederick, Duke of Württemberg-Mömpelgard = Anna Eleanor of Nassau-Weilberg, daughter of John Casimir, Count of Nassau-Weilberg (and Elizabeth of Hesse-Darmstadt), son of Albert, Count of Nassau-Weilberg and Anna of Nassau-Dillenburg, sister of William the Silent, Prince of Orange, d. 1564, 1st Stadholder of the Netherlands

7. George, Duke of Württemberg-Mömpelgard = Anne de Coligny

8. Leopold Eberhard, Duke of Württemberg-Mömpelgard, d. 1723 = (1) Anna Sabina Hedwiger, Countess von Sponeck; (2) Henrietta Hedwige Curie, Baroness von l'Esperance

9. (by 2) Karl Leopold, = 9. (by 1) Leopoldine
Baron von l'Esperance   Eberhardine,
and Sandersleben, Count   Countess von Sponeck
of Coligny

(This extraordinary marriage, and that of one of his sisters to one of her brothers, was of a half-brother and a half-sister)

10. Anna Elizabeth de Sandersleben, Countess of Coligny = Thomas de Pillot, seigneur de Chenecey, Marquis de Coligny

11. Charles Ignace de Pillot, Marquis de Coligny = Marie Anne Claude de Bernard de Sassenay

12. (Charles Francois) Emmanuel (Edwige) de Pillot, Marquis de Coligny = Charlotte Victorine Clémentine Angélique de Messey Beaupré

13. (Marie Simone) Léopoldine de Pillot = (Louis Joseph) Léonce Dedons, Marquis de Pierrefeu

14. (Louis Dolorès Emmanuel) Alphonse Dedons, Count de Pierrefeu = (Aline) Anne de Quérangal

15. **Alain Dedons, Count de Pierrefeu** of Mass. = Elsa Tudor (their daughters Dolores and Katharine Dedons de Pierrefeu married respectively Arthur Noyes Daniels and Horace Durham Gilbert, New Hampshire businessmen treated in *Who's Who in America*).

Sources: Henri, Baron de Woelmont de Brumagne, *Notices Généalogiques,* 6th ser. (1930), pp. 470-73 (Dedons de Pierrefeu); *GAdeF,* vol. 5, p. 288 (Pillot); *ES,* charts for the illegitimate agnate progeny of Leopold Eberhard, Duke of Württemberg-Mömpelgard (new ser., vol. 3, part 2, table 268) and for Württemberg, Nassau, Anhalt, Brandenburg, and Denmark.

The Royal Descents of 500 Immigrants

1. Casimir IV, King of Poland, d. 1492 = Elizabeth of Austria

2. Sophie of Poland = Frederick, Margrave of Brandenburg-Ansbach

3. Barbara of Brandenburg-Anspach = George, Landgrave of Leuchtenberg

4. Elizabeth of Leuchtenberg = John I, Count of Nassau-Dillenburg, brother of William the Silent, Prince of Orange, d. 1584, 1st Stadholder of The Netherlands

5. John II, Count of Nassau-Siegen = Magdalena of Waldeck

6. Elizabeth of Nassau-Siegen = Christian, Count of Waldeck-Wildungen

7. Louise Sybil of Waldeck-Wildungen = Gerhard Ludwig, Baron von Effern

8. Charlotte Dorothea, Countess von Effern = Augustin von Steuben

9. Wilhelm Augustin von Steuben = Maria Justina Dorothea von Jagow

10. **Friedrich Wilhelm Ludolf Gerhard Augustin, Baron von Steuben** (1730-1794), Prussian soldier, American Revolutionary commander, d. unm.

Sources: *DGA*, vol. 1 (1939), pp. 259, 264-65; *ES*, tables for Poland, Brandenburg-Anspach, Leuchtenberg, Nassau-Dillenburg, Nassau-Siegen, and Waldeck-Wildungen.

The Royal Descents of 500 Immigrants

1. Charles VII, King of France, d. 1461 = Marie of Anjou

2. (illegitimate by Agnes Sorèl) Charlotte de Valois = Jacques de Brezé, Count de Maulévrier

3. Louis de Brezé, Count de Maulévrier = Diane de Poitiers, Duchess de Valentinois, mistress of Henry II, King of France

4. Francoise de Brezé = Robert de la Marck, Duc de Bouillon

5. Diane de la Marck = Henri de Clermont, Count de Tonnerre

6. Charles Henri de Clermont, Count de Clermont et de Tonnerre = Catherine Marie d'Escoubleau de Sourdis

7. Isabeau de Clermont = Jacques de Beauvau, Seigneur du Rivau

8. Francoise de Beauvau = Jacques de Voyer, Vicomte de Paulmy

9. Jean Armand de Voyer, Marquis de Paulmy = Radegonde de Mauroy

10. Marie Francoise Céleste de Voyer = Charles Yves Jacques de La Rivière, Marquis de Paulmy, Count de La Rivière

11. Charles Yves Thibault de La Rivière, Marquis de La Rivière = Julie Célestine Barberin de Reignac

12. Julie Louise Céleste de La Rivière = Joseph Yves Thibault Hyacinthe de La Rivière, Marquis de La Rivière

13. Marie Louise Julie de La Rivière = Michel Louis Christophe Roch Gilbert Motier, Marquis de La Fayette

14. **Marie Joseph Paul Yves Roch Gilbert Motier, Marquis de La Fayette (Lafayette)** (1757-1834), the American revolutionary general and French statesman = Marie Adrienne Francoise de Noailles, ARD, SETH.

15. Anastasie Louise Pauline Motier = Just Charles César de Fay, Count de la Tour-Maubourg

16. Adrienne Jenny Florimonde de Fay = Charles Joseph Maurice Hector, Count Perrone di San Martino

17. Louise Perrone di San Martino = Félix Henri Victor Gaspard Edouard Alexandre, Count Rignon

18. Maria Cristina Giovanna Luigia Rignon = Augusto Filippo Stanislas Gazelli di Rossana

19. Luisa Albertina Cristina Giovanna Gazelli di Rossana = Fulco Antonio Francesco Benjamino, 1st Prince Ruffo di Calabria

20. Paola Margherita Giuseppina Maria Consiglia Ruffo di Calabria (Queen Paola of the Belgians) = Albert II, King of the Belgians (since August 1993), b. 1934

21. Philippe Leopold Louis Marie, Prince of the Belgians, b. 1960

21. Laurent Benoit Baudouin Marie, Prince of the Belgians, b. 1963

21. Astrid Josephine Charlotte Fabrizia Elisabeth Paola Maria, Princess of the Belgians, b. 1962 = Lorenz Otto Carl Amadeus Thadeus Maria Pius Andreas Marcus d'Aviano, Archduke of Austria, grandson of Charles I, Emperor of Austria.

Sources: Arnaud Chaffonjon, *La Fayette et sa Descendance* (1976), pp. 73-75 (generations 4-14), 99-101, 131-33, 143, 155-56, 160-61 (generations 15-21); *Anselme*, vol. 7, pp. 168-69 (de la Marck), vol. 8, pp. 271-72 (Brezé).

The Royal Descents of 500 Immigrants

1. James II, King of Scotland, d. 1460 = Mary of Guelders
2. Mary Stewart = James Hamilton, 1st Baron Hamilton
3. James Hamilton, 1st Earl of Arran = (1) Elizabeth Home; (2) Janet Beaton
4. (illegitimate by ----) Sir John Hamilton of Samuelston = Janet Home
5. Margaret Hamilton = David Douglas, 7th Earl of Angus
6. Margaret Douglas = Sir Walter Scott of Buccleuch

7. Mary Scott = William Elliot of Larriston

7. Walter Scott, 1st Baron Scott of Buccleuch = Margaret Kerr

8. Jean Eliot = Thomas Rutherford of Edgerston

8. Walter Scott, 1st Earl of Buccleuch = Mary Hay

9. Robert Rutherford of Edgerston = Marion Riddell

9. (illegitimate by ----) Francis Scott of Mangerton = ----

10. John Rutherford of Edgerston = Barbara Abernethy

10. Elizabeth Scott = Sir John Scott, 1st Bt.

11. Barbara Rutherford = Archibald Bennet of Chesters

11. Margaret Scott of Ancrum = John Murray of Bowhill

12. Andrew Bennet of Chesters = Dorothy Collingwood

12. Anne = Bennet

12. John Murray of Unthank

13. **Barbara Bennet** of N.C. = 13. **James Murray** of N.C. & Mass.

14. Elizabeth Murray = Edward Hutchinson Robbins
15. Anne Jean Robbins = Joseph Lyman (III)
16. Catherine Robbins Lyman = Warren Delano, Jr.

17. Sara Delano = James Roosevelt
18. Franklin Delano Roosevelt (1882-1945), 32nd U.S. President = (Anna) Eleanor Roosevelt

11. **John Scott** of N.Y. (brother of Mrs. Murray) = Magdalen Vincent.

13. **Barbara Murray** of N.C. (sister of James Murray of N.C. and Mass.) = Thomas **Clarke.**
13. John Murray = Mary Boyles
14. **John Boyles Murray** of N.Y. = Martha McClenachan.

11. Thomas Rutherford of Edgerston (brother of Barbara) = Susanna Riddell
12. Sir John Rutherford of Edgerston = Elizabeth Cairncross
13. **Walter Rutherford** of N.Y. = Catherine Alexander.
13. John Rutherford of Edgerston (and N.Y.) = Eleanor Elliot, ARD, SETH (John's family returned to Scotland but a great-grandson, Archibald Russell, SETH, also immigrated to N.Y. and married Helen Rutherford Watts, a great-granddaughter of John's brother Walter).

Sources: *DAB* (John Morin Scott), M.S.B. Chance & M.A.E. Smith, *Scott Family Letters* (1930), p. 318 esp. and N.M. Tiffany, *Letters of James Murray, Loyalist* (1901), pp. 292-94 esp.; *MGH*, 4th ser., vol. 2 (1906-7):166-68 (Scotts, Murrays, and Bennets); T.H. Cockburn-Hood, *The Rutherfords of That Ilk & Their Cadets* (1884), chart at end esp., Livingston Rutherfurd, *Family Records and Events* [Rutherfurd family] (1894), chapters 2-3 (pp. 85-256) and chart at end esp., and *Rutherfurd*, vol. 1, pp. 27, 31, 37-38, 47, 57, 70-71, 73-74; *Douglas*, p. 217 (Scott of Ancrum); *SP*, articles on the Scotts of Buccleuch, Douglases of Angus, and Hamiltons of Arran.

The Royal Descents of 500 Immigrants

1. James II, King of Scotland, d. 1460 = Mary of Guelders
2. Mary Stewart = James Hamilton, 1st Baron Hamilton
3. James Hamilton, 1st Earl of Arran = Janet Beaton
4. Jean Hamilton = Alexander Cunyngham, 5th Earl of Glencairn
5. William Cunyngham, 6th Earl of Glencairn = Janet Gordon
6. Elizabeth Cunyngham = (1) James Crawford of Crosbie; (2) Alexander Cunyngham of Craigends
7. (by 1) Jane Crawford = Patrick Crawford of Auchenames
8. Elizabeth Crawford = Robert Hunter of Hunterston
9. James Hunter = Margaret Spalding
10. **Robert Hunter** (d. 1734), colonial governor of N.Y. and N.J., lt. gov. of Va., governor of Jamaica, soldier, dramatist = Elizabeth Orby.

7. (by 2) William Cunyngham of Craigends = Elizabeth Stewart
8. William Cunyngham of Craigends = Elizabeth Napier, daughter of John Napier, the mathematician and inventor of logarithms, and Ann Chisolm
9. Alexander Cunyngham of Craigends = Janet Cunyngham
10. Rebecca Cunyngham = John Hamilton of Grange
11. Alexander Hamilton of Grange = Elizabeth Pollok
12. James Hamilton of Nevis, B.W.I.
13. (illegitimate by Mrs. Rachel Faucette Levine) **Alexander Hamilton** (1755 or 1757–1804) of N.Y., the statesman, 1st U.S. Secretary of the Treasury = Elizabeth Schuyler.

Sources: *BLG*, 18th ed., vol. 3 (1972), p. 473 (Hunter of Hunterston) and *BLG* 1939, p. 505 (Craufurd of Auchenames); *SP* and *CP* (Glencairn, Arran, Hamilton); *Hamilton*, pp. 1069-70, 221; Roberdeau Buchanan, *Genealogy of the Roberdeau Family* (1876), p. 20 (Cunyngham of Craigends), *BP* and *SP* (Napier).

The Royal Descents of 500 Immigrants

1. James II, King of Scotland, d. 1460 = Mary of Guelders
2. Mary Stewart = James Hamilton, 1st Baron Hamilton
3. Elizabeth Hamilton = Matthew Stewart, 2nd Earl of Lennox
4. John Stewart, 3rd Earl of Lennox = Anne Stewart
5. John Stewart, lord of Aubigny = Anne de la Queuille
6. Esmé Stewart, 1st Duke of Lennox, Scottish political leader = Catherine de Balsac
7. Mary Stewart = John Erskine, 2nd Earl of Mar
8. Sir Charles Erskine = Mary Hope
9. Mary Erskine = William Hamilton of Wishaw
10. Katherine Hamilton = David Pitcairn
11. **John Pitcairn** (1722-1775), British commander at the Battle of Lexington in April 1775 = Elizabeth Dalrymple.

Sources: *DAB;* Constance Pitcairn, *The History of the Fife Pitcairns* (1905), pp. 409-53 (esp. 419); *SP, BP* and *CP* (Belhaven, Rosslyn, Mar, Lennox, Hamilton -- under Arran in *SP*).

The Royal Descents of 500 Immigrants

1. James II, King of Scotland, d. 1460 = Mary of Guelders
2. Margaret Stewart = William Crichton, 3rd Baron Crichton
3. (of debated legitimacy, but certain maternity) Sir James Crichton = Catherine Borthwick
4. Margaret Crichton = John Robertson of Muirton
5. Gilbert Robertson of Muirton = Janet Reid
6. David Robertson of Muirton = ---- Innes
7. William Robertson of Muirton = Isabel Petrie
8. William Robertson of Gledney = ---- Mitchell (parents of William and Mary Robertson, who married Eleanor Pitcairn and William Adam respectively and grandparents of William Robertson [IV], the historian, and Robert Adam, the classical architect)
9. Jean Robertson = Alexander Henry
10. **John Henry** of Va. = Mrs. Sarah Winston Syme (parents of Patrick Henry, 1736-1799, the revolutionary statesman and editor).

Sources: W.T.J. Gun, *Studies in Hereditary Ability* (1928), pp. 170-81 and Mary Selden Kennedy, *Seldens of Virginia and Allied Families,* vol. 2 (1911), pp. 387-92; *BLG* 1937, p. 2452 (Robertson, under Williamson of Lawers); *DNB* (William Robertson and Robert Adam); *SP* and *CP* (Crichton).

The Royal Descents of 500 Immigrants

1. James I, King of Scotland, d. 1437 = Joan Beaufort
2. Annabella Stewart = George Gordon, 2nd Earl of Huntly
3. Alexander Gordon, 3rd Earl of Huntly, whose maternity may be uncertain = Janet Stewart, daughter of John Stewart, 1st Earl of Atholl (and Margaret Douglas), son of Sir James Stewart, the "Black Knight of Lorne" and Joan Beaufort, Dowager Queen of Scotland, above and SETH
4. Jean Gordon = Colin Campbell, 3rd Earl of Argyll
5. Archibald Campbell, 4th Earl of Argyll = Margaret Graham
6. Janet Campbell = Hector MacLean of Duart, chief of the Clan MacLean
7. Marion MacLean = Hector Roy MacLean of Coll, a cousin
8. Lachlan MacLean of Coll = Florence MacLeod of MacLeod
9. Neil MacLean of Drimnacross = Florence MacDonald of Morrer
10. Allan MacLean of Grisiboll = Catherine MacLean of Balliphetrish
11. **Neil MacLean (McLean)** of Conn. = Mrs. Hannah Stillman Caldwell.
11. **Allan MacLean (McLean)** of Conn. = (1) Susanna Beauchamp; (2) Mary Loomis. John MacLean, a brother of the immigrants Neil and Allan, married Anne MacLean of Kilmore in Mull and was the father of John MacLean, a merchant of Norfolk, Va., said to have married there and left a daughter, but for whom I can find no NDTPS.

10. Florence MacLean (sister of Allan of Grisiboll) = Charles MacLean of Borreray
11. Archibald MacLean = Susanna Campbell of Scamadall
12. John MacLean = Anne Long or Lang

13. **John MacLean** (1771-1814) of N.J., chemist, educator = Phebe Bainbridge. Their son, another John MacLean (1800-1886), was 10th president of the College of New Jersey, later Princeton University.

12. Margaret MacLean (sister of John) = Neil McLeod (MacLeod)

13. **Alexander McLeod** (MacLeod) (1774-1833) of N.Y., Reformed Presbyterian clergyman, author and editor = Maria Anne Agnew.

Sources: J.P. MacLean, *A History of the Clan MacLean* (1889), pp. 90-91, 285-87, 295-96, 273-74, *DAB* (John MacLean and Alexander McLeod), and *SP* and *CP* (Argyll, Huntly, Atholl). See also John J. McLean, *A Brief History of the Ancestry and Posterity of Doctor Neil McLean of Hartford, Conn., U.S.A.* (1900), and Mary McLean Hardy, *A Brief History of the Ancestry and Posterity of Allan MacLean, 1715-1786, Vernon, Colony of Connecticut, New England, U.S.A.* (1905). These immigrants were first brought to my attention by Thomas Frederick Gede of Davis, California.

The Royal Descents of 500 Immigrants

1. James I, King of Scotland, d. 1437 = Joan Beaufort

2. Joan Stewart = James   2. Annabella Stewart =
   Douglas, 1st Earl of   George Gordon, 2nd
   Morton   Earl of Huntly

3. John Douglas, 3. Elizabeth Gordon 3. Isabel Gordon =
   2nd Earl of   = William Keith,   William Hay,
   Morton   2nd Earl   3rd Earl of
   = Janet   Marischal   Erroll
   Crichton

4. Elizabeth   = 4. Robert, Lord   4. Thomas Hay =
   Douglas   Keith   Margaret Logie

5. William Keith, 3rd Earl   5. George Hay, 7th Earl of
   Marischal = Margaret,   Erroll = Margaret
   Keith, a cousin   Robertson

6. William, Lord Keith   =   6. Elizabeth Hay

7. Margaret Keith = Sir William Keith of Ludquhairn

8. Sir William Keith, 1st Bt. = ----

9. Sir Alexander Keith, 2nd Bt. = Margaret Bannerman

10. Sir William Keith, 3rd Bt. = Jean Smith

11. **Sir William Keith**, 4th Bt. (1680-1749), colonial
    governor of Pa. and Del. = Anne Newbury.

7. George Keith, 4th Earl Marischal (brother of Lady
   William Keith) = Margaret Ogilvy

8. Sir James Keith of Benholm = Margaret Lindsay

9. Elizabeth Keith = Sir Archibald Primrose, 1st Bt.

10. Margaret Primrose = Sir John Foulis, 1st Bt.

11. Elizabeth Foulis = Alexander Gibson of Durie

12. Archibald Gibson, Baron von Gibson in Prussia =
    Renata Clark

13. Helen Gibson = Otto Ernst, Count von Keyserlingk

14. Otto Alexander Heinrich Dietrich, Count von
    Keyserlingk = Emilie Alexandrine, Countess von Dönhoff

15. Friederike Caroline Alexandrine Emma, Countess von
    Keyserlingk = Gustav Friedrich Eugen von Below (their
    son, Friedrich Karl Bogislav von Below, married Maria
    Karoline Elizabeth von der Goltz and was the father of
    [Anton] Georg Hugo von Below, German historian)

16. Karl Emil Gustav von Below = Eleonore Melitta Behrend

17. Marie Eleonore Dorothea von Below = Wernher Theodor
    August Friedrich Wilhelm von Quistorp

18. Emmy Melitta Cécile von Quistorp = Magnus Alexander
    Maximilian, Freiherr (Baron) von Braun

19. **Wernher Magnus Maximilian, Freiherr (Baron) von
    Braun** (1912-1977) of Huntsville, Ala., the rocket
    scientist = 19. **Maria Irmengard Emmy Luise Gisela von
    Quistorp** of Ala., his first cousin, daughter of 18.
    Alexander August Gustav Henric Achim Albrecht von
    Quistorp (son of generation 17 above) and Theda
    Elisabeth Klementine Franziska von Falkenhayn.

Sources: *DAB, GPFPM* 472-80, *CB* (Keith of Ludquhairn); *SP* and
CP (Marischal, Huntly, Morton, Erroll) (Sir William Keith, 4th Bt.);
GH des A, vol. 21 (Freiherrl Häuser A, Band III, 1959), pp. 519-28,
and *Ahnentafeln Berühmter Deutscher,* vol. 4 (1938), for Georg von
Below, esp. tafeln 1 and 7, pp. 284, 288 (von Braun).

The Royal Descents of 500 Immigrants

1. James I, King of Scotland, d. 1437 = Joan Beaufort
2. Joan Stewart = James Douglas, 1st Earl of Morton
3. Janet Douglas = Patrick Hepburn, 1st Earl of Bothwell
4. Janet Hepburn = George Seton, 3rd Baron Seton
5. George Seton, 4th Baron Seton = Elizabeth Hay
6. John Seton of Cariston = Isabel Balfour
7. George Seton of Cariston = Margaret Ayton
8. George Seton of Cariston = Cecilia Kynynmond
9. Isabella Seton = Sir George Seton of Parbroath
10. Robert Seton = ----
11. James Seton = Margaret Newton
12. John Seton = Elizabeth Seton of Belsies
13. **William Seton** of N.Y. = (1) Rebecca Curson, daughter of Richard Curson of Md., ARD, SETH, and Elizabeth Becker (their son, William Magee Seton, married Elizabeth Ann Bayley, known as Mother [Elizabeth Ann Bayley] Seton, foundress of the American Sisters of Charity); (2) Anna Maria Curson.
13. **Margaret Seton** of N.Y. = Andrew **Seton** (of Barnes, almost certainly a kinsman).

Sources: Monsignor Robert Seton, *An Old Family or the Setons of Scotland and America* (1899), pp. 176-78, 197-98, 239-73, 312-13 esp.; *SP* and *CP* (Seton [under Winton in *SP*], Bothwell, Morton).

The Royal Descents of 500 Immigrants

1. James I, King of Scotland, d. 1437 = Joan Beaufort
2. Annabella Stewart = George Gordon, 2nd Earl of Huntly
3. Elizabeth Gordon = William Keith, 3rd Earl Marischal
4. Agnes Keith = Sir Archibald Douglas of Glenbervie
5. William Douglas, 9th Earl of Angus = Egidia Graham
6. Sir Robert Douglas of Glenbervie = Elizabeth Auchinleck
7. Margaret Douglas = Sir Thomas Burnet, 1st Bt.
8. Catherine Burnet = Robert Gordon of Pitlurg
9. **Thomas Gordon**, chief justice of N.J. = (1) Helen ----; (2) Janet Mudie.

6. Margaret Douglas (sister of Sir Robert) = William Forbes of Monymusk
7. Sir William Forbes, 1st Bt. = Elizabeth Wishart
8. Robert Forbes of Barnes = ---- ----
9. Jean Forbes = Alexander Forbes of Ballogie
10. ---- Forbes = Robert Burnett of N.J.
11. **Isabel Burnett** of N.J. = William **Montgomery** of N.J., ARD, SETH.

Sources: *AR7*, line 256 (Thomas Gordon, generations 7-9), *Burnett of Leys,* pp. 32-72, *CB* and *BP* (Burnet of Leys and Douglas of Glenbervie, baronets); *SP* and *CP* (Angus, Marischal, Huntly); *Montgomery,* pp. 79-83 and *Forbes,* pp. 301-2, 410.

The Royal Descents of 500 Immigrants

1. James I, King of Scotland, d. 1437 = Joan Beaufort
2. Annabella Stewart = George Gordon, 2nd Earl of Huntly
3. Sir William Gordon of Gight = Janet Ogilvy
4. John Gordon of Gight = Marjory Gordon of Lesmoir
5. William Gordon of Gight = Isabel Ochterlony
6. John Gordon of Ardlogie = ---- Keir
7. John Gordon of Ardlogie = Isabel Innes
8. Elizabeth Gordon = John Innes of Edingight
9. John Innes of Edingight = Helen Strachan
10. John Innes of Edingight = Jean Duff
11. John Innes of Edingight = Elizabeth Grant
12. Elizabeth Innes = George Robinson of Gask
13. William Rose Robinson of Clermiston = Mary Douglas
14. **Douglas Robinson** of N.Y. = Fanny Monroe, great-niece of James Monroe, 5th U.S. President.

Sources: *BLG* 1952, pp. 2171-72 (Robertson of Orchardton); *BP* (Innes of Balvenie, baronets); *Gordon*, vol. 1 (1903), Gordon of Gight section, pp. 9-21, 33-51; *SP* and *CP* (Huntly).

The Royal Descents of 500 Immigrants

1. James I, King of Scotland, d. 1437 = Joan Beaufort
2. Joan Stewart = James Douglas, 1st Earl of Morton
3. Janet Douglas = Patrick Hepburn, 1st Earl of Bothwell
4. Janet Hepburn = George Seton, 3rd Baron Seton
5. George Seton, 4th Baron Seton = Elizabeth Hay
6. Beatrix Seton = Sir George Ogilvy of Dunlugas
7. Janet Ogilvy = William Forbes of Tolquhon
8. Thomas Forbes of Waterton = Jean Ramsay
9. Grizel Forbes = John Douglas of Inchmarlo
10. John Douglas of Tilquhillie = Agnes Horn
11. Euphemia Douglas = Charles Irvine of Over Boddam
12. **John Irvine** of Ga. = Ann Elizabeth Baillie.
13. Anne Irvine = James Bulloch
14. James Stephens Bulloch = Martha Stewart
15. Martha Bulloch = Theodore Roosevelt
16. Theodore Roosevelt, Jr. (1858-1919), 26th U.S. President = (1) Alice Hathaway Lee; (2) Edith Kermit Carow

Sources: *MCS4*, line 93; *BSIC*, pp. 85-87; *TSA* 8(1893-94):40-42; *Forbes*, pp. 396-97, 416; *SP*, articles on Ogilvys (of Dunlugas, later Lords Banff), Setons (Lords Seton, later Earls of Winton), Hepburns (Earls of Bothwell) and Douglases (Earls of Morton).

The Royal Descents of 500 Immigrants

1. Charles VI, King of France, d. 1422 = Isabella of Bavaria (parents of Catherine of France, wife of Henry V, King of England, and of Sir Owen Tudor, and paternal grandmother of Henry VII, King of England)

2. Joanna of France = John VI, Duke of Brittany

3. Isabel of Brittany = Guy XIV, Count of Laval

4. Louise de Laval = Jean III de Brosse, Count of Penthièvre

5. Isabel de Brosse = Jean IV, Sire de Rieux and de Rochefort, Count of Harcourt

6. Jean de Rieux, Seigneur de Châteauneuf = Béatrix de Jonchères

7. René de Rieux, Seigneur de Sourdéac = Susanne de Sainte Melaine

8. Marie de Rieux = Sébastien de Plöeuc, Marquis de Timeur (great-great-great-grandparents of Donatien Alphonse Francois de Sade, Count de Sade, the infamous Marquis de Sade, the erotic writer)

9. Marie de Plöeuc = Guillaume de Penancoët, Seigneur de Kéroualle

10. Henriette Mauricette de Penancoët de Kéroualle (sister of Louise Renée de Penancoët de Kéroualle, Duchess of Portsmouth and mistress of Charles II, King of England, SETH) = Philip Herbert, 7th Earl of Pembroke

11. Charlotte Herbert = John Jeffreys, 2nd Baron Jeffreys

12. Henrietta Louisa Jeffreys = Thomas Fermor, 1st Earl of Pomfret

13. **Lady Juliana Fermor** = Thomas **Penn** (1702-1775), proprietor of Pa., son of William Penn, the founder of Pennsylvania, and Hannah Callowhill.

Sources: *DAB* (Thomas Penn) and *GPFPGM* 2:566-70; *CP* (Pomfret, Jeffreys, Pembrooke, Portsmouth); *D de la N*, vol. 15, pp. 628-29 (Penancoët de Kéroualle), 954 (Plöeuc); *Anselme*, vol. 6, pp. 767-68, 771-73 (Rieux), vol. 5, pp. 574-75 (Brosse); *ES*, tables for Laval, Brittany, and France.

The Royal Descents of 500 Immigrants

1. Henry IV, King of England, d. 1413 = Mary Bohun

2. Humphrey Plantagenet, Duke of Gloucester = (1) Jacqueline of Bavaria; (2) Eleanor Cobham (probably the mother of Antigone)

3. (illegitimate) Antigone Plantagenet = Henry Grey, 2nd Earl of Tankerville

4. Elizabeth Grey = Sir Roger Kynaston

5. Mary Kynaston = Hywel ap Jenkin

6. Humphrey ap Hywel = Anne Herbert

7. Jane ferch Humphrey ap Hywel = Gruffudd Nannau ap Hywel

8. John ap Gruffudd (John Nannau) = Elsbeth ferch Dafydd Llwyd

9. Lewys ap John Gruffudd = Elen ferch Hywel ap Gruffudd

10. Rees Lewys ap John Gruffudd = Catrin ferch Elisha ap Dafydd

10. Owain ap Lewys = Mary ferch Tudur Vaughn

11. Ellis ap Rees (alias Ellis Price) = Anne Humphrey, ARD, SETH

11. Robert ab Owain = Margaret ferch John ap Lewys

12. **Rowland Ellis** of Pa. = (2) = (1) Margaret ferch Ellis Morris

12. **Margaret Roberts** of Pa.

12. Lewis ap Robert (brother of Mrs. Margaret Roberts Ellis of Pa.) = Mary ----

13. **Ellis Lewis** of Pa. = (1) Elizabeth Newlin; (2) Mrs. Mary (----) Baldwin.

Sources: *Merion,* pp. 216-29, 235-37; *WFP1,* p. 116, footnote 1 and chart between pp. 116-17; *Bartrum 2,* pp. 131, 1428, 148 (generations 4-7).

Note: Ellis Lewys, a third son of Lewys ap John Gruffudd and Elen ferch Hywel ap Gruffudd, married Elen ferch Gruffudd ap Hywel and left a daughter, Elen Ellis, who married Thomas ap Robert. Their son, Robert ap Thomas, by Catrin ----, his wife, left a son, Thomas Roberts, bp. 19 April 1691 at Mallwyn, Merionethshire, suggested in *CVR*, pp. 224-33 as the immigrant Thomas Roberts of Milford, Pa. (= Alice ----).

The Royal Descents of 500 Immigrants

1. Henry IV, King of England, d. 1413 = Mary Bohun
2. Humphrey Plantagenet, Duke of Gloucester = (1) Jacqueline of Bavaria; (2) Eleanor Cobham (probably the mother of Antigone)
3. (illegitimate) Antigone Plantagenet = Henry Grey, 2nd Earl of Tankerville
4. Elizabeth Grey = Sir Roger Kynaston
5. Humphrey Kynaston = Elsbeth ferch Maredudd ap Hywel
6. Margaret Kynaston = John ap Ieuan ab Owain
7. Humphrey Wynn = Mawd ferch Oliver ap Thomas Pryce
8. Catrin Wynn = John Lloyd
9. Charles Lloyd = Elizabeth Stanley
10. **Thomas Lloyd** (1640-1694), dep. gov. of Pa., physician, colonial statesman = (1) Mary Jones of Pa., ARD, SETH; (2) Mrs. Patience Gardiner Story.

10. Charles Lloyd (brother of Dep. Gov. Thomas) = Elizabeth Lort, see below
11. Sampson Lloyd = Mary Crowley
12. Sampson Lloyd = Rachel Champion
13. Charles Lloyd = Mary Farmer
14. Anna Lloyd = Isaac Braithwaite
15. Joseph Bevan Braithwaite = Martha Gillett
16. **Anna Lloyd Braithwaite** of Md. = Richard Henry **Thomas** (1854-1904), physician, Quaker minister, author.

1. Henry VIII, King of England, d. 1547
2. (possibly an illegitimate son by Mary Berkeley, daughter of James Berkeley and Susan Viell, and granddaughter of Maurice Berkeley and Isabel Mead, SETH; possibly also, however, a son of Mary Berkeley and Sir Thomas Perrott, her 1st husband) Sir John Perrott = Jane Pollard
3. Anne Perrott = Sir John Phillips, 1st Bt.

4. Olive Phillips = Sampson Lort
5. Elizabeth Lort = Charles Lloyd, see above

Sources: *MCS4*, line 31, *Merion*, pp. 340–42 (Lloyd) and Charles F.H. Evans and Irene Haines Leet, *Thomas Lloyd, Dolobran to Pennsylvania* (1982) (including an ancestor table of Dep. Gov. Thomas Lloyd for 8 generations); *Bartrum 2*, pp. 131, 21 (generations 4–7); *RLNGF* 2:15–20 (Mrs. Thomas); *DNB* (Sir John Perrott) and *CB* (Phillips of Picton Castle).

The Royal Descents of 500 Immigrants

1. Henry IV, King of England, d. 1413 = Mary Bohun

2. Humphrey Plantagenet, Duke of Gloucester = (1) Jacqueline of Bavaria; (2) Eleanor Cobham (probably the mother of Antigone)

3. (illegitimate) Antigone Plantagenet = Henry Grey, 2nd Earl of Tankerville

4. Elizabeth Grey = Sir Roger Kynaston

5. Jane Kynaston = Roger Thornes

6. John Thornes = Elizabeth Astley

7. Richard Thornes = Margaret ---- or Joan ferch Evan Lloyd

8. Alice Thornes = John Lyttelton (Littleton)

9. Sir Edward Lyttelton (Littleton) = Mary Walter

10. **Nathaniel Littleton** of Va. = Anne South(e)y.

Sources: *AR7*, line 1A, and sources cited therein, esp. *Transactions of the Shropshire Archaeological and National History Society*, 4th ser., vol. 3 (1913), pp. 302-32 (Littleton) and George Grazebrook and J.P. Rylands, *Visitation of Shropshire, 1623*, vol. 2 (*HSPVS*, vol. 29, 1889), pp. 458-60 (Thornes), 295 (Kynaston). See also *NEHGR* 41(1887):364-68 and *AP&P*, pp. 577-78.

The Royal Descents of 500 Immigrants

1. Henry IV, King of England, d. 1413 = Mary Bohun

2. Humphrey Plantagenet, Duke of Gloucester = (1) Jacqueline of Bavaria; (2) Eleanor Cobham (probably the mother of Antigone)

3. (illegitimate) Antigone Plantagenet = Henry Grey, 2nd Earl of Tankerville

4. Elizabeth Grey = Sir Roger Kynaston

5. Margaret Kynaston = Richard Hanmer

6. Sir Thomas Hanmer = Jane Brereton

7. Sir Thomas Hanmer = Catherine Salter

8. John Hanmer = Jane Salisbury

9. Sir Thomas Hanmer = Catherine Mostyn

10. Sir John Hanmer, 1st Bt. = Dorothy Trevor

11. Sir Thomas Hanmer, 2nd Bt. = Susan Hervey

12. William Hanmer = Peregrine North

13. Susan Hanmer = Sir Henry Bunbury, 3rd Bt.

14. Isabella Bunbury = John Lee

15. **Charles Lee** (1731-1782), soldier of fortune, U.S. revolutionary general, d. unm.

Sources: *DAB* and *DNB* (Charles Lee); *Ormerod*, vol. 1, pp. 630-31 (Lee), vol. 2, pp. 395-96 (Bunbury); *CB* and *BP* (Bunbury of Stanney and Hanmer of Hanmer, baronets); Calvert Hanmer, *The Hanmers of Marton and Montford Salop* (1916), pp. 41-44 and chart at end entitled "Extract from the Pedigree of the Hanmers of Hanmer, showing their connection with the families of Bunbury and Lee."

The Royal Descents of 500 Immigrants

1. Robert III, King of Scotland, d. 1406 = Annabella Drummond
2. Mary Stewart = George Douglas, 1st Earl of Angus
3. William Douglas, 2nd Earl of Angus = Margaret Hay
4. George Douglas, 4th Earl of Angus = Isabel Sibbald
5. Archibald Douglas, 5th Earl of Angus = Elizabeth Boyd
6. Sir William Douglas of Glenbervie = Elizabeth Auchinleck
7. Sir Archibald Douglas of Glenbervie = Elizabeth Irvine
8. John Douglas (half-brother of William Douglas, 9th Earl of Angus) = ----
9. John Douglas of Leith = ----
10. Rev. William Douglas of Aboyne = ----
11. Rev. William Douglas of Midmar = ----
12. Robert Douglas of Blackmiln = Barbara Farquharson
13. Francis Douglas of Aberdeen and Paisley = Elizabeth Ochterloney
14. Bethiah Douglas = Hugh Cochrane of Glanderston
15. John Cochrane of Glanderston = Isabella Ramsay
16. **Alexander Cochrane** of Mass. = Margaret Rae.

Sources: Walter Kendall Watkins, *The Cochranes of Renfrewshire, Scotland: The Ancestry of Alexander Cochrane of Billerica and Malden, Mass., U.S.A.* (1904) and Cochrane tabular pedigree compiled by same (TP COC 735 at NEHGS), which contains some errors; *NEHGR* 56(1902):192 (reprinted in *EO* 2:2:802) and *SP* and *CP* (Angus).

The Royal Descents of 500 Immigrants

1. Robert III, King of Scotland, d. 1406 = Annabella Drummond
2. Mary Stewart = James Kennedy of Dunure
3. Gilbert Kennedy, 1st Baron Kennedy = Katherine Maxwell
4. John Kennedy, 2nd Baron Kennedy = Elizabeth Montgomery
5. David Kennedy, 1st Earl of Cassilis = Agnes Borthwick
6. Gilbert Kennedy, 2nd Earl of Cassilis = Isabel Campbell
7. Gilbert Kennedy, 3rd Earl of Cassilis = Margaret Kennedy
8. Sir Thomas Kennedy of Culzean = Elizabeth Makgill
9. Sir Alexander Kennedy of Culzean = Agnes Kennedy
10. Alexander Kennedy of Craigoch and Kilhenzie = Anna Crawford
11. **Archibald Kennedy** (c. 1685-1763) of N.Y., British colonial official (collector of customs and provincial councillor) = (1) --- Massan (by whom he was the father of Archibald Kennedy, 11th Earl of Cassilis); (2) Mrs. Mary Walter Schuyler.

Sources: *BP* (Ailsa), *SP* and *CP* (Cassilis).

1. Robert III, King of Scotland, d. 1406 = Annabella Drummond

2. Mary Stewart = George Douglas, 1st Earl of Angus

3. Elizabeth Douglas = Alexander Forbes, 1st Baron Forbes

4. James Forbes, 2nd Baron Forbes = Egidia Keith

5. Duncan Forbes of Corsindae = Christian Mercer

5. Margaret Forbes = Malcolm Forbes of Tolquhon

6. William Forbes of Corsindae = Margaret Lumsden

6. William Forbes of Tolquhon = ---- Leith

7. James Forbes of Corsindae = Janet Gordon

7. Alexander Forbes of Tolquhon = Alison Anderson

8. William Forbes of Tolquhon = Elizabeth Gordon

8. John Forbes of Bandley = Elizabeth Keith

8. William Forbes of Corsindae = 9. Janet Forbes

9,10. James Forbes of Corsindae = Katherine Mortimer

10,11. Janet Forbes = 9. Duncan Forbes of Culloden
(Their daughter, Elizabeth Forbes, married William Baillie of Dunain and was the mother of the Alexander Baillie of Dunain who married Jean Mackenzie and of the Mary Baillie who married William Mackintosh of Borlum, both SETH.)

10-12. John Forbes of Culloden = Anna Dunbar

11-13. John Forbes of Pittencrieff = Elizabeth Graham

12-14. **John Forbes** (c.1710-1759) of Pa., British army officer, hero of Fort Duquesne = ----.

Sources: *DNB*, supp.; *Forbes,* pp. 406-7 (Pittencrieff), 403 (Culloden), 394-95 (Tolquhon), 294-97 (Corsindae), 25-42 (1st and 2nd barons Forbes); *SP* and *CP* (Forbes, Angus).

The Royal Descents of 500 Immigrants

1. Robert III, King of Scotland, d. 1406 = Annabella Drummond
2. Margaret Stewart = Archibald Douglas, 4th Earl of Douglas
3. Elizabeth Douglas = William Sinclair, 3rd Earl of Orkney, 1st Earl of Caithness
4. Elizabeth Sinclair = Sir Andrew Leslie, master of Rothes
5. William Leslie, 3rd Earl of Rothes = Janet Balfour
6. Hon. John Leslie of Parkhill = Euphemia Moncreiff
7. Joan Leslie = Sir Alexander Dunbar of Cumnock
8. Margaret Dunbar = Robert Munro, 14th baron of Foulis
9. George Munro of Katewell = ---
10. George Munro of Katewell = Euphemia Munro of Pittonachy
11. David Munro of Katewell = Agnes Munro of Durness
12. **Rev. John Munro** of Va. = Christian Blair (their daughter, Mary Munro, married John Blair, her 1st cousin, colonial governor of Va. and president of its council). Rev. John's brother, Rev. Andrew Munro of Isle of Wight Co., Va., married Mrs. Sarah Smith Pitt and left issue but probably no NDTPS. Rev. Andrew was *not*, however, the Andrew Munroe/Munro of St. Mary's Co., Md., and Westmoreland Co., Va., patrilineal great-great-grandfather of U.S. President James Monroe.

Sources: *Clan Munro Magazine,* no. 6 (1959-60):14-18, R.W. Munro, ed., *The Munro Tree: A Genealogy and Chronology of the Munros of Foulis and Other Families of the Clan, a Manuscript Compiled in 1734 Edited with Introduction and Notes* (1978), pp. 15, 17 and notes Q, Q45-48, and Alexander Mackenzie, *History of the Munros of Fowlis* (1898), pp. 40-43, 480-81; *Douglas,* pp. 120-21 (Dunbar of Cumnock); *SP* and *CP* (Rothes, Caithness, Douglas).

The Royal Descents of 500 Immigrants

1. Robert III, King of Scotland, d. 1406 = Annabella Drummond
2. Mary Stewart = George Douglas, 1st Earl of Angus
3. Elizabeth Douglas = Alexander Forbes, 1st Baron Forbes
4. James Forbes, 2nd Baron Forbes = Egidia Keith
5. William Forbes, 3rd Baron Forbes = Christian Gordon
6. John Forbes, 6th Baron Forbes = Christian Lundin
7. Elizabeth Forbes = Alexander Dunbar of Conzie and Kilbuyack
8. William Dunbar of Hempriggs = Margaret Anderson
9. John Dunbar of Hempriggs = ---- ----
10. James Dunbar of Newton = ---- ----
11. Archibald Dunbar of Newton and Thunderton = Elizabeth Hacket
12. Robert Dunbar of Newton and Thunderton = Margaret Mackenzie
13. (Sir) Archibald Dunbar of Newton and Thunderton (*de jure* 4th Bt. of Northfield) = Anne Bayne
14. **William Dunbar** (1749-1810) of Natchez, Mississippi, planter and scientist = Dinah Clark.

Sources: Mrs. Dunbar Rowland, *The Life, Letters and Papers of William Dunbar* (1930), pp. 14-15 esp.; *BP* and *CB* (Dunbar of Northfield [or Hempriggs]); *SP* and *CP* (Forbes, Angus).

The Royal Descents of 500 Immigrants

1. Robert III, King of Scotland, d. 1406 = Annabella Drummond
2. Mary Stewart = George Douglas, 1st Earl of Angus
3. Elizabeth Douglas = Alexander Forbes, 1st Baron Forbes
4. James Forbes, 2nd Baron Forbes = Egidia Keith
5. Duncan Forbes of Corsindae = Christian Mercer
6. James (Jacob) Forbes of Sweden = Helen Lundie
7. Mattias (Matthew) Forbes = Margareta Penters
8. Ernald Forbes = Carin Björnram
9. Arvid (Forbes), Baron Forbus = Margareta Boije
10. Sofia Juliana, Baroness Forbus = Axel Julius, Count de la Gardie
11. Magnus Julius, Count de la Gardie = Hedwig Catharina, Countess Lillie
12. Hedwig Catharina, Countess de la Gardie = Frederick Axel, Count von Fersen
13. **Hans Axel, Count von Fersen** (1755-1810), Swedish soldier, aide-de-camp to Rochambeau during the American Revolution, favorite and benefactor of Marie Antoinette, Queen of France, d. unm.

Sources: *DAB* and *ES*, vol. 8, tables 153-154 (de la Gardie); *Elgenstierna*, vol. 2, pp. 686 (von Fersen), 227-28 (de la Gardie), 787-88, 792-93 (Forbes, Forbus); *SP* (Forbes, Angus). See also *Forbes*, pp. 469-71.

The Royal Descents of 500 Immigrants

1. Robert II, King of Scotland, d. 1390 = (2) Euphemia of Ross

2. Katherine (also called Jean or Elizabeth) Stewart = David Lindsay, 1st Earl of Crawford

3. Elizabeth Lindsay = Robert Erskine, 1st Baron Erskine

4. Christian Erskine = Patrick Graham, 1st Baron Graham

5. Elizabeth Graham = William Livingston of Kilsyth

6. William Livingston of Kilsyth = Janet Bruce

7. Alexander Livingston of Over and Nether Inches = Barbara Forrester

8. Barbara Livingston = Alexander Livingston, rector of Monyabroch

9. William Livingston, rector of Monyabroch = Agnes Livingston

10. John Livingston, rector of Ancrum = Janet Fleming

11. **Robert Livingston the elder** (1654-1728) of N.Y., 1st lord of Livingston Manor, landowner, merchant, public official = Mrs. Alida Schuyler Van Rensselaer.

12. Gilbert Livingston = Cornelia Beekman

13. James Livingston = Judith Newcomb

14. Gilbert James Livingston = Susanna Lewis

15. Judith Livingston = Samuel Herrick Butler

16. Courtland Philip Livingston Butler = Elizabeth Slade Pierce

17. Mary Elizabeth Butler = Robert Emmet Sheldon

18. Flora Sheldon = Samuel Prescott Bush

19. Prescott Sheldon Bush, U.S. Senator = Dorothy Walker

20. George Herbert Walker Bush (b. 1924), 41st U.S. President = Barbara Pierce

11. James Livingston (brother of Robert the elder) = ----

12. **Robert Livingston the younger** of N.Y. = Margareta Schuyler.

7. Elizabeth Livingston (sister of Alexander) = Gabriel Cunyngham of Craigends

8. James Cunyngham of Achenyeard = Margaret Fleming

9. William Cunyngham, clerk of the Signet of Edinburgh = Rebecca Muirhead

10. Richard Cunyngham of Glengarnock = Elizabeth Heriot

11. Robert Cunyngham of St. Christopher, B.W.I. = Judith Elizabeth de Bonneson

12. Mary Cunyngham = Isaac Roberdeau

13. **Daniel Roberdeau** (c. 1727-1795) of Pa., merchant, revolutionary patriot = (1) Mary Bostwick; (2) Jane Milligan.

Sources: *MCS4*, lines 42, 42B, 43 and sources cited therein, esp. Florence Van Rensselaer, *The Livingston Family in America and Its Scottish Origins* (1949), pp. 5-7, 45-46, 49-50, 52, 81, 301 and E.B. Livingston, *The Livingstons of Callendar and Their Principal Cadets* (1920), pp. 446-49, 212-17 (the Robert Livingstons); *SP* and *CP* (Graham or Montrose, Erskine or Mar, Crawford); *LDBR* 1:227-28 and Roberdeau Buchanan, *Genealogy of the Roberdeau Family* (1876), chart opposite p. 9 (which contains some errors) and pp. 19, 21-102.

The Royal Descents of 500 Immigrants

1. Robert II, King of Scotland, d. 1390 = (2) Euphemia of Ross

2. Katherine (also called Jean or Elizabeth) Stewart = David Lindsay, 1st Earl of Crawford

3. Elizabeth Lindsay = Robert Erskine, 1st Baron Erskine

4. Thomas Erskine, 2nd Baron Erskine = Janet Douglas

5. Alexander Erskine, 3rd Baron Erskine = Christian Crichton

6. Robert Erskine, 4th Baron Erskine = Isabel Campbell

7. James Erskine of Little Sauchie and Balgownie = Christian Stirling

8. Alexander Erskine of Shielfield = Elizabeth Haliburton

9. Ralph Erskine of Shielfield = (1) Isabella Cairncross; (2) Janet Wilson

10. (probably by 2) Henry Erskine of Chirnside = Margaret Halcro

11. Ralph Erskine of Dunfermline = Margaret Simpson

12. **Robert Erskine** (1735-1780) of N.J., geographer and hydraulic engineer = Elizabeth ----.

10. (by 1) John Erskine of Shielfield = Margaret Haliburton

11. James Erskine of Shielfield = Elizabeth Carre

12. ---- Erskine (daughter) = Patrick Haliburton of Muirhouselaw

13. George Haliburton, Lord Provost of Edinburgh = Jean Clark

14. Jean Haliburton = Edward Burd of Ormiston

15. **James Burd** of Pa. = Sarah Shippen.

Sources: *DAB* (Robert Erskine) and *DNB* (Henry and Ralph Erskine); Ebenezer Erskine Scott, *The Erskine-Halcro Genealogy*, 2nd ed. (1895), charts I and V, part 2, and p. 51 (R. Erskine); *PSECD* 3:85-87 (undocumented), W.K. and A.C. (Zimmerman) Rutherford, *Genealogical History of the Halliburton Family*, rev. ed., vol. 1 (1983), pp.

12, 21, 23, 41-42, plus materials on the Erskines of Shielfield and Chirnside submitted to the Order of the Crown of Charlemagne by Ann Naile Phelps (according to Timothy Field Beard) (James Burd); *SP* and *CP* (Erskine or Mar, Crawford).

The Royal Descents of 500 Immigrants

1. Robert II, King of Scotland, d. 1390 = (1) Elizabeth Mure
2. Robert Stewart, 1st Duke of Albany = Margaret Graham, Countess of Menteith
3. Marjory Stewart = Duncan Campbell, 1st Baron Campbell
4. Hon. Archibald Campbell = Elizabeth Somerville
5. Colin Campbell, 1st Earl of Argyll = Isabel Stewart
6. Helen Campbell = Hugh Montgomery, 1st Earl of Eglinton
7. Sir Neil Montgomery of Lainshaw = Margaret Mure
8. Sir Neil Montgomery of Lainshaw = Jean Lyle
9. Sir Neil Montgomery of Lainshaw = Elizabeth Cunyngham
10. William Montgomery of Brigend = Jean Montgomery
11. John Montgomery of Brigend = Elizabeth Baxter
12. Hugh Montgomery of Brigend = Katharine Scott
13. **William Montgomery** of N.J. = Isabel Burnett, daughter of Robert Burnett and Mrs. ---- Forbes Burnett of N.J., ARD, SETH.

7. Margaret Montgomery = William Sempill, 2nd Baron Semphill
8. Robert Sempill, 3rd Baron Semphill = Isabel Hamilton
9. Margaret Sempill = David Hamilton of Broomhill
10. Katherine Hamilton = James Hamilton of Torrence
11. Robert Hamilton of Torrence = Beatrix Hamilton
12. Janet Hamilton = John Hamilton of Airdrie
13. Gavin Hamilton of Airdrie = Jane Montgomery
14. William Hamilton, professor of divinity and principal, University of Edinburgh = Mary Robertson
15. **Alexander Hamilton** (1712-1756) of Md., physician and social historian = Margaret Dulany.

Sources: *Montgomery,* pp. 55-58, 62-68, 71-83; *SP* and *CP* (Semphill, Eglinton, Argyll, Campbell, Albany); *Hamilton,* pp. 704-9, 853-56, 187 and *BP* (Stirling-Hamilton of Preston, baronets).

1. Robert II, King of Scotland, d. 1390 = (2) Euphemia of Ross

2. Katherine (also called Jean or Elizabeth) Stewart = David Lindsay, 1st Earl of Crawford

3. Elizabeth Lindsay = Robert Erskine, 1st Baron Erskine

4. Thomas Erskine, 2nd Baron Erskine = Janet Douglas

5. Alexander Erskine, 3rd Baron Erskine = Christian Crichton

6. Christian Erskine = David Stewart of Rosyth

7. Christian Stewart = John Bethune of Balfour

8. John Bethune of Balfour = Agnes Anstruther

9. Margaret Bethune = John Row

10. John Row = Grizel Ferguson

11. John Row = Elspeth Gillespie

12. Lilias Row = John Mercer (the three John Rows and John Mercer, plus William Mercer below, were all ministers)

13. Thomas Mercer of Todlaw = Isabel Smith

14. William Mercer = Anne Munro

15. **Hugh Mercer** (1726-1777) of Va., physician and revolutionary officer = Isabel Gordon.

10. Catherine Row (sister of the second John) = William Rigg

11. William Rigg of Aithernie = Sarah Inglis

12. Thomas Rigg of Aithernie = Bethia Carstairs

13. Margaret Rigg = George Scott of Pitlochie, writer on America

14. **Euphan Scott** of N.J. = John **Johnstone**.

Sources: *MCS4*, line 91B (generations 14-22) and sources cited therein, esp. J.T. Clark, ed., *Genealogical Collections Concerning Families in Scotland made by Walter Macfarlane, 1750-1751*, vol. 1 (1900), pp. 11-12, 21 (Bethune of Balfour) (for Hugh Mercer);

TSA 5(1891):5 (Stewart of Rosyth); *SP* (Mar) and *CP* (Erskine, Crawford); *NYGBR* 33 (1902):246-47, *DNB* (George Scott or Scot, d. 1685) and Rev. Walter Wood, *The East Neuk of Fife, Its History and Antiquities,* 2nd ed. (1887), pp. 40-41 (Rigg) (for Mrs. Johnstone). Macfarlane (and Wood, p. 375) state that Christian Stewart, wife of John Bethune of Balfour, was a daughter of the laird of Rosyth. Chronology and naming patterns (the 3 Christians) make the above descent almost certain; a full monograph centered on Christian Stewart, however, would be welcome.

The Royal Descents of 500 Immigrants

1. Robert II, King of Scotland, d. 1390 = (1) Elizabeth Mure

2. Robert Stewart, 1st Duke of Albany = Margaret Graham, Countess of Menteith

3. Marjory Stewart = Duncan Campbell, 1st Baron Campbell

3. Joan Stewart = Robert Stewart, 1st Baron Lorne, brother of Sir James Stewart, the "Black Knight of Lorne," 2nd husband of Joan Beaufort, Dowager Queen of Scotland, SETH

4. Hon. Archibald Campbell = Elizabeth Somerville

4. John Stewart, 2nd Baron Lorne = Agnes of the Isles

5. Colin Campbell, 1st Earl of Argyll

= 5. Isabel Stewart (see also p. 96)

6. Archibald Campbell, 2nd Earl of Argyll = Elizabeth Stewart

7. Donald Campbell, Abbott of Coupar Angus

8. (illegitimate, allegedly by Margaret ----) Nicholas Campbell, Dean of Lismore Cathedral = Katherine Drummond

9. Margaret Campbell = Alexander McGruder

10. **Alexander Magruder (McGruder) of Md.** = (1) Sarah ----; (2) Elizabeth ----.

Sources: *PSECD* 3:202-4 (undocumented); *Yearbook of the American Clan Gregor Society*, 52(1978):55-65, 53(1979):53-71 ("The Ancestral History of Margaret Campbell of Keithick" and "The McGruder Lineage in Scotland to Magruder Family in America," both by Dr. Charles G. Kurz, based on research of Thomas Garland Magruder, Jr.), kindly brought to my attention by Brice McAdoo Clagett of Washington, D.C.; *SP* and *CP* (Argyll, Campbell, Lorn [Innermeath in *SP*], and Albany [Stewart]). For the marriage of John Stewart, 2nd Baron Lorne, to Agnes of the Isles, see A.I. Dunlop and David MacLauchlan, *Calendar of Scottish Supplications to Rome, Volume IV, 1433-1447* (1983), p. 295, item 1192.

The Royal Descents of 500 Immigrants

1. Robert II, King of Scotland, d. 1390 = (2) Euphemia of Ross

2. Katherine (also called Jean or Elizabeth) Stewart = David Lindsay, 1st Earl of Crawford

3. Alexander Lindsay, 2nd Earl of Crawford = Marjory ----

4. David Lindsay, 3rd Earl of Crawford = Marjory Ogilvy

5. Sir Walter Lindsay of Beaufort and Edzell = Isabel Livingston

6. Sir David Lindsay of Beaufort and Edzell = Katherine Fotheringham

7. Sir Walter Lindsay of Beaufort and Edzell = ---- Erskine

8. Alexander Lindsay of Haltoun (younger brother of the 9th earl of Crawford) = ---- Barclay

9. David Lindsay, Bishop of Ross = Janet Ramsay (their daughter Rachel Lindsay married John Spotswood, Archbishop of St. Andrews, and was the mother of Sir Robert Spotswood of Dunipage, husband of Bethia Morrison, SETH)

10. Sir Jerome Lindsay of Annatland and the Mount = Margaret Colville

11. **Rev. David Lindsay** of Va. = (1) ----; (2) Susanna ----.

Sources: *MCS4*, line 43 (and 43A for the Spotswood connection); Margaret Isabella Lindsay, *The Lindsays of America* (1889), charts opp. 8 and 22 esp.

The Royal Descents of 500 Immigrants

1. Robert II, King of Scotland, d. 1390 = (1) Elizabeth Mure

2. Alexander Stewart, 1st Earl of Buchan = Euphemia, Countess of Ross

3. (illegitimate prob. by Mariot Athyn) Margaret Stewart = Robert Sutherland, 6th Earl of Sutherland

4. John Sutherland, 7th Earl of Sutherland = Margaret Baillie

5. Janet Sutherland = Alexander Dunbar of Conzie and Kilbuyack

6. James Dunbar of Conzie and Kilbuyack = Ellen Innes

7. Marjory Dunbar = John Rose of Ballivat

8. John Rose of Ballivat = Janet Urquhart

9. John Rose of Ballivat = Margaret Falconer

10. Hugh Rose of Logie = Katherine Ord

11. Patrick Rose of Lochiehills = Margaret ----

12. John Rose of Lochiehills = Margaret Grant

13. **Rev. Robert Rose** of Va. = (1) Mary Tarent; (2) Anne Fitzhugh. John Rose (= Anne Cuming), Rev. Charles Rose (= Catharine Brooke), and Alexander Rose (prob. = Nelly Grant), brothers of Rev. Robert, also immigrated to Va. but left no NDTPS.

Sources: Christine Rose, *Ancestors and Descendants of the Brothers Rev. Robert Rose and Rev. Charles Rose of Colonial Virginia and Wester Alves, Morayshire, Scotland* (1985), pp. 6-7, 13-14, 17-38, 243-46, 267-68, 273-76 esp.; *BLG* 1952, p. 2199 (Rose); *BP* (Dunbar of Mochrum, baronets) and *Drummond*, vol. 2 (Dunbar); *SP* and *CP* (Sutherland, Buchan [Stewart]). W.G. Stanard, *A Chart of the Ancestors and Descendants of Rev. Robert Rose* (1895), with various errors, has been superseded by the above.

The Royal Descents of 500 Immigrants

1. Robert II, King of Scotland, d. 1390 = (1) Elizabeth Mure

2. Robert Stewart, 1st Duke of Albany = Margaret Graham, Countess of Menteith

3. Margaret Stewart = Sir John Swinton of that Ilk

4. Sir John Swinton of that Ilk = Marjory Dunbar

5. Sir John Swinton of that Ilk = ----

6. Sir John Swinton of that Ilk = Katherine Lauder

7. John Swinton of that Ilk = Marion Home

8. John Swinton of that Ilk = Katherine Lauder, a cousin

9. Robert Swinton of that Ilk = Jean Hepburn

10. Sir Alexander Swinton of that Ilk = Margaret Home

11. Sir Alexander Swinton of Mersington = Alison Skene

12. Elizabeth Swinton = Sir Alexander Cuming, 1st Bt.

13. **Sir Alexander Cuming, 2nd Bt.** (c. 1690-1775), English agent who persuaded the Creek and Cherokee Indians to accept British sovereignty in 1730, treated in the *DAB* = Amy Whitehall.

Sources: *CB* (Cuming of Culter); *BLG,* 18th ed., vol. 3 (1972), p. 878 (Swinton); *SP* and *CP* (Albany).

The Royal Descents of 500 Immigrants

1. Charles II, King of Navarre, d. 1387 = Joanna of France, daughter of John II, King of France, and Bona of Bohemia

2. Joanna of Navarre = John V, Duke of Brittany (Joanna married secondly Henry IV, King of England)

3. Margaret of Brittany = Alain IX, Vicomte de Rohan

4. Catherine de Rohan = Jean d'Albret, Vicomte de Tartas

5. Alain d'Albret, Count of Dreux = Francoise de Châtillon-Blois (their children included Jean d'Albret, King of Navarre, and Charlotte d'Albret, wife of Cesare Borgia, Duc de Valentinois, tyrant of Italy, son of Pope Alexander VI and brother of Lucretia Borgia, Duchess of Modena and Ferrara)

6. Isabel d'Albret = Gaston II de Foix, Count of Benauges, son of John de Foix, 1st Earl of Kendal, and Margaret de Kerdeston, SETH. Gaston II de Foix, Count of Benauges married firstly Catherine de Foix, a cousin, and left a daughter, Anne de Foix, who married Ladislaus V, King of Bohemia and Hungary. Their daughter, Anne of Bohemia, married Ferdinand I, Holy Roman Emperor, and is an ancestress of many later European kings.

7. Louise de Foix = Francois de Melun, Baron d'Antoing

8. Hugh de Melun, Prince d'Epinoy = Yolande de Barbancon

9. Pierre de Melun, Prince d'Epinoy = Hippolite de Montmorency

10. Anne de Melun = Alexander de Bournonville, Duc de Bournonville

11. Ambrose Francois de Bournonville, Duc de Bournonville = Lucrèce Francoise de la Vieuville

12. Marie Francoise de Bournonville = Anne Jules de Noailles, Duc de Noailles. Their daughter, Marie Victoire Sophie de Noailles, married secondly Louis Alexandre de Bourbon, Count of Toulouse, legitimized son of Louis XIV, King of France, and Francoise

Athénaïs de Rochechouart, Marquise de Montespan, and was a great-grandmother of Louis Philippe, King of the French.

13. Adrien Maurice de Noailles, Duc de Noailles, French soldier and statesman = Francoise Charlotte Amable d'Aubigné (niece of Francoise d'Aubigné, Marquise [known as Madame] de Maintenon, mistress and 2nd wife of Louis XIV, King of France)

14. Louis de Noailles, Duc de Noailles = Catherine Francoise Charlotte de Cossé

15. Jean Louis Francois Paul de Noailles, Duc de Noailles = Henriette Anne Louise d'Aguesseau

16. **Marie Adrienne Francoise de Noailles** = Marie Joseph Paul Yves Roch Gilbert **Motier**, Marquis de La Fayette (Lafayette) (1757-1834), the American revolutionary general and French statesman, ARD, SETH.

16. **Anne Jeanne Baptiste Pauline Adrienne Louise Catherine Dominique de Noailles** = Louis Marie **de Noailles,** Vicomte de Noailles (1756-1804), leader in the American and French revolutions and in the American emigré community of the 1790s, his wife's 1st cousin once removed, see below.

14. Philippe de Noailles, Duc de Mouchy (brother of Louis de Noailles, Duc de Noailles) = Anne Claudine Louise d'Arpajon

15. **Louis Marie de Noailles, Vicomte de Noailles** (1756-1804), leader in the American and French revolutions and in the American emigré community of the 1790s (fought at the battles of Savannah and Yorktown, resided in Philadelphia from 1793 to 1800) = Anne Jeanne Baptiste Pauline Adrienne Louise Catherine Dominique de Noailles, see above.

13. Marie Christine de Noailles (sister of Adrien Maurice) = Antoine IV de Gramont, 3rd Duc de Gramont

14. Louis de Gramont, 5th Duc de Gramont = Geneviève de Gontaut

15. Antoine Adrien Charles de Gramont, Count d'Aster = Marie Louise Sophie de Faoucq

16. Antoine Louis Marie de Gramont, 8th Duc de Gramont = Louise Gabrielle Aglaé de Polignac, see below

17. Antoine Héraclius Geneviève Agénor de Gramont, 9th Duc de Gramont = Anna Quintana Albertine Ida Grimod

18. Antoine Alfred Agénor de Gramont, 10th Duc de Gramont, foreign minister of Napoleon III = Emma Mary Mackinnon

19. Antoine Alfred Agénor de Gramont, 11th Duc de Gramont = Maria Ruspoli

20. Count Gabriel Antoine Armand de Gramont = Marie Negroponte

21. **Sanche Armand Gabriel de Gramont** (b. 1932), known as **Ted Morgan** (pseudonym), of N.Y., historian, biographer of Churchill, FDR, Somerset Maugham, and William S. Burroughs = (1) Margaret Kinnicutt; (2) Nancy Ryan.

13. Anne Louise de Noailles (sister of Adrien Maurice and Marie Christine) = Jacques Hippolyte Mancini-Mazarini, Marquis de Mancini, a 1st cousin of Eugène, Prince of Savoy, Austrian commander in the War of the Spanish Succession, and great-nephew of both Cardinal Jules (Giulio) Mazarin(i), minister of Louis XIII, King of France, and Francoise Athénaïs de Rochechouart, Marquise de Montespan, see above, mistress of Louis XIV, King of France

14. Diane Adélaide Zéphirine Mancini-Mazarini = Louis Melchior Armand de Polignac, Marquis de Chalencon

15. Armand Jules Francois de Polignac, 1st Duc de Polignac = Gabrielle Yolande Claude Martine de Polastron

16. Louise Gabrielle Aglaé de Polignac (sister of Auguste Jules Armand, Prince de Polignac, minister of

The Royal Descents of 500 Immigrants

Charles X, King of France) = Antoine Louis Marie de Gramont, 8th Duc de Gramont, see above

Sources: Arnaud Chaffanjon, *La Fayette et sa Descendance* (1976), pp. 58-64, and *Anselme* (and Potier de Courcy), vol. 9, part 2, pp. 242-44 (Noailles), vol. 5, pp. 837-39 (Bournonville), 231-32 (Melun), vol. 3, pp. 383-84 (Foix), vol. 6, pp. 213-15 (Albret), vol. 4, pp. 55-56 (Rohan); *ES,* tables for Navarre, Brittany, Rohan, Albret, Foix, Melun, and Noailles. See also *TG* 6(1985):160-65; 3(1982):30, 32, 41-42, 44, 190-91, 194, 2(1981):166, 168, on Margaret de Kerdeston and her immediate ancestry and royal progeny. For Sanche de Gramont (Ted Morgan), see his own *On Becoming American* (1978), plus *GHdesA,* Fürstliche Häuser, vol. 3 (1955), pp. 353-56, *Anselme,* vol. 9, part 2, pp. 233-34 (Gramont), part 1, pp. 854-55 (Polignac), vol. 4, pp. 582-83 (Gramont), vol. 5, pp. 463-64 (Mancini), and Jean, Due de Polignac, *La Maison de Polignac: Etude d'Une Evolution Sociale de la Noblesse* (1975), p. 243 and *passim.*

The Royal Descents of 500 Immigrants

1. Edward III, King of England, d. 1377 = Philippa of Hainault
2. John of Gaunt, Duke of Lancaster = Catherine Roet
3. John Beaufort, Marquess of Somerset and Dorset = Margaret Holand
4. Joan Beaufort, Dowager Queen of Scotland = Sir James Stewart, the "Black Knight of Lorne"
5. James Stewart, 1st Earl of Buchan = Margaret Ogilvy
6. ---- Stewart (daughter) = Alexander Abernethy, 4th Baron Saltoun
7. Beatrix Abernethy = Alexander Forbes of Pitsligo
8. Marion Forbes = Alexander Gordon of Lesmoir
9. Katherine Gordon = Alexander Burnet of Leys
10. Robert Burnet = Rachel Johnston
11. Gilbert Burnet, Bishop of Salisbury, the historian = Mary Scott
12. **William Burnet** (1688-1729), colonial governor of N.Y., N.J., Mass. and N.H. = (1) Maria Stanhope; (2) Anna Maria Van Horne.

11. Sir Thomas Burnet (brother of the Bishop of Salisbury) = Janet Bruce
12. Helen Burnet = Ralph Dundas of Manour
13. John Dundas of Manour = Anne Murray
14. **James Dundas** of Pa. = Elizabeth Moore.
14. **Thomas Dundas** of Pa. = ----, sister of Mrs. Hannah Russell.

9. Sir James Gordon, 1st Bt. (brother of Katherine) = Rebecca Keith
10. Sir James Gordon of Lesmoir = Helen Urquhart
11. Katherine Gordon = John Abercromby of Glassaugh
12. Alexander Abercromby of Glassaugh = Katherine Dunbar

13. Alexander Abercromby of Glassaugh = Helen Meldrum
14. **James Abercromby** (1706-1781), British commander in America during the French and Indian wars, the loser at Ticonderoga = Mary Duff.

Sources: *DAB* (William Burnet), *Burnett of Leys,* pp. 32-40, 130-42, *Gordon,* vol. 2, Lesmoir section, pp. 37-61, *Forbes,* p. 346, and *SP* and *CP* (Forbes of Pitsligo, Saltoun, Buchan) (Burnet); *CRLA,* vol. 8 (1941), pp. 143-45 (Dundas) and Francis de Sales Dundas, *Dundas, Hesselius* (1938), pp. 15-16, 35-45 esp; *DAB* (James Abercromby) and Cavendish D. Abercromby, *The Family of Abercromby* (1927), pp. 61, 87-89 and chart opposite p. 86.

The Royal Descents of 500 Immigrants

1. Edward III, King of England, d. 1377 = Philippa of Hainault
2. John of Gaunt, Duke of Lancaster = Catherine Roet
3. John Beaufort, Marquess of Somerset and Dorset = Margaret Holand
4. Joan Beaufort, Dowager Queen of Scotland = Sir James Stewart, the "Black Knight of Lorne"
5. John Stewart, 1st Earl of Atholl = Eleanor Sinclair
6. John Stewart, 2nd Earl of Atholl = Janet Campbell
6. Elspeth Stewart = Robert Innes of Innermarkie
7. Elizabeth Stewart = Sir Kenneth Mackenzie of Kintail
7. Robert Innes of Monycabok = Marion Ogilvy
8. Agnes Mackenzie = Lachlan Mackintosh of Mackintosh
8. Robert Innes of Innermarkie = Margaret Innes of that Ilk
9. Robert Innes of Innermarkie = Jean Barclay
9. William Mackintosh of Borlum = 10. Elizabeth Innes
10,11. Lachlan Mackintosh of Borlum = Helen Gordon
11,12. **Col. Henry Mackintosh (McIntosh) of Mass. and R.I. =** Elizabeth Byfield.
12,13. Elizabeth Mackintosh (McIntosh) = Lachlan Mackintosh (McIntosh) of Mass., her cousin, see below.

11,12. William Mackintosh of Borlum (brother of Col. Henry of Mass.) = Mary Baillie, sister of the Alexander Baillie of Dunain who married Jean Mackenzie, SETH
12,13. William Mackintosh of Borlum = Mary Reade, see below
13,14. **Lachlan Mackintosh (McIntosh) of R.I. =** Elizabeth Mackintosh (McIntosh), his cousin, see above.

12,13. Lachlan Mackintosh of Knocknagel (brother of the younger William) = Mary Lockhart

13,14. **John Mohr Mackintosh (McIntosh)** of Ga. = Marjory Fraser.

4. Edmund Beaufort, 1st Duke of Somerset (brother of Joan Beaufort, Queen of Scotland) = Eleanor Beauchamp

5. Anne Beaufort = Sir William Paston

6 Anne Paston = Sir Gilbert Talbot

7. Elizabeth Talbot = John Lyttelton

8. Sir John Lyttelton = Bridget Pakington

9. Sir Gilbert Lyttelton = Elizabeth Coningsby

10. Anne Lyttelton = Sir Thomas Cornewall

11. Mary Cornewall = Sir Thomas Reade

12. Edward Reade = Ellen Allen

13. Mary Reade = William Mackintosh of Borlum, see above

Sources: Walter H. McIntosh, *A Genealogical Record of Families in New England Bearing the Name McIntosh* (1981), p. 40, and *McIntosh, Mackintosh Families of Scotland and America* (1982), pp. 26, 49-51; Alexander M. Mackintosh, *The Mackintoshes and Clan Chattan* (1903), pp. 141-92, 377-83; *SP* (Seaforth [Mackenzie] and Atholl) and *BP* (Innes of Balvenie, baronets, including Innes of Innermarkie); Compton Reade, *A Record of the Redes of Barton Court, Berks.* (1899), pp. 26-30, 40, 44, 61-64, 67-69; *Cornewall*, pp. 217-25, 228-30. See also *NEXUS* 8(1991):146-47, 150.

The Royal Descents of 500 Immigrants

1. Edward III, King of England, d. 1377 = Philippa of Hainault
2. John of Gaunt, Duke of Lancaster = Catherine Roet
3. John Beaufort, Marquess of Somerset and Dorset = Margaret Holand
4. Joan Beaufort, Dowager Queen of Scotland = Sir James Stewart, the "Black Knight of Lorne"
5. James Stewart, 1st Earl of Buchan = Margaret Ogilvy
6. (illegitimate by Margaret Murray) James Stewart of Traquair = Catherine Rutherford
7. William Stewart of Traquair = Christian Hay
8. James Stewart of Traquair = Katherine Kerr
9. Sir Robert Stewart of Schillinglaw = Alice Cockburn
10. Christian Stewart = John Cranston of Bold
11. James Cranston, a chaplain to King Charles I = ----
12. **John Cranston** (c. 1626-1680), physician, colonial governor of R.I. = Mary Clarke, daughter of Jeremiah Clarke, acting governor of R.I., ARD, SETH, and Mrs. Frances Latham Dungan.

9. Janet Stewart (sister of Sir Robert) = John Veatch of Peebles
10. Malcolm Veatch of Muirdeen = ---- ----
11. **James Veatch** of Md. = Mary Gakerlin.

Sources: *MCS4*, lines 41, 91 and *AR7*, line 1 (Cranston); *TAG* 53 (1977):152-53 and William Robert Veitch, *In Search of Yesterday* (Veatch/Veitch family), c. 1969.

1. Edward III, King of England, d. 1377 = Philippa of Hainault

2. John of Gaunt, Duke of Lancaster = Catherine Roet

3. John Beaufort, Marquess of Somerset and Dorset = Margaret Holand

4. Joan Beaufort, Dowager Queen of Scotland = Sir James Stewart, "The Black Knight of Lorne"

5. John Stewart, 1st Earl of Atholl = Eleanor Sinclair

6. John Stewart, 2nd Earl of Atholl = Janet Campbell

7. Jean Stewart = James Arbuthnott of Arbuthnott

8. Isabel Arbuthnott = Sir Robert Maule of Panmure

9. William Maule of Glaster = Bethia Guthrie

10. Eleanor Maule = Sir Alexander Morrison of Prestongrange

11. Bethia Morrison = Sir Robert Spotswood of Dunipage

12. Robert Spotswood = Catherine Mercer

13. **Alexander Spotswood** (1676-1740), colonial (lt.) governor of Va. = Anne Butler Brayne.

14. Dorothea Spotswood = Nathaniel West Dandridge

15. Martha Dandridge = Archibald Payne

16. Catherine Payne = Archibald Bolling

17. Archibald Bolling, Jr. = Anne E. Wigginton

18. William Holcombe Bolling = Sallie Spiers White

19. Edith Bolling = (1) Norman Galt; (2) (Thomas) Woodrow Wilson (1856-1924), 28th U.S. President

10. Isabel Maule (sister of Eleanor) = James Dundas of Doddington

11. Bethia Dundas = James Hume

12. Isabel Hume = Patrick Logan

13. **James Logan** (1674-1751) of Pa., colonial statesman, jurist, Indian trader and scholar = (1) Sarah Read; (2) Amy Child.

Sources: *MCS4*, lines 43A, 111A, 91A, 91, 90, 161 and sources cited therein, especially *CP* and *SP* (Spotswood); *MCS4*, line 111B and C.P. Keith, *The Provincial Councillors of Pennsylvania* (1883), pp. 1-14 (Logan), *Drummond*, vol. 2 (Dundas and Hume pedigrees), and *SP* (Maule, earls of Panmure).

The Royal Descents of 500 Immigrants

1. Edward III, King of England, d. 1377 = Philippa of Hainault
2. John of Gaunt, Duke of Lancaster = Catherine Roet
3. John Beaufort, Marquess of Dorset and Somerset = Margaret Holand
4. Joan Beaufort = Sir James Stewart, "The Black Knight of Lorne"
5. John Stewart, 1st Earl of Atholl = Eleanor Sinclair
6. John Stewart, 2nd Earl of Atholl = Janet Campbell
7. Elizabeth Stewart = Sir Kenneth Mackenzie of Kintail
8. Colin Mackenzie of Kintail = Barbara Grant
9. (illegitimate by Mary Mackenzie) Alexander Mackenzie of Coul = Christian Munro
10. Sir Kenneth Mackenzie, 1st Bt. = Jean Chisolm
11. Jean Mackenzie = Alexander Baillie of Dunain
12. John Baillie "of Balrobert" (almost certainly son or son-in-law [the husband of Jean Baillie] of the above)
13. **Col. Kenneth Baillie of Ga.** = Elizabeth Mackay.
14. Ann Elizabeth Baillie = John Irvine of Ga., ARD, SETH
15. Anne Irvine = James Bulloch
16. James Stephens Bulloch = Martha Stewart
17. Martha Bulloch = Theodore Roosevelt
18. Theodore Roosevelt, Jr. (1858-1919), 26th U.S. President = (1) Alice Hathaway Lee; (2) Edith Kermit Carow.

Sources: *Baillie*, pp. 3-6, 12-25, 40-46; *CB*, vol. 4, p. 296 (Mackenzie of Coul); *SP*, articles on Mackenzies (of Kintail, later Earls of Seaforth) and Stewarts (Earls of Atholl). Documentary proof of the identity of John Baillie "of Balrobert" would be welcome.

The Royal Descents of 500 Immigrants

1. Edward III, King of England, d. 1377 = Philippa of Hainault
2. John of Gaunt, Duke of Lancaster = Catherine Roet
3. John Beaufort, Marquess of Somerset and Dorset = Margaret Holand
4. Edmund Beaufort, 1st Duke of Somerset = Eleanor Beauchamp
5. Eleanor Beaufort = Sir Robert Spencer
6. Margaret Spencer = Thomas Cary
7. William Cary = Mary Boleyn, sister of Anne Boleyn, 2nd Queen of Henry VIII, and aunt of Elizabeth I, Queen of England
8. Mary Cary = Sir Francis Knollys
9. Anne Knollys = Thomas West, 2nd Baron Delaware (de la Warr)
10. **Thomas West, 3rd Baron Delaware** (de la Warr) (1577-1618), colonial governor of Va. = Cecily Shirley, ARD, SETH.
10. **Hon. Francis West** (1586-1634), colonial governor of Va. = (1) Mrs. Margaret Blayney; (2) Lady Temperance Flowerdew Yeardley, widow of Sir George Yeardley, colonial governor of Va.; (3) Jane Davye.
10. **Hon. John West**, colonial governor of Va. = Anne ---.
11. John West, Jr. = Unity Croshaw
12. Nathaniel West = Martha Woodward
13. Unity West = William Dandridge, uncle of First Lady Mrs. Martha Dandridge Custis Washington
14. Nathaniel West Dandridge = Dorothea Spotswood
15. Martha Dandridge = Archibald Payne
16. Catherine Payne = Archibald Bolling
17. Archibald Bolling, Jr. = Anne E. Wigginton
18. William Holcombe Bolling = Sallie Spiers White
19. Edith Bolling = (1) Norman Galt, = (2) (Thomas) Woodrow Wilson (1856-1924), 28th U.S. President

10. Hon. Elizabeth West (sister of the 3rd Baron Delaware, Hon. Francis and Hon. John) = Herbert Pelham (who = (1) Catherine Thatcher)

11. Elizabeth Pelham = John Humphrey, dep. gov. of Mass. (who = (3) Lady Susan Clinton, sister of Lady Arabella Clinton Johnson)

12. **Anne Humphrey** of Mass. = (1) William **Palmes**; (2) Rev. John **Myles**.

10. Hon. Penelope West (sister of the 3rd Baron Delaware, Hon. Francis, Hon. John, and Hon. Elizabeth) = Herbert Pelham (Jr., son of Herbert Pelham and Catherine Thatcher)

11. **Herbert Pelham** of Mass., 1st treasurer of Harvard College = (1) Jemima Waldegrave; (2) Mrs. Elizabeth Bosvile Harlakenden of Mass. Both of his wives were ARD, SETH.

11. **Penelope Pelham** of Mass. = Richard **Bellingham** (c. 1592-1672), colonial governor of Mass. ARD, SETH. Note: Hon. Nathaniel West, another son of Thomas West, 2nd Baron Delaware (de la Warr) and Anne Knollys, also immigrated to Va., and = Frances Greville, but his only known child returned to England and left no NDTPS.

9. Catherine Knollys (sister of Anne) = Sir Philip Boteler

10. Sir John Boteler = Anne Spencer

11. Sir Philip Boteler = Elizabeth Langham

12. **Anne Boteler** of Md. = Lionel **Copley** (d. 1693), colonial governor of Md., ARD, SETH.

9. Sir Thomas Knollys (brother of Anne and Catherine) = Ottilia de Merode

10. Lettice Knollys = Sir Rowland Rugeley

11. Mary Rugeley = John Wiseman

12. Elizabeth Wiseman = Richard Clagett

13. Wiseman Clagett = Martha Clifton

14. **Wiseman Clagett** (1721-1784) of N.H., lawyer, King's Attorney for and Solicitor-General of N.H. = Lettice Mitchell.

9. Richard Knollys (brother of Anne, Catherine and Sir Thomas) = Jane Heigham

10. Francis Knollys = Alice Beecher

11. Dorothy Knollys = William Byam

12. Edward Byam = Lydia Thomas

13. William Byam = Anne Gunthorpe

14. William Byam = Mary Burgh

15. Edward Samuel Byam = Eleanor Prior

16. (illegitimate, perhaps by Clara Parker) **Amelia Jane Byam** of N.Y. = John **Ericsson** (1803-1889), engineer, builder of the *Monitor* (for the U.S.) in 1861.

Sources: *AR7*, lines 1, 228, 229, *MCS4*, lines 4, 80, *AP&P*, pp. 665-61 (West), *TAG* 16(1939-40):129-32, 201-5, 18(1941-42):137-46, 210-18, 19(1942-43):197-202 (Pelham, Humphrey) and sources cited therein, esp. *CP* (generations 1-5, 8-9); *DAB* (Lionel Copley), *Clutterbuck,* vol. 2, p. 477 (Boteler), and *CP* VII, 239 (Gerald FitzGerald, Lord Gerald).

For **Wiseman Clagett** *DAB* (Clagett); research by Brice McAdoo Clagett to appear in his forthcoming Clagett genealogy, citing, among other sources, *NGSQ* 62(1974):207, L.B. McQuiston, *The McQuiston, McCuiston, and McQuesten Families, 1620-1937* (1937), pp. 138-39, *Morant,* vol. 2, p. 559 (Clagett, Wiseman), W.C. Metcalfe, ed., *Visitations of Essex 1552, 1558, 1570, 1612 and 1634,* vol. 1 (*HSPVS,* vol. 13, 1878), p. 528 (Wiseman); *MGH,* new ser., 3 (1878-80):201-2 (Rugeley, Knollys), *DNB* (Sir Francis and Thomas Knollys), and the lengthy inscription of the sepulchral monument of Mary (Rugeley) Wiseman in the Windish, Essex, parish church.

For **Mrs. Ericsson:** Ruth White, *Yankee From Sweden: The Dream and the Reality in the Days of John Ericsson* (1960), pp.

40-41; V.L. Oliver, *History of the Island of Antigua*, vol. 1 (1894), pp. 97-99 (Byam, Knollys); *DAB* (Sir Francis and Richard Knollys) and J.B. Burke, *The Royal Families of England, Scotland, and Wales, with Their Descendants, Sovereigns, and Subjects*, vol. 1 (1851), pedigree CXCVI (an unreliable work, seemingly good in this instance). Some printed sources confuse the brothers Robert and Richard Knollys, sons of Sir Francis.

The Royal Descents of 500 Immigrants

1. Edward III, King of England, d. 1377 = Philippa of Hainault
2. Lionel of Antwerp, Duke of Clarence = Elizabeth de Burgh
3. Philippa Plantagenet = Edmund Mortimer, 3rd Earl of March
4. Elizabeth Mortimer = Sir Henry "Hotspur" Percy
5. Elizabeth Percy = John Clifford, 7th Baron Clifford
6. Mary Clifford = Sir Philip Wentworth
7. Sir Henry Wentworth = Anne Saye
8. Sir Richard Wentworth = Anne Tyrrell
9. Thomas Wentworth, 1st Baron Wentworth = Margaret Fortescue
10. Philip Wentworth = Elizabeth Corbett
11. Jane Wentworth = John Harleston (their daughter, Affra Harleston, married John Comin/g and immigrated to S.C., but left no children)
12. John Harleston = Elizabeth ----
13. **John Harleston** of S.C. = Elizabeth Willis.
13. **Elizabeth Harleston** of S.C. = Elias **Ball**.

9. Dorothy Wentworth (sister of the 1st Baron Wentworth) = Sir Lionel Tollemache
10. Lionel Tollemache = Susan Jermyn
11. Sir Lionel Tollemache, 1st Bt. = Elizabeth Cromwell, daughter of Henry Cromwell, 2nd Baron Cromwell, and Mary Paulet, see below
12. Sir Lionel Tollemache, 2nd Bt. = Elizabeth Stanhope
13. Susan Tollemache = Sir Henry Felton, 2nd Bt.
14. **Susan Felton** = (1) Philip Harbord; (2) Francis **Howard**, 5th Baron Howard of Effingham, colonial governor of Va., ARD, SETH.

10. Mary Tollemache (sister of Lionel) = John Jermyn

11. Thomas Jermyn = Sarah Stephens
12. Jane Jermyn = Thomas Wright
13. Jermyn Wright = Anne Blatchford
14. Sir Robert Wright = Susan Wren, a 1st cousin of Sir Christopher Wren, the architect
15. **Robert Wright**, chief justice of S.C. = Mrs. Isabella Wright Pitts, possibly a cousin (parents of Sir James Wright, 1st Bt., colonial governor of Ga. = Sarah Maidman).

8. Margery Wentworth (sister of Sir Richard) = Sir John Seymour (parents of Jane Seymour, 3rd Queen of Henry VIII, King of England, and maternal grandparents of Edward VI, King of England, d. 1553)
9. Edward Seymour, 1st Duke of Somerset, Lord Protector = Anne Stanhope
10. Anne Seymour = Sir Edward Unton
11. Cecilia Unton = John Wentworth
12. Anne Wentworth = Sir Edmund Gostwick, 2nd Bt.
13. Mary Gostwick = Nicholas Spencer
14. **Nicholas Spencer**, acting colonial governor of Va., president of its council = Frances Mottrom.

10. Mary Seymour (sister of Lady Anne) = Francis Cosby
11. Alexander Cosby = Dorcas Sidney
12. Richard Cosby = Elizabeth Pigott
13. Francis Cosby = Anne Loftus
14. Alexander Cosby = Elizabeth L'Estrange
15. **William Cosby** (c. 1690-1735/6), colonial governor of N.Y. and N.J. = Grace Montagu, ARD, SETH.

9. Sir Henry Seymour (brother of the 1st Duke of Somerset) = Barbara Morgan
10. Jane Seymour = Sir John Rodney

11. William Rodney = Alice Caesar
12. William Rodney, sometime of New York City = Rachel
    ----
13. **William Rodney** of Del. and Pa. = (1) Mary Hollyman;
    (2) Sarah Jones.

 9. Elizabeth Seymour (sister of the 1st Duke of Somerset
    and of Sir Henry) = Gregory Cromwell, 1st Baron
    Cromwell
10. Henry Cromwell, 2nd Baron Cromwell = Mary Paulet
11. Edward Cromwell, 3rd Baron Cromwell = Frances Rugge
12. Frances Cromwell = Sir John Wingfield
13. John Wingfield = Mary Owen
14. **Thomas Wingfield** of Va. = (1) Mary ----; (2) Mary
    ----.

10. Frances Cromwell (sister of the 2nd Baron Cromwell) =
    Richard Strode
11. Sir William Strode = Mary Southcott
12. Juliana Strode = Sir John Davie, 1st Bt.
13. **Humphrey Davie** of Mass. = (1) Mary White; (2) Mrs.
    Sarah Gibbon Richards.

Sources: *TG* 9(1988):163-225, esp. 179-88, 190, 211-19, and sources
cited therein (Harlestons); *CP* (Effingham), *CB* (Felton, Tollemache),
Walter C. Metcalfe, ed., *Visitations of Suffolk 1561, 1577, and 1612*
(1882), p. 71 (Talmache or Tollemache), and *Wentworth*, vol. 1, pp.
38-42; *DNB* (Sir James Wright, 1st Bt., and Sir Robert Wright), *MCS4*,
line 37, *SMF* 2:256 (Wright, Jermyn); *VM* 2(1894-95):32-34
(Spencer), *EB* and *CB* (Gostwick), W.H. Rylands, ed., *Four Visitations
of Berkshire 1532, 1566, 1623 and 1665-6*, vol. 2 (*HSPVS*, vol. 57,
1908), p. 222 (Unton) and *BP* and *CP* (Somerset); *BLGI*, 1958, p.
181 (Cosby of Stradbally) and W.G. Duke, *Henry Duke, Councilor,
His Descendants and Connections* (1949), pp. 294-99 (Cosby); *MCS4*,

line 38, *WC*, pp. 447-55, *TAG* 64(1989):97-111 (Rodney) and *Collins*, vol. 1, pp. 149-50 (Seymour); *MCS4*, line 21, *GVFVM5*:822-26, 840-41 (Wingfield) and *EP* and *CP* (Cromwell); *TAG* 23 (1946-47):206-10 and *CB* (Davie), *VD*, pp. 270 (Davie), 718-19 (Strode) and F.A. Crisp, ed., *Visitation of England and Wales, Notes*, vol. 12 (1917), pp. 121, 127 (Strode, Cromwell).

The Royal Descents of 500 Immigrants

1. Edward III, King of England, d. 1377 = Philippa of Hainault
2. John of Gaunt, Duke of Lancaster = Catherine Roet
3. Joan Beaufort = Ralph Neville, 1st Earl of Westmoreland
4. Edward Neville, 1st Baron Abergavenny = Catherine Howard
5. Margaret Neville = John Brooke, 7th Baron Cobham
6. Thomas Brooke, 8th Baron Cobham = Dorothy Heydon
7. Elizabeth Brooke = Sir Thomas Wyatt, poet
8. Sir Thomas Wyatt, conspirator = Jane Hawte
9. George Wyatt = Jane Finch
10. **Sir Francis Wyatt** (1588-1644), colonial governor of Va. = Margaret Sandys of Va., ARD, SETH.
10. **Rev. Hawte Wyatt** of Va. = (1) Barbara Mitford; (2) Elizabeth ----; (3) Anne Cox.

9. Jane Wyatt (sister of George) = Charles Scott, son of Sir Reginald Scott and Mary Tuke, SETH
10. Deborah Scott = William Fleete
11. **Henry Fleete** of Va. = Mrs. Sarah --- Burden.
    Reginald, Edward and John Fleete, brothers of Henry, immigrated to Md. and served in its assembly, but left no NDTPS.

9. Anne Wyatt (sister of George and Jane) = Roger Twisden
10. Margaret Twisden = Henry Vane
11. Sir Henry Vane, English Secretary of State = Frances Darcy
12. **Sir Henry Vane** (1613-1662), Puritan statesman, colonial governor of Mass. = Frances Wray, ARD, SETH.
12. Margaret Vane = Sir Thomas Pelham, 2nd Bt.
13. **Philadelphia Pelham** = Francis **Howard**, 5th Baron Howard of Effingham, colonial governor of Va., ARD, SETH.

7. George Brooke, 9th Baron Cobham (brother of Elizabeth) = Anne Bray

8. William Brooke, 10th Baron Cobham = Frances Newton

9. Margaret Brooke = Sir Thomas Sondes

10. Frances Sondes = Sir John Leveson

11. Christian Leveson = Sir Peter Temple, 2nd Bt.

12. Sir Richard Temple, 3rd Bt. = Mary Knapp

13. Christian Temple = Sir Thomas Lyttelton, 4th Bt.

14. **William Henry Lyttelton, 1st Baron Lyttelton** (1724-1808), colonial governor of S.C. and Jamaica, diplomat = (1) Mary Macartney; (2) Caroline Bristow.

Sources: *DNB* (Sir Francis and both Sir Thomas Wyatts, both Sir Henry Vanes), J. Cave-Browne, *The History of Boxley Parish, Including an Account of the Wiat Family* (1892), chart opp. p. 133 esp., *MCS4*, line 72, *AP+P*, pp. 718-20 (Wyatt), 284-86 (Fleete), and *VGE*, pp. 623-33 (Wyatt), 567-68 (Fleete); *Berry's Kent*, p. 310 (Twisden); *CB* (Pelham, Temple and Lyttelton, baronets); *CP* or *BP* (Howard of Effingham or Effingham, Chichester [Pelham], Barnard [Vane], Lyttelton, viscounts and barons Cobham, Abergavenny).

The Royal Descents of 500 Immigrants

1. Edward III, King of England, d. 1377 = Philippa of Hainault
2. John of Gaunt, Duke of Lancaster = Catherine Roet
3. Joan Beaufort = Ralph Neville, 1st Earl of Westmoreland
4. Richard Neville, 1st Earl of Salisbury = Alice Montagu
4. Edward Neville, 1st Baron Abergavenny = Elizabeth Beauchamp
5. Alice Neville = Henry FitzHugh, 5th Baron FitzHugh
5. George Neville, 2nd Baron Abergavenny = Margaret Fenne
6. Elizabeth FitzHugh = Nicholas Vaux, 1st Baron Vaux of Harrowden
6. Sir Edward Neville = Eleanor Windsor
7. Katherine Vaux = Sir George Throckmorton
8. Clement Throckmorton =   7. Katherine Neville
8,9. Katherine Throckmorton = Thomas Harby
9,10. Katherine Harby = Daniel Oxenbridge
10,11. **Rev. John Oxenbridge** (1608/9-1674) of Mass., Puritan clergyman = (1) Jane Butler; (2) Frances Woodward; (3) Mary Hackshaw; (4) Susanna ---- (his daughter by 2, Theodora Oxenbridge, married Rev. Peter Thacher of Milton, Mass., noted theologian and Congregational clergyman)
10,11. Elizabeth Oxenbridge = Caleb Cockcroft
11,12. Elizabeth Cockcroft = Nathaniel Hering
12,13. Oliver Hering = Elizabeth Hughes
13,14. Oliver Hering = Anna Maria Morris
14,15. Julines Hering = Mary Inglis
15,16. **Mary Helen Hering** of S.C. = Henry **Middleton** (1770-1846), governor of S.C., congressman, diplomat.

9,10. Emma Harby (sister of Katherine) = Robert Charlton
10,11. Catherine Charlton = Richard Coke

11,12. Richard Coke = Elizabeth Robie

12,13. **John Coke** of Va. = Sarah Hoge.

8,9. Martha Throckmorton (sister of Katherine) = George Lynne

9,10. George Lynne = Isabel Forrest

10,11. Martha Lynne = John Blennerhasset

11,12. Robert Blennerhasset = Avice Conway

12,13. John Blennerhasset = Elizabeth Cross

13,14. Conway Blennerhasset = Elizabeth Harman

14,15. Conway Blennerhasset = Elizabeth Lacy

15,16. **Harman Blennerhasset** (1765-1831) of Va., adventurer, "western empire" associate of Aaron Burr = 16,17. **Margaret Agnew** of Va., his niece, daughter of Robert Agnew and 15,16. Catherine Blennerhasset.

12,13. Catherine Blennerhasset (sister of John) = Richard McLaughlin

13,14. Avice McLaughlin = John Mason

14,15. James Mason = Catherine Power

15,16. Elizabeth Mason = Robert Emmet

16,17. **Thomas Addis Emmet** (1764-1827) of N.Y., lawyer, Irish patriot = Jane Patten.

17,18. John Patten Emmet = Mary Byrd Farley Tucker of Va., ARD, SETH.

Sources: *DNB* (Rev. John Oxenbridge), *AR7*, lines 201 and 78, *TAG* 31(1955):60, and *NEHGR* 108(1954):178 (reprinted in *EO* 1:3:776), plus *Throckmorton*, pp. 105-6, 165-66, *EP, BP* or *CP* (Vaux of Harrowden, FitzHugh, Salisbury, Abergavenny); J.A. Inglis, *The Family of Inglis of Auchindenny and Redhall* (1914), pp. 72-77, John Britton, *Graphical and Literary Illustrations of Fonthill Abbey, Wiltshire, with Heraldical and Genealogical Notices of the Beckford Family* (1823), pp. 64-65 (table VII -- Hering), *DNB* (Oliver

St. John, d. 1673, second husband of Elizabeth [Oxenbridge] Cockcroft) (for Mrs. Middleton); *MCS4*, line 94A and *BLG*, 18th ed., vol. 1, 1965, pp. 147-48 (Coke); *BIFR*, pp. 136-37, 140 (Blennerhasset), Rev. H.I. Longden, ed., *Visitation of Northamptonshire*, 1681 (*HSPVS*, vol. 87, 1935), pp. 127-28 (Lynne); Thomas Addis Emmet II, *A Memoir of John Patten Emmet* (1898) (Emmet pedigree) and *Memoir of Thomas Addis and Robert Emmet*, 2 vols. (1915) (vol. 1, p. 175 and vol. 2, pp. 360-61 for Mason esp.).

The Royal Descents of 500 Immigrants

1. Edward III, King of England, d. 1377 = Philippa of Hainault

2. Lionel of Antwerp, Duke of Clarence = Elizabeth de Burgh

3. Philippa Plantagenet = Edmund Mortimer, 3rd Earl of March

4. Elizabeth Mortimer = Sir Henry "Hotspur" Percy

5. Elizabeth Percy = John Clifford, 7th Baron Clifford

6. Thomas Clifford, 8th Baron Clifford = Joan Dacre

7. Matilda Clifford = Sir Edmund Sutton (or/alias Dudley), who = (1) Joyce Tiptoft, SETH

8. Dorothy Sutton = Richard Wrottesley

9. Walter Wrottesley = Isabella Harcourt

10. Eleanor Wrottesley = Richard Lee

11. Dorothy Lee = Thomas Mackworth

12. Richard Mackworth = Dorothy Cranage

13. **Agnes Mackworth** = (1) Richard **Watts**; (2) William **Crowne** (ca. 1617-1683) of Mass., adventurer and land speculator.

9. Margery Wrottesley (sister of Walter) = James Leveson

10. Elizabeth Leveson = Sir Walter Aston

11. Elizabeth Aston = Basil Fielding, son of Sir William Fielding and Dorothy Lane, sister of Virginia colonist Sir Ralph Lane, SETH

12. William Fielding, 1st Earl of Denbigh = Susan Villiers

13. George Fielding, 1st Earl of Desmond = Bridget Stanhope

14. John Fielding = Bridget Cokayne

15. Edmund Fielding = Sarah Gould

16. Henry Fielding, the novelist = Charlotte Craddock

17. **Henrietta Fielding** = James Gabriel **Montrésor** (1702-1776), British military engineer who served in the American colonies from 1754 to 1760 (father by Mary

Haswell, his 1st wife, of John Montrésor, also a British military engineer who served in the American colonies, who married Frances Tucker of N.Y., ARD, SETH).

9. Eleanor Wrottesley (sister of Walter and Margery) = Sir Henry Long

10. Margery Long = Robert Hungerford

11. Walter Hungerford = Frances Cocke

12. Anne Hungerford = William Gostlett

13. Charles Gostlett = Marie, widow of ---- Short

14. Benjamin Gostlett = Elizabeth Chetwynd

15. Helena Gostlett = John Harington

16. Henry Harington = Mary Backwell

17. Henry Harington = Martha Musgrave

18. Susanna Isabella Harington = Josiah Thomas, Archdeacon of Bath. Their daughter, Jane Anne Thomas, married Edward Musgrave Harington (her first cousin, son of Henry Harington and Esther Lens, and grandson of 17 above) and was the mother of Edward Templer Harington, father (by Ada Drew) of Ada Constance Helen Harington, wife of John Gerhard Tiarks. John Gerhard Edward Tiarks, a son of these last, married Evelyn Florence Cripps and left a daughter, Anne Patricia Tiarks, wife of Peter William Garside Phillips and mother of Mark Antony Peter Phillips, first husband of H.R.H. Princess Anne (Elizabeth Alice Louise) of Great Britain, The Princess Royal, daughter of H.M. Queen Elizabeth II.

19. George Hudleston Thomas = Mary Anne Broadhurst

20. Edgar Hastings Thomas = Christian Jean Wallace

21. **Hilda Margaret Rose Thomas** of Calif. = (Theodor) Ernst (Heinrich) **Otto**, brother of (Karl Ludwig) Rudolf Otto, German theologian and philosopher of religion. Gerhard Gottfried (Gerald Godfrey) Otto, son of Ernst and Hilda, married Jean Blackman and was the father of

Julie Helen Otto (b. 1954), co-editor of the *NEHGS NEXUS*, who drew the charts in *Ancestors of American Presidents*.

8. Thomas Dudley (brother of Dorothy Sutton) = Grace Threlkeld

9. Richard Dudley = Dorothy Sanford
9. Lucy Dudley = Albany Featherstonehaugh

10. Edmund Dudley = Catherine Hutton
10. Henry Featherstone-haugh = Dorothy Wybergh

11. Dorothy Dudley = Bernard Kirkbride
11. Sir Timothy Featherstone-haugh, royalist = Bridget Patrickson

12. Richard Kirkbride = Bridget Maplate

13. Bernard Kirkbride = 12. Jane Featherstonehaugh

13,14. Matthew Kirkbride = Magdalen Dalston

14,15. **Joseph Kirkbride** of Pa. = (1) Phebe Blackshaw; (2) Sarah Stacy; (3) Mrs. Mary Fletcher Yardley.

11. Mary Dudley (sister of Dorothy) = Thomas Ferrand

12. Eleanor Ferrand = Thomas Heber

13. Martha Heber = George Clapham

14. Sir Christopher Clapham = Margaret Oldfield

15. Margaret Clapham = Sir William Craven

16. **Christopher Craven**, colonial governor of S.C. = Elizabeth Staples.

Sources: *MCS4*, lines 39, 36, 161, *AR7*, lines 198, 5 and sources cited therein, plus *NEHGR* 108 (1954):176-77 (reprinted in *EO* 1:3:774-75) (Mrs. Mackworth, and see below); *DNB* (J.G. Montrésor), *BLG* 1894, p. 1418, *BP* (Denbigh), *CP* (Desmond and Denbigh), *Tixall*, pp. 149-50 (Aston), *Salt*, new ser., 12(1909):79, 1912:34A (chart)

The Royal Descents of 500 Immigrants

(Leveson) and George Wrottelsey, *History of the Family of Wrottesley of Wrottesley, co. Stafford* (1903), pp. 244-57, 400 (for Mrs. Montrésor), 266-75 (for Walter Wrottesley and Eleanor [Wrottesley] Lee behind Mrs. Mackworth); research of Julie Helen Otto, Rev. Francis J. Poynton, *Memoranda, Historical and Genealogical, Relating to the Parish of Kelston in the County of Somerset*, part IV (1885), pp. 53-56, 1-4, 110 (Benjamin Gostlett to Edgar Hastings Thomas), F.W. Todd, *Humphrey Hooke of Bristol and His Family and Descendants in England and America During the Seventeenth Century* (1938), charts opposite pp. 10 and 141 and T.F. Fenwick and Walter C. Metcalfe, eds., *Visitation of the County of Gloucester, 1682-83* (1884), pp. 73-74 (Gostlett), G.D. Squibb, ed., *Wiltshire Visitation Pedigrees, 1623* (*HSPVS*, vol. 105-6, 1954), pp. 94 (Hungerford), 117 (Long), plus *GM* 17(1972-74):407-19 (Edward III to Mark Phillips) (for Mrs. Otto); *LDBR* 3:210-13, *Taylor*, pp. 114-17, 121, 132 (Kirkbride, Dudley), *DNB* (Sir Timothy Fe[a]therstonehaugh) and *TCWAAS*, new ser., 14(1914):220-23 (Fe[a]therstonehaugh), 9(1888):318 (and chart opp.)-23 (Dudley) (for Joseph Kirkbride); *BP* (Craven), *DVY*2:475-76, 378 (Clapham, Heber), 3:96 (Ferrand).

The Royal Descents of 500 Immigrants

1. Edward III, King of England, d. 1377 = Philippa of Hainault

2. John of Gaunt, Duke of Lancaster = Catherine Roet

2. Thomas of Woodstock, 1st Duke of Gloucester = Eleanor Bohun

3. Joan Beaufort = Ralph Neville, 1st Earl of Westmoreland

3. Anne Plantagenet = William Bourchier, Count of Eu

4. George Neville, 1st Baron Latymer = Elizabeth Beauchamp

4. John Bourchier, Baron Berners = Margery Berners

5. Sir Henry Neville   =   5. Joan Bourchier

6. Richard Neville, 2nd Baron Latymer = Anne Stafford

7. Margaret Neville = Edward Willoughby

8. Elizabeth Willoughby = Sir Fulke Grevile

9. Robert Grevile = Blanche Whitney

10. Fulke Grevile = Mary Copley

11. Dorothy Grevile = Sir Arthur Haselrige, 2nd Bt., Puritan leader

12. **Catherine Haselrige** = George **Fenwick** (1603-1656/7), colonist, a founder of Saybrook, Connecticut, ARD, SETH.

9. Katherine Grevile (sister of Robert) = Giles Reed

10. Elizabeth Reed = Richard Brent

11. **Margaret Brent** (1600-1670/1) of Md., feminist, d. unm.

11. **Giles Brent** of Va. and Md., dep. gov. of Md. = (1) Kittamaquund, an Indian; (2) Mrs. Frances Whitgreaves Harrison.

11. George Brent = Mariana Peyton (parents also of Robert Brent of Va., who = Anne Baugh but left no NDTPS)

12. **George Brent** of Va. = (1) Elizabeth Greene; (2) Mrs. Mary Sewall Chandler, daughter of Henry Sewall,

secretary of Md., and Lady Jane Lowe Sewall Calvert, Baroness Baltimore, of Md., ARD, SETH.

12. **Mary Brent** of Va. = (1) Giles **Brent** Jr., her 1st cousin, son of Giles Brent, dep. gov. of Md., and Kittamaquund; (2) Francis Hammersley.

Sources: *DNB* (Fenwick, Haselrige [Hesilrige]), *CB* (Hasilrigg), *BP* (Warwick) or *Collins*, vol. 4, pp. 337-43 (Grevile), *CP* (Willoughby de Broke, Latymer, Berners, Eu, etc.); *DAB* (Margaret Brent), *LDBR* 5:492-95, 666-73, and Chester Horton Brent, *The Descendants of Colonel Giles Brent, Capt. George Brent, and Robert Brent, Gent., Immigrants to Maryland and Virginia* (1946), pp. 42-89.

The Royal Descents of 500 Immigrants

1. Edward III, King of England, d. 1377 = Philippa of Hainault
2. John of Gaunt, Duke of Lancaster = Catherine Roet
3. Henry Beaufort, Cardinal Beaufort
4. (illegitimate by Alice FitzAlan, who = John Cherleton, 4th Baron Cherleton of Powis) Jane Beaufort = Sir Edward Stradling
5. Sir Henry Stradling = Elizabeth Herbert
6. Thomas Stradling = Janet Mathew
7. Sir Edward Stradling = Elizabeth Arundel
8. Jane Stradling = Alexander Popham
9. Edward Popham = Jane Norton
10. **George Popham** (d. 1608), Maine colonist, = ----.

9. Catherine Popham (sister of Edward) = Sir William Pole
10. Sir William Pole, antiquary = Mary Periham
11. **William Poole** of Mass. = Mary ----.

8. Catherine Stradling (sister of Jane) = Sir Thomas Palmer
9. John Palmer = Elizabeth Verney
10. Catherine Palmer = Sir Thomas Hinton
11. Sir John Hinton = Elizabeth Dilke
12. James Hinton = ---- (parents also of James and William Hinton of N.C., who left no NDTPS)
13. **John Hinton** of N.C. = Mary Hardy.

8. (illegitimate, perhaps by Felice Gwyn ferch John ap Llwyd Kemeys) Elizabeth Stradling (half-sister of Jane and Catherine) = Edmund Morgan, son of Thomas Morgan and Elizabeth Vaughan, daughter of Sir Roger Vaughan and Joan Whitney, SETH
9. Mary Morgan = John Thomas
10. William Thomas = Joan Lewis

11. Thomas Thomas = Dorothy Carew
12. Elizabeth Thomas = William Aubrey
13. **Barbara Aubrey** of Pa. = John **Bevan** of Pa., ARD, SETH.

Sources: *DAB* (George Popham), *BLG* 1952 (Buller-Leyborne-Popham of Huntstrete) and F.T. Colby, *Visitation of Somerset, 1623* (*HSPVS*, vol. 11, 1876), p. 87 (Popham); *MCS4*, line 27, and sources cited therein, esp. *TAG* 31 (1955):171-72, 32(1956):9-12 and *M&G*, pp. 435-36 (Stradling) (for William Poole); *LDBR* 1:153-55 and *Wilson*, pp. 89-91, 107-8, 110-11 (Hinton); *Keeler-Wood*, pp. 415-19 (partly corrected or confirmed by *M&G*, pp. 435-36, 241, 311, 317, 31-32, 347 and *Bartrum 2*, p. 1623, which gives no mother for Elizabeth Stradling, wife of Edmund Morgan) and S.W. Pennypacker, *The Descent of Samuel Whitaker Pennypacker...From the Ancient Counts of Holland* (1898), pp. 10-16 (Mrs. Bevan). A fully documented Hinton monograph would be welcome.

The Royal Descents of 500 Immigrants

1. Edward III, King of England, d. 1377 = Philippa of Hainault
2. John of Gaunt, Duke of Lancaster = Catherine Roet
3. Joan Beaufort = Ralph Neville, 1st Earl of Westmoreland
4. Richard Neville, 1st Earl of Salisbury = Alice Montagu
5. Catherine Neville = William Bonville, Baron Harington and Bonville
6. Cecily Bonville, Baroness Harington and Bonville = Thomas Grey, 1st Marquess of Dorset
7. Thomas Grey, 2nd Marquess of Dorset = Margaret Wotton
8. Lord John Grey = Mary Browne
9. Jane Grey = Sir Edward Grevile, son of Sir Fulke Grevile and Elizabeth Willoughby, SETH
10. Margaret Grevile = Godfrey Bosvile
11. **Elizabeth Bosvile** of Mass. = (1) Roger **Harlakenden**; (2) Herbert **Pelham** of Mass., 1st treasurer of Harvard College, ARD, SETH.

8. Anne Grey (sister of Lord John) = Sir Henry Willoughby
9. Margaret Willoughby = Sir Matthew Arundell, son of Sir Thomas Arundell (and Margaret Howard), son of Sir John Arundell and Eleanor Grey, daughter of Thomas Grey, 1st Marquess of Dorset, and Cecily Bonville above
10. Thomas Arundell, 1st Baron Arundell of Wardour = Anne Philipson
11. **Hon. Anne Arundell** = Cecil **Calvert**, 2nd Baron Baltimore, proprietor of Md., ARD, SETH.
12. Charles Calvert, 3rd Baron Baltimore (1637–1715), colonial governor of Md. = (1) Mary Darnall; (2) Mrs. Jane Lowe Sewall of Md., ARD, SETH; (3) Mrs. Mary Banks Thorpe; (4) Margaret Charleton
13. (by 2) Benedict Leonard Calvert, 4th Baron Baltimore, proprietor of Md. = Lady Charlotte Lee, ARD, SETH.

7. Dorothy Grey (sister of the 2nd Marquess of Dorset) = William Blount, 4th Baron Mountjoy

8. Dorothy Blount = John Bluet

9. Richard Bluet = Mary Chichester

10. Arthur Bluet = Joan Lancaster

11. John Bluet = Elizabeth Portman

12. Anne Bluet = Cadwallader Jones

13. Cadwallader Jones = Elizabeth Creswick

14. William Jones = Martha Smith

15. **John Jones** of Mass. = Hannah Francis.

8. Mary Blount (sister of Dorothy) = Sir Robert Dennis

9. Anne Dennis = Sir John Chichester

10. Sir Robert Chichester = Ursula Hill

11. Sir John Chichester, 1st Bt. = Mary Colley

12. Sir Arthur Chichester, 3rd Bt. = Elizabeth Drewe

13. Anne Chichester = Francis Fulford

14. Francis Fulford = Ellen Edgcombe

15. **Mary Fulford** of N.Y. = Joseph **Lovecraft**. Their son, George Lovecraft, married Helen Allgood; their son, Winfield Scott Lovecraft, married Sarah Susan Phillips and was the father of science fiction author Howard Phillips (H.P.) Lovecraft (1890-1937).

Sources: *MCS4*, line 95 and sources cited therein (esp. *PCF Yorkshire* -- Bosvile pedigree), *Collins*, vol. 4, p. 342 and *BP* (Grevile, later earls of Warwick, and Greys, earls of Stamford) and *CP* (Dorset, Bonville, Salisbury, Westmoreland) (for Mrs. Pelham); *MG* 1:138-40, *MCS4*, line 63, and Joseph Jackson Howard and H. Seymour Hughes, *Genealogical Collections Illustrating the History of Roman Catholic Families of England, Based on the Lawson Manuscript*, part III (Arundell) (1887?), pp. 226, 229, 233-34 (for Lady A.A. Calvert, Baroness Baltimore); *NEHGR* 113 (1959):216-21 (reprinted in *EO* 2:2:570-75), *VD*, pp. 93-94 (Bluet), 102 (Blount, Grey) and *CP* (Mountjoy) (John Jones); *NEHGR* 133(1979):180, correspondence from Henry L.P. Beckwith, Jr., of Wickford, R.I., citing information outlined by George Lovecraft, her son, accepted by the Heraldry Committee of NEHGS, *BLG,* 18th ed., vol. 1 (1965), p. 295 (Fulford), *BP* (Chichester, baronets), and *VD,* pp. 380-81, 174, 280 (Fulford, Chichester, Dennis) (for Mrs. Lovecraft).

The Royal Descents of 500 Immigrants

1. Edward III, King of England, d. 1377 = Philippa of Hainault
2. Lionel of Antwerp, Duke of Clarence = Elizabeth de Burgh
3. Philippa Plantagenet = Edmund Mortimer, 3rd Earl of March
4. Elizabeth Mortimer = Sir Henry "Hotspur" Percy
5. Elizabeth Percy = John Clifford, 7th Baron Clifford
6. Thomas Clifford, 8th Baron Clifford = Joan Dacre
7. John Clifford, 9th Baron Clifford = Margaret Bromflete
8. Henry Clifford, 10th Baron Clifford = Anne St. John
9. Elizabeth Clifford = Sir Ralph Bowes
10. Sir George Bowes = Muriel Eure
11. Elizabeth Bowes = John Blakiston
12. Marmaduke Blakiston = Margaret James
13. **George Blakiston** of Md. = Barbara Lawson.
13. John Blakiston, regicide = Susan Chambers
14. **Nehemiah Blakiston** of Md. = Elizabeth Gerard, daughter of Thomas Gerard of Md., ARD, SETH, and Susannah Snow. Elizabeth m. (2) Ralph Rymer, (3) Joshua Guibert.
14. John Blakiston = Phebe Johnston
15. **Nathaniel Blakiston**, colonial governor of Md. = ---.
15. **Margaret Blakiston** of Va. = Edward Nott, colonial governor of Va., ARD, SETH.

Sources: *MG* 1:48-55; *Surtees*, vol. 4, pp. 107-8 (Bowes); *Collins*, vol. 6, pp. 516-20 (Clifford); *CP* (Clifford, Northumberland, March).

The Royal Descents of 500 Immigrants

1. Edward III, King of England, d. 1377 = Philippa of Hainault

2. Lionel of Antwerp, Duke of Clarence = Elizabeth de Burgh

3. Philippa Plantagenet = Edmund Mortimer, 3rd Earl of March

4. Elizabeth Mortimer = Sir Henry "Hotspur" Percy

5. Henry Percy, 2nd Earl of Northumberland = Eleanor Neville

6. Henry Percy, 3rd Earl of Northumberland = Eleanor Poynings

7. Henry Percy, 4th Earl of Northumberland = Maud Herbert

8. Eleanor Percy = Edward Stafford, 3rd Duke of Buckingham, son of Henry Stafford, 2nd Duke of Buckingham, and Catherine Woodville, sister of Elizabeth Woodville, Queen of Edward IV

9. Mary Stafford = George Neville, 3rd Baron Abergavenny (their progeny shares the entire known ancestry of Elizabeth Plantagenet of York, Queen of Henry VII)

10. Ursula Neville = Sir Warham St. Leger

11. Anne St. Leger = Thomas Digges, mathematician

12. Sir Dudley Digges, diplomat, judge = Mary Kempe

13. **Edward Digges**, colonial governor of Va. = Elizabeth Page.

11. Sir Anthony St. Leger (brother of Anne) = Mary Scott

12. Sir Warham St. Leger = Mary Heyward

13. **Katherine St. Leger** of Va. = Thomas **Colepepper (Culpeper)** of Va., ARD, SETH. Their daughter, Frances Colepepper (Culpeper), married (1) Samuel Stephens, colonial governor of N.C.; (2) Sir William Berkeley (1608-1677), colonial governor of Va., ARD, SETH; and (3) Philip Ludwell (d. 1717), planter, Virginia councilor, colonial governor of N.C. and S.C.

13. Ursula St. Leger = Daniel Horsmanden

14. **Warham Horsmanden** of Va. = Susanna Beeching. Their
    daughter, Mary Horsmanden, married (1) Samuel Filmer;
    (2) William Byrd I (1652-1704), Virginia planter, Indian
    trader, merchant and councilor. A son, Rev. Daniel
    Horsmanden, married Mrs. Susanna Woolston Bowyer
    and was the father of Daniel Horsmanden, Jr.
    (1694-1778), last chief justice of the province of New
    York, who married Mrs. Mary Reade Vesey and Anne
    Jevon.

13. Mary St. Leger = William Codd

14. **St. Leger Codd** of Va. = (1) Mrs. Anne Mottrom Wright
    Fox; (2) Mrs. Anne Bennett Bland; (3) Mrs. Anne
    Hynson Randall Wickes.

Sources: *MCS4*, lines 48, 47, 44, 36, 161, *AR7*, lines 3, 19, 5, *AP&P*,
pp. 247-50 (Digges), 523-30 (St. Leger), *DAB* (Berkeley, Ludwell,
Byrd, Horsmanden), *DNB* (Sir Warham St. Leger) and sources cited
in all, especially *CP* (for generations 1-9).

The Royal Descents of 500 Immigrants

1. Edward III, King of England, d. 1377 = Philippa of Hainault
2. Lionel of Antwerp, Duke of Clarence = Elizabeth de Burgh
3. Philippa Plantagenet = Edmund Mortimer, 3rd Earl of March
4. Elizabeth Mortimer = Sir Henry "Hotspur" Percy
5. Henry Percy, 2nd Earl of Northumberland = Eleanor Neville
6. Catherine Percy = Edmund Grey, 1st Earl of Kent
7. Anne Grey = John Grey, 8th Baron Grey of Wilton
8. Edmund Grey, 9th Baron Grey of Wilton = Florence Hastings
9. Tacy Grey (possibly by an earlier wife than Florence Hastings) = John Guise
10. William Guise = Mary Rotsy
11. John Guise = Joan Pauncefort
12. Elizabeth Guise = Robert Haviland
13. **Jane Haviland** of Mass. = William **Torrey.**

7. George Grey, 2nd Earl of Kent (brother of Lady Anne) = Catherine Herbert
8. Anne Grey = John Hussey, 1st Baron Hussey
9. Bridget Hussey = Sir Richard Morrison
10. Elizabeth Morrison = Henry Clinton, 2nd Earl of Lincoln
11. Sir Henry Clinton alias Fynes = Elizabeth Hickman
12. William Clinton = Elizabeth Kennedy
13. James Clinton = Elizabeth Smith
14. **Charles Clinton** of N.Y. = Elizabeth Denniston. Their sons included U.S. Vice-President George Clinton (1739-1812), also governor of N.Y., and General James Clinton (1733-1812), noted revolutionary soldier and father by Mary DeWitt of Republican statesman

DeWitt Clinton (1769-1828), U.S. senator, governor of N.Y., and promoter of the Erie Canal.

14. **Christiana Clinton** of N.Y. = John **Beatty.**

Sources: *AR7*, lines 197, 207, 19, 5 and *NEHGR* 108(1954):177-78, 110(1956):232, reprinted in *EO 1*:3:775-77 (Mrs. Torrey); *NYGBR* 51 (1920):360-62, 66(1935):330-35, *EP* and *CP* (Lincoln, Hussey, Kent) (Clinton and Mrs. Beatty).

The Royal Descents of 500 Immigrants

1. Edward III, King of England, d. 1377 = Philippa of Hainault
2. Lionel of Antwerp, Duke of Clarence = Elizabeth de Burgh
3. Philippa Plantagenet = Edmund Mortimer, 3rd Earl of March
4. Elizabeth Mortimer = Sir Henry "Hotspur" Percy
5. Henry Percy, 2nd Earl of Northumberland = Eleanor Neville
6. Henry Percy, 3rd Earl of Northumberland = Eleanor Poynings
7. Margaret Percy = Sir William Gascoigne
8. Sir William Gascoigne = Alice Frognall
9. Sir William Gascoigne = Margaret Wright
10. Alice Gascoigne = John Haselwood
11. Alice Haselwood = Francis Bernard
12. Francis Bernard = Mary Woolhouse
13. **Col. William Bernard** of Va. = Mrs. Lucy Higginson Burwell.

12. Richard Bernard (brother of Francis) = Elizabeth Woolhouse (sister of Mary)
13. **Richard Bernard** of Va. = (1) Dorothy Alwey; (2) Anna Cordray of Va., ARD, SETH.

12. Thomas Bernard (brother of Francis and Richard) = Sarah ---
13. Francis Bernard = Sarah ----
14. Francis Bernard = Margery Winslowe
15. **Sir Francis Bernard**, 1st Bt. (1712-1779), barrister, colonial governor of N.J. and Mass. = Amelia Offley of Mass., ARD, SETH.

Sources: *MCS4*, line 46 and sources cited therein, esp. *MGH*, 5th ser., 7(1929-31):304-6 (Richard) and *Bernards of Abington*, vol. 1, pp.

34-43 and chapters 5, pp. 95-117, and 8-9, pp. 170-212 (Haselwood, line of Sir Francis); *PCF Yorkshire* (Gascoigne pedigree); *BP* and *CP* (Northumberland, March) and *MP*, tables I-II, XXX, pp. 1-2, 33. See also *NEXUS* 4(1987):24-28.

1. Edward III, King of England, d. 1377 = Philippa of Hainault
2. Thomas of Woodstock, 1st Duke of Gloucester = Eleanor Bohun
3. Anne Plantagenet = William Bourchier, Count of Eu
4. John Bourchier, Baron Berners = Margery Berners
5. Sir Humphrey Bourchier = Elizabeth Tilney
6. John Bourchier, Baron Berners = Catherine Howard
7. Jane Bourchier = Sir Edmund Knevet
8. John Knevet = Agnes Harcourt
9. Abigail Knevet = Sir Martin Sedley
10. Muriel Sedley = Brampton Gurdon
11. **Muriel Gurdon** of Mass. = Richard **Saltonstall** (c. 1610-1694) of Mass., colonial official, ARD, SETH.

8. Elizabeth Knevet (sister of John) = Francis Bohun
9. Nicholas Bohun = Audrey Coke
10. Edmund Bohun = Dorothy Baxter
11. Baxter Bohun = Margaret Lawrence
12. **Edmund Bohun**, chief justice of S.C. = Mary Brampton.

7. (illegitimate by Elizabeth Bacon) Sir James Bourchier (half-brother of Lady Knevet) = Mary Banister
8. Sir Ralph Bourchier = Elizabeth Hall, daughter of Francis Hall (and Ursula Sherington), son of Francis Hall and Elizabeth Wingfield, SETH
9. Sir John Bourchier = Elizabeth ----
10. **Mary Bourchier** of Va. = Jabez **Whitaker** of Va., ARD, SETH.

Sources: *AR7*, line 4, *MCS4*, line 18, *SMF* 1:286-88 (Gurdon) and *PSECD* 2, pp. xcviii-cxix (Mrs. Saltonstall); S. Wilton Rix, ed., *The Diary and Autobiography of Edmund Bohun, Esq., with an*

Introductory Memoir, Notes and Illustrations (1853), pp. vii (and pedigree opposite)-xxxii; *MCS4,* line 73, Sarah C.W. Cantey, *Our Children's Ancestry* [Whitaker family] (1935), pp. 59 (and chart opposite)-64, and Rev. A.R. Maddison, ed., *Lincolnshire Pedigrees,* vol. 2 (*HSPVS,* vol. 51, 1903), p. 441 (Hall) (for Mrs. Whitaker).

The Royal Descents of 500 Immigrants

1. Edward III, King of England, d. 1377 = Philippa of Hainault
2. Lionel of Antwerp, Duke of Clarence = Elizabeth de Burgh
3. Philippa Plantagenet = Edmund Mortimer, 3rd Earl of March
4. Elizabeth Mortimer = Sir Henry "Hotspur" Percy
5. Henry Percy, 2nd Earl of Northumberland = Eleanor Neville
6. Henry Percy, 3rd Earl of Northumberland = Eleanor Poynings
7. Anne Percy = Sir Thomas Hungerford
8. Mary Hungerford = Edward Hastings, 2nd Baron Hastings
9. Anne Hastings = Thomas Stanley, 2nd Earl of Derby
10. Margaret Stanley = Robert Radcliffe, 1st Earl of Sussex
11. Jane Radcliffe = Anthony Browne, 1st Viscount Montagu
12. Hon. Anthony Browne = Mary Dormer
13. Dorothy Browne = Edmund Lee
14. Dorothy Lee = Sir John Temple
15. Mary Temple = Robert Nelson
16. **John Nelson** (c. 1654-1734) of Mass., merchant, proponent of French expulsion from North America, and public official = Elizabeth Tailer.
17. Rebecca Nelson = Henry Lloyd
18. Margaret Lloyd = William Henry Smith
19. Rebecca Smith = John Aspinwall
20. John Aspinwall, Jr. = Susan Howland
21. Mary Rebecca Aspinwall = Isaac Roosevelt
22. James Roosevelt = Sara Delano
23. Franklin Delano Roosevelt (1882-1945), 32nd U.S. President = (Anna) Eleanor Roosevelt

16. **Margaret Nelson** (sister of John Nelson of Mass.) said to be of Va. and to have = Rev. Thomas **Teackle**.

15. Dorothy Temple (sister of Mary) = John Alston
16. William Alston = Thomasine Brooke
17. **John Alston of S.C.** = Mrs. Elizabeth Turgis Harris.

Sources: *TG* 2(1981):123-28, and sources cited therein, especially the works of Temple Prime and John Alexander Temple; John A. Upshur, *Upshur Family in Virginia* (1955), pp. 24-25 (Mrs. Teackle); *Lineage Book, Descendants of the Illegitimate Sons and Daughters of the Kings of Britain*, #212 (John Alston of S.C.), and sources cited therein.

The Royal Descents of 500 Immigrants

1. Edward III, King of England, d. 1377 = Philippa of Hainault
2. Lionel of Antwerp, Duke of Clarence = Elizabeth de Burgh
3. Philippa Plantagenet = Edmund Mortimer, 3rd Earl of March
4. Elizabeth Mortimer = Sir Henry "Hotspur" Percy
5. Henry Percy, 2nd Earl of Northumberland = Eleanor Neville
6. Henry Percy, 3rd Earl of Northumberland = Eleanor Poynings
7. Henry Percy, 4th Earl of Northumberland = Maud Herbert
8. Eleanor Percy = Edward Stafford, 3rd Duke of Buckingham, son of Henry Stafford, 2nd Duke of Buckingham, and Catherine Woodville, sister of Elizabeth Woodville, Queen of Edward IV
9. Elizabeth Stafford = Thomas Howard, 3rd Duke of Norfolk
10. Henry Howard, Earl of Surrey, the poet = Frances Vere
11. Catherine Howard = Henry Berkeley, Baron Berkeley
12. Mary Berkeley = Sir John Zouche
13. Sir John Zouche = Isabel Lowe, sister of Vincent Lowe, husband of Anne Cavendish, SETH
14. Elizabeth Zouche = Devereux Wolseley
15. Anne Wolseley = Rev. Thomas Knipe, headmaster of Westminster School
16. Anne Knipe = Michael Arnold
17. **Alicia Arnold** of Md. = John **Ross**.

11. Thomas Howard, 4th Duke of Norfolk (brother of Lady Berkeley) = Margaret Audley
12. Thomas Howard, 1st Earl of Suffolk = Catherine Knevet

13. Theophilus Howard, 2nd Earl of Suffolk = Elizabeth Home

14. James Howard, 3rd Earl of Suffolk = Barbara Villiers

15. Elizabeth Howard = Sir Thomas Felton, 4th Bt.

16. Elizabeth Felton = John Hervey, 1st Earl of Bristol

17. John Hervey, 1st Baron Hervey of Ickworth, man of letters = Mary Lepell

18. Mary Hervey = George Fitzgerald

19. Charles Lionel Fitzgerald = Dorothea Butler

20. Edward Thomas Fitzgerald = Emma Green

21. Lionel Charles Henry William Fitzgerald = Sarah Caroline Brown

22. **Desmond Fitzgerald** (1846-1926) of R.I. and Mass., hydraulic engineer = Elizabeth Parker Clark Salisbury.

10. Thomas Howard, 1st Viscount Howard of Bindon (brother of the Earl of Surrey) = Gertrude Lyte

11. Charles Lyte-Howard = Rebecca Webb

12. Catherine Howard = Sir Thomas Thynne

13. Anne Thynne = Sir Thomas Nott

14. **Edward Nott**, colonial governor of Va. = Margaret Blakiston of Va., ARD, SETH.

Sources: *AP+P*, pp. 729-31, *MP*, tables I-II, XXI, pp. 1-2, 22, 434, *Lives of the Berkeleys*, vol. 2, pp. 402-3 esp. and *NGSQ* 51 (1963):36-37 esp. (Lowe) (for Mrs. Ross); *MP*, tables I-II, XXI, pp. 1-2, 22-23, 336-37, and Desmond Fitzgerald, *Family Notes* (1911), pp. 6-8, 31, 71-136 esp. (for Fitzgerald); *MG*1:50, *VGE*, pp. 171-72, *DNB* (Sir Thomas Nott), *CP* (Howard of Bindon -- vol. 6, p. 584, note (c) esp.) and *MP*, tables I-II, XXI, XXIV, pp. 1-2, 22, 26, 440 (for Nott).

The Royal Descents of 500 Immigrants

1. Edward III, King of England, d. 1377 = Philippa of Hainault

2. Lionel of Antwerp, Duke of Clarence = Elizabeth de Burgh

3. Philippa Plantagenet = Edmund Mortimer, 3rd Earl of March

4. Elizabeth Mortimer = Sir Henry "Hotspur" Percy

5. Henry Percy, 2nd Earl of Northumberland = Eleanor Neville

6. Henry Percy, 3rd Earl of Northumberland = Eleanor Poynings

7. Margaret Percy = Sir William Gascoigne

8. Agnes Gascoigne = Sir Thomas Fairfax

9. Sir Nicholas Fairfax = Jane Palmes

10. Mary Fairfax = Sir Henry Curwen

11. Mabel Curwen = 12. Sir William Fairfax, see below

12,13. Sir Philip Fairfax = Frances Sheffield

13,14. Sir William Fairfax, Parliamentary general in the English Civil War = Frances Chaloner

14,15. Isabella Fairfax = Nathaniel Bladen

15,16. **William Bladen** (1673-1718), colonial publisher, attorney-general of Md. = Anne Swearingen.

16,17. Anne Bladen = Benjamin Tasker, president of the council (and act. gov.) of Md.

17,18. Anne Tasker = 16,17. Samuel Ogle (c. 1702-1752), colonial governor of Md., see below.

8. Margaret Gascoigne (sister of Agnes) = Ralph Ogle, 3rd Baron Ogle

9. Dorothy Ogle = Sir Thomas Forster

10. Eleanor Forster = George Craster

11. Edmund Craster = Alice Mitford

12. Isabel Craster = Luke Ogle, a cousin

13. Nicholas Ogle = ----
14. Luke Ogle = Katherine Graham
15. Samuel Ogle = 16. Ursula Markham, see below
16,17. **Samuel Ogle** (c. 1702-1752), colonial governor of Md. = 17,18. Anne Tasker, see above.

10. Thomas Forster (brother of Eleanor) = Florence Wharton
11. Thomas Forster = Isabel Brewster
12. Phyllis Forster = John Forster, a cousin
13. Dorothy Forster = George Fenwick
14. **George Fenwick** (1603-1656/7), colonist, a founder of Saybrook, Conn. = (1) Alice Apsley, ARD, SETH; (2) Catherine Haselrige, ARD, SETH.

5. Elizabeth Percy (sister of the 2nd Earl of Northumberland) = John Clifford, 7th Baron Clifford
6. Thomas Clifford, 8th Baron Clifford = Joan Dacre
7. John Clifford, 9th Baron Clifford = Margaret Bromflete
8. Elizabeth Clifford = Sir Robert Aske
9. John Aske = Eleanor Ryther
10. Robert Aske = (1) Eleanor Markenfield; (2) Anne Sutton
11. (by 2) Elizabeth Aske = Gabriel Fairfax
12. Sir William Fairfax = 11. Mabel Curwen, see above

11. (by 1) Robert Aske (half-brother of Elizabeth) = Elizabeth Dawney
12. Helen Aske = Thomas Fairfax, 1st Baron Fairfax
13. Ferdinando Fairfax, 2nd Baron Fairfax, Parliamentary general in the English Civil War = Mary Sheffield
14. Frances Fairfax = Sir Thomas Widdrington, Speaker of the House of Commons
15. Mary Widdrington = Sir Robert Markham, 3rd Bt.
16. Ursula Markham = 15. Samuel Ogle, see above

Sources: *LDBR* 2:763-64 and *MG* 1:43-47 (Bladen), *PCF Yorkshire* (Fairfax and Gascoigne pedigrees), William Jackson, *Papers and Pedigrees Mainly Relating to Cumberland and Westmorland*, vol. 1 (1892), chart at end (Curwen) and *BP* and *CP* (Northumberland, March) (for William Bladen); Sir H.A. Ogle, 7th Bt., *Ogle and Bothal, or a History of the Baronies of Ogle, Bothal and Hepple, and of the Families of Ogle and Bertram* (1902), passim (and chart between pp. 220 and 221), *NF* 2:148-49, 154-55, 197, 199-299, 203-5 (Ogle), 259-60, 264 (Craster), 131 (Widdrington) and *NHN*, vol. 1 (1893), pp. 228, 276 (Forster), vol. 7 (1904), p. 473 (Fenwick) (for Samuel Ogle and George Fenwick); *DNB* (Sir William and the 2nd baron Fairfax, Sir Thomas Widdrington) and *CB* (Markham of Sedgebrooke, baronets), *Foster's V of Yorkshire*, pp. 118-19 (Aske) and *Collins*, vol. 6, pp. 516-18 (Clifford).

The Royal Descents of 500 Immigrants

1. Edward III, King of England, d. 1377 = Philippa of Hainault
2. John of Gaunt, Duke of Lancaster = Catherine Roet
3. John Beaufort, Marquess of Somerset and Dorset = Margaret Holand
4. Edmund Beaufort, 1st Duke of Somerset = Eleanor Beauchamp
5. Henry Beaufort, 2nd Duke of Somerset, d. unm.
6. (illegitimate by Joan Hill) Charles Somerset, 1st Earl of Worcester = Elizabeth Herbert
7. Henry Somerset, 2nd Earl of Worcester = Elizabeth Browne, daughter of Sir Anthony Browne and Lucy Neville, daughter of John Neville, 1st Marquess of Montagu (and Isabel Ingoldsthorpe), son of Richard Neville, 1st Earl of Salisbury and Alice Montagu, SETH
8. Lucy Somerset = John Neville, 4th Baron Latymer
9. Dorothy Neville = Thomas Cecil, 1st Earl of Exeter, son of William Cecil, 1st Baron Burghley, minister of Elizabeth I
10. Dorothy Cecil = Sir Giles Alington
11. Susan Alington = Sir Robert Crane, 1st Bt.
12. Elizabeth Crane = Sir Edmund Bacon, 4th Bt.
13. Frances Bacon = Walter Norborne
14. Elizabeth Norborne = John Symmes Berkeley
15. **Norborne Berkeley, 1st Baron Botetourt** (c. 1718-1770), colonial governor of Va., d. unm.

11. Katherine Alington (sister of Susan) = Zouche Tate
12. William Tate = Mary Stedman
13. Bartholomew Tate = Mary Noel
14. Mary Tate = Samuel Long
15. **Catherine Maria Long** of N.Y. = Sir Henry **Moore**, 1st Bt. (1713-1769), colonial governor of N.Y.

9. Elizabeth Neville (sister of Dorothy) = Sir John Danvers
10. Dorothy Danvers = Sir Peter Osborne
11. Sir John Osborne, 1st Bt. = Eleanor Danvers, a cousin
12. Sir John Osborne, 2nd Bt. = Elizabeth Strode
13. **Sir Danvers Osborne, 3rd Bt.**, colonial governor of N.Y. = Lady Mary Montagu, ARD, SETH.

Sources: *DAB, EP* and *CP* (Botetourt), *CB* (Bacon of Redgrave, Crane of Chilton), *BP* and *CP* (Exeter, Latymer, Worcester [under Beaufort in *BP*], Somerset, plus the *CP* entry for Edward Devereux, 8th Viscount Hereford, 1st husband of Elizabeth Norborne) (for Botetourt); Robert Mowbray Howard, *Records and Letters of the Family of the Longs of Longville, Jamaica, and Hampton Lodge, Surrey,* vol. 1 (1925), pp. 113, 120, 185 esp. (for Lady Moore); *BP* and *CB* (Osborn[e] of Chicksands Priory, baronets), and F.N. McNamara, *Memorials of the Danvers Family* (1895), chart opposite p. 103 and pp. 284-86 (for Osborne).

The Royal Descents of 500 Immigrants

1. Edward III, King of England, d. 1377 = Philippa of Hainault

2. Edmund of Langley, 1st Duke of York = Isabel of Castile

3. Constance Plantagenet = Thomas le Despencer, 1st Earl of Gloucester

4. (illegitimate by Edmund Holand, 4th Earl of Kent) Eleanor Holand = James Touchet, 2nd Baron Audley

5. Constance Touchet (or Audley) = Robert Whitney

6. Eleanor Whitney = John Puleston

7. Jane Puleston = Sir William Griffith

8. Sybil Griffith = Owen ap Hugh

9. Jane Owen = Hugh Gwyn

10. Sybil Gwyn = John Powell

11. Elizabeth Powell = Humphrey ap Hugh

12. Owen Humphrey = (1) Margaret Vaughan; (2) Elizabeth Thomas

13. (maternity uncertain) **Joshua Owen** of N.J. = Martha Shinn.

13. (maternity uncertain) **Rebecca Owen** (sometimes called Rebecca Humphrey[s]) of Pa. = Robert **Owen** of Pa., ARD, SETH (John Owen and Elizabeth Owen, wife of John Roberts, a brother and sister of Joshua and Rebecca, also came to Pa. John Owen seems to have died unmarried. Mrs. Elizabeth Owen Roberts left no NDTPS).

12. Samuel Humphrey = Elizabeth Rees

13. **Daniel Humphrey(s)** of Pa. = Hannah Wynne, daughter of Dr. Thomas Wynne of Pa., physician, 1st speaker of the Pennsylvania Provincial Assembly, ARD, SETH, and Martha Buttall. (All of Daniel's siblings also came to Pa. -- Lydia Humphrey, wife of Ellis Ellis; Joseph Humphrey = Elizabeth Medford; Benjamin Humphrey = Mary Llewelyn; Rebecca Humphrey = Edward Rees; Anne Humphrey = Edward Roberts; Goditha Humphrey;

and Elizabeth Humphrey = Thomas Abel. To date I
have found NDTPS only for Daniel.)

12. Anne Humphrey = Ellis ap Rees (alias Ellis Price),
ARD, SETH (parents of Rowland Ellis of Pa.) (John
Humphrey, a brother of Owen, Samuel and Anne also
came to Pa. = Jane Humphrey, and d.s.p.)

Sources: *WFP* 1, pedigree IV, pp. 44-47, and chart facing p. 44, plus
Merion, pp. 241-51. See also *Whitney*, pp. 114-15 esp. and *PACF*,
pp. 275, 185, 58, 273 (Puleston, Griffith, Owen, Gwyn [later Wynn]).

The Royal Descents of 500 Immigrants

1. Edward III, King of England, d. 1377 = Philippa of Hainault
2. John of Gaunt, Duke of Lancaster = Catherine Roet
3. Joan Beaufort = Ralph Neville, 1st Earl of Westmoreland
4. Edward Neville, 1st Baron Abergavenny = Elizabeth Beauchamp
5. George Neville, 2nd Baron Abergavenny = Margaret Fenne
6. Elizabeth Neville = Thomas Berkeley
7. Alice Berkeley = George Whetenhall
8. Thomas Whetenhall = Dorothy Vane
9. Susanna Whetenhall = William Tilghman
10. Oswald Tilghman = Elizabeth Packham
11. **Richard Tilghman** of Md. = Mary Foxley.

8. Anna Whetenhall (sister of Thomas) = John Sanders
9. Anna Sanders = Christopher Tilghman, cousin of William Tilghman above
10. Christopher Tilghman = ----
11. **Christopher Tilghman** of Va. = ----.

7. Anne Berkeley (sister of Alice) = John Brent
8. Margaret Brent = John Dering
9. Richard Dering = Margaret Twisden
10. Benetta Dering = John Fisher, whose sister Thomazine Fisher married John Epes and was the mother of William, Francis and Peter Epes, all of Va.
11. **John Fisher** of Va. = Elizabeth ----.

Sources: *LDBR* 5:847-48 (Christopher Tilghman) and *MG* 2:444-48 (Richard Tilghman) and sources cited therein; S.F. Tillman, *Spec Alit Agricolam* [Tilghman Family] (1962), pp. 1-2, 72, W. Bruce Bannerman, *Visitations of Kent, 1530-1, 1574 and 1592*, vol. 2

(*HSPVS*, vol. 75, 1924), p. 116 (Whetenhall), *Lives of the Berkeleys*, vol. 1, p. 354 and *Collins*, vol. 5, pp. 157-62 (Neville, barons Abergavenny); unpublished John Fisher article by John Anderson Brayton of Winston-Salem, N.C., *AP+P*, pp. 279-80, 256 (Fisher, Epes), Robert Hovenden, ed., *Visitation of Kent, 1619-1621* (*HSPVS*, vol. 42, 1898), pp. 159, 207, 212 (Fisher, Dering, Brent) and *Berry's Kent*, pp. 324, 398-99 (Fisher, Dering).

The Royal Descents of 500 Immigrants

1. Edward III, King of England, d. 1377 = Philippa of Hainault
2. John of Gaunt, Duke of Lancaster = Blanche Plantagenet
3. Elizabeth Plantagenet = John Holand, 1st Duke of Exeter, half-brother of Richard II, King of England
4. Constance Holand = Sir John Grey of Ruthin
5. Alice Grey = Sir William Knyvett (Knevet)
6. Anne Knyvett (Knevet) = John Thwaites
7. Christopher Thwaites = Joan ----
8. William Thwaites = Alice Garneys
9. Winifred Thwaites = Sir George Pierpont
10. Isabella Pierpont = Sir John Harpur
11. Jane Harpur = Patrick Lowe
12. Vincent Lowe = Anne Cavendish, illegitimate daughter (by ----) of Henry Cavendish (husband of Grace Talbot), son of Sir William Cavendish and Elizabeth Hardwick, the well-known "Bess of Hardwick," Countess of Shrewsbury, adventuress (Sir William was the second of four husbands), daughter of John Hardwick and Elizabeth Leke, ARD, SETH
13. **Jane Lowe** of Md. = (1) Henry **Sewall**, secretary of Md., nephew of Sir William Dugdale the antiquarian and genealogist; (2) Charles **Calvert**, 3rd Baron Baltimore (1637-1715), colonial governor of Md., ARD, SETH.
13. John Lowe = Catherine Pilkington
14. **Nicholas Lowe** of Md. = Mrs. Elizabeth Roe Combes.
14. **Henry Lowe** of Md. = Mrs. Susannah Maria Bennett Darnall, daughter of Richard Bennett, Jr., governor of Va. and Md., and Henrietta Maria Neale, daughter of James Neale of Md., ARD, SETH, and Anna Maria Gill.
    (Note: Nicholas and Vincent Lowe, younger brothers of Lady Baltimore, also came to Md., and Vincent married Elizabeth Foster. Neither brother, however, left NDTPS).

Sources: *NGSQ* 51(1963):32-43 (Lowe) and *The Reliquary* 22 (1881-82):241-42 (Hardwick); *Glover*, vol. 2, pp. 184-85 (Harpur), *Thoroton*, vol. 1, p. 176 (Pierpont) plus Thwaites and Knyvett (Knevet) research in English primary sources, esp. wills, by Brice McAdoo Clagett and Neil D. Thompson, to be incorporated into the former's forthcoming *Seven Centuries: Ancestors for Twenty Generations of John Brice de Treville Clagett and Ann Calvert Brooke Clagett*, and likely also to be published as a separate monograph; Rev. G.H. Dashwood, *Visitation of Norfolk in the Year 1563*, vol. 1 (1878) pp. 118-19 (Thwaites), plus *Calendar of Inquisitions Post Mortem*, 2nd ser., vol. III, *1504-1509* (1955), pp. 168-70 (1506 IPM of John Thwaites) and Walter C. Metcalfe, ed., *Visitations of Suffolk, 1561, 1577 and 1612* (1882) p. 32 (Garneys); *Blomefield*, vol. 1, pp. 378-79 (Knevet); *CP* (Grey of Ruthin, Exeter).

The Royal Descents of 500 Immigrants

1. Edward III, King of England, d. 1377 = Philippa of Hainault
2. Thomas of Woodstock, 1st Duke of Gloucester = Eleanor Bohun
3. Anne Plantagenet = William Bourchier, Count of Eu
4. William Bourchier, Baron Fitzwarin = Thomasine Hankford
5. Fulk Bourchier, Baron Fitzwarin = Elizabeth Dinham
6. John Bourchier, 1st Earl of Bath = Cecily Daubeney
7. Dorothy Bourchier = Sir John Fulford
8. Sir John Fulford = Anne Dennis
9. Thomas Fulford = Ursula Bamfield
10. **Mary Fulford** = (1) Thomas **Achims**; (2) Sir Ferdinando **Gorges** (c. 1565-1647), founder and lord proprietor of Maine, ARD, SETH.

8. Andrew Fulford (brother of Sir John) = Eleanor ----
9. Faith Fulford = John Davis, Elizabethan navigator and explorer
10. Philip Davys or Davis = Agnes Horton
11. Nathaniel Davis = Mary ----
12. **Margaret Davis** of Pa. = Thomas **Bye** of Pa., ARD, SETH.

Sources: *Ligon,* vol. 1, pp. 178-80 (Gorges), *VD*, pp. 379-80, 106-7 (Fulford, Bourchier) and *CP* (Bath, Fitzwarin, Eu) (for Lady Gorges); *LDBR* 4:228-30 and *Bye,* pp. 268-79 (for Mrs. Bye). A fully documented detailed monograph on the immediate ancestry of Mrs. Bye would be welcome.

1. Edward III, King of England, d. 1377 = Philippa of Hainault

2. Lionel of Antwerp, Duke of Clarence = Elizabeth de Burgh

3. Philippa Plantagenet = Edmund Mortimer, 3rd Earl of March

4. Elizabeth Mortimer = Sir Henry "Hotspur" Percy

5. Henry Percy, 2nd Earl of Northumberland = Eleanor Neville

6. Henry Percy, 3rd Earl of Northumberland = Eleanor Poynings

7. Margaret Percy = Sir William Gascoigne

8. Dorothy Gascoigne = Sir Ninian Markenfield

9. Alice Markenfield = Robert Mauleverer

10. Dorothy Mauleverer = John Kaye

11. Robert Kaye = Anne Flower

12. Grace Kaye = Sir Richard Saltonstall, a founder of the Massachusetts Bay Colony

13. **Richard Saltonstall** (c. 1610-1694) of Mass., colonial official = Muriel Gurdon of Mass., ARD, SETH.

10. Sir Edmund Mauleverer (brother of Dorothy) = Mary Danby

11. William Mauleverer = Eleanor Aldeborough

12. James Mauleverer = Beatrice Hutton

13. Edmund Mauleverer = Anne Pearson

14. **Anne Mauleverer** of N.J. = John Abbott.

Sources: *AR7*, lines 3, 19 and 5, *Saltonstall*, pp. 7-8, 12-13, 1st chart opposite p. 84 (Kaye), *PCF Yorkshire* (Mauleverer and Gascoigne pedigrees), C.B. Norcliffe, ed., *Visitation of Yorkshire, 1563-64* (*HSPVS,* vol. 16, 1881), p. 197 (Markenfield) and *MP,* charts I-II, XXX, pp. 1-2, 33 (for Saltonstall); *LDBR* 5, pp. 782-84, *CRLA,* vol. 15 (1950), pp. 240-41, *Yorkshire Archaeological Journal* 16(1902): 196-203 and sources cited therein (for Mrs. Abbott).

The Royal Descents of 500 Immigrants

1. Edward III, King of England, d. 1377 = Philippa of Hainault
2. John of Gaunt, Duke of Lancaster = Catherine Roet
3. Henry Beaufort, Cardinal Beaufort
4. (illegitimate by Alice FitzAlan, who = John Cherleton, 4th Baron Cherleton of Powis) Jane Beaufort = Sir Edward Stradling
5. Sir Henry Stradling = Elizabeth Herbert
6. Thomas Stradling = Janet Mathew
7. Jane Stradling = Sir William Griffith
8. Dorothy Griffith = William Williams
9. Jane Williams = William Coytmore
10. Rowland Coytmore = Mrs. Katherine Miles Gray of Mass.
11. **Elizabeth Coytmore** of Mass. = William **Tyng**.
12. Anna Tyng = Thomas Shepard, Jr.
13. Anna Shepard = Daniel Quincy
14. John Quincy = Elizabeth Norton
15. Elizabeth Quincy = William Smith, Jr.
16. Abigail Smith = John Adams, Jr. (1735-1826), 2nd U.S. President
17. John Quincy Adams (1767-1848), 6th U.S. President = Louisa Catherine Johnson

13. Thomas Shepard (III) (brother of Anna) = Mary Anderson
14. Anna Shepard = Henry Smith
15. William Henry Smith = Margaret Lloyd
16. Rebecca Smith = John Aspinwall
17. John Aspinwall, Jr. = Susan Howland
18. Mary Rebecca Aspinwall = Isaac Roosevelt
19. James Roosevelt = Sara Delano
20. Franklin Delano Roosevelt (1882-1945), 32nd U.S. President = (Anna) Eleanor Roosevelt

10. Alice Coytmore (sister of Rowland) = Hugh Wynne
11. William Wynne = ----
12. Sarah Wynne = Archibald Hamilton
13. Sarah Hamilton = John Kenrick
14. John Kenrick = Mary Quarrell
15. **Sarah Kenrick** of Pa. = Ralph **Eddowes** of Pa., ARD, SETH. John Kenrick, brother of Mrs. Eddowes and an American resident for about three years, married Sarah Savage and left two sons, Samuel Savage Kenrick and Edward Kenrick, who settled in Hillsdale, Mich., but probably left no NDTPS.

Sources: *AR7*, lines 199, 199A, 234; *MCS4*, lines 103, 104; *TAG* 32 (1956):9-23 (reprinted in *JIC* 136-49), 24(1948):219-22.

The Royal Descents of 500 Immigrants

1. Edward III, King of England, d. 1377 = Philippa of Hainault
2. Edmund of Langley, 1st Duke of York = Isabel of Castile
3. Constance Plantagenet = Thomas le Despencer, 1st Earl of Gloucester
4. (illegitimate by Edmund Holand, 4th Earl of Kent) Eleanor Holand = James Touchet, 2nd Baron Audley
5. Constance Touchet (or Audley) = Robert Whitney
6. Eleanor Whitney = John Puleston
7. Sir Robert Puleston = Jane ferch Richard Thomas
8. Margaret Puleston = Lewys Owen
9. Robert Owen = Elsbeth ferch Robert ap Morgan
10. Humphrey Owen = ---
11. **Robert Owen** of Pa. = Jane Vaughan of Pa., see below.

9. Edward Owen (brother of Robert) = Elen Llwyd ferch Robert ap Morgan
10. Margred Owen = Hywel Vaughan ap Gruffudd ap Hywel
11. Robert Vaughan, antiquary = Catherine Nannau
12. **Jane Vaughan** of Pa. = Robert **Owen** of Pa., her 2nd cousin once removed, see above.

Sources: *WFP* 1, pedigree V, pp. 50-56 and chart facing p. 50. See also *Whitney*, pp. 114-15 esp. and *PACF,* p. 275 (Puleston).

The Royal Descents of 500 Immigrants

1. Edward III, King of England, d. 1377 = Philippa of Hainault

2. Edmund of Langley, 1st Duke of York = Isabel of Castile

3. Constance Plantagenet = Thomas le Despencer, 1st Earl of Gloucester

4. Eleanor Holand (illegitimate by Edmund Holand, 4th Earl of Kent) = James Touchet, 2nd Baron Audley

5. Constance Touchet = Robert Whitney

6. Eleanor Whitney = John Puleston

7. Sir John Puleston = Gainor ferch Robert ap Maredudd

8. Jane Puleston = Rhys Thomas

9. Gainor Thomas = Richard Pugh

10. Elizabeth Pugh = Rowland Owen

11. Thomas Owen = ---

12. Harry Thomas Owen = ---

13. **Daniel Harry** of Pa. = Sybil ----.

13. **Hugh Harry** of Pa. = Elizabeth Brinton.

14. John Harry = Frances ---

15. Miriam Harry = Record Hussey

16. Lydia Hussey = Jacob Griffith

17. Amos Griffith = Edith Price

18. Elizabeth Price Griffith = Joshua Vickers Milhous

19. Franklin Milhous = Almira Park Burdg

20. Hannah Milhous = Francis Anthony Nixon

21. Richard Milhous Nixon, (b. 1913), 37th U.S. President = Thelma Catherine (Pat) Ryan

Sources: *WFP* 1, pedigree XX, pp. 136-38, chart between pp. 138 and 139, and sources cited therein, data reprinted or absorbed in Robert Jesse Harry, *The Ancestors and Descendants of Hugh Harry and Elizabeth Brinton* (1987).

The Royal Descents of 500 Immigrants

1. Edward III, King of England, d. 1377 = Philippa of Hainault
2. John of Gaunt, Duke of Lancaster = Catherine Roet
3. Joan Beaufort = Ralph Neville, 1st Earl of Westmoreland
4. Edward Neville, 1st Baron Abergavenny = Catherine Howard
5. Catherine Neville = Robert Tanfield
6. William Tanfield = Isabel Stavely
7. Francis Tanfield = Bridget Cave
8. Anne Tanfield = Clement Vincent
9. Elizabeth Vincent = Richard Lane
10. Dorothy Lane = William Randolph
11. **Henry Randolph** of Va. = (1) Elizabeth ----; (2) Judith Soane.
11. Richard Randolph = Elizabeth Ryland
12. **William Randolph** (c. 1651-1711) of Va., planter, merchant and colonial official = Mary Isham, daughter of Henry Isham of Va., ARD, SETH, and Mrs. Katherine Banks Royall.
13. Isham Randolph = Jane Rogers
14. Jane Randolph = Peter Jefferson
15. Thomas Jefferson (1743-1826), 3rd U.S. President = Mrs. Martha Wayles Skelton

15. Mary Jefferson (sister of Thomas) = John Bolling (III), a great-great-great-grandson of Pocahontas and John Rolfe
16. Archibald Bolling = Catherine Payne
17. Archibald Bolling, Jr. = Anne E. Wigginton
18. William Holcombe Bolling = Sallie Spiers White
19. Edith Bolling = (1) Norman Galt; (2) (Thomas) Woodrow Wilson (1856-1924), 28th U.S. President

Sources: *MCS4*, lines 71, 47, 45 (plus *AR7*, lines 1, 2, and *LDBR* 5: 315-16), and sources cited therein; Wassell Randolph, *Pedigree of the Descendants of Henry Randolph I (1623-1673) of Henrico County, Virginia* (1957), pp. 2-7. See also *DAB* (William Randolph), *Isham*, pp. 81-89 (Randolph), *Nichols*, vol. 4, part 2, p. 870 (Vincent), and *Baker*, vol. 2, p. 276 (Tanfield).

The Royal Descents of 500 Immigrants

1. Edward III, King of England, d. 1377 = Philippa of Hainault
2. John of Gaunt, Duke of Lancaster = Catherine Roet
3. Joan Beaufort = Ralph Neville, 1st Earl of Westmoreland
4. Richard Neville, 1st Earl of Salisbury = Alice Montagu
5. Alice Neville = Henry FitzHugh, 5th Baron FitzHugh
6. Elizabeth FitzHugh = Sir William Parr
7. William Parr, 1st Baron Parr = Mary Salisbury
8. Maud Parr = Sir Ralph Lane
9. **Sir Ralph Lane** (c. 1530-1603), Virginia colonist (commander of the Roanoke Island settlement 1585-86), d. unm.

8. Elizabeth Parr (sister of Maud) = Sir Nicholas Woodhull
9. Anne Woodhull = Richard Burnaby
10. Thomas Burnaby = Elizabeth Sapcotts
11. Susan Burnaby = Stephen Agard
12. Katherine Agard = Josias Bull
13. **Stephen Bull** of S.C. = ----.

Sources: *DNB* (Sir Ralph Lane) (and sources listed therein), *TAG* 52 (1976):15-17 (Parr, Woodhull) and *AR7*, lines 78, 2 (generations 1-7); Henry DeSaussure Bull, *The Family of Stephen Bull of Kinghurst Hall, County Warwick, England, and Ashley Hall, South Carolina, 1600-1960* (1961), pp. 4-11, 92-94 esp.; Walter C. Metcalfe, ed., *Visitations of Northamptonshire, 1564 and 1618-19* (1887), p. 172 (Burnaby), and Rev. A.R. Maddison, ed., *Lincolnshire Pedigrees*, vol. 3 (*HSPVS*, vol. 52, 1904), p. 853 (Sapcotts).

The Royal Descents of 500 Immigrants

1. Edward III, King of England, d. 1377 = Philippa of Hainault
2. Lionel of Antwerp, Duke of Clarence = Elizabeth de Burgh
3. Philippa Plantagenet = Edmund Mortimer, 3rd Earl of March
4. Elizabeth Mortimer = Sir Henry "Hotspur" Percy
5. Henry Percy, 2nd Earl of Northumberland = Eleanor Neville
6. Henry Percy, 3rd Earl of Northumberland = Eleanor Poynings
7. Henry Percy, 4th Earl of Northumberland = Maud Herbert
8. Henry Algernon Percy, 5th Earl of Northumberland = Catherine Spencer
9. Sir Thomas Percy = Eleanor Harbottle
10. Henry Percy, 8th Earl of Northumberland = Katherine Neville
11. **Hon. George Percy** (1580-1632), colonial governor of Va., d. unm.

10. Joan Percy (sister of the 8th Earl of Northumberland) = Arthur Harris
11. William Harris = Anne Ruther
12. Christopher Harris = Mary Gedge
13. Sir William Harris = Frances Astley
14. Frances Harris = Oliver Raymond
15. St. Clere Raymond = Anne Warkham
16. Samuel Raymond = ----
17. William Raymond = ----
18. Samuel Raymond = Isabella Child
19. Samuel Raymond = Margaretta Bridges
20. Isabella Raymond = Henry Yeats Smythies

21. Emily Smythies = Edward Greene (her sister, Margaretta Smythies, married John Greene, Edward's brother, and was a great-grandmother of [Henry] Graham Greene, the novelist)

22. Emily Smythies Green = Frederic Machell Smith

23. Kathleen Machell Smith = Francis Edward Bradshaw-Isherwood

24. **Christopher William Bradshaw-Isherwood, known as Christopher Isherwood** (1904-1986), of Calif., man of letters, d. unm.

Sources: *DNB* (Hon. George Percy) and *MP*, tables I-III, pp. 1-4, 122, 125-27 (Percy and Isherwood).

The Royal Descents of 500 Immigrants

1. Edward III, King of England, d. 1377 = Philippa of Hainault
2. Lionel of Antwerp, Duke of Clarence = Elizabeth de Burgh
3. Philippa Plantagenet = Edmund Mortimer, 3rd Earl of March
4. Elizabeth Mortimer = Sir Henry "Hotspur" Percy
5. Henry Percy, 2nd Earl of Northumberland = Eleanor Neville
6. Henry Percy, 3rd Earl of Northumberland = Eleanor Poynings
7. Henry Percy, 4th Earl of Northumberland = Maud Herbert
8. Henry Algernon Percy, 5th Earl of Northumberland = Catherine Spencer
9. Margaret Percy = Henry Clifford, 1st Earl of Cumberland
10. Henry Clifford, 2nd Earl of Cumberland (who = (1) Eleanor Brandon, granddaughter of Henry VII, SETH) = Anne Dacre (his second wife)
11. Frances Clifford = Philip Wharton, 3rd Baron Wharton
12. Frances Wharton = Sir Richard Musgrave, 1st Bt.
13. Sir Philip Musgrave, 2nd Bt. = Juliana Hutton
14. Sir Christopher Musgrave, 4th Bt. = Mary Cogan
15. Philip Musgrave = Mary Legge
16. Sir Christopher Musgrave, 5th Bt. = Julia Chardin
17. Anne Musgrave = Henry Aglionby
18. Mary Aglionby = John Orfeur Yates
19. **John Yates** of Va. = Julia Lovell.

11. Francis Clifford, 4th Earl of Cumberland (brother of Lady Wharton) = Grisold Hughes
12. Frances Clifford = Sir Gervase Clifton, 1st Bt.
13. Sir Clifford Clifton = Frances Finch

14. Catherine Clifton = Sir John Parsons, 2nd Bt.

15. Sir William Parsons, 3rd Bt. = Frances Dutton

16. Grace Parsons = Thomas Lambarde

17. Mary Lambarde = John Hallward

18. John Hallward = Emily Jane Leslie

19. Charles Berners Hallward = Elizabeth Anne Morgan

20. Reginald Francis Hallward = Adelaide Caroline Bloxam

21. **Reginald Michael Bloxam Hallward** of Calif. = Jeannie McDougall, actress under the name Jean Grahame (parents of the actress Gloria Grahame, 1925-1981, born Gloria Hallward, wife of Stanley Clements, film director Nicholas Ray, 1911-1978, Cy Howard, and Anthony Ray [her step-son]).

Sources: *MP,* tables I-II, VIII, X, XII, pp. 1-2, 9, 11, 13, 207 (for Yates); *MP,* tables I-II, VIII, IX, pp. 1-2, 9-10, 137 and Charles Kidd, *Debrett Goes to Hollywood* (1986), pp. 124-28 (for R.M.B. Hallward).

The Royal Descents of 500 Immigrants

1. Edward III, King of England, d. 1377 = Philippa of Hainault
2. John of Gaunt, Duke of Lancaster = Catherine Roet
3. Joan Beaufort = Sir Robert Ferrers
4. Elizabeth Ferrers = John de Greystock, 4th Baron Greystock
5. Joan de Greystock = John Darcy
6. Richard Darcy = Eleanor Scrope
7. Sir William Darcy = Eupheme Langton
8. Thomas Darcy, 1st Baron Darcy of Darcy = Dowsabel Tempest
9. Sir Arthur Darcy = Mary Carew, daughter of Sir Nicholas Carew and Elizabeth Bryan, SETH
10. Sir Edward Darcy = Elizabeth Astley
11. Isabella Darcy = John Launce
12. **Mary Launce** of Mass. = Rev. John **Sherman** (1613-1685), Puritan theologian and mathematician.

Sources: *AR7*, lines 13, 62, 2 and sources cited therein, esp. *TAG* 21 (1944-45):169-77.

The Royal Descents of 500 Immigrants

1. Edward III, King of England, d. 1377 = Philippa of Hainault
2. John of Gaunt, Duke of Lancaster = Catherine Roet
3. Joan Beaufort = Ralph Neville, 1st Earl of Westmoreland
4. Richard Neville, 1st Earl of Salisbury = Alice Montagu
5. Eleanor Neville = Thomas Stanley, 1st Earl of Derby
6. George Stanley, Baron Strange = Joan Strange, daughter of John Strange, 8th Baron Strange of Knokyn and Jacquetta Woodville, sister of Elizabeth Woodville, Queen of Edward IV, King of England
7. Sir James Stanley = Anne Hart
8. Henry Stanley = Margaret Stanley
9. Margaret Stanley (possibly illegitimate) = Richard Houghton
10. Evan Houghton = Ellen Parker
11. Katherine Houghton = William Henshaw
12. **Joshua Henshaw** of Mass. = Elizabeth Sumner.

Sources: *NEHGR* 22(1868):105-115 (115 esp.), reprinted in *EO* 2:2:329-39, *Chetham Society Publications* 51 (1860):95-97 (1598 will of Henry Stanley of Bickerstrath, which does not mention a daughter Margaret, wife of Richard Houghton), 82(1871):111 (a Stanley of Bickerstrath pedigree, again with no mention of Margaret, wife of Richard Houghton), *BP* (Derby-Crosshall, Aughton and Bickerstrath cadet line) and *CP* (Derby, Strange, Salisbury, Westmoreland). The 1701 pedigree reproduced in *NEHGR* 22:115 cites a marriage settlement between Richard Houghton and "Margaret, daughter of Henry Stanley of Bickerstagh" dated 8 Oct. 1585 and as reported in 1980 by Michael J. Wood to W. Charles Barnard, Richard Houghton and his wife enfeoffed Edward, James and William Stanley (sons of Henry, of whom William was illegitimate) with lands in Great Carleton, etc. (William Farrer and John Brownbill, eds., *The Victoria History of the County of Lancaster,* vol. 3 [1907, rep. 1966], p. 278, note 8 and vol. 7 [1913, rep. 1966], p. 230, note 29). Very likely Margaret Stanley, wife of Richard Houghton, was also illegitimate, despite her forename. A definitive monograph on this descent would be welcome.

The Royal Descents of 500 Immigrants

1. Edward III, King of England, d. 1377 = Philippa of Hainault
2. John of Gaunt, Duke of Lancaster = Catherine Roet
3. Joan Beaufort = Sir Robert Ferrers
4. Mary Ferrers = Sir Ralph Neville, her step-brother
5. John Neville = Elizabeth Newmarch
6. Jane Neville = Sir William Gascoigne
7. Margaret Gascoigne = Sir Christopher Ward
8. Anne Ward = Sir Ralph Neville, a cousin
9. Katherine Neville = Sir Walter Strickland
10. Walter Strickland = (1) Agnes (Hamerton?); (2) Alice Tempest
11. (prob. by 1) Ellen Strickland = John Carleton
12. Walter Carleton = Jane Gibbon
13. **Edward Carleton** of Mass. = Ellen Newton of Mass., ARD, SETH.

Sources: *AR7*, line 2 and sources cited therein, esp. Walter Lee Sheppard, Jr., "The Ancestry of Edward Carleton and Ellen Newton, his wife" (microfilm, 1978), which incorporates much data from *Moriarty*, plus much research also by John G. Hunt.

The Royal Descents of 500 Immigrants

1. Edward III, King of England, d. 1377 = Philippa of Hainault
2. Edmund of Langley, 1st Duke of York = Isabel of Castile
3. Constance Plantagenet = Thomas le Despencer, 1st Earl of Gloucester
4. (illegitimate by Edmund Holand, 4th Earl of Kent) Eleanor Holand = James Touchet, 2nd Baron Audley
5. Constance Touchet (or Audley) = Robert Whitney
6. Joan Whitney = Sir Roger Vaughan
7. Watkyn Vaughan = Joan ferch Ieuan ap Gwilym Fychan
8. Sir William Vaughan = Catrin ferch Jenkin ap Havard
9. Catrin Vaughan = David Evans
10. Mary Evans = Thomas Basset
11. Catrin Basset = Richard ap Ieuan
12. Jane Richards = Ieuan ap John
13. **John Bevan** of Pa. = Barbara Aubrey of Pa., ARD, SETH.

Sources: *TAG* 59(1983):1-2, *Merion*, pp. 168-69, corrected by *M&G*, p. 241, and *Whitney*, pp. 114-15 and chart opposite p. 216. See also *Keeler-Wood*, pp. 403-5, 413 (ignore 412, which repeats the error in *Merion*, p. 168-69, that the mother of Watkyn Vaughan was Eleanor Somerset. She was instead Joan Whitney, as above).

1. Edward III, King of England, d. 1377 = Philippa of Hainault

2. Lionel of Antwerp, Duke of Clarence = Elizabeth de Burgh

3. Philippa Plantagenet = Edmund Mortimer, 3rd Earl of March

4. Elizabeth Mortimer = Sir Henry "Hotspur" Percy

5. Elizabeth Percy = John Clifford, 7th Baron Clifford

6. Thomas Clifford, 8th Baron Clifford = Joan Dacre

7. Margaret Clifford = Robert Carre

8. Anne Carre = Roger Tempest

9. Catherine Tempest = Thomas Maude

10. Christopher Maude = Grace ----

11. John Maude = Alice Brome

12. John Maude = Jane ----

13. John Maude = Sarah ----

14. Joshua Maude = Elizabeth ----

15. **Margery Maude** of Del. = Thomas **Fisher**.

Sources: *LDBR* 1, pp. 46-47; Anna Wharton Smith, *Genealogy of the Fisher Family* (1896), pp. 14-20 and Joseph Hunter, *Familiae Minorum Gentium,* vol. 2 (*HSPVS,* vol. 38, 1895), pp. 618-19 (Maude); *DVY,* vol. 1, p. 121 (Tempest); *TG* 3(1878-79): 195, 202-3 (Carre); *Collins,* vol. 6, pp. 516-17 (Clifford); *CP* (Clifford, Northumberland, March).

The Royal Descents of 500 Immigrants

1. Edward III, King of England, d. 1377 = Philippa of Hainault

2. Edmund of Langley, 1st Duke of York = Isabel of Castile

3. Constance Plantagenet = Thomas le Despencer, 1st Earl of Gloucester

4. (illegitimate by Edmund Holand, 4th Earl of Kent) Eleanor Holand = James Touchet, 2nd Baron Audley

5. Margaret Touchet (or Audley) = (1) Sir Roger Vaughan; (2) Richard Grey, Baron Grey of Powis, son of Henry Grey, 2nd Earl of Tankerville, and Antigone Plantagenet, SETH

6. Elizabeth Vaughan or Grey (her paternity is uncertain) = Sir John Ludlow

7. Anne Ludlow = Thomas Vernon

8. Eleanor Vernon = Francis Curson

9. George Curson = ----

10. Francis Curson = Isabel Symonds

11. Samuel Curson = Elizabeth Stevens

12. Samuel Curson = Susanna ----

13. Samuel Curson = Rebecca Clark

14. **Richard Curson** of Md. = Elizabeth Becker.

Sources: J. Hall Pleasants, *The Curzon Family of New York and Baltimore* (1919), pp. 13-41 and chart opp. pp. 51 esp.; *Collins,* vol. 7, p. 401 (Vernon); *CP* (Grey of Powis, Audley and Kent, esp. vol. 6, appendix C, pp. 697-701).

The Royal Descents of 500 Immigrants

1. Edward III, King of England, d. 1377 = Philippa of Hainault
2. Thomas of Woodstock, 1st Duke of Gloucester = Eleanor Bohun
3. Anne Plantagenet = William Bourchier, Count of Eu
4. John Bourchier, Baron Berners = Margery Berners
5. Sir Humphrey Bourchier = Elizabeth Tilney
6. Margaret Bourchier = Sir Thomas Bryan
7. Elizabeth Bryan = Sir Nicholas Carew
8. Isabel Carew = Nicholas Saunders
9. Mary Saunders = Robert Beville
10. John Beville = Mary Clement
11. **Essex Beville** of Va. = Mrs. Amy --- Butler.

Sources: Asselia Strobhar Lichliter, *700 Years of the Beville Family: The Lives and Times of 18 Generations of the Beville Family of Huntingdonshire, England* (1976), passim, esp. pp. 343-44, 399; Sir Henry Ellis, ed., *Visitation of Huntingdon*[shire, 1613] (Camden Society Publications, No. 43, 1849), p. 9 (Beville); W. Bruce Bannerman, ed., *Visitations of Surrey, 1530, 1572, and 1623* (*HSPVS*, vol. 43, 1899), pp. 69 (Saunders), 17, 214 (Carew); *DNB* (Sir Francis Bryan and Sir Nicholas Carew); S.C.W. Allen, *Our Children's Ancestry* [Whitaker family] (1935), pp. 59 (and chart opposite)-60 (Bourchier) and *AR7*, line 4.

The Royal Descents of 500 Immigrants

1. Edward III, King of England, d. 1377 = Philippa of Hainault
2. Lionel of Antwerp, Duke of Clarence = Elizabeth de Burgh
3. Philippa Plantagenet = Edmund Mortimer, 3rd Earl of March
4. Elizabeth Mortimer = Sir Henry "Hotspur" Percy
5. Henry Percy, 2nd Earl of Northumberland = Eleanor Neville
6. Henry Percy, 3rd Earl of Northumberland = Eleanor Poynings
7. Margaret Percy = Sir William Gascoigne
8. Elizabeth Gascoigne = Sir George Talboys
9. Anne Talboys = Sir Edward Dymoke
10. Frances Dymoke = Sir Thomas Windebank
11. Mildred Windebank = Robert Reade
12. **Col. George Reade** of Va. = Elizabeth Martiau.
13. Mildred Reade = Augustine Warner Jr.
14. Mildred Warner = Lawrence Washington
15. Augustine Washington = Mary Ball
16. George Washington (1731/2-1799), 1st U.S. President = Mrs. Martha Dandridge Custis

Sources: *MCS4*, lines 86, 108; *LDBR* 5:101-2; *AR7*, lines 3, 19, 5, plus sources cited in all three.

The Royal Descents of 500 Immigrants

1. Edward III, King of England, d. 1377 = Philippa of Hainault
2. John of Gaunt, Duke of Lancaster = Catherine Roet
3. Joan Beaufort = Ralph Neville, 1st Earl of Westmoreland
4. George Neville, 1st Baron Latymer = Elizabeth Beauchamp
5. Sir Henry Neville = Joan Bourchier (see p. 132)
6. Richard Neville, 2nd Baron Latymer = Anne Stafford
7. Dorothy Neville = Sir John Dawney
8. Anne Dawney = Sir George Conyers
9. Sir John Conyers = Agnes Bowes
10. Eleanor Conyers = Lancelot Strother
11. William Strother = Elizabeth ---
12. **William Strother,** allegedly the immigrant to Va. = Dorothy --.
13. William Strother, Jr. = Margaret Thornton
14. Francis Strother = Susannah Dabney
15. William Strother = Sarah Bayly
16. Sarah Dabney Strother = Richard Taylor
17. Zachary Taylor (1784-1850), 12th U.S. President = Margaret Mackall Smith

Sources: *Lineage Book, Descendants of the Illegitimate Sons and Daughters of the Kings of Britain,* no. 76, which cites pp. 25-26 of a Strother manuscript I cannot locate; *CP.* Latymer article, and *AR7,* line 2. The above-given parentage and grandparentage of the immigrant William Strother first appeared, perhaps, in George Norbury Mackenzie's *Colonial Families of the United States of America,* vol. 5 (1915, rep. 1966), pp. 492-93.

The Royal Descents of 500 Immigrants

1. Edward III, King of England, d. 1377 = Philippa of Hainault

2. Lionel of Antwerp, Duke of Clarence = Elizabeth de Burgh

3. Philippa Plantagenet = Edmund Mortimer, 3rd Earl of March

4. Elizabeth Mortimer = Sir Henry "Hotspur" Percy

5. Elizabeth Percy = John Clifford, 7th Baron Clifford

6. Thomas Clifford, 8th Baron Clifford = Joan Dacre

7. Elizabeth Clifford = Sir William Plumpton

8. Elizabeth Plumpton = John Sotehill

9. Henry Sotehill = Joan Empson

10. Elizabeth Sotehill = Sir William Drury

11. Bridget Drury = Henry Yelverton

12. Sir William Yelverton, 1st Bt. = Dionysia Stubbs

13. Sir William Yelverton, 2nd Bt. = Ursula Richardson

14. Elizabeth Yelverton = Thomas Peyton

15. **Robert Peyton** of Va. = ----.

Sources: *LDBR* 4:525-30, *EB*, pp. 410, 594 and *CB* (Yelverton of Rougham), plus *Chester of Chicheley*, vol. 1, pp. 238-43 (Peyton) and Rev. G.H. Dashwood, ed., *Visitation of Norfolk, 1563*, vol. 1 (1878), pp. 267-68 (Yelverton); *SMF* 1:354 (Drury of Hawstead); J.W. Walker, ed., *Yorkshire Pedigrees, G-S* (*HSPVS*, vol. 95, 1943), p. 345 (Soothill); *PCF Yorkshire* (Plumpton pedigree); *Collins*, vol. 6, pp. 516-17 (Clifford); *CP* (Clifford, Northumberland, March).

The Royal Descents of 500 Immigrants

1. Edward III, King of England, d. 1377 = Philippa of Hainault

2. Lionel of Antwerp, Duke of Clarence = Elizabeth de Burgh

3. Philippa Plantagenet = Edmund Mortimer, 3rd Earl of March

4. Elizabeth Mortimer = Sir Henry "Hotspur" Percy

5. Henry Percy, 2nd Earl of Northumberland = Eleanor Neville

6. Henry Percy, 3rd Earl of Northumberland = Eleanor Poynings

7. Henry Percy, 4th Earl of Northumberland = Maud Herbert

8. Henry Algernon Percy, 5th Earl of Northumberland = Catherine Spencer

8. Eleanor Percy = Edward Stafford, 3rd Duke of Buckingham, son of Henry Stafford, 2nd Duke of Buckingham, and Catherine Woodville, sister of Elizabeth Woodville, Queen of Edward IV

9. Margaret Percy = Henry Clifford, 1st Earl of Cumberland

9. Elizabeth Stafford = Thomas Howard, 3rd Duke of Norfolk

10. Catherine Clifford = John Scrope, 8th Baron Scrope of Bolton

10. Henry Howard, Earl of Surrey, the poet = Frances Vere

11. Henry Scrope, 9th Baron Scope of Bolton = 11. Margaret Howard

12. Thomas Scrope, 10th Baron Scrope of Bolton = Philadelphia Carey

13. Emanuel Scrope, 1st Earl of Sunderland = Elizabeth Manners

14. (illegitimate by Martha Jeanes) Annabella Scrope = John Grubham Howe

15. Scrope Howe, 1st Viscount Howe = Juliana Alington, daughter of William Alington, 2nd Baron Alington (and Juliana Noel), son of William Alington, 1st Baron Alington, and Elizabeth Tollemache, daughter of Sir Lionel Tollemache, 2nd Bt., and Elizabeth Stanhope, SETH

16. Emanuel Scrope Howe, 2nd Viscount Howe = 6. Sophie Charlotte Marie von Kielmansegge, see below

7,17. **George Augustus Howe, 3rd Viscount Howe** (c. 1724-1758), British commander in America during the French & Indian wars, d. unm.

1. Christian III, King of Denmark, d. 1559 = Dorothea of Saxe-Lauenburg

2. Dorothea of Denmark = William, Duke of Brunswick-Lüneburg

3. George, Duke of Brunswick-Kalenberg = Anna Eleanor of Hesse-Darmstadt

4. Ernest Augustus, Elector of Hanover (father by Sophie of the Palatinate of George I, King of England and Sophie Charlotte of Hanover, wife of Frederick I, King of Prussia); by Klara Elisabeth von Meysenbug, wife of Franz Ernst, Count von Platen and Hallermund, Ernest Augustus is now thought to be the father of

5. Sophia Charlotte, Countess von Platen and Hallermund, Countess of Leinster and Darlington = Johann Adolf, Baron von Kielmansegge

6. Sophie Charlotte Marie von Kielmansegge = 16. Emanuel Scrope Howe, 2nd Viscount Howe, see above.

Sources: *MP*, tables I-II, VIII, XIII, XXI, pp. 1-2, 9, 14, 22; *EP, BP* or *CP* (Howe, Sunderland, Scrope, Alington, etc.); Ragnhild Hatton, *George I, Elector and King* (1978), *passim*, esp. pp. 23-24, 157, 340-41, 412 (Howe, Kielmansegge, Hanover); *ES*, charts for Denmark, Brunswick-Lüneburg (Hanover) and Platen-Hallermund.

The Royal Descents of 500 Immigrants

1. Edward III, King of England, d. 1377 = Philippa of Hainault
2. John of Gaunt, Duke of Lancaster = Catherine Roet
3. Joan Beaufort = Ralph Neville, 1st Earl of Westmoreland
4. Richard Neville, 1st Earl of Salisbury = Alice Montagu
5. Eleanor Neville = Thomas Stanley, 1st Earl of Derby
6. Margaret Stanley = Sir John Osbaldeston
7. Edward Osbaldeston = Maud Halsall
8. Geoffrey Osbaldeston, Chief Justice of Connaught = Lucy Warren
9. Deborah Osbaldeston = Walter Lyster
10. Anthony Lyster = Christiana Killkeny
11. Thomas Lyster = ---- O'Kelly
12. John Lyster = Elizabeth Coddington
13. John Lyster = Jane Ducasse
14. William John Lyster = Martha Hatton
15. **Rev. William Narcissus Lyster** of Mich. = Ellen Emily Cooper (parents of Henry Francis LeHunte Lyster, 1837-1894, noted physician). W.N.'s brother, Armstrong Lyster, who married Anne Isabella Isdell, also immigrated to the U.S. but left no NDTPS.

Sources: Rev. H.L.L. Denny, *Memorials of an Ancient House: A History of The Family of Lister or Lyster* (1913), pp. 19-22 (and chart opposite), 32-33, 61, 94-100. See also *BLGI*, 1912, pp. 426-27 (Lyster) and *CP* (Derby, Salisbury, Westmoreland).

The Royal Descents of 500 Immigrants

1. Edward III, King of England, d. 1377 = Philippa of Hainault
2. John of Gaunt, Duke of Lancaster = Catherine Roet
3. Joan Beaufort = Ralph Neville, 1st Earl of Westmoreland
4. Richard Neville, 1st Earl of Salisbury = Alice Montagu
5. Alice Neville = Henry FitzHugh, 5th Baron FitzHugh
6. Elizabeth FitzHugh = Nicholas Vaux, 1st Baron Vaux of Harrowden
7. Anne Vaux = Sir Thomas Le Strange
8. Richard Le Strange = Anne Astley
9. Thomas Le Strange = Elizabeth ----
10. Hamon Le Strange = Dorothy Moore
11. Thomas Le Strange = ----
12. Henry Le Strange = Elizabeth Sandes
13. Thomas L'Estrange = Frances Atkinson

14. George L'Estrange = Anne Crosbie	14. Henry L'Estrange = Elizabeth Malone
15. William L'Estrange = Anne Atkinson, a cousin	15. Henry Peisley L'Estrange = Mary Carleton
16. Edmund L'Estrange =	16. Henrietta Maria L'Estrange

17. William L'Estrange = Caroline Stewart Atkinson, a cousin
18. **Sarah L'Estrange** of Mich. = George Charles **Mahon** of Mich., ARD, SETH. Their daughter, Jane Caroline Mahon, married Louis Crandall Stanley and was the mother of Alice Caroline Stanley, wife of Dean Gooderham Acheson (1893-1991), U.S. Secretary of State.

Sources: George C. Mahon, "Family History of L'Estrange of Kilcummin, King's County, Ireland" (typescript, 1885, now owned by G.C. and Sarah's great-granddaughter, Helen Jefferson Sanford, former trustee of NEHGS), pp. 14-22 esp.; *BIFR*, pp. 722-25 (L'Estrange), 39-41 (Atkinson); *BLG*, 18th ed., vol. 3 (1972), p. 533 (Le Strange of Hunstanton); Godfrey Anstruther, *Vaux of Harrowden, A Recusant Family* (1953), pp. 7-8; *AR7*, lines 201, 78, 2.

The Royal Descents of 500 Immigrants

1. Edward III, King of England, d. 1377 = Philippa of Hainault
2. Lionel of Antwerp, Duke of Clarence = Elizabeth de Burgh
3. Philippa Plantagenet = Edmund Mortimer, 3rd Earl of March
4. Elizabeth Mortimer = Sir Henry "Hotspur" Percy
5. Elizabeth Percy = John Clifford, 7th Baron Clifford
6. Thomas Clifford, 8th Baron Clifford = Joan Dacre
7. John Clifford, 9th Baron Clifford = Margaret Bromflete
8. Henry Clifford, 10th Baron Clifford = Florence Pudsey
9. Dorothy Clifford = Sir Hugh Lowther
10. Sir Richard Lowther = Frances Middleton
11. Sir Christopher Lowther = Eleanor Musgrave
12. Sir John Lowther = Eleanor Fleming
13. Sir John Lowther, 1st Bt. = Mary Fletcher
14. Eleanor Lowther = Sir Christopher Wandesford, 1st Bt.
15. Frances Wandesford = Robert Maude
16. Anthony Maude = Alice Hartstonge
17. Anne Maude = Jerome Ryves, Dean of St. Patrick's
18. Alice Ryves = Thomas Le Hunte
19. Anne Le Hunte = Abraham Symes
20. Anne Symes = 10. Henry Mahon, see below

11,21. **George Charles Mahon** of Mich. = Sarah L'Estrange of Mich., ARD, SETH.

1. Henry VIII, King of England, d. 1547
2. (possibly an illegitimate son by Mary Berkeley, daughter of James Berkeley and Susan Viell, and granddaughter of Maurice Berkeley and Isabel Mead, SETH; possibly also, however, a son of Mary Berkeley and Sir Thomas Perrott, her 1st husband) Sir John Perrott = Jane Pollard
3. Anne Perrott = Sir John Phillips, 1st Bt.

190

4. Dorothy Phillips = Francis Annesley, 1st Viscount Valentia

5. Hon. John Annesley = Charity Warren

6. Maurice Annesley = Sarah Blayney

7. Elizabeth Annesley = Sir Arthur Gore, 2nd Bt.

8. Anne Gore = John Browne, 1st Earl of Altamont

9. Anne Browne = Ross Mahon

10. Henry Mahon = 20. Anne Symes, see above.

Sources: George C. Mahon, "Family History of Mahon of Castlegar, County of Galway, Ireland" (typescript, 1889) and further notes and data gathered by his granddaughter, Mrs. Dean Gooderham Acheson (Alice Caroline Stanley, wife of the U.S. Secretary of State and daughter of Louis Crandall Stanley and Jane Caroline Mahon) and by his great-granddaughter, Helen Jefferson Sanford, former trustee of NEHGS; *BP* (Mahon of Castlegar, baronets; Hawarden [for Maudes]; Lonsdale [for Lowthers]; Sligo [for Brownes, Earls of Altamont]; Arran [for Gores]; Valentia [for Annesleys]) and John O'Hart, *Irish Pedigrees,* 5th ed., vol. 1 (1892, reprint 1976), p. 579 (Mahon); *CP* (Altamont, Valentia, Clifford, Northumberland, March), *CB* (Wandesford of Kirklington, Gore of Newtown Gore, Phillips of Picton Castle) and *DNB* (Sir John Perrott); *Collins,* vol. 6, pp. 516-21 (Clifford) and *Lodge,* vol. 7, pp. 277-78 (Maude, Ryves), vol. 4, pp. 109-19 (Annesley), vol. 3, pp. 115-16 (Gore); *BLG* 4th ed. (1863), p. 856 (Le Hunte).

The Royal Descents of 500 Immigrants

1. Edward III, King of England, d. 1377 = Philippa of Hainault

2. Edmund of Langley, 1st Duke of York = Isabel of Castile

3. Constance Plantagenet = Thomas le Despencer, 1st Earl of Gloucester

4. (illegitimate by Edmund Holand, 4th Earl of Kent) Eleanor Holand = James Touchet (or Audley), 2nd Baron Audley

5. Constance Touchet (or Audley) = Robert Whitney

6. Eleanor Whitney = John Puleston

7. Jane Puleston = Sir William Griffith

8. Mary Griffith = Sir Randall Brereton

9. Jane Brereton = Nicholas Robinson, Bishop of Bangor

10. Piers Robinson alias Norris = Margaret Fowke, daughter of John Fowke and Dorothy Cupper, SETH

11. Eleanor Robinson alias Norris = John Maudit

12. Isaac Maudit = Elizabeth Berryman

13. Jasper Maudit = Elizabeth King, daughter of Thomas King (and Anne Roberts), son of Richard King and Martha Goddard, sister of William Goddard of Mass., SETH

14. Elizabeth Maudit = Thomas Wright

15. Anne Wright = Samuel Lawford

16. Samuel Lawford = Margaret Sarah Acland

17. Thomas Acland Lawford = Janet Turing Bruce

18. Sir Sydney Turing Barlow Lawford = Mrs. May Somerville Bunny Cooper Aylen

19. **Peter (Sydney Ernest [Aylen, later]) Lawford**, known as **Peter Lawford** (1923-1984) of Calif., actor = (1) Patricia Kennedy, daughter of Joseph Patrick Kennedy, the financier and diplomat, and sister of John Fitzgerald Kennedy, 35th U.S. President, of Robert Francis Kennedy, U.S. Senator and Attorney-General, of Edward Moore Kennedy, U.S. Senator, and of

Mrs. (Robert) Sargent Shriver, Jr. (Eunice Mary Kennedy), wife of the Democratic vice-presidential candidate in 1972; (2) Mary Anne Rowan; (3) Deborah Gould; (4) Patricia Seaton.

Sources: Will of Sir Sydney T.B. Lawford of Los Angeles, dated 4 Aug. 1932, with a codicil of 8 Sept. 1950, probated in London 7 Sept. 1953, at Somerset House, London, birth record (17 Sept. 1923) of Peter Sydney Ernest Aylen, later Lawford, and *The [London] Times* of Thurs., 21 Feb. 1924, p. 5, col. 4 (report of the Lawford and Aylen divorce cases of Lawford's parents); *BP* (Sir S.T.B. Lawford in the "Knightage" section post 1918); *TG*, new ser., 8 (1891-92): chart between pp. 184 and 185 (Lawford); *TG* 1 (1877):135, 4(1880):87-88 (Maudit, Wright, Lawford); Reginald Ames, *Genealogical Memoranda of the Family of Ames* (1889), chart entitled "Seize Quartier [sic] of Elizabeth, Sister of Eleanor Maudit, Drawn upon her Marriage with a German Nobleman," pp. 12-13, 16 (Maudit, King, Goddard, Robinson, Brereton, Griffith, Fowke); *PACF*, pp. 23, 185, 275 (Robinson, Griffith, Puleston); *Whitney*, pp. 114-15 esp.

The Royal Descents of 500 Immigrants

1. John II, King of France, d. 1364 = Bona of Bohemia

2. Philip I, Duke of Burgundy = Margaret of Flanders

3. John, Duke of Burgundy = Margaret of Bavaria

4. Mary of Burgundy (great-aunt of another Mary of Burgundy, wife of Maximilian I, Holy Roman Emperor, through whom the Hapsburgs inherited the "Spanish" Netherlands) = Adolf I, Duke of Cleves

5. Elizabeth of Cleves = Henry XXVI, Count of Schwarzburg-Blankenburg

6. Günther XXVIII, Count of Schwarzburg-Blankenburg = Katharina von Querfurt

7. Henry XXXI, Count of Schwarzburg-Blankenburg = Magdalen von Honstein

8. Günther XL, Count of Schwarzburg-Blankenburg = Elizabeth of Isenburg-Kelsterbach

9. Albert VII, Count of Schwarzburg-Rudolstadt = Juliane of Nassau-Dillenburg, sister of William the Silent, Prince of Orange, d. 1584, 1st Stadholder of the Netherlands

10. Magdalena of Schwarzburg-Rudolstadt = Henry II, Count Reuss-Gera

11. Henry X, Count Reuss-Lobenstein = Marie Sybil of Reuss-Obergreiz

12. Henry X, Count Reuss-Ebersdorf = Erdmuthe Benigna of Solms-Laubach

13. Henry XXIX, Count Reuss-Ebersdorf = Sophie Theodora of Castell-Remlingen, daughter of Wolfgang Dietrich, Count of Castell-Remlingen (also a descendant, via Limpurg-Speckfield, of Henry XXVI, Count of Schwarzburg-Blankenburg and Elizabeth of Cleves, 5 above) and Dorothea Renata von Zinzendorf, Countess of Zinzendorf and Pottendorf, daughter of Maximilian Erasmus von Zinzendorf, Count of Zinzendorf and Pottendorf, and Anna Amelia of Dietrichstein-Hollenburg, SETH. Henry XXIX and Sophie Theodora were the parents of Henry XXIV, Count

Reuss-Ebersdorf, who married Caroline Ernestine of Erbach-Schönburg and left a daughter, Augusta of Reuss-Ebersdorf, who married Francis, Duke of Saxe-Coburg-Saalfield and was both the mother of Leopold I, King of the Belgians, and the maternal grandmother of Victoria, Queen of Great Britain.

14. Joanna Dorothea, Countess Reuss-Ebersdorf = Christoph Friedrich Levin von Trotta genannt Treyden

15. Frederica Theodora Elizabeth von Trotta genannt Treyden = Friedrich Ludwig von Tschirschky und Bögendorff

16. Franz Ludwig von Tschirschky und Bögendorff = Wilhelmine Maximiliane Luise Marina von Schönberg

17. **Amalie Joanna Lydia von Tschirschky und Bögendorff** of Pa. = Edmund Alexander **de Schweinitz** (1825-1887), Moravian Bishop and historian, see below.

16. Augusta Theodora von Tschirschky und Bögendorff (sister of Franz Ludwig) = Heinrich August von Gersdorff

17. **Ernst Bruno von (de)Gersdorff** of Mass. = Caroline Choate.

13. Erdmuthe Dorothea, Countess Reuss-Ebersdorf (sister of Henry XXIX) = Nicholas Ludwig von Zinzendorf, Count of Zinzendorf and Pottendorf (1700-1760), religious reformer, founder of the Moravian brotherhood, American resident Dec. 1741-Jan. 1743, ARD, SETH.

14. Henrietta Benigna Justina von Zinzendorf, Countess of Zinzendorf and Pottendorf = Johann Michael, Baron von Watteville

15. **Anna Dorothea Elizabeth, Baroness von Watteville,** of Pa. = Hans Christian Alexander **von Schweinitz.**

16. Lewis David von Schweinitz (1780-1834), Moravian clergyman, botanist, pioneer mycologist = Louise Amalia Ledoux

The Royal Descents of 500 Immigrants

17. Edmund Alexander de Schweinitz (1825-1887), Moravian Bishop and historian = (1) 17. Amalie Joanna Lydia von Tschirschky und Bögendorff of Pa., ARD, SETH, see above; (2) Isabel Allen Bogge.

Sources: *ES*, tables for France, Burgundy, Cleves, Schwarzburg-Blankenburg and Schwarzburg-Rudolstadt, Nassau-Dillenburg, Reuss-Gera, Reuss-Lobenstein, Reuss-Ebersdorf, Saxe-Coburg-Saalfeld, Belgium, and Great Britain; Dr. Walter von Boetticher, *Geschichte des Oberlausitzischen Adels und Seiner Güter, 1635-1815*, vol. 2 (1913), pp. 1004-5 (Trotta genannt Treyden); *Gothaisches Genealogisches Taschenbuch der Uradeligen Häuser* (1913), pp. 726-28 (von Tschirschky und Bögendorff), (1923), p. 263 (von Gersdorff) and *GHdesA*, vol. 15 (Adelige Häuser A, vol. 3, 1957), p. 218 (E.B. von [de] Gersdorff); *DAB* (N.L. von Zinzendorf and L.D. and E.A. von [de] Schweinitz); Gerhard Meyer, *Nikolas Ludwig von Zinzendorf, Eine Genealogische Studie mit Ahnen und Nachfahrenliste* (1966). See also Gerald Paget, *The Lineage and Ancestry of H.R.H. Prince Charles, Prince of Wales*, vol. 2 (1977), pp. 21 (J457-8), etc.

The Royal Descents of 500 Immigrants

1. John II, King of France, d. 1364 = Bona of Bohemia
2. John, Duke of Berry = Joanna of Armagnac
3. Marie of Berry = John I, Duke of Bourbon
4. Louis, Count of Montpensier = Gabrielle de la Tour d'Auvergne
5. Charlotte of Bourbon-Montpensier = Wolfart VI von Borsselen, Count of Grandpré
6. Joanna von Borsselen = Wolfgang IV von Polheim
7. Magdalena von Polheim = George VI of Liechtenstein-Steieregg
8. Susanna of Liechtenstein-Steieregg = George Hartmann of Liechtenstein-Feldsberg
9. Hartmann II of Liechtenstein-Feldsberg = Anna Maria of Ortenburg
10. Judith of Liechtenstein-Feldsberg = Johann Joachim von Zinzendorf, Baron von Zinzendorf and Pottendorf (their daughter, Anna von Zinzendorf, married Conrad, Count von Starhemberg, and was the mother of [Heinrich] Ernst Rüdiger, Count von Starhemberg, defender of Vienna against the Turks in 1683)
11. Otto Henry von Zinzendorf, Baron von Zinzendorf and Pottendorf = Anna Apollonia von Zelking
12. Maximilian Erasmus von Zinzendorf, Count of Zinzendorf and Pottendorf = Anna Amelia of Dietrichstein-Hollenburg
13. George Louis von Zinzendorf, Count of Zinzendorf and Pottendorf (brother of Dorothea Renata von Zinzendorf, Countess of Zinzendorf and Pottendorf, wife of Wolfgang Dietrich, Count of Castell-Remlingen, a great-great-grandmother of Leopold I, King of the Belgians, and a great-great-great-grandmother of Victoria, Queen of Great Britain) = Carlotta Justina von Gersdorff
14. **Nicholas Ludwig von Zinzendorf, Count of Zinzendorf and Pottendorf** (1700-1760), religious reformer, founder

of the Moravian brotherhood, American resident Dec. 1741-Jan. 1743 = Erdmuthe Dorothea, Countess Reuss-Ebersdorf, ARD, SETH.

Sources: Meyer and Paget as per immediately preceding chart (for Erdmuthe Dorothea, etc.); *ES*, tables for France, Bourbon, Borsselen, Liechtenstein-Steieregg and Liechtenstein-Feldsburg; *DGA*, vol. 1 (1939), p. 117 (Starhemberg). Generations 4-12 of this line are followed by Gerald Paget (see p. 196), #s K919-920, L1837-1838, M3673-3674, N7347-7348, O14693-14694 (N3175-3176), O6351-6352, P12703-12704, Q25407-25408 (Q19031-19032).

The Royal Descents of 500 Immigrants

1. John II, King of France, d. 1364 = Bona of Bohemia
2. John, Duke of Berry = Joanna of Armagnac
3. Marie of Berry = John I, Duke of Bourbon
4. Charles I, Duke of Bourbon = Agnes of Burgundy
5. (illegitimate by Jeanne de Souldet), Sidoine alias Edmée de Bourbon = René du Bus, Seigneur de Tizon
6. Renée du Bus = Claude d'Anlezy, Seigneur de Menetou-Couture
7. Robert d'Anlezy, Seigneur de Menetou-Couture = Charlotte de Chastellux
8. Francoise d'Anlezy alias de Menetou = Francois de Celle, Seigneur du Puy
9. Gabrielle de Celle = Gilbert de Besse, Seigneur de la Richardie
10. Marguerite de Besse = Jerôme de Laizer, Seigneur de Siougeat
11. Louise de Laizer = Jean Baptiste de Saignes, Seigneur de Grizols
12. Louise de Saignes = Francois des Rosiers, Seigneur de Moncelet
13. Charles Annet des Rosiers, Seigneur de Moncelet = Anne de Bonnet de la Chabanne
14. Jean Charles de Moncelet alias Moslé = Catharine Elisabeth Koehler
15. Alexander Samuel Mosle = Dorothea Catharina Rendorff
16. Georg Rudolf Mosle = Charlotte Amalie Schultze
17. **George Mosle** of N.Y. = Caroline Durnford Dunscomb. Their daughter, Marie Caroline Mosle, married Keyes Winter, President Justice of the New York Municipal Court, and was the mother of Henry Mosle (H.M.) West Winter (b. 1915, married Elizabeth Tatham Dick), Pepsi-Cola executive, economic consultant, and author of *The Descendants of Charlemagne (800-1400)*, 10 vols. (1987-91), covering sixteen generations.

The Royal Descents of 500 Immigrants

Sources: H.M. West Winter (who compiled and contributed this line), "Genealogy of Hawtayne and West of Banbury (Oxon.) and London" (1965-70, typescript at NEHGS), pp. 144-45, "Magill and Dunscomb of Middletown, Conn., Chicago and New York" (1980, also a typescript at NEHGS), pp. 38-42, and "Durnford Family Records in Hampshire, Wiltshire, Dorset, Somerset and Canada" (1981, another typescript at NEHGS), pp. 31-33 (generations 13-17); A.G. Mosle, *Die Familie Mosle* (1912), pp. 1-11, and Otto Lasius, *Aus dem literarischen Nachlasse von Johann Ludwig Mosle, Grossherzoglich-Oldenburgischem Generalmajor* (1879), vol. 1, pp. 1-2 (de Moncelet alias Moslé); Dr. de Ribier, *Preuves de noblesse des pages auvergnats admis dans les écuries du roi*, vol. 1 (1909), pp. 229, 231 (de Saignes and des Rosiers); *D de la N* (Laizer); Comte Jean de Remacle, *Généalogies des familles nobles de la Basse-Auvergne* (mms. at Family History Library in Salt Lake City, microfilm 661,782, no date or pagination) (de Besse) and *Dictionnaire des fiefs de la Basse-Auvergne,* in *Mémoires de l'Académie des Sciences Belles-Lettres and Arts de Clermont-Ferrand,* vol. 42/1 (1941), col. 642 (de Celle); Hugues A. Desgranges, *Nobiliaire de Berry,* vol. 1 (1965), p. 222 (du Bus and d'Anlezy); *ES,* tables for France, Berry, and Bourbon, and illegitimate children of the Bourbon house.

The Royal Descents of 500 Immigrants

1. Philip III, King of Navarre, d. 1343 = Joanna of France, daughter of Louis X, King of France, d. 1316, and Margaret of Burgundy

2. Joanna of Navarre = Jean I, Vicomte de Rohan

3. Charles de Rohan, Seigneur de Guémené = Catherine de Guesclin

4. Louis I de Rohan, Seigneur de Guémené = Marie de Montauban

5. Pierre de Rohan, Seigneur de Gié = Francoise de Penhoët

6. Charles de Rohan, Seigneur de Gié = Jeanne de Saint-Severin

7. Francois de Rohan, Seigneur de Gié = Catherine de Silly

    (5. Pierre de Rohan was also Count de Marle, 6. Charles de Rohan was also Vicomte de Fronsac, and 7. Francois de Rohan was also Baron de Château-du-Loir)

8. Francoise (called Diane) de Rohan = Francois de Maillé de la Tour-Landry, Baron de la Tour-Landry, Count de Châteauroux

9. Madeleine de Maillé de la Tour-Landry = Francois de Menon, Seigneur de Turbilly

10. Urbain de Menon, Seigneur de Turbilly, Count de Brestau = Marie de Chahannai

11. Elizabeth de Menon = René IV de Vimeur, Seigneur de Rochambeau

12. Joseph Charles I de Vimeur, Seigneur de Rochambeau = Marie Magdalene Brachet

13. Joseph Charles II de Vimeur, Marquis de Rochambeau = Marie Claire Thérèse Bégon

14. **Jean Baptiste Donatien de Vimeur, Count de Rochambeau** (1725-1807), commander of the French expeditionary army in America during the last three years of the American Revolution, treated in the *DAB* = Jeanne Thérèse Tellez d'Acosta

The Royal Descents of 500 Immigrants

Sources: *Armorial General, ou Registres de la Noblesse de France*, vol. 2, pt. 2 (1742), pp. 13-18 (de Vimeur de Rochambeau) and *ES*, charts for Maillé and Rohan (new ser., vol. 10, 1986) and Navarre. See also *D de la N* (Vimeur de Rochambeau and Maillé) and *Anselme* (Rohan and Navarre).

The Royal Descents of 500 Immigrants

1. Robert I, King of Scotland, d. 1329 = (2) Elizabeth de Burgh
2. Matilda Bruce = Thomas Isaac or Ysac
3. Joanna Isaac or Ysac = John de Ergadia of Lorne
4. Isabel de Ergadia = Sir John Stewart of Innermeath and Lorne
5. Jean Stewart = Sir David Bruce of Clackmannan
6. John Bruce of Clackmannan = Elizabeth Stewart
7. Sir David Bruce of Clackmannan = Mariot Herries
8. Sir David Bruce of Clackmannan = Janet Blackadder
9. Edward Bruce of Blairhall = Alison Reid
10. Sir George Bruce of Carnock = Margaret Primrose
11. Margaret Bruce = Francis Nichols (Nicolls)
12. **Richard Nichols** (Nicolls) (c. 1624-1672), 1st English colonial governor of N.Y.; d. unm.

Sources: *DNB; Drummond*, vol. 1 (Bruce) and *BP* (Bruce, earls of Elgin); *BP* (recent editions, Moray -- for Stewart of Lorne); *CP* (Lorn) and *MCS4*, line 42. See also *TAG* 68(1993):113-14.

The Royal Descents of 500 Immigrants

1. Edward I, King of England, d. 1307 = Margaret of France
2. Thomas of Brotherton, Earl of Norfolk = Alice de Hales
3. Margaret Plantagenet, Duchess of Norfolk = John de Segrave, 4th Baron Segrave
4. Elizabeth de Segrave = John Mowbray, 4th Baron Mowbray
5. Thomas Mowbray, 1st Duke of Norfolk = Elizabeth FitzAlan
6. Isabel Mowbray = James Berkeley, 6th Baron Berkeley
7. Maurice Berkeley = Isabel Mead
8. Anne Berkeley = Sir William Dennis, son of Sir Walter Dennis (and Agnes Danvers), son of Morris Dennis and Katherine Stradling, daughter of Sir Edward Stradling, who had various illegitimate children, probably including Katherine, but whose wife was Jane Beaufort, SETH, a great-granddaughter of Edward III, King of England, d. 1377, and Philippa of Hainault
9. Eleanor Dennis = William Lygon
10. Thomas Lygon = 11. Frances Dennis, see below
11,12. Thomas Lygon = Elizabeth Pratt
12,13. **Col. Thomas Ligon (Lygon) of Va.** = Mary Harris.

7. Isabel Berkeley (sister of Maurice) = William Trye
8. William Trye = Anne Baynham
9. Edward Trye = Sybil Mornington
10. Katherine Trye = Hugh Dennis, nephew of Sir William Dennis, above
11. Frances Dennis = Thomas Lygon, see above

10. Cecily Lygon (sister of the first Thomas Lygon) = Edward Gorges, SETH
11. **Sir Ferdinando Gorges** (c. 1565-1647), founder and lord proprietor of Maine, = (1) Anne Bell, ARD, SETH; (2)

Mrs. Mary Fulford Achims, ARD, SETH; (3) Elizabeth Gorges, ARD, SETH; (4) Lady Elizabeth Gorges Smith, ARD, SETH.

10. Margaret Lygon (sister of Thomas and Cecily) = Sir Henry Berkeley

11. Sir Maurice Berkeley = Elizabeth Killigrew

12. **Sir William Berkeley** (1608-1677), colonial governor of Va. = Mrs. Frances Colepepper (Culpeper) Stephens, daughter of Thomas Colepepper (Culpeper) of Va., ARD, SETH, and Mrs. Katherine St. Leger Colepepper (Culpeper) of Va., ARD, SETH.

10. Katherine Lygon (sister of Thomas, Cecily, and Margaret) = Thomas Foliot

11. Sir John Foliot = Elizabeth Aylmer

12. **Rev. Edward Foliot** of Va. = ----.

9. Isabel Dennis (sister of Eleanor) = Sir John Berkeley

10. Elizabeth Berkeley = Henry Lygon (brother of William Lygon above)

11. Elizabeth Lygon = Edward Bassett

12. Jane Bassett = John Deighton

13. **Katherine Deighton** of Mass. = (1) Samuel **Hackburne**; (2) Thomas **Dudley** (1576-1653), colonial governor of Mass., ARD, SETH; (3) Rev. John **Allyn**.

13. **Frances Deighton** of Mass. = Richard **Williams**.

13. **Jane Deighton** of Mass. = (1) John **Lugg**; (2) Jonathan **Negus**.

10. Sir Richard Berkeley (brother of Elizabeth) = Elizabeth Reade

11. Elizabeth Berkeley = Sir Thomas Throckmorton

12. **Elizabeth Throckmorton** of Va. = Sir Thomas **Dale** (d. 1619), colonial governor of Va.

11. Mary Berkeley (sister of Elizabeth [Lady Throckmorton]) = Sir John Hungerford

12. Bridget Hungerford = Sir William Lisle

13. John Lisle, regicide = Alice Beckenshaw

14. **Bridget Lisle** of Mass. = (1) Leonard **Hoar** (c. 1630-1675), 3rd president of Harvard College; (2) Hezekiah **Usher**.

Sources: *MCS4*, lines 66 (Ligon), 69 (Sir Wm. Berkeley), 70 (Foliot), 29 (Gorges), 28, 28B (Deighton sisters) and *AR7*, lines 16 (generations 1-5), 209 (Gorges), 84, 187 (Deightons); *TVG* 32(1978):253-55, 33(1979):80 (Ligon); *TG* 6(1985):195-97, 216-18 (Deightons); *Ligon*, *passim*, esp. pp. 196-97, 211-12 (Trye), 177-80 (Gorges), 219-20, 222, 229-34 (Sir Wm. Berkeley), 45-46, 101-2 (Foliot), 861-62 (Deightons), 214-15 (Sir Richard Berkeley); *Gorges*, pp. 119-40, 163-65 and chart at end esp.; *DAB* (Sir Thomas Dale) and *Lives of the Berkeleys*, vol. 2, pp. 178, 180-81 (Lady Dale); *DNB* (Leonard Hoar, John and Alice Lisle), W.H. Rylands, ed., *Visitations of Hampshire, 1530, 1575, and 1622-34* (*HSPVS*, vol. 64, 1913), pp. 52-53 (Lisle[y]), and Sir John MacLean and W.C. Heane, *Visitation of Gloucester, 1623* (*HSPVS*, vol. 21, 1885), p. 89 (Hungerford) (for Mrs. Hoar), pp. 49-51 (Dennis). See also *Ligon*, vols. 2 and 3, *passim*, *M&G*, p. 435 (Stradling) and G.T. Clark, *Cartae et Alia Munimenta quae ad Dominium de Glamorgancia pertinent*, vol. 5 (1910), pp. 1845-47.

Note: Elizabeth Lygon, another daughter of William Lygon and Eleanor Dennis, married William Norwood; their son, Henry Norwood, married Elizabeth Rodney and was the father of two immigrants to Virginia, Henry Norwood, treasurer of the colony, 1661-73, and Charles Norwood, clerk of the Virginia Assembly, 1654-56. Both Henry and Charles returned to England and left no NDTPS. See *MCS4*, line 68 and *Ligon*, pp. 102-3.

The Royal Descents of 500 Immigrants

1. Edward I, King of England, d. 1307 = Margaret of France
2. Thomas of Brotherton, Earl of Norfolk = Alice de Hales
3. Margaret Plantagenet, Duchess of Norfolk = John de Segrave, 4th Baron Segrave
4. Elizabeth de Segrave = John Mowbray, 4th Baron Mowbray
5. Eleanor Mowbray = John de Welles, 5th Baron Welles
6. Eudo de Welles = Maud de Greystock
7. Lionel de Welles, 6th Baron Welles = Joan Waterton
8. Eleanor de Welles = Thomas Hoo, 1st Baron Hoo
9. Eleanor Hoo = James Carew
10. Sir Richard Carew = Malyn Oxenbridge
11. Margaret Carew = John St. John
12. Nicholas St. John = Elizabeth Blount
13. Elizabeth Blount = Sir Richard St. George
14. Sir George St. George = Catherine Gifford
15. Mary St. George = Richard Coote, 1st Baron Coote of Coloony
16. **Richard Coote, 1st Earl of Bellomont** (1636-1701), colonial governor of N.Y., Mass. and N.H. = Catherine Nanfan, ARD, SETH.
16. Letitia Coote = Robert Molesworth, 1st Viscount Molesworth
17. Hon. William Molesworth = Anne Adair
18. Richard Molesworth = Catherine Cobb
19. John Molesworth = Louise Tomkyns
20. Margaret Letitia Molesworth = Charles Richard de Havilland
21. Walter Augustus de Havilland = Lilian Augusta Ruse
22. **Olivia (Mary) de Havilland** (b. 1916) of Calif., actress, recipient of the Academy Award in 1946 and 1949 = (1) Marcus Aurelius Goodrich; (2) Pierre Paul Galante.

22. **Joan de Beauvoir de Havilland,** known as Joan Fontaine (b. 1917) of Calif., actress, recipient of the Academy Award in 1941 = (1) Brian de Lacey Aherne (1902-1986), actor; (2) William Dozier; (3) Collier Young; (4) Alfred Wright, Jr.

14. Sir Henry St. George (brother of Sir George) = Mary Dayrell
15. Frances St. George = George Tucker of Bermuda
16. Henry Tucker = Jehoiadden ----
17. Frances Tucker = Matthew Witter
18. **Thomas Witter** of N.Y. = (1) Mary Lewis; (2) Catherine Van Zandt.

16. St. George Tucker (brother of Henry) = Jane Hubbard
17. Henry Tucker = Frances Tudor
18. Henry Tucker (Jr.) = Anne Butterfield
19. **St. George Tucker** (1752-1827) of Va., revolutionary soldier, Virginia jurist, professor of law at William and Mary = (1) Frances Bland; (2) Lelia Skipwith.
19. Henry Tucker (III) = Frances Brune
20. Henry St. George Tucker = Jane Bosewell
21. William Thornhill Tucker = ----
22. **Frederick St. George de Lautour (Tucker,** later) **Booth-Tucker,** Salvation Army officer = Emma Moss Booth, known as Mrs. Emma Moss Booth-Tucker (1860-1903), Salvation Army officer, American resident from 1896 to 1903, daughter of William Booth, founder of the Salvation Army (and Catherine Mumford).

19. Frances Tucker (sister of Henry III and St. George) = Henry Tucker, a cousin
20. John Henry Tucker = Eliza Jane Tucker, a cousin
21. **Mary Byrd Farley Tucker** of Va. = John Patten **Emmet,** SETH.

18. Thomas Tucker (brother of Henry, Jr.) = Mary Nichols
19. **Frances Tucker** of N.Y. = John **Montrésor** (1736-1799), British military engineer who served in the American colonies from 1754 to 1778, son of James Gabriel Montrésor, also a noted British military engineer who served in the American colonies, SETH, by Mary Haswell, his 1st wife.

14. Richard St. George (brother of Sir George and Sir Henry) = Anne Pinnock
15. Henry St. George = Anne Hatfield
16. George St. George = Elizabeth Bligh
17. Sir Richard St. George, 1st Bt. = Sarah Persse
18. Sir Richard Bligh St. George, 2nd Bt. = Bridget Blakeney
19. Robert St. George = Sophia Madelina Olivia Mahon, daughter of James Mahon, Dean of Dromore (and Frances Catherine Ker), son of Ross Mahon and (Lady) Anne Browne, SETH
20. Howard Bligh St. George = Florence Evelyn Baker of N.Y.
21. **George Baker Bligh St. George** of N.Y. = Katherine Delano Price Collier, known as Mrs. Katherine D.P.C. St. George (1896-1893), congresswoman from N.Y.

Sources: *CP* (Bellomont, Coote of Coloony, Hoo, Welles), *EP* and *BP* (St. George, in *BP* to G.B.B. St. George, plus *BLGI* 1912, p. 452 for Mahon), *BP* (Bolingbroke) *Manning and Bray*, vol. 2, chart opp. p. 532 (Carew), *Horsham*, pp. 70-71 (Copley), and *AR7*, lines 202, 16; *BP* (Molesworth) and *BLG*, 18th ed., vol. 1 (1965), pp. 196-97 (de Havilland and Fontaine); Thomas Addis Emmet II, *A Memoir of John Patten Emmet* (1898), Tucker pedigrees esp., F.A. Mackenzie, *Booth-Tucker: Sadhu and Saint* (1930), pp. 1-9, 22, and W.P. Bacon, *Ancestry of Albert Gallatin and Hannah Nicholson* (c. 1916), pp. 45-48 (Witter) (for Witter, St. George Tucker, Booth-Tucker, Mrs. Emmet and Mrs. Montrésor).

The Royal Descents of 500 Immigrants

1. Edward I, King of England, d. 1307 = Eleanor of Castile
2. Joan Plantagenet = Gilbert de Clare, 3rd Earl of Gloucester, 7th Earl of Hertford
3. Margaret de Clare = Piers de Gaveston, 1st Earl of Cornwall
4. Amy de Gaveston = John de Driby
5. Alice de Driby = Sir Anketil Malory
6. Sir William Malory = ---
7. Margaret Malory = Robert Corbet
8. Mary Corbet = Robert Charlton
9. Richard Charlton = Anne Mainwaring
10. Anne Charlton = Randall Grosvenor
11. Elizabeth Grosvenor = Thomas Bulkeley
12. Edward Bulkeley = Olive Irby
13. Sarah Bulkeley = Sir Oliver St. John
14. **Elizabeth St. John** of Mass. = Samuel **Whiting**.
15. Samuel Whiting, Jr. = Dorcas Chester
16. Samuel Whiting (III) = Elizabeth Read
17. Katherine Whiting = John Lane, Jr.
18. Susanna Lane = Nathaniel Davis
19. Nathaniel Davis, Jr. = Lydia Harwood
20. Mary Davis = John Moor
21. Hiram D. Moor = Abigail Franklin
22. Victoria Josephine Moor = John Calvin Coolidge
23. (John) Calvin Coolidge (Jr.) (1872-1933), 30th U.S. President = Grace Anna Goodhue

13. **Rev. Peter Bulkeley** (1582/3-1658/9) of Mass., Puritan clergyman, a founder and first minister of Concord, Mass. = (1) Jane Allen (died in England), ARD, SETH; (2) Grace Chetwode of Mass., ARD, SETH
14. (by 1) Edward Bulkeley = Lucian ---

210

15. Peter Bulkeley = Rebecca Wheeler
16. Rebecca Bulkeley = Jonathan Prescott, Jr.
17. Abel Prescott = Abigail Brigham
18. Lucy Prescott, sister of Dr. Samuel Prescott, who completed Paul Revere's "Midnight Ride" of 19 Apr. 1775 = Jonathan Fay, Jr.
19. Samuel Prescott Phillips Fay = Harriet Howard
20. Samuel Howard Fay = Susan Shellman
21. Harriet Eleanor Fay = James Smith Bush
22. Samuel Prescott Bush = Flora Sheldon
23. Prescott Sheldon Bush, U. S. Senator = Dorothy Walker
24. George Herbert Walker Bush (b. 1924), 41st U.S. President = Barbara Pierce

13. **Elizabeth Bulkeley** of Mass. = (1) Richard **Whittingham**; (2) Atherton **Haugh**.
13. **Martha Bulkeley** of Mass. = Abraham **Mellowes**.
13. Frances Bulkeley = Richard Welby
14. **Olive Welby** of Mass. = Henry **Farwell**.
13. Dorcas Bulkeley = Anthony Ingoldsby
14. Olive Ingoldsby = Rev. Thomas James, sometime of Charlestown, Mass. and New Haven, Conn.
15. **Rev. Thomas James**, first minister of Southampton, L.I., N.Y. = (1) Ruth Jones; (2) Katherine Blux.

10. William Charlton (brother of Anne) = Alicia Horde
11. Cecily Charlton = Richard Morton
12. Margery Morton - Roger Fowke, son of John Fowke and Anne Bradshaw, SETH
13. Joyce Fowke = Walter Grosvenor
14. Gawen Grosvenor = Dorothy Pudsey
15. Winifred Grosvenor = Thomas Corbin

16. **Henry Corbin** of Va. = Mrs. Alice Eltonhead Burnham
of Va., ARD, SETH.

Sources: *AR7*, lines 85, 31, 203, 29B, 16A, 9, *TAG* 35(1959):100-6,
37(1961):45-51, 40(1964):95-99, plus items listed in *NEHGR* 141
(1987):100, esp. *Blackman*, pp. 57, 60, 62-134, 138-58 (Bulkeleys;
see also *Bulkeley*, pp. 2-36, and *Hawes, Freeman and James*);
LDBR 5: 874 and *Ligon*, vol. 1, pp. 160-63, 806-11 (Corbin);
GVFVM 2:313 esp. (Grosvenor); *Shaw*, vol. 2, part I, p. 60 (Fowke);
George Grazebrook and J.P. Rylands, eds., *Visitation of Shropshire,
1623* (*HSPVS*, vols. 28-29, 1889), pp. 368 (Morton), 101 (Charlton).

The Royal Descents of 500 Immigrants

1. Edward I, King of England, d. 1307 = Margaret of France
2. Thomas of Brotherton, Earl of Norfolk = Alice de Hales
3. Margaret Plantagenet, Duchess of Norfolk = John de Segrave, 4th Baron Segrave
4. Elizabeth de Segrave = John Mowbray, 4th Baron Mowbray
5. Eleanor Mowbray = John de Welles, 5th Baron Welles
6. Eudo de Welles = Maud de Greystock
7. Lionel de Welles, 6th Baron Welles = Joan Waterton
8. Margaret de Welles = Sir Thomas Dymoke
9. Sir Lionel Dymoke = Joanna Griffith
10. Alice Dymoke = Sir William Skipwith
11. Henry Skipwith = Jane Hall, daughter of Francis Hall (and Ursula Sherington), son of Francis Hall and Elizabeth Wingfield, SETH
12. Sir William Skipwith = Margaret Cave, daughter of Roger Cave and Margaret Cecil, sister of William Cecil, 1st Baron Burghley, minister of Elizabeth I
13. Sir Henry Skipwith, 1st Bt. = Amy Kempe, daughter of Sir Thomas Kempe and Dorothy Thompson, SETH
14. **Sir Grey Skipwith, 3rd Bt.,** of Va. = Elizabeth ----.
14. **Diana Skipwith** of Va. = Edward **Dale.**

11. John Skipwith (brother of Henry) = Eleanor Kingston
12. Mary Skipwith = John Newcomen
13. Eleanor Newcomen = William Asfordby
14. John Asfordby = Alice Wolley
15. **William Asfordby** of N.Y. = Martha Burton.

11. Mary Skipwith (sister of Henry and John) = 13. George FitzWilliam, son of 12. John FitzWilliam (and Margaret Wygersley), son of 11. Thomas FitzWilliam (and Joan Gunby), son of 10. John FitzWilliam (and Joan Britt),

son of Thomas FitzWilliam and 9. Margaret Dymoke, daughter of Sir Thomas Dymoke and 8. Margaret de Welles, above

12, 14. Frances FitzWilliam = Thomas Massingberd

13, 15. Thomas Massingberd = Frances Halton

14, 16. Sir Dra(y)ner Massingberd = Anne Mildmay

15, 17. **Elizabeth Massingberd** of S.C. = Edward **Hyrne**.

10. Anne Dymoke (sister of Alice) = John Goodrick

11. Lionel Goodrick = Winifred Sapcott

12. Anne Goodrick = Benjamin Bolles

13. Thomas Bolles = (1) Elizabeth Perkins; (2) Mary Witham, Baronetess of Nova Scotia

14. (by 1) **Joseph Bolles** of Me. = Mary (Howell?).

14. (by 2) Anne Bolles = Sir William Dalston, 1st Bt.

15. Sir John Dalston, 2nd Bt. = Margaret Ramsden

16. Sir Charles Dalston, 3rd Bt. = Susan Blake

17. **Catherine Dalston** of Va. = Francis **Fauquier** (c. 1704-1768), colonial (lt.) governor of Va.

Sources: *LDBR* 1:143-45, *MCS4*, line 85, *BP* and *CB* (Skipwith of Prestwould, baronets), J.L. Miller, *The Descendants of Capt. Thomas Carter of "Barford," Lancaster County, Virginia* (1912), pp. 12-35, and J.B. Price and Harry Hollingsworth, *The Price, Blakemore, Hamblen, Skipwith and Allied Lines* (1992), pp. 15-43 (Skipwith and Mrs. Dale); Rev. A.R. Maddison, ed., *Lincolnshire Pedigrees* (*HSPVS*, vols. 50-52, 55, 1902-4, 1906), pp. 889-90 (Skipwith), 441 (Hall), 1204 (Dymoke), 716 (Newcomen), 46 (Asfordby), 357-58 (FitzWilliam), 657-58, 660 (Massingberd), 416 (Goodrick); *MCS4*, line 84 and Frank Allaben, *The Ancestry of Leander Howard Crall* (1908), pp. 92-93, 153-54, 191-92, 203-6, 350-65 (Asfordby); *SCG* 2:397-401 (Mrs. Hyrne); *AR7*, line 202, George E. Williams, *A Genealogy of the Descendants of Joseph Bolles of Wells, Maine*, vol. 1 (1970), pp. 1-10, 14-21, *CB* (Dalston of Dalston, Bolles of Osberton), W.H. Bowles, *Records of the Bowles Family* (1918), pp. 158-59, C.A. Goodricke, *History of the Goodricke Family* (1885), pp. 4-5, *DAB* (Francis Fauquier), *TCWAAS*, new ser. 10(1910):221-27 (Dalston), and J.W. Walker, ed., *Yorkshire Pedigrees, G-S* (*HSPVS*, vol. 95, 1943), pp. 254, 256-57 (Witham, Bolles, Dalston) (for Bolles and Mrs. Fauquier). Much material on the ancestry of Joseph Bolles was also collected by the late Augustine H. Ayers.

The Royal Descents of 500 Immigrants

1. Edward I, King of England, d. 1307 = Margaret of France

2. Thomas of Brotherton, Earl of Norfolk = Alice de Hales

3. Margaret Plantagenet, Duchess of Norfolk = John de Segrave, 4th Baron Segrave

4. Elizabeth de Segrave = John Mowbray, 4th Baron Mowbray

5. Eleanor Mowbray = John de Welles, 5th Baron Welles

6. Eudo de Welles = Maud de Greystock

7. Sir William de Welles, Lord Deputy of Ireland = Anne Barnewall

8. Elizabeth de Welles = Christopher Plunkett, 2nd Baron Killeen

8. Eleanor de Welles = Walter Chevers

9. Genet Plunkett = Nicholas St. Lawrence, 16th Baron Howth

9. Margaret Chevers = Bartholomew Aylmer

10. Alison St. Lawrence = (1) John Netterville (2) Patrick White

10. Anne Aylmer = Sir Thomas Luttrell

11. (by 2) Margaret White = Walter Foster

11. (by 1) Lucas = Netterville

11. Margaret Luttrell

12. Margaret Foster = Sir John Dongan

12. Margaret Netterville = John Netterville, a cousin

13. Sir Walter Dongan, 1st Bt. = Jane Rochfort

13. Alison Netterville = Sir William Talbot, 1st Bt.

14. Sir John Dongan, 2nd Bt. =

14. Mary Talbot

15. **Thomas Dongan, 2nd Earl of Limerick** (1634–1715), colonial governor of N.Y., soldier = Mary ----.

10. Sir Gerald Aylmer, Lord Chief Justice of Ireland (brother of Lady Thomas Luttrell) = Alison Fitzgerald

11. Bartholomew Aylmer = Ellen Warren

12. Christopher Aylmer = ----

13. Gerald Aylmer = ----

14. Sir Christopher Aylmer, 1st Bt. = Margaret Plunkett

15. Catherine Aylmer = Michael Warren

16. **Sir Peter Warren** (1703-1752) of N.Y., naval officer in the American colonies, 1730-47 = Susannah De Lancey.

16. Anne Warren = Christopher Johnson

17. **Sir William Johnson, 1st Bt.** (1715-1774) of N.Y., Mohawk Valley pioneer and superintendant of Indian affairs in the American colonies = Catherine Weissenburg.

18. Mary Johnson = 18. Guy Johnson (c. 1740-1788) of N.Y., northern superintendent of Indian affairs, 1774-82, loyalist, her first cousin, see below.

17. John Johnson (brother of Sir William, 1st Bt.) = Catherine Nangle

18. **Guy Johnson** (c. 1740-1788) of N.Y., northern superintendent of Indian affairs, 1774-82 = 18. Mary Johnson, his first cousin, see above.

18. Anne Johnson = Walter Dowdall

19. **Matilda Cecilia Dowdall** of N.J. = Thomas **Shedden**.

Sources: *CP* (Limerick, Howth, Killeen, Howth), *CB* (Dongan of Castletown and Talbot of Carton), *Lodge*, vol. 4, pp. 204-7 (Netterville), vol. 3, pp. 189-91 (St. Lawrence), 408-9 (Luttrell), vol. 7, pp. 44-45 (Aylmer), *BIFR*, p. 228 (Chevers), *Forebears* 15, #2 (Spring 1972):103-6, and *The Colonial Genealogist* 8, #4(1977):200-12 (for Thomas Dongan, 2nd Earl of Limerick, but see *TG* 4[1983]:187-202 for disproof of the royal descent of William Dungan of St. Martin-in-the-Fields, first husband of Mrs. Frances Latham Dungan Clarke Vaughan of R.I. [whose second husband was Act. Gov. Jeremiah Clarke of R.I., ARD, SETH] and father of Thomas Dungan of Pa., Mrs. Barbara Dungan Barker of R.I., and Mrs. Frances Dungan

Holden of R.I.); *DNB* (Guy and Sir Wm. Johnson, Sir Peter Warren), *CB* (Johnson or Johnston of N.Y., Aylmer of Balrath) and Franz V. Recum, *The Families of Warren and Johnson of Warrenstown, County Meath* (1950) (for Warren, the Johnsons, and Mrs. Shedden). See also *DNB* (Sir William de Welles under Lionel, Leo, or Lyon de Welles, 6th Baron Welles) and *CP* 12, part I, p. 9 (for the forename of Anne Barnewall).

The Royal Descents of 500 Immigrants

1. Edward I, King of England, d. 1307 = Margaret of France
2. Thomas of Brotherton, Earl of Norfolk = Alice de Hales
3. Margaret Plantagenet, Duchess of Norfolk = John de Segrave, 4th Baron Segrave
4. Elizabeth de Segrave = John Mowbray, 4th Baron Mowbray
5. Eleanor Mowbray = John de Welles, 5th Baron Welles
6. Eleanor de Welles = Sir Hugh Poynings
7. Constance Poynings = Sir John Paulet
8. John Paulet = Eleanor Ros
9. Sir John Paulet = Alice Paulet, a cousin
10. Eleanor Paulet = Sir William Gifford
11. John Gifford = Joan Bruges
12. Anne Gifford = Thomas Goddard
13. Richard Goddard = Elizabeth Walrond
14. Edward Goddard = Priscilla D'Oyley
15. **William Goddard** of Mass. = Elizabeth Miles.
16. Josiah Goddard = Rachel Davis
17. Rachel Goddard = Obadiah Coolidge, Jr.
18. Josiah Coolidge = Mary Jones
19. John Coolidge = Hannah Priest
20. Calvin Coolidge = Sarah Thompson
21. Calvin Galusha Coolidge = Sarah Almeda Brewer
22. John Calvin Coolidge = Victoria Josephine Moor
23. (John) Calvin Coolidge (Jr.) (1872-1933), 30th U.S. President = Grace Anna Goodhue

10. William Paulet, 1st Marquess of Winchester, lord treasurer (brother of Eleanor) = Elizabeth Capell
11. Lord Thomas Paulet = Mary Moore
12. George Paulet = Alice Pacy (or Plesey)

219

13. Rachel Paulet = Sir Philip de Carteret

14. Rachel de Carteret = Benjamin La Cloche

15. Rachel La Cloche = Helier de Carteret, atty. gen. of Jersey

16. **Philip de Carteret** (1639-1682), 1st colonial governor of N.J. = Mrs. Elizabeth Smith Lawrence, widow of William Lawrence of L.I. She married (3) Richard Towneley of N.J. Both of her other husbands were ARD, SETH.

16. **Peter de Carteret**, colonial governor of N.C. = ----.

14. Susan de Carteret (sister of Rachel) = Abraham Dumaresq

15. Elias Dumaresq = Jane Payne

16. Elias Dumaresq = Frances de Carteret, see below

17. **Philip Dumaresq** of Mass. = Susan Ferry.

10. Sir George Paulet (brother of Eleanor and the 1st Marquess of Winchester) = Barbara Hamden

11. Sir Hamden Paulet = ----

12. Elizabeth Paulet = Sir Francis Dowse

13. Anne Dowse = 14. Sir Philip de Carteret (brother of Rachel and Susan)

14. Francis de Carteret, atty gen. of Jersey = Anne Seale

15. Frances de Carteret = 16. Elias Dumaresq, see above

Sources: Mss. autobiography of Edward Goddard (1675-1754) at the American Antiquarian Society in Worcester, Mass. (notably pp. 2-3); Frederick Arthur Crisp, *Visitation of England and Wales, Notes,* vol. 6 (1906), pp. 109-16, *UGHM* 21(1930):59-66, and W.H. Rylands, ed., *Visitations of Hampshire, 1530, 1575, and 1622-4 (HSPVS,* vol. 64, 1913), p. 16 (all three of which sources contain errors) (Goddard and Gifford; a definitive monograph on the family of Gifford of Itchell, Hampshire, is badly needed); *MGH,* 5th ser., 9(1935-37):88-90, 142-46 (Paulet), 44-48 (Welles), 162-68 (Plantagenet, Segrave, Mowbray); *(Journal of) North Carolina*

Genealogy 16(1970):2537-52 and *BLG* (1952), pp. 638, 1685-86 (de Carteret); *Collins,* vol. 2, pp. 369-73 (Paulet); *NEHGR* 17 (1863):317-18 (reprinted in *EO* 2:1: 693-96) (Dumaresq) and W.B.H. Dowse, *Lawrence Dowse of Legbourne, England, His Ancestors, Descendants, and Connections in England, Massachusetts and Ireland* (1926), pp. 71-73.

The Royal Descents of 500 Immigrants

1. Edward I, King of England, d. 1307 = Eleanor of Castile

2. Joan Plantagenet = Gilbert de Clare, 3rd Earl of Gloucester, 7th Earl of Hertford

3. Elizabeth de Clare = Roger Damory, 1st Baron Damory

4. Elizabeth Damory = John Bardolf, 3rd Baron Bardolf

5. William Bardolf, 4th Baron Bardolf = Agnes Poynings

6. Cecily Bardolf = Sir Brian Stapleton

7. Sir Miles Stapleton = Catherine de la Pole

8. Elizabeth Stapleton = Sir William Calthorpe

9. Anne Calthorpe = Sir Robert Drury, Speaker of the House of Commons

10. Anne Drury = George Waldegrave

11. Edward Waldegrave = Joan Acworth

12. Margery Waldegrave = William Clopton

13. **Thomasine Clopton** = John **Winthrop** (1587/8-1649), the colonial statesman, founder and governor of the Massachusetts Bay Colony (his second wife; Winthrop married thirdly Margaret Tyndal/Tindal of Mass., ARD, SETH).

13. Walter Clopton = Margaret Maidstone

14. William Clopton = Elizabeth Sutcliffe

15. **William Clopton** of Va. = Mrs. Anne Booth Dennett.

11. Sir William Waldegrave (brother of Edward) = Juliana Raynsford

12. Dorothy Waldegrave = Arthur Harris

13. Dorothy Harris = Robert Kempe

14. **Richard Kempe**, secretary and acting governor of Va. = Elizabeth Wormeley (who married secondly Sir Thomas Lunsford of Va., royalist army officer, ARD, SETH), niece of Ralph Wormeley, second husband of (Lady) Agatha Eltonhead (Kellaway) Wormeley (Chichele) of Va., ARD, SETH. Of Richard Kempe's brothers Edmund and Edward Kempe, and possibly John Kempe,

also came to Virginia; the secretary mentioned a nephew Edmund Kempe in his will, and Matthew Kempe of Gloucester Co., Va., may have been a nephew as well.

11. Phyllis Waldegrave (sister of Edward and Sir William) = Thomas Higham

12. Bridget Higham = Thomas Burrough

13. George Burrough = Frances Sparrow

14. **Nathaniel Burrough of Mass. and Md.**, who returned to England = Rebecca Style.

15. Rev. George Burroughs of Mass., executed for witchcraft at Salem, 19 Aug. 1692 = (1) Hannah ----; (2) Mrs. Sarah Ruck Hathorne; (3) Mary ----.

Sources: *MCS4*, lines 5 (Mrs. Winthrop and Clopton), 74, 75 (Burroughs, Kempe), 49, 40; *AR7*, lines 200 (Burroughs), 257, 11; *William Clopton*, esp. pp. 12-18, 49-50, 57-58, 71-73, 75-78 (generations 5-15, Bardolf-Clopton); *Kempe*, section II, pp. 32-36, *HSF*, vol. 10 (1966), pp. 164-69, 11(1967), pp. 156-58; *SMF* 1:354, 144, 26, 311 esp. (Drury, Clopton, Winthrop, Burrough), *SMF* 2:237 (Kempe); *TAG* 48(1972):140-46, 56(1980):43-45, 60(1984):140-42 (for Nathaniel Burrough and Rev. George Burroughs).

The Royal Descents of 500 Immigrants

1. Edward I, King of England, d. 1307 = Eleanor of Castile
2. Joan Plantagenet = Gilbert de Clare, 3rd Earl of Gloucester, 7th Earl of Hertford
3. Margaret de Clare = Hugh de Audley, 1st Earl of Gloucester
4. Margaret de Audley = Ralph Stafford, 1st Earl of Stafford
5. Hugh Stafford, 2nd Earl of Stafford = Philippa Beauchamp
6. Katherine Stafford = Michael de la Pole, 2nd Earl of Suffolk
7. Isabel de la Pole = Thomas Morley, 5th Baron Morley
8. Anne Morley = Sir John Hastings
9. Elizabeth Hastings = Sir Robert Hildyard
10. Katherine Hildyard = William Girlington
11. Isabel Girlington = Christopher Kelke
12. William Kelke = Thomasine Skerne
13. Cecily Kelke = John Farrar
14. **William Farrar** of Va. = Mrs. Cecily ---- Jordan.

10. Margery Hildyard (sister of Katherine) = Sir William Ayscough
11. Sir William Ayscough = Elizabeth Wrottesley
12. Jane Ayscough = Richard Disney
13. Susan Disney = Alexander Amcotts
14. Sir Richard Amcotts = Jane Fulnetby
15. Martha Amcotts = Robert Cracroft
16. John Cracroft (of Hackthorn, Lincolnshire) = ----
17. (very probably) **John Cra(y)croft** of ("Hackthorn Heath"), Md. = Anne ----

14. Frances Amcotts (sister of Sir Richard) = William Bellingham

15. **Richard Bellingham** (c. 1592-1672), colonial governor of Mass. = Penelope Pelham of Mass., ARD, SETH.

10. Peter Hildyard (brother of Katherine and Margery) = Joan de la See

11. Katherine Hildyard = William Holme

12. John Holme = Anne Aislaby

13. Catherine Holme = Marmaduke Constable

14. Frances Constable = Sir John Rodes

15. Sir Francis Rodes, 1st Bt. = Elizabeth Lascelles

16. John Rodes = Elizabeth Jason

17. **Charles Rodes** of Va. = Frances ----.

Sources: Alvahn Holmes, *The Farrar's Island Family and its English Ancestry*, vol. 1 (1977), chapters 1-3 and Farrar and Kelke charts at end esp.; Rev. A.R. Maddison, ed., *Lincolnshire Pedigrees* (*HSPVS*, vols. 50-52, 55, 1902-4, 1906), pp. 404-5 (Girlington), 279-80 (Cracroft), 15-16 (Amcotts), 306 (Disney), 60-61 (Ayscough) 118 (Bellingham) and Cracroft research by Brice McAdoo Clagett, discussed in the Cracroft bibliographical note in his forthcoming *Seven Centuries: Ancestors for Twenty Generations of John Brice de Treville Clagett and Ann Calvert Brooke Clagett*; *PCF Yorkshire* (Hildyard pedigree); *Foster's V of Yorkshire*, pp. 372-73 (Hastings), *CP* (Hastings, Morley, Suffolk, Stafford, Gloucester) and *AR7*, lines 8-10; *PSECD* 3:241-43 (undocumented), *GVFVM*5:188-90 and Joseph Hunter, *Familiae Minorum Gentium*, vol. 2 (*HSPVS*, vol. 38, 1895), pp. 585-86 (Rodes); *DVY*, vol. 2, pp. 118-19 (Holme), vol. 3, p. 48 (Constable). See also *DAB* and *DNB* for Governor Bellingham.

The Royal Descents of 500 Immigrants

1. Edward I, King of England, d. 1307 = Eleanor of Castille
2. Joan Plantagenet = Gilbert de Clare, 3rd Earl of Gloucester, 7th Earl of Hertford
3. Margaret de Clare = Hugh de Audley, 1st Earl of Gloucester
4. Margaret de Audley = Ralph Stafford, 1st Earl of Stafford
5. Katherine Stafford = Sir John Sutton
6. Sir John Sutton = Jane ---
7. Sir John Sutton = Constance Blount
8. John Sutton, 1st Baron Dudley = Elizabeth Berkeley
9. Jane Sutton = Thomas Mainwaring
10. Cecily Mainwaring = John Cotton
11. Sir George Cotton = Mary Onley
12. Richard Cotton = Mary Mainwaring, see below
13. Frances Cotton = George Abell
14. **Robert Abell** of Mass. = Joanna ---.
15. Caleb Abell = Margaret Post
16. Experience Abell = John Hyde
17. James Hyde = Sarah Marshall
18. Abiah Hyde = Aaron Cleveland (IV)
19. William Cleveland = Margaret Falley
20. Richard Falley Cleveland = Anne Neal
21. (Stephen) Grover Cleveland (1837-1908), 22nd and 24th U.S. President = Frances Folsom

10. George Mainwaring (brother of Cecily) = ---- Moore
11. Joan Mainwaring = Robert Mainwaring, a cousin
12. Margery Mainwaring = Edward Lodge
13. Jasper Lodge = Eleanor Grosvenor
14. Elizabeth Lodge = John Kenrick
15. Matthew Kenrick = Rebecca Percival

16. Elizabeth Kenrick = David Clarkson

17. **Matthew Clarkson**, provincial secretary of N.Y. = Katherine Van Schaick.

 2. Elizabeth Plantagenet (sister of Joan) = Humphrey de Bohun, 4th Earl of Hereford and Essex

 3. William de Bohun, 1st Earl of Northampton = Elizabeth Badlesmere

 4. Elizabeth de Bohun = Richard FitzAlan, 10th Earl of Arundel

 5. Joan FitzAlan = William Beauchamp, Baron Abergavenny

 6. Joan Beauchamp = James Butler, 4th Earl of Ormonde

 7. Elizabeth Butler = John Talbot, 2nd Earl of Shrewsbury

 8. Anne Talbot = Sir Henry Vernon

 9. Elizabeth Vernon = Sir Robert Corbet

10. Dorothy Corbet = Sir Richard Mainwaring

11. Sir Arthur Mainwaring = Margaret Mainwaring, a cousin, daughter of Sir Randall Mainwaring (and Elizabeth Brereton), son of Sir John Mainwaring and Katherine Hondford, SETH

12. Mary Mainwaring = Richard Cotton, above

10. Sir Roger Corbet (brother of Dorothy) = Anne Windsor, daughter of Andrews Windsor, 1st Baron Windsor, and Elizabeth Blount, SETH

11. Margaret Corbet = Sir Francis Palmes

12. Sir Francis Palmes = Mary Hadnall

13. Andrew Palmes = Elizabeth ----

14. **Edward Palmes** of Conn. = (1) Lucy Winthrop, daughter of John Winthrop, Jr., colonial governor of Conn. (and Elizabeth Reade), son of John Winthrop, the colonial statesman, founder and governor of the Massachusetts Bay Colony, and Mary Forth, his first wife; (2) Mrs. Sarah Farmer Davis.

Sources: H.A. and L.P. Abell, *The Abell Family in America* (1940), pp. 41-46, *AR7*, lines 56A, 7, 120, 15, 81, 9 and *TG* 5(1984):131-39, 150-51, 154-56, 158-71, 9(1988):89 (R. Abell); J.R.T. Craine and H.W. Hazard, *The Ancestry and Posterity of Matthew Clarkson (1664-1702)* (1971), pp. 7-12, plus, for initial collaboration, George Grazebrook and J.P. Rylands, *Visitation of Shropshire, 1623,* vol. 2 (*HSPVS*, vol. 29, 1889), pp. 285 (Kenrick, Lodge), 348 (Mainwaring); *NEHGR* 11(1857):28, 28(1874):90 (reprinted in *EO* 2:2:964), 65(1911): 379, *PCF Yorkshire* (Palmes pedigree) and *Nichols*, vol. 2, p. 295 (E. Palmes); A.E.B. Corbet, *The Family of Corbet,* vol. 2 (1920), chart at end, and *Roger Ludlow,* pp. 2193-2209 (Windsor).

The Royal Descents of 500 Immigrants

1. Edward I, King of England, d. 1307 = Eleanor of Castile
2. Elizabeth Plantagenet = Humphrey de Bohun, 4th Earl of Hereford and Essex
3. Margaret de Bohun = Hugh Courtenay, 2nd Earl of Devon
4. Elizabeth Courtenay = Sir Andrew Luttrell
5. Sir Hugh Luttrell = Catherine Beaumont
6. Elizabeth Luttrell = John Stratton
7. Elizabeth Stratton = John Andrews
8. Elizabeth Andrews = Thomas Windsor
9. Andrews Windsor, 1st Baron Windsor = Elizabeth Blount
10. Edith Windsor = George Ludlow
11. Thomas Ludlow = Jane Pyle
12. Gabriel Ludlow = Phyllis ---
13. **Sarah Ludlow** of Va. = John **Carter.**
14. Robert "King" Carter = Elizabeth Landon
15. Anne Carter = Benjamin Harrison (IV)
16. Benjamin Harrison (V), Signer of the Declaration of Independence = Elizabeth Bassett
17. William Henry Harrison (1773-1841), 9th U.S. President = Anna Tuthill Symmes
18. John Scott Harrison = Elizabeth Ramsey Irwin
19. Benjamin Harrison (1833-1901), 23rd U.S. President = (1) Caroline Lavinia Scott; (2) Mrs. Mary Scott Lord Dimmick

12. **Roger Ludlow** (1590-1666, brother of Gabriel), of Mass. and Conn., dep. gov. of Mass., author of the Fundamental Orders of Connecticut = Mary Cogan (almost certainly the parents of Sarah, wife of Rev. Nathaniel Brewster of Brookhaven, L.I.). George Ludlow, a brother of Roger and Gabriel, also immigrated to Massachusetts, and later settled in Virginia, but apparently left no descendants.

12. Thomas Ludlow (brother of Gabriel and Roger) = Jane Bennett

13. Gabriel Ludlow = Martha ----

14. **Gabriel Ludlow** of N.Y. = Sarah Hanmer.

Sources: *AR7*, lines 12, 6 and *MCS4*, line 88; *Roger Ludlow*.

The Royal Descents of 500 Immigrants

1. Edward I, King of England, d. 1307 = Eleanor of Castile
2. Joan Plantagenet = Gilbert de Clare, 3rd Earl of Gloucester, 7th Earl of Hertford
3. Eleanor de Clare = Hugh le Despencer, 1st Baron Despencer
4. Sir Edward Despencer = Anne Ferrers
5. Edward Despencer, 3rd Baron Despencer = Elizabeth Burghersh
6. Elizabeth Despencer = John FitzAlan, 2nd Baron Arundel
7. Sir Thomas Arundel = Joan Moyns
8. Eleanor Arundel = Sir Thomas Browne
9. Sir Robert Browne = Mary Malet
10. Eleanor Browne = Sir William Kempe
11. Sir Thomas Kempe = (1) Catherine Cheney; (2) Anne Moyle
12. (by 1) Anne Kempe = Sir Thomas Shirley
13. **Cecily Shirley** = Thomas **West**, 3rd Baron Delaware (de la Warr) (1577-1618), colonial governor of Va., ARD, SETH.

12. (by 2) Sir Thomas Kempe (half brother of Lady Shirley) = Dorothy Thompson
13. Dorothy Kempe = Sir Thomas Chichele
14. **Sir Henry Chichele**, colonial deputy-governor of Va. = Mrs. Agatha Eltonhead Kellaway Wormeley of Va., ARD, SETH.

11. Edward Kempe (brother of Sir Thomas) = Elizabeth Wilmot
12. Thomas Kempe = Mary Oglander
13. Frances Kempe = Henry Bromfield
14. **Edward Bromfield** of Mass. = (1) Mrs. Elizabeth ---- Brading; (2) Mary Danforth.

The Royal Descents of 500 Immigrants

Sources: *CP* (de la Warr), *Shirleiana*, pp. 235, 256-58 esp.; *Kempe*, section I, pp. 24-31, 34-38, charts opp. pp. 14 and 20, and section IV, p. 32 and chart opp. p. 20, *CP* (Arundel, Despencer, Gloucester), and *AR7*, lines 8, 74; *VGE*, pp. 421-23 (for Sir Henry Chichele); *NEHGR* 25 (1871):182-85, 329-35, reprinted in *EO* 2:1:316-26, E.E. Salisbury, *Family Memorials* (1885), Bromfield pedigree post p. 610 (for Edward Bromfield).

The Royal Descents of 500 Immigrants

1. Edward I, King of England, d. 1307 = Eleanor of Castile
2. Joan Plantagenet = Gilbert de Clare, 3rd Earl of Gloucester, 7th Earl of Hertford
3. Eleanor de Clare = Hugh le Despencer, 1st Baron Despencer
4. Isabel Despencer = Richard FitzAlan, 9th Earl of Arundel
5. Isabel FitzAlan = John le Strange, 4th Baron Strange of Blackmere
6. Ankaret le Strange = Richard Talbot, 4th Baron Talbot, a great-grandson of Elizabeth Plantagenet, wife of Humphrey de Bohun, 4th Earl of Hereford and Essex, and younger daughter of Edward I and Eleanor of Castile, see *AR7*, lines 14, 13, 7
7. Mary Talbot = Sir Thomas Greene
8. Sir Thomas Greene = Philippa Ferrers, daughter of Robert de Ferrers, 5th Baron Ferrers of Chartley, and Margaret Despencer, SETH
9. Elizabeth Greene = William Raleigh
10. Sir Edward Raleigh = Margaret Verney
11. Edward Raleigh = Anne Chamberlayne
12. Bridget Raleigh = Sir John Cope
13. Elizabeth Cope = John Dryden
14. Bridget Dryden = Francis Marbury, son of William Marbury and Agnes Lenton, SETH
15. **Katherine Marbury** of R.I. = Richard **Scott**.
15. **Anne Marbury, known as Mrs. Anne Hutchinson** (1591-1643), the religious reformer, heretic and founder of R.I. = William **Hutchinson**.
16. Edward Hutchinson = Catherine Hamby of Mass., ARD, SETH
17. Elisha Hutchinson = (1) Hannah Hawkins; (2) Elizabeth Clarke
18. (by 2) Edward Hutchinson = Lydia Foster
19. Elizabeth Hutchinson = Nathaniel Robbins

20. Edward Hutchinson Robbins = Elizabeth Murray

21. Anne Jean Robbins = Joseph Lyman (III)

22. Catherine Robbins Lyman = Warren Delano, Jr.

23. Sara Delano = James Roosevelt

24. Franklin Delano Roosevelt (1882-1945), 32nd U.S. President = (Anna) Eleanor Roosevelt

18. (by 1) Hannah Hutchinson = John Ruck

19. Hannah Ruck = Theophilus Lillie

20. John Lillie = Abigail Breck

21. Anna Lillie = Samuel Howard

22. Harriet Howard = Samuel Prescott Phillips Fay

23. Samuel Howard Fay = Susan Shellman

24. Harriet Eleanor Fay = James Smith Bush

25. Samuel Prescott Bush = Flora Sheldon

26. Prescott Sheldon Bush, U.S. Senator = Dorothy Walker

27. George Herbert Walker Bush (b. 1924), 41st U.S. President = Barbara Pierce

17. Elizabeth Hutchinson (sister of Elisha) = Edward Winslow

18. Anne Winslow = John Taylor

19. Elizabeth Taylor = Nathaniel Greene, Jr.

20. John Greene - Azubah Ward

21. Lucretia Greene = 20. Elijah Mason, son of 19. Peleg Sanford Mason (and Mary Stanton), son of John Mason and 18. Anne Sanford, daughter of 17. Peleg Sanford, governor of R.I. (and Mary Coddington), son of John Sanford, acting governor of R.I., and 16. Bridget Hutchinson, daughter of William Hutchinson and 15. Anne Marbury, the famed Mrs. Anne Hutchinson, above

21,22. Arabella Mason = Zebulon Rudolph

22,23. Lucretia Rudolph = James Abram Garfield (1831-1881), 20th U.S. President

12. George Raleigh (brother of Bridget) = ----, widow of Sir Thomas Fitzgerald

13. Bridget Raleigh = Sir William Kingsmill

14. Sir Francis Kingsmill = --- Clifford (their daughter Dorothea Kingsmill married Alexander Marchant, Sieur de St. Michel and was the mother of Elizabeth Marchant, wife of the diarist Samuel Pepys)

15. William Kingsmill = Dorothy St. Leger

16. Levina Kingsmill = Matthew Pennefather

17. Kingsmill Pennefather = Elizabeth Bolton

18. Richard Bennefather = Charity Graham

19. Mary Pennefather = John Croker

20. Henry Croker = Harriet Dillon

21. **Eyre Coote Croker** of N.Y. = Frances Welstead (parents of Tammany Hall "boss" Richard Welstead Croker, 1841-1922, who married Elizabeth Frazier and Beula Benton Edmondson).

Sources: *AR7*, lines 14, 8, *Marbury*, and *NEHGR* 123(1969):180-81, reprinted in *EO* 2:2:483-84; *BIFR*, pp. 295-96 (Croker), *BLGI* 1958, pp. 568-70 (Pennefather), 1912, p. 370 (Kingsmill), plus John Fetherston, ed., *Visitations of Warwickshire, 1619* (*HSPVS*, vol. 12, 1877), p. 77 and *NEHGR* 145(1991):14-21 (Raleigh).

The Royal Descents of 500 Immigrants

1. Edward I, King of England, d. 1307 = Eleanor of Castile
2. Joan Plantagenet = Gilbert de Clare, 3rd Earl of Gloucester, 7th Earl of Hertford
3. Eleanor de Clare = Hugh le Despencer, 1st Baron Despencer
4. Isabel Despencer = Richard FitzAlan, 9th Earl of Arundel
5. Sir Edmund FitzAlan = Sybil Montagu
6. Philippa FitzAlan = Sir Richard Sergeaux
7. Philippa Sergeaux = Sir Robert Pashley
8. Anne Pashley = Edward Tyrrell
9. Philippa Tyrrell = Thomas Cornwallis
10. William Cornwallis = Elizabeth Stanford
11. Sir John Cornwallis = Mary Sulyard
12. Elizabeth Cornwallis = John Blennerhasset
13. Elizabeth Blennerhasset = Lionel Throckmorton
14. Bassingborne Throckmorton = Mary Hill
15. **John Throckmorton** of R.I. = Rebecca ---.
16. John Throckmorton, Jr. = Alice Stout
17. Patience Throckmorton = Hugh Coward
18. John Coward = Alice Britton
19. Deliverance Coward = James FitzRandolph
20. Isaac FitzRandolph = Eleanor Hunter
21. Rebecca Longstreet FitzRandolph = Isaac Stockton Keith Axson
22. Samuel Edward Axson = Margaret Jane Hoyt
23. Ellen Louise Axson = (Thomas) Woodrow Wilson (1856-1924), 28th U.S. President

11. Affra Cornwallis (sister of Sir John) = Sir Anthony Aucher
12. Edward Aucher = Mabel Wroth

13. Elizabeth Aucher = Sir William Lovelace
14. Sir William Lovelace = Anne Barne
15. **Francis Lovelace** (c. 1621-1675), colonial governor of N.Y., d. umn.
15. **Anne Lovelace** of Va. (progeny in Md.) = Rev. John **Gorsuch**. Thomas and Dudley Lovelace, brothers of Francis and Mrs. Gorsuch, also immigrated to N.Y. Thomas married Mary --- and Dudley may have married also, but neither brother left NDTPS.

Sources: *AR7*, line 208, *NEHGR* 98(1944):67-72, 111-23, 271-79, 117(1963):234 (Throckmorton, Blennerhasset), 110(1956):122-27 (Cornwallis), 109(1955):17-31, 236 (Tyrrell) (reprinted in *EO* 2:3: 478-98, *EO* 1:2:765-73, 3:240-45, 204-19), plus *Moriarty*; *MCS4*, lines 117, 113B, 113A, 134, 34; *AP&P*, pp. 401-403 (Lovelace), *NYGBR* 51(1920):175-94 (Francis Lovelace and his brothers) and *WV*, end packet, "A Chart of the Ancestry of Anne Lovelace, Wife of The Reverend John Gorsuch."

The Royal Descents of 500 Immigrants

1. Edward I, King of England, d. 1307 = Eleanor of Castile
2. Elizabeth Plantagenet = Humphrey de Bohun, 4th Earl of Hereford and Essex
3. William de Bohun, 1st Earl of Northampton = Elizabeth Badlesmere
4. Elizabeth de Bohun = Richard FitzAlan, 10th Earl of Arundel
5. Elizabeth FitzAlan = Sir Robert Goushill
6. Joan Goushill = Thomas Stanley, 1st Baron Stanley
7. Catherine Stanley = Sir John Savage
8. Elizabeth Savage = John Leeke
9. Muriel Leeke = Sir Robert Waterton
10. Sir Thomas Waterton = Joan Tempest
11. Thomas Waterton = Beatrix Restwolde
12. Anne Waterton = Sir Cotton Gargrave
13. Elizabeth Gargrave = William Fenwick
14. **John Fenwick** (1618-1683), colonist, founder of Salem, N.J. = (1) Elizabeth Covert, ARD, SETH; (2) Mary Marten, sister of the younger Sir Henry Marten, regicide.
14. Edward Fenwick = Sarah Neville
15. Robert Fenwick = Anne Culcheth
16. **John Fenwick** of S.C. = Elizabeth Gibbes, daughter of Robert Gibbes, gov. of S.C., ARD, SETH, and --- Davis.

14. Priscilla Fenwick (sister of John of N.J. and of Edward) = Roland Nevet
15. Elizabeth Nevet = Roger Eddowes
16. Ralph Eddowes = Eleanor Carter
17. John Eddowes = Catherine Moulson
18. **Ralph Eddowes** of Pa. = Sarah Kenrick of Pa., ARD, SETH.

Sources: *DAB* (John Fenwick of N.J.), *MCS4*, line 65 and *SCG* 2: 188-91 (John Fenwick of S.C.), *Foster's V of Yorkshire*, p. 69 (Gargrave), *PCF Yorkshire* (Waterton pedigree), *The Reliquary* 10 (1869-70):70 (Leeke), *Ormerod*, vol. 1, p. 713 (Savage) and *AR7*, lines 57, 20, 15; Joseph Hunter, *Familiae Minorum Gentium*, vol. 1 (*HSPVS*, vol. 37, 1894), pp. 109-13 (Eddowes) and unpublished research by John Insley Coddington (whose manuscript collection is now at NEHGS) showing that his ancestor, Elizabeth Nevet, wife of Roger Eddowes, was a daughter of Rev. Roland Nevet, d. 1675, rector of Stanton-on-Hine Heath and Oswestry, Shropshire, and Priscilla Fenwick, sister of John Fenwick of N.J. (for Ralph Eddowes).

The Royal Descents of 500 Immigrants

1. Edward I, King of England, d. 1307 = Margaret of France
2. Thomas of Brotherton, Earl of Norfolk = Alice de Hales
3. Margaret Plantagenet, Duchess of Norfolk = John de Segrave, 4th Baron Segrave
4. Elizabeth de Segrave = John Mowbray, 4th Baron Mowbray
5. Thomas Mowbray, 1st Duke of Norfolk = Elizabeth FitzAlan
6. Margaret Mowbray = Sir Robert Howard
7. John Howard, 1st Duke of Norfolk = Katherine Moleyns
8. Margaret Howard = Sir John Wyndham
9. Sir Thomas Wyndham = Eleanor Scrope
10. Margaret Wyndham = Sir Andrew Luttrell
11. Sir John Luttrell = Mary Ryce
12. Catherine Luttrell = Sir Thomas Copley
13. William Copley = Magdalen Prideaux
14. **Thomas Copley** (1595–c. 1652) of Md., Jesuit missionary, d. unm.

11. Margaret Luttrell (sister of Sir John) = Peter Edgcumbe
12. Margaret Edgcumbe = Sir Edward Denny
13. Henry Denny = Mary Fitch
14. Peter Denny = Anne Hill
15. Hill Denny = Abigail Berners
16. **William Denny**, lt. gov. of Pa., gov. of Del. = Mary Hill.

10. Mary Wyndham (sister of Margaret) = Erasmus Paston
11. Frances Paston = Thomas le Gros
12. Sir Thomas le Gros = Elizabeth Cornwallis
13. Anne le Gros = Nathaniel Bacon
14. Thomas Bacon = Elizabeth Brooke

15. **Nathaniel Bacon** (1647-1676), colonial governor of Va.,
leader of Bacon's Rebellion = Elizabeth Duke.

Sources: *DNB* (Copley and Bacon); *Horsham,* pp. 71-72 (Copley of
Roughey and Gatton), *VD,* pp. 537, 539 (Luttrell), Walter Rye, ed.,
Visitation of Norfolk, 1563, 1589 and 1613 (*HSPVS,* vol. 32, 1891),
pp. 324 (Wyndham), 217 (Paston), 186 (le Gros), *BP* and *CP* (Norfolk)
and *AR7,* lines 16, 22 (for Thomas Copley); *PMHB* 44(1920):97-121,
MGH, 4th ser., 5(1914):367-71, *BP* (Denny of Castle Moyne,
baronets), and M.C.D. Dixon and E.C.D. Vann, *Denny Genealogy,*
vol. 1 (1944), pp. 47-55, 64, 68 (all for Denny), plus *VC,* p. 142
(Edgcombe); W.H. Rylands, ed., *Visitation of Suffolk, 1664-8*
(*HSPVS,* vol. 61, 1910), p. 39 (Bacon) and A.W. Hughes Clarke and
Arthur Campling, eds., *Visitation of Norfolk, 1664* (*HSPVS,* vol. 85,
1933), p. 120 (le Gros). See also *Dunster,* vol. 1, pp. 134-65 and
H.A. Wyndham, *A Family History, 1440-1688, the Wyndhams of
Norfolk and Somerset* (1939), pp. 22-46.

The Royal Descents of 500 Immigrants

1. Edward I, King of England, d. 1307 = Eleanor of Castile
2. Joan Plantagenet = Gilbert de Clare, 3rd Earl of Gloucester, 7th Earl of Hertford
3. Eleanor de Clare = Hugh le Despencer, 1st Baron Despencer
4. Isabel Despencer = Richard FitzAlan, 9th Earl of Arundel
5. Sir Edmund FitzAlan = Sybil Montagu
6. Philippa FitzAlan = Sir Richard Sergeaux
7. Philippa Sergeaux = Sir Robert Pashley
8. Sir John Pashley = Elizabeth Woodville
9. Sir John Pashley = Lowys Gower
10. Elizabeth Pashley = Reginald Pympe
11. Anne Pympe = Sir John Scott
12. Sir Reginald Scott = Mary Tuke
13. Mary Scott = Richard Argall
14. **Sir Samuel Argall** (c. 1572-1626), colonial governor of Va., d. unm.
14. Elizabeth Argall = Sir Edward Filmer (parents of Sir Robert Filmer, political writer, author of *Patriarcha*)
15. **Henry Filmer** of Va. = Elizabeth ----.
15. Katherine Filmer = Robert Barham
16. **Charles Barham** of Va. = Elizabeth Ridley.

Sources: *MCS4*, line 134, *AR7*, lines 8, 28, *DAB* (Argall), and *LDBR* 1:66-67 (Filmer), 435-36 (Barham) and sources cited therein; *VGE*, pp. 199-200, 346-47, 394-96, 583, 664-66; *GVFVM* 4:528-32 (Barham); *Scot of Scots Hall*, pp. 170-71, 185, 254 esp.

The Royal Descents of 500 Immigrants

1. Edward I, King of England, d. 1307 = Margaret of France
2. Edmund of Woodstock, Earl of Kent = Margaret Wake
3. Joan Plantagenet = Thomas Holand, 1st Earl of Kent
4. Thomas Holand, 2nd Earl of Kent = Alice FitzAlan
5. Eleanor Holand = Edward Cherleton, 4th Baron Cherleton of Powis
6. Joyce Cherleton = John Tiptoft (Tibetot), 1st Baron Tiptoft
7. Joyce Tiptoft = Sir Edmund Sutton (or Dudley)
8. Sir John Sutton = --- Charroll
9. Margaret Sutton = John Butler
10. William Butler = Margaret Greeke
11. Margaret Butler = Lawrence Washington
12. Lawrence Washington = Amphyllis Twigden
13. **Lawrence Washington** of Va. (second son) = (1) Mary Jones; (2) Mrs. Joyce ---- Fleming.
13. **Col. John Washington of Westmoreland County, Va.** = (1) Anne Pope; (2) Mrs. Anne Gerard Broadhurst Brett; (3) Mrs. Frances Gerard Speake Peyton Appleton (2 and 3, who left no issue, were daughters of Thomas Gerard of Md., ARD, SETH, and Susannah Snow).
14. (by 1) Lawrence Washington = Mildred Warner
15. Augustine Washington = Mary Ball
16. George Washington (1731/2-1799), 1st U.S. President = Mrs. Martha Dandridge Custis

12. Richard Washington (brother of Lawrence) = Frances Browne
13. **John Washington**, probably the immigrant to Surry Co., Va. = Mrs. Mary ---- Blunt Ford.

Sources: *MCS4*, lines 30, 30A, 94, 90, 114 (plus *AR7*, lines 47, 155); *BLG* (1939), whose American section was reprinted in 1971 as *Prominent Families in America with British Ancestry*, pp. 2959-63; *HSF* 4:149-55; *TAG* 53(1977):15.

The Royal Descents of 500 Immigrants

1. Edward I, King of England, d. 1307 = Margaret of France

2. Thomas of Brotherton, Earl of Norfolk = Alice de Hales

3. Margaret Plantagenet, Duchess of Norfolk = John de Segrave, 4th Baron Segrave

4. Elizabeth de Segrave = John Mowbray, 4th Baron Mowbray

5. Thomas Mowbray, 1st Duke of Norfolk = Elizabeth FitzAlan

6. Margaret Mowbray = Sir Robert Howard

7. John Howard, 1st Duke of Norfolk = Katherine Moleyns

8. Anne Howard = Sir Edmund Gorges

9. Sir Edward Gorges = Mary Poyntz

10. Edward Gorges = Anne Walsh

10. Sir William Gorges = Winifred Butshead

10. Sir Thomas Gorges = Helen Bååt (Snakenborg)

11. Edward Gorges = Cecily Lygon, SETH

11. Tristram Gorges = Elizabeth Cole

12. Sir Ferdinando Gorges (c. 1565-1647) founder and lord proprietor of Maine = (1) Anne Bell, ARD, SETH; (2) Mrs. Mary Fulford Achims, ARD, SETH.

12. (3) **Elizabeth Gorges**

11. (4) **Elizabeth Gorges** = (1) Sir Hugh Smith

Sources: *Gorges,* esp. pp. 43-51, 86-109, 114-15, 119-39 and chart at end, and *Ligon,* pp. 172-80; *BP* and *CP* (Norfolk) and *AR7,* lines 16, 22.

The Royal Descents of 500 Immigrants

1. Edward I, King of England, d. 1307 = Eleanor of Castile
2. Elizabeth Plantagenet = Humphrey de Bohun, 4th Earl of Hereford and Essex
3. William de Bohun, 1st Earl of Northampton = Elizabeth Badlesmere
4. Elizabeth de Bohun = Richard FitzAlan, 10th Earl of Arundel
5. Elizabeth FitzAlan = Sir Robert Goushill
6. Joan Goushill = Thomas Stanley, 1st Baron Stanley
7. Margaret Stanley = Sir John Boteler
8. Sir Thomas Boteler = Margaret Delves
9. Margery Boteler = Sir Thomas Southworth
10. Sir John Southworth = Mary Ashton
11. Thomas Southworth = Rosamond Lister
12. Edward Southworth, probably the Leyden Pilgrim = Alice Carpenter of Mass.
13. **Constant Southworth** of Mass. = Elizabeth Collier.
13. **Thomas Southworth** of Mass. = Elizabeth Reynor.
14. Elizabeth Southworth = Joseph Howland
15. Nathaniel Howland = Martha Cole
16. Nathaniel Howland, Jr. = Abigail Burt
17. Joseph Howland = Lydia Bill
18. Susan Howland = John Aspinwall, Jr.
19. Mary Rebecca Aspinwall = Isaac Roosevelt
20. James Roosevelt = Sara Delano
21. Franklin Delano Roosevelt (1882-1945), 32nd U.S. President = (Anna) Eleanor Roosevelt

Sources: *AR7*, lines 9, 46, 20, 15, and sources cited therein. Clinching proof (or disproof) that Edward Southworth, son of Thomas Southworth and Rosamond Lister, was the Leyden Pilgrim of that name would be welcome.

The Royal Descents of 500 Immigrants

1. Edward I, King of England, d. 1307 = Margaret of France

2. Thomas of Brotherton, Earl of Norfolk = Alice de Hales

3. Margaret Plantagenet, Duchess of Norfolk = John de Segrave, 4th Baron Segrave

4. Elizabeth de Segrave = John Mowbray, 4th Baron Mowbray

5. Thomas Mowbray, 1st Duke of Norfolk = = Elizabeth FitzAlan

6. Margaret Mowbray = Sir Robert Howard

7. John Howard, 1st Duke of Norfolk = Katherine Moleyns

8. Isabel Howard = Sir Robert Mortimer

9. (almost certainly) Elizabeth Mortimer = George Guilford

5. Eleanor Mowbray = John de Welles, 5th Baron Welles

6. Eudo de Welles = Maud de Greystock

7. Lionel de Welles, 6th Baron Welles = Joan Waterton

8. Eleanor de Welles = Thomas Hoo, 1st Baron Hoo

9. Anne Hoo = Sir Roger Copley

10. Eleanor Copley = Thomas West, 8th Baron Delaware (de la Warr)

10. Sir John Guilford = 11. Barbara West

11,12. Dorothy Guilford = Sir Thomas Walsingham

12,13. Barbara Walsingham = Anthony Shirley

13,14. Thomas Shirley = Jane Essex

14,15. Thomas Shirley = Elizabeth Stapley

15,16. William Shirley = ---- Oglander

16,17. William Shirley = Elizabeth Godman

17,18. **William Shirley** (c. 1694-1771), colonial governor of Mass. and of the Bahamas = Frances Barker.

11. Sir George West (brother of Lady Guilford) = Elizabeth Morton

12. Sir Thomas West = ---- Huttoft

13. Elizabeth West = Sir John Leigh, son of John Leigh (and Margaret Saunders), son of Ralph Leigh (and Margaret Ireland), son of Ralph Leigh and Joyce Colepepper (Culpeper), SETH

14. Thomas Leigh = Mary Fleming, daughter of Sir Thomas Fleming and Dorothy Cromwell, aunt of Oliver Cromwell, the Lord Protector

15. Anne Leigh = Joseph Stockman

16. **John Stockman** of Mass. = Mrs. Sarah Pike Bradbury.

Sources: *Lewes,* pp. 261-65 (Shirley of Wiston and Preston), *Manning and Bray,* vol. 2, p. 540 (Walsingham), W.B. Bannerman, ed., *Visitations of Kent, 1530-1, 1574, and 1596,* vol. 1 (*HSPVS* vol. 74, 1923), p. 77 and *Mary Isaac,* pp. 92-93 (Guilford, plus Mortimer), *CP* (de la Warr, Hoo, Welles, Norfolk), *Horsham,* pp. 70-71 (Copley) and *AR7,* lines 22, 16, 202 (for Governor Shirley); Katharine Dickson, *The Stockman Story: The English Ancestry of Mr. John Stockman of Salisbury, Massachusetts* (1992), esp. pp. 126-28 and sources cited therein, including W.H. Rylands, ed., *Visitations of Hampshire, 1530, 1575, and 1622-34* (*HSPVS,* vol. 64, 1913), pp. 158 (Leigh), 59 (West) (or *Berry's Hants,* pp. 294 [Leigh], 200 [West]). See also, for Stockman, the Heraldry Committee of NEHGS, *Third Part of A Roll of Arms* (1936), p. 8 and *NEHGR* 125(1971):263.

1. Edward I, King of England, d. 1307 = Eleanor of Castile
2. Joan Plantagenet = Gilbert de Clare, 3rd Earl of Gloucester, 7th Earl of Hertford
3. Elizabeth de Clare = Sir Theobald de Verdun
4. Isabel de Verdun = Henry Ferrers, 2nd Baron Ferrers of Groby
5. William Ferrers, 3rd Baron Ferrers of Groby = Margaret Ufford
6. Henry Ferrers, 4th Baron Ferrers of Groby = Joan de Hoo
7. William Ferrers, 5th Baron Ferrers of Groby = Philippa Clifford
8. Sir Thomas Ferrers = Elizabeth Freville
9. Sir Henry Ferrers = Margaret Heckstall
10. Elizabeth Ferrers = James Clerke
11. George Clerke = Elizabeth Wilsford
12. James Clerke = Mary Saxby
13. William Clerke = Mary Weston, sister of Richard Weston, 1st Earl of Portland, Lord Treasurer under Charles I
14. **Jeremiah Clarke**, acting governor of R.I. = Mrs. Frances Latham Dungan. Their daughter, Mary Clarke, married (1) John Cranston (1625-1680), physician, colonial governor of R.I., ARD, SETH; (2) Philip Jones; (3) Robert Stanton.

8. Elizabeth Ferrers (sister of Sir Thomas) = Sir William Colepepper (Culpeper)
9. Richard Colepepper (Culpeper) = Isabel Worsley
10. Joyce Colepepper (Culpeper) = (1) Ralph Leigh; (2) Lord Edmund Howard
11. (by 1) Isabel Leigh (half-sister of Katherine Howard, 5th Queen of Henry VIII) = Sir Edward Baynton
12. Henry Baynton/Bainton = Anne Cavendish, daughter (by Margaret Bostock, a first wife) of Sir William Cavendish,

husband of Elizabeth Hardwick, the well-known "Bess of Hardwick," later Countess of Shrewsbury, adventuress, SETH

13. Ferdinando Bainton = Joan Weare alias Browne

14. **Anne Bainton** of Mass. = Christopher **Batt** of Mass., ARD, SETH.

Sources: *AR7*, lines 11 and 8 (Clarke), 248 (Mrs. Batt); *NEHGR* 74 (1920):68-76, 130-40, reprinted in *EO* 1:1:570-88, and *Jeremy Clarke*, pp. 10-54 (34-35 esp.) (for Jeremiah Clarke); Rev. Henry Norris, *Baddesley Clinton, its Manor, Church, and Hall, with Some Account of the Family of Ferrers from the Norman Conquest to the Present Day* (1897), pp. 112-17 esp. and *CP* (Ferrers of Groby); *AL*, pp. 201-47 (241 esp.), 183-88 and *Mary Isaac*, pp. 343-54 (for Mrs. Batt).

The Royal Descents of 500 Immigrants

1. Edward I, King of England, d. 1307 = Eleanor of Castile

2. Joan Plantagenet = Gilbert de Clare, 3rd Earl of Gloucester, 7th Earl of Hertford

3. Margaret de Clare = Hugh de Audley, 1st Earl of Gloucester

4. Margaret de Audley = Ralph Stafford, 1st Earl of Stafford

5. Katherine Stafford = Sir John Sutton

6. Sir John Sutton = Jane ---

7. Sir John Sutton = Constance Blount

8. John Sutton, 1st Baron Dudley = Elizabeth Berkeley

9. John Dudley = Elizabeth Bramshot

10. Edmund Dudley, minister of Henry VII = Elizabeth Grey

11. (illegitimate by ----) Simon Dudley = Emma Saunders

12. John Dudley = (1) Elizabeth Leighton

13. Roger Dudley (possibly illegitimate, no proof of parentage) = Susanna Thorne, see below

14. **Thomas Dudley** (1576-1653), colonial governor of Mass. = Dorothy Yorke.

15. Anne Dudley, known as Mrs. Anne Bradstreet, poet = Simon Bradstreet, Governor of Mass.

16. Dudley Bradstreet = Anne Wood

17. Margaret Bradstreet = Job Tyler

18. Hannah Tyler = John Spofford (IV)

19. Phoebe Spofford = John Grout, Jr.

20. Phoebe Grout = Jacob Winn (III)

21. Endymia Winn = Thomas Sherwood

22. Lucinda Sherwood = John Minthorn

23. Theodore Minthorn = Mary Wasley

24. Hulda Randall Minthorn = Jesse Clark Hoover

25. Herbert Clark Hoover (1874-1964), 31st U.S. President = Lou Henry

10. Elizabeth Dudley (sister of Edmund) = Thomas Ashburnham

11. Helen Ashburnham = Sir Walter Henley

12. Anne Henley = Richard Covert

13. John Covert = Charity Bowes

14. Anne Covert = Sir Walter Covert, a cousin

15. **Elizabeth Covert** (died in England) = John **Fenwick** (1618-1683), colonist, founder of Salem, N.J., ARD, SETH.

Sources: *MCS4*, lines 50, 149B, *AR7*, lines 81, 9, *TAG* 44(1968): 129-37, and *TG* 5(1984):131-39, 150-51, 154-56 (Gov. Dudley); *Ardingly*, pp. 183-86 (Covert); W.B. Bannerman, ed., *Visitations of Kent, 1530-1, 1574, and 1592*, vol. 2 (*HSPVS*, vol. 75, 1924), p. 104 (Henley), and *Visitations of Sussex, 1530 and 1633-4* (*HSPVS*, vol. 53, 1905), p. 18 (Ashburnham); Dean Dudley, *The History of the Dudley Family* (1886-98), esp. p. 60 (Elizabeth Dudley). As the parentage of Roger Dudley remains unproved, the best royal descent of Gov. Thomas Dudley through his mother, Susanna Thorne, is outlined below.

1. John "Lackland," King of England, d. 1216 = (2) Isabel of Angoulême

2. (illegitimate by --- de Warenne) Richard FitzRoy = Rohese of Dover

3. Lorette de Dover = Sir William Marmion

4. John Marmion, 1st Baron Marmion = Isabel ---

5. John Marmion, 2nd Baron Marmion = Maud Furnival

6. Avice Marmion = John Grey, 1st Baron Grey of Rotherfield

7. Maud Grey = Sir Thomas Harcourt

8. Sir Thomas Harcourt = Jane Franceys

9. Sir Richard Harcourt = Edith St. Clair

10. Alice Harcourt = William Bessiles

11. Elizabeth Bessiles = Richard Fettiplace
12. Anne Fettiplace = Edward Purefoy
13. Mary Purefoy = Thomas Thorne
14. Susanna Thorne = Roger Dudley, see above
15. **Thomas Dudley** (1576-1653), colonial governor of Mass. = Dorothy Yorke.

Sources: *AR7*, lines 50, 30, 219, 218, and sources cited therein.

The Royal Descents of 500 Immigrants

1. Edward I, King of England, d. 1307 = Eleanor of Castile
2. Elizabeth Plantagenet = Humphrey de Bohun, 4th Earl of Hereford and Essex
3. William de Bohun, 1st Earl of Northampton = Elizabeth Badlesmere
4. Elizabeth de Bohun = Richard FitzAlan, 10th Earl of Arundel
5. Elizabeth FitzAlan = Sir Robert Goushill
6. Joan Goushill = Thomas Stanley, 1st Baron Stanley
7. Catherine Stanley = Sir John Savage
8. Sir Christopher Savage = Anne Stanley
9. Christopher Savage = Anne Lygon, sister of the William Lygon who married Eleanor Dennis, and of the Henry Lygon who married Elizabeth Berkeley, SETH
10. Francis Savage = Anne Sheldon
11. Walter Savage = Elizabeth Hall
12. Ralph Savage = ----
13. **Anthony Savage**, possibly the husband of Sarah Constable and immigrant to Va.
14. Alice Savage = Francis Thornton
15. Elizabeth Thornton = Edwin Conway, Jr.
16. Francis Conway = Rebecca Catlett
17. Eleanor Rose Conway = James Madison
18. James Madison, Jr. (1750/1-1836), 4th U.S. President = Mrs. Dorothea "Dolly" Payne Todd

15. Margaret Thornton (sister of Elizabeth) = William Strother, Jr.
16. Francis Strother = Susannah Dabney
17. William Strother = Sarah Bayly
18. Sarah Dabney Strother = Richard Taylor
19. Zachary Taylor (1784-1850), 12th U.S. President = Margaret Mackall Smith

10. Bridget Savage (sister of Francis) = Anthony Bonner

11. Mary Bonner = William Yonge

12. Bridget Yonge (died in England) = George Wyllys, colonial governor of Conn.

13. **Amy Wyllys** of Mass. = John **Pynchon** (c. 1626-1702/3), colonial industrialist and public official, son of William Pynchon, founder of Springfield, Mass., and Anne Andrew.

Sources: Ongoing Savage research by Brice M. Clagett and Neil D. Thompson, plus *Ligon,* vol. 1, pp. 38-41 and *GVFT* 3:474-79; *AR7*, lines 57, 20, 15, 6 and *TAG* 39(1963):86-89 (Mrs. Pynchon).

The Royal Descents of 500 Immigrants

1. Edward I, King of England, d. 1307 = Eleanor of Castile
2. Elizabeth Plantagenet = Humphrey de Bohun, 4th Earl of Hereford and Essex
3. William de Bohun, 1st Earl of Northampton = Elizabeth Badlesmere
4. Elizabeth de Bohun = Richard FitzAlan, 10th Earl of Arundel
5. Elizabeth FitzAlan = Sir Robert Goushill
6. Joan Goushill = Thomas Stanley, 1st Baron Stanley
7. Sir John Stanley   7. Catherine Stanley = Sir John Savage
   = Elizabeth Weever

8. Margery Stanley   8. Margaret Savage   8. Ellen Savage =
   = Sir William   = Sir Edmund   Sir Peter
   Torbock   Trafford   Legh
9. Thomas Torbock   9. Margery   9. Peter Legh =
   = Elizabeth   Trafford = Sir   Jane Gerard
   Moore   Thomas Gerard
                     10. Sir Thomas Gerard   = 10. Jane Legh

10. William Torbock = 11. Catherine Gerard
11,12. Margaret Torbock = Oliver Mainwaring
12,13. Oliver Mainwaring = Prudence Esse
13,14. **Oliver Mainwaring** of Conn. = Hannah Raymond
12,13. **Mary Mainwaring** (sister of the 2nd Oliver), prob. of Md. = Benjamin **Gill** of Md. Whether Mary died in England or immigrated to Md. is uncertain.
13,14. Anna Maria Gill = James Neale of Md., ARD, SETH.

10. William Gerard (brother of Sir Thomas) = Constance ----
11. Thomas Gerard = Jane ----
12. John Gerard = Isabel ----
13. **Thomas Gerard** of Md. = (1) Susannah Snow; (2) Mrs. Rose Tucker.

Sources: *NEHGR* 141(1987):104-5 and sources cited therein, including *NEHGR* 79(1925):110-11 (reprinted in *EO* 2:2:677), *Devon and Cornwall Notes and Queries* 5 (1908-9):50-62, 9(1916-17):3-4, *Transactions of the Historic Society of Lancashire and Cheshire (for the Year 1915)* 67(new ser., 31)(1916):212 (Mainwaring articles by Howard M. Buck), Matthew Gregson, *Portfolio of Fragments Relative to the History and Antiquities, Topography and Genealogies of the County Palatine and Duchy of Lancaster* (1869), p. 242 and *The Reliquary* 11(1870-1), chart opp. p. 97 (Torbock), *PCF Lancashire* (Stanley, Gerard, Trafford and Legh pedigrees), *Ormerod*, vol. 1, p. 713 (Savage), William Farrer and John Brownbill, eds., *The Victoria History of the County of Lancaster*, vol. 3 (1907, rep. 1966), p. 180 (Stanley) and *AR7*, lines 20, 15, 6 (for Oliver Mainwaring, materials assembled and brought to my attention by Robert Behra of Newport, Rhode Island; see also an unpublished monograph by Glenn H. Goodman, "The Ancestry of Oliver Mainwaring of New London, Ct., compiled from Published Sources," n.d.); unpublished Gill research by Brice McAdoo Clagett, to be incorporated into his forthcoming *Seven Centuries: Ancestors for Twenty Generations of John Brice de Treville Clagett and Ann Calvert Brooke Clagett*; *AR7*, line 233A and primary sources cited therein esp., and *MG1*:478-503 (for Thomas Gerard).

The Royal Descents of 500 Immigrants

1. Edward I, King of England, d. 1307 = Margaret of France
2. Thomas of Brotherton, Earl of Norfolk = Alice de Hales
3. Margaret Plantagenet, Duchess of Norfolk = John de Segrave, 4th Baron Segrave
4. Elizabeth de Segrave = John Mowbray, 4th Baron Mowbray
5. Thomas Mowbray, 1st Duke of Norfolk = Elizabeth FitzAlan
6. Isabel Mowbray = James Berkeley, 6th Baron Berkeley
7. Alice Berkeley = Richard Arthur
8. John Arthur = Margaret Butler
9. Margaret Arthur = Roger Porter
10. Arthur Porter = Alice Arnold
11. Isabel Porter = Giles Codrington
12. Richard Codrington = Joyce Burlace
13. Robert Codrington = Henningham Drury
14. (very probably) Robert Codrington of Barbados = Elizabeth ----
15. Henningham Codrington = Paul Carrington
16. **George Carrington** of Va. = Anne Mayo
16. Paul Carrington = Jane (Mellowes)?
17. **Elizabeth Hannah Carrington** of Pa. = Charles **Willing**.

Sources: *NGSQ* 70(1982):248-70 (252-53 esp., an article that errs, however, in the parentage of Robert Codrington, husband of Henningham Drury); V.L. Oliver, *History of the Island of Antiqua*, vol. 1 (1894), pp. 143-75 (147-48 esp.), *Bristol and Gloucestershire Archaeological Society Transcactions* 21(1898):301-45, esp. pp. 340-42 (Codrington plus Porter, Arthur and Berkeley, p. 340, as abstracted from *Lives of the Berkeleys*). Clinching proof of the parentage of Robert Codrington of Barbados would be welcome.

The Royal Descents of 500 Immigrants

1. Edward I, King of England, d. 1307 = Eleanor of Castile
2. Joan Plantagenet = Gilbert de Clare, 3rd Earl of Gloucester, 7th Earl of Hertford
3. Margaret de Clare = Hugh de Audley, 1st Earl of Gloucester
4. Margaret de Audley = Ralph Stafford, 1st Earl of Stafford
5. Katherine Stafford = Sir John Sutton
6. Sir John Sutton = Jane ----
7. Sir John Sutton = Constance Blount
8. John Sutton, 1st Baron Dudley = Elizabeth Berkeley
9. Eleanor Sutton = George Stanley
10. Anne Stanley = John Wolseley
11. Anthony Wolseley = Margaret Blith
12. Erasmus Wolseley = Cassandra Giffard
13. Sir Thomas Wolseley = Ellen Broughton, daughter of Edward Broughton and Anne Dixwell, SETH
14. **Anne Wolseley** of Md. = Hon. Philip **Calvert**, colonial governor of Md., half-brother of Cecil Calvert, 2nd Baron Baltimore, proprietor of Md. and of Hon. Leonard Calvert, also a colonial governor of Md., both ARD, SETH. Winifred Wolseley of Md., a sister of Anne, married Rev. William Mullet but left no issue.
14. Walter Wolseley = Mary Beauchamp
15. **Mary Wolseley** of Md. = Roger **Brooke** (who = (1) Dorothy Neale, daughter of James Neale of Md., ARD, SETH and Anna Maria Gill), son of Gov. Robert Brooke of Md., ARD, SETH, and Mary Mainwaring.

Sources: *TG* 5(1984):131-48, 150-52, 154-57. See also *MD* 1:138 (Calvert), 96-97 (Brooke), *LDBR* 2:332-33 (Mrs. Mary Wolseley Brooke) and *AR7*, lines 81, 9, 8.

The Royal Descents of 500 Immigrants

1. Edward I, King of England, d. 1307 = Eleanor of Castile
2. Elizabeth Plantagenet = Humphrey de Bohun, 4th Earl of Hereford and Essex
3. Eleanor de Bohun = James Butler, 1st Earl of Ormonde
4. James Butler, 2nd Earl of Ormonde = Elizabeth Darcy
5. James Butler, 3rd Earl of Ormonde = Anne de Welles
   5. Joan Butler = Teige O'Carroll
   5. Eleanor Butler = Gerald FitzGerald, 3rd Earl of Desmond
6. Sir Richard Butler = Catherine O'Reilly
   6. Mulroona O'Carroll = Bibiana O'Dempsey
   6. James FitzGerald 6th Earl of Desmond = Mary Burke
7. Sir Edmund = Butler
   7. Shile O'Carroll
   7. Joan FitzGerald = Thomas FitzGerald, 7th Earl of Kildare
8. Sir James Butler = Sabina MacMorough Kavanagh
   8. Gerald FitzGerald, 8th Earl of Kildare = Alison Eustace
9. Piers Butler, 8th Earl of Ormonde =
   9. Margaret FitzGerald
10. James Butler, 9th Earl of Ormonde = 10. Joan FitzGerald, daughter of 9. James FitzGerald, 10th Earl of Desmond (and Amy Brien), son of 8. Maurice FitzGerald, 9th Earl of Desmond (and Ellen Roche), son of 7. Thomas FitzGerald, 7th Earl of Desmond (and Ellice Barry), son of 6. James FitzGerald, 6th Earl of Desmond and Mary Burke, see above
11. Sir Edmund Butler = Eleanor Eustace
12. (illegitimate by ----) Sir Thomas Butler, 1st Bt. = Anne Colclough
13. Sir Edmund Butler, 2nd Bt. = Juliana Hyde
14. Sir Thomas Butler, 3rd Bt. = Jane Boyle
    14. Eleanor Butler = Sir Nicholas Loftus
15. James Butler =
    15. Eleanor Loftus

16. Sir Richard Butler, 5th Bt. = Henrietta Percy

17. **Pierce Butler** (1744-1822) of S.C., planter, legislator, one of the first two U.S. senators from S.C. = Mary Middleton, daughter of Thomas Middleton and Mary Bull, daughter of John Bull (and Mary Branford), son of Stephen Bull of S.C., ARD, SETH, and ----.

10. Ellen Butler (sister of the 9th Earl of Ormonde) = Donough O'Brien, 2nd Earl of Thomond

11. Margaret O'Brien = Richard Burke, 2nd Earl of Clanricarde

12. Mary Burke = Sir John Moore

13. Jane Moore = Sir Lucas Dillon

14. Mary Dillon = 13. John O'Carroll, son of 12. Mulroona O'Carroll (and Margaret O'Doyne), son of 11. Teige O'Carroll (and ----), son of 10. Sir William O'Carroll (and Morny Dulcante), son of 9. Ferganainm O'Carroll (and ----), son of 8. Mulroona O'Carroll (and ---- MacMorough Kavanagh), son of 7. John O'Carroll (and ---- O'Kennedy Finn), son of 6. Mulroona O'Carroll and Bibiana O'Dempsey, see above

14, 15. Charles O'Carroll = Clare Dunne (O'Doyne)

15, 16. **Dr. Charles Carroll** of Annapolis, Md. = (1) Dorothy Blake; (2) Anne Plater.

Sources: *DAB* (Pierce Butler), *SCG*3:155 (Middleton, Butler), *BP* and *CB* (Butler of Cloughgrenan), *Lodge,* vol. 7, pp. 265-66 (Loftus), *BP* and *CP* (Ormonde), *CP* (Kildare, Desmond) and *AR7,* lines 6, 7; *Journal of the Butler Society,* vol. 3, #3(1991):352-62 (including an ancestor table, complete for #s 1-16 and with only two omissions through #31, of Dr. Charles Carroll's Butler descents), plus sources cited therein, including the forthcoming *Seven Centuries: Ancestors for Twenty Generations of John Brice de Treville Clagett and Ann Calvert Brooke Clagett,* by Brice McAdoo Clagett (author also of the Carroll-Butler article). The above chart outlines only a selection of the descents of Dr. Charles Carroll from James Butler, 2nd Earl of Ormonde -- the three lines through the 8th Earl of Ormonde and his wife, plus the patrilineal descent from Teige O'Carroll and Lady Joan Butler. The remaining Ormonde to Carroll lines are all treated in the cited article.

The Royal Descents of 500 Immigrants

1. Edward I, King of England, d. 1307 = Eleanor of Castile
2. Elizabeth Plantagenet = Humphrey de Bohun, 4th Earl of Hereford and Essex
3. William de Bohun, 1st Earl of Northampton = Elizabeth Badlesmere
4. Elizabeth de Bohun = Richard FitzAlan, 10th Earl of Arundel
5. Elizabeth FitzAlan = Sir Robert Goushill
6. Elizabeth Goushill = Sir Robert Wingfield
7. Elizabeth Wingfield = Sir William Brandon
8. Anne Brandon = Nicholas Sidney
9. Sir William Sidney = Anne Pagenham
10. Lucy Sidney = Sir James Harington
11. Sir Henry Harington = Ruth Pilkington
12. Elizabeth Harington = Sir Richard Moryson
13. **Francis Moryson**, deputy and acting colonial governor of Va. = ---- (Richard [= Winifred ----] and Robert Moryson, brothers of Dep. and Acting Gov. Francis Moryson, also immigrated to Va. but left no NDTPS).

11. Frances Harington (sister of Henry) = Sir William Leigh
12. Sir Francis Leigh = Mary Egerton, see below
13. Juliana Leigh = Sir Richard Newdigate, 1st Bt.
14. Sir Richard Newdigate, 2nd Bt. = Mary Bagot
15. **Mary Newdigate** = William **Stephens**, colonial governor of Ga.

6. Joan Goushill (sister of Lady Wingfield) = Thomas Stanley, 1st Baron Stanley
7. Sir John Stanley = Elizabeth Weever
8. Anne Stanley = Ralph Ravenscroft
9. George Ravenscroft = Eleanor ferch Richard ap Howell
10. Thomas Ravenscroft = Katherine Grosvenor

11. Elizabeth Ravenscroft = Thomas Egerton, 1st Viscount Brackley, Lord Chancellor
12. Mary Egerton = Sir Francis Leigh, see above

Sources: *VM* 2(1894-95):383-85, *VGE*, pp. 320-21 (Moryson), *DAB* (Sir Richard Moryson, under Fynes Moryson; Sir Henry Sidney), *BP* (Harington, baronets) and G.J. Armitage, ed., *Visitation of Rutland, 1618-19* (*HSPVS*, vol. 3, 1870), pp. 38-39 (Harington), *NEHGR* 103 (1949):102-7, 287-95 (reprinted in *EO* 1:3:82-96 (Brandon, Wingfield) and *AR7*, lines 15, 6 (for Dep. and Act. Gov. Francis Moryson); *DNB* (William Stephens), *EB* and *CB* (Newdigate of Arbury), *CP* (Chichester [Leigh] and Brackley [Egerton]) and *EP*, p. 187 (Egerton), *MGH*, 5th ser., 1(1916):212-17 (Ravenscroft), *PCF Lancashire* (Stanley pedigree) and *AR7*, lines 20, 15, 6 (for Mrs. Stephens).

The Royal Descents of 500 Immigrants

1. Edward I, King of England, d. 1307 = Eleanor of Castile
2. Joan Plantagenet = Gilbert de Clare, 3rd Earl of Gloucester, 7th Earl of Hertford
3. Margaret de Clare = Hugh de Audley, 1st Earl of Gloucester
4. Margaret de Audley = Ralph Stafford, 1st Earl of Stafford
5. Katherine Stafford = Sir John Sutton
6. Sir John Sutton = Jane ---
7. Sir John Sutton = Constance Blount
8. John Sutton, 1st Baron Dudley = Elizabeth Berkeley
9. Eleanor Sutton = Sir Henry Beaumont
10. Constance Beaumont = John Mitton
11. Joyce Mitton = John Harpersfield
12. Edward Harpersfield alias Mitton = Anna Skrimshire
13. Katherine Mitton = Roger Marshall
14. **Elizabeth Marshall** of Maine = Thomas **Lewis** of Maine, ARD, SETH.
15. Judith Lewis = James Gibbins
16. Hannah Gibbins = --- Hibbert
17. Mary Hibbert = Joseph Jewett
18. Nathan Jewett = Deborah Lord
19. David Jewett = Sarah Selden
20. Elizabeth Jewett = Anselm Comstock
21. Betsey Comstock = Daniel Butler
22. George Selden Butler = Elizabeth Ely Gridley
23. Amy Gridley Butler = George Manney Ayer
24. Adele Augusta Ayer = Levi Addison Gardner
25. Dorothy Ayer Gardner = (1) Leslie Lynch King, m. (2) Gerald Rudolf Ford

26. Leslie Lynch King, Jr., whose name was changed to
    Gerald Rudolph Ford, Jr. (b. 1913), 38th U.S. President
    = Mrs. Elizabeth Ann (Betty) Bloomer Warren

Sources: *AR7*, lines 17, 221, 81, 9; *ND* 137-88; *TG* 5 (1984):131-41,
150-51, 154-56.

The Royal Descents of 500 Immigrants

1. Edward I, King of England, d. 1307 = Eleanor of Castile
2. Elizabeth Plantagenet = Humphrey de Bohun, 4th Earl of Hereford & Essex
3. William de Bohun, 1st Earl of Northampton = Elizabeth Badlesmere
4. Elizabeth de Bohun = Richard FitzAlan, 10th Earl of Arundel
5. Elizabeth FitzAlan = Sir Robert Goushill
6. Elizabeth Goushill = Sir Robert Wingfield
7. Elizabeth Wingfield = Sir William Brandon
8. Eleanor Brandon = John Glemham
9. Anne Glemham = Henry Pagrave
10. Thomas Pagrave = Alice Gunton
11. Edward Palgrave = ---
12. **Dr. Richard Palgrave** of Mass. = Anna --.
13. Sarah Palgrave = John Alcock
14. Joanna Alcock = Ephraim Hunt, Jr.
15. Elizabeth Hunt = Lemuel Pope
16. Mercy Pope = Caleb Church
17. Joseph Church = Deborah Perry
18. Deborah Church = Warren Delano
19. Warren Delano, Jr. = Catherine Robbins Lyman
20. Sara Delano = James Roosevelt
21. Franklin Delano Roosevelt (1882-1945), 32nd U.S. President = (Anna) Eleanor Roosevelt

13. Mary Palgrave (sister of Sarah) = Roger Wellington
14. Benjamin Wellington = Elizabeth Sweetman
15. Elizabeth Wellington = John Fay, Jr.
16. John Fay (III) = Hannah Child
17. Jonathan Fay = Joanna Phillips
18. Jonathan Fay, Jr. = Lucy Prescott

The Royal Descents of 500 Immigrants

19. Samuel Prescott Phillips Fay = Harriet Howard
20. Samuel Howard Fay = Susan Shellman
21. Harriet Eleanor Fay = James Smith Bush
22. Samuel Prescott Bush = Flora Sheldon
23. Prescott Sheldon Bush, U.S. Senator = Dorothy Walker
24. George Herbert Walker Bush (b. 1924), 41st U.S. President = Barbara Pierce

Sources: *AR7,* line 15 and sources cited therein, esp. *NEHGR* 102 (1948):87-98, 312-13, 103(1949):102-7, 287-95, 116(1962):79, all reprinted in *EO* 1:3:60-72, 82-96; *Moriarty.*

1. Edward I, King of England, d. 1307 = Eleanor of Castile
2. Elizabeth Plantagenet = Humphrey de Bohun, 4th Earl of Hereford and Essex
3. Margaret de Bohun = Hugh Courtenay, 2nd Earl of Devon
4. Sir Philip Courtenay = Anne Wake
5. Sir John Courtenay = Joan Champernowne
6. Sir Philip Courtenay = Elizabeth Hungerford
7. Sir Philip Courtenay = Elizabeth Hyndeston
8. Philip Courtenay = Jane Fowell
9. Elizabeth Courtenay = William Strode
10. Elizabeth Strode = Walter Hele
11. Frances Hele = John Snelling
12. **John Snelling** of Mass. = Sarah ----.

Sources: *NEHGR* 52(1898):342-46 (reprinted in *EO* 2:3:274-78), 108(1954):179; *VD*, pp. 694 (Snelling), 462 (Hele), 718 (Strode), 244, 246, 251 (Courtenay); *AR7*, lines 51, 6. Further proof of the immigrant's identification as John Snelling, baptized 17 Jan. 1624/5 at Plympton St. Mary, Devon, son of John Snelling and Frances Hele, and nephew of William Snelling of Newbury and Boston, Mass., for whom I can find no NDTPS, would be desirable.

The Royal Descents of 500 Immigrants

1. Edward I, King of England, d. 1307 = Eleanor of Castile
2. Elizabeth Plantagenet = Humphrey de Bohun, 4th Earl of Hereford and Essex
3. William de Bohun, 1st Earl of Northampton = Elizabeth Badlesmere
4. Elizabeth de Bohun = Richard FitzAlan, 10th Earl of Arundel
5. Elizabeth FitzAlan = Sir Robert Goushill
6. Joan Goushill = Thomas Stanley, 1st Baron Stanley
7. Margaret Stanley = Sir William Troutbeck
8. Adam Troutbeck = Margaret Boteler
9. Margaret Troutbeck = 9. Sir John Talbot, see below
10. Anne Talbot = Thomas Needham
11. Robert Needham = Frances Ashton
12. Dorothy Needham = Sir Richard Chetwode
13. **Grace Chetwode** of Mass. = Rev. Peter **Bulkeley** (1582/3-1658/9) of Mass., a founder and 1st minister of Concord, Mass., ARD, SETH.

5. Joan FitzAlan (sister of Elizabeth) = William Beauchamp, Baron Abergavenny
6. Joan Beauchamp = James Butler, 4th Earl of Ormonde
7. Elizabeth Butler = John Talbot, 2nd Earl of Shrewsbury
8. Sir Gilbert Talbot = Audrey Cotton
9. Sir John Talbot = 9. Margaret Troutbeck, see above.

Sources: *AR7*, lines 7, 120, 20, 15, 6; *Bulkeley*, pp. 54-89.

The Royal Descents of 500 Immigrants

1. Edward I, King of England, d. 1307 = Margaret of France
2. Thomas of Brotherton, Earl of Norfolk = Alice de Hales
3. Margaret Plantagenet, Duchess of Norfolk = John de Segrave, 4th Baron Segrave
4. Elizabeth de Segrave = John Mowbray, 4th Baron Mowbray
5. Eleanor Mowbray = John de Welles, 5th Baron Welles
6. Eudo de Welles = Maud de Greystock
7. Lionel de Welles, 6th Baron Welles = Joan Waterton
8. Eleanor de Welles = Thomas Hoo, 1st Baron Hoo
9. Anne Hoo = Sir Roger Copley
10. Margaret Copley = Edward Lewknor
11. Edward Lewknor = Dorothy Wroth
12. Mary Lewknor = Matthew Machell
13. (probably) Mary Machell = Ralph Cudworth
14. **James Cudworth** of Mass. = ----.

Sources: Ongoing research by Debrett Ancestry Research commissioned by Miss Jane E. Grunwell (these reports have so far proved James Cudworth's parentage but disproved that his mother was a daughter of John Machell and Jane Woodruff; probably she was John's sister, and royally descended as above); W.J. Calder and A.G. Cudworth, Jr., *Records of the Cudworth Family: A History of the Ancestors and Descendants of James Cudworth of Scituate, Mass.* (1974), pp. 4-7, 22 esp.; Machell pedigree (an oversize tabular chart at NEHGS, described in *NEHGR* 30[1876]:464, reprinted in *EO* 2:1:633), corrected by the Debrett reports as indicated above; *Lewes*, pp. 159-60 (Lewknor) and *Horsham*, pp. 70-71 (Copley); *CP* (Hoo, Welles) and *AR7*, lines 202, 16.

The Royal Descents of 500 Immigrants

1. Edward I, King of England, d. 1307 = Eleanor of Castile
2. Joan Plantagenet = Gilbert de Clare, 3rd Earl of Gloucester, 7th Earl of Hertford
3. Elizabeth de Clare = Roger Damory, 1st Baron Damory
4. Elizabeth Damory = John Bardolf, 3rd Baron Bardolf
5. William Bardolf, 4th Baron Bardolf = Agnes Poynings
6. Cecily Bardolf = Sir Brian Stapleton
7. Sir Miles Stapleton = Catherine de la Pole
8. Elizabeth Stapleton = Sir William Calthorpe
9. Anne Calthorpe = Sir Robert Drury, Speaker of the House of Commons
10. Elizabeth Drury = Sir Philip Boteler
11. Sir John Boteler = Grizel Roche
12. Sir Henry Boteler = Catharine Waller
13. John Boteler, 1st Baron Boteler of Bramfield = Elizabeth Villiers, half-sister of George Villiers, 1st Duke of Buckingham, favorite of James I, King of England
14. Helen Boteler = Sir John Drake
15. Elizabeth Drake = Sir Winston Churchill
16. Charles Churchill, English soldier (brother of John Churchill, 1st Duke of Marlborough, English commander during the War of the Spanish Succession and hero of the Battle of Blenheim, and of Arabella Churchill, wife of Charles Godfrey and mistress of James II, King of England) = Mary Gould
17. (illegitimate by ----) **Harriet Churchill** = (1) Sir Everard **Fawkener**; (2) Thomas **Pownall** (1722-1805), colonial governor of Mass.

Sources: *DNB* (Thomas Pownall, Sir Everard Fawkener, and Charles Churchill); *Chester of Chicheley,* vol. 1, pp. 139-46 (Boteler and generations 1-13 on pp. 140-41); *SMF* 1:354 (Drury); *AR7*, lines 257, 11, 8, and sources cited therein.

The Royal Descents of 500 Immigrants

1. Edward I, King of England, d. 1307 = Margaret of France

2. Thomas of Brotherton, Earl of Norfolk = Alice de Hales

3. Margaret Plantagenet, Duchess of Norfolk = John de Segrave, 4th Baron Segrave

4. Elizabeth de Segrave = John Mowbray, 4th Baron Mowbray

5. Eleanor Mowbray = John de Welles, 5th Baron Welles

6. Eudo de Welles = Maud de Greystock

7. Lionel de Welles, 6th Baron Welles = Joan Waterton

8. Margaret de Welles = Sir Thomas Dymoke

9. Margaret Dymoke = Thomas FitzWilliam

10. Elizabeth FitzWilliam = Robert Eyre

11. Jane Eyre = Thomas Meverell

12. Elizabeth Meverell = William Basset

13. Anne Basset (whose maternity as shown above is highly probable for chronological and other reasons, but unproved) = Thomas Alsop

14. Anne Alsop = John Alsop, a cousin

15. Anthony Alsop = Jane Smith

16. John Alsop = Temperance Gilbert (Timothy and George Alsop, sons of John and Temperance and husbands of Eliza Heires and Dorothy Bentley respectively, also immigrated to Connecticut but apparently left no American descendants)

17. **Elizabeth Alsop** of Conn. = (1) Richard **Baldwin**; (2) William **Fowler**.

18. Sarah Baldwin (by first husband) = Samuel Riggs

19. Ebenezer Riggs = Lois Hawkins

20. John Riggs = Hannah Johnson

21. John Riggs, Jr. = Abigail Peet

22. James Riggs = Sarah Clark

23. George Riggs = Phebe Caniff

24. Maria Riggs = Eli Doud
25. Royal Houghton Doud = Mary Cornelia Sheldon
26. John Sheldon Doud = Elivera Mathilda Carlson
27. Mamie Geneva Doud = Dwight David Eisenhower (1890-1969), 34th U.S. President

Sources: *NEHGR* 46(1892):366-69 (reprinted in *EO* 2:1:15-18) and *TG*, new ser., 7(1890-91):1 (Alsop); *Shaw*, vol. 2, part 1, p. 13 (Basset of Blore); *Salt*, new ser., 12(1909):167 (Meverell); Joseph Hunter, *Familiae Minorum Gentium*, vol. 2 (*HSPVS*, vol. 38, 1895), p. 551 (Eyre); *PCF Yorkshire* (FitzWilliam pedigree); Rev. A.R. Maddison, ed., *Lincolnshire Pedigrees*, vol. 4 (*HSPVS*, vol. 55, 1906), p. 1204 (Dymoke); *AR7*, lines 202, 16. An authoritative monograph on the Bassets of Blore is much needed.

The Royal Descents of 500 Immigrants

1. Edward I, King of England, d. 1307 = Eleanor of Castile
2. Elizabeth Plantagenet = Humphrey de Bohun, 4th Earl of Hereford and Essex
3. William de Bohun, 1st Earl of Northampton = Elizabeth Badlesmere
4. Elizabeth de Bohun = Richard FitzAlan, 10th Earl of Arundel
5. Elizabeth FitzAlan = Sir Robert Goushill
6. Joan Goushill = Thomas Stanley, 1st Baron Stanley
7. Catherine Stanley = Sir John Savage
8. Margaret Savage = John Hondford
9. Katherine Hondford = Sir John Mainwaring
10. Katherine Mainwaring = William Newton
11. William Newton = Parnell Davenport
12. William Newton = Margaret Mere
13. William Newton = Margery Wright
14. Anne Newton = Anthony Rudyard
15. **Thomas Rudyard,** deputy governor of East Jersey = Alice ----.

Sources: *NYGBR* 121(1990):193-97 and John Sleigh, *A History of the Ancient Parish of Leek in Staffordshire,* 2nd ed. (1883), p. 129 (Rudyard); *Earwaker,* vol. 1, pp. 127-28 (Newton), 251 (Hondford), *Ormerod,* vol. 1, pp. 482 (Mainwaring), 713 (Savage); *AR7,* lines 57, 20, 15, 6, plus *TG* 5(1984):164-65, 171. Henry Bainbridge Hoff, editor of *NYGBR,* reports that further research undertaken since publication of the 1990 Rudyard article confirms the above identification of the immigrant's mother.

The Royal Descents of 500 Immigrants

1. Edward I, King of England, d. 1307 = Eleanor of Castile
2. Joan Plantagenet = Gilbert de Clare, 3rd Earl of Gloucester, 7th Earl of Hertford
3. Elizabeth de Clare = Roger Damory, 1st Baron Damory
4. Elizabeth Damory = John Bardolf, 3rd Baron Bardolf
5. William Bardolf, 4th Baron Bardolf = Agnes Poynings
6. Cecily Bardolf = Sir Brian Stapleton
7. Sir Miles Stapleton = Catherine de la Pole
8. Elizabeth Stapleton = Sir William Calthorpe
9. Anne Calthorpe = Sir Robert Drury, Speaker of the House of Commons
10. Bridget Drury = Sir John Jernegan
11. George Jernegan = Ela Spelman
12. Ela Jernegan = Arthur Jenney
13. Francis Jenney = Anne Reade
14. Sir Arthur Jenney = Helen Stonard
15. **Isabel Jenney** = John **Talbot** (c. 1645-1727) of N.J., Anglican missionary clergyman, ARD, SETH.

Sources: A.W.H. Clarke and Arthur Campling, eds., *Visitation of Norfolk, 1664*, vol. 1 (*HSPVS*, vol. 85, 1933), p. 109 (Jenney); Joan Corder, ed., *Visitation of Suffolk, 1561, Part II* (*HSPVS*, new ser., vol. 3, 1984), pp. 299-300 (Jenney), 335-36 (Jernegan); *SMF* 1:354 (Drury); *AR7*, lines 257, 11, 8.

The Royal Descents of 500 Immigrants

1. Edward I, King of England, d. 1307 = Eleanor of Castile
2. Elizabeth Plantagenet = Humphrey de Bohun, 4th Earl of Hereford and Essex
3. William de Bohun, 1st Earl of Northampton = Elizabeth Badlesmere
4. Elizabeth de Bohun = Richard FitzAlan, 10th Earl of Arundel
5. Elizabeth FitzAlan = Sir Robert Goushill
6. Elizabeth Goushill = Sir Robert Wingfield
7. Sir Henry Wingfield = Elizabeth Rokes
8. Robert Wingfield = Margery Quarles
9. Robert Wingfield = Elizabeth Cecil, sister of William Cecil, 1st Baron Burghley, minister of Elizabeth I
10. Dorothy Wingfield = Adam Claypoole
11. John Claypoole = Mary Angell
12. **James Claypoole** of Pa. = Helen Mercer.

Sources: *TAG* 67(1992):97-107, 47(1971):204-5, 18(1941-42):201-6 and sources cited therein, esp. J.M. Wingfield, *Some Records of the Wingfield Family* (1925), pp. 7-17, 23-26 and chart opp. p. 252 and R.I. Graff, *Genealogy of the Claypoole Family* (1893), pp. 11-52; *AR7*, lines 15, 6. See also *BLG* 1952, pp. 2762-63 (Parry-Wingfield of Tichencote).

The Royal Descents of 500 Immigrants

1. Edward I, King of England, d. 1307 = Eleanor of Castile

2. Joan Plantagenet = Gilbert de Clare, 3rd Earl of Gloucester, 7th Earl of Hertford

3. Margaret de Clare = Hugh de Audley, 1st Earl of Gloucester

3. Eleanor de Clare = Hugh le Despencer, 1st Baron Despencer

4. Margaret de Audley = Ralph Stafford, 1st Earl of Stafford

4. Sir Edward Despencer = Anne Ferrers

5. Elizabeth Stafford = John de Ferrers, 4th Baron Ferrers of Chartley

5. Edward Despencer, 3rd Baron Despencer = Elizabeth Burghersh

6. Robert de Ferrers, 5th Baron Ferrers of Chartley = 6. Margaret Despencer

7. Sir Edmund Ferrers = Ellen Roche

8. Sir William Ferrers = Elizabeth Belknap

9. Anne Ferrers = Walter Devereux, 1st Baron Ferrers of Chartley (of the second creation)

10. Elizabeth Devereux = Sir Richard Corbet

11. Anne Corbet = Sir Thomas Cornewall

12. Eleanor Cornewall = Roger Vaughan

13. Anne Vaughan = Richard Salway

14. Alice Salway = William Penrhyn

15. Gainor Penrhyn = Humphrey Jones

16. Gilbert Jones = Joan Moore

17. Gilbert Jones = Mary ----

18. **Mary Jones** of Pa. = Thomas **Lloyd** (1640-1694), dep. gov. of Pa., physician, colonial statesman, ARD, SETH.

Sources: Charles F.H. Evans and Irene Haines Leet, *Thomas Lloyd, Dolobran to Pennsylvania* (1982), pp. 4, 14 (Jones); Rev. W.V. Lloyd, *The Sheriffs of Montgomeryshire* (1876), pp. 294, 153 (Penrhyn,

Salway); *Bartrum 2*, p. 457 (Vaughan); *Cornewall*, pp. 189, 203-8; A.E. Corbet, *The Family of Corbet*, vol. 2 (1920), p. 253 esp.; *AR7*, lines 56B, 61, 9, 70, 74, 8.

The Royal Descents of 500 Immigrants

1. Edward I, King of England, d. 1307 = Eleanor of Castile
2. Elizabeth Plantagenet = Humphrey de Bohun, 4th Earl of Hereford and Essex
3. Margaret de Bohun = Hugh Courtenay, 2nd Earl of Devon
4. Margaret Courtenay = John Cobham, 3rd Baron Cobham
5. Joan Cobham = Sir John de la Pole
6. Joan de la Pole, Baroness Cobham = Sir Reginald Braybrooke
7. Joan Braybrooke = Sir Thomas Brooke
8. Elizabeth Brooke = John St. Maure
9. Joan St. Maure = Walter Blewett
10. Nicholas Blewett = Joan Fitzjames
11. Edith Blewett = John Bonville
12. Humphrey Bonville = Joanna Wynslade
13. Edmund Bonville = Jane Tregion
14. Richard Bonville = ----
15. Agnes Bonville = Hugh Croker
16. Francis Croker = ---- Pascoe
17. George Croker = Anstice Tripp
18. Tabitha Croker = Francis Fox
19. **Mary Fox** of Pa. = Andrew **Ellicott.**

Sources: *MG*1:273-94; *VD*, pp. 254 (Croker), 103 (Bonville), 92 (Blewett, St. Mawr); *EP* and *CP* (Cobham, Devon) and *AR7*, line 6. A thorough monograph on the above Blewett and Bonville families would be welcome.

The Royal Descents of 500 Immigrants

1. Edward I, King of England, d. 1307 = Margaret of France
2. Edmund of Woodstock, 1st Earl of Kent = Margaret Wake
3. Joan Plantagenet, "The Fair Maid of Kent" = Thomas Holand, 1st Earl of Kent (she later = Edward, "The Black Prince" of Wales and was the mother of Richard II, King of England)
4. Thomas Holand, 2nd Earl of Kent = Alice FitzAlan
5. Eleanor Holand = Edward Cherleton, 4th Baron Cherleton of Powis
6. Joyce Cherleton = John Tiptoft (Tibetot), 1st Baron Tiptoft
7. Philippa Tiptoft = Thomas de Ros, Baron Ros
8. Eleanor de Ros = Sir Robert Manners
9. Elizabeth Manners = Sir William Fairfax
10. Sir William Fairfax = Isabel Thwaits
11. Anne Fairfax = Sir Henry Everingham
12. Eleanor Everingham = Gervase Cressy
13. Anne Cressy = William Copley
14. Lionel Copley = Frisalina Warde
15. **Lionel Copley** (d. 1693), colonial governor of Md. = Anne Boteler of Md., ARD, SETH.

Sources: *DAB* (Lionel Copley); *DVY*, vol. 2, pp. 53-54 (Copley), vol. 3, p. 118 (Cressy); *Foster's V of Yorkshire*, p. 38 (Everingham); *PCF Yorkshire* (Fairfax pedigree); *NF* 2:247 (Manners); *BP*, *EP* or *CP* (Rutland, Ros, Tiptoft, Cherleton of Powis, Kent), *AR7*, lines 155, 236, 47 and *MCS4*, lines 30, 94.

The Royal Descents of 500 Immigrants

1. Edward I, King of England, d. 1307 = Eleanor of Castile
2. Elizabeth Plantagenet = Humphrey de Bohun, 4th Earl of Hereford and Essex
3. William de Bohun, 1st Earl of Northampton = Elizabeth Badlesmere
4. Elizabeth de Bohun = Richard FitzAlan, 10th Earl of Arundel
5. Elizabeth FitzAlan = Sir Robert Goushill
6. Elizabeth Goushill = Sir Robert Wingfield
7. Sir John Wingfield = Elizabeth Fitz Lewis
8. Sir Richard Wingfield = Bridget Wiltshire
9. Thomas Maria Wingfield = ---- Kerry
10. **Edward Maria Wingfield** (c. 1570-post 1613), adventurer, 1st president of the Virginia Colony, d. unm.

Sources: *DAB* and *MCS4*, lines 18-20; *GVFVM* 5:822-25.

The Royal Descents of 500 Immigrants

1. Edward I, King of England, d. 1307 = Margaret of France

2. Thomas of Brotherton, Earl of Norfolk = Alice de Hales

3. Margaret Plantagenet, Duchess of Norfolk = John de Segrave, 4th Baron Segrave

4. Elizabeth de Segrave = John Mowbray, 4th Baron Mowbray

5. Thomas Mowbray, 1st Duke of Norfolk = Elizabeth FitzAlan

6. Isabel Mowbray = James Berkeley, 6th Baron Berkeley

7. Thomas Berkeley = Margaret Guy

8. Richard Berkeley = Margaret Dyer

9. William Berkeley = Elizabeth Burghill

10. Rowland Berkeley = Catherine Heywood

11. William Berkeley = Margaret Chettle

12. Jane Berkeley = William Jeffreys

13. **Sir Herbert Jeffreys,** colonial governor of Va. = Susanna ----.

Sources: E.M. Jefferys, *Jefferys of Worcestershire, Nevis, [and] Philadelphia* (1939), pp. 6, 14-15, *BLG,* 1863, pp. 89-90 (Berkeley) and *Lives of the Berkeleys,* vol. 2, pp. 82-83, 86-88 esp.; *MCS4,* lines 66, 63 and *AR7,* line 16.

The Royal Descents of 500 Immigrants

1. Edward I, King of England, d. 1307 = Margaret of France
2. Thomas of Brotherton, Earl of Norfolk = Alice de Hales
3. Margaret Plantagenet, Duchess of Norfolk = John de Segrave, 4th Baron Segrave
4. Elizabeth de Segrave = John Mowbray, 4th Baron Mowbray
5. Thomas Mowbray, 1st Duke of Norfolk = Elizabeth FitzAlan
6. Margaret Mowbray = Sir Robert Howard
7. John Howard, 1st Duke of Norfolk = Katherine Moleyns
8. Thomas Howard, 2nd Duke of Norfolk = Agnes Tilney
9. William Howard, 1st Baron Howard of Effingham = Margaret Gamage
10. Sir William Howard = Frances Gouldwell
11. Sir Francis Howard = Jane Monson
12. Sir Charles Howard = Frances Courthope
13. **Francis Howard, 5th Baron Howard of Effingham,** colonial governor of Va. = (1) Philadelphia Pelham, ARD, SETH; (2) Susan Felton, ARD, SETH.

Sources: *BP* and *CP* (Effingham or Howard of Effingham, Norfolk); *AR7*, line 16.

The Royal Descents of 500 Immigrants

1. Edward I, King of England, d. 1307 = Eleanor of Castile
2. Elizabeth Plantagenet = Humphrey de Bohun, 4th Earl of Hereford and Essex
3. William de Bohun, 1st Earl of Northampton = Elizabeth Badlesmere
4. Elizabeth de Bohun = Richard FitzAlan, 10th Earl of Arundel
5. Joan FitzAlan = William Beauchamp, Baron Abergavenny
6. Joan Beauchamp = James Butler, 4th Earl of Ormonde
7. Thomas Butler, 7th Earl of Ormonde = Anne Hankford
8. Margaret Butler = Sir William Boleyn
9. Margaret Boleyn (aunt of Anne Boleyn, 2nd Queen of Henry VIII, and great-aunt of Elizabeth I, Queen of England) = John Sackville
10. Mary Sackville = John Lunsford
11. Sir John Lunsford = Barbara Lewknor
12. Thomas Lunsford = Katherine Fludd
13. **Sir Thomas Lunsford** (c. 1610-c. 1653) of Va., royalist army officer = (1) Anne Hudson; (2) Katherine Neville; (3) Elizabeth Wormeley, widow of Richard Kempe, secretary and act. gov. of Va., ARD, SETH, and niece of Ralph Wormeley, 2nd husband of (Lady) Agatha Eltonhead (Kellaway) Wormeley (Chichele) of Va., ARD, SETH.

Sources: *MCS4*, lines 88A, 17A, 17, 19, 18 (and *AR7*, lines 120, 15, 6) and sources cited therein, esp. *Collectanea Topographica et Genealogica* 4 (1837):141-42, and *VM* 17(1909):26-33; E.L. Lomax, *Genealogy of the Virginia Family of Lomax* (1913), pp. 57-63 (Lunsford).

The Royal Descents of 500 Immigrants

1. Edward I, King of England, d. 1307 = Eleanor of Castile
2. Elizabeth Plantagenet = Humphrey de Bohun, 4th Earl of Hereford and Essex
3. William de Bohun, 1st Earl of Northampton = Elizabeth Badlesmere
4. Elizabeth de Bohun = Richard FitzAlan, 10th Earl of Arundel
5. Elizabeth FitzAlan = Sir Robert Goushill
6. Elizabeth Goushill = (1) Sir Robert Wingfield; (2) Sir William Hardwick

7. (by 1) Sir John Wingfield = Elizabeth FitzLewis	7. (by 2) Roger Hardwick = Nicola Barlow
8. Sir John Wingfield = Anne Touchet	8. John Hardwick = Elizabeth Bakewell
9. Sir Anthony Wingfield = Elizabeth Vere	9. John Hardwick = Elizabeth Pinchbeck
	10. John Hardwick = Elizabeth Leke
10. Richard Wingfield =	11. Mary Hardwick

11,12. Henry Wingfield = Elizabeth Risby

12,13. Mary Wingfield = William Dade

13,14. **Francis Dade** of Va. = Behethland Bernard

Sources: *GVFVM*2:657-63; Sir Henry Ellis, *Visitation of Huntingdon, 1613* (Camden Society Publications, vol. 43, 1849), pp. 125-28 (Wingfield); *The Reliquary* 22(1881-82):241-42 (Hardwick); *AR7*, lines 15, 6.

The Royal Descents of 500 Immigrants

1. Edward I, King of England, d. 1307 = Margaret of France
2. Thomas of Brotherton, Earl of Norfolk = Alice de Hales
3. Margaret Plantagenet, Duchess of Norfolk = John de Segrave, 4th Baron Segrave
4. Elizabeth de Segrave = John Mowbray, 4th Baron Mowbray
5. Thomas Mowbray, 1st Duke of Norfolk = Elizabeth FitzAlan
6. Isabel Mowbray = James Berkeley, 6th Baron Berkeley
7. Maurice Berkeley = Isabel Mead
8. Thomas Berkeley, 8th Baron Berkeley = Eleanor Constable
9. Joan Berkeley = Sir Nicholas Poyntz
10. Sir Nicholas Poyntz = Anne Verney
11. Mary Poyntz = John Sydenham
12. Anne Sydenham = John Poyntz
13. Newdigate Poyntz = Sarah Foxley
14. Dorothea Poyntz = John Owsley
15. **Thomas Owsley of Va.** = Anne ----.

Sources: Harry Bryan Owsley, *Genealogical Facts of the Owsley Family in England and America* (1890), chapters 2-6; *BLG*, 18th ed., vol. 1 (1965), pp. 580-82 (Poyntz); *Lives of the Berkeleys*, vol. 2, pp. 235-36 esp; *MCS4*, lines 66, 63 and *AR7*, line 16.

The Royal Descents of 500 Immigrants

1. Edward I, King of England, d. 1307 = Eleanor of Castile
2. Joan Plantagenet = Gilbert de Clare, 3rd Earl of Gloucester, 7th Earl of Hertford
3. Eleanor de Clare = Hugh le Despencer, 1st Baron Despencer
4. Isabel Despencer = Richard FitzAlan, 9th Earl of Arundel
5. Sir Edmund FitzAlan = Sybil Montagu
6. Philippa FitzAlan = Sir Richard Sergeaux
7. Elizabeth Sergeaux = Sir William Marney
8. Emma Marney = Sir Thomas Tyrrell

9. Humphrey Tyrrell = Isabel Helion

9. Sir Robert Tyrrell = Christian Hartshorn

10. Anne Tyrrell = Sir Roger Wentworth

10. Joyce Tyrrell = Thomas Appleton

11. Margery Wentworth = John Berney

11. Roger Appleton = 9. Anne Sulyard, see below

12. John Berney = Margaret Read

12. Henry Appleton = Margaret Roper

13. Roger Appleton = Agnes Clarke

13. Henry Berney   =   14. Alice Appleton
14,15. Sir Thomas Berney = Juliana Gawdy
15,16. Frances Berney = Sir Edward Barkham, 1st Bt.
16,17. Margaret Barkham = Sir Edmund Jennings. Their daughter, Elizabeth Jennings, married Sir Roger Beckwith, 1st Bt. and was the mother of Sir Marmaduke Beckwith, 3rd Bt., of Va., ARD, SETH.
17,18. **Edmund Jennings**, acting colonial governor of Va., president of its council = Frances Corbin, daughter of Henry Corbin of Va., ARD, SETH and Mrs. Alice Eltonhead Burnham Corbin (Creek) of Va., ARD, SETH.

2. Elizabeth Plantagenet = Humphrey de Bohun, 4th Earl of Hereford and Essex

3. Margaret de Bohun = Hugh Courtenay, 2nd Earl of Devon

4. Elizabeth Courtenay = Sir Andrew Luttrell

5. Sir Hugh Luttrell = Catherine Beaumont

6. Elizabeth Luttrell = John Stratton

7. Elizabeth Stratton = John Andrews

8. Anne Andrews = Sir John Sulyard

9. Anne Sulyard = 11. Roger Appleton, above

Sources: *HSF* 4:129-30 and *VGE*, pp. 93-97, 365-66; *CB* (Barkham); Walter Rye, ed., *Visitations of Norfolk, 1563, 1589, and 1613* (*HSPVS*, vol. 32, 1891), pp. 16-17 (Berney); *Wentworth*, vol. 1, pp. 34-36; Walter C. Metcalfe, ed., *Visitations of Essex, 1552, 1558, 1570, 1612 and 1634*, vol. 1 (*HSPVS*, vol. 13, 1878), pp. 134-35 (Appleton), 300-1 (Tyrrell); Frederic Chancellor, *The Ancient Sepulchral Monuments of Essex* (1890), pp. 173-74 (Tyrrell), 20 (Marney); Sir John MacLean, *The Parochial and Family History of the Deanery of Trigg Manor in the County of Cornwall*, vol. 2 (1876), p. 507 (Marney, Sergeaux) and *MCS4*, lines 134, 34; Walter C. Metcalfe, ed., *Visitations of Suffolk, 1561, 1577, and 1612* (1882), p. 69 (Sulyard); *Roger Ludlow*, pp. 2322-24 (Andrews) and *AR7*, lines 12, 6.

The Royal Descents of 500 Immigrants

1. Edward I, King of England, d. 1307 = Eleanor of Castile
2. Elizabeth Plantagenet = Humphrey de Bohun, 4th Earl of Hereford and Essex
3. William de Bohun, 1st Earl of Northampton = Elizabeth Badlesmere
4. Elizabeth de Bohun = Richard FitzAlan, 10th Earl of Arundel
5. Elizabeth FitzAlan = Sir Robert Goushill
6. Elizabeth Goushill = Sir Robert Wingfield
7. Sir John Wingfield = Elizabeth FitzLewis
8. Elizabeth Wingfield = Francis Hall
9. Alice Hall = Sir Henry Sutton
10. William Sutton = Anne Rodney
11. Sir William Sutton = Susan Cony
12. Susan Sutton = William Oglethorpe
13. Sutton Oglethorpe = Frances Mathews
14. Sir Theophilus Oglethorpe = Eleanor Wall
15. **James Edward Oglethorpe** (1696-1785), soldier, the founder of Georgia = Elizabeth Wright.
15. Eleanor Oglethorpe = Eugène Marie de Béthisy, Marquis de Mézières
16. Catherine Eléonore Eugénie de Bethisy = Charles de Rohan, Prince of Rohan-Montauban
17. Louise Julie Constance de Rohan = Charles Louis of Lorraine, Prince of Lambesc, Count of Brionne
18. Marie Therese Josephe of Lorraine-Brionne = Victor Amadeus II of Savoy, Prince of Carignan
19. Charles Emanuel of Savoy, Prince of Carignan = Marie of Saxony
20. Charles Albert, King of Sardinia = Maria Teresa of Tuscany, Archduchess of Austria
20. Elizabeth of Savoy = Rainier, Archduke of Austria, son of Leopold II, Holy Roman Emperor

21. Victor Emanuel II, = (1)   21. Adelaide, Archduchess
King of Sardinia,   of Austria
1st King of United Italy
(1820-1878) = (2) Rosa
Teresa Vercellana,
Countess di Mirafiori and
Fontanafredda (among his
grandsons or great-grandsons
were kings of Italy, of the
Bulgarians, and of Portugal).

Sources: *NEXUS* 9(1992):62-65 and sources cited therein; *DNB* (James Edward and Sir Theophilus Oglethorpe); *DVY*, vol. 2, pp. 299-300 (Oglethorpe); G.W. Marshall, ed., *Visitations of the County of Nottingham, 1569 and 1614* (*HSPVS*, vol. 4, 1871), p. 143 (Sutton); Rev. A.R. Maddison, *Lincolnshire Pedigrees*, vol. 2 (*HSPVS*, vol. 51, 1903), pp. 441-42 (Hall); J.M. Wingfield, *Some Records of the Wingfield Family* (1925), pp. 7-22 and chart at end; *MCS4*, lines 18-20 and *AR7*, lines 15, 6. For the Oglethorpe descent of the kings of Italy, see *Courcelles*, vol. 1, pp. 8-12 (Béthisy), *Anselme* (and Potier de Courcy), vol. 4, p. 63, vol. 9, part 2, pp. 204 (Rohan-Montauban), 182-83 (Lorraine-Brionne); *ES*, charts for Rohan, Lorraine-Brionne, Savoy-Carignan and Italy; and *BRFW* 1:360, 364-68 (Italy), 59 (Bulgaria), 449 (Portugal).

The Royal Descents of 500 Immigrants

1. Edward I, King of England, d. 1307 = Eleanor of Castile
2. Joan Plantagenet = Gilbert de Clare, 3rd Earl of Gloucester, 7th Earl of Hertford
3. Margaret de Clare = Hugh de Audley, 1st Earl of Gloucester
4. Margaret de Audley = Ralph Stafford, 1st Earl of Stafford
5. Hugh Stafford, 2nd Earl of Stafford = Philippa Beauchamp
6. Katherine Stafford = Michael de la Pole, 2nd Earl of Suffolk
7. Elizabeth de la Pole = Sir Thomas de Kerdeston
8. Margaret de Kerdeston = John de Foix, 1st Earl of Kendal (their son, Gaston III de Foix, Count of Benauges, married firstly Catherine de Foix, his cousin, niece of the half blood of Ferdinand I, 1st King of united Spain, and was the father of Anne de Foix, wife of Ladislaus V, King of Bohemia and Hungary and mother of Anne of Bohemia, wife of Ferdinand I (Hapsburg), Holy Roman Emperor. Descendants of Anne and Ferdinand include all later Holy Roman or Austrian emperors; all kings of France after Henry IV; all kings of Spain after Philip II; Charles II, James II, Mary II, William III, and Anne of England/Great Britain, plus George III and all later (post-George III) British sovereigns; Ivan VI, Peter III, Catherine II and all later (post-Catherine) czars of Russia; all kings of Prussia and German emperors; all kings of Portugal after Peter II; all kings of the Netherlands, Belgium, Sardinia, the two Sicilies and Italy; all Kings of Denmark after Christian V; Swedish sovereigns from Christina through Charles XIII and after Oscar II; all modern kings of Norway and Greece; etc.)
9. Jean de Foix, Vicomte de Meille = Anne de Villeneuve
10. Marthe de Foix = Claude de Grasse, Seigneur du Bar
11. Claude de Grasse, Count du Bar = Jeanne de Brancas

12. Annibal de Grasse, Count du Bar = Claire d'Alagonia

13. Honoré de Grasse, Seigneur de Valette = Marguerite de Flotte-d'Agoult

14. Jean Pierre Charles de Grasse, Seigneur de Valette = Angélique de Rouxel

15. Francois de Grasse-Rouville, Seigneur de Valette = Véronique de Villeneuve-Trans

16. **Francois Joseph Paul de Grasse, Count de Grasse, Marquis de Tilly** (1722-1788), French admiral, commander of the French fleet in Chesapeake Bay that helped force Cornwallis's surrender at Yorktown = (1) Antoinette Rosalie Accaron; (2) Catherine de Pien; (3) Christine de Cibon. Sylvie de Grasse, a daughter by (1), married Francois de Pau and left descendants in America, including a daughter, Caroline de Grasse de Pau, who married Henry Walter Livingston, Jr., nephew of Harriet Livingston, wife of steamboat inventor Robert Fulton.

Sources: Le Marquis de Grasse and M. Emile Isnard, *Histoire de la Maison de Grasse,* 2 vols. (1933), passim, and *D de la N* (de Grasse, de Foix); *Anselme,* vol. 3, pp. 382-83, 387-88 (Foix); *TG*6(1985): 160-65 (Margaret de Kerdeston); *CP* (Suffolk, Stafford, Gloucester, Hertford) and *AR7,* lines 8-10. This line was brought to my attention by Henry Bainbridge Hoff of New York City.

The Royal Descents of 500 Immigrants

1. Przemysl Ottokar II, King of Bohemia, d. 1278 = (1) Margaret of Austria; (2) Kunigunde of Halicz

2. (illegitimate by ----) Nicholas I, Duke of Troppau = Adelaide ----

3. Nicholas II, Duke of Troppau = Anna of Silesia-Ratibor

4. Euphemia of Troppau = Ziemowit III, Duke of Mazovia

5. John I, Duke of Mazovia = Anna of Lithuania

6. Boleslaw IV, Duke of Mazovia = Barbara ----

7. Conrad III, Duke of Mazovia = Anna, Princess Radziwill

8. Anna of Mazovia = Stanislaus Odrowaz

9. Sophia Odrowazowna = Jan Kostka

10. Anna Kostczanka = Alexander, Prince Ostrogski, son of Constantine Basil, Prince Ostrogski (and Sophia, Countess Tarnowska), son of Constantine, Prince Ostrogski, and Alexandra, Princess Sluka, daughter of Siemion, Prince Olelkowicz-Slucky (and Anastasia, Princess Mscislawska), son of Michael, Prince Olelkowicz-Slucky (and Anna ----), son of Alexander Olelko, Prince of Kiev, and Anastasia of Moscow, daughter of Basil II, Grand Prince of Moscow (and Sophie of Lithuania), son of Dimitri IV, Grand Prince of Moscow, and Eudoxia of Susdal, both ARD, SETH

11. Sophia, Princess Ostrogska = Stanislaus, Prince Lubomirski

12. George (Jerzy) Sebastian, Prince Lubomirski = Konstance z Bobrku Ligezianka

13. Alexander Michael, Prince Lubomirski = Katherine Anne, Princess Sapieha

14. George Alexander, Prince Lubomirski = (1) Joanna von Starzhausen; (2) Aniela Teresa Michowska

15. (maternity uncertain) Stanislaus, Prince Lubomirski = Louisa Honorata Pociejowna

16. Josef, Prince Lubomirski = Louisa Sosnowska

17. Frederick, Prince Lubomirski = Francoise, Countess Zaluska
18. Casimir, Prince Lubomirski = Zeneide Holynska
19. Marie, Princess Lubomirska = René Lannes de Montebello
20. George Ernest Casimir Lannes de Montebello = Emilie d'Aviles
21. Andre Roger Lannes de Montebello = Germaine Wiener de Croisset
22. **Guy Philippe Lannes de Montebello** (b. 1936), of N.Y., museum curator, head of the Metropolitan Museum of New York = Edith Bradford Myles.

Sources: *GH des A,* Fürstliche Häuser, vol. 5 (1959), pp. 507-8 (Lannes de Montebello) and various Almanachs de Gotha (for example, 1855, pp. 182-83) (Lubomirski), Wlodzimierz Dworzaczek, *Genealogia* (1959), charts for Lubomirski, Ostrogski, Kostkowie, Odrowazowie, and Olelkowicz (vol. 2, #s 143, 165, 127, 109 and 161); *ES,* charts for Mazovia (Masowien), Moscow, Troppau and Bohemia.

The Royal Descents of 500 Immigrants

1. Henry III, King of England, d. 1272 = Eleanor of Provence
2. Edmund Plantagenet, 1st Earl of Lancaster = Blanche of Artois
3. Henry Plantagenet, 3rd Earl of Lancaster = Maud Chaworth
4. Eleanor Plantagenet = Richard FitzAlan, 9th Earl of Arundel
5. John FitzAlan, 1st Baron Arundel = Eleanor Maltravers
6. Joan FitzAlan = Sir William Echyngham
7. Joan Echyngham, said to = Sir John Baynton
8. Henry Baynton = ----
9. (said to be) Joan Baynton = Thomas Prowse
10. Mary Prowse = Robert Gye
11. Robert Gye = Grace Dowrish
12. **Mary Gye** of Mass. = Rev. John **Maverick**.

Sources: *NEHGR* 115(1961):248-53, 122(1968):282-83 (reprinted in *EO* 1:3:359-66); *AL*, pp. 221-23; *AR7*, lines 261 (which covers, with connections to lines 30-32, 127, 125, 124, 66, 53, etc., lesser royal descents for Mrs. Maverick through Dowrish, Farringdon, Stukeley, and FitzRoger families), 59, 21, 17. Further documentary proof of generations 7-9 would be desirable.

The Royal Descents of 500 Immigrants

1. Henry III, King of England, d. 1272 = Eleanor of Provence
2. Beatrix Plantagenet = John I, Duke of Brittany
3. Marie of Brittany = Guy III de Châtillon, Count of St. Pol
4. Isabel de Châtillon = William (Guillaume) de Coucy, Seigneur de Coucy
5. Aubert de Coucy, Seigneur de Dronai = Jeanne de Ville-Savoir
6. Marie de Coucy = Gilles VI de Mailly, Baron de Mailly
7. Colart (Nicholas) de Mailly, Baron de Mailly = Marie de Mailly, Dame de Lorsignol, a cousin
8. Jean II de Mailly, Baron de Mailly = Catherine de Mamez
9. Antoinette de Mailly = Philippe de Noyelles, Vicomte de Langle
10. Nicole de Noyelles = Jean de Villers
11. Isabella de Villers = Jan de Carpentier
12. Roelant de Carpentier = Josina van Hecke
13. Jan de Carpentier = Sophia van Culenburg (or Culemburg)
14. **Maria de Carpentier** of Del. = Jean (Jan) Paul **Jaquet.**

Sources: Edwin Jacquett Sellers, *De Carpentier Allied Ancestry: Ancestry of Maria de Carpentier, Wife of Jean Paul Jaquet* (1928); *ES,* charts for Coucy, Chatillon-St. Pol, and Brittany.

The Royal Descents of 500 Immigrants

1. (St.) Louis IX, King of France, d. 1270 = Margaret of Provence

2. Robert of France, Count of Clermont = Beatrix of Burgundy and Bourbon

3. Louis I, Duke of Bourbon = Marie of Hainault

4. Margaret of Bourbon = Jean II, Sire de Sully

5. Louis, Sire de Sully = Isabel de Craon

6. Marie de Sully = Guy V, Sire de la Trémoille

7. George, Seigneur de la Trémoille, Count of Guines = Catherine d'Isle-Bouchard

8. Louis I de la Trémoille, Vicomte de Thouars = Marguerite d'Amboise

9. Antoinette de la Trémoille = Charles de Husson, Count de Tonnerre

10. Madeleine de Husson = Jean d'Estampes, Seigneur de la Ferté-Nabert

11. Marguerite d'Estampes = Nectaire de Senneterre, Seigneur de Saint-Nectaire

12. Marguerite de Senneterre = Francois de Morlhon, Seigneur d'Asprières

13. Marguerite de Morlhon = Jean III de Lupé, Seigneur de Maravat

14. Percide de Lupé = Pierre II de Rapin, Baron de Maivers

15. Jacob de Rapin, Seigneur de Thoyras = Jeanne de Pelisson

16. Paul de Rapin, Seigneur de Thoyras, historian = Marie Anne Testard

17. Susanne Esther de Rapin = Jean de Coninck

18. Frederic de Coninck = Marie de Joncourt

19. Marie Henriette de Coninck = Christian Wilhelm Duntzfelt

20. Cecile Olivia Duntzfelt = Jacques Louis Garrigue

21. **Rudolph Pierre Garrigue** of N.Y. (born in Copenhagen, died in Vienna) = Charlotte Lydia Whiting. Their

daughter, Charlotte Garrigue, married Tomas Jan (later Tomas Garrigue) Masaryk (1850-1937), president of Czechoslovakia, 1918-35. Their son, Jan Garrigue Masaryk (1886-1948), who married Mrs. Frances Anita Crane Leatherbee of Chicago, was Czech foreign minister, 1940-48 (of the provisional government in London during World War II).

Sources: *NEXUS* 5(1988):94-98, Ruth Crawford Mitchell, *Alice Garrigue Masaryk, 1879-1966* (1980), pp. 3-16, C.H.N. Garrigues, *Silhouetten Garrigues'scher und Einiger Anderer Profile* (1930) and Patricia Wright Strati, *Our Garrigues Ancestors: French Huguenots with Connections to Charlemagne & European Royalty* (1992), pp. 116-21, 141-42 esp., confirmed by *ES* (charts for France and Bourbon), *Anselme* (vol. 2, pp. 858-59 for Sully; vol. 4, 4th ed., pp. 135-39 for de la Trémoille, pp. 842-43 for Saint-Nectaire), *Courcelles* (vol. 4, pp. 44-46 for Lupé), *DNB* (Paul de Rapin) and *Der Deutsche Herold* 55 (1924):20-22 (generations 1-16). Generations 1-18 of this descent are also outlined in *Généalogie Magazine* #76 (Oct. 1989), p. 37, which cites *Les de Coninck*, Mulhouse, 1978.

The Royal Descents of 500 Immigrants

1. (St.) Louis IX, King of France, d. 1270 = Margaret of Provence

2. Robert of France, Count of Clermont = Beatrix of Burgundy and Bourbon

3. Louis I, Duke of Bourbon = Marie of Hainault

4. James I, Count of la Marche = Jeanne de Châtillon-St. Pol

5. John I, Count of la Marche and Vendôme = Catherine of Vendôme

6. Jean I de Bourbon, Seigneur de Carency = Jeanne de Vendômois

7. Pierre de Bourbon, Seigneur de Carency = Philippote de Plaines

8. (illegitimate by ----) Jeanne Catherine de Bourbon = Bertrand de Sallmard, Seigneur de Ressiz and de la Fay

9. Claude I de Sallmard, Seigneur de Ressiz and de la Fay = Charlotte de Sarron

10. Claude II de Sallmard, Seigneur de Ressiz and de la Fay = Marguerite de Tenay

11. Geoffrey I de Sallmard, Seigneur de Ressiz, de la Fay, and Montfort = Madeleine de Foudras

12. Geoffrey II de Sallmard, Seigneur de Ressiz and de la Fay = Eléonore de Guillens

13. Jean de Sallmard, Seigneur de Montfort = (1) Claude de Virieux; (2) Just Madeleine de Grammont

14. (probably by 2) Louis de Sallmard, Seigneur de Montfort = Isabeau de Vangelet

15. Philippe Guillaume de Sallmard, Seigneur de Ressiz, Montfort and Roche-Pingolet = Francoise de Guillet

16. Raymond I de Sallmard, Seigneur de Ressiz, Montfort, and Roche-Pingolet = Marie Jeanne Francoise de Ponchon

17. Raymond II de Sallmard, Vicomte de Ressiz = Marie Anne de Chabrières

18. Pauline de Sallmard = Jean Baptiste Joseph, Count de Sibour

19. **Jean Antonin Gabriel, Vicomte de Sibour,** of Washington, D.C., French consular officer = Mary Louisa Johnson. Their younger son was noted architect Jules Gabriel Henri de Sibour, also of Washington, D.C., who married Margaret Marie Clagett.

Sources: Alfred Johnson, *History and Genealogy of One Line of Descent From Captain Edward Johnson* (1914), pp. 111-12, 125-27 (de Sibour); *Saint-Allais,* vols. 2, pp. 155-57 (de Sallmard), 8, pp. 279-80 (de Sibour); *ES,* tables for France, Bourbon, Bourbon-Vendome, Bourbon-Carency and illegitimate children of the Bourbon house (new ser., vol. 2, 1984, table 12, vol. 3, part I, 1984, tables 72, 74, 76, and vol. 3, part 2, 1983, table 331). This line was suggested to me by Mr. Brice McAdoo Clagett of Washington, D.C.

The Royal Descents of 500 Immigrants

1. Ferdinand III, King of Castile, d. 1252 = (2) Joan of Dammartin, Countess of Ponthieu

2. Ferdinand of Castile, Count of Aumale = Laure de Montfort

3. John I, Count of Aumale = Ida of Meullent

4. Laure of Ponthieu = Guy IV de Mauvoisin, Seigneur de Rosny

5. Guy V de Mauvoisin, Seigneur de Rosny = Roberta de Baumez

6. Laure de Mauvoisin = Robert de Beaussart, Seigneur de Wingles

7. Béatrix de Beaussart = Hugh de Melun, Seigneur d'Antoing

8. Philippa de Melun = Jacques I, Seigneur de Montmorency, a descendant of Louis VII, King of France, d. 1180, and Eleanor of Aquitaine (see *ES*, tables for Montmorency, Brienne, and Champagne)

9. Jean II, Seigneur de Montmorency = Jeanne de Fosseux

10. Louis de Montmorency, Seigneur de Fosseux = Marguerite de Wastines

11. Ogier de Montmorency, Baron de Wastines = Anne de Vendégies

12. Jean de Montmorency, Baron de Wastines = Anne de Blois

13. Jeanne de Montmorency = Antoine de Montigny, Seigneur de Noyelle

14. Georges de Montigny, Seigneur de Noyelle = Charlotte de Nouvelles

15. Anne de Montigny = Paul de Carondelet, Seigneur de Mousty, Baron de Noyelle

16. Antoine de Carondelet, Baron de Noyelle, Vicomte de la Hestre = Jeanne Louise, Countess de Lannoy

17. Alexandre de Carondelet, Baron de Noyelle, Vicomte de la Hestre = Marie Bonne de Bacquehem

18. Jean Louis de Carondelet, Baron de Noyelle, Vicomte de la Hestre and du Langue = Marie Angelique Bernard de Rasoir

19. **Francois Luis Hector de Carondelet and de Noyelle, Vicomte de la Hestre and du Langue** (c. 1748-1807), Spanish governor of Louisiana and West Florida = Maria Castanos Aragorri Uriarte y Olivide.

Sources: *New Orleans Genesis* 16(1977):123-36; *ES*, charts for Montmorency (old ser., vol. 3, 1956, tables 122, 119 and 113), Melun (new ser., vol. 7, 1979, table 55), Aumale (new ser., vol. 3, part 1, 1984, table 124B) and Castile; Lindsay L. Brook, ed., *Studies in Genealogy and Family History in Tribute to Charles Evans on the Occasion of his Eightieth Birthday* (1989), pp. 381-82 (#40), 389 (#66), 396 (#103), 398 (#112) (generations 1-5) and *D de la N* (Mauvoisin).

The Royal Descents of 500 Immigrants

1. Alphonso IX, King of Leon, d. 1230 = Berengaria of Castile, daughter of Alphonso VIII, King of Castile, d. 1214, and Eleanor Plantagenet, daughter of Henry II, King of England, d. 1189, and Eleanor of Aquitaine

2. Berengaria of Leon = John de Brienne, King of Jerusalem and Emperor of Constantinople, d. 1237

3. Jean de Brienne = Jeanne de Châteaudun

4. Blanche de Brienne = Sir William de Fienes

5. Margaret de Fienes = Edmund Mortimer, 1st Baron Mortimer

6. Maud Mortimer = Theobald de Verdun, 2nd Baron Verdun

7. Margery de Verdun = Sir John Crophull

8. Thomas Crophull = Sybil Delabere

9. Agnes Crophull = Sir Walter Devereux

10. Sir Walter Devereux = Elizabeth Bromwich

11. Elizabeth Devereux = John Milborne

12. Sir Simon Milborne = Jane Baskerville

13. Anne Milborne = William Rudhall

14. Elizabeth Rudhall = William Hugford

15. John Hugford = Elizabeth Fettiplace

16. Margaret Hugford = John Hugford, a cousin

17. Margaret Hugford = William Laurence

18. Elizabeth Laurence = George Gwinnett

19. George Gwinnett = Elizabeth Randle

20. George Gwinnett = Elizabeth Coxe

21. Samuel Gwinnett = Anne Emes

22. **Button Gwinnett** (c. 1735-1777), president (governor) of Ga., merchant, planter, signer of the Declaration of Independence = Anne Bourne.

Sources: Charles Francis Jenkins, *Button Gwinnett, Signer of the Declaration of Independence* (1926), pp. 7-16; T.F. Fenwick and W.C.

Metcalfe, eds., *Visitation of Gloucester, 1682-83* (1884), pp. 84-86 (Gwinnett), 110 (Laurence); John Fetherston, ed., *Visitation of Warwickshire, 1619* (*HSPVS*, vol. 12, 1877), p. 337 and Sir John Maclean and W.C. Heane, eds., *Visitation of Gloucestershire, 1623* (*HSPVS*, vol. 21, 1885), p. 86 (Hugford); F.W. Weaver, *Visitation of Herefordshire, 1569* (1886), pp. 93 (Rudhall), 90-91 (Milborne); *MGH*, 5th ser. , vol. 3 (1918-19), pp. 198-99 and *Whitney*, appendix XI (Milborne); *BP* (Devereux, viscounts Hereford); George F. Farnham, *Leicestershire Medieval Pedigrees* (1925), p. 31 (Crophull); *CP* (Verdun, Mortimer) and *AR7*, lines 114, 120.

The Royal Descents of 500 Immigrants

1. John "Lackland," King of England, d. 1216 = (2) Isabel of Angoulême

2. (illegitimate by Clemence, possibly Clemence Dauntsey, wife of Nicholas de Verdun) Joan Plantagenet = Llywelyn Fawr ap Iorwerth, Prince of North Wales

3. David, Prince of North Wales (Dafydd ap Llywelyn Fawr) = Isabel de Braose

4. (illegitimate by ----) Llywelyn ap Dafydd, constable of Rhuddlau = ----

5. Cynwrig ap Llywelyn = Angharad ferch Thomas ap Gwion

6. Dafydd Llwyd ap Cynwrig = Annes ferch Gwyn ap Madog

7. Mawd ferch Dafydd Llwyd = Dafydd Goch ap Trahaearn Goch ap Madog

8. Ieuan Goch ap Dafydd Goch = Efa ferch Einion ap Celynin

9. Madog Goch ap Ieuan Goch = (perhaps) Ales ferch Ieuan ap Madog Gwenwys

10. Deicws Ddu ap Madog Goch = Gwen ferch Ieuan Dew ap Meurig

11. Einion ap Deicws Ddu = Morfudd ferch Mathew ap Llywarch

12. Hywel ab Einion = Mali Llwyd ferch Llywelyn ap Ieuan

13. Gruffudd ap Hywel = Gwenllian ferch Einion ap Ieuan Llwyd

14. Lewys ap Gruffudd = Ellyw ferch Edward ap Ieuan

15. Robert Lewis = Gwerful ferch Llywelyn ap Dafydd

16. Hugh Roberts = ----

17. Robert Pugh
= Elizabeth Williams
of Pa., ARD, SETH

16. Evan Robert Lewis =
Jane, daughter of
Cadwaladr ap Maredudd
(and ----), son of
Maredudd ap Ieuan and
Elen, daughter of
Cadwaladr ap Robert
and Jane ferch Maredudd
ap Ieuan, SETH

17. John ap Evan (son of Evan Robert Lewis and Jane ferch Cadwaladr ap Maredudd) = ----

18. **Jane John** of Pa. = Robert **Cadwalader**, ARD, SETH, of Pa. (their children and descendants took the surname Roberts)

18. Margaret John = David Evans

19. **Gwen Evans** of Pa. = Thomas **Foulke**, son of Edward Foulke of Pa., ARD, SETH, and Mrs. Ellen Hughes Foulke, ARD, SETH

17. Owen ap Evan (brother of John ap Evan) = Gainor John

18. **Robert Owen** of Pa. = Rebecca Owen (sometimes called Rebecca Humphrey[s]) of Pa., ARD, SETH.

18. **Jane Owen** of Pa. = Hugh **Roberts** of Pa., ARD, SETH, son of Robert Pugh (see above) and Mrs. Elizabeth Williams Pugh of Pa., ARD, SETH.

18. Ellen Owen = Cadwalader Thomas

19. **John Cadwalader** of Pa. = Martha Jones, daughter of Edward Jones and Mary Wynne, daughter of Dr. Thomas Wynne of Pa., ARD, SETH, and Martha Buttall.

17. Griffith ap Evan (brother of John and Owen ap Evan) = ----

18. Edward Griffith = ----

19. **Jane Edward** of Pa. = John **Jones**, son of Rees Jones and Mrs. Hannah Price Jones David Evans of Pa., ARD, SETH.

17. Evan Lloyd Evan (brother of John, Owen, and Griffith ap Evan) = ----

18. **Thomas Evans** of Pa. = (1) Anne ----; (2) Mrs. Hannah Price Jones David of Pa. (Thomas and Hannah left no NDTPS).

18. **Cadwalader Evans** of Pa. = Ellen Morris of Pa., ARD, SETH.

Immigrant members of this family who left no NDTPS include the following:

1-5. Robert and Griffith John or Jones, brothers of Mrs. Jane John Cadwalader; Gwen Jones, their sister, wife of John ---- and John Humphrey; Margaret Evans, their neice (and a sister of Mrs. Gwen Evans Foulke), who married Robert Humphrey; and William John, their half-brother (son of John ap Evan and Margaret John), who married Jane Pugh or Hughes, sister of Mrs. Ellen Hughes Foulke

6-10. Hugh Griffith (= Mary ----) and Catherine Griffith, wife of John Williams, an uncle and aunt of Mrs. Jane Edward Jones; Griffith Edward (= Lowry Evans) and Margaret Edward, wife of David George, a brother and sister of Mrs. Jane Edward Jones; and Catherine Robert, wife of William Morgan and daughter (by ----) of Robert Griffith, a brother of Hugh and Mrs. Williams and an uncle of Mrs. Jones, Griffith Edward, and Mrs. George

11-14. Robert Evans and Sarah Evans, wife of Evan Pugh, a brother and sister of Thomas and Cadwalader Evans; and Robert Jones (= Gainor Lloyd, widow of Rowland ---- and sister of Robert Lloyd of Pa., ARD, SETH) and Cadwalader Jones, brothers, sons of John ---- and Ellen Evans, sister of the half-blood of Thomas and Cadwalader Evans (both wives of Evan Lloyd Evan are unknown).

Sources: *WFP* 2, "Owen, Evans and Alled Families," esp. pp. 75-100, 108 (generations 7-19, Mawd ferch Dafydd Llwyd to the progeny of Evan Robert Lewis); *WFP* 1, pedigree XXIV, p. 220 (Robert Pugh and family) and pedigree I, pp. 15-21 and chart facing (John Cadwalader); *Bartrum 1*, pp. 446-47, 867-68, *Bartrum 2*, p. 1657 (generations 1-14). For the identification of Clemence, mother of Joan, Princess of Wales, see a forthcoming article in *TG* by Douglas Richardson of Tucson, Arizona; this identification is repeated on several subsequent charts.

The Royal Descents of 500 Immigrants

1. John "Lackland," King of England, d. 1216 = (2) Isabel of Angoulême

2. (illegitimate by Clemence, possibly Clemence Dauntsey, wife of Nicholas de Verdun) Joan Plantagenet = Llywelyn Fawr ap Iorwerth, Prince of North Wales

3. David, Prince of North Wales (Dafydd ap Llywelyn Fawr) = Isabel de Braose

4. (illegitimate by ----) Llywelyn ap Dafydd, constable of Rhuddlau = ----

5. Cynwrig ap Llywelyn = Angharad ferch Thomas ap Gwion

6. Dafydd Llwyd ap Cynwrig = Annes ferch Gwyn ap Madog

7. Mawd ferch Dafydd Llwyd = Dafydd Goch ap Trahaearn Goch ap Madog

8. Ieuan Goch ap Dafydd Goch = Efa ferch Einion ap Celynin

9. Morfudd ferch Ieuan Goch = Maredudd ap Hywel ap Tudur

10. Ieuan ap Maredudd = Lleucu ferch Hywel ap Meurig Fychan

11. Maredudd ap Ieuan = Margred ferch Einion ap Ithel

12. John ap Maredudd = Gwenhwyfar ferch Gronwy ap Ieuan

13. Elen ferch John = Hywel Fychan ap Hywel ap Gruffudd

14. Mallt ferch Hywel Fychan ap Hywel = Hywel Llwyd ap Dafydd o'r Bala, son (by Lowri ferch Dafydd ap Ieuan or Gwenllian ferch William ap Gruffudd) of Dafydd o'r Bala ap Maredudd, SETH

15. Thomas Gethin ap Hywel Llwyd = Catrin ferch Dafydd ap Gethin

16. Margred ferch Thomas Gethin = Huw ap Thomas

17. William ap Huw = ----

18. Ellis Williams (Ellis William ap Huw) = Margaret John

19. Gwen Williams = Hugh ap Cadwaladr ap Rhys
20. **Ellen Hughes** (Hugh or Pugh) of Pa. = Edward **Foulke** of Pa., ARD, SETH. John Pugh and Jane Pugh or Hughes, wife of William John, a brother and sister of Mrs. Ellen Hughes Foulke, also immigrated to Pa., but left no NDTPS.
19. Eleanor Williams (sister of Gwen) = John Morris
20. **Ellen Morris** of Pa. = Cadwalader **Evans** of Pa., ARD, SETH.

15. Lowri ferch Hywel Llwyd (sister of Thomas Gethin) = Edward ap John Wyn, whose mother was not, according to Bartrum, Catrin, daughter of Hywel ap Jenkin and Mary Kynaston, as claimed in *WFP* 1, pedigree XVIII, p. 116 and chart following
16. Watkyn ap Edward = Grace, daughter of Cadwaladr ap Robert and Jane ferch Maredudd ap Ieuan, SETH
17. Edward ap Watkyn = ---- ferch Thomas ap Robert ap Gruffudd
18. John ab Edward = Jane ----
18. Agnes Edwards = William Owen
19. Edward ap John = ----
19. Elizabeth Williams of Pa. = Robert Pugh, ARD, SETH
20. **William Edwards** of Pa. = (1) = (2) Jane Jones.
20. Katherine Roberts (she left no NDTPS)
20. **John Edwards** of Pa. = ----.
20. Evan ab Edward (brother of William and John Edwards) = ----
21. **John Evans** of Pa. = Mary Hughes.

19. Gainor John (sister of Edward ap John) = John Thomas Ellis
20. **Hugh Jones** of Pa. = (1) ---- ----; (2) Margaret David; (3) Anne Williams; (4) Margaret Edwards.

20. **Hugh Roberts** of Pa. (brother of Mrs. Katherine Roberts Edwards) = Jane Owen of Pa., a cousin, ARD, SETH.

20. **Gainor Roberts** of Pa. (sister of Katherine and Hugh) = John **Roberts** of (Pencoyd, Lower Merion) Pa., ARD, SETH.

Sources: *WFP* 1, pedigree XXII, pp. 141-42 (progeny of Ellis Williams), pedigree XVIII, pp. 117-25 (Edwards and Evans), p. 149 and pedigree XXIV, p. 220 (plus *Merion,* pp. 98-105) (Roberts) and chart between pp. 116-17 (generations 9-17, Edward ap Watkyn); W.W. Harrison, *The Royal Ancestry of George Leib Harrison of Philadelphia* (1914), pp. 7-10 (Jones): *Bartrum 1,* pp. 446-47, 867, 457, *Bartrum 2,* pp. 845-46, 23, 1481, 1479 (generations 1-15).

The Royal Descents of 500 Immigrants

1. John "Lackland," King of England, d. 1216 = (2) Isabel of Angoulême

2. (illegitimate by Clemence, possibly Clemence Dauntsey, wife of Nicholas de Verdun) Joan Plantagenet = Llywelyn Fawr ap Iorwerth, Prince of North Wales

3. David, Prince of North Wales (Dafydd ap Llywelyn Fawr) = Isabel de Braose

4. (illegitimate by ----) Annes ferch Dafydd = Elise ap Iorwerth ab Owain Brogyntyn

5. Madog ab Elise = (1) ----; (2) ---- ferch Llywelyn

6. (maternity uncertain) Efa ferch Madog = Gruffudd ap Llywelyn ap Cynwrig

7. Einion ap Gruffudd = Tangwystl ferch Rhydderch ap Ieuan Llwyd

8. Gruffudd ab Einion = Lowri, daughter of Tudur ap Gruffudd Fychan (and Mawd ferch Ienaf ab Abba), brother of Welsh hero Owen Glendower and son of Gruffudd Fychan ap Gruffudd o'r Rhuddallt, SETH, and Elen ferch Thomas

9. Elise ap Gruffudd = Margred ferch Jenkin ap Ieuan

10. Dafydd Llwyd ab Elise = Gwenhwyfar ferch Richard Llwyd

11. John Wyn = Elsbeth Mostyn

12. (illegitimate by Agnes Lloyd) David Yale = Frances Lloyd

13. Thomas Yale = Anne Lloyd, later of Conn., ARD, SETH

14. **David Yale** of Conn. = Ursula Knight (parents of Elihu Yale, 1649-1721, official of the East India Company and benefactor of Yale College, for whom it was named).

14. **Thomas Yale** of Conn. = Mary Turner.

14. **Anne Yale** of Conn. = Edward **Hopkins** (c. 1600-1657), colonial governor of Conn.

10. Lowri ferch Elise (sister of David Llwyd ab Elise) = Rheinallt ap Gruffudd ap Rhys

11. Mary ferch Rheinallt = Robert ap Dafydd Llwyd

12. Thomas ap Robert = Catrin ferch Robert ap Gruffudd

13. Ieuan ap Thomas = Dorothea Evans

14. Thomas ap Ieuan = Catrin ferch William Dafydd

15. Foulke ap Thomas = Lowri ferch Edward ap Dafydd

16. **Edward Foulke** of Pa. = Ellen Hughes (Hugh or Pugh) of Pa., ARD, SETH.

13. Mary ferch Thomas ap Robert (sister of Ieuan ap Thomas) = Richard of Tyddin Tyfod

14. Rhys ap Richard = ----

15. Gruffudd ap Rhys = ----

16. Richard Price = ----

17. **Hannah Price** of Pa. = (1) Rees **Jones**; (2) Ellis **David**; (3) Thomas **Evans** of Pa., ARD, SETH. Edward Price (= Mably Owen) and Jane Price, wife of Cadwalader Morgan, a brother and sister of Hannah, also immigrated to Pa., but left no NDTPS.

Sources: *AR7*, line 251 and *TAG* 32(1976):71-80, 56(1980):101-5 (Yales); *CVR*, pp. 69-82 (with some errors) (Foulke); *Merion*, pp. 80-81 (also with some errors), 94-95 (Foulke and Mrs. Evans); *Bartrum 1*, pp. 446-47, 51, 727, *Bartrum 2*, pp. 1415, 1416, 116, 1486 (generations 1-11 and 1-12).

The Royal Descents of 500 Immigrants

1. John "Lackland," King of England, d. 1216 = (2) Isabel of Angoulême

2. (illegitimate by ---- de Warenne) Richard FitzRoy = Rohese of Dover

3. Lorette de Dover = Sir William Marmion

4. John Marmion, 1st Baron Marmion = Isabel ----

5. John Marmion, 2nd Baron Marmion = Maud Furnival

6. Avice Marmion = John Grey, 1st Baron Grey of Rotherfield

7. Sir Robert Grey, later Marmion = Lora St. Quentin

8. Elizabeth Marmion = Henry FitzHugh, 3rd Baron FitzHugh

9. William FitzHugh, 4th Baron FitzHugh = Margery Willoughby

10. Lora FitzHugh = Sir John Constable

11. Isabel Constable = Stephen Thorpe

12. Margaret Thorpe = John Newton

13. John Newton = Margaret Grimston

14. John Newton = Mary ----

15. Lancelot Newton = Mary Lee

16. **Ellen Newton** of Mass. = Edward **Carleton** of Mass., ARD, SETH.

11. Joan Constable (sister of Isabel) = Sir William Mallory

12. Sir John Mallory = Margaret Thwaites

13. Sir William Mallory = Jane Norton

14. Sir William Mallory = Ursula Gale

15. Thomas Mallory, Dean of Chester = Elizabeth Vaughan

16. Thomas Mallory = (1) Jane ----; (2) Frances ----

17. (prob. by Jane) **Roger Mallory** of Va. = ----. His brother, Thomas Mallory of Charles City Co., Va., left no NDTPS. Rev. Philip Mallory of York Co., Va., son

of 15 above and uncle of Roger and Thomas, returned to England and also left no NDTPS.

16. Martha (or Katherine) Mallory (sister of Thomas) = John Batte

17. **Thomas Batte** of Va. = (1) Mary ----; (2) Mrs. Amy ---- Butler.

17. **Henry Batte** of Va. = Mary Lounds. William Batte, a brother of Thomas and Henry, also came to Va., but left no NDTPS.

Sources: *AR7*, lines 121D, 219, 218, 26 and *MCS4*, line 109; Walter Lee Sheppard, Jr., "The Ancestry of Edward Carleton and Ellen Newton, His Wife" (microfilm, 1978), see under Edward Carleton; *VHG*, pp. 103-16, *GVFVM* 4:250-70 and *VGE*, pp. 100-4 (Mallory, Batte).

The Royal Descents of 500 Immigrants

1. John "Lackland," King of England, d. 1216 = (2) Isabel of Angoulême
2. (illegitimate by ---- de Warenne) Richard FitzRoy = Rohese of Dover
3. Lorette de Dover = Sir William Marmion
4. John Marmion, 1st Baron Marmion = Isabel ----
5. John Marmion, 2nd Baron Marmion = Maud Furnival
6. Joan Marmion = Sir John Bernacke
7. Maud Bernacke = Ralph Cromwell, 2nd Baron Cromwell
8. Maud Cromwell = Sir William FitzWilliam
9. Sir John FitzWilliam = Eleanor Greene
10. John FitzWilliam = Helen Villiers
11. Sir William FitzWilliam = Anne Hawes
12. Anne FitzWilliam = Sir Anthony Cooke (their daughters Mildred and Jane Cooke married respectively William Cecil, 1st Baron Burghley, the statesman and minister of Elizabeth I, and Sir Nicholas Bacon, the Lord Keeper and Lord Chancellor; a grandson was Francis Bacon, 1st Viscount St. Albans, the philosopher, scientist, and politician)
13. Sir Richard Cooke = Anna Caunton
14. Philippa Cooke = Hercules Meautys
15. Frances Meautys = Francis Shute, son of Robert Shute and Thomasine Burgoyne, SETH
16. Francis Shute = ----
17. Benjamin Shute = Patience (or Anne) Caryl
18. **Samuel Shute** (1662-1742), colonial governor of Mass., d. unm.
18. Anne Shute = Stephen Offley
19. **Amelia Offley** of Mass. = Sir Francis **Bernard**, 1st Bt. (1712-1779), barrister, colonial governor of N.J. and Mass., ARD, SETH.

Sources: *MCS4*, line 128A and sources cited therein, esp. *Lodge*, vol. 5, pp. 200-1; Walter C. Metcalfe, ed., *Visitations of Essex, 1552, 1558, 1570, 1612 and 1634*, vol. 1 (*HSPVS*, vol. 13, 1878), pp. 77, 247 (Meautys), 39 (Cooke), 198-99 (FitzWilliam); *PCF Yorkshire* (FitzWilliam pedigree); *AR7*, lines 210, 218, 26.

The Royal Descents of 500 Immigrants

1. John "Lackland," King of England, d. 1216 = (2) Isabel of Angoulême

2. Richard Plantagenet, King of the Romans = (1) Isabel Marshall; (2) Sancha of Provence; (3) Beatrix of Valkenburg

3. (illegitimate by Joan de Vautort or Valletort) Richard de Cornwall = Joan ----

4. Joan de Cornwall = Sir John Howard

5. Sir John Howard = Alice de Boys

6. Sir Robert Howard = Margery Scales

7. Sir John Howard = Alice Tendring

8. Henry Howard (brother of Sir Robert Howard, husband of Margaret Mowbray, and uncle of John Howard, 1st Duke of Norfolk) = Mary Hussey

9. Elizabeth Howard = Sir Henry Wentworth, son of Sir Roger Wentworth and Margery Despencer, ARD, SETH

10. Margery Wentworth = Sir William Waldegrave

11. Anthony Waldegrave = Elizabeth Gray

12. Thomas Waldegrave = Elizabeth Gurdon, aunt of Brampton Gurdon, husband of Muriel Sedley, SETH, and half-sister of Thomas Appleton, husband of Mary Isaac, SETH

13. Thomas Waldegrave = Margaret Holmstead

14. **Jemima Waldegrave** = Herbert **Pelham** of Mass., 1st treasurer of Harvard College, ARD, SETH.

11. Margaret Waldegrave (sister of Anthony) = Sir John St. John

12. Alice St. John = Edmund Elmes

13. Elizabeth Elmes = Sir Edward Apsley

14. **Alice Apsley** = (1) Sir John **Boteler**; (2) George **Fenwick** (1603-1656/7), colonist, a founder of Saybrook, Conn.

The Royal Descents of 500 Immigrants

Sources: *MCS4*, line 75A, *AR7*, lines 200, 258 and *TAG* 18 (1941-42):139-44 (for Mrs. Pelham); *BP* (Norfolk), *Cornewall*, p. 157, and *NEHGR* 119(1965):98, 101-2; D.G.C. Elwes, *A History of the Castles, Mansions, and Manors of Western Sussex* (1876), chart opp. p. 250 (Apsley), Walter C. Metcalfe, ed., *Visitations of Northamptonshire, 1564 and 1618-19* (1887), p. 18 (Elmes), F.A. Blaydes, ed., *Visitations of Bedfordshire 1566, 1582 and 1634* (*HSPVS*, vol. 19, 1884), p. 53 (St. John), Walter C. Metcalfe, ed., *Visitations of Essex, 1552, 1558, 1570, 1612 and 1634*, vol. 1 (*HSPVS*, vol. 13, 1878), pp. 120, 122, 309-10, 515 (Waldegrave), and *Wentworth*, vol. 1, pp. 27-28. Further documentation of the identity and parentage of Joan de Cornwall, wife of Sir John Howard, would be welcome.

The Royal Descents of 500 Immigrants

1. John "Lackland," King of England, d. 1216 = (2) Isabel of Angoulême
2. (illegitimate by ----) Isabel la Blanche = Sir Robert FitzUva
3. Richard FitzUva = ----
4. Isabel FitzUva = Sir Belym Heligan
5. Richard Heligan = Margaret Prideaux
6. Isabel Heligan = John Petit
7. Sir John Petit = Joanna Carminow
8. Michael Petit = Amicia Bloyou
9. John Petit = Margaret Roscarrock
10. John Petit = Margaret Trenowith
11. John Petit = Jane Anthorne
12. Jane Petit = (1) Thomas Trevanion; (2) John Killigrew
13. (by 2) Elizabeth Killigrew = Thomas Treffry
14. John Treffry = Emilyn Tresithny
15. Martha Treffry = Thomas Dyckwood, alias Peters
16. **Hugh Peter(s)** (1598-1660) of Mass., Puritan clergyman and Cromwellian politician = (1) Mrs. Elizabeth Cooke Reade; (2) Deliverance Sheffield.

13. (by 1) John Trevanion (half-brother of Elizabeth Killigrew) = Janet Treffry
14. Sir William Trevanion = Anne Edgcombe
15. Sir Hugh Trevanion = Elizabeth Pollard
16. Richard Trevanion = Margaret Chamond
17. Richard Trevanion = Mary Rolle
18. Nathaniel Trevanion = Elizabeth Sawle
19. Richard Trevanion = ---- Maunder
10. Sir Nicholas Trevanion = Elizabeth ----
21. Arabella Trevanion = William Barlow
22. ---- Barlow (daughter) = George Smith

23. **Arabella Maria Smith** of Pa. = Alexander James **Dallas** (1759-1817), lawyer, secretary of the treasury.

Sources: *DAB* (Peter[s]), *VC,* pp. 459-60 (misnumbered 559-60 -- Treffry), 267-68, 494-95, 30 (Killigrew, Petit, Heligan, FitzUva), 501, 504-6 (Trevanion); Raymond Walters, Jr., *Alexander James Dallas, Lawyer, Politician, Financier, 1759-1817* (1943), pp. 9-11 (and Mrs. Dallas's *Autobiographical Memoir for Her Children,* mentioned on p. 240). Further documentation concerning Isabel la Blanche, wife of Sir Robert FitzUva and said to be an illegitimate daughter of King John, as shown above (and see *NEHGR* 119[1965]: 98, 101 [footnote 41]), would be desirable.

The Royal Descents of 500 Immigrants

1. John "Lackland," King of England, d. 1216 = (2) Isabel of Angoulême

2. (illegitimate by Clemence, possibly Clemence Dauntsey, wife of Nicholas de Verdun) Joan Plantagenet = Llywelyn Fawr ap Iorwerth, Prince of North Wales

3. David, Prince of North Wales (Dafydd ap Llywelyn Fawr) = Isabel de Braose

4. (illegitimate by ----) Llywelyn ap Dafydd, constable of Rhuddlau = ----

5. Cynwrig ap Llywelyn = Angharad ferch Thomas ap Gwion

6. Dafydd Llwyd ap Cynwrig = Annes ferch Gwyn ap Madog

7. Mawd ferch Dafydd Llwyd = Dafydd Goch ap Trahaearn Goch ap Madog

8. Ieuan Goch ap Dafydd Goch = Efa ferch Einion ap Celynin

9. Maredudd ap Ieuan Goch = Morfudd ferch Gruffudd ap Llywelyn Fychan

10. Lleucu ferch Maredudd = Gruffudd ap Cynwrig ap Bleddyn Llwyd

11. Dafydd Llwyd ap Gruffudd = Gwen ferch Gruffudd Goch ap Ieuan

12. Dyddgu ferch Dafydd Llwyd = Llywelyn ap Gruffudd Llwyd ap Robin

13. Maredudd Llwyd ap Llywelyn = Jonet ferch Gwilym ap Llywelyn Llwyd

14. John ap Maredudd Llwyd = Margred ferch Morus Gethin ap Rhys

15. Maredudd Llwyd ap John = Jonet Conwy

16. George Lloyd, Bishop of Chester = Anne Wilkinson

17. **Anne Lloyd** of Conn. = (1) Thomas **Yale**, ARD, SETH (their three children came to Conn. with their mother and step-father; (2) Theophilus **Eaton** (c. 1590-1657/8),

colonial statesman and merchant, governor of the New Haven Colony.

Sources: *TAG* 52(1976):142-44; *Bartrum 1*, pp. 446-47, 867, 869, 512; *Bartrum 2*, pp. 975, 1288-89 (generations 1-15).

The Royal Descents of 500 Immigrants

1. John "Lackland," King of England, d. 1216 = (2) Isabel of Angoulême

2. (illegitimate by Clemence, possibly Clemence Dauntsey, wife of Nicholas de Verdun) Joan Plantagenet = Llywelyn Fawr ap Iorwerth, Prince of North Wales

3. David, Prince of North Wales (Dafydd ap Llywelyn Fawr) = Isabel de Braose

4. (illegitimate by ----) Annes ferch Dafydd = Elise ap Iorwerth ab Owain Brogyntyn

5. Madog ab Elise = (1) ----; (2) ---- ferch Llywelyn

6. (maternity uncertain) Efa ferch Madog = Gruffudd ap Llywelyn ap Cynwrig

7. Einion ap Gruffudd = Tangwystl ferch Rhydderch ap Ieuan Llwyd

8. Ieuan ab Einion = Angharad ferch Dafydd

9. Mali ferch Ieuan = Dafydd ap Rhys ap Ieuan

10. Lowri ferch Dafydd = Gruffudd ap Hywel ap Madog

11. Margred ferch Gruffudd = Morus ap Gruffudd ap Ieuan

12. Thomas ap Morus = ---- (Bartrum gives him only a daughter, Jonet Anwyl, by Catrin ferch Edward ap Gruffudd)

13. Robert Thomas Morris = ----

14. Richard Roberts = Margaret Evans

15. **John Roberts** of (Pencoyd, lower Merion) Pa. = Gainor Roberts of Pa., ARD, SETH.

Sources: *Merion*, pp. 100-5 (generations 11-15); *CRFP*, vol. 1, pp. 451-54 (generations 5-15); *Bartrum 1*, pp. 446-47, 51, 727-28, *Bartrum 2*, pp. 117, 807, 803 (generations 1-12). Further research should be undertaken to confirm the parentage of Robert Thomas Morris.

The Royal Descents of 500 Immigrants

1. John "Lackland," King of England, d. 1216 = (2) Isabel of Angoulême

2. (illegitimate by Clemence, possibly Clemence Dauntsey, wife of Nicholas de Verdun) Joan Plantagenet = Llywelyn Fawr ap Iorwerth, Prince of North Wales

3. David, Prince of North Wales (Dafydd ap Llywelyn Fawr) = Isabel de Braose

4. (illegitimate by ----) Annes ferch Dafydd = Elise ap Iorwerth ab Owain Brogyntyn

5. Madog ab Elise = (1) ----; (2) ---- ferch Llywelyn

6. (maternity uncertain) Lleucu ferch Madog = Gronwy Llwyd ab Y Penwyn

7. Margred ferch Gronwy Llwyd = Hywel y Gadair ap Gruffudd ap Madog

8. Gronwy ap Hywel y Gadair = (1) Gwen ferch Gruffudd; (2) ---- ferch Gronwy

9. (maternity uncertain) Tudur ap Gronwy = Gwerful ferch Ieuan ab Einion

10. (not by Gwerful) Mali ferch Tudur = Madog ap Ieuan

11. Dafydd ap Madog = Mali ferch Gruffudd (Dafydd and Mali left two daughters and a son, Thomas, according to Bartrum, but no Dafydd Fychan)

12. Dafydd Fychan ap Dafydd = ----

13. Huw ap Dafydd Fychan = ----

14. Ellis ap Huw = ----

15. William Ellis = ----

16. William ap William = ----

17. **John Williams** of Pa. = (1) Mary Evans; (2) Mrs. Catherine ---- Edwards.

Sources: *CVR*, pp. 301-5 (generations 10-17); *Bartrum 1*, pp. 446-47, 51, 694, 751-52, *Bartrum 2*, p. 155 (generations 1-11). Further research should be undertaken to confirm the last seven generations of this descent (the immigrant's patrilineal descent from Dafydd ap Madog).

The Royal Descents of 500 Immigrants

1. John "Lackland," King of England, d. 1216 = (2) Isabel of Angoulême
2. (illegitimate by ---- de Warenne) Richard FitzRoy = Rohese of Dover
3. Lorette de Dover = Sir William Marmion
4. John Marmion, 1st Baron Marmion = Isabel ----
5. John Marmion, 2nd Baron Marmion = Maud Furnival
6. Avice Marmion = John Grey, 1st Baron Grey of Rotherfield
7. Maud Grey = Sir Thomas Harcourt
8. Sir Thomas Harcourt = Jane Franceys
9. Sir Robert Harcourt = Margaret Bryan
10. John Harcourt = Anne Norris
11. Sir Robert Harcourt = Agnes Limerick
12. Agnes Harcourt = Sir William Cope
13. Stephen Cope = Anne Saunders
14. Sir Anthony Cope = Anne Stafford
15. Edward Cope = Maud ----
16. John Cope = Margaret ----
17. John Cope = Elizabeth ----
18. **Oliver Cope** of Pa. = Rebecca ----.

Sources: *LDBR* 1, p. 158 (ignore the erroneous descent from Edward I; for Sir Humphrey Stafford and Elizabeth Aylesbury, great-great-grandparents of Anne Stafford above, see *AR7*, lines 55, 187); J.C. Biddle-Cope, *Memoirs of the Copes of Wiltshire* (1881) and *MGH*, 3rd ser., 4(1902):208-10 (Cope); *Salt*, new ser., 35 (1914), pp. 196-204 and chart opposite p. 187 (Harcourt); *AR7*, lines 50, 30, 219, 218.

The Royal Descents of 500 Immigrants

1. John "Lackland," King of England, d. 1216 = (2) Isabel of Angoulême

2. (illegitimate by Clemence, possibly Clemence Dauntsey, wife of Nicholas de Verdun) Joan Plantagenet = Llywelyn Fawr ap Iorwerth, Prince of North Wales

3. David, Prince of North Wales (Dafydd ap Llywelyn Fawr) = Isabel de Braose

4. (illegitimate by ----) Annes ferch Dafydd = Elise ap Iorwerth ab Owain Brogyntyn

5. Madog ab Elise = (1) ----; (2) ---- ferch Llywelyn

6. (maternity uncertain) Lleucu ferch Madog = Gronwy Llwyd ab Y Penwyn

7. Margred ferch Gronwy Llwyd = Hywel y Gadair ap Gruffudd ap Madog

8. Gronwy ap Hywel y Gadair = (1) Gwen ferch Gruffudd; (2) ---- ferch Gronwy

9. (maternity uncertain) Tudur ap Gronwy = Gwerful ferch Ieuan ab Einion

10. Ieuan ap Tudur = ----

11. Gwenhwyfar ferch Ieuan = Maredudd ap Hywel ap Tudur

12. Dafydd o'r Bala ap Maredudd = Annes ferch Rhys ap Maredudd

13. Huw ap Dafydd o'r Bala = ---- (no wife or children are given by Bartrum)

14. Ieuan ap Huw = ----

15. Rhydderch ap Ieuan = ----

16. Ieuan Llwyd ap Rhydderch = ----

17. Thomas Lloyd, poet = Lowry, perhaps a sister of Edward Foulke of Pa., ARD, SETH

18. **Robert Lloyd** of Pa. = Lowry Jones, daughter of Rees Jones and Mrs. Hannah Price Jones David Evans of Pa., ARD, SETH. Thomas Lloyd and Mrs. Gainor Lloyd ---- Jones, wife of Rowland ---- and Robert Jones, a

brother and sister of Robert Lloyd, also immigrated to
Pa., but left no NDTPS.

Sources: *WFP1*, pedigree XXVI, pp. 226-28 (Robert Lloyd) and chart
between pp. 116-17 (generations 8-12); *Bartrum 1*, pp. 446-47, 51,
694, 751-52, *Bartrum 2*, p. 1481 (generations 1-13). Further research
should be undertaken to confirm the above line from Huw ap Dafydd
o'r Bala.

The Royal Descents of 500 Immigrants

1. John "Lackland," King of England, d. 1216 = (2) Isabel of Angoulême

2. (illegitimate by Clemence, possibly Clemence Dauntsey, wife of Nicholas de Verdun) Joan Plantagenet = Llywelyn Fawr ap Iorwerth, Prince of North Wales

3. David, Prince of North Wales (Dafydd ap Llywelyn Fawr) = Isabel de Braose

4. (illegitimate by ----) Llywelyn ap Dafydd, constable of Rhuddlau = ----

5. Cynwrig ap Llywelyn = Angharad ferch Thomas ap Gwion

6. Dafydd Llwyd ap Cynwrig = Annes ferch Gwyn ap Madog

7. Mawd ferch Dafydd Llwyd = Dafydd Goch ap Trahaearn Goch ap Madog

8. Ieuan Goch ap Dafydd Goch = Efa ferch Einion ap Celynin

9. Morfudd ferch Ieuan Goch = Maredudd ap Hywel ap Tudur

10. Ieuan ap Maredudd = Lleucu ferch Hywel ap Meurig Fychan

11. Maredudd ap Ieuan = Margred ferch Einion ap Ithel

12. John ap Maredudd = Gwenhwyfar ferch Gronwy ap Ieuan

13. Morus ap John = Angharad ferch Elise ap Gruffudd

14. Margred ferch Morus = Maredudd ap Ieuan ap Robert

15. Jane ferch Maredudd = Cadwaladr ap Robert

16. Hywel ap Cadwaladr (Hywel Fychan) = ----

17. Robert ap Hywel = ----

18. Cadwaladr ap Robert = ----

19. **Robert Cadwalader** of Pa. = Jane John of Pa., ARD, SETH (their children and descendants took the surname Roberts).

The Royal Descents of 500 Immigrants

Sources: *WFP* 2, "Roberts of Gwynedd," esp. pp. 24-26, 43-46 (generations 15-19); *Bartrum 1*, pp. 446-47, 867, 457, *Bartrum 2*, pp. 845-47, 851 (generations 1-15).

The Royal Descents of 500 Immigrants

1. William I the Lion, King of Scotland, d. 1214 = Ermengarde de Beaumont

2. (illegitimate by a daughter of Richard Avenal) Isabel of Scotland = Robert de Ros, Magna Charta Surety

3. Sir William de Ros = Lucy FitzPiers

4. Sir William de Ros = Eustache FitzHugh

5. Lucy de Ros = Sir Robert Plumpton

6. Sir William Plumpton = Christiana ---

7. Alice Plumpton = (1) Sir Richard Sherburne; (2) Sir John Boteler

8. (by 1) Margaret Sherburne = Richard Bayley

9. Richard Bayley alias Sherburne = Agnes Stanley

10. Richard Sherburne = Matilda Hamerton

11. Isabel Sherburne = John Towneley

12. Lawrence Towneley = ---

13. Henry Towneley = ---

14. Lawrence Towneley = Helen Hesketh

15. Lawrence Towneley = Margaret Hartley

16. Lawrence Towneley = Jennet Halstead

17. **Mary Towneley** of Va. = Augustine **Warner.**

18. Augustine Warner, Jr. = Mildred Reade

19. Mildred Warner = Lawrence Washington

20. Augustine Washington = Mary Ball

21. George Washington (1731/2-1799), 1st U.S. President = Mrs. Martha Dandridge Custis

17. Lawrence Towneley (brother of Mrs. Warner) = Alice Calvert

18. **Lawrence Towneley** of Va. = Sarah Warner, his first cousin, daughter of Augustine Warner and Mary Towneley of Va., see above.

17. Elizabeth Towneley (sister of Mrs. Warner) = Christopher Smith

18. **Lawrence Smith**, almost certainly the immigrant to Va. = Mary (Hitchen?). Mary Towneley, a second sister of Mrs. Warner, married Samuel Hoyle and left a son, Edward Hoyle, who also immigrated to Va. and married Ann Debnam but left no NDTPS.

12. Grace Towneley (sister of Lawrence) = Roger Nowell

13. John Nowell = Elizabeth Kay

14. Elizabeth Nowell = Thomas Whitaker

15. William Whitaker, master of St. John's College, Cambridge = ---- Culverwell

16. **Alexander Whitaker** (c. 1585-1616/7) of Va., Anglican clergyman, d. unm.

16. **Jabez Whitaker** of Va. = Mary Bourchier of Va., ARD, SETH.

8. (by 2) Sir William Boteler = Elizabeth Standish

9. Sir John Boteler = Isabel Harington, daughter of Sir William Harington and Margaret de Neville, SETH

10. Elizabeth Boteler = Hamon Mascy

11. Margaret Mascy = John Holcroft

12. Margaret Holcroft = James Gerard

13. William Gerard = Dorothy Page

14. Dorothy Gerard = Thomas Waller

15. Edmund Waller (not the poet of the same name, who was a second cousin of the half blood of this Edmund) = Mary Smith

16. Thomas Waller = Anne Keate (their son, Thomas Waller, immigrated to Va., married Elizabeth ----, and left issue, but no NDTPS)

17. John Waller = Mary Pomfrett

18. **Col. John Waller** of Va. = Dorothy King.

18. **Mary Waller,** prob. of Va., prob. = Edward **Herndon,** son of William Herndon and Catherine ----, apparently not Digges and not a daughter of Edward Digges, colonial governor of Va., ARD, SETH, and Elizabeth Page, as claimed by J.G. Herndon (see citation below). The 1691 estate division of Mrs. Elizabeth Page Digges (*AP&P,* pp. 248-50) lists no daughter Catherine or her heirs.

19. Edward Herndon, Jr. = Elizabeth (Stubblefield?)

20. Joseph Herndon = Mary Minor

21. Dabney Herndon = Elizabeth Hull

22. William Lewis Herndon = Frances Elizabeth Hansbrough

23. Ellen Lewis Herndon = Chester Alan Arthur (1829-1886), 21st U.S. President

 8. Alice Boteler (full sister of Sir William) = John Gerard

 9. Constance Gerard = Sir Alexander Standish

10. Oliver Standish = ----

11. Grace Standish = Ralph Faircloth

12. Lawrence Faircloth = Elizabeth ----

13. Thomas Faircloth = Millicent Barr

14. Mary Faircloth = Thomas Allen

15. **Jane Allen,** who died in England = Rev. Peter **Bulkeley** of Mass.

16. Edward Bulkeley = Lucian ----

17. Peter Bulkeley = Rebecca Wheeler

18. Rebecca Bulkeley = Jonathan Prescott, Jr.

19. Abel Prescott = Abigail Brigham

20. Lucy Prescott, sister of Dr. Samuel Prescott, who completed Paul Revere's "Midnight Ride" of 19 Apr. 1775 = Jonathan Fay, Jr.

21. Samuel Prescott Phillips Fay = Harriet Howard

22. Samuel Howard Fay = Susan Shellman

23. Harriet Eleanor Fay = James Smith Bush
24. Samuel Prescott Bush = Flora Sheldon
25. Prescott Sheldon Bush, U.S. senator = Dorothy Walker
26. George Herbert Walker Bush (b. 1924), 41st U.S. President = Barbara Pierce

Sources: *GVFVM* 5:538-90; *Baines 1*, vol. 3, chart between pp. 572 and 573 (Sherburne); *AR7*, line 170; David A. Avant, Jr., *Some Southern Colonial Families*, vol. 1(1983), pp. 316-25 (Lawrence Smith); Sarah C.W. Allen, *Our Children's Ancestry* [Whitaker family] (1935), pp. 31-65 (Whitaker, Nowell, Towneley) and *DAB* (Alexander Whitaker); *PCF Lancashire* (Whitaker, Nowell, Towneley and Gerard pedigrees); *GVFVM* 5:703-18, 762, *GVFWM* 5:345-49 (Waller) and J.G. Herndon, *The Herndon Family of Virginia, vol. 1 (The First Three Generations)* (1947), pp. 1-10; *Berry's Bucks*, pp. 5, 7 (Waller); Sir G.J. Armytage, Bt., *Middlesex Pedigrees as Collected by Richard Mundy* (*HSPVS*, vol. 65, 1914), pp. 19-21 (Waller, Gerard); J.P. Earwaker, *Local Gleanings Relating to Lancashire and Cheshire*, vol. 2 (1877-78), #620, p. 121 (Holcroft); *Baines 2*, vol. 4, p. 414 (Mascy); William Beamont, *Annals of the Lords of Warrington, Part 1* (Publications of the Chetham Society, vol. 86, 1872), pp. 199-262 (Boteler); *MCS4*, lines 116, 116A, *Bulkeley*, pp. 38-51, *TAG* 42 (1966):129-35, and F.L. Weis, *The Families of Standish, Lancashire, England* (1959), pp. 14-15 (Mrs. Bulkeley). Further proof of the marriage of Mary Waller and Edward Herndon, first claimed by Moncure D. Conway and argued by J.G. Herndon (but not accepted by others) would be desirable.

The Royal Descents of 500 Immigrants

1. William I the Lion, King of Scotland, d. 1214 = Ermengarde de Beaumont

2. (illegitimate by a daughter of Richard Avenal) Isabel of Scotland = Robert de Ros, Magna Charta Surety

3. Sir William de Ros = Lucy FitzPiers

4. Sir Robert de Ros = Isabel d'Aubigny

5. Mary de Ros = William de Braose

6. William de Braose = Eleanor de Bavant

7. Sir Peter de Braose = Joan de Percy

8. Beatrix de Braose = Sir Hugh Shirley

9. Sir Ralph Shirley = Joan Basset

10. Ralph Shirley = Margaret Staunton

11. John Shirley = Eleanor Willoughby, a daughter of Sir Hugh Willoughby and Margaret Freville (who later married Sir Richard Bingham), SETH

12. Robert Shirley = ----

13. Ralph Shirley = Amee Lolle

14. Eleanor Shirley = Nicholas Browne

15. Sir William Browne = Mary Savage

16. Percy Browne = Anne Rich

17. **Nathaniel Browne** of Conn. = Eleanor Watts.

12. Hugh Shirley (brother of Robert) = Anne Hevyn

13. Thomas Shirley = Margaret Wroth

14. Joyce Shirley = Richard Abington (or Habington)

15. Mary Abington (or Habington) = Richard Barnaby

16. Winifred Barnaby = Henry Davenport

17. **Rev. John Davenport** (1597-1669/70) of Conn., non-conformist clergyman, author, founder of the New Haven Colony = Elizabeth ----.

10. Beatrix Shirley (sister of Ralph) = John Brome

11. Nicholas Brome = Katherine Lampeck

12. Elizabeth Brome = Thomas Hawes

13. William Hawes = Ursula Colles

14. Edmond Hawes = Jane Porter

15. **Edmond Hawes** of Mass. = ----. His only child, John Hawes, married Desire Gorham, daughter of John Gorham and Desire Howland, daughter of John and Elizabeth (Tilley) Howland of the *Mayflower*.

13. Constance Hawes (sister of William) = Thomas Shepherd

14. Thomas Shepherd = Amphyllis Chamberlain alias Spicer

15. Constance Shepherd = Edmund Bressie

16. **Thomas Bressie** of Conn. = (1) Hannah Hart; (2) Phebe Bisby. John Bressie, a brother of Thomas, was also in New Haven in the 1640s but returned to England by 1649 and left no NDTPS.

Sources: *MCS4*, lines 122-122D, 116-117, *AR7*, lines 230-230B, and sources cited therein, esp. *TAG* 22(1945-46):158-63, 23(1946-47):109, 60(1984):91 (Nathaniel Browne), 52(1976):216-17 (Rev. John Davenport) and *TG* 7-8(1986-1987):132-36 (Edmond Hawes and Thomas Bressie); *Shirleiana*, pp. 2-44; *Edmond Hawes*; Henry James Young, *George Eldridge, Hydrographer, and Eliza Jane, His Wife: Their Ancestors and Their Descendants* (1982, which includes an ancestor table of Edmond Hawes for 33 generations, with a full bibliography) and *Hawes, Freeman and James*; *NEHGR* 112(1958):27-44, 118(1964):251-62 (reprinted in *EO* 2:1:286-304 and *EO* 1:3:398-409) (Bressey and Shepherd articles by W.G. Davis).

The Royal Descents of 500 Immigrants

1. William I the Lion, King of Scotland, d. 1214 = Ermengarde de Beaumont

2. (illegitimate by a daughter of Richard Avenal) Isabel of Scotland = Robert de Ros, Magna Charta Surety

3. Sir William de Ros = Lucy FitzPiers

4. Sir Robert de Ros = Isabel d'Aubigny

5. William de Ros, 1st Baron Ros of Helmsley = Maud Vaux

6. Agnes de Ros = Pain de Tibetot, 1st Baron Tibetot

7. John de Tibetot, 2nd Baron Tibetot = (2) Elizabeth Aspall

8. Sir Pain de Tibetot = Agnes Wrothe

9. Elizabeth de Tibetot = Sir John Daneys

10. Elizabeth Daneys = William Haselden

11. John Haselden = Elizabeth Cheney

12. Anthony Haselden = Jane Marshall

13. Beatrice Haselden, said to = Robert Freville

14. Thomasine Freville = Christopher Burgoyne

15. Thomasine Burgoyne = Robert Shute

16. Anne Shute = John Leete

17. **William Leete** (c. 1613-1683), colonial governor of Conn. = (1) Anna Payne; (2) Sarah Rutherford; (2) Mrs. Mary Newman Street.

7. Ada de Tibetot (sister of the 2nd Baron Tibetot) = John de Mohun, 1st Baron Mohun

8. William de Mohun = Maud Polyslinche

9. Margaret de Mohun = Thomas Penkeville

10. John Penkeville = Isabel Tregarrack

11. John Penkeville = Isabel Raynward

12. Philip Penkeville = Joan Hernance

13. Isabel Penkeville = Richard Goode

14. Richard Goode = Joan Downe

15. Richard Goode = ----

16. **John Goode** of Va. = (1) Frances Mackarness; (2) Anne Bennett. Richard Goode, a brother of John, also immigrated to Va., but left no NDTPS.

Sources: *MCS4*, line 128 (generations 12-15: Freville, Burgoyne, Shute, Leete); E.A. Stratton, *Applied Genealogy* (1988), pp. 70-72, 74, 165, 170 (disproof of the Peyton descent and of the identification of Rose Peyton as the wife of Robert Freville and mother of Thomasine [Freville] Burgoyne); S.T. Bindoff, *The House of Commons*, vol. 2 (1982), pp. 173-74, "Pedigree of the Family of Freville" (TP FRE 8905 in the tabular pedigree collection at NEHGS), and *Chester of Chicheley*, vol. 1, pp. 214-17 (Haselden); *Blore*, pp. 61, 44 (Daneys, Tybetot [Tiptoft]); *AR7*, line 89 and *MCS4*, line 2; *LDBR*1, pp. 87-89 (Goode), George Brown Goode, *Virginia Cousins: A Study of the Ancestry and Posterity of John Goode of Whitby* (1887), pp. 20-24, 27-32, and *VC*, pp. 189 (Goode), 414 (Penkevill); *CP* (Mohun, Tybetot, Ros). The subject of Robert Freville's wife merits a thorough monograph, and I should like to see further documentation also for the parentage of the immigrant John Goode. Possibly problematic as well are the parentage and maternal grandparentage of William de Mohun of Puswith, husband of Maud Polyslinche, which are not confirmed in *Dunster*, vol. 1, pp. 38-43.

The Royal Descents of 500 Immigrants

1. William I the Lion, King of Scotland, d. 1214 = Ermengarde de Beaumont

2. (illegitimate by a daughter of Richard Avenal) Isabel of Scotland = Robert de Ros, Magna Charta Surety

3. Sir William de Ros = Lucy FitzPiers

4. Sir Robert de Ros = Isabel d'Aubigny

5. William de Ros, 1st Baron Ros of Helmsley = Maud Vaux

6. Agnes de Ros = Pain de Tibetot, 1st Baron Tibetot

7. John de Tibetot, 2nd Baron Tibetot = (1) Margaret Badlesmere, daughter of Bartholomew Badlesmere, 1st Baron Badlesmere, and Margaret de Clare, daughter of Thomas de Clare and Juliana FitzMaurice, SETH

8. Robert de Tibetot, 3rd Baron Tibetot = Margaret Deincourt

9. Elizabeth de Tibetot = Sir Philip Despencer

10. Margery Despencer = Sir Roger Wentworth

11. Margaret Wentworth = Sir William Hopton

12. Margaret Hopton = Sir Philip Booth

13. Audrey Booth = Sir William Lytton

14. Sir Robert Lytton = Frances Cavalery

15. Anne Lytton = Sir John Borlase

16. Anne Borlase = Sir Euseby Isham

17. William Isham = Mary Brett

18. **Henry Isham** of Va. = Mrs. Katherine Banks Royall.

19. Mary Isham = William Randolph

20. Isham Randolph = Jane Rogers

21. Jane Randolph = Peter Jefferson

22. Thomas Jefferson (1743-1826), 3rd U.S. President = Mrs. Martha Wayles Skelton, see below

22. Mary Jefferson (sister of Thomas) = John Bolling (III), a great-great-great-grandson of Pocahontas and John Rolfe

23. Archibald Bolling = Catherine Payne

24. Archibald Bolling, Jr. = Anne E. Wigginton
25. William Holcombe Bolling = Sallie Spiers White
26. Edith Bolling = (1) Norman Galt; (2) (Thomas) Woodrow Wilson (1856-1924), 28th U.S. President

19. Anne Isham (sister of Mary) = Francis Epes (III)
20. Francis Epes (IV) = Sarah ---
21. Martha Epes = John Wayles
22. Martha Wayles = (1) Bathurst Skelton; (2) 22 Thomas Jefferson (1743-1826), 3rd U.S. President, her 3rd cousin, see above. For Martha's Isham line see *AP&P*, pp. 263-64 and J.F. Dorman, *Ancestors and Descendants of Francis Epes I of Virginia (Epes-Eppes-Epps)*, vol. 1 (1992), pp. 150-53.

15. Elizabeth Lytton (sister of Anne) = Edward Barrett
16. Anne Barrett = Thomas Corbett
17. Catherine Corbett = Sir John Mede
18. Jane Mede = Thomas Talbot
19. **John Talbot** (c. 1645-1727) of N.J., Anglican missionary clergyman = (1) Isabel Jenney, ARD, SETH; (2) Mrs. Anne Herbert.

Sources: *TG* 9(1988):194-96, 223-25; *AR7*, lines 200, 65A, 89, 54, and *MCS4*, lines 2, 1, 117, 116, 74 (Isham -- see also *Isham*, pp. 32-35, 44-45, 50-55; *TG*, new ser., 2[1885]:228-30 [Borlase]; and *Clutterbuck*, vol. 2, p. 377 [Lytton]). For John Talbot see *DAB;* A.W. H. Clarke and Arthur Campling, eds., *Visitation of Norfolk, 1664*, vol. 2 (*HSPVS*, vol. 86, 1934), p. 214 (Talbot); Walter C. Metcalfe, ed., *Visitations of Essex, 1552, 1558, 1570, 1612 and 1634*, vol. 1 (*HSPVS*, vol. 13, 1878), pp. 448 (Me[a]de), 146 (Barrett); Walter Rye, ed., *Visitations of Norfolk, 1563, 1589, and 1613* (*HSPVS*, vol. 32, 1891), pp. 84-85 (Corbett).

The Royal Descents of 500 Immigrants

1. William I the Lion, King of Scotland, d. 1214 = Ermengarde de Beaumont

2. (illegitimate by a daughter of Richard Avenal) Isabel of Scotland = Robert de Ros, Magna Charta Surety

3. Sir William de Ros = Lucy FitzPiers

4. Sir Robert de Ros = Isabel d'Aubigny

5. William de Ros, 1st Baron Ros of Helmsley = Maud Vaux

6. Agnes de Ros = Pain de Tibetot, 1st Baron Tibetot

7. John de Tibetot, 2nd Baron Tibetot = (1) Margaret Badlesmere, daughter of Bartholomew Badlesmere, 1st Baron Badlesmere, and Margaret de Clare, daughter of Thomas de Clare and Juliana FitzMaurice, SETH

8. Robert de Tibetot, 3rd Baron Tibetot = Margaret Deincourt

9. Elizabeth de Tibetot = Sir Philip Despencer

10. Margery Despencer = Sir Roger Wentworth

11. Agnes Wentworth = Sir Robert Constable

12. Sir William Constable = Joan Fulthorpe

13. Robert Constable = ---- Arden

14. Francis Constable = Margaret Brigham

15. ---- Constable (daughter) = Walter Fenwick

16. George Fenwick = Margaret ----

17. Walter Fenwick = Magdalen Hunt

18. **Thomas Fenwick** of Del. = (1) Mrs. Mary Savill Porter Lawson; (2) Mary ----.

12. Anne Constable (sister of Sir William) = Sir William Tyrwhit

13. Sir Robert Tyrwhit = Maud Talboys

14. Anna Tyrwhit = Edward Kaye

15. Lucy Kaye = John Pickering

16. Elizabeth Pickering = Robert Throckmorton

17. Gabriel Throckmorton = Alice Bedell

18. **Robert Throckmorton** of Va. = (1) Anne Chace; (2) Judith Hetley.

Sources: Edwin Jaquett Sellers, *Fenwick Allied Ancestry: Ancestry of Thomas Fenwick of Sussex County, Delaware* (1916) and *Supplement to Genealogies* (1922), pp. 40-49; *AR7*, lines 200, 65A, 89, 54 and *MCS4*, lines 2, 1, 117, 116, 74, 76, 8B (generations 1-11 and 13-18 for Throckmorton); *BP* (Throckmorton of Ellington and Virginia, under the baronets of Coughton, in editions since 1928), *Throckmorton*, pp. 273-76, 287-91, 295-303, *NGSQ* 60(1974):22-24 (and sources cited therein -- Pickering, Kaye, Tyrwhit); Rev. A.R. Maddison, *Lincolnshire Pedigrees*, vol. 3 (*HSPVS*, vol. 52, 1904), p. 1019 (Tyrwhit); *DVY* 2:289, 3:47-48 (Constable).

The Royal Descents of 500 Immigrants

1. William I the Lion, King of Scotland, d. 1214 = Ermengarde de Beaumont

2. (illegitimate by a daughter of Richard Avenal) Isabel of Scotland = Robert de Ros, Magna Charta Surety

3. Sir William de Ros = Lucy FitzPiers

4. Sir Robert de Ros = Isabel d'Aubigny

5. William de Ros, 1st Baron Ros of Helmsley = Maud Vaux

5. Isabel de Ros = Walter de Fauconberg, 2nd Baron Fauconberg

6. Alice de Ros = Nicholas de Meinell, 3rd Baron Meinell

6. John de Fauconberg, 3rd Baron Fauconberg = Eve (Bulmer?)

7. Elizabeth de Meinell = John Darcy, 2nd Baron Darcy

7. Joan de Fauconberg = Sir William Colville

8. Alice Darcy = 8. Sir John Colville

9. Isabel Colville = John Wandesford

10. Thomas Wandesford = Idonea ----

11. Joan Wandesford = John Tichborne

12. John Tichborne = Margaret Martin

13. Nicholas Tichborne = Anne White

14. Nicholas Tichborne = Elizabeth Rythe

15. Jane Tichborne = Francis Yate

16. Thomas Yate = Mary Tregian

17. John Yate = Mary Tattershall

18. **George Yate** of Md. = Mrs. Mary Wells Stockett.

Sources: *NGSQ* 64(1976):176-80, esp. note 26, p. 180; W.H. Rylands, ed., *Visitations of Hampshire, 1520, 1575, and 1622-34* (*HSPVS*, vol. 64, 1913), pp. 125-26 and *BP* (Tichborne, baronets); *Moriarty*, vol. 12, pp. 90-94 (Wandesford); *AR7*, lines 208, 89 and *CP* (Ros, Meinell, Darcy and Fauconberg).

The Royal Descents of 500 Immigrants

1. Frederick I Barbarossa, Holy Roman Emperor, d. 1190 = (2) Beatrix of Burgundy

2. Otto of Hohenstaufen, Palatine Count of Burgundy = Margaret of Blois, daughter of Theobald V, Count of Blois, and Alix of France, daughter of Louis VII, King of France, d. 1180, and Eleanor of Aquitaine (who = (2) Henry II, King of England)

3. Beatrix of Hohenstaufen and Burgundy = Otto I, Duke of Merania

4. Alix of Merania and Burgundy = Hugh de Châlon, Count Palatine of Burgundy

5. Hypolite of Burgundy = Aymar III de Poitiers, Count of Valentinois

6. Constance de Poitiers = Hugh III Adhémar, Seigneur de la Garde

7. Lambert III Adhémar, co-Seigneur de Monteil = Douce Gaucelme

8. Hugh IV Adhémar, Seigneur de la Garde = Mabile du Puy

9. Louis Adhémar, co-Seigneur de Monteil = Dauphine de Glandevez

10. Marguerite Adhémar = Berthold di Baschi, Seigneur en parti di Vitozzo

11. Thadée de Baschi, Seigneur de Saint-Estève = Jeanne de Barras

12. Louis de Baschi, Seigneur de Saint-Estève = Melchionne de Matheron

13. Louis de Baschi, Seigneur d'Auzet = Louise de Varas

14. Balthazard de Baschi, Seigneur de Saint-Estève = Marguerite du Faur

15. Louis de Baschi, Baron d'Aubais = Anne de Rochemore

16. Louise de Baschi = Jacques des Vignolles, Seigneur de Prades

17. Charles des Vignolles, Seigneur de Prades = Gabrielle de Sperandieu (generations 17-19 were, before Louis Nicola's immigration to Pa., Huguenot refugees in Ireland)

18. Charlotte des Vignolles = Charles Nicola (or Nicholas)

19. **Louis Nicola** (c. 1717-1807) of Pa., revolutionary soldier, public official, editor, merchant = (1) Christiana D'Oyly; (2) Jane Bishop.

Sources: *TAG* 57(1981):139-44, and sources cited therein and listed on p. 144. The accent marks are from W.A. Reitwiesner's original draft of this article.

The Royal Descents of 500 Immigrants

1. Henry II, King of England, d. 1189 = Eleanor of Aquitaine
2. (illegitimate by Ida, later wife of Roger Bigod, 2nd Earl of Norfolk) William Longespee, Earl of Salisbury = Ela, Countess of Salisbury, a descendant of Robert II, King of France, d. 1031, and Constance of Provence, see *AR7*, lines 108, 101
3. Stephen Longespee = Emmeline de Riddleford
4. Ela Longespee = Sir Roger la Zouche
5. Alan la Zouche, 1st Baron Zouche of Ashby = Eleanor de Segrave
6. Maud la Zouche = Robert Holand, 1st Baron Holand
7. Elizabeth Holand = Sir Henry FitzRoger
8. John FitzRoger = Alice ----
9. Elizabeth FitzRoger = (1) John Bonville; (2) Richard Stukeley
10. (by 1) William Bonville, 1st Baron Bonville = (1) Margaret ----; (2) Elizabeth Courtenay
11. (illegitimate by Isabella Kirkby) John Bonville = Alice Dennis
12. Isabella Bonville = Edmund Larder
13. Ursula Larder = William Hull
14. Henry Hull = ----
15. Ursula Hull = Peter Colleton
16. Sir John Colleton, 1st Bt. = Katherine Amy
17. **James Colleton**, colonial governor of S.C. = Anne Kendall.

10. (by 2) Hugh Stukeley (half-brother of the 1st Baron Bonville) = Katherine de Affeton
11. Nicholas Stukeley = Thomasine Cockworthy
12. Joan Stukeley = Philip Baynard
13. Robert Baynard = Anne Blake

14. Thomas Baynard = Elizabeth Barnes
15. Henry Baynard = Anne Hobbes
16. Thomas Baynard = Martha Prickman
17. Thomas Baynard = Mary Bennett
18. **John Baynard** of Md. = Elizabeth Blackwell.

11. Alice Stucley (sister of Nicholas) = Sir Thomas Beaumont
12. Hugh Beaumont = Thomasine Wise
13. Margaret Beaumont = John Chichester
14. Elizabeth Chichester = Nicholas Pyne
15. John Pyne = Honor Penfound
16. George Pyne = Joan Darte
17. John Pyne = Anstice Rich
18. John Pyne = Alice ----
19. John Pyne = Charity White
20. John Pyne = Mary Hammett
21. John Pyne = Mary Craze
22. **Thomas Pyne** of N.Y. = (1) Sarah Gainesford; (2) Anna Rivington.

16. John Pyne (brother of George) = ----
17. Josias Pyne = Christian Heydon
18. Philip Pyne = Anne ----, widow of James Oxenham
19. John Pyne = Joan Hunt
20. Cornelius Pyne = Margaret Markham
21. John Pyne = Isabella Pyne
22. **John Pyne** of S.C. = Honora Smith

Sources: *SCG* 2:3-7 (Colleton), *VD*, pp. 218 (Colleton), 492 (Hull), 524 (Larder), 101-3 (Bonville), *NGSQ* 59(1971):254-62, 60(1972): 25-35 (FitzRoger, Holand), *AR7*, lines 261, 30-32 and *CP* (Bonville); *MCS4*, lines 90-90A, 142, 144, *NGSQ* 71(1983):37-40 (Baynard) and sources cited in both, esp. G.D. Squibb, ed., *Wiltshire Visitation Pedigrees, 1623* (*HSPVS*, vol. 105-6, 1954), pp. 15-16 (Baynard) and *VD*, p. 721 (Stucley); M. Taylor Pyne, *Memorials of the Pyne Family* (1919), pp. 120-26, 170-203, 228-54, F.W. Pyne, *The John Pyne Family in America, Being the Comprehensive Genealogical Record of the Descendants of John Pyne (1766-1813) of Charleston, South Carolina* (1992), pp. 16-35, 180-83 esp., *BLG*, 1939 ed., p. 2875, 1952 ed., p. 2103 (Pyne), and *VD*, pp. 632 (Pyne), 173 (Chichester), 65 (Beaumont). For the identification of the mother of William Longespee, Earl of Salisbury see a forthcoming Countess Ida monograph by Douglas Richardson, plus Vera C.M. London, ed., *The Cartulary of Bradenstoke Priory* (*Publications of the Wiltshire Record Society*, vol. 35, 1979), pp. 8-9 and *TG* 3(1982):265-66; the above identification of Countess Ida is repeated on each of the next nine charts.

The Royal Descents of 500 Immigrants

1. Henry II, King of England, d. 1189 = Eleanor of Aquitaine

2. (illegitimate by Ida, later wife of Roger Bigod, 2nd Earl of Norfolk) William Longespee, Earl of Salisbury = Ela, Countess of Salisbury

3. Stephen Longespee = Emmeline de Riddleford

4. Ela Longespee = Sir Roger la Zouche

5. Alan la Zouche, 1st Baron Zouche of Ashby = Eleanor de Segrave

6. Maud la Zouche = Robert Holand, 1st Baron Holand

7. Maud Holand = Sir Thomas Swinnerton

8. Sir Robert Swinnerton = Elizabeth Beke

9. Maud Swinnerton = Sir John Savage

10. Sir John Savage = Eleanor Brereton

11. (probably, although *which* Sir John Savage was Alice's father remains problematic) Alice (or Dulcia) Savage = Sir Henry Bold

12. Maud Bold = Thomas Gerard

13. Jennet Gerard = Richard Eltonhead, son of John Eltonhead (and Elizabeth Birkenhead), son of John Eltonhead (and Margaret Lancaster), son of Nicholas Eltonhead and ---- Harington, daughter of Nicholas Harington of Huyton (and Margaret Lathom), son of Sir Nicholas Harington and Isabel English, SETH

14. William Eltonhead = Anne Bowers

15. Richard Eltonhead = Anne Sutton

16. **Martha Eltonhead** of Va. = Edwin **Conway.**

17. Edwin Conway, Jr. = Elizabeth Thornton

18. Francis Conway = Rebecca Catlett

19. Eleanor Rose Conway = James Madison

20. James Madison, Jr. (1750/1-1836), 4th U.S. President = Mrs. Dorothea "Dolly" Payne Todd

16. **Alice Eltonhead** of Va. = (1) Rowland **Burnham**; (2) Henry **Corbin** of Va., ARD, SETH; (3) Henry **Creek**.

16. **Jane Eltonhead** of Md. = (1) Robert **Moryson**; (2) Cuthbert **Fenwick** of Md., probably ARD, SETH.

16. **Agatha Eltonhead** of Va. = (1) William **Kellaway**; (2) Ralph **Wormeley**; (3) Sir Henry **Chichele**, colonial (deputy) governor of Va., ARD, SETH. Eleanor Eltonhead, a 4th sister, also immigrated to Va. and married (1) William Brocas; (2) John Carter (who later married Sarah Ludlow of Va., ARD, SETH); Katherine Eltonhead, a 5th sister married "Thomas Mease of Burras, Ireland," thought by H.E. Hayden to be probably Thomas Mears, later of Va.; and William Eltonhead of Md. (d. 1655, m. Jane ----), was thought by Hayden to be a brother of these five sisters, although omitted (because dead and childless?) from the 1664 visitation of Lancashire. Neither Eleanor, Katherine, nor William left NDTPS.

Sources: *HVG*, pp. 227-30 (Eltonhead); *Baines 2*, vol. 4, pp. 375-76 (Gerard), vol. 5, pp. 25 (Bold), 74 (Harington); various Savage sources, none satisfactory, including *Ormerod*, vol. 1, pp. 712-13, *Salt*, new ser., vol. 12 (1909), p. 144, and J.P. Rylands, ed., *Visitation of Cheshire, 1580* (*HSPVS*, vol. 18, 1882), p. 203; *AR7*, lines 30-32, 34. See also Corbin, Cuthbert Fenwick, and Chichele sources cited elsewhere.

1. Henry II, King of England, d. 1189 = Eleanor of Aquitaine

2. (illegitimate by Ida, later wife of Roger Bigod, 2nd Earl of Norfolk) William Longespee, Earl of Salisbury = Ela, Countess of Salisbury

3. Stephen Longespee = Emmeline de Riddleford

4. Ela Longespee = Sir Roger la Zouche

5. Alan la Zouche, 1st Baron Zouche of Ashby = Eleanor de Segrave

6. Maud la Zouche = Robert Holand, 1st Baron Holand

7. Maud Holand = Sir Thomas Swinnerton

8. Alice Swinnerton = Sir John Gresley

9. Sir Nicholas Gresley = Thomasine Wasteneys

10. Sir Thomas Gresley = Margaret Walsh

11. Sir John Gresley = Elizabeth Clarell

12. Thomasine Gresley = Hugh Wrottesley

13. Sir Walter Wrottesley = Joan Baron

14. Joan Wrottesley = Richard Cresset

15. Margaret Cresset = Thomas More

16. Jasper More = Elizabeth Smalley

17. Katherine More = Samuel More, a cousin; by Jacob Blakeway she was the mother of

18. **Richard More** (1614-1693/4-96) of Mass., a passenger on the *Mayflower* = (1) Christian Hunt(er?); (2) Mrs. Jane --- Crumpton. Ellen More (b. 1612), Jasper More (b. 1613) and undoubtedly Mary More (b. 1616), siblings of Richard More, were also passengers on the *Mayflower* but died before reaching adulthood.

11. Margaret Gresley (sister of Sir John) = Sir Thomas Blount

12. Sir Thomas Blount = Agnes Hawley

13. Anne Blount = William Marbury

14. Robert Marbury = Katherine Williamson

15. William Marbury = Agnes Lenton (parents of Francis Marbury, husband of Bridget Dryden, SETH, and father of the noted Mrs. Anne Marbury Hutchinson and Mrs. Katherine Marbury Scott, both of R.I., both ARD, SETH)

16. Katherine Marbury = Christopher Wentworth

17. William Wentworth = Susanna Carter

18. **William Wentworth** of N.H. = (1) ----; (2) Elizabeth Knight.

17. Anne Wentworth (sister of William) = John Lawson

18. **Christopher Lawson** of Mass. = Elizabeth James.

Sources: *NEHGR* 114(1960):163-68, 124(1970):85-87 (reprinted in *EO* 2:2:763-71 and *GMF* 2:743-51) and Robert M. Sherman, ed., *Mayflower Families Through Five Generations,* vol. 2 (1978), pp. 121-25 (Richard More); *Gresleys of Drakelowe,* pp. 299 (Wrottesley), 225-26 (Gresley) esp.; *Salt* 7, pt. 2 (1886):24, 40-41 esp. (Swinnerton) and *AR7*, lines 30-32, esp. note at end of 32; *MCS4*, lines 78A, 78 (Wentworth, Lawson), *Marbury*, pp. 23-25, 44-47 esp., *TAG* 67 (1992):201-10, and *Wentworth*, vol. 1, pp. 60-109 esp. For the identification above of Alice Swinnerton, wife of Sir John Gresley, as a daughter of Sir Thomas and Maud, I depend on Canon Bridgeman's conclusion to that effect in *Salt* 7, pt. 2, p. 41.

1. Henry II, King of England, d. 1189 = Eleanor of Aquitaine

2. (illegitimate by Ida, later wife of Roger Bigod, 2nd Earl of Norfolk) William Longespee, Earl of Salisbury = Ela, Countess of Salisbury

3. Ida Longespee = William de Beauchamp

4. Beatrice de Beauchamp = Sir Thomas FitzOtho or FitzOtes

5. Maud (or Matilda) FitzThomas = John de Botetourte, 1st Baron Botetourte, formerly thought to be an illegitimate son of Edward I, King of England, d. 1307, but see *TAG* 63(1988):145-53

6. Thomas de Botetourte = Joan de Somery

7. John de Botetourte, 2nd Baron Botetourte = Joyce la Zouche de Mortimer

8. Joyce de Botetourte = Sir Baldwin Freville

9. Sir Baldwin Freville = Maud ----

10. Margaret Freville = Sir Richard Bingham

11. Margery Bingham = Hugh Hercy

12. Humphrey Hercy = Jane Stanhope

13. Humphrey Hercy = Elizabeth Digby, daughter of Sir John Digby and Catherine Griffin, ARD, SETH (their daughter, Anne Hercy married Nicholas Denman; their son, Francis Denman, married Anne Blount; their daughter, Anne Denman, married Sir Thomas Aylesbury, 1st Bt.; their daughter, Frances Aylesbury, married Edward Hyde, 1st Earl of Clarendon, statesman and historian; and their daughter, Anne Hyde, Duchess of York, was the first wife of James II, King of England, and mother of Mary II and Anne, Queens of England)

14. Alice Hercy = Henry Hatfield

15. Elizabeth Hatfield = Thomas Whalley

16. Richard Whalley = Frances Cromwell, aunt of Oliver Cromwell, the Lord Protector

17. **Edward Whalley** (d. 1674 or 1675), English army officer and regicide, later a resident of Mass. and Conn.; (1) Judith Duffell; (2) Mary Middleton. Frances Whalley, a daughter by Judith, married William Goffe, also an English army officer and regicide and later a resident of Mass. and Conn.

14. Barbara Hercy (sister of Alice) = George Neville

15. John Neville = Gertrude Whalley

16. Hercy Neville = Bridget Saville

17. Gilbert Neville = Margaret Bland

18. Edward Neville = Mary Scott

19. Mary Neville = William Lovelace

20. **John Lovelace, 4th Baron Lovelace,** colonial governor of N.Y. = Charlotte Clayton.

Sources: *DNB* (Whalley and Lovelace); Mark Noble, *Memoirs of the Protectoral House of Cromwell,* 3rd ed., vol. 2 (1787), pp. 139-41, 143-53 (Whalley); G.W. Marshall, ed., *Visitations of the County of Nottingham, 1569 and 1614* (*HSPVS,* vol. 4, 1871), pp. 117-18 (Whalley, Hatfield), 15 (Hercy), 121 (Bingham), 65-66 (Neville); *GM* 21(1983-85):185-90 (Freville); *AR7,* lines 216, 122A, 30; *Thoroton,* vol. 3, pp. 262-63 (Neville), *CP* (Lovelace) and *NYGBR* 51(1920):179, footnote 1. See also *Nichols,* vol. 2, p. 261*** (Digby) and *TG,* new ser., 8(1892):44 (Hercy to Anne Hyde). Margery Bingham, wife of Hugh Hercy, was the daughter of Sir Richard Bingham probably, but perhaps not certainly, by Margaret Freville, widow of Sir Hugh Willougby; further documentation is needed.

The Royal Descents of 500 Immigrants

1. Henry II, King of England, d. 1189 = Eleanor of Aquitaine

2. (illegitimate by Ida, later wife of Roger Bigod, 2nd Earl of Norfolk) William Longespee, Earl of Salisbury = Ela, Countess of Salisbury

3. Sir William Longespee = Idoine de Camville

3. Stephen Longespee = Emmeline de Riddleford

4. Ela Longespee = James de Audley

4. Emmeline Longespee = Maurice FitzMaurice

5. Hugh de Audley, 1st Baron Audley = Isolde Mortimer

5. Juliana FitzMaurice = Thomas de Clare

6. Alice de Audley = Ralph Neville, 2nd Baron Neville

6. Maud de Clare = Robert Clifford, 1st Baron Clifford

7. Idoine Clifford = Henry Percy, 2nd Baron Percy

7. John Neville, 3rd Baron Neville   =   8. Maud Percy

8,9. Eleanor Neville = Ralph Lumley, 1st Baron Lumley

9,10. Sir John Lumley = Felicia Redman

10,11. Thomas Lumley, 2nd Baron Lumley = Margaret Harington

11,12. Joan Lumley = Bertram Harbottle

12,13. Agnes Harbottle = Sir Roger Fenwick

13,14. Sir Ralph Fenwick = Margery Corbet

14,15. Anthony Fenwick = Isabel Selby

15,16. Stephen Fenwick = Elizabeth Haggerston

16,17. George Fenwick = Barbara Mitford

17,18. **Cuthbert Fenwick**, probably the Cuthbert Fenwick of Md. = (1) ----; (2) Mrs. Jane Eltonhead Moryson of Md., ARD, SETH.

9,10. Katherine Lumley (sister of Sir John) = Sir John Chidiock

10,11. Katherine Chidiock = Sir John Arundell

11,12. Margaret Arundell = Sir William Capel

12,13. Sir Giles Capel = Isabel Newton

13,14. Margaret Capel = Robert Ward

14,15. Henry Ward = Margaret Ugges

15,16. Tobias Ward = Thomasine Fisher

16,17. (almost certainly) George Ward = Dionis Burrow

17,18. **Thomasine Ward** of Mass. = (1) John **Thompson**; (2) Robert **Buffum.**

Sources: *Catholic Historical Review* 5(1919):156-74 (Cuthbert Fenwick); Joseph Foster, *Visitation Pedigrees of Northumberland* (1891), pp. 50-51 (Fenwick of Langshawes and Stanton); *NHN*, vol. 12, chart opp. p. 352 (Fenwick of Hartington), vol. 9, pp. 266-67 (Harbottle); J.W. Clay, *Extinct and Dormant Peerages of the Northern Counties of England* (1913), pp. 129, 145-46 (Lumley, Neville); *AR7*, lines 207, 122, 30, 205, 64, 178, 31; Owen A. Perkins, *Buffum Family, Volume II* (1983), pp. 1-5 and *DW*, p. 120; Walter Rye, *Norfolk Families* (1913), p. 988, Walter Rye, ed., *Visitations of Norfolk, 1563, 1589, and 1613* (*HSPVS*, vol. 32, 1891), pp. 305-6 and Rev. G.H. Dashwood, ed., *Visitation of Norfolk, 1563*, vol. 1 (1878), pp. 31-33 (Ward); Walter C. Metcalfe, ed., *Visitations of Essex, 1552, 1558, 1570, 1612 and 1634*, vol. 1 (*HSPVS*, vol. 13, 1878), p. 171 (Capel); J.J. Howard and H.S. Hughes, *Genealogical Collections Illustrating the History of Roman Catholic Families of England, Based on the Lawson Manuscript, Part III: Arundell* (1887?), pp. 224, 226-27 (Arundell, Chidiock). The descent of Mrs. Buffum was first developed (and brought to my attention) by Michael J. Wood of London. Clinching proof of George Ward's parentage, asserted by Rye in *Norfolk Families* and highly probable from naming patterns and chronology alone, would be welcome.

The Royal Descents of 500 Immigrants

1. Henry II, King of England, d. 1189 = Eleanor of Aquitaine
2. (illegitimate by Ida, later wife of Roger Bigod, 2nd Earl of Norfolk) William Longespee, Earl of Salisbury = Ela, Countess of Salisbury

3. Stephen Longespee = Emmeline de Riddleford

3. Sir William Longespee = Idoine Camville

4. Ela Longespee = Sir Roger la Zouche

4. (prob. -- but poss. a 2nd Ida/Idoine, dau of 2.) Ida Longespee = Sir Walter FitzRobert

5. Alan la Zouche, 1st Baron Zouche of Ashby = Eleanor de Segrave

5. Ela FitzRobert = William de Odingsells

6. Maud la Zouche = Robert Holand, 1st Baron Holand

6. Ida de Odingsells = John de Clinton, 1st Baron Clinton

7. Maud Holand = Sir Thomas Swinnerton

7. John de Clinton, 2nd Baron Clinton = Margaret Corbet

8. Sir Robert Swinnerton = Elizabeth Beke

8. John de Clinton, 3rd Baron Clinton = Idonea de Say

9. Maud Swinnerton = Sir John Savage

9. Margaret de Clinton = Sir Baldwin Montfort

10. Margaret Savage = Sir John Dutton

10. Sir William Montfort = Margaret ----

11. Maud Dutton = Sir William Booth

11. Robert Montfort = ----

12. Sir George Booth = 12. Katherine Montfort
13. Sir William Booth = Ellen Montgomery
14. Jane Booth = Sir Thomas Holford
15. Dorothy Holford = John Bruen
16. John Bruen = Anne Fox
17. **Obadiah Bruen** of Conn. = Sarah ----.

11. Eleanor Dutton (sister of Maud) = Edward Langford

12. Janet Langford = Simon Thelwall

13. Alice Thelwall = Harri ap Cynric

14. John Wynne ap Harri = Katherine ferch Ithel ap Jenkin

15. Rees ap John Wynne = ----

16. John ap Rees Wynne = Grace Morgan

17. Thomas ap John Wynne = ----

18. **Dr. Thomas Wynne** of Pa., physician, 1st speaker of the Pennsylvania Provincial Assembly = (1) Martha Buttall; (2) Mrs. Elizabeth ---- Rawden Maude. John Wynne, a brother of Dr. Thomas, also came to Pa. (and practiced law in Sussex Co., now Del.) but left no NDTPS.

Sources: *AR7*, lines 30-33, 86, 122 and *TAG* 26(1950):12-25 (Bruen); *PSECD* 2:329-31 (Wynne, undocumented), *WFP1*, pedigree XVII, pp. 95-102, *GPFPGM* 3:396-99 (Mrs. Elizabeth Wynne) and *Ormerod*, vol. 1, p. 649 (Dutton). *Bartrum 2*, p. 1135, makes Janet (Jonet) Langford, wife of Simon Thelwall, an aunt, not daughter, of the Edward Langford who married Eleanor Dutton; more research may be required, but chronologically the descent above seems likely.

The Royal Descents of 500 Immigrants

1. Henry II, King of England, d. 1189 = Eleanor of Aquitaine

2. (illegitimate by Ida, later wife of Roger Bigod, 2nd Earl of Norfolk) William Longespee, Earl of Salisbury = Ela, Countess of Salisbury

3. Stephen Longespee = Emmeline de Riddleford

4. Ela Longespee = Sir Roger la Zouche

5. Alan la Zouche, 1st Baron Zouche of Ashby = Eleanor de Segrave

6. Maud la Zouche = Robert Holand, 1st Baron Holand

7. Maud Holand = Sir Thomas Swinnerton

8. Sir Robert Swinnerton = Elizabeth Beke

9. Maud Swinnerton = Sir John Savage

10. Sir John Savage = Eleanor Brereton

11. Margaret Savage = Randall Mainwaring

12. Margery Mainwaring = Thomas Davenport

13. Thomas Davenport = Katherine Radcliffe

14. Thomas Davenport = Elizabeth Fitton

15. Katherine Davenport = William Leversage

16. William Leversage = Eleanor Sheffield

17. Eleanor Leversage = John Weld

18. Jane Weld = John Lowndes

19. Charles Lowndes = Sarah ----

20. **Charles Lowndes** of S.C. = Ruth Rawlins.

19. Richard Lowndes (brother of Charles) = Alice ----

20. Richard Lowndes = Margaret Poole

21. **Christopher Lowndes** of Md. = Elizabeth Tasker, daughter of Benjamin Tasker, president of the council (and act. gov.) of Md., and Anne Bladen, daughter of William Bladen of Md., colonial publisher and attorney-general of Md., ARD, SETH, and Anne Swearingen.

The Royal Descents of 500 Immigrants

Sources: *NEHGR* 30(1876):141-46, *MG* 2:187-88, *BLG*, 18th ed., vol. 3 (1972), pp. 553-54 (Lowndes of Hassall) and John Parsons Earwaker, *The History of the Ancient Parish of Sandbach* (1890), pp. 121-23 (Weld, Lowndes), 102-3 (Leversage); *Ormerod*, vol. 3, pp. 707-8 (Davenport of Henbury), 80 (Mainwaring of Kermincham) and vol. 1, pp. 712-13 (Savage, plus vol. 3, p. 89 for Elizabeth Brereton as the wife of Sir John Savage); *AR7*, lines 30-32.

The Royal Descents of 500 Immigrants

1. Henry II, King of England, d. 1189 = Eleanor of Aquitaine

2. (illegitimate by Ida, later wife of Roger Bigod, 2nd Earl of Norfolk) William Longespee, Earl of Salisbury = Ela, Countess of Salisbury

3. Stephen Longespee = Emmeline de Riddleford

4. Ela Longespee = Sir Roger la Zouche

5. Alan la Zouche, 1st Baron Zouche of Ashby = Eleanor de Segrave

6. Maud la Zouche = Robert Holand, 1st Baron Holand

7. Maud Holand = Sir Thomas Swinnerton

8. Sir Robert Swinerton = Elizabeth Beke

9. Maud Swinnerton = Sir William Ipstones

10. Alice Ipstones = Sir Randall Brereton

11. Randall Brereton = Katherine Bulkeley

12. Randall Brereton = Emma Carrington

13. Sir Randall Brereton = Eleanor Dutton

14. John Brereton = Alicia ----

15. William Brereton = Elizabeth Green

16. Cuthbert Brereton = Joan House or Howes

17. **Rev. John Brereton** or **Brierton** (fl. 1572-1619) of Me., explorer, author of the first English work dealing with New England = Margaret ----.

Sources: *DAB* and Robert Maitland Brereton, *The Breretons of Cheshire, 1100 to 1904 A.D.* (1904), pp. 97-98, 112-13 esp.; Walter Rye, ed., *Visitations of Norfolk, 1563, 1589, and 1613* (*HSPVS*, vol. 32, 1891), p. 53 and *Ormerod*, vol. 2, pp. 686-87 (Brereton); *Salt* 7, pt. 2 (1886), pp. 24, 36-47 (Ipstones, Swinnerton); *AR7*, lines 30-32.

The Royal Descents of 500 Immigrants

1. Henry II, King of England, d. 1189 = Eleanor of Aquitaine

2. (illegitimate by Ida, later wife of Roger Bigod, 2nd Earl of Norfolk) William Longespee, Earl of Salisbury = Ela, Countess of Salisbury

3. Ida Longespee = William de Beauchamp

4. Beatrice de Beauchamp = Sir Thomas FitzOtho or FitzOtes

5. Maud (or Matilda) FitzThomas = John de Botetourte, 1st Baron Botetourte, formerly thought to be an illegitimate son of Edward I, King of England, d. 1307, but see *TAG* 63(1988):145-53.

6. Thomas de Botetourte = Joan de Somery

7. John de Botetourte, 2nd Baron Botetourte = Joyce la Zouche de Mortimer

8. Joyce de Botetourte = Sir Baldwin Freville

9. Sir Baldwin Freville = Maud ---

10. Joyce Freville = Sir Roger Aston

11. Sir Robert Aston = Isabella Brereton

12. John Aston = Elizabeth Delves

13. Sir John Aston = Joan Lyttleton

14. Sir Edward Aston = Joan Bowles

15. Leonard Aston = Elizabeth Barton

16. Walter Aston = Joyce Nason

17. **Col. Walter Aston** of Va. = Hannah Jordan.

18. Mary Aston = Richard Cocke

19. Richard Cocke the younger (of two brothers both named Richard) = Elizabeth (Littleberry?)

20. Anne Cocke = Robert Bolling, Jr.

21. Elizabeth Bolling = James Munford

22. Robert Munford/Montfort = Anne Brodnax

23. Clarissa Montfort = John Shellman, Jr.

24. Susan Shellman = Samuel Howard Fay

25. Harriet Eleanor Fay = James Smith Bush

26. Samuel Prescott Bush = Flora Sheldon

27. Prescott Sheldon Bush, U. S. Senator = Dorothy Walker

28. George Herbert Walker Bush (b. 1924), 41st U.S. President = Barbara Pierce

Sources: *MCS 4*, lines 101, 101A and *VHG*, pp. 272-78 (but note the Burley correction in *MCS4*); *VGE*, pp. 390-92 and *Tixall*, pp. 146-49 (Aston); *GM* 21(1983-85):185-90 (Freville); *AR7*, lines 216, 122A, 30.

The Royal Descents of 500 Immigrants

1. Henry II, King of England, d. 1189 = Eleanor of Aquitaine

2. (illegitimate by Ida, later wife of Roger Bigod, 2nd Earl of Norfolk) William Longespee, Earl of Salisbury = Ela, Countess of Salisbury

3. Ida Longespee = William de Beauchamp

4. Beatrice de Beauchamp = Sir Thomas FitzOtho or FitzOtes

5. Maud (or Matilda) FitzThomas = John de Botetourte, 1st Baron Botetourte, formerly thought to be an illegitimate son of Edward I, King of England, d. 1307, but see *TAG* 63(1988):145-53.

6. Thomas de Botetourte = Joan de Somery

7. John de Botetourte, 2nd Baron Botetourte = Joyce la Zouche de Mortimer

8. Joyce de Botetourte = Sir Baldwin Freville

9. Sir Baldwin Freville = Maud ---

10. Joyce Freville = Sir Roger Aston

11. Sir Robert Aston = Isabella Brereton

12. John Aston = Elizabeth Delves

13. Margaret Aston = John Kinnersley

14. Isabel Kinnersley = John Bradshaw

15. Anne Bradshaw = John Fowke

16. Francis Fowke = Jane Raynsford

17. John Fowke = Dorothy Cupper, daughter of John Cupper and Audrey Peto, daughter of John Peto (and Margaret Baynham), son of Edward Peto (and Goditha Throckmorton), son of John Peto (and Eleanor Mantfield), son of William Peto and Katherine Gresley, daughter of Sir John Gresley and Elizabeth Clarell, SETH

18. Roger Fowke = Mary Bayley

19. **Col. Gerard Fowke** of Va. = Anne Thoroughgood.

20. Elizabeth Fowke = William Dent

21. Peter Dent = Mary Brooke

22. Peter Dent, Jr. = Mary Eleanor ---
23. George Dent = Susannah Dawson
24. Frederick Fayette Dent = Ellen Bray Wrenshall
25. Julia Boggs Dent = Ulysses Simpson Grant (1822-1885), 18th U.S. President

Sources: *Shaw*, vol. 2, part 1, p. 60, *VGE*, pp. 583-85, *HVG*, pp. 154-56, 743-44 and E.W. Schieffelin, *In Search of a Magna Carta Signer, A Tale of Adventure* (1990) (Fowke); T.F. Kynnersley, *A History of the Family of Kynnersley of Leighton, Shropshire* (1897), chart at end; *Tixall*, pp. 146-48 (Aston); *GM* 21(1983-85):185-91 (Freville); *AR7*, lines 216, 122A, 30 and *MCS4*, line 101A. A definitive monograph on the Aston-Kinnersley-Bradshaw-Fowke link would be welcome. Documentation for the Cupper-Peto-Gresley alternate descent, outlined in *PSECD* 3:160, is discussed by Mrs. Schieffelin; see also Rev. Herbert Barnett, *Glympton: The History of an Oxfordshire Manor* (Publications of the Oxfordshire Record Society, vol. 5, 1923), p. 23 (Cupper), Sir William Dugdale, *The Antiquities of Warwickshire*, 2nd ed., vol. 1 (1730), p. 472 (Peto), and *Gresleys of Drakelowe*, pp. 225-26.

The Royal Descents of 500 Immigrants

1. Louis VII, King of France, d. 1180 = (1) Eleanor of Aquitaine (who = (2) Henry II, King of England)

2. Marie of France = Henry I, Count of Champagne

3. Marie of Champagne = Baldwin IX, Count of Flanders, King of Constantinople, d. 1205

4. Margaret of Flanders = Bouchard d'Avesnes

5. John I, Count of Hainault = Adelaide of Holland, a great-great-granddaughter of Stephen, King of England, d. 1154, and Matilda of Boulogne, and of Henry of Scotland, Earl of Huntingdon, and Ada de Warenne, SETH (see *AR7*, lines 100, 170, 155, 165, 169)

6. John II, Count of Hainault (paternal grandfather of Philippa of Hainault, wife of Edward III, King of England) = Philippa of Luxemburg

7. (illegitimate by ----) William (Willem) de Cuser = Ida van Oosterwijk

8. Coenraad Cuser van Oosterwijk = Clementia Gerrit Boelendochter

9. Ida Cuser van Oosterwijk = Jan Herpertsz. van Foreest

10. Catryn van Foreest = Frank van der Meer

11. Arend van der Meer = Jacomina Jacob Claesdr. van Ruyven

12. Pieter van der Meer = Liedewey de Wilt van Bleyswyck

13. Frank van der Meer = Clara van Berendrecht

14. Joost van der Meer van Berendrecht = Machteld van der Dussen

15. Sophia van der Meer van Berendrecht = Cornelis van Lodensteyn

16. Jan van Lodensteyn = Geertruy (Gertrude) Jansdr. van Ilpendam

17. **Sophia van Lodensteyn** of N.Y. = Carel **de Beauvois** or **Debevoise**.

The Royal Descents of 500 Immigrants

Sources: *NYGBR* 66(1935):376-83; Adriaan Willem Eliza Dek, *Genealogie der Graven van Holland* (1954?), pp. 29-31, 40-41 esp. For the full ancestry of John II, Count of Hainault, see George Andrews Moriarty, "The Plantagenet Ancestry of King Edward III and Queen Philippa," mss. at NEHGS and elsewhere, and Roderick W. Stuart, *Royalty for Commoners: The Complete Known Lineage of John of Gaunt, Son of Edward III, King of England, and Queen Philippa,* 2nd ed. (1992).

The Royal Descents of 500 Immigrants

1. David I, King of Scotland, d. 1153 = Matilda of Northumberland, widow of Simon de St. Liz, SETH

2. Henry of Scotland, Earl of Huntingdon = Ada de Warenne, a great-granddaughter of Henry I, King of France, d. 1060, and Anne of Kiev, see *AR7*, lines 89, 50, 53

3. David of Scotland, Earl of Huntingdon (brother of Malcolm IV and William the Lion, Kings of Scotland) = Maud de Meschines, daughter of Hugh Kevelioc, 3rd Earl of Chester, SETH, and Bertrade de Montfort

4. Isabel of Scotland = Robert Bruce, lord of Annandale

5. Robert Bruce, lord of Annandale = Isabel de Clare

6. Robert Bruce, Earl of Carrick = (1) Marjorie of Carrick; (2) Eleanor ----

7. (maternity uncertain) Isabel Bruce (sister of Robert I, King of Scotland) = Thomas Randolph

8. Thomas Randolph, 1st Earl of Moray = Isabel Stewart

9. Isabel Randolph = Sir Patrick Dunbar

10. Sir David Dunbar of Cumnock and Blantyre = ----

11. Sir Patrick Dunbar of Cumnock and Mochrum = ----

12. Cuthbert Dunbar of Blantyre and Enterkine = ----

13. John Dunbar of Blantyre and Enterkine = ----

14. John Dunbar of Blantyre and Enterkine = Agnes Mure

15. Alexander Dunbar of Machermore = ----

16. Antoine Dunbar of Machermore = (1) Mary Montgomery; (2) ---- Stewart

17. (maternity uncertain) John Dunbar of Machermore = (1) Jean Murdoch; (2) Agnes McDowall

18. (maternity uncertain) Jean Dunbar = Andrew Heron of Kirrouchtrie

19. Andrew Heron of Bargaly = Mary Graham

20. Patrick Heron = Anne Vining

21. **Benjamin Heron** of N.C. = Mary Howe.

Sources: *LDBR*1, pp. 755, 757-58; P.H. McKerlie, *History of the Lands and Owners in Galloway*, vol. 4 (1878), pp. 423-24, 448-50 (Heron), 435-39 (Dunbar); *The Herald and Genealogist* 6(1871): 309-11, *SP*, vol. 3, pp. 260-61 and *Drummond*, vol. 2 (Dunbar); *SP* and *CP* (Moray). A thorough monograph on this descent would be welcome.

The Royal Descents of 500 Immigrants

1. David I, King of Scotland, d. 1153 = Matilda of Northumberland, widow of Simon de St. Liz, SETH

2. Henry of Scotland, Earl of Huntingdon = Ada de Warenne, a great-granddaughter of Henry I, King of France, d. 1060, and Anne of Kiev, see *AR7*, lines 89, 50, 53

3. David of Scotland, Earl of Huntingdon (brother of Malcolm IV and William the Lion, Kings of Scotland) = Maud de Meschines, daughter of Hugh Kevelioc, 3rd Earl of Chester, SETH, and Bertrade de Montfort

4. Isabel of Scotland = Robert Bruce, lord of Annandale

5. Robert Bruce, lord of Annandale = Isabel de Clare

6. Robert Bruce, Earl of Carrick = Marjorie of Carrick (parents of Robert I, King of Scotland)

7. Mary Bruce = Sir Alexander Fraser of Philorth

7. Maud Bruce = Hugh Ross, 4th Earl of Ross, SETH (he = (2) Margaret Graham)

8. Sir William Fraser of Philorth = Margaret Moray

8. William Ross, 5th Earl of Ross = Mary of the Isles

9. Sir Alexander Fraser of Philorth =

9. Joanna Ross

10. Sir William Fraser of Philorth = Eleanor Douglas

11. Agnes Fraser = Sir William Forbes of Pitsligo

12. Sir Alexander Forbes of Pitsligo = Maria Hay

13. William Forbes of Pitsligo = Mariota Ogilvy

14. William Forbes of Daach = Elizabeth Forbes of Brux

15. Alexander Forbes of Newe = Jean Lumsden

16. William Forbes of Newe = Margaret Gordon

17. John Forbes of Newe = Isabel Burnett

18. Alexander Forbes of Newe = Janet Robertson

18. William Forbes of Culquhonny = Isabel Gordon

19. William Forbes of Newe = 19. Helen Forbes of
Culquhonny

20. John Forbes of Deskrie = Margaret Farquharson

21. Archibald Forbes of Deskrie = Agnes Lumsden

22. **Rev. John Forbes** (c. 1740-1783), Anglican clergyman
and magistrate in East Florida = Dorothy Murray,
daughter of James Murray of N.C. and Mass. and Mrs.
Barbara Bennet Murray of N.C., both ARD, SETH.

Sources: *Forbes*, pp. 345-46, 365-66, 384, 388; *SP* (Forbes of Pitsligo,
Saltoun [Fraser], Carrick) and *CP* (Ross, Carrick).

The Royal Descents of 500 Immigrants

1. David I, King of Scotland, d. 1153 = Matilda of Northumberland, widow of Simon de St. Liz, SETH

2. Henry of Scotland, Earl of Huntingdon = Ada de Warenne, a great-granddaughter of Henry I, King of France, d. 1060, and Anne of Kiev, see *AR7*, lines 89, 50, 53

3. David of Scotland, Earl of Huntingdon (brother of Malcolm IV and William the Lion, Kings of Scotland) = Maud de Meschines, daughter of Hugh Kevelioc, 3rd Earl of Chester, SETH, and Bertrade de Montfort

4. Margaret of Scotland = Alan, lord of Galloway

5. Devorguilla of Galloway = John Baliol

6. Cecily Baliol (sister of John Baliol, King of Scotland 1292-96) = Sir John de Burgh

7. Hawise de Burgh = Sir Robert de Grelle

8. Joan de Grelle = John de la Warre, 2nd Baron de la Warre

9. Catherine de la Warre = Warin le Latimer, 2nd Baron Latimer of Braybrooke, son of Thomas le Latimer, 1st Baron Latimer of Braybrooke, and Lora Hastings, daughter of Sir Henry Hastings (and Joan de Cantilupe), son of Sir Henry Hastings and Ada of Scotland, daughter of David of Scotland, Earl of Huntingdon, and Maud de Meschines, above

10. Elizabeth le Latimer = Sir Thomas Griffin

11. Richard Griffin = Anna Chamberlain

12. Nicholas Griffin = Margaret Pilkington

13. Nicholas Griffin = Catherine Curzon

14. Catherine Griffin = Sir John Digby

15. William Digby = Rose Prestwich

16. Simon Digby = Anne Grey

17. Everard Digby = Katherine Stockbridge

18. Elizabeth Digby = Enoch Lynde

19. **Simon Lynde** of Mass. = Hannah Newgate.

14. Isabel Griffin (sister of Catherine) = Thomas Neville

15. Thomas Neville = Alice Wauton

16. Anne Neville, illegitimately by Sir John St. John (husband of Margaret Waldegrave, SETH) had

17. Cresset St. John = John Boteler

18. John Boteler = Jane Elliott

19. **Thomas Boteler** (Butler) of Md. = Mrs. Joan Christopher Mountstephen.

19. **Elizabeth Boteler** of Va. = William **Claiborne** (1600-c. 1677/8) dep. gov. and secretary of state for Va. John Boteler (Butler), a brother of Thomas and Elizabeth, also came to Md. but left no NDTPS.

Sources: *AR7*, lines 99, 94, 93, 170, 89, 50, 53, and sources cited therein, esp. E.E. Salisbury, *Family Histories and Genealogies*, vol. 1, part II (1892), pp. 359-471 (Lynde, Digby, Griffin), vol. 3 (*Supplement*), pedigree VIII (Lynde), and *CP* (Latimer, de la Warre, Hastings); *MCS4*, line 61 (Thomas Boteler and Mrs. Claiborne), *VHG*, pp. 18-26, 36-39 and *VM* 56(1948):458-60; F.A. Blaydes, ed., *Visitations of Bedfordshire, 1566, 1582 and 1634* (*HSPVS*, vol. 19, 1884), pp. 53 (St. John), 168-69 (Neville of Holt); George F. Farnham, *Leicestershire Medieval Pedigrees* (1925), p. 36 (Neville of Holt); Walter C. Metcalfe, ed., *Visitations of Northamptonshire, 1564 and 1618-19* (1887), pp. 23-24 (Griffin).

The Royal Descents of 500 Immigrants

1. David I, King of Scotland, d. 1153 = Matilda of Northumberland, widow of Simon de St. Liz, SETH

2. Henry of Scotland, Earl of Huntingdon = Ada de Warenne, a great-granddaughter of Henry I, King of France, d. 1060, and Anne of Kiev, see *AR7*, lines 89, 50, 53

3. David of Scotland, Earl of Huntingdon (brother of Malcolm IV and William the Lion, Kings of Scotland) = Maud de Meschines, daughter of Hugh Kevelioc, 3rd Earl of Chester, SETH, and Bertrade de Montfort

4. Ada of Scotland = Sir Henry Hastings

5. Sir Henry Hastings = Joan de Cantilupe

6. John Hastings, 1st Baron Hastings = Isabel de Valence, daughter of William de Valence, Earl of Pembroke (and Joan Munchensy), son of Hugh X de Lusignan, Count of la Marche, and Isabel of Angoulême, widow of John "Lackland," King of England, SETH

7. Elizabeth Hastings = Roger de Grey, 1st Baron Grey of Ruthyn

8. Reginald de Grey, 2nd Baron Grey of Ruthyn = Eleanor le Strange

9. Reginald de Grey, 3rd Baron Grey of Ruthyn = Joan Astley

10. Robert Grey = Eleanor Lowe

11. Humphrey Grey = Anne Fielding

12. Mary Grey = John Dixwell

13. William Dixwell = Elizabeth Knight

14. Charles Dixwell = Abigail Herdson

15. William Dixwell = Elizabeth Brent

16. **John Dixwell** (c. 1607-1688/9), English regicide and Cromwellian politician, later a resident of New Haven, Conn. = (1) Mrs. Joanna ---- Ling; (2) Bathsheba Howe.

14. Humphrey Dixwell (brother of Charles) = Ellen Lowe (their daughter Elizabeth Dixwell was the 1st wife of Sampson Erdeswick, historian of Staffordshire)
15. Anne Dixwell = Edward Broughton
16. Edward Broughton = Helen Pell
17. **Thomas Broughton** of Mass. = Mary Biscoe.

12. Margery Grey (sister of Mary) = Richard St. Barbe
13. Thomas St. Barbe = Joan ----
14. Alice St. Barbe = Christopher Batt
15. Thomas Batt = Joan Byley
16. **Christopher Batt** of Mass. = Anne Bainton of Mass, ARD, SETH.

8. Mary de Grey (sister of the 2nd Baron Grey of Ruthyn) = Sir William Disney
9. Sir William Disney = Lucy Felton
10. John Disney = Katherine Leake
11. Richard Disney = Jane Middleton
12. Emeline Disney = Hamon Sutton
13. Mary Sutton = Thomas Yorke
14. Mary Yorke = Thomas Randes
15. Mary Randes = George Merriton (Meriton, Meryton), Dean of York, chaplain of Anne of Denmark, Queen of James I, King of England
16. Anne Merriton = Francis Wright
17. **Richard Wright** of Va. = Anne Mottrom.

8. Juliane de Grey (sister of the 2nd Baron Grey of Ruthyn and of Lady Disney) = John Talbot
9. John Talbot = Katherine ----
10. Elizabeth Talbot = Sir Warin l'Archdeacon
11. Eleanor l'Archdeacon = Henry Barrett

12. William Barrett = Margred ferch Hugh Howel

13. Sinet (Jenet) Barrett = Jenkin Elliot

14. John ap Jenkin Elliot = Sined (Jane) Perrott

15. Elizabeth Elliot = John Butler

16. John Butler = Ann Travers

17. Grace Butler = John Neale

18. Raphael Neale = Jane Baker

19. **James Neale** of Md. = Anna Maria Gill, daughter of Benjamin Gill of Md. by Mary Mainwaring, probably also of Md., ARD, SETH.

Sources: *DAB, DNB* and *EB,* pp. 161-62 (Dixwell), John Fetherston, ed., *Visitation of Warwickshire, 1619* (*HSPVS,* vol. 12, 1877), pp. 297, 41 (Dixwell), 43 (Grey), *Shaw,* vol. 2, p. 268 (Grey of Enville) and *AR7,* lines 93A, 93, 170 (for Dixwell); *Salt 5,* pt. 2 (1884) (H.S. Grazebrook, ed., *Heraldic Visitations of Staffordshire, 1614 and 1663-64),* p. 61, Sir G.J. Armytage and W.H. Rylands, eds., *Staffordshire Pedigrees, 1664-1700* (*HSPVS,* vol. 63, 1912), p. 38, *NEHGR* 40(1886):106, and *GDMNH,* p. 113 (Broughton); *AL,* pp. 175-98 (Batt, St. Barbe); *PSECD* 3:284-85 (undocumented) and Timothy Field Beard, *How to Find Your Family Roots* (1977), p. 174 (Richard Wright), *DVY,* vol. 3, p. 456 (Wright), vol. 2, pp. 485-86 (Meryton), Rev. A.R. Maddison, *Lincolnshire Pedigrees,* vol. 3 (*HSPVS,* vol. 52, 1904), pp. 810 (Randes), 1125 (Yorke), 940 (Sutton), vol. 1 (*HSPVS,* vol. 50, 1902), p. 303 (Disney) and Walter C. Metcalfe, ed., *Visitations of Essex, 1552, 1558, 1570, 1612 and 1634,* vol. 2 (*HSPVS,* vol. 14, 1879), p. 654 (Disney); *Maryland Genealogical Society Bulletin* 31(1989-1990):137-53 (James Neale, including an ancestor table for 9 generations), plus Neale, Butler, Elliot, Barrett, l'Archdeacon and Talbot sources cited therein and the forthcoming *Seven Centuries: Ancestors for Twenty Generations of John Brice de Treville Clagett and Ann Calvert Brooke Clagett* by Brice McAdoo Clagett (author also of the James Neale monograph and AT); *CP* (l'Arcedekne, Talbot of Richard's Castle, Grey of Ruthin). The Neale-Gill-Mainwaring connection was first noted by Robert Behra of Newport, Rhode Island.

The Royal Descents of 500 Immigrants

1. David I, King of Scotland, d. 1153 = Matilda of Northumberland, widow of Simon de St. Liz, SETH

2. Henry of Scotland, Earl of Huntingdon = Ada de Warenne, a great-granddaughter of Henry I, King of France, d. 1060, and Anne of Kiev, see *AR7*, lines 89, 50, 53

3. David of Scotland, Earl of Huntingdon (brother of Malcolm IV and William the Lion, Kings of Scotland) = Maud de Meschines, daughter of Hugh Kevelioc, 3rd Earl of Chester, SETH, and Bertrade de Montfort

4. Ada of Scotland = Sir Henry Hastings

5. Hilaria Hastings = Sir William Harcourt

6. Sir Richard Harcourt = Margaret Beke

7. Sir John Harcourt = Ellen la Zouche

8. Matilda Harcourt = Henry Crispe

9. John Crispe = Anne Phillips (or Fettiplace)

10. Henry Crispe = Joan Dyer

11. John Crispe = Joan Sevenoaks

12. John Crispe = Agnes Queke

13. John Crispe = Avice Denne

14. Margaret Crispe = (1) John Crayford; (2) John Blechynden

15. (by 1) Edward Crayford = Mary Atsea

16. Sir William Crayford = Anne Norton

17. Anne Crayford = John Warren

18. William Warren = Catherine Gookin, niece of Daniel Gookin of Newport News, Va.

19. **Thomas Warren** of Va. = Jane ----.

15. (by 2) Alice Blechynden (half-sister of Edward Crayford) = Thomas Tournay

16. Jane Tournay = Stephen Gibbes

17. Robert Gibbes of Barbados = Mary Coventry

18. **Robert Gibbes,** colonial governor of S.C. = ---- Davis.

18. **Thomas Gibbes** of S.C. = Elizabeth ----.

18. Basil Gibbes = Ann Murrey

19. **John Gibbes,** very probably the immigrant to Goose Creek, S.C. = Elizabeth ----.

Sources: *PSECD* 3:308-11 and *LDBR* 1, pp. 186-89 (Thomas Warren); *VHG*, pp. 232-49 (Warren, Crayford), *HSF* 2:87-90 (Crispe) and *AR7*, lines 93, 170; Brice McAdoo Clagett, "The Gibbes Family of St. Andrew Parish, Barbados: Its English Ancestry in Co. Kent, England, and its Beginnings in South Carolina" (1987), unpublished mss. scheduled to be a forthcoming article in *TG*. See also W. Bruce Bannerman, ed., *Visitations of Kent, 1574 and 1592* (*HSPVS*, vol. 75, 1924), p. 146 (Torney or Tournay) and F.A. Crisp, *Collections Relating to the Family of Crispe,* new ser. (1913), vol. 1, p. 34 (Blechynden) and passim (Crispe).

The Royal Descents of 500 Immigrants

1. Louis VI, King of France, d. 1137 = Adela of Savoy

2. Peter of France, lord of Courtenay = Elizabeth of Courtenay

3. Alice of Courtenay = Aymer I, Count of Angoulême

4. Isabel of Angoulême, widow of John "Lackland," King of England = Hugh X de Lusignan, Count of la Marche

5. Alice de Lusignan = John de Warenne, 6th Earl of Surrey

6. William de Warenne = Joan de Vere

7. John de Warenne, 7th Earl of Surrey = (1) Joan of Bar; (2) Joanna of Strathern

8. (illegitimate by Maud de Nerford) Sir Edward Warren = Cecily de Eton

9. Sir John Warren = Margaret Stafford

10. Nicholas Warren = Agnes Winnington

11. Sir Lawrence Warren = Margaret Bulkeley

12. Joan Warren = Sir Nicholas Longford

13. Joan Longford = Sir Nicholas Montgomery

14. Margaret Montgomery = John Kniveton

15. John Kniveton = Anne Dethick

16. Barbara Kniveton (daughter certainly of 16 or 17, probably 17) = Richard Weston

17. Ralph Weston = Anna Smyth

18. **Thomas Weston** (c. 1576, bp. 1584-1647) of Mass., ironmonger, merchant adventurer, agent of the London syndicate that underwrote the sailing of the Pilgrims to Plymouth in 1620, a New England resident for an unknown period post 1622, = Elizabeth Weaver.

Sources: *DAB, DNB, NGSQ* 62(1974):163-72 and Sampson Erdeswick, *A Survey of Staffordshire* (1844), chart opposite p. 164 (Weston); *TG*, new ser. 7 (1890-91):226-27 (Kniveton); *The Reliquary* 15 (1874-75):chart opposite p. 7 (Montgomery of Cubley); *Transactions of the Historic Society of Lancashire and Cheshire for the Year 1934*, 86(1935):47-65 (Longford) plus, for a crucial chronological correction, the Longford bibliographical note in the forthcoming *Seven Centuries: Ancestors for Twenty Generations of John Brice de Treville Clagett and Ann Calvert Brooke Clagett,* by Brice McAdoo Clagett; *Ormerod,* vol. 3, p. 685 (Warren of Poynton); *AR7,* lines 231, 83, 153, 117. See *NEHGR* 141(1987): 99-100 for the chronological reasons (and suggestive naming patterns) leading to my conclusion that Barbara Kniveton, wife of Richard (not Ralph) Weston, was almost certainly a daughter of John Kniveton the younger and Anne Dethick. A definitive Kniveton monograph would be welcome.

The Royal Descents of 500 Immigrants

1. Louis VI, King of France, d. 1137 = Adela of Savoy

2. Robert I, Count of Dreux = Agnes de Baudemont

3. Alix of Dreux = Raoul I, Sire de Coucy

4. Agnes de Coucy = Gilles de Beaumez, Châtelain de Bapaulme

5. Gilles de Beaumez, Châtelain de Bapaulme = ---- de Bailleul

6. ---- de Beaumez (daughter) = Jean I de Sombreffe

7. Jean II de Mareau, Sire de Sombreffe = ----

8. Johann III, Sire de Sombreffe = Jutta von Wevelinghoven

9. Wilhelm I von Sombreffe = Margarethe von Kerpen

10. (illegitimate by ----) Maria von Sombreffe = Heinrich Typoets

11. Thonis Typoets = Beater van Beele

12. Maria Typoets = Jan Pijpelinckx

13. Hendrik Pijpe alias Pijpelinckx = Clara de Thovion

14. Maria Pijpelinckx = Jan Rubens

15. Peter Paul Rubens (1577-1640), the Baroque painter = (1) Isabelle Brant; (2) Hélène Fourment

16. (by 1) Nicolas Rubens, Seigneur of Rameyen = Constance Helman

17. Hélène Rubens = Jean Baptiste Lunden

18. Jeanne Catherine Lunden = Jean Jacques du Mont dit de Brialmont

19. Hélène Francoise du Mont dit de Brialmont = Jean Baptiste de la Bistrate, Seigneur of Laer and Neerwinde

20. Isabelle Hélène de la Bistrate = Albert Jean Stier

21. **Henri Joseph Stier**, Seigneur of Aertselaer, of Md. = Marie Louise Peeters.

Sources: *TG* 9(1988):45-73, Hervé Douxchamps, *Rubens et ses Descendants,* vol. 4 (1985), *passim,* and Robert Winder Johnson, *The Ancestry of Rosalie Morris Johnson,* vol. 1 (1905), chart at beginning and pp. 196-211 (P.P. Rubens to H.J. Stier); *Archiv für Sippenforschung* 43(1977):263-66 (generations 8-15); *ES*, charts for Sombreffe (new ser., 11, table 14), Coucy, Dreux and France; H.M. West Winter, *The Descendants of Charlemagne (800-1400), Part I, "Brandenburg Updated," Generations I-XIV* (1987) and *Part II, The Continental Descendants, Generations XV-XVI* (1991), generations 12-87, 13-147, 14-250, 14-835, 15-1180, and 16-1589 (generations 1-6).

The Royal Descents of 500 Immigrants

1. Henry I, King of England, d. 1135 = Matilda of Scotland
2. (illegitimate by Sybil Corbet) Reginald FitzRoy or de Mortain, Earl of Cornwall = Mabel FitzWilliam
3. Maud FitzReginald = Robert de Beaumont, Count of Meulan, great-great-grandson of Henry I, King of France, d. 1060, and Anne of Kiev (see *AR7*, lines 53, 50)
4. Maud de Beaumont = William de Vernon, 5th Earl of Devon
5. Mary de Vernon = Sir Robert Courtenay
6. Sir John Courtenay = Isabel de Vere
7. Sir Hugh Courtenay = Eleanor le Despencer
8. Eleanor Courtenay = Henry Grey, 1st Baron Grey of Codnor
9. Richard Grey, 2nd Baron Grey of Codnor = Joan FitzPayn
10. Robert FitzPayn (formerly Grey), Baron FitzPayn = Elizabeth de Brian
11. Isabel FitzPayn = Richard Poynings, 3rd Baron Poynings
12. Joan Poynings = Sir Richard Camoys
13. Margaret Camoys = Ralph Radmylde
14. Margaret Radmylde = John Goring
15. John Goring = Joan Hewster
16. John Goring = Constance Dyke
17. Constance Goring = Sir John Kingsmill
18. Mary Kingsmill = Edward Goddard
19. Bridget Goddard = William Cordray
20. **Anna Cordray** of Va. = Richard **Bernard** of Va., ARD, SETH.
20. Bridget Cordray = Samuel Ironmonger
21. **Francis Ironmonger** of Va. = Elizabeth ----.
21. **William Ironmonger** of Va. = Elizabeth Jones.

18. Alice Kingsmill (sister of Mary) = James Pilkington, Bishop of Durham

19. Deborah Pilkington = Walter Dunch

20. **Deborah Dunch,** known as **Lady Deborah Moody** (d. c. 1659), founder of a colony at Gravesend, L.I. = Sir Henry **Moody,** 1st Bt.

13. Eleanor Camoys (sister of Margaret) = Sir Roger Lewknor, son of Sir Thomas Lewknor and Philippa Dalyngridge, ARD, SETH

14. Elizabeth Lewknor = John Wroth

15. Thomas Wroth = Joan Newdigate

16. Robert Wroth = Jane Hawte

17. Sir Thomas Wroth = Mary Rich

18. Elizabeth Wroth = George Mynne

19. Anne Mynne = George Calvert, 1st Baron Baltimore (c. 1578/9-1632), promoter of Md.

20. **Cecil Calvert, 2nd Baron Baltimore,** proprietor of Md. = Hon. Anne Arundell, ARD, SETH.

20. **Hon. Leonard Calvert** (1606-1647), colonial governor of Md. = ----. Note: Hon. Grace and Hon. Helen or Ellen Calvert, daughters of George Calvert, 1st Baron Baltimore and Anne Mynne, married respectively Sir Robert Talbot, 2nd Bt., and James Talbot, and left sons Sir William Talbot, 3rd Bt., secretary of Md. (= Anne Nugent) and George Talbot (son of Helen), surveyor general of Md. (= Sarah ----). Both returned to Ireland, Sir William died childless and George left no NDTPS.

18. Judith Wroth (sister of Elizabeth) = Robert Burgoyne

19. Roger Burgoyne = Mary Wendy

20. Judith Burgoyne = Onslow Winch

21. Sir Humphrey Winch, 1st Bt. = Rebecca Browne

22. Mary Winch = Sir Francis Bickley, 3rd Bt.

The Royal Descents of 500 Immigrants

23. **Joseph Bickley** of Va. = Mrs. Sarah Shelton Gissage.

Sources: *TG* 1(1980):113, 124, 2(1981):249, 255, *VGE*, pp. 414-15, *LDBR* 1, pp. 642-43, and *LDBR* 3, pp. 42-44 (Sir Richard Camoys and Joan Poynings to William and Francis Ironmonger; Sir Richard Camoys was a son of Thomas Camoys, 1st Baron Camoys, not, however, by his second wife, Elizabeth Mortimer, widow of Sir Henry "Hotspur" Percy, but by his first wife, Elizabeth de Louches); G.D. Squibb, ed., *Wiltshire Visitation Pedigrees, 1623* (*HSPVS*, vol. 105-6, 1954), p. 40 (Cordray), W.H. Rylands, ed., *Visitations of Hampshire, 1530, 1575, 1622 and 1634* (*HSPVS*, vol. 64, 1913), p. 168 (Goddard); *Berry's Hants*, pp. 44-45 (Kingsmill); *BP* (Goring, baronets and Camoys); *CP* (Camoys, Poynings, FitzPayn, Grey of Codnor); *AR7*, lines 50, 121 and *TG* 9(1988):226-27; *NAW* (Lady Deborah Moody), *CB* (Moody of Garesdon), *MGH*, 3rd ser., 2 (1898):43 (Dunch), and John Pilkington, *History of the Pilkington Family of Lancashire*, 3rd ed. (1912), pp. 104-110, 268-72, 297 and chart in pocket at end; *AP&P*, pp. 153-58, 161-63, *MG* 1:132-38, 143-44 (Calvert, Mynne), *DAB* (Leonard Calvert), *Mary Isaac*, pp. 177-78, *Archaeologia Cantiana* 12(1878):315, F.W. Weaver, *Visitations of Somerset, 1531 and 1573* (1885), p. 93, and J.C. Wedgwood, *History of Parliament: Biographies of Members of the Commons House, 1439-1509* (1936), p. 974 (Wroth), plus *Lewes*, pp. 149-53 (Lewknor); *TVG* 27(1983):32-49, *CB* (Bickley and Winch), and F.A. Blaydes, ed., *Visitations of Bedfordshire, 1566, 1582, and 1634* (*HSPVS*, vol. 19, 1884), pp. 199 (Winch), 88 (Burgoyne). A definitive Kingsmill monograph is much needed.

The Royal Descents of 500 Immigrants

1. Henry I, King of England, d. 1135 = Matilda of Scotland
2. (illegitimate by ----) Elizabeth = Fergus, lord of Galloway
3. Uchtred of Galloway = Gunnild of Dunbar, a descendant of Ethelred II the Unready, King of England, d. 1016, see *AR7*, lines 38, 34
4. Roland, lord of Galloway = Elena de Morville
5. Alan, lord of Galloway = --- de Lacy
6. Helen of Galloway = Roger de Quincy, 2nd Earl of Winchester, a descendant of Henry I, King of France, d. 1060, see *AR7*, line 53
7. Elizabeth de Quincy = Alexander Comyn, 2nd Earl of Buchan
8. Elizabeth Comyn = Gilbert de Umfreville, 1st Earl of Angus
9. Robert de Umfreville, 2nd Earl of Angus = Eleanor ----
10. Thomas de Umfreville = Joan de Roddam
11. Sir Thomas de Umfreville = Agnes (de Grey?)
12. Elizabeth de Umfreville = Sir William Elmeden
13. Joan Elmeden = Thomas Forster
14. Thomas Forster = Elizabeth de Etherstone
15. Thomas Forster = --- Fetherstonhaugh
16. Sir Roger Forster = Joan Hussey
17. Thomas Forster = Margaret Browning
18. Sir Thomas Forster = Susan Foster
19. Susan Forster = Thomas Brooke
20. **Robert Brooke**, acting governor of Md. = (1) Mary Baker; (2) Mary Mainwaring.
21. (by 1) Thomas Brooke = Eleanor Hatton
22. Thomas Brooke, Jr. = Anne ---
23. Thomas Brooke (III) = Lucy Smith
24. Mary Brooke = Peter Dent
25. Peter Dent, Jr. = Mary Eleanor ---

26. George Dent = Susannah Dawson
27. Frederick Fayette Dent = Ellen Bray Wrenshall
28. Julia Boggs Dent = Ulysses Simpson Grant (1822–1885), 18th U.S. President

19. Catherine Forster (sister of Susan) = Francis Towneley, son of Edmund Towneley and Catherine Curson, daughter of Richard Curson and Anne Giffard, daughter of William Giffard (and ---- Vachell), son of John Giffard and Agnes Winslow, ARD, SETH
20. Nicholas Towneley = Joanna White
21. **Richard Towneley** of N.J. = Mrs. Elizabeth Smith Lawrence de Carteret, widow of William Lawrence of L.I. and Philip de Carteret, 1st colonial governor of N.J., both ARD, SETH.

20. Francis Towneley (brother of Nicholas) = Anne Elborough
21. Francis Towneley = ----
22. Jeremiah Towneley = Frances Andrews
23. **Margaret Frances Towneley** of Md. = Richard **Chase.**

Sources: *AR7*, lines 224, 38, 121B, and *MCS4*, lines 108, 109, 110; Bennet B. Browne, *Pedigree Chart of Robert Brooke and Mary Baker, His First Wife* (1912); W. L. Sheppard, Jr., *The Ancestry of Edward Carleton and Ellen Newton, His Wife* (microfilm, 1978- generations 1-11); *MG* 1:91-94 (Brooke); F.A. Hill, *The Mystery Solved: Facts Relating to the "Lawrence-Towneley," "Chase-Towneley" Marriages and Estate Question* (1888), chart in packet esp. (Towneley and Mrs. Chase), W.H. Turner, ed., *Visitations of Oxfordshire, 1566, 1574, and 1634* (*HSPVS*, vol. 5, 1871), p. 131 (Curson) and *NEHGR* 75 (1921):135 (reprinted in *EO* 1:1:631) (Giffard). Brice McAdoo Clagett questions the de Umfreville-Elmeden-Forster descent (generations 11-13) on chronological grounds; a thorough Elmeden monograph is much needed.

The Royal Descents of 500 Immigrants

1. Henry I, King of England, d. 1135 = Matilda of Scotland
2. (illegitimate by ----) Robert of Caen, 1st Earl of Gloucester = Mabel FitzHamon
3. William Fitz Robert, 2nd Earl of Gloucester = Hawise de Beaumont
4. (illegitimate by ----) Mabel of Gloucester = Gruffudd ab Ifor Bach
5. Hywel Felyn ap Gruffudd = Sara le Sore
6. Madog ap Hywel Felyn = Iwerydd ferch Lewys ap Rhys
7. Joan ferch Madog = Dafydd ap Owain Fychan
8. Goleuddydd ferch Dafydd = Rhys Llwyd, son of Adam (and Elen ferch Llywelyn o'r Cwmwd ap Hywel Hen), son of Rhys ab Einion Sais and Gwladys, daughter of Llywelyn (and ----), son of Hywel Felyn ap Gruffudd, 5. above, and Sara le Sore
9. Gwilym ap Rhys Llwyd = Margred ferch John ap Jenkin
10. Gwenllian ferch Gwilym = Jenkin Gunter
11. Margred Gunter = Roger ap John
12. John ap Roger = Mawd Aubrey
13. Alice ferch John = Owain ap Jenkin
14. Gruffudd Bowen = Anne Berry
15. Philip Bowen = Elsbeth Vaughan
16. Francis Bowen = Ellen Franklyn
17. **Griffith Bowen** of Mass. = Margaret Fleming of Mass, ARD, see below.
18. Henry Bowen = Elizabeth Johnson
19. John Bowen = Hannah Brewer
20. Abigail Bowen = Caleb Kendrick
21. Benjamin Kendrick = Sarah Harris
22. Anna Kendrick = Benjamin Pierce, Jr.
23. Franklin Pierce (1804-1869), 14th U.S. President = Jane Means Appleton

9. Isabel ferch Rhys Llwyd (sister of Gwilym ap Rhys Llwyd) = Gruffudd ap Cadwgon Fychan

10. Mallt ferch Gruffudd = Maredudd ap Henry Dwnn

11. Mabli ferch Maredudd = Gruffudd ap Nicholas

12. Owain ap Gruffudd = Alison Malefaunt

13. Elen ferch Owain = William Barrett

14. William Barrett = Agnes ferch Philip ap Maredudd

15. Henry Barrett = Catrin ferch Trahaearn ap Morgan

16. Margaret Barrett = William Dawkin

17. Jenkin Dawkin = Elizabeth Jenkin

18. Alice Dawkin = Henry Fleming

19. **Margaret Fleming** of Mass. = Griffith **Bowen** of Mass., ARD, see above.

Sources (for this and ten [possibly twenty-one] other lines from Gruffudd ab Ifor Bach to either Griffith Bowen or his wife Margaret Fleming): *AR7*, lines 179, 124, *NGSQ* 67 (1979):163-66, *CN*19 (1986-87):335-41, 588-96, and *Lineage Book, Descendants of the Illegitimate Sons and Daughters of the Kings of Britain*, no. 156; AT of Griffith Bowen and Margaret Fleming compiled by William Addams Reitwiesner of Washington, D.C., based largely on *M&G* (pp. 386, 483 etc.), on *Bartrum 1* (pp. 209, 210, 248, 107-9, 618, 616, 330 for the lines above), *Bartrum 2* (pp. 1650, 248, 649, 51, 450 for the lines above, to generations 14 and 16 respectively) and on correspondence among Bartrum, William C. Rogers and General Herman Nickerson, Jr. of Jacksonville, N.C.

The Royal Descents of 500 Immigrants

1. Henry I, King of England, d. 1135 = Matilda of Scotland
2. (illegitimate by ----) Robert of Caen, 1st Earl of Gloucester = Mabel FitzHamon
3. Maud of Gloucester = Ranulph de Gernon, 2nd Earl of Chester
4. Hugh Kevelioc, 3rd Earl of Chester = Bertrade de Montfort
5. Mabel of Chester = William d'Aubigny, 3rd Earl of Arundel, Magna Charta surety
6. Nicole d'Aubigny = Roger de Somery
7. Joan de Somery = John le Strange (IV) of Knokyn
8. John le Strange (V), 1st Baron Strange of Knokyn = Maud de Wauton
9. Elizabeth le Strange = Gruffudd o'r Rhuddallt ap Madog Fychan ap Madog Crupl
10. Gruffudd Fychan ap Gruffudd o'r Rhuddallt = Elen ferch Thomas, great-aunt of Sir Owen Tudor, founder of the Tudor dynasty and husband of Katherine of France, widow of Henry V, King of England (Elen was **not**, according to Bartrum, a descendant of Llywelyn Fawr ap Iorwerth, Prince of North Wales, and Joan Plantagenet)
11. Lowri ferch Gruffudd Fychan (sister of Owen Glendower, the Welsh rebel hero) = Robert Puleston
12. Angharad Puleston = Edwart (Iorwerth) Trevor ap Dafydd ab Ednyfed Gam
13. Rose Trevor = Sir Otewell Worsley
14. Margaret Worsley = Adrian Whetehill
15. Sir Richard Whetehill = Elizabeth Muston
16. Margery Whetehill = Edward Isaac
17. Mary Isaac = Thomas Appleton
18. **Samuel Appleton** of Mass. = Judith Everard of Mass., ARD, SETH.
19. John Appleton = Priscilla Glover

20. Priscilla Appleton = Joseph Capen
21. Mary Capen = Thomas Baker, Jr.
22. Priscilla Baker = Tarrant Putnam, Jr.
23. Priscilla Putnam = Adam Brown, Jr.
24. Israel Putnam Brown = Sally Briggs
25. Sally Brown = Israel C. Brewer
26. Sarah Almeda Brewer = Calvin Galusha Coolidge
27. John Calvin Coolidge = Victoria Josephine Moor
28. (John) Calvin Coolidge (Jr.) (1872-1933), 30th U.S. President = Grace Anna Goodhue

14. Joyce Worsley (sister of Margaret) = Richard Lee
15. Richard Lee = Eleanor ----
16. Geoffrey Lee = Agnes Conyers
17. Richard Lee = Elizabeth Crispe
18. Mary Lee = Henry Drake
19. **Robert Drake** of Va. = Joan Gawton.

Sources: *AR7*, lines 249, 124-26 and sources cited therein, esp. *Mary Isaac* (Appleton); *PSECD* 3:122-23, *LDBR* 5, p. 381, and W.B. Bannerman, ed., *Visitations of Surrey, 1530, 1572, and 1623* (*HSPVS*, vol. 43, 1899), p. 102 (Drake) plus Robert Hovenden, *Visitation of Kent, 1619-1621* (*HSPVS*, vol. 42), p. 56 (Lee). See also, for Drake, Mrs. Henrietta Dawson Ayres Sheppard, *Ayres-Dawson and Allied Families*, vol. 1 (1961), pp. 149-85.

The Royal Descents of 500 Immigrants

1. Henry I, King of England, d. 1135 = Matilda of Scotland

2. (illegitimate by ----) Robert of Caen, 1st Earl of Gloucester = Mabel FitzHamon

3. William FitzRobert, 2nd Earl of Gloucester = Hawise de Beaumont

4. (illegitimate by ----) Mabel of Gloucester = Gruffudd ab Ifor Bach

5. Mawd ferch Gruffudd = Hywel ap Madog

6. Cynwrig ap Hywel of Radur = Angharad ferch Lewys

7. Hywel ap Cynwrig of Radur = (1) ---- Maelog; (2) ---- ferch Ieuan

8. (maternity uncertain) Meurig ap Hywel of Radur = Crisli ferch Adam Fychan

9. Dafydd ap Meurig of Radur = Ela ferch Hopkin

10. Gwladys ferch Dafydd = Ieuan ap Rhys

11. Mawd ferch Ieuan = Llywelyn ap Hywel Fychan

12. Sir Dafydd Gam = Gwenllian ferch Gwilym ap Hywel Grach (their daughter Gwladys married Sir William ap Thomas and was the mother of William Herbert, 1st Earl of Pembroke, father illegitimately, by Mawd ferch Adam Turberville, of Richard Herbert of Ewyas, father by Margaret Cradock of William Herbert, 1st Earl of Pembroke of the second creation, and Thomas Herbert of Abergavenny. Alice Herbert, an illegitimate daughter of Thomas Herbert of Abergavenny, married William Jenkin and was the mother of Elizabeth Jenkin, wife of Jenkin Dawkin, SETH, and maternal grandmother of Mrs. Margaret Fleming Bowen of Mass., SETH)

13. Thomas ap Dafydd Gam = ---- (*Bartrum 1*, p. 104 gives him only a son, Sir Dafydd Gam, d.s.p., no daughters)

14. Gwenhwyfar ferch Thomas = Ieuan Goch ap Ieuan Ddu

15. Rhys ap Ieuan Goch = ----

16. Tudur ap Rhys = ----

17. Rhys Goch ap Tudur = ----

18. Ieuan ap Rhys Goch = ----

19. Huw ap Ieuan = ----

20. Thomas ap Huw = ---- (a son, Cadwalader Thomas, married Ellen Owen, SETH, and was the father of John Cadwalader of Pa., SETH)

21. John Thomas = (1) Anne Lloyd; (2) Katherine Robert of Pa.

22. (by 2) **Robert Jones** of Pa. = Ellen Jones.

22. (by 1) Elizabeth Jones = Rees Evan

23. **Sidney Rees** of Pa. = Robert **Roberts,** son of John Roberts of (Pencoyd) Pa., ARD, SETH, and Mrs. Gainor Pugh Roberts, ARD, SETH.

Members of this family who also immigrated to Pa. but left no NDTPS include:

1. Thomas Jones, son of John Thomas and Anne Lloyd and husband of Anne Griffith

2-3. Cadwalader Jones and Katherine Jones, wife of Robert Roberts (son of Hugh Roberts of Pa., ARD, SETH, and Mrs. Jane Owen Roberts, ARD, SETH), son and daughter of John Thomas and Katherine Robert

4-5. Evan Rees and David Rees, brothers of Mrs. Sidney Rees Roberts

6-7. Elizabeth and Mably Owen, sisters, wives respectively of Thomas Andrews (no issue) and Edward Price, and daughters of Owen ap Huw (and ----), brother of 20. Thomas ap Huw above.

Sources: *WFP* 1, pedigrees I and II, pp. 7-23, 36-39 esp.; *Merion,* pp. 252-60, 294-303; *NGSQ* 67(1979):165 esp., plus citations to Bartrum as given on p. 166. Further research should be undertaken to confirm the above line from Thomas ap Dafydd Gam to Thomas ap Huw.

The Royal Descents of 500 Immigrants

1. Henry I, King of England, d. 1135 = Matilda of Scotland

2. (illegitimate by ----) Elizabeth = Fergus, lord of Galloway

3. Uchtred of Galloway = Gunnild of Dunbar, a descendant of Ethelred II the Unready, King of England, d. 1016, see *AR7*, lines 38, 34

4. Roland, lord of Galloway = Elena de Morville

5. Alan, lord of Galloway = --- de Lacy

6. Helen of Galloway = Roger de Quincy, 2nd Earl of Winchester, a descendant of Henry I, King of France, d. 1060, see *AR7*, line 53

7. Elizabeth de Quincy = Alexander Comyn, 2nd Earl of Buchan

8. Elizabeth Comyn = Gilbert de Umfreville, 1st Earl of Angus

9. Robert de Umfreville, 2nd Earl of Angus = Lucy de Kyme

10. Elizabeth de Umfreville = Gilbert de Boroughdon

11. Eleanor de Boroughdon, Baroness Kyme = Henry Talboys

12. Walter Talboys, Baron Kyme = Margaret ---	12. Joan Talboys = Andrew Luttrell, Baron Luttrell
13. Sir John Talboys = Agnes Cokefield	13. Hawise Luttrell, Baroness Luttrell = Sir Godfrey Hilton
14. John Talboys = Katherine Gibthorpe	14. Godfrey Hilton, Baron Luttrell = Margery ---
15. Margaret Talboys = John Ayscough	15. Elizabeth Hilton = Richard Thimbleby
16. Elizabeth Ayscough = William Booth	
17. John Booth =	16. Anne Thimbleby

17,18. Eleanor Booth = Edward Hamby

The Royal Descents of 500 Immigrants

18,19. William Hamby = Margaret Blewett

19,20. Robert Hamby = Elizabeth Arnold

20,21. **Catherine Hamby** of Mass. = Edward **Hutchinson.**

21,22. Elisha Hutchinson = (1) Hannah Hawkins; (2) Elizabeth Clarke

22,23. (by 2) Edward Hutchinson = Lydia Foster

23,24. Elizabeth Hutchinson = Nathaniel Robbins

24,25. Edward Hutchinson Robbins = Elizabeth Murray

25,26. Anne Jean Robbins = Joseph Lyman (III)

26,27. Catherine Robbins Lyman = Warren Delano, Jr.

27,28. Sara Delano = James Roosevelt

28,29. Franklin Delano Roosevelt (1882-1945), 32nd U.S. President = (Anna) Eleanor Roosevelt

22,23. (by 1) Hannah Hutchinson = John Ruck

23,24. Hannah Ruck = Theophilus Lillie

24,25. John Lillie = Abigail Breck

25,26. Anna Lillie = Samuel Howard

26,27. Harriet Howard = Samuel Prescott Phillips Fay

27,28. Samuel Howard Fay = Susan Shellman

28,29. Harriet Eleanor Fay = James Smith Bush

29,30. Samuel Prescott Bush = Flora Sheldon

30,31. Prescott Sheldon Bush, U.S. Senator = Dorothy Walker

31,32. George Herbert Walker Bush (b. 1924), 41st U.S. President = Barbara Pierce

21,22. Elizabeth Hutchinson (sister of Elisha) = Edward Winslow

22,23. Anne Winslow = John Taylor

23,24. Elizabeth Taylor = Nathaniel Greene, Jr.

24,25. John Greene - Azubah Ward

25,26. Lucretia Greene = Elijah Mason

26,27. Arabella Mason = Zebulon Rudolph

27,28. Lucretia Rudolph = James Abram Garfield (1831–1881), 20th U.S. President

Sources: *AR7*, lines 224A, 224, 38, 121B, 74A, *NEHGR* 145(1991): 99–121, 258–68, and sources cited therein, esp. those listed in *NEHGR* 141(1987):96–97.

The Royal Descents of 500 Immigrants

1. Henry I, King of England, d. 1135 = Matilda of Scotland
2. (illegitimate by ----) Robert of Caen, 1st Earl of Gloucester = Mabel FitzHamon
3. Mabira de Caen = Jordan de Cambernon
4. Henry de Chambernon = Isabel ---
5. Henry de Chambernon = Rose de Tracy, daughter of Sir William de Tracy, one of four murderers of Thomas à Becket, Archbishop of Canterbury (by probably --- de Pomeroy), son of William de Tracy (and ---), also an illegitimate son, by an unknown mistress, of Henry I, King of England, above
6. Oliver de Chambernon = Wymarca ---
7. Sir Henry de Chambernon = Dionisia English
8. Richard de Chambernon = Joan Okeston
9. Sir Richard Champernowne = ---
10. Sir Richard Champernowne = Joan de Valletort
11. Sir Thomas Champernowne = Eleanor de Rohart
12. Sir Richard Champernowne = Katherine Daubeny
13. John Champernowne = Margaret Spriggy
14. Richard Champernowne = Mary Hamley
15. Elizabeth Champernowne = William Fortescue, son of John Fortescue and Joan Prutteston, SETH
16. Jane Fortescue = John Cobleigh
17. Margaret Cobleigh = Sir Roger Giffard
18. Jane Giffard = Amyas Chichester
19. Frances Chichester = John Wyatt
20. **Margaret Wyatt** of Conn. = Matthew **Allyn.**
21. Thomas Allyn = Abigail Warham
22. Abigail Allyn = John Williams
23. Elijah Williams = Lydia Dwight
24. Abigail Williams = Thomas Williams, a cousin
25. Abigail Williams = Alexander Bliss

26. Margaret Bliss = Nathan Hoyt
27. Margaret Jane Hoyt = Samuel Edward Axson
28. Ellen Louise Axson = (Thomas) Woodrow Wilson (1856-1924), 28th U.S. President

21. Mary Allyn (sister of Thomas) = Benjamin Newberry
22. Mary Newberry = John Moseley
23. Joseph Moseley = Abigail Root
24. Abigail Moseley = John Lyman (III)
25. Mindwell Lyman = Ebenezer Pomeroy (III)
26. Eunice Pomeroy = Ebenezer Clark (III)
27. Jerusha Clark = Samuel Gates, Jr.
28. George Williams Gates (Vt. to Mo.) = Sarah D. Todd
29. George Porterfield Gates = Elizabeth Emery
30. Margaret (Madge) Gates = David Willick Wallace
31. Elizabeth Virginia "Bess" Wallace = Harry S Truman (1884-1972), 33rd U.S. President

23. Mary Moseley (sister of Joseph) = Eleazer Weller, Jr.
24. Mary Weller = Daniel Sackett
25. Daniel Sackett, Jr. = Mehitable Cadwell
26. Mehitable Sackett = Luke Francis
27. Manning Francis = Elizabeth Robbins Root
28. Frederick Augustus Francis = Jessie Anne Stevens
29. Anne Ayers Francis = John Newell Robbins
30. Kenneth Seymour Robbins = Edith Luckett, who = (2) Dr. Loyal Edward Davis, who adopted his step-daughter
31. Anne Francis Robbins, whose name was changed to Nancy Davis = Ronald Wilson Reagan (b. 1911), 40th U.S. President

Sources: *AR7*, lines 52, 25, 246F, 124A, 222 and sources cited therein, plus *VD*, pp. 160, 162.

The Royal Descents of 500 Immigrants

1. Henry I, King of England, d. 1135 = Matilda of Scotland
2. (illegitimate by ----) Robert of Caen, 1st Earl of Gloucester = Mabel FitzHamon
3. Maud of Gloucester = Ranulph de Gernon, 2nd Earl of Chester
4. Hugh Kevelioc, 3rd Earl of Chester = Bertrade de Montfort
5. (illegitimate by ----) Amicia de Meschines = Ralph de Mainwaring
6. Bertrade de Mainwaring = Henry de Audley
7. Emma de Audley = Gruffudd ap Madog, Prince of Powys Fadog
8. Angharad ferch Gruffudd = William le Boteler
9. William le Boteler, 1st Baron Boteler of Wemme = Ela de Herdeberg
10. Denise le Boteler = Hugh de Cokesey
11. Cecily de Cokesey = Thomas Cassy
12. Agnes Cassy = Walter de Hodington
13. Thomas de Hodington = Margery Thurgrym
14. Joan de Hodington = Roger Wynter
15. Robert Wynter = Margery ----
16. Anne Wynter = Thomas Underhill
17. Hugh Underhill = ----
18. Thomas Underhill = Magdalen ----
19. John Underhill = Honor Pawley
20. **John Underhill** (c. 1597-1672) of N.Y., colonial military leader and magistrate = (1) Helena de Hooch; (2) Elizabeth Feake, great-niece of John Winthrop, the colonial statesman, founder and governor of the Massachusetts Bay Colony.

Sources: *Delafield*, vol. 2, pp. 538-40, 557-59, 562-63, 566-69, 575-78, 582-84, 592-97 esp.; Edwin R. Deats and Harry Macy, Jr.,

The Royal Descents of 500 Immigrants

Underhill Genealogy, vol. 5 (1980), pp. 18-55; *AR7*, lines 124-25.
The late Ludlow Elliman told me that research he sponsored had
disproved this line; this research has not yet, however, appeared in
print.

The Royal Descents of 500 Immigrants

1. Henry I, King of England, d. 1135 = Matilda of Scotland
2. (illegitimate by ----) Robert of Caen, 1st Earl of Gloucester = Mabel FitzHamon
3. Maud of Gloucester = Ranulph de Gernon, 2nd Earl of Chester
4. Hugh Kevelioc, 3rd Earl of Chester = Bertrade de Montfort
5. Agnes de Meschines = William de Ferrers, 4th Earl of Derby
6. William de Ferrers, 5th Earl of Derby = Margaret de Quincy
7. Agnes de Ferrers = Sir Robert de Muscegros
8. Hawise de Muscegros = Sir John de Bures
9. Catherine de Bures = Giles Beauchamp
10. Roger Beauchamp, 1st Baron Beauchamp of Bletsoe = Sybil Patshull
11. Roger Beauchamp = ----
12. Roger Beauchamp, 2nd Baron Beauchamp of Bletsoe = Joan Clopton
13. John Beauchamp, 3rd Baron Beauchamp of Bletsoe = Esther Stourton
14. Margaret Beauchamp = (1) Sir Oliver St. John; (2) John Beaufort, 1st Duke of Somerset (by whom she left a daughter, Margaret Beaufort, wife firstly of Edmund Tudor, 1st Earl of Richmond and mother of Henry VII, King of England, d. 1509)
15. (by 1) Sir John St. John = Alice Bradshaw
16. Sir John St. John = Sybil ferch Morgan ap Jenkin
17. Margaret St. John = Sir Thomas Gamage
18. Robert Gamage = Joan Champernoun
19. Mary (or Eleanor) Gamage = William Lewis
20. Joan Lewis = Edward Kemeys
21. Edward Kemeys = Alice Thomas

22. Edward Kemeys = Margaret Morgan
23. Lewis Kemeys = Mary ----
24. Nicholas Kemeys = Mary Witty
25. Edward Kemeys = Hannah Fowler
26. **William Kemeys** of N.Y. = Elizabeth Thornton.

Sources: *BLG*, 18th ed., vol. 2 (1969), pp. 363-64 (Kemeys); *M&G*, pp. 407-8 (Kemeys), 330 (Lewis), 390 (Gamage); F.A. Blaydes, ed., *Visitations of Bedfordshire, 1566, 1582 and 1634* (*HSPVS*, vol. 19, 1884), pp. 52-53 (St. John); *AR7*, lines 85, 189, 127, 125, 124, plus sources cited therein, esp. *CP*, and *TG* 4(1983):148, 6(1985):149.

The Royal Descents of 500 Immigrants

1. Henry I, King of England, d. 1135 = Matilda of Scotland

2. (illegitimate by ----) Robert of Caen, 1st Earl of Gloucester = Mabel FitzHamon

3. Maud of Gloucester = Ranulph de Gernon, 2nd Earl of Chester

4. Hugh Kevelioc, 3rd Earl of Chester = Bertrade de Montfort

5. (illegitimate by ----) Amicia de Meschines = Ralph de Mainwaring

6. Roger de Mainwaring = ----

7. Sir Thomas de Mainwaring = ----

8. Warin de Mainwaring = Agnes Arderne

9. Matilda de Mainwaring = Sir William Trussell

10. Sir Warin Trussell = ----

11. Lawrence Trussell = Matilda de Charnells

12. Sir William Trussell = Margery Ludlow

13. Isabel Trussell = Thomas Wodhull

14. John Wodhull = Joan Etwell

15. Fulk Wodhull = Anne Newenham

16. Lawrence Wodhull = Elizabeth Hall

17. Fulk Wodhull = Alice Wickliffe

18. Thomas Wodhull = Margaret ----

19. Alice Wodhull = William Elkington

20. Joseph Elkington = Ann ----

21. **George Elkington** of N.J. = (1) ----; (2) Mrs. Mary Humphries Core.

Sources: *TG* 7-8(1986-87):4-127, esp. 34-41, 48-68, 96-101, 107-22 (Col. Charles M. Hansen), which corrects Arthur Adams, *The Elkington Family of England and America, Being the Ancestry and Descendants of George Elkington of Burlington County, New Jersey* (1945).

The Royal Descents of 500 Immigrants

1. Henry I, King of England, d. 1135 = Matilda of Scotland
2. (illegitimate by Sybil Corbet) Reginald FitzRoy or de Mortain, Earl of Cornwall = Mabel FitzWilliam
3. Maud FitzReginald = Robert de Beaumont, Count of Meulan, great-great-grandson of Henry I, King of France, d. 1060, and Anne of Kiev (see *AR7*, lines 53, 50)
4. Maud de Beaumont = William de Vernon, 5th Earl of Devon
5. Mary de Vernon = Sir Robert Courtenay
6. Sir John Courtenay = Isabel de Vere
7. Sir Hugh Courtenay = Eleanor le Despencer
8. Hugh Courtenay, 1st Earl of Devon = Agnes St. John
9. Sir Thomas Courtenay = Muriel de Moels
10. Margaret Courtenay = Sir Thomas Peverell
11. Catherine Peverell = Walter Hungerford, 1st Baron Hungerford
12. Sir Edmund Hungerford = Margaret Burnell
13. Sir Thomas Hungerford = Christian Hall
14. Sir John Hungerford = Margaret Blount
15. Sir Anthony Hungerford = Dorothy Danvers
16. Anne Hungerford = John Blagrave
17. Anne Blagrave = John Bye
18. Anthony Bye = ----
19. Thomas Bye = Elizabeth Alliston
20. **Thomas Bye** of Pa. = Margaret Davis of Pa., ARD, SETH.

Sources: *LDBR 5*, pp. 480-81 and *Bye*, pp. 223-24, 227, 233-42, 252-61 esp.; G.D. Squibb, ed., *Wiltshire Visitation Pedigrees, 1623* (*HSPVS*, vol. 105-6, 1954), pp. 90-92 (Hungerford); *VD*, pp. 243-44 (Courtenay); *AR7*, lines 50, 51, 121 and *TG* 9(1988):226-27.

The Royal Descents of 500 Immigrants

1. Henry I, King of England, d. 1135 = Matilda of Scotland
2. (illegitimate by ----) Robert of Caen, 1st Earl of Gloucester = Mabel FitzHamon
3. William FitzRobert, 2nd Earl of Gloucester = Hawise de Beaumont
4. (illegitimate by ----) Mabel of Gloucester = Gruffudd ab Ifor Bach
5. (probably) Nest ferch Gruffudd = Hywel ap Trahaearn of Llan-gors
6. Gwenllian ferch Hywel = Gruffudd ab Ednyfed Fychan, brother of Gronwy ab Ednyfed Fychan, patrilineal great-great-great-grandfather of Sir Owen Tudor, founder of the Tudor dynasty and husband of Katherine of France, widow of Henry V, King of England
7. Sir Hywel ap Gruffudd = Tangwystl ferch Dafydd Goch
8. Gruffudd ap Hywel = Nest Fechen ferch Gwrwared
9. Sir Rhys Hen ap Gruffudd = (1) Joan Somerville; (2) Isabel Stackpole
10. (maternity uncertain) Margred ferch Rhys Hen = Philip Dorddu ap Hywel
11. Cadwgon ap Philip Dorddu = Ela ferch Llywelyn Crugeryr
12. Philip ap Cadwgon = ---- ferch Hywel ap Meurig
13. Cadwgon Fychan ap Philip = ----
14. Philip ap Cadwgon Fychan = ---- ferch Dafydd ap Maredudd
15. Hywel ap Philip = Joan ferch Richard ap Twmlyn
16. Owain Philips = Margred ferch James ap Ieuan Gwyn
17. Elen Philips = Edward Gwyn ap Hywel
18. Morgan ab Edward = ----
19. Lewys Morgan = ----
20. Morgan Lewys = ----
21. James Morgan = Jane ----

22. **John Morgan** of Pa. = Sarah Evans, daughter of John Evans of Pa., ARD, SETH, and Mary Hughes.

Sources: *WFP 1*, pedigree XIX, pp. 130-33 esp. (generations 16-22); *Bartrum 1*, pp. 209, 85, 681-82, 381, 383 (and 671, 678-80 for the connection to Sir Owen Tudor) and *Bartrum 2*, p. 703 (generations 1-16).

The Royal Descents of 500 Immigrants

1. Henry I, King of England, d. 1135 - Matilda of Scotland
2. (illegitimate by ----) Robert of Caen, 1st Earl of Gloucester = Mabel FitzHamon
3. William FitzRobert, 2nd Earl of Gloucester = Hawise de Beaumont
4. Amice of Gloucester = Richard de Clare, 3rd Earl of Hertford, Magna Charta surety
5. Maud de Clare = William de Braose
6. Maud de Braose = Henry de Tracy
7. Eve de Tracy = Guy de Brian
8. Maud de Brian = Geoffrey de Canville, 1st Baron Canville
9. Amicia de Canville = Sir Henry de la Pomeray
10. Sir Henry de la Pomeray = Joan de Moels
11. Thomas de la Pomeray = ----
12. Edward de la Pomeray = Margaret Bevile
13. Henry de la Pomeray = Alice Raleigh
14. Sir Richard Pomeroy = Elizabeth Densell
15. Sir Edward Pomeroy = Joan Sapcot(es)
16. Sir Thomas Pomeroy = Joan Edgecumbe (Edgcomb)
17. Thomas Pomeroy = Honor Rolle
18. Edward Pomeroy = Wilmot Periman (Peryam)
19. Samuel Pomeroy = Martha Smith
20. Martha Pomeroy = William Holmes
21. Thomas Holmes Pomeroy = Andriah Towgood
22. **George (Holmes) Pomeroy** of Pa. = Margaret ----.

Sources: William McL. and J. Nevin Pomeroy, publishers, *History and Genealogy of the Pomeroy Family and Collateral Lines, England-Ireland-America, Comprising the Ancestors and Descendants of George Pomeroy of Pennsylvania* (1958), pp. xxviii-xxix, 10-81, 147-48 and sources cited therein (English and Irish research by Margaret Dickson Falley); *AR7*, lines 63A, 63, 124.

The Royal Descents of 500 Immigrants

1. Henry I, King of England, d. 1135 = Matilda of Scotland
2. (illegitimate by ----) Robert of Caen, 1st Earl of Gloucester = Mabel FitzHamon
3. Maud of Gloucester = Ranulph de Gernon, Earl of Chester
4. Hugh Kevelioc, 3rd Earl of Chester = Bertrade de Montfort
5. (illegitimate by ----) Amicia de Meschines = Ralph de Mainwaring
6. Bertrade de Mainwaring = Henry de Audley
7. Emma de Audley = Gruffudd ap Madog, Prince of Powys Fadog
8. Margred ferch Gruffudd = Sir John Arderne
9. Agnes Arderne = Sir John Whetenhall
10. Margaret Whetenhall = Adam Bostock
11. Adam Bostock = Janet Bradshaw
12. Sir Ralph Bostock = Isabel Lawton
13. Sir Adam Bostock = Elizabeth Venables
14. Nicholas Bostock = Catherine Mobberly
15. Hugh Bostock = Joan Del Heath
16. George Bostock = Joan Horne
17. Joan Bostock = William Jennings
18. Thomas Jennings = Alice Bright
19. Catherine Jennings = William Branch
20. Lionel Branch = Valentia Sparkes
21. **Christopher Branch** of Va. = Mary Addie.
22. Christopher Branch, Jr. = ---
23. Mary Branch = Thomas Jefferson
24. Thomas Jefferson, Jr. = Mary Field
25. Peter Jefferson = Jane Randolph
26. Thomas Jefferson (1743-1826), 3rd U.S. President = Mrs. Martha Wayles Skelton

26. Mary Jefferson (sister of Thomas) = John Bolling (III), a great-great-great-grandson of Pocahontas and John Rolfe

27. Archibald Bolling = Catherine Payne

28. Archibald Bolling, Jr. = Anne E. Wigginton

29. William Holcombe Bolling = Sallie Spiers White

30. Edith Bolling = (1) Norman Galt; (2) (Thomas) Woodrow Wilson (1856-1924), 28th U.S. President

Sources: *GVFVM* 1:208-32 (Branch); W. H. Rylands, ed., *Four Visitations of Berkshire, 1532, 1566, 1623 and 1665-6*, vol. 2 (*HSPVS*, vol. 57, 1908), pp. 76-78 (Bostock, Jennings); *Ormerod*, vol. 3, p. 259 (Bostock), vol. 2, pp. 195 (Whetenhall), 85, 77 (Arderne, Powys Fadog); *Delafield*, vol. 2, pp. 589-97 (Powys Fadog, Audley and Mainwaring); *AR7*, lines 125, 124.

The Royal Descents of 500 Immigrants

1. Henry I, King of England, d. 1135 = Matilda of Scotland

2. (illegitimate by ----) Robert of Caen, 1st Earl of Gloucester = Mabel FitzHamon

3. Maud of Gloucester = Ranulph de Gernon, 2nd Earl of Chester

4. Hugh Kevelioc, 3rd Earl of Chester = Bertrade de Montfort

5. Mabel of Chester = William d'Aubigny, 3rd Earl of Arundel, Magna Charta surety

6. Nicole d'Aubigny = Roger de Somery

7. Joan de Somery = John le Strange (IV) of Knokyn

8. John le Strange (V), 1st Baron Strange of Knokyn = Maud de Wauton

9. Elizabeth le Strange = Gruffudd o'r Rhuddallt ap Madog Fychan ap Madog Crupl

10. Gruffudd Fychan ap Gruffudd o'r Rhuddallt = Elen ferch Thomas, great-aunt of Sir Owen Tudor, founder of the Tudor dynasty and husband of Katherine of France, widow of Henry V, King of England (Elen was **not**, according to Bartrum, a descendant of Llywelyn Fawr ap Iorwerth, Prince of North Wales, and Joan Plantagenet)

11. Owen Glendower (Owain ap Gruffudd Fychan), the Welsh rebel hero = Margaret Hanmer

12. Janet ferch Owain = Sir John de Croft

13. William de Croft = Margaret Walwyn

14. Richard Croft the younger = Anne Fox

15. Anne Croft = Sir John Rodney, son of Thomas Rodney (and Isabel ----), son of Sir Walter Rodney and Margaret Hungerford, son of Walter Hungerford, 1st Baron Hungerford, and Catherine Peverell, SETH

16. George Rodney = Elizabeth Kirton

17. Agatha Rodney = Thomas Hodges

18. George Hodges = Eleanor Rosse

19. George Hodges = Anne Mansell
20. Jane Hodges = John Strachey, son of William Strachey (and Elizabeth Cross) son of William Strachey, historian and 1st secretary of the Virginia Colony, ARD, SETH, and Frances Forster
21. John Strachey = Elizabeth Elletson
22. **John Strachey** of Va. = Elizabeth Vernon.

Sources: *AP+P*, pp. 590-93, *Strachey*, pp. 41-62, 296-97 esp. (and footnote 4, pp. 43-44 for Hodges); *WC*, pp. 444-46 (Rodney); O.G.S. Croft, *The House of Croft of Croft Castle* (1949), pp. 28-39, 148-53, and G.D. Squibb, ed., *Wiltshire Visitation Pedigrees, 1623* (*HSPVS*, vol. 105-6, 1954), p. 90 (Hungerford); *AR7*, lines 251, 124-26.

The Royal Descents of 500 Immigrants

1. Wladislaw I, King of Poland, d. 1102 = (2) Judith of Germany, daughter of Henry III, Holy Roman (German) Emperor, d. 1056, and Agnes of Poitou
2. ---- of Poland (daughter) = Jaroslaw I, Prince of Wladimir
3. George, Prince of Turow = ---- of Gorodno
4. Anna of Turow = Rurik I, Prince of Owrutsch, Grand Prince of Kiev
5. Predslawa of Owrutsch = Roman, Prince of Wolhynien and Galicia
6. ---- of Galicia (daughter) = Michael, Prince of Tschernigow, Grand Prince of Kiev
7. Maria of Tschernigow = Wassilko, Prince of Rostow
8. Boris, Prince of Rostow = Marie of Murom
9. Constantine II, Prince of Rostow and Uglitsch = ---- (1st wife)
10. Vassili, Prince of Rostow = ----
11. Constantine III, Prince of Rostow = Maria of Moscow, daughter of Ivan I, Grand Prince of Moscow (and Helene ----), son of Daniel, Prince of Perejaslawl (and ----), son of Alexander Nevsky, Grand Prince of Kiev and Wladimir, the Russian hero, and Praskowia of Polotzk
12. Anna of Rostow = Dimitri IV, Prince of Susdal and Wladimir
13. Semyon, Prince of Susdal = Alexandra ----
13. Maria of Susdal = Nicholas Veliaminov
14. Vassili, Prince Shuisky = ----
14. Xenia Veliaminov = Ivan, Prince Vsevoloje
15. Ivan, Prince Gorbaty-Shuisky = ----
15. Ivan, Prince Vsevoloje = -----
16. Ivan, Prince Gorbaty-Shuisky = ----
16. Vassilissa, Princess Vsevoleje = Daniel, Prince Kholmsky

411

17. Boris, Prince Gorbaty-Shuisky = ----

        17. Anna, Princess Kholmsky = Ivan Golovine

        18. Peter Golovine = Maria, Princess Odoevsky

18. Alexander, Prince = Gorbaty-Shuisky

        19. Anastasia Golovine

19, 20. Eudoxia, Princess Gorbaty-Shuisky = Nikita Romanov, brother of Anastasia Romanov, 1st wife of Ivan IV, the Terrible, Czar of Russia. Fedor Romanov, son of Nikita and Eudoxia, married Xenia Chestov and was the father of Michael III, Czar of Russia, d. 1645.

20, 21. Anastasia Romanov = Boris, Prince Lykov-Obolensky

21, 22. Elena, Princess Lykov-Obolensky = Fedor, Prince Khvorostinine

22, 23. Maria, Princess Khvorostinine = Boris, Prince Golitsyn, Russian minister under Peter the Great, son of Alexei, Prince Golitsyn and Irina, Princess Khilkov, see below. Alexei, Prince Golitsyn, son of Maria and Boris, married Anna Soukine; their daughter, Maria, Princess Golitsyn, married Vassili, Count Saltykov, and was the mother of Sergei, Count Saltykov, paramour of Catherine (II) the Great, Czarina of Russia and, some authorities think, likely father of Paul, Czar of Russia.

23, 24. Anastasia, Princess Golitsyn = Andrei, Prince Romodanovsky

24, 25. Ekaterina, Princess Romodanovsky = Ivan Ladyjensky

25, 26. Anastasia Ladyjensky = Vassili, Prince Dolgoroukov

26, 27. Paul, Prince Dolgoroukov = Henriette Adolfina de Bandré-du Plessis

27, 28. Elena, Princess Dolgoroukov = Andrei Fadeev (their daughter, Ekaterina Fadeev, married Julius von Witte and was the mother of Sergei, Count Witte, the Russian statesman)

28, 29. Elena Fadeev = Peter Hahn

29, 30. **Helena Petrovna Hahn,** known as **Madame Blavatsky** (1831-1891), founder of the Theosophical movement, a resident of New York City from 1873 to 1878 = (1) Nikifor Vassilievitch **Blavatsky**; (2) M.C. **Betanelly.**

13. Eudoxia of Susdal (sister of Semyon and Maria) = Dimitri IV, Grand Prince of Moscow, son of Ivan II, Grand Prince of Moscow (and Alexandra ----), brother of Maria of Moscow, wife of Constantine III, Prince of Rostow, above. Basil II, Grand Prince of Moscow, son of Dimitri and Eudoxia, married Sophie of Lithuania and was the father of Basil III, Grand Prince of Moscow, who married Maria of Borowsk and was the father in turn of Ivan III, 1st Czar of Russia, d. 1505.

14. Anna of Moscow = Youri, son of Patrick (and ----), son of Narimond, Prince of Pinsk (son of Gedymin, Grand Duke of Lithuania, and Eva), allegedly by Maria, daughter of Toktai, Khan of the Golden Horde (a great-great-great-grandson of Genghis Khan) and Maria Palaeologina, illegitimate daughter of Andronicus II, Byzantine Emperor

15. Vassili Patrikeev = Maria ----

15. Ivan Grozdj Patrikeev = Eudoxia Khovrine

16. Ivan Boulgak Patrikeev = 16. Xenia, Princess Vsevoloje, daughter of 15. Ivan, Prince Vsevoloje (and ----), above

16. Irina Patrikeev = Semen Khripoun Riapolovsky

17. Michael, Prince Golitsyn = ----

17. Ivan Khripounov = ----

18. Youri, Prince Golitsyn = Xenia ----

18. Ivan, Prince Khilkov = -----

19. Ivan, Prince Golitsyn = Eudoxia ----

19. Dimitri, Prince Khilkov = ----

20. Andrei, Prince Golitsyn = Anna ----

20. Vassili, Prince Khilkov = ----

21. Andrei, Prince Golitsyn
= Euphemia Piliemanov-
Sabourov

21. Andrei, Prince
Khilkov = ----

22. Fedor, Prince
Khilkov = ----

22. Alexei, Prince Golitsyn =

23. Irina, Princess Khilkov

23, 24. Ivan, Prince Golitsyn = Anastasia, Princess Prozorovsky

24, 25. Alexei, Prince Golitsyn = Doria, Princess Gagarin

25, 26. Dimitri, Prince Golitsyn = Adelaide Amalia, Countess
von Schmettau

26, 27. **Demetrius Augustine, Prince Golitzin** (or **Gallitzin**)
(1770-1840) of Md. and Pa., Roman Catholic clergyman,
colony founder, and writer, d. unm.

Sources: *DAB* (Madame Blavatsky and Gallitsin); *DGA*, vol. 1 (1939), p. 297 (Sergei, Count Witte, 1st cousin of Mme. Blavatsky); Nicolas Ikonnikov, *La Noblesse de Russie*, 1st ed., (at least) 11 vols., 1933-40, and 2nd ed., 26 vols., 1957-66 (Fadeev, Dolgoroukov, Ladyjensky, Golitsyn, Lykov-Obolensky, Romanov, Golovine, Khilkov, Saltykov, descendants of Rurik and Gedymin); *ES*, charts for Poland and descendants of Rurik, covering generations 1-15 (Gorbaty-Shuisky). See also Gerald Paget, *The Lineage and Ancestry of H.R.H. Prince Charles, Prince of Wales*, vol. 2 (1977), pp. 70 (M 1057-8), etc.

The Royal Descents of 500 Immigrants

1. Donald III Bane, King of Scotland, d. 1099 (uncle of Duncan II, King of Scotland, who d. 1094) = ----

2. Bethoc of Scotland = Uchtred of Tynedale

3. Hextilda of Tynedale = Richard Comyn

4. William Comyn, 1st Earl of Buchan = Sarah FitzHugh (see *CP* 11:143)

5. Jean Comyn = William Ross, 2nd Earl of Ross

6. William Ross, 3rd Earl of Ross = Eupheme ----

7. Hugh Ross, 4th Earl of Ross = Margaret Graham

8. Hugh Ross of Balnagown = Margaret de Barclay

9. William Ross of Balnagown = Christian (Livingston?)

10. Walter Ross of Balnagown = Katherine McTyre

11. Hugh Ross of Balnagown = ----

12. William Ross of Little Allan = Grizel McDonald

13. Walter Ross of Shandwick = Janet Tulloch

14. Hugh Ross of Balmachy = ----

15. Donald Ross of Balmachy = Margaret Innes

16. Walter Ross of Balmachy = Jean Douglas

17. Hugh Ross of Balmarchy = Katherine Macleod

18. George Ross of Balmachy = Margaret McCulloch

19. Andrew Ross of Balbair = ----

20. David Ross of Balbair = Margaret Stronach

21. **Rev. George Ross** of Del. = (1) Joanna Williams; (2) Catherine Van Gezel (father by 2 of George Ross, Jr., 1730-1779, signer of the Declaration of Independence, Pennsylvania patriot and jurist, and of Gertrude Ross, wife of Isaac Till and George Read, 1733-1798, also a signer of the Declaration of Independence, Federalist statesman and U.S. senator).

Sources: Harmon Pumpelly Read, *Rossiana: Ross, Read and Related Families* (1908), pp. 2-6, 8-10, 31, 40-45 (a revision of Francis Neville Reid, *The Earls of Ross and Their Descendants* [1894], pp. 2-5, 8-9, 26-27, 35-36); *CP* and *SP* (Ross), *SP* 1:504-5 (Comyn); *AR7*, line 121A.

The Royal Descents of 500 Immigrants

1. Duncan II, King of Scotland, d. 1094 = Ethelreda of Northumberland, daughter of Gospatrick I, Earl of Northumberland and Dunbar, SETH, and ----, sister of Edmund

2. William FitzDuncan, Earl of Moray = Alice de Romilly

3. Amabel of Moray = Reginald de Lucy

4. Richard de Lucy = Ada de Morville

5. Alice de Lucy = Alan de Multon, called de Lucy

6. John de Lucy = ----

7. Margaret de Lucy = Sir Hugh Lowther

8. Sir Hugh Lowther = Margaret Whale

9. Sir Hugh Lowther = Maud Tilloul

9. Alice Lowther = Sir Gilbert Curwen

10. John Lowther = Maud (?) ----

10. William Curwen = Margaret Croft

11. Sir Robert Lowther = Margaret Strickland

11. Sir Christopher Curwen = Elizabeth Huddleston

12. Anne Lowther =

12. Sir Thomas Curwen

13. Sir Christopher Curwen = Anne Pennington

14. Margaret Curwen = William Curwen, a cousin

15. Thomas Curwen, a priest = ----

16. Thomas Curwen = ----

17. Henry Curwen = ----

18. John Curwen = ----

19. **George Curwen** of Mass. = (1) Mrs. Elizabeth Herbert White; (2) Mrs. Elizabeth Winslow Brooks, daughter of Edward Winslow, Governor of Plymouth Colony, and Mrs. Susanna ---- White.

Sources: *AR7*, lines 37 (generations 30-40), 40 (generations 22-26) and sources cited therein, plus J.F. Curwen, *The Ancient Family of Curwen of Workington* (1928); *TCWAAS*, new. ser., 14 (1914) chart opp. 432, 16 (1916), pedigree 2 opp. 168, plus parts of the preceding articles (Curwen, Lowther, Lucy) and Hugh Owen, *The Lowther Family* (1990), chart on pp. 7-8 esp.

The Royal Descents of 500 Immigrants

1. William I, the Conqueror, King of England, d. 1087 = Matilda of Flanders

2. Adela of England = Stephen II, Count of Blois

3. William of Champagne, Seigneur de Sully (elder brother of Stephen, King of England) = Agnes de Sully

4. Margaret of Champagne = Henry, Count of Eu

5. John, Count of Eu = Alice d'Aubigny, daughter of William d'Aubigny, 1st Earl of Arundel, and Adeliza of Louvain, widow of Henry I, King of England

6. Ida of Eu = William Hastings

7. Thomas Hastings = ----

8. Hugh Hastings = Helen Alveston

9. Thomas Hastings = Amicia ----

10. Sir Nicholas Hastings = Emeline Heron

11. Sir Hugh Hastings = Beatrix ----

12. Sir Nicholas Hastings = Agnes ----

13. Sir Ralph Hastings = Margaret Herle

14. Sir Ralph Hastings = Isabel Sadington

15. Margaret Hastings = Sir Roger Heron

16. Isabel Heron = Thomas Hesilrig

17. Thomas Hesilrig = Elizabeth Brocket

18. William Hesilrig = Elizabeth Staunton

19. Thomas Hesilrig = Lucy Entwisle

20. Anne Hesilrig = Edward Catesby

21. Michael Catesby = Anne Odim

22. Kenelm Catesby = Alice Rudkin

23. Mark Catesby = ----

24. John Catesby = Elizabeth Jekyll

25. **Mark Catesby** (c. 1679-1749), naturalist, traveler to and writer on the South (Va., S.C., Ga., and Fla.), d. unm.

25. **Elizabeth Catesby** of Va. = William **Cocke**, Secretary of Va.

Sources: *DAB* (Mark Catesby), Sir A.R. Wagner, *English Genealogy,* 3rd ed. (1983), p. 226, and L.H. Jones, *Captain Roger Jones of London and Virginia* (1891), pp. 117-23 (Catesby and Cocke); G.A. Armytage, ed., *Visitation of Rutland, 1618-19 (HSPVS*, vol. 3, 1870), p. 33 (Catesby); John Fetherston, ed., *Visitations of Leicestershire, 1619 (HSPVS,* vol. 2, 1870), p. 15 (Hesilrig); George F. Farnham, *Leicestershire Medieval Pedigrees* (1925), chart opp. p. 57 (Hesilrig, Heron, Hastings); *Collins,* vol. 6, pp. 643-48 (Hastings); *MGH,* 4th ser., 3(1908-9):18-19 (Counts of Eu) and *AR7,* lines 139, 169. A new monograph on this Hastings line would be welcome.

The Royal Descents of 500 Immigrants

1. Henry I, King of France, d. 1060 = Anne of Kiev
2. Hugh Magnus, Duke of France and Burgundy = Adelaide of Vermandois
3. Isabel of Vermandois = Robert de Beaumont, 1st Earl of Leicester
4. Maud de Beaumont = William de Lovel
5. William de Lovel = Isabel ----
6. John de Lovel = Katherine Basset
7. John de Lovel = Maud Sydenham
8. Maud de Lovel = Sir Ralph de Gorges
9. Sir Ralph de Gorges = Eleanor (Ferre?)
10. Eleanor de Gorges = Sir Theobald Russell
11. Sir Theobald Gorges alias Russell = Agnes Wyke
12. Thomas Gorges = Agnes Beauchamp
13. Sir Theobald Gorges = Jane Hankford
14. Elizabeth Gorges = Thomas Grenville
15. Sir Thomas Grenville = Isabella Gilbert
16. Jane Grenville = Sir John Chamond
17. Richard Chamond = Margaret Trevener
18. Gertrude Chamond = Walter Porter
19. Mary Porter = Richard Penhallow
20. Chamond Penhallow = Anne Tamlyn
21. **Samuel Penhallow** (1665-1726) of N.H., merchant, jurist, historian and public official = (1) Mary Cutts; (2) Mrs. Abigail Atkinson Winslow Osborn.

16. Philippa Grenville (sister of Jane) = Francis Harris
17. William Harris = Catherine Esse
18. Jane Harris = John Harris, a cousin
19. Frances Harris = Thomas Kestell
20. Frances Kestell = Nicholas Morton
21. **Charles Morton** (c. 1627-1698) of Mass., Puritan clergyman and schoolmaster = Joan ----.

11. Sir Ralph Russell (brother of Sir Theobald Gorges alias Russell) = Alice ----

12. Sir Morris Russell = Isabel ----

13. Isabel Russell = Stephen Hatfield

14. Lawrence Hatfield = Agnes Marshall

15. Agnes Hatfield = Thomas Cranmer

16. Edmund Cranmer (brother of Thomas Cranmer, Archbishop of Canterbury) = Alice Sandes

17. Alice Cranmer = Thomas Norton

18. **Walter Norton** of Mass. = (1) Mrs. Jane Reeve Reynolds; (2) Eleanor ----.

18. Henry Norton = Sarah Lawson

19. **Henry Norton** of Maine = Margaret ----.

Sources: *MCS4*, line 23 and sources cited therein, esp. *VC*, pp. 360-61 (Penhallow), 383 (Porter), 84 (Chamond), 190-91 (Grenville) (for virtual disproof of the Courtenay line, and lack of proof for the Bonville alternative [*MCS4*, lines 22, 90A, 90, 144, 142] see Charles Fitch-Northen, "A Revision of the Grenville Pedigree" in *Devon and Cornwall Notes and Queries* 34[1978-81]:154-61); *Gorges*, pp. 13-40 and chart at end, and *AR7*, lines 215, 50, 53; *DAB* (Penhallow and Morton) and *VC*, pp. 264 (Kestell), 206, 209 (Harris); *TAG* 16 (1939-40):107-9, 112-15 (Norton), *Chester of Chicheley*, vol. 2, pp. 368-69, 396-98, 444-45, 448 esp. (Cranmer) and J.W. Walker, ed., *Hunter's Pedigrees* (*HSPVS*, vol. 88, 1936), p. 91 (Hatfield). A thorough monograph on the above Isabel Russell, wife of Sir John Drayton and Stephen Hatfield, would be welcome. Note: John Drake of Windsor, Conn. (see *MCS4*, line 22, and *AR7*, line 234) has now been proved *not* to be the son of William Drake and Philippa Dennis; an article on this immigrant's immediately pre-American history is now being prepared by Douglas Richardson of Tucson, Arizona.

The Royal Descents of 500 Immigrants

1. Henry I, King of France, d. 1060 = Anne of Kiev
2. Hugh Magnus, Duke of France and Burgundy = Adelaide of Vermandois
3. Isabel of Vermandois = Robert de Beaumont, 1st Earl of Leicester
4. Isabel de Beaumont = Gilbert de Clare, 1st Earl of Pembroke
5. Richard de Clare ("Strongbow"), 2nd Earl of Pembroke = Eve of Leinster, daughter of Dermot MacMurrough (Diarmait MacMurchada), King of Leinster, d. 1171, and Mor Ua Tuathail
6. Isabel de Clare = William Marshall, 1st Earl of Pembroke
7. Eve Marshall = William de Braose
8. Eve de Braose = Sir William de Cantilupe
9. Milicent de Cantilupe = Eudo la Zouche
10. Elizabeth la Zouche = Sir Nicholas Poyntz
11. Nicholas Poyntz = ----
12. Nicholas Poyntz = ----
13. Pontius Poyntz = Eleanor ----
14. Sir John Poyntz = Maud ----
15. John Poyntz = Matilda Perth
16. William Poyntz = Elizabeth Shaw
17. Thomas Poyntz = Anne Calva
18. Susanna Poyntz = Sir Richard Saltonstall, uncle of the Sir Richard Saltonstall who married Grace Kaye, SETH
19. Elizabeth Saltonstall = Richard Wyche
20. Henry Wyche = Ellen Bennett
21. **Henry Wyche** of Va. = ----.

19. Judith Saltonstall (sister of Elizabeth) = Edward Rich
20. Edward Rich = Susan Percy
21. Sir Peter Rich = Anne Evans

22. Edward Rich = ----
23. **Anne Rich** of Va. = Francis **Willis**.

17. Margaret Poyntz (sister of Thomas) = John Barley
18. John Barley = Philippa Bradbury
19. Margaret Barley = Edward Bell
20. **Anne Bell** = Sir Ferdinando **Gorges** (c. 1565-1647), founder and lord proprietor of Maine, ARD, SETH.

Sources: *MCS4*, lines 60-60A, *AR7*, lines 253, 66, 50, 53, 175 and sources cited therein, esp. *GVFWM* 5:596-600 (Wyche), *Saltonstall*, pp. 6-7, 12, Sir John MacLean, *Historical and Genealogical Memoir of the Family of Poyntz* (1886, rep. 1983), pp. 18-21, 29-38, 47-48 (for generations 11-15 above, I have followed the chart on 47-48, which differs somewhat from *MCS4*), *TAG* 21(1944-45): 237-38 (Mrs. Willis), 52(1976):176-77, 247 (Lady A.B. Gorges). Further documentation for generations 11-16 would be desirable.

The Royal Descents of 500 Immigrants

1. Henry I, King of France, d. 1060 = Anne of Kiev
2. Hugh Magnus, Duke of France and Burgundy = Adelaide of Vermandois
3. Isabel of Vermandois = Robert de Beaumont, 1st Earl of Leicester
4. Isabel de Beaumont = Gilbert de Clare, 1st Earl of Pembroke
5. Richard de Clare ("Strongbow"), 2nd Earl of Pembroke = Eve of Leinster, daughter of Dermot MacMurrough (Diarmait MacMurchada), King of Leinster, d. 1171, and Mor Ua Tuathail
6. Isabel de Clare = William Marshall, 1st Earl of Pembroke
7. Maud Marshall = Hugh Bigod, 3rd Earl of Norfolk
8. Sir Hugh Bigod = Joan de Stuteville
9. Sir John Bigod = Isabel ----
10. Sir Roger Bigod = Joan ----
11. Joan Bigod = Sir William Chauncey
12. John Chauncey = Margaret Giffard
13. John Chauncey = Anne Leventhorp
14. John Chauncey = Alice Boyce
15. John Chauncey = Elizabeth Proffit
16. Henry Chauncey = Lucy ----
17. George Chauncey = Anne Welsh
18. **Rev. Charles Chauncey** (1592-1671/2) of Mass., nonconformist clergyman, 2nd president of Harvard College = Catherine Eyre.

15. William Chauncey (son of John and Alice Boyce) = ---- Garland
16. Henry Chauncey = Joan Tenderyng
17. Elizabeth Chauncey = Richard Huberd
18. Edward Huberd = Jane Southall

423

19. Margaret Huberd = Richard Harlakenden

20. **Mabel Harlakenden** of Mass. = (1) John **Haynes** (c. 1594-1653/4), colonial governor of Mass. and Conn.; (2) Samuel **Eaton**. Roger Harlakenden, a brother of Mabel, also came to Mass. and married (1) Emlin ---- and (2) Elizabeth Bosvile (of Mass., ARD, SETH, who later married Herbert Pelham of Mass., 1st treasurer of Harvard College, also ARD, SETH) but left no NDTPS.

Sources: *AR7*, lines 69A, 69, 66, 53, 175, *MCS4*, lines 3, 148, 145, 89, 89A and sources cited therein; W.C. Fowler, *Memorials of the Chaunceys* (1858), 1st chart opposite p. 54 esp. and *Clutterbuck*, vol. 2, pp. 400-1 (Chauncey); *Yorkshire Archaeological Journal* 32 (1934-36):172-82, 187-89, 201 (Bigod); *NEHGR* 15(1861):327-29, 120(1966):243-47, reprinted in *EO* 2:2:210-12, 215-19 (Harlakenden).

The Royal Descents of 500 Immigrants

1. Henry I, King of France, d. 1060 = Anne of Kiev

2. Hugh Magnus, Duke of France and Burgundy = Adelaide of Vermandois

3. Isabel of Vermandois = Robert de Beaumont, 1st Earl of Leicester

4. Isabel de Beaumont = Gilbert de Clare, 1st Earl of Pembroke

5. Richard de Clare ("Strongbow"), 2nd Earl of Pembroke = Eve of Leinster, daughter of Dermot MacMurrough (Diarmait MacMurchada), King of Leinster, d. 1171, and Mor Ua Tuathail

6. Isabel de Clare = William Marshall, 1st Earl of Pembroke

7. Maud Marshall = Hugh Bigod, 3rd Earl of Norfolk

8. Sir Simon Bigod = Maud de Felbrigg

9. Sir Roger Bigod = Cecilia ----

10. John Bigod alias Felbrigg = Lucia

11. Roger Bigod alias Felbrigg = ----

12. Sir George Felbrigg = Margery Aspale

13. Sir John Felbrigg = Margaret (Waldegrave?)

14. Margery Felbrigg = Thomas Sampson

15. George Sampson = ----

16. Thomas Sampson = ----

17. Margery Sampson = Robert Felton

18. Thomas Felton = Cecily Seckford

19. Cecily Felton = John Stratton

20. Thomas Stratton = Dorothy Nicolls (their son, Joseph Stratton, mariner, settled in James City, Va., married Joan ---- and may have left descendants through his *possible* son, Edward Stratton of Henrico Co.)

21. John Stratton = Anne Derehaugh of Mass.

22. **John Stratton** of Mass. = ---- (a daughter, Anne Stratton, married William Lake and William Stevens).

22. **Elizabeth Stratton** of Mass. = John **Thorndike** (Dorothy Stratton, a sister of John and Elizabeth, also came to Mass. but her later history is uncertain).

Sources: *NEHGR* 135(1981):287-90, reprinted in *EO* 2:3:378-81 (Stratton), Harriet Russell Stratton, *A Book of Strattons,* vol. 1 (1908), pp. 43-60, 75-83 and chart opposite p. 42, and Morgan Hewitt Stafford, *Descendants of John Thorndike of Essex County, Massachusetts* (1960), pp. 1-12; Walter C. Metcalfe, ed., *Visitations of Suffolk, 1561, 1577 and 1612* (1882), p. 190 (Felton); *Proceedings of the Suffolk Institute of Archaeology and Natural History* 4 (1874):14-41 (Felton, Sampson, Felbrigg, Bigod); Charles Parkin, *An Essay Toward a Topographical History of the County of Norfolk,* vol. 8(1808), pp. 107-11 (Felbrigg, Bigod); *AR7,* lines 232, 69, 66, 50, 53, 175. This descent was first developed and brought to my attention by Dr. David A. Sandmire of Madison, Wisc. Further record evidence for the Sampsons (beyond the above and data in Lilla Sampson Briggs, *The Sampson Family* [1914], pp. 19-20) would be desirable.

The Royal Descents of 500 Immigrants

1. Henry I, King of France, d. 1060 = Anne of Kiev

2. Hugh Magnus, Duke of France and Burgundy = Adelaide of Vermandois

3. Isabel of Vermandois = Robert de Beaumont, 1st Earl of Leicester

4. Isabel de Beaumont = Gilbert de Clare, 1st Earl of Pembroke

5. Richard de Clare ("Strongbow"), 2nd Earl of Pembroke = Eve of Leinster, daughter of Dermot MacMurrough (Diarmait MacMurchada), King of Leinster, d. 1171, and Mor Ua Tuathail

6. Isabel de Clare = William Marshall, 1st Earl of Pembroke

7. Maud Marshall = Hugh Bigod, 3rd Earl of Norfolk

8. Sir Simon Bigod = Maud de Felbrigg

9. Sir Roger Bigod = Cecilia ----

10. Sir Simon Bigod alias Felbrigg = Alice Thorpe

11. Sir Roger Bigod alias Felbrigg = Elizabeth Scales

12. Sir Simon de Felbrigg = Margaret, probably a daughter (perhaps illegitimate) of Przemysl I Nosak, Duke of Teschen and Glogau

13. Helena de Felbrigg = Sir William Tyndal

14. Sir Thomas Tyndal = Margaret Yelverton

15. Sir William Tyndal = Mary Mondeford

16. Sir John Tyndal = Amphyllis Coningsby

17. Sir Thomas Tyndal = Anne Fermor

18. Sir John Tyndal = Anna Egerton

19. **Margaret Tyndal** (Tindal) of Mass. = John **Winthrop** (1587/8-1649), the colonial statesman, founder and governor of the Massachusetts Bay Colony (his third wife; Winthrop married secondly Thomasine Clopton, ARD, SETH).

20. Samuel Winthrop of Antigua = Elizabeth ----

21. Joseph Winthrop = Catherine Slicer

22. Sarah Winthrop = George Thomas
23. **Sir George Thomas, 1st Bt.** (c. 1695-1774), colonial governor of Pa. and Del. = Elizabeth King.

Sources: *DAB* (Sir George Thomas, 1st Bt. and John Winthrop); Ellery Kirke Taylor, *The Lion and the Hare* [Winthrop family] (1939), chart Q, *BIFR*, pp. 643, 648-49 and Robert Charles Winthrop, *Evidences of the Winthrops of Groton* (1894-96, later vol. 1 of *SMF*), pp. 26, 28, 153 esp. (Winthrop, Tyndal, Felbrigge, Bigod); *AR7*, lines 232, 69, 66, 50, 53, 175. See also *Chester of Chicheley*, vol. 1, pp. 252-59, 263-64, 276-83 (Tindal) and *Blackmansbury* 2(1965-66):3-7 (on Margaret of Teschen).

The Royal Descents of 500 Immigrants

1. Henry I, King of France, d. 1060 = Anne of Kiev

2. Hugh Magnus, Duke of France and Burgundy = Adelaide of Vermandois

3. Isabel of Vermandois = (1) Robert de Beaumont, 1st Earl of Leicester; (2) William de Warenne, 1st Earl of Surrey

4. (by 1) Robert de Beaumont, 2nd Earl of Leicester = Amicia de Gael

4. (by 2) Gundred de Warenne = Roger de Newburgh, 2nd Earl of Warwick

5. Isabel de Beaumont = Simon de St. Liz, Earl of Huntingdon and Northampton, son of Simon de St. Liz, Earl of Huntingdon and Northampton, and Matilda of Northumberland, SETH, who later married David I, King of Scotland

5. Waleran de Newburgh, 4th Earl of Warwick = Alice de Harcourt

6. Isabel de St. Liz = William Mauduit

7. William Mauduit = ----

8. Robert Mauduit = Isabel Basset

9. William Maudit   =   6. Alice de Newburgh

7, 10. Isabel Mauduit = William de Beauchamp

8, 11. William de Beauchamp, 9th Earl of Warwick = Maud FitzJohn, daughter of Sir John FitzGeoffrey and Isabel Bigod, daughter of Hugh Bigod, 3rd Earl of Norfolk, and Maud Marshall, SETH, also descended from 3. Isabel of Vermandois above

9, 12. Guy de Beauchamp, 10th Earl of Warwick = Alice de Toeni

10, 13. Maud de Beauchamp = Geoffrey de Say, 2nd Baron Say

11, 14. Joan de Say = Sir William Fiennes

12, 15. Sir William Fiennes = Elizabeth Batisford

13, 16. James Fiennes, 1st Baron Saye and Sele = Emmeline Cromer

14, 17. Elizabeth Fiennes = William Cromer, probably a cousin

15, 18. Sir James Cromer = Catherine Cantilupe

16, 19. Anne Cromer = Wiliam Whetenhall

17, 20. Rose Whetenhall = Thomas Wilsford

18, 21. Cecily Wilsford = Edwin Sandys, Archbishop of York

19, 22. **George Sandys** (1577/8-1643/4), poet, treasurer of Va., d. unm.

19, 22. Sir Samuel Sandys = Mercy Colepepper (Culpeper)

20, 23. **Margaret Sandys** of Va. = Sir Francis **Wyatt** (1588-1644), colonial governor of Va., ARD, SETH.

Sources: *PCF Lancashire* (Sandys pedigree); *Berry's Kent,* p. 134 (Wilsford); W.B Bannerman, ed., *Visitations of Kent, 1530-1, 1574, and 1592,* vol. 2 (*HSPVS,* vol. 75, 1924), p. 116 (Whetenhall), vol. 1 (*HSPVS,* vol. 74, 1923), p. 43 (Cromer); *Collins,* vol. 7, pp. 17-19 (Say and Fiennes); *CP* (Say and Sele, Say, Warwick, Huntingdon, Leicester, Surrey) and *AR7,* lines 86, 84, 50, 53, 72, 69-70, 66; *The Herald and Genealogist* 7(1873):384-95 and *The Ancestor* 5(1903): 207-10 (Mauduit).

The Royal Descents of 500 Immigrants

1. Robert II, King of France, d. 1031 = Constance of Provence
2. Adela of France = Baldwin V, Count of Flanders
3. Baldwin VI, Count of Flanders (and I, Count of Hainault; brother of Matilda of Flanders, wife of William I the Conqueror, King of England, d. 1087) = Richilde ----
4. Baldwin II, Count of Hainault = Ida of Louvain
5. Baldwin III, Count of Hainault = Yolande of Guelders
6. Ida of Hainault = Roger III de Toeni
7. Godeheut de Toeni = William de Mohun
8. Yolande de Mohun = Ralph FitzWilliam
9. ---- (daughter) = ----
10. Isabel ---- (granddaughter and co-heiress of Ralph FitzWilliam) = Nicholas Martin
11. Avice Martin = Sir Nicholas Carew
12. Nicholas Carew = Lucy Willoughby
13. Elizabeth Carew = Sir Roger Lewknor
14. Sir Thomas Lewknor = Philippa Dalyngridge
15. Nicholas Lewknor = Elizabeth Radmylde
16. Edward Lewknor = Anne Everard
17. Eleanor Lewknor = Sir William Wroughton
18. Sir Thomas Wroughton = Anna Berwick
19. Gertrude Wroughton = Sir Ralph Gibbs
20. Sir Henry Gibbs = Elizabeth Temple
21. **Robert Gibbs** of Mass. = Elizabeth Sheafe.

15. Jane (or Joan) Lewknor (sister of Nicholas) = Thomas Goodere
16. John Goodere = Alice Brent
17. John Goodere = Alice Frowick
18. Henry Goodere = Jane Greene

19. Anne Goodere = Henry Cooke

20. Edmund Cooke = Elizabeth Nichols

21. Theodora Cooke = Sir Thomas Josselyn

22. **John Josselyn** (c. 1608-post 1675), traveler (to New England), author and naturalist, d. unm. His brother Henry Josselyn (= Mrs. Margaret ---- Cammock) was dep. gov. of Maine but is not known to have left any children.

20. Mary Cooke (sister of Edmund) = William Strachey

21. **William Strachey** (c. 1572-post 1618), 1st secretary of the Virginia Colony = Frances Forster.

22. William Strachey = Eleanor Read

23. **William Strachey** of Va. = (1) Mary Miller; (2) Martha ----. John Strachey, his half-brother (son of Elizabeth Cross) married Jane Hodges, ARD, SETH, and was the paternal grandfather of John Strachey of Va., ARD, SETH.

15. Beatrix Lewknor (sister of Nicholas and Jane) = Ralph Roper

16. Agnes Roper = Walter Colepepper (Culpeper)

17. Sir John Colepepper (Culpeper) = Agnes Gainsford

18. Walter Colepepper (Culpeper) = Anne Aucher

19. William Colepepper (Culpeper) = Cecilia Barrett

20. John Colepepper (Culpeper) = Elizabeth Sidley

21. John Colepepper (Culpeper) = Ursula Woodcock

22. **Thomas Colepepper** (Culpeper) of Va. = Katherine St. Leger of Va., ARD, SETH. Their daughter, Frances Colepepper (Culpepper) married (1) Samuel Stephens, colonial governor of Ga.; (2) Sir William Berkeley (1608-1677), colonial governor of Va., ARD, SETH; and (3) Philip Ludwell (d. 1717), planter, Virginia councilor, colonial governor of N.C. and S.C. A son, John Colepepper (Culpeper) of N.C., participated in the 1677

Culpeper Rebellion (named after him) against Act. Gov. Thomas Miller (of Albemarle).

21. Thomas Colepepper (Culpeper) (brother of John II) = Anne Slaney

22. John Colepepper (Culpeper), 1st Baron Colepepper (Culpeper) = Judith Colepepper (Culpeper), his 2nd cousin, see below

23. **Thomas Colepepper** (Culpeper), **2nd Baron Colepepper** (Culpeper) (1635-1689), colonial governor of Va., returned to England = Margaret van Hesse (parents of Catherine Colepepper [Culpeper], wife of Thomas Fairfax, 5th Baron Fairfax, ARD, SETH, and mother of Thomas Fairfax, 6th Baron Fairfax, of Va., proprietor of the Northern Neck of Virginia, ARD, SETH).

20. Francis Colepepper (Culpeper) (brother of John I) = Joan Pordage

21. Sir Thomas Colepepper (Culpeper) = Elizabeth Cheney

22. Judith Colepepper (Culpeper) = John Colepepper (Culpeper), 1st Baron Colepepper (Culpeper), her 2nd cousin, see above

Sources: Walter Kendall Watkins, *The Robert Gibbs House, Boston* (1932, an excerpt from *Old-Time New England* 22[1931-32]:193-96), *NEHGR* 19(1865):208-9, *Heraldic Journal* 3(1867):165-66 (Gibbs) and Josiah Willard Gibbs, *Memoir of the Gibbs Family of Warwickshire, England, and* [The] *United States of America* (1879), pp. 12-13, 48-49 esp.; G.D. Squibb, ed., *Wiltshire Visitation Pedigrees, 1623* (*HSPVS*, vol. 105-6, 1954), pp. 219-20 (Wroughton); *Lewes*, pp. 149-50, 158-59 (Lewknor); *Berry's Surrey*, pp. 3-4 and *VC*, p. 68 (Carew); *Proceedings of the Somersetshire Archaeological and Natural History Society* 65(1920, for the year 1919):15-21 (FitzMartin) and *CP* (Martin); *TG* 9(1988):4-5, 26 (Mohun); *ES*, charts for Hainault, Flanders and France and *AR7*, lines 163, 128.

The Mohun-FitzWilliam-Martin-Carew descent was first brought to my attention by Mr. Douglas Richardson of Tucson, Arizona.

For **John Josselyn**: *AR7,* line 211 (generations 42-43 only) and *NEHGR* 71(1917):248-50, reprinted in *EO* 1:1:488-90 (Josselyn); Robert Hovenden, ed., *Visitation of Kent, 1619-21* (*HSPVS*, vol. 62, 1898), pp. 117-18 (Cooke); Sir G.J. Armytage, Bt., ed., *Middlesex Pedigrees* (*HSPVS*, vol. 65, 1914) pp. 23-24 (Goodere).

For **William Strachey**: *AP&P*, pp. 590-93 and *Strachey*, pp. 10-27, 296.

For the **Colepeppers** (**Culpepers**): *GVFVM2:*400, 408-87, 493-509, 520-48, *MCS4*, line 16D and *Sussex Archaeological Collections* 47(1904):57-74 (and charts opp. pp. 56 and 72 esp.] (Colepepper/ Culpeper); *Berry's Kent*, p. 214 (Roper).

Identification of the parents of Isabel, granddaughter and co-heiress of Ralph FitzWilliam and wife of Nicholas Martin, would be welcome, as would a definitive monograph on the Goodere family.

The Royal Descents of 500 Immigrants

1. Ethelred II the Unready, King of England, d. 1016 = (1) Alfflaed
2. Elgiva of England = Uchtred, Earl of Northumberland
3. Edith of Northumberland = Maldred, lord of Carlisle and Allendale
4. Gospatrick I, Earl of Northumberland and Dunbar = ----, sister of Edmund
5. Gospatrick II, 2nd Earl of Dunbar = Sybil Morel
6. Juliana of Dunbar = Ralph de Merlay
7. Roger de Merlay = Alice de Stuteville
8. Agnes de Merlay = Richard Gobion
9. Hugh Gobion = Matilda ----
10. Joan Gobion = John de Morteyn
11. Sir John de Morteyn = Joan de Rothwell
12. Lucy de Morteyn = Sir John Giffard
13. Sir Thomas Giffard = Elizabeth de Missenden
14. Roger Giffard = Isabel Stretle
15. Thomas Giffard = Eleanor Vaux
16. John Giffard = Agnes Winslow
17. Roger Giffard = Mary Nanseglos
18. Nicholas Giffard = Agnes Master
19. Margaret Giffard = Hugh Sargent
20. Roger Sargent = Ellen Makerness
21. **Rev. William Sargent** of Mass. = (1) Hannah ----; (2) Mary ----; (3) Sarah ----.

17. Thomas Giffard (brother of Roger) = Joan Langston
18. Amy Giffard = Richard Samwell
19. Susanna Samwell = Peter Edwards
20. Edward Edwards = Ursula Coles
21. Margaret Edwards = Henry Freeman

22. **Alice Freeman** of Mass. and (presumably) Conn. = (1) John **Thompson**; (2) Robert **Parke**. Alice and both her husbands (Dorothy Thompson, her daughter by 1, married Thomas Parke, son of Robert Parke and Martha Chaplin, his 1st wife) are ancestors of H.R.H. The Princess of Wales and her sons, H.R.H. Prince William and H.R.H. Prince Henry of Wales. See p. 469 of this volume, G.B. Roberts and W.A. Reitwiesner, *American Ancestors and Cousins of The Princess of Wales* (1984), pp. 21-32, 143-44, and *TG* 4(1983):176-82, 184-86.

23. Mary Thompson = Joseph Wise

24. Sarah Wise = Stephen Williams

25. Joseph Williams = Abigail Davis

25. Stephen Williams, Jr. = Mary Capen

26. Joseph Williams, Jr. = Martha Howell

26. Mary Williams = Benjamin May

27. Joseph Williams (III) = 27. Susanna May

28. Benjamin Williams = Sarah Copeland Morton

29. Susan May Williams = **Jerome Napoleon Bonaparte**, a native of Camberwell, Surrey, England, later a resident of Baltimore, son of Jerome Bonaparte, King of Westphalia (1807-1813), Prince of Montfort, sometime of Baltimore, d. 1860 (youngest brother of Napoleon I, Emperor of the French) and his first wife, Elizabeth Patterson of Baltimore. The younger son of Susan and Jerome was Charles Joseph Bonaparte (1851-1921), U.S. Attorney General and Secretary of the Navy (under Theodore Roosevelt), civil service reformer, who was of Napoleonic imperial descent through his father but of earlier royal ancestry only as outlined above.

Sources: *AR7*, lines 41-43, 34, 29A and sources cited therein, esp. *NEHGR* 74(1920):231-37, 267-83, 75(1921):57-63, 129-42, 79(1925): 358-78 (reprinted in *E01:*1:595-638 and *EO* 2:2:18-38), plus *Moriarty* (Sargent); *MCS4*, line 63, *TAG* 13(1936-37):1-8, 14(1937-38):145-46, 29(1953):215-18, *Blackman,* pp. 55-134, 138-58 (an ancestor table of Mrs. Parke for 32 generations, with an extensive bibliography), *Hawes, Freeman and James,* and *NEHGR* 141(1987):105. For the line from Mrs. Parke to the Bonapartes see *TAG* 56(1980):80-82, F.L. Weis, "Robert Williams of Roxbury, Massachusetts, and some of His Descendants" (typescript, 1945), pp. 21-23, 52-54, 127-39, 320-21, Christopher Johnston, ed., *Society of Colonial Wars in the State of Maryland* (1905), p. 125 (pedigree of John Savage Williams), and G.N. Mackenzie, *Colonial Families of the United States of America* (rep. 1966), vols. 1(1907), pp. 598-603 (Williams), 5(1915), pp. 68-71 (Bonaparte).

The Royal Descents of 500 Immigrants

1. Ethelred II the Unready, King of England, d. 1016 = (1) Alfflaed

2. Elgiva of England = Uchtred, Earl of Northumberland

3. Edith of Northumberland = Maldred, lord of Carlisle and Allendale

4. Gospatrick I, Earl of Northumberland and Dunbar = ----, sister of Edmund

5. Gospatrick II, 2nd Earl of Dunbar = Sybil Morel

6. Juliana of Dunbar = Ralph de Merlay

7. Roger de Merlay = Alice de Stuteville

8. Agnes de Merlay = Richard Gobion

9. Hugh Gobion = Matilda ----

10. Joan Gobion = John de Morteyn

11. Sir John de Morteyn = Joan de Rothwell

12. Lucy de Morteyn = Sir John Giffard, whose patrilineal descent from Osbern de Bolebec and Avelina, sister of Gunnora, wife of Richard I, Duke of Normandy (and great-grandmother of William I, the Conqueror, King of England) is treated in *EO* 2:1:622-28

13. (maternity uncertain -- possibly by Sir John's second wife, Alice de Montfort, a likely illegitimate daughter, by Lora Astley, of Peter [or Piers] de Montfort, 3rd Baron Montfort, son of John de Montfort, 1st Baron Montfort [and Alice de la Plaunche, a kinswoman of Eleanor of Castile, wife of Edward I, King of England -- see J.C. Parsons, *The Court and Household of Eleanor of Castile in 1290* (1977), pp. 48-50], son of Piers de Montfort and Alice de Audley, daughter of Hugh de Audley and Bertrade de Mainwaring, SETH) Alice Giffard = Sir John Anne

14. Alice Anne = William Raynsford

15. John Raynsford = Alice Danvers

16. George Raynsford = Katherine Taverner

17. Richard Raynsford = Anne Meade

18. Robert Raynsford = Mary Kirton
19. **Edward Raynsford** of Mass. = (1) ----; (2) Elizabeth
    ----.

Sources: *NEHGR* 139(1985):229-38, 296-301 (Raynsford); J.W. Walker, ed., *Yorkshire Pedigrees, A-F* (*HSPVS*, vol. 94, 1942), pp. 13, 17-18 (Anne); *Moriarty,* vol. 4, p. 268 (noting the kinship between Catholic chantry priest Alexander Ann and his "well beloved cosyn Roger Giffard"); *Publications of the Bedfordshire Historical Record Society* 14(1931):68-70 and *Berks, Bucks & Oxon Archaeological Journal,* new ser., 5(1899-1900):21, 44 (on Alice de Montfort and her four husbands); *AR7,* lines 42, 41, 34 and sources cited therein (generations 1-12 above), *CP* (Montfort) and *Delafield,* vol. 2, pp. 592-97 (Audley, Mainwaring). A monograph on Alice (Giffard) Anne is much needed.

1. Ethelred II the Unready, King of England, d. 1016 = (1) Alfflaed

2. Elgiva of England = Uchtred, Earl of Northumberland

3. Edith of Northumberland = Maldred, lord of Carlisle and Allendale

4. Gospatrick I, Earl of Northumberland and Dunbar = ----, sister of Edmund

4. Maldred = ----

5. Gunnilda of Northumberland = Orm of Kendal

5. Uchtred Fitz Maldred of Raby = ----

6. Gospatrick of Workington = Egeline (Engaine?)

6. Dolfin Fitz Uchtred of Raby = ----

7. Thomas of Workington = Grace ----

7. Maldred Fitz Dolfin of Raby = ---- de Stuteville

8. Ada of Workington = William le Fleming

8. Robert Fitz Maldred = Isabel de Neville

9. Sir Michael le Fleming = Agatha Fitz Hervey

9. Geoffrey de Neville = Joan (of Monmouth?)

10. William le Fleming = ----

10. Geoffrey de Neville = Margaret de Lungvilliers

11. Eleanor le Fleming = Sir Richard Cansfield

11. Robert de Neville = Isabel Byron

12. Agnes Cansfield = Sir Robert Haverington

12. Sir Robert de Neville = Joan de Atherton

13. Sir John Harington = Joan (Dacre?)

13. Sir Robert de Neville = Margaret de la Pole

14. Sir John Harington = Katherine Banastre

15. Sir Nicholas Harington = Isabel English

16. Sir William Harington   =   14. Margaret de Neville

440

15, 17. Margaret Harington = Richard Braddyll

16, 18. John Braddyll = Emote Pollard

17, 19. Edward Braddyll = Jennett Crombock

18, 20. John Braddyll = Jennett Foster

19, 21. Edward Braddyll = Anne Ashton

20, 22. Dorothy Braddyll = John Talbot

21, 23. John Talbot = Mabel Carleton

22, 24. George Talbot = Anne Ryley

23, 25. **George Talbot, Jr.,** known as **Peter Talbot,** of Mass. = (1) Mrs. Mary Gold Wodell; (2) Mrs. Hannah Clarke Frizzell.

Sources: Joseph Gardner Bartlett, *The English Ancestry of Peter Talbot of Dorchester, Massachusetts* (1917), pp. 35-85 esp. (Talbot, Braddyll); James Croston, *County Families of Lancashire and Cheshire* (1887), pp. 253-55 esp. (Harrington of Farleton); F.L. Weis, *500 Ancestors of John Prescott of Lancaster and of James Prescott of Hampton* (1960, a work that does not, however, prove the parentage of the immigrants it treats), charts covering the ancestry of Sir William Harington of Farleton and Hornby and Margaret de Neville (#s28 and 30 esp.); *AR7,* lines 34, 35, 247 and *TG* 4(1983):184, note 25.

The Royal Descents of 500 Immigrants

1. Ethelred II the Unready, King of England, d. 1016 = (1) Alfflaed

2. Elgiva of England = Uchtred, Earl of Northumberland

3. Edith of Northumberland = Maldred, lord of Carlisle and Allendale

4. Gospatrick I, Earl of Northumberland and Dunbar = ----, sister of Edmund

5. Gospatrick II, 2nd Earl of Dunbar = Sybil Morel

6. Edgar of Dunbar = Alice de Greystoke

7. Agnes of Dunbar = Anselm le Fleming

8. Eleanor le Fleming = Ralph d'Eyncourt

9. Sir Ralph d'Eyncourt = Alice ----

10. Elizabeth d'Eyncourt = Sir William de Strickland

11. Joan de Strickland = Robert Washington

12. Robert Washington = Agnes le Gentyl

13. John Washington = Joan de Croft

14. John Washington = ----

15. Robert Washington = Margaret ----

16. Robert Washington = ---- Westfield

17. John Washington = Margaret Kitson

18. Lawrence Washington = Amy Pargiter (their son Robert Washington married Elizabeth Light and was the father of Lawrence Washington, husband of Margaret Butler, SETH)

19. Magdalen Washington = Anthony Humphrey

20. Alice Humphrey = Thomas Watts

21. John Watts = Elizabeth ----

22. Anthony Watts = Joanna Bennett

23. Elizabeth Watts = Henry Addington

24. Anthony Addington = Mary Hiley

25. Henry Addington, 1st Viscount Sidmouth, British Prime Minister = Ursula Mary Hammond

26. Frances Addington = George Pellew
27. **Henry Edward Pellew, 6th Viscount Exmouth** (title never assumed) (1828-1923) of N.Y. (and Washington, D.C.), philanthropist, treated in the DAB = (1) Eliza Jay; (2) Augusta Jay (sisters).

Sources: *BP* and *CP* (Sidmouth, Exmouth); Eversley M.G. Belfield, *The Annals of the Addington Family* (1959), pp. 18-26 and chart at end esp.; George Horace Sydney Lee Washington, *The Earliest Washingtons and Their Anglo-Saxon Connections* (1964), chart opp. p. 24, part II esp.; *AR7*, lines 41, 34, and *TG* 4(1983):184, note 25. See also *Burke's Presidential Families of the U.S.A.*, 2nd ed. (1981), pp. 14-15 (Washington).

The Royal Descents of 500 Immigrants

1. Hugh Capet, King of France, d. 996 = Adelaide of Poitou
2. Edith of France = Rainier IV, Count of Hainault
3. Beatrix of Hainault = Ebles I, Count of Roucy
4. Alice of Roucy = Hildouin IV, Count of Montdidier
5. Margaret of Montdidier = Hugh I, Count of Clermont
6. Adeliza of Clermont = Gilbert de Clare
7. Richard de Clare = Adeliza de Meschines
8. Roger de Clare, 2nd Earl of Hertford = Maud de St. Hilaire
9. Aveline de Clare = Geoffrey FitzPiers
10. Hawise FitzGeoffrey = Sir Reynold de Mohun
11. Alice de Mohun = Robert de Beauchamp
12. Sir Humphrey de Beauchamp = Sybil Oliver
13. Sir John Beauchamp = Joan de Nonant
14. Sir John Beauchamp = Margaret Whalesburgh
15. Elizabeth Beauchamp = William Fortescue
16. William Fortescue = Matilda Falwell
17. John Fortescue = Joan Prutteston
18. Joan Fortescue = Thomas Hext
19. Thomas Hext = Wilmot Poyntz
20. Margery Hext = John Collamore
21. Peter Collamore = Edith ---
22. Thomas Collamore = Agnes Adams (their son, Peter Collamore, was almost certainly the immigrant of that name to Mass., who married Mary ---- and died without surviving issue; his chief heir was his nephew ["cousin"] Anthony, below)
23. John Collamore = Mary Nicholl
24. (very probably) **Anthony Collamore** of Mass. = Sarah Chittenden.
25. Elizabeth Collamore = Timothy Symmes
26. Timothy Symmes, Jr. = Mary Cleves

444

27. John Cleves Symmes = Anna Tuthill
28. Anna Tuthill Symmes = William Henry Harrison (1773-1841), 9th U.S. President
29. John Scott Harrison = Elizabeth Ramsey Irwin
30. Benjamin Harrison (1833-1901), 23rd U.S. President = (1) Caroline Lavinia Scott; (2) Mrs. Mary Scott Lord Dimmick

21. Henry Collamore (brother of Peter) = Margaret Blight
22. Elizabeth Collamore = Bartholomew Harris
23. **Agnes Harris** of Conn. = (1) William **Spencer**; (2) William **Edwards.**

Sources: *AR7*, lines 106, 151, 246, 246B, 246E, *TAG* 63(1988):33-45, *TG* 9(1988):6-9, 27-30 esp., and for Anthony Collamore, unpublished research of Douglas Richardson of Tucson, Arizona, based partly on *VD*, pp. 216-17, Charles Hatch, *Genealogy of the Descendants of Anthony Collamore of Scituate, Massachusetts* (1915), pp. 9-25, and the Northam, Devon, parish register.

The Royal Descents of 500 Immigrants

1. Hugh Capet, King of France, d. 996 = Adelaide of Poitou

2. Edith of France = Rainier IV, Count of Hainault

3. Beatrix of Hainault = Ebles I, Count of Roucy

4. Alice of Roucy = Hildouin IV, Count of Montdidier

5. Margaret of Montdidier = Hugh I, Count of Clermont

6. Adeliza of Clermont = Gilbert de Clare

7. Alice de Clare = Aubrey de Vere

8. Juliana de Vere = Hugh Bigod, 1st Earl of Norfolk

9. Roger Bigod, 2nd Earl of Norfolk = Ida ---

10. Mary Bigod = Ranulf FitzRobert

11. Ranulf FitzRanulf = Bertrama ---

12. Ralph FitzRanulf = Theophania (or Tiffany) de Lascelles

13. Ranulf FitzRalph = Isabel ---

14. John FitzRanulf = Maud de Campania

15. Randall FitzJohn = ---

16. Sir John FitzRandall = ---

17. Sir Ralph FitzRandall = Elizabeth ---

18. John FitzRandolph = Joan Conyers

19. John FitzRandolph = ---

20. Christopher FitzRandolph = Jane Langton

21. Christopher FitzRandolph = ---

22. Edward FitzRandolph = Frances Howis

23. **Edward FitzRandolph** of Mass. and N.J. = Elizabeth Blossom.

24. Benjamin FitzRandolph = Sarah Dennis

25. Isaac FitzRandolph = Rebecca Seabrook

26. James FitzRandolph = Deliverance Coward

27. Isaac FitzRandolph = Eleanor Hunter

28. Rebecca Longstreet FitzRandolph = Isaac Stockton Keith Axson

29. Samuel Edward Axson = Margaret Jane Hoyt

30. Ellen Louise Axson = (Thomas) Woodrow Wilson
(1856-1924), 28th U.S. President

Sources: *MCS4*, lines 164 (and notes and sources therein), 155, 154; *AR7*, lines 246, 151, 106. See also Oris H.F. Randolph, *Edward FitzRandolph Branch Lines: Allied Families and English and Norman Ancestry*, 2nd ed. (1980), pp. 583-89.

The Royal Descents of 500 Immigrants

1. Hugh Capet, King of France, d. 996 = Adelaide of Poitou
2. Edith of France = Rainier IV, Count of Hainault
3. Beatrix of Hainault = Ebles I, Count of Roucy
4. Alice of Roucy = Hildouin IV, Count of Montdidier
5. Margaret of Montdidier = Hugh I, Count of Clermont
6. Adeliza of Clermont = Gilbert de Clare
7. Richard de Clare = Adeliza de Meschines
8. Roger de Clare, 2nd Earl of Hertford = Maud de St. Hilaire
9. Aveline de Clare = Geoffrey FitzPiers
10. Hawise FitzGeoffrey = Sir Reynold de Mohun
11. Alice de Mohun = Robert de Beauchamp
12. Sir Humphrey de Beauchamp = Sybil Oliver
13. Eleanor Beauchamp = John Bampfield
14. John Bampfield = Isabel Cobham
15. John Bampfield = Joan Gilbert
16. Thomas Bampfield = Agnes Coplestone
17. Agnes Bampfield = John Prowse
18. Richard Prowse = Margaret Norton
19. John Prowse = Joan Orchard
20. Robert Prowse = ---
21. John Prowse = Alice White
22. John Prowse = Elizabeth Collack alias Colwyck
23. Agnes Prowse = John Trowbridge
24. **Thomas Trowbridge** of Conn. = Elizabeth Marshall.
25. Thomas Trowbridge, Jr. = Sarah Rutherford
26. Thomas Trowbridge (III) = Mary Winston
27. Sarah Trowbridge = John Russell
28. Rebecca Russell = Ezekiel Hayes
29. Rutherford Hayes = Chloe Smith
30. Rutherford Hayes, Jr. = Sophia Birchard

31. Rutherford Birchard Hayes (1822-1893), 19th U.S.
President = Lucy Ware Webb

Sources: *AR7*, lines 246G, 246B, 246, 151, 106 and *TG* 9(1988):3-39
(Charles Fitch-Northen), based largely on *TAG* 18(1941-42):129-37,
57(1981):31-33, primary sources cited in both, and printed sources
cited in *NEHGR* 141 (1987):99.

The Royal Descents of 500 Immigrants

1. Hugh Capet, King of France, d. 996 = Adelaide of Poitou

2. Edith of France = Rainier IV, Count of Hainault

3. Beatrix of Hainault = Ebles I, Count of Roucy

4. Alice of Roucy = Hildouin IV, Count of Montdidier

5. Margaret of Montdidier = Hugh I, Count of Clermont

6. Adeliza of Clermont = Gilbert de Clare

7. Alice de Clare = Aubrey de Vere

8. Juliana de Vere = Hugh Bigod, 1st Earl of Norfolk

9. Roger Bigod, 2nd Earl of Norfolk = Ida ----

10. Margaret Bigod = Sir John Jermy

11. Sir William Jermy = Ellen Lampett

12. Sir John Jermy = Joan Halys

13. Sir Thomas Jermy = Isabel St. Aubin

14. Sir William Jermy = Elizabeth Hunhall

15. John Jermy = Margaret Multney

16. Sir John Jermy = Elizabeth Wroth

17. Elizabeth Jermy = Henry Repps

18. Henry Repps = Elizabeth Grimstone

19. Anne Repps = Sir William Woodhouse

20. Sir Henry Woodhouse = Anne Bacon, daughter of Sir Nathaniel Bacon, lord keeper, by Jane Ferneley, and half-sister of Francis Bacon, 1st Viscount St. Albans, the lord keeper, lord chancellor, philosopher and scientist

21. **Henry Woodhouse** of Va., governor of Bermuda = Mrs. Judith (Manby?) Haen.

Sources: *LDBR* 1, pp. 92-93 and *AP&P*, pp. 699-700; G.H. Dashwood, ed., *Visitation of Norfolk, 1563*, vol. 1 (1878), pp. 195-96 (Repps), 107 (Jermy); Walter Rye, ed., *Visitations of Norfolk, 1563, 1589 and 1613* (*HSPVS*, vol. 32, 1891), pp. 321 (Woodhouse), 230-31 (Repps), 172-73 (Jermy); *MCS* 4, lines 153-5 and *AR7*, lines 246, 151, 106.

The Royal Descents of 500 Immigrants

1. Hugh Capet, King of France, d. 996 = Adelaide of Poitou
2. Edith of France = Rainier IV, Count of Hainault
3. Beatrix of Hainault = Ebles I, Count of Roucy
4. Alice of Roucy = Hildouin IV, Count of Montdidier
5. Margaret of Montdidier = Hugh I, Count of Clermont
6. Adeliza of Clermont = Gilbert de Clare
7. Richard de Clare = Adeliza de Meschines
8. Roger de Clare, 2nd Earl of Hertford = Maud de St. Hilaire
9. Aveline de Clare = Geoffrey FitzPiers
10. Hawise Fitz Geoffrey = Sir Reynold de Mohun
11. Alice de Mohun = Robert de Beauchamp
12. Sir Humphrey de Beauchamp = Sybil Oliver
13. Sir John Beauchamp = Joan de Nonant
14. Jane (or Joan) Beauchamp = John Chudleigh
15. Sir James Chudleigh = Agnes Champernoun
16. James Chudleigh = Radigond ----
17. John Chudleigh = Thomasine Kirkham
18. Sir James Chudleigh = (1) Margaret (or Mary) Stourton; (2) Margaret Tremayne
19. (probably by 1) Petronell Chudleigh = Anthony Pollard
20. Mary Pollard = John Ayre (Eyre)
21. Margery Ayre (Eyre) = George Damerie (Amory)
22. John Damerie (Amory) = Emmot Thomas
23. Joan Damerie (Amory) = Samuel Butler
24. Almeric (Amory) Butler = ----
26. **Mary Butler** of Va. = William **Underwood**, Jr. Rev. Amory Butler, Rev. William Butler, and John Butler, brothers of Mary, also immigrated to Va., but I can find no evidence that they left descendants.

Sources: *PSECD* 2:72-73 (undocumented), *AR7*, lines 217, 246B, 246, 151, 106 and *TG* 9(1988):6-9, 27-30; F.L. Weis, *The Colonial Clergy of Virginia, North Carolina, and South Carolina* (1955), p. 9 (Amory and William Butler), John and J.A. Venn, *Alumni Cantabrigienses,* part 1, vol. 1 (1922), pp. 271, 274 (Almeric [Amory] and William Butler), and *VD*, pp. 15, 31, 597, 189 (Amory [Damerie], Ayre (Eyre), Pollard, Chudleigh) (sources that confirm *PSECD*).

The Royal Descents of 500 Immigrants

1. Hugh Capet, King of France, d. 996 = Adelaide of Poitou
2. Edith of France = Rainier IV, Count of Hainault
3. Beatrix of Hainault = Ebles I, Count of Roucy
4. Alice of Roucy = Hildouin IV, Count of Montdidier
5. Adelaide of Montdidier = Fulk de Grandson
6. Ebles de Grandson = Adelaide ----
7. Barthélemy de Grandson, Seigneur de la Sarraz and Belmont = ----
8. Jordan de Grandson, Seigneur of Belmont = Petronelle ----
9. Columba de Grandson = Rodolphe, Count of Gruyères
10. Beatrix de Gruyères = Aymon de Blonay, Seigneur de St. Paul
11. Jeannette de Blonay = Guillaume de Langin
12. Rodolphe de Langin = Isabelle de Pontverre
13. (of uncertain maternity) Marguerite de Langin = Henri d'Allinges, Seigneur de Coudrée
14. Nicolette d'Allinges = Francois de Greysier
15. Marguerite de Greysier = Jean de Rovorée, Seigneur du Crest and La Roche d'Ollon
16. Jean de Rovorée, Seigneur de Bonneveaux = Isabelle de Dompierre
17. Jean de Rovorée, co-Seigneur de Saint-Triphon and des Ormonts = Marie de Confignon
18. Guigues de Rovorée, Seigneur de Saint-Triphon and des Ormonts = (perhaps) Guillauma de Montvuagnard
19. Pierre de Rovorée, Seigneur de Granges (in Valais) = two or three times
20. (of uncertain maternity) Guigues de Rovéréaz = twice
21. (of uncertain maternity) Claudia Antonia de Rovéréaz = Georges de Ville
22. Marie de Ville = Abraham Gignilliat
23. **Jean Francois Gignilliat** of S.C. = Suzanne Le Serrurier.

The Royal Descents of 500 Immigrants

Sources: *TAG* 53(1977):129-31 and sources cited therein, esp. Comte E. Amédée de Foras, *Armorial et Nobiliaire de l'Ancien Duché de Savoie* (1863-1938); *ES*, new ser., vol. 11 (1986), table 153 (Grandson) and *AR7*, lines 151, 106.

The Royal Descents of 500 Immigrants

1. Louis IV, King of France, d. 954 (probable grandson maternally of Edward the Elder, King of England, d. 924) = Gerberga, daughter of Henry I the Fowler, German Emperor, d. 936

2. Charles, Duke of Lower Lorraine = Adelaide ----

3. Gerberga of Lower Lorraine = Lambert, Count of Louvain

4. Maud of Louvain = Eustace I, Count of Boulogne

5. Lambert, Count of Lens = Adeliza of Normandy, sister of William I, the Conqueror, King of England, and widow of Enguerrand II, Count of Ponthieu, for whose ancestry see G.A. Moriarty, *The Plantagenet Ancestry (Ancestry of Edward III and Queen Philippa)*, mss. widely available on microfilm, pp. 113-14, etc., Roderick W. Stuart, *Royalty for Commoners*, 2nd ed. (1992), lines 131, 244, and H.M. West Winter, *The Descendants of Charlemagne (800-1400), Part I, "Brandenburg Updated," Generations I-XIV* (1987), XII 75a, etc. Enguerrand II was a son of Hugh III, Count of Ponthieu (and Bertha of Aumale), son of Enguerrand I, Count of Ponthieu (and Adela, possibly of Westfriesland), son of Hugh I, Count of Ponthieu and (almost certainly) Gisela, daughter of Hugh Capet, King of France, and Adelaide of Poitou. Adeliza's own descent from Charlemagne, and that of William the Conqueror, her brother, is also fully covered by H.M. West Winter and outlined in *AR7*, lines 130, 121, 118, 50.

6. Judith of Lens (paternity uncertain, possibly a daughter of Enguerrand II; see Sir A.R. Wagner, *Pedigree and Progress* [1975], p. 253, and sources cited therein) = Waltheof II, Earl of Huntingdon, Northampton, and Northumberland

7. Matilda of Northumberland = Simon de St. Liz, Earl of Huntingdon and Northampton

8. Matilda de St. Liz = Robert de Clare

9. Walter FitzRobert = Maud de Lucy

10. Alice FitzWalter (sister of Robert FitzWalter, leader of the Magna Charta barons) = Gilbert Pecche

11. Hamon Pecche = Eve ----

12. Gilbert Pecche = Joan de Creye

13. Gilbert Pecche, 1st Baron Pecche = Iseult ---

14. Gilbert Pecche, 2nd Baron Pecche = Joan --

15. Katherine Pecche = Thomas Notbeam

16. Margaret Notbeam = John Hinkley

17. Cecily Hinkley = Henry Caldebeck

18. Thomasine Caldebeck = Thomas Underhill

19. Anne Underhill = Thomas Knighton

20. Joan Knighton = Charles Bull

21. Richard Bull = Alice Hunt

22. Elizabeth Bull = John Lawrence

23. Thomas Lawrence = Joan Antrobus of Mass., who m. (2) John Tuttle

24. **Jane Lawrence** of Mass. = George **Giddings.**

25. Joseph Giddings = Susanna Rindge

26. Joseph Giddings, Jr. = Grace Wardwell

27. Susanna Giddings = William Torrey

28. Joseph Torrey = Deborah Holbrook

29. William Torrey = Anna Davenport

30. Samuel Davenport Torrey = Susan Holman Waters

31. Louisa Maria Torrey = Alphonso Taft, diplomat, U.S. Secretary of War and Attorney General

32. William Howard Taft (1857-1930), 27th U.S. President = Helen Herron

24. **John Lawrence** of Flushing, Long Island, N.Y. = Susanna ----.

24. **Thomas Lawrence** of Newtown, Long Island, N.Y. = Mary ----.

25. Mary Lawrence (very probably, see *TAG* 17 [1940-41]:74-78) = Thomas Walton

26. William Walton = Mary Santvoort

27. Jacob Walton = Maria Beekman

28. Abraham Walton = Grace Williams

29. Maria Eliza Walton = James Roosevelt

30. Isaac Roosevelt = Mary Rebecca Aspinwall

31. James Roosevelt = Sara Delano

32. Franklin Delano Roosevelt (1882-1945), 32nd U.S. President = (Anna) Eleanor Roosevelt

24. **William Lawrence** of Flushing, Long Island, N.Y. = (1) Elizabeth ----; (2) Elizabeth Smith (She = (2) Philip de Carteret, 1st colonial governor of N.J. and (3) Richard Towneley of N.J. Both of her later husbands were ARD, SETH.).

24. **Mary Lawrence** of Mass. = Thomas **Burnham**.

Sources: Unpublished, copyrighted research by David L. Greene, co-editor of *TAG*, based in part on *AR7*, line 148, the Pecche article in *CP* (vol. 10, pp. 333-38), Joan Corder, ed., *Visitation of Suffolk, 1561, Part I* (*HSPVS*, new ser., vol. 2, 1981), pp. 78, 86, 88 esp. (Pecche to Knighton) and Walter C. Metcalfe, ed., *Visitation of Hertfordshire, 1634* (*HSPVS* vol. 22, 1896), p. 34 (Bull). Mr. Greene's Lawrence monograph, to incorporate research in numerous English record sources, will appear in a future issue of *TG*; see also Consuelo Furman, "St. Albans Origin of John Lawrence of New Amsterdam, Thomas Lawrence of Newtown, L.I., William Lawrence of Flushing, L.I." (typescript, revised 1955), pp. 2-4 (but ignore her identification of John Lawrence's wife, paternal grandmother of the immigrants), 9-41.

The Royal Descents of 500 Immigrants

1. Louis IV, King of France, d. 954 (probable grandson maternally of Edward the Elder, King of England, d. 924) = Gerberga, daughter of Henry I the Fowler, German Emperor, d. 936

2. Charles, Duke of Lower Lorraine = Adelaide ----

3. Gerberga of Lower Lorraine = Lambert, Count of Louvain

4. Maud of Louvain = Eustace I, Count of Boulogne

5. Lambert, Count of Lens = Adeliza of Normandy, sister of William I, the Conqueror, King of England, and widow of Enguerrand II, Count of Ponthieu, for whose ancestry see G.A. Moriarty, *The Plantagenet Ancestry (Ancestry of Edward III and Queen Philippa)*, mss. widely available on microfilm, pp. 113-14, etc., Roderick W. Stuart, *Royalty for Commoners*, 2nd ed. (1992), lines 131, 244, and H.M. West Winter, *The Descendants of Charlemagne (800-1400), Part I, "Brandenburg Updated," Generations I-XIV* (1987), XII 75a, etc. Enguerrand II was a son of Hugh III, Count of Ponthieu (and Bertha of Aumale), son of Enguerrand I, Count of Ponthieu (and Adela, possibly of Westfriesland), son of Hugh I, Count of Ponthieu and (almost certainly) Gisela, daughter of Hugh Capet, King of France, and Adelaide of Poitou. Adeliza's own descent from Charlemagne, and that of William the Conqueror, her brother, is also fully covered by H.M. West Winter and outlined in *AR7*, lines 130, 121, 118, 50.

6. Judith of Lens (paternity uncertain, possibly a daughter of Enguerrand II; see Sir A.R. Wagner, *Pedigree and Progress* [1975], p. 253, and sources cited therein) = Waltheof II, Earl of Huntingdon, Northampton, and Northumberland

7. Matilda of Northumberland = Simon de St. Liz, Earl of Huntingdon and Northampton

8. Matilda de St. Liz = Robert de Clare

9. Walter FitzRobert = Maud de Lucy

10. Alice FitzWalter (sister of Robert FitzWalter, leader of the Magna Charta barons) = Gilbert Pecche

11. Hamon Pecche = Eve ----

12. Gilbert Pecche = Joan de Creye

13. Gilbert Pecche, 1st Baron Pecche = Iseult ---

14. Sir Simon Pecche = Agnes Holme

15. Margaret Pecche = John Hunt

16. Iodena Hunt = Thomas Cornish

17. John Cornish = ---

18. John Cornish = Agnes Walden

19. Mary Cornish = Thomas Everard

20. Henry Everard = ---

21. Thomas Everard = Margaret Wiseman

22. John Everard = Judith Bourne

23. **Judith Everard** of Mass. = Samuel **Appleton** of Mass., ARD, SETH.

24. John Appleton = Priscilla Glover

25. Priscilla Appleton = Joseph Capen

26. Mary Capen = Thomas Baker, Jr.

27. Priscilla Baker = Tarrant Putnam, Jr.

28. Priscilla Putnam = Adam Brown, Jr.

29. Israel Putnam Brown = Sally Briggs

30. Sally Brown = Israel C. Brewer

31. Sarah Almeda Brewer = Calvin Galusha Coolidge

32. John Calvin Coolidge = Victoria Josephine Moor

33. (John) Calvin Coolidge (Jr.) (1872-1933), 30th U.S. President = Grace Anna Goodhue

18. Margaret Cornish (sister of the 2nd John) = Thomas Mildmay

19. Walter Mildmay = Mary Everard (sister of Thomas Everard who married Mary Cornish)

20. Thomas Mildmay = Anne Reade

21. John Mildmay = Frances Rainbow

22. Thomas Mildmay   22. Thomasine Mildmay
    = Olive Nuttal   = John Boddie

23. Mary Mildmay   =   23. Thomas Boddie

24. John Boddie = Mary ----

25. **William Boddie** of Va. = (1) Anna ----; (2) Elizabeth;
(3) Mrs. Mary (----) Griffin.

21. Thomasine Mildmay (sister of John) = Anthony Bourchier

22. Thomas Bourchier = ----

23. Anne Bourchier = Thomas Rich

24. Susan Rich = Edward Bathurst

25. **Lancelot Bathurst** of Va. = ----

Sources: *TAG* 27(1951):208-10, *FNE*, pp. 315, 391-410, *VHG*, pp. 230-33, *HSF* 1:338, Pecche article in *CP* and *AR7*, line 148 (Mrs. Appleton and Boddie); *HSF* 8:135-37 (Bathurst); T.F. Fenwick and W.C. Metcalfe, eds., *Visitation of Gloucester, 1682-3* (1884), pp. 142-43 (Rich), 20 (Bourchier); W.C. Metcalfe, ed., *Visitations of Essex, 1552, 1558, 1570, 1612 and 1634*, vol. 1 (*HSPVS*, vol. 13, 1878), pp. 250-51, 452 (Mildmay). A thorough monograph on the immediate ancestry of William Boddie of Va. would be welcome since J.B. Boddie gives few details. See also J.T. and J.B. Boddie, *Boddie and Allied Families* (1918), introductory data and charts.

The Royal Descents of 500 Immigrants

1. Louis IV, King of France, d. 954 (probable grandson maternally of Edward the Elder, King of England, d. 924) = Gerberga, daughter of Henry I the Fowler, German Emperor, d. 936

2. Charles, Duke of Lower Lorraine = Adelaide ----

3. Adelaide of Lower Lorraine = Albert I, Count of Namur

4. Albert II, Count of Namur = Regelinde of Lower Lorraine

5. Albert III, Count of Namur = Ida of Saxony

6. Godfrey, Count of Namur = Sybil of Château-Porcien

7. Elizabeth of Namur = Gervais, Count of Réthel

8. Milicent of Réthel = Robert Marmion

9. Robert Marmion = ----

10. William Marmion = ----

11. Geoffrey Marmion = Rosamond ----

12. William Marmion = Matilda (le Justice?)

13. John Marmion = Margery de Nottingham

14. Thomas Marmion = Agnes ----

15. Alice Marmion = William Harlyngrugge

16. Cecilia Harlyngrugge = John Rede

17. Joan Rede = Walter Cotton

18. William Cotton = Alice Abbott

19. Catherine Cotton = Thomas Heigham

20. Clement Heigham = Matilda Cooke

21. Clement Heigham = Anne Munnings

22. Elizabeth Heigham = Henry Eden

23. Anne Eden = William Bradbury

24. Wymond Bradbury = Elizabeth Whitgift, niece of John Whitgift, Archbishop of Canterbury

25. **Thomas Bradbury** of Mass. = Mary Perkins.

Sources: *AR7*, lines 246A, 148-149 and sources cited therein, esp. *TAG* 55(1979):1-4, 57(1981):98-99; John Brooks Threlfall, *The Ancestry of Thomas Bradbury (1611-1695) and His Wife Mary (Perkins) Bradbury (1615-1700) of Salisbury, Massachusetts* (1988). Criticism of the linkage between generations 9 and 10 was published in *TG* 9(1988):80-87 and answered by a note at the end of *AR7*, line 246A. Further articles on Marmions or other Bradbury forebears may be forthcoming.

The Royal Descents of 500 Immigrants

1. Louis IV, King of France, d. 954 (probable grandson maternally of Edward the Elder, King of England, d. 924) = Gerberga, daughter of Henry I the Fowler, German Emperor, d. 936

2. Charles, Duke of Lower Lorraine = Adelaide ----

3. Gerberga of Lower Lorraine = Lambert, Count of Louvain

4. Maud of Louvain = Eustace I, Count of Boulogne

5. Lambert, Count of Lens = Adeliza of Normandy, sister of William I, the Conqueror, King of England, and widow of Enguerrand II, Count of Ponthieu, for whose ancestry see sources cited on pp. 455, 458 herein, esp. H.M. West Winter, *The Descendants of Charlemagne (800-1400), Part I, "Brandenburg Updated," Generations I-XIV* (1987), XII 75a, etc. Enguerrand II was a son of Hugh III, Count of Ponthieu (and Bertha of Aumale), son of Enguerrand I, Count of Pontieu (and Adela, possibly of Westfriesland), son of Hugh I, Count of Ponthieu and (almost certainly) Gisela, daughter of Hugh Capet, King of France, and Adelaide of Poitou. Adeliza's own descent from Charlemagne, and that of William the Conqueror, her brother, is also fully covered by H.M. West Winter and outlined in *AR7*, lines 130, 121, 118, 50.

6. Judith of Lens (paternity uncertain, possibly a daughter of Enguerrand II; see Sir A.R. Wagner, *Pedigree and Progress* [1975], p. 253, and sources cited therein) = Waltheof II, Earl of Huntingdon, Northampton, and Northumberland

7. Matilda of Northumberland = Simon de St. Liz, Earl of Huntingdon and Northampton

8. Matilda de St. Liz = Robert de Clare

9. Walter FitzRobert = Maud de Lucy

10. Alice FitzWalter (sister of Robert FitzWalter, leader of the Magna Charta barons) = Gilbert Pecche

11. Hamon Pecche = Eve ----

12. Gilbert Pecche = Joan de Creye

13. Margery Pecche = Sir Nicholas de Criol

14. Sir Nicholas de Criol = Rohesia ----

15. Sir John de Criol = Lettice ----

16. Ida de Criol = Sir John Brockhull

17. William Brockhull = Margaret ----

18. Nicholas Brockhull = Katherine Wood

19. William Brockhull = Elizabeth Hever

20. John Brockhull = ----

21. Edward Brockhull = Mildred Ellis

22. Marion Brockhull = Thomas Harfleet

23. Henry Harfleet = Mary Slaughter

24. Martha Harfleet = John Halsnode

25. John Halsnode = Margaret Ladd

26. **Margaret Halsnode of N.J. = John Denn(e)**.

Sources: *LDBR* 1, pp. 5-6, and Salem, N.J., Quaker Monthly Meeting records, which show that John and Margaret Denn(e) were in Salem by 1679 (Vital data for their children are recorded at St. Alphage, Canterbury and the Quaker records of Folk(e)stone, Kent. Their daughter Elizabeth, born 19 Mar. 1662/3, died 18 Oct. 1666; the wife of Richard Hancock of Salem, N.J., was probably their daughter Margaret, born 4 Dec. 1664); Arthur Adams, *Richard Hancock and The Founding of Bridgeton, New Jersey* (1936, reprinted from *Proceedings of the New Jersey Historical Society* 54[1936]:209-17); James Robinson Planché, *A Corner of Kent, or Some Account of the Parish of Ash-Next-Sandwich* (1864), pp. 339-40, 347 (Harfleet); *Berry's Kent*, p. 106 (Brockhull); *MGH*, 5th ser., 6(1926-28):255-56 and *Publications of the Bedfordshire Historical Record Society* 14(1931):chart opp. p. 133 esp. (Criol); *CP* (Pecche) and *AR* 7, line 148. Material on the immediate family of Mrs. Margaret Halsnode Denn(e) is being collected (for a possible future monograph) by Mary Ann Nicholson of Belmont, Mass. A detailed examination by Col. Charles M. Hansen of the Pecche to Halsnode descent, an article which includes John Brockhull, generation 20 above, will appear in a forthcoming issue of *TAG*.

The Royal Descents of 500 Immigrants

1. Cynfyn, Prince of Powys = Angharad II, Queen of Powys
2. Rhywallon, Prince of Powys, d. 1070 = ---
3. Sionet of Powys = Ednyfed ap Llywarch Gam
4. Rhys Sais ab Ednyfed = Efa ferch Gruffudd Hir
5. Elidir ap Rhys Sais = Nest ferch Lles
6. Sandde ab Elidir = ---
7. Hwfa ap Sandde = ---
8. Hwfa Gryg ap Hwfa = ---
9. Hwfa Fychan ap Hwfa Gryg = ---
10. Iorwerth ap Hwfa Fychan = ---
11. Madog Foel ap Iorwerth = ---
12. (possibly illegitimate) Rheinallt ap Madog Foel = --
13. Owain ap Rheinallt = ---
14. Robert ab Owain = ---
15. William Coetmor = ---
16. Ieuan Coetmor = ---
17. Lewys ab Ieuan = Anne Wilson
18. Andrew Lewis = Mary Herring
19. **Thomas Lewis** of Maine = Elizabeth Marshall of Maine, ARD, SETH.
20. Judith Lewis = James Gibbins
21. Hannah Gibbins = --- Hibbert
22. Mary Hibbert = Joseph Jewett
23. Nathan Jewett = Deborah Lord
24. David Jewett = Sarah Selden
25. Elizabeth Jewett = Anselm Comstock
26. Betsey Comstock = Daniel Butler
27. George Selden Butler = Elizabeth Ely Gridley
28. Amy Gridley Butler = George Manney Ayer
29. Adele Augusta Ayer = Levi Addison Gardner

30. Dorothy Ayer Gardner = (1) Leslie Lynch King, m. (2) Gerald Rudolf Ford

31. Leslie Lynch King, Jr., whose name was changed to Gerald Rudolph Ford, Jr. (b. 1913), 38th U.S. President = Mrs. Elizabeth Ann (Betty) Bloomer Warren

Sources: *NEHGR* 101(1947):3-23, reprinted in *EO* 2:2:627-48; *ND*, pp. 105-25; *Bartrum 1*, pp. 47, 870, 887, 889, 890 and *Bartrum 2*, p. 1699 (generations 1-17).

Appendix

From Kings via the American Colonies to Recent Sovereigns:
Lines from Royally Descended Immigrants to
the Present British Royal Family,
Princes of Monaco, and Queen Geraldine of the Albanians

13. Richard Bernard of Va. (see p. 144) = (2) 20. Anna Cordray of Va. (see p. 382)

17. Mary Towneley of Va. (see p. 330) = Augustine Warner

12. Col. George Reade of Va. (see p. 183) = Elizabeth Martiau

14,21. Anne Bernard = John Smith

18. Augustine Warner, Jr.

= 13. Mildred Reade

15,22. John Smith, Jr. = 14,19. Mary Warner

15,16,20,23. Mildred Smith = Robert Porteus

16,17,21,24. Robert Porteus, native of Va. who returned to England (with his father), 1730 graduate of Peterhouse College, Cambridge, rector of Cockayne Hatley, Bedfordshire = Judith Cockayne

17,18,22,25. Mildred Porteus = Robert Hodgson

18,19,23,26. Robert Hodgson, Dean of Carlisle = Mary Tucker

19,20,24,27. Henrietta Mildred Hodgson = Oswald Smith

20,21,25,28. Frances Dora Smith = Claude Bowes-Lyon, 13th Earl of Strathmore and Kinghorne

21,22,26,29. Claude George Bowes-Lyon, 14th Earl of Strathmore and Kinghorne = Nina Cecilia Cavendish-Bentinck

22,23,27,30. Lady Elizabeth Angela Marguerite Bowes-Lyon, H.M. Queen Elizabeth The Queen Mother (b. 1900) = H.M. George VI (1895-1952), King of Great Britain, 1936-1952

23,24,28,31. H.M. Queen Elizabeth II (b. 1926), Queen of Great Britain since 1952 = H.R.H. Prince Philip of Greece and Denmark, Duke of Edinburgh (b. 1921)

24,25,29,32. H.R.H. Prince Charles Philip Arthur George of Great Britain, Prince of Wales (b. 1948) = Lady Diana Frances Spencer, now H.R.H. The Princess of Wales (b. 1961), see next page

25,26,30,33. H.R.H. Prince William Arthur Philip Louis of Wales, b. 1982.

25,26,30,33. H.R.H. Prince Henry Charles Albert David of Wales, b. 1984.

Sources: *NEXUS* 4(1987):24-28 and sources cited therein, plus *GM* 23(1989-91):263-64, 338.

22. Alice Freeman of Mass. and (presumably) Conn. (see p. 436) = (1) John Thompson; (2) Robert Parke

23. (by 1) Dorothy Thompson = Thomas Parke, her step-brother

24. Dorothy Parke = Joseph Morgan

25. Margaret Morgan = Ebenezer Hibbard

26. Keziah Hibbard = Caleb Bishop

27. Lucy Bishop = Benajah Strong

28. Dr. Joseph Strong = Rebecca Young

29. Eleanor Strong = John Wood

30. Ellen Wood = Frank(lin H.) Work

31. Frances Eleanor (Ellen) Work = James Boothby Burke Roche, 3rd Baron Fermoy

32. Edmund Maurice Burke Roche, 4th Baron Fermoy = Ruth Sylvia Gill

33. Frances Ruth Burke Roche = Edward John Spencer, 8th Earl Spencer

34. Lady Diana Frances Spencer, now H.R.H. The Princess of Wales (b. 1961) = H.R.H. Prince Charles Philip Arthur George of Great Britain, Prince of Wales (b. 1948), see preceding page

35. H.R.H. Prince William Arthur Philip Louis of Wales, b. 1982

35. H.R.H. Prince Henry Charles Albert David of Wales, b. 1984.

Sources: G.B. Roberts and W.A. Reitwiesner, *American Ancestors and Cousins of The Princess of Wales* (1984), pp. 21-32, 143-44 esp.

10,11. Rev. John Oxenbridge (1608/9-1674) of Mass., Puritan clergyman (see p. 125) = (1) Jane Butler

11,12. Bathshua Oxenbridge = Richard Scott of Jamaica

12,13. Bathshua Scott = 12,13. Julines Hering of Jamaica, son of 11,12. Nathaniel Hering and Elizabeth Cockcroft, see p. 125

13,14. Bathshua Hering = Peter Beckford, Speaker of the House of Assembly of Jamaica

14,15. William Beckford, alderman and Lord Mayor of London = Maria Hamilton

15,16. William Beckford, art collector and man of letters, author of *Vathek* = Margaret Gordon, daughter of Charles Gordon, 4th Earl of Aboyne (and Margaret Stewart, sister-in-law of John Murray, 4th Earl of Dunmore, colonial governor of N.Y. and Va., and daughter of Alexander Stewart, 6th Earl of Galloway, and Catherine Cochrane, ARD, SETH), son of John Gordon, 3rd Earl of Aboyne, and Grace Lockhart, daughter of George Lockhart of Carnwath and Euphemia Montgomery, ARD, SETH

16,17. Susan Euphemia Beckford = Alexander Hamilton, 10th Duke of Hamilton, 7th Duke of Brandon, son of Archibald Hamilton, 9th Duke of Hamilton, 6th Duke of Brandon, and Harriet Stewart, also a daughter of Alexander Stewart, 6th Earl of Galloway, and Catherine Cochrane, ARD, SETH

17,18. William Alexander Anthony Archibald Hamilton, 11th Duke of Hamilton, 8th Duke of Brandon = Princess Marie Amelie Elizabeth Caroline of Baden

18,19. Lady Mary Victoria Douglas-Hamilton = (1) Albert I (Honoré Charles Grimaldi), sovereign Prince of Monaco (1848-1922)

19,20. Louis II (Honoré Charles Antoine Grimaldi), sovereign Prince of Monaco (1870-1949) = Ghislaine Marie Francoise Dommanget

20,21. (by Marie Juliette Louvet) Charlotte (Louise Juliette Grimaldi), hereditary Princess of Monaco, Duchess of Valentinois = Count Pierre (Marie Xavier Raphael Antoine Melchior) de Polignac

21,22. Rainer III (Louis Henry Maxence Bertrand), sovereign Prince of Monaco, b. 1923 = Grace (Patricia) Kelly, the American actress

22,23. Albert (Alexandre Louis Pierre), hereditary Prince of Monaco, b. 1958.

Sources: *TAG* 31(1955):60-62, reprinted in *JIC*, pp. 133-36; John Britton, as per p. 126; *CP* (Aboyne, Galloway, Hamilton); *BRFW* 1: 408-9, 198.

24. Thomas Trowbridge of Conn. (see p. 448) = Elizabeth Marshall
25. James Trowbridge = Margaret Atherton
26. Elizabeth Trowbridge = John Merrick
27. Sarah Merrick = Jonathan Fuller
28. Sarah Fuller = Edward Learned
29. Edward Learned, Jr. = Sarah Pratt
30. Mary Learned = Seth Harding
31. Edward Learned Harding = Lucy Booker Ramsay
32. Mary Virginia Ramsay Harding = John Henry Steuart
33. Gladys Virginia Steuart = (1) Julius, Count Apponyi de Nagy-Appony
34. Geraldine, Countess Apponyi de Nagy-Appony, Queen of the Albanians (b. 1915) = 1938 Zog I, King of the Albanians (formerly Ahmed Bey Zogu) (1895-1961, king 1928-39)
35. Leka I, styled King of the Albanians since 1961 (b. 1939) = Susan Barbara Cullen-Ward.

Sources: *TAG* 53(1977):18-20 and *BRFW* 1:8 (generations 30-35); W.L. Learned, *The Learned Family* (1898), pp. 52-54, 86-87 and E.L. James, *The Learned Family in America, 1630-1967* (1967), pp. 16-17, 34-35; W.H. Fuller, *Genealogy of Some Descendants of Captain Matthew Fuller, John Fuller of Newton...* (1914), p. 129; G.B. Merrick, *Genealogy of the Merrick-Mirick-Myrick Family of Massachusetts, 1636-1902* (1902), pp. 101-2; F.B. Trowbridge, *The Trowbridge Genealogy* (1908), pp. 39-48, 503-6.

LIST OF ABBREVIATED SOURCES

AL W.G. Davis, *The Ancestry of Abel Lunt* (1963)

Anselme Père Anselme de Sainte-Marie, *Histoire Généalogique et Chronologique de la Maison Royale de France, des Pairs, Grands Officiers de la Couronne et de la Maison du Roy, et des Anciens Barons du Royaume* (3rd ed., 8 vols., 1726-33, reissued in 9 volumes 1879-82, partial revision by Pol Potier de Courcy [of vols. 4 and 9])

AP+P Virginia M. Meyer and J.F. Dorman, *Adventurers of Purse & Person, Virginia 1607-1624/5,* 3rd ed. (1987)

AR7 F.L. Weis, W.L. Sheppard, Jr., and David Faris, *Ancestral Roots of Certain American Colonists Who Came to America Before 1700,* 7th ed. (1992)

ARD <u>A</u>lso of <u>R</u>oyal <u>D</u>escent

Ardingly, Horsham, Lewes John Comber, *Sussex Genealogies* (*Ardingly Centre,* 1932; *Horsham Centre,* 1931; *Lewes Centre,* 1933)

AT ancestor table

Baillie J.G.B. Bulloch, *Genealogical and Historical Records of The Baillies of Inverness, Scotland, and Some of their Descendants in the United States of America* (1923)

Baines1 Edward Baines, *History of the County Palatine and Duchy of Lancaster,* 4 vols. (1836)

473

Baines2	Edward Baines and James Croston, *The History of the County Palatine and Duchy of Lancaster*, rev. ed., 5 vols. (1888-93)
Baker	George Baker, *The History and Antiquities of the County of Northampton*, 2 vols. (1822-41)
Bartrum 1,2	P.C. Bartrum, *Welsh Genealogies, A.D. 300-1400*, 8 vols. (1974) and *Welsh Genealogies, A.D. 1400-1500*, 18 vols. (1983)
Bernards of Abington	Mrs. Napier Higgins, *The Bernards of Abington and Nether Winchendon, A Family History*, 4 vols. (1903-4)
Berry's Bucks	William Berry, *Pedigrees of Buckinghamshire Families* (1837)
Berry's Hants	William Berry, *Pedigrees of the Families in the County of Hants* (1833)
Berry's Kent	William Berry, *Pedigrees of the Families in the County of Kent* (1830)
Berry's Surrey	William Berry, *Pedigrees of Surrey Families* (1837)
BIFR	*Burke's Irish Family Records* (1976)
Blackman	H.J. Young, *The Blackmans of Knight's Creek: Ancestors and Descendants of George and Maria (Smith) Blackman*, rev. ed. (1980)
BLG	*Burke's Landed Gentry (Burke's Genealogical and Heraldic History of the Landed Gentry [of Great Britain])* (often further identified by publication year, edition, and/or page)
BLGI	*Burke's Genealogical and Heraldic History of the Landed Gentry of Ireland* (4 editions -- 1899, 1904, 1912 and 1958)

The Royal Descents of 500 Immigrants

Blomefield	Francis Blomefield and Rev. Charles Parkin, *An Essay Towards a Topographical History of the County of Norfolk*, 2nd ed., 11 vols. (1805-10)
Blore	Thomas Blore, *The History and Antiquities of the County of Rutland* (1811)
BP	*Burke's Peerage (Burke's Genealogical and Heraldic History of the Peerage, Baronetage, and Knightage)*, various editions
BRB	Marquis of Ruvigny and Raineval, *The Blood Royal of Britain, Being a Roll of the Living Descendants of Edward IV and Henry VII, Kings of England, and James III, King of Scotland* (1903)
BRFW	*Burke's Royal Families of the World, Volume 1, Europe and Latin America* (1977)
BSIC	J.G.B. Bulloch, *A History and Genealogy of the Families of Bulloch and Stobo and of Irvine of Cults* (1911)
Bulkeley	D.L. Jacobus, *The Bulkeley Genealogy* (1933)
Burnett of Leys	George Burnett, *The Family of Burnett of Leys* (1901)
Bye	A.E. Bye, *History of the Bye Family and Some Allied Families* (1956)
CB	G.E. Cokayne, *Complete Baronetage*, 5 vols. (1900-6)
Chester of Chicheley	R.E.C. Waters, *Genealogical Memoirs of the Extinct Family of Chester of Chicheley, Their Ancestors and Descendants*, 2 vols. (1878)
Clarence	Marquis of Ruvigny and Raineval, *The Plantagenet Roll of The Blood Royal: The*

	Clarence Volume, Containing the Descendants of George, Duke of Clarence (1905)
Jeremy Clarke	A.R. Justice, *Ancestry of Jeremy Clarke of Rhode Island and Dungan Genealogy* (1922)
William Clopton	Lucy L. Erwin, *The Ancestry of William Clopton of York County, Virginia, with Records of Some of his Descendants* (1939)
Clutterbuck	Robert Clutterbuck, *The History and Antiquities of the County of Hertford*, 3 vols. (1815-27)
CN	*The Connecticut Nutmegger*
Collins	Sir Egerton Brydges, ed., *Collins' Peerage of England*, 9 vols. (1812)
Cornewall	C.G. Savile Foljambe, 4th Earl of Liverpool, and Compton Reade, *The House of Cornewall* (1908)
Courcelles	M. le Chevalier de Courcelles, *Histoire Généalogique et Héraldique des Pairs de France*, 12 vols. (1822-33)
CP	Vicary Gibbs, etc., *The* [New] *Complete Peerage*, 13 vols. (1910-59)
CRFP	J.W. Jordan, ed., *Colonial and Revolutionary Families of Pennsylvania*, 3 vols. (1911, rep. 1978)
CRLA	American Historical Company, Inc., *Colonial and Revolutionary Lineages of America*, 25 vols. (1939-68)
CVR	Clarence V. Roberts, *Ancestry of Clarence V. Roberts and Frances A. (Walton) Roberts* (1940)
DAB	*Dictionary of American Biography*, 20 vols. plus index (1928-37), and eight

	supplements (to deaths through 1970) and *Comprehensive Index* (1944-90)
D de la N	Francois Alexandre Aubert de la Chenaye-Desbois et Badier, *Dictionnaire de la Noblesse,* 19 vols., 1863-76 (a reprint of the last 18th cent. [3rd] ed.)
Delafield	J.R. Delafield, *Delafield: The Family History,* 2 vols. (1945)
DGA	Heinrich Banniza von Bazan and Richard Müller, *Deutsche Geschichte in Ahnentafeln,* 2 vols. (1939-42)
DNB	*Dictionary of National* [British] *Biography,* 21 vols. plus 4 supplements (1908-12, orig. pub. 1885-1900). Nine further supplements, published 1927-93, cover figures who died from 1912 through 1985, plus *Missing Persons.*
Douglas	Sir Robert Douglas of Glenbervie, 6th Bt., *The Baronage of Scotland* (1798)
DP	*Debrett's Peerage and Baronetage* or *Debrett's Peerage, Baronetage, Knightage and Companionage,* various editions
Drummond	Henry Drummond, *History of Noble British Families,* 2 vols., 1846 (vol. 1 - Ashburnham, Arden, Compton, Cecil, Harley, Bruce; vol. 2 - Perceval, Dunbar, Hume, Dundas, Drummond, Neville)
Duncumb	John Duncumb and W.H. Cooke, *Collections Toward the History and Antiquities of the County of Hereford,* 5 vols. (1804-97)
Dunster	Sir H.C. Maxwell Lyte, *A History of Dunster and of the Families of Mohun & Luttrell,* 2 vols. (1909)

DVY	J.W. Clay, ed., *Dugdale's Visitation of Yorkshire with Additions*, 3 vols. (1899, 1907, 1917)
DW	W.G. Davis, *The Ancestry of Dudley Wildes* (1959)
Earwaker	J.P. Earwaker, *East Cheshire: Past and Present; or a History of the Hundred of Macclesfield in the County Palatine of Chester*, 2 vols. (1877–80)
Edmond Hawes	See under Hawes
Elgenstierna	Gustaf Elgenstierna, *Den Introducerade Svenska Adelns Ättartavlor Med Tillägg Och Rättelser*, 9 vols. (1925–36)
EO 1,2	*English Origins of New England Families From The New England Historical and Genealogical Register*, 1st ser. (3 vols., 1984), 2nd ser. (3 vols., 1985)
EP	Sir Bernard Burke, *A Genealogical History of the Dormant, Abeyant, Forfeited, and Extinct Peerages of the British Empire*, new ed., 1883 (rep. 1962, 1969)
ES	Wilhelm Karl, Prinz von Isenburg, Frank, Baron Freytag von Loringhoven, and Detlev Schwennicke, *Europäische Stammtafeln: Stammtafeln zur Geschichte der Europäischen Staaten*, old ser., 5 vols. (1936, 1937, 1956, 1957, 1978), new ser., vols. 1–15 (vol. 3 in 4 parts) (1978–93)
Essex	Marquis of Ruvigny and Raineval, *The Plantagenet Roll of The Blood Royal: The Isabel of Essex Volume, Containing the Descendants of Isabel (Plantagenet), Countess of Essex and Eu* (1908)

Exeter	Marquis of Ruvigny and Raineval, *The Plantagenet Roll of the Blood Royal: The Anne of Exeter Volume, Containing the Descendants of Anne (Plantagenet), Duchess of Exeter* (1907)
FNE	Ernest Flagg, *Genealogical Notes on the Founding of New England* (1926, rep. 1973)
Forbes	Alistair and Henrietta Tayler, *The House of Forbes* (1937)
Foster's V of Yorkshire	Joseph Foster, ed., *Visitations of Yorkshire, 1584-5 and 1612* (1875)
G A de F	Henri Jougla de Morenas, *Grand Armorial de France*, 6 vols. (1934-49)
GDMNH	C.T. Libby, Sybil Noyes, and W.G. Davis, *Genealogical Dictionary of Maine and New Hampshire* (1928-1929, rep. 1972)
G H des A	*Genealogisches Handbuch des Adels*, 1951- (70+ vols. to date)
Glover	Stephen Glover and Thomas Noble, *The History and Gazetteer of the County of Derby*, 2 vols. (1829-33)
GM	*Genealogists' Magazine*
Gordon	J.M. Bulloch, ed., *The House of Gordon*, 3 vols. (1903-12)
Gorges	Raymond Gorges, *The Story of a Family Through Eleven Centuries, Being a History of the Gorges Family* (1944)
GPFPGM	*Genealogies of Pennsylvania Families From The Pennsylvania Genealogical Magazine*, 3 vols. (1982)
GPFPM	*Genealogies of Pennsylvania Families From The Pennsylvania Magazine of History and Biography*, 1 vol. (1981)

Gresleys of Drakelowe	Falconer Madan, *The Gresleys of Drakelowe* (1899)
GVFT	*Genealogies of Virginia Families From Tyler's Quarterly Historical and Genealogical Magazine*, 4 vols. (1981)
GVFVM	*Genealogies of Virginia Families From The Virginia Magazine of History and Biography*, 5 vols. (1981)
GVFWM	*Genealogies of Virginia Families From the William and Mary College Quarterly Magazine*, 5 vols. (1982)
Hamilton	George Hamilton, *A History of the House of Hamilton* (1933)
Edmond Hawes	J.W. Hawes, *Edmond Hawes of Yarmouth, Massachusetts, an Emigrant to America in 1635, His Ancestors, Including the Allied Families of Brome, Colles, Greswold, Porter, Rody, Shirley, and Whitfield, and Some of His Descendants* (1914)
Hawes, Freeman and James	H.J. Young, *The Carolingian Ancestry of Edmond Hawes, Alice Freeman, and Thomas James* (1983) and *Some Ancestral Lines of Edmond Hawes, Alice Freeman, and Thomas James* (1984)
HSF	J.B. Boddie, *Historical Southern Families*, 23 vols. (1957–80)
HSPVS	*Harleian Society Publications, Visitations Series* (ongoing)
HVG	Rev. H.E. Hayden, *Virginia Genealogies* (1891, rep. 1959)
Mary Isaac	W.G. Davis, *The Ancestry of Mary Isaac* (1955)

The Royal Descents of 500 Immigrants

Isham   H.W. Brainerd, *A Survey of the Ishams in England and America* (1938)

Jeremy Clarke   See under Clarke

JIC   N.D. Thompson and R.C. Anderson, *A Tribute to John Insley Coddington on the Occasion of the Fortieth Anniversary of the American Society of Genealogists* (Association for the Promotion of Scholarship in Genealogy, Ltd., Occasional Publication No. One, 1981)

Keeler-Wood   Josephine C. Frost, *Ancestors of Evelyn Wood Keeler, Wife of Willard Underhill Taylor* (1939)

Kempe   Frederick Hitchin-Kemp, *A General History of the Kemp and Kempe Families of Great Britain and Her Colonies* (1902)

LDBR 1,2,3,4,5   H.H. d'Angerville, *Living Descendants of Blood Royal,* 5 vols. (1959-73)

Ligon   W.D. Ligon and E.L. Whittington, *The Ligon Family and Connections,* 3 vols. (1947, rep. 1988; 1957; 1973)

Lives of the Berkeleys John Smyth of Nibley, *The Lives of the Berkeleys, Lords of the Honour, Castle, and Manor of Berkeley in the County of Gloucester from 1066 to 1618,* Sir John MacLean, ed., 3 vols. (1883-85)

Lodge   John Lodge and Mervyn Archball, *The Peerage of Ireland,* 7 vols. (1789)

Roger Ludlow   H.F. Seversmith, *The Ancestry of Roger Ludlow* (1964) (vol. 5 of *Colonial Families of Long Island, New York, and Connecticut*)

Manning and Bray   Rev. Owen Manning and William Bray, *The History and Antiquities of the County of Surrey,* 3 vols. (1795-1814)

481

Marbury	M.B. Colket, Jr., *The English Ancestry of Anne Marbury Hutchinson and Katherine Marbury Scott* (1936)
Mary Isaac	See under Isaac
MCS4	F.L. Weis, W.L. Sheppard, Jr., and David Faris, *The Magna Charta Sureties, 1215,* 4th ed. (1991)
Merion	T.A. Glenn, *Merion in the Welsh Tract* (1896, rep. 1970)
M+G	G.T. Clark, *Limbus Patrum Morganiae et Glamorganiae* (1886)
MG	*Maryland Genealogies: A Consolidation of Articles from the Maryland Historical Magazine,* 2 vols. (1980)
MGH	*Miscellanea Genealogica et Heraldica*
Montgomery	T.H. Montgomery, *A Genealogical History of the Family of Montgomery, Including the Montgomery Pedigree* (1863)
Morant	Philip Morant, *The History and Antiquities of the County of Essex,* 2nd ed., 2 vols. (1768)
Moriarty	George Andrews Moriarty, Jr., "Ancestry of [same]," 19 vol. mss collection at NEHGS, covering virtually the entire known medieval ancestry of Edward and Mrs. Ellen (Newton) Carleton, Dr. Richard Palgrave, Rev. William Sargent, and John Throckmorton
MP	Marquis of Ruvigny and Raineval, *The Plantagenet Roll of the Blood Royal: The Mortimer-Percy Volume, Containing the Descendants of Lady Elizabeth Percy, née Mortimer* (1911)

NAW   *Notable American Women, 1607-1950, A Biographical Dictionary,* 3 vols. (1971), and *Notable American Women: The Modern Period: A Biographical Dictionary* (1980)

ND   W.G. Davis, *The Ancestry of Nicholas Davis* (1956)

NDTPS   Notable Descendants Treated in Printed Sources

NEHGR   *The New England Historical and Genealogical Register*

NEXUS   *NEHGS NEXUS* (since 1983)

NF 1,2   W.P. Hedley, *Northumberland Families,* 2 vols. (1968-70)

NGSQ   *National Genealogical Society Quarterly*

NHN   *A* [New] *History of Northumberland,* 15 vols. (1893-1940)

Nichols   John Nichols, *The History and Antiquities of the County of Leicester,* 4 vols. in 8 (1795-1815)

NYGBR   *The New York Genealogical and Biographical Record*

Ormerod   George Ormerod and Thomas Helmsby, *The History of the County Palatine and City of Chester,* 2nd ed., 3 vols. (1882)

PACF   J.E. Griffith, *Pedigrees of Anglesey and Carnarvonshire Families* (1914)

PCF Lancashire   Joseph Foster, *Pedigrees of the County Families of England, Vol. 1 - Lancashire* (1873)

PCF Yorkshire   Joseph Foster, *Pedigrees of the County Families of Yorkshire,* 2 vols. (1874)

PMHB	*The Pennsylvania Magazine of History and Biography*
PSECD 2,3	J.O. Buck, A.E. Langston, and T.F. Beard, eds., *Pedigrees of Some of the Emperor Charlemagne's Descendants,* vols. 2-3 (1974-78). Undocumented, cited as seldom as possible, and always with at least one other source.
RHS	A.C. Addington, *The Royal House of Stuart: The Descendants of King James VI of Scotland, James I of England,* 3 vols. (1969-76)
RLNGF	Joseph Foster, *The Royal Lineage of Our Noble and Gentle Families,* vol. 1 (1883), vol. 2 (1884)
Roger Ludlow	See under Ludlow
Rutherford	W.K. and A.C.Z. Rutherford, *Genealogical History of the Rutherford Family,* 2 vols. (1969), rev. ed., 2 vols. (1979) and 2nd rev. ed., 2 vols. (1986)
Saint Allais	M. de Saint Allais, *Nobiliaire Universel de France, ou Recueil Général des Généalogies Historiques des Maisons Nobles de ce Royaume,* 21 vols. (rep. 1872-77)
Salt	William Salt Archaeological Society, *Collections for a History of Staffordshire* (ongoing journal)
Saltonstall	Leverett Saltonstall, *Ancestry and Descendants of Sir Richard Saltonstall, First Associate of the Massachusetts Bay Colony and Patentee of Connecticut* (1897)
SCG	*South Carolina Genealogies: Articles from the South Carolina Historical (and Genealogical) Magazine,* 5 vols. (1983)

The Royal Descents of 500 Immigrants

Scott of Scots Hall	J.R. Scott, *Memorials of the Family of Scott of Scots Hall in the County of Kent* (1876)
SETH	See Elsewhere in This Volume
Shaw	Rev. Stebbing Shaw, *History and Antiquities of Staffordshire*, 2 vols. (1798-1801)
Shirleiana	E.P. Shirley, *Stemmata Shirleiana* (1873)
SMF 1,2,3	J.J. Muskett, *Suffolk Manorial Families*, 3 vols. (1900-10)
SP	Sir J.B. Paul, *The Scots Peerage*, 9 vols. (1904-14)
Strachey	C.R. Sanders, *The Strachey Family, 1588-1932, Their Writings and Literary Associations* (1953)
Surtees	Robert Surtees, *The History and Antiquities of the County Palatine of Durham*, 4 vols. (1816-40)
TAG	*The American Genealogist*
Taylor	A.E. Bye, *A Friendly Heritage Along the Delaware: The Taylors of Washington Crossing and Some Allied Families in Bucks County* (1959)
TCWAAS	*Transactions of the Cumberland & Westmorland Antiquarian & Archaeological Society*
TG	*The Genealogist* (London, 1877-1922; New York and Salt Lake City, 1980-present)
Thoroton	John Throsby, *Thoroton's History of Nottinghamshire*, 3 vols. (1797)
Throckmorton	C.W. Throckmorton, *A Genealogical and Historical Account of the Throckmorton*

	Family in England and the United States with Brief Notes on Some of the Allied Families (1930)
Tixall	Sir Thomas Clifford, 1st Bt., and Arthur Clifford, *A Topographical and Historical Description of the Parish of Tixall in the County of Stafford* (1817)
TM	*Tyler's Quarterly Historical and Genealogical Magazine*
TSA	*The Scottish Antiquary*
TVG	*The Virginia Genealogist*
UGHM	*The Utah Genealogical and Historical Magazine*
VC	J.L. Vivian, *The Visitations of Cornwall, Comprising the Heralds' Visitations of 1520, 1573, and 1620, with Additions* (1887)
VD	J.L. Vivian, *The Visitations of the County of Devon* (1895)
VGE	Lothrop Withington, *Virginia Gleanings in England: A Consolidation of Articles from The Virginia Magazine of History and Biography* (1980)
VHG	J.B. Boddie, *Virginia Historical Genealogies* (1954, rep. 1965)
VM	*The Virginia Magazine of History and Biography*
WC	G.E. McCracken, *The Welcome Claimants: Proved, Disproved and Doubtful, With an Account of Some of Their Descendants* (1970, Publications of the Welcome Society of Pennsylvania, Number 2)

Wentworth	John Wentworth, *The Wentworth Genealogy, English and American,* 2nd ed., 3 vols., (1878)
WFP 1,2	T.A. Glenn, *Welsh Founders of Pennsylvania,* 2 vols. (1911-13, rep. 1970)
Whitney	Henry Melville, *The Ancestry of John Whitney* (1896)
William Clopton	See under Clopton
Wilson	Y.L. Wilson, *A Carolina-Virginia Genealogy* [Wilson Family] (1962)
WV	Clayton Torrence, *Winston of Virginia and Allied Families* (1927)

Index

Numbers below refer to pages. Men are listed under their surnames and each title noted herein; women are listed under both maiden and married surnames, and any title they bear in their own right, but not under titles they bear through their husbands. Kings, queens, princes, princesses, archdukes, grand dukes, margraves, landgraves, counts, and other members of sovereign or mediatized houses are listed by first names (those by which they are known) and sovereignty or place (kingdom, duchy, county, etc.). The prefixes "de," "d'," "du," "de la," "la," "le," "l'," "les," "von," "von der," "van," "van de," and "van der" are generally ignored in the alphabetization itself, unless, as with LaFayette and most New York Dutch families, the figure or family is usually alphabetized *with* the prefix. Welsh names before the use of surnames (Gruffudd ap Llywelyn, Elen ferch Ieuan) are listed under first names only. Scottish lairds (but not, generally, peers, baronets, or clergymen) are designated as, for example, "of Blairhall," but indexed under only their surnames. Lord or Hon. for younger sons of dukes and marquesses, or earls, viscounts, and barons, is usually retained on both charts and index, but knighthood ("Sir") supersedes "Hon." and "Lady" is used only among the 570 themselves for wives of knights or daughters of earls, marquesses or dukes. Cross references denote *some* common surname variations. Usually, however, I have followed my sources and related surnames (for example, Le Strange and L'Estrange on p. 189) are not generally combined. Names in the acknowledgments (except for my own descents from Col. Thomas Ligon/Lygon of Virginia and Act. Gov. Jeremiah Clarke of Rhode Island), introduction, and list of references at the end of each chart, are not indexed.

The Royal Descents of 500 Immigrants

----
ferch Dafydd ap
Maredudd 404
ferch Gronwy 324,
326
ferch Hywel ap
Meurig 404
ferch Ieuan 391
ferch Llywelyn 311,
323, 324, 326
ferch Thomas ap
Robert ap Gruffudd
309

ABBOTT
Alice 461
Anne (Mauleverer)
164
John 164

ABEL
Elizabeth (Humphrey)
158
Thomas 158

ABELL
Caleb 226
Experience 226
Frances (Cotton) 226
George 226
Joanna (----) 226
Margaret (Post) 226
Robert 226

ABERCROMBY
Alexander of
Glassaugh 107, 108
Helen (Meldrum) 108
James 108
John of Glassaugh 107
Katherine (Dunbar)
107
Katherine (Gordon)
107
Mary (Duff) 108

ABERDEEN
William Gordon, 2nd
Earl of 11

ABERGAVENNY
Edward Neville, 1st
Baron 123, 125,
159, 169
George Neville, 2nd
Baron 125, 159
George Neville, 3rd
Baron 140
Henry Neville, 6th
Baron 42
William Beauchamp,
Baron 227, 269, 284

ABERNETHY
---- (Stewart) 107
Alexander, 4th Baron
Saltoun 107
Barbara 66
Beatrix 107

ABINGTON
Joyce (Shirley) 334
Mary 334
Richard 334

**ABINGTON also
HABINGTON**

ABOYNE
Charles Gordon, 4th
Earl of 470
John Gordon, 3rd Earl
of 470

ACCARON
Antoinette Rosalie 292

ACHESON
Alice Caroline
(Stanley) 189
Dean Gooderham 189
Margaret 55

ACHIMS
Mary (Fulford) 163,
205, 244
Thomas 163

ACLAND
Elizabeth 25
Margaret Sarah 192

ACWORTH
Joan 222

ADA
of Scotland 371, 373,
376
of Workington 440

ADAIR
Ann 207

ADAM
ap Rhys 387
Mary (Robertson) 70
Robert 70
William 70

ADAMS
Abigail (Smith) 165
Agnes 444
John Jr. 165
John Quincy 165
Louisa Catherine
(Johnson) 165

ADDIE
Mary 407

ADDINGTON
Anthony 442
Elizabeth (Watts) 442
Frances 443
Henry 442
Henry, 1st Viscount
Sidmouth 442
Mary (Hiley) 442
Ursula Mary
(Hammond) 442

ADELA
of England 417
of France 431
of Savoy 378, 380
of Westfriesland 455,
458, 463

ADELAIDE
Archduchess of
Austria 290
of Holland 365
of Lower Lorraine 461
of Montdidier 453

of Poitou 444, 446,
448, 450, 451, 453,
455, 458, 463
of Vermandois 419,
421, 423, 425, 427,
429

ADELIZA
of Clermont 444, 446,
448, 450, 451
of Louvain 417
of Normandy 455,
458, 463

ADHEMAR
Constance (de Poitiers)
343
Dauphine (de
Glandevez) 343
Douce (Gaucelme) 343
Hugh III, Seigneur de
la Garde 343
Hugh IV, Seigneur de
la Garde 343
Lambert III, co-
Seigneur de Monteil
343
Louis, co-Seigneur de
Monteil 343
Mabile (du Puy) 343
Marguerite 343

ADOLF
Duke of Cleves 194

AERTSELAER
Henri Joseph Stier,
Seigneur of 380

de AFFETON
Katherine 345

AGARD
Katherine 171
Stephen 171
Susan (Burnaby) 171

AGLIONBY
Anne (Musgrave) 174
Henry 174
Mary 174

AGNELLI
Clara 7
Edoardo 7
Giovanni 7
Virginia (Bourbon del
Monte) 7

AGNES
ferch Philip ap
Maredudd 388
of Barby 61
of Burgundy 199
of Poitou 411
of the Isles 99

AGNEW
Catherine
(Blennerhasset) 126
Margaret 126
Maria Anne 72
Robert 126

d'AGUESSEAU
Henriette Ann Louise
104

The Royal Descents of 500 Immigrants

AHERNE
Brian de Lacey 208
Joan de Beauvoir (de Havilland) 208
AINSLIE
Frances Anne 10
John 28
Mary (Mackenzie) Clarke Drayton, Lady 28
AIRLIE
David Graham Drummond Ogilvy, 7th Earl of 8
AISLABY
Anne 225
AITKEN
Janet Gladys 23
d'ALAGONIA
Claire 292
ALAN
lord of Galloway 371, 385, 393
ALBANIANS, KING OF THE
Leka I 472
Zog I (Ahmed Bey Zogu) 472
ALBANIANS, QUEEN OF THE
Geraldine, Countess Apponyi de Nagy-Appony 472
ALBANY
Robert Stewart, 1st Duke of 96, 99, 102
ALBERT
(Alexandre Louis Pierre), Prince of Monaco 471
Count of Nassau-Weilberg 61
(Honore Charles Grimildi), Prince of Monaco 470
Prince of Prussia 3
Prince of Saxe-Coburg and Gotha 1
ALBERT I
Count of Namur 461
ALBERT II
Count of Namur 461
King of the Belgians 65
ALBERT III
Count of Namur 461
ALBERT VII
Count of Schwarzburg-Rudolstadt 194
ALBERTINE JOHANNETTE
of Nassau-Hadamar 14
d'ALBRET
Alain, Count of Dreux 103

Catherine (de Rohan) 103
Charlotte 103
Francoise (de Châtillon-Blois) 103
Isabel 103
Jean, King of Navarre 103
Jean, Vicomte de Tartas 103
Jeanne Baptiste 5
ALCOCK
Joanna 266
John 266
Sarah (Palgrave) 266
ALDEBOROUGH
Eleanor 164
ALES
ferch Ieuan ap Madog Gwenwys 305
ALEXANDER
---- 59
Catherine 55, 67
Margaret (Stirling) Forbes 59
ALEXANDER I
King of Yugoslavia 2
ALEXANDER VI
Pope 103
ALEXANDER NEVSKY
Grand Prince of Kiev and Wladimir 411
ALEXANDER OLELKO
Prince of Kiev 293
ALEXANDRA
Mother 1
ALEXANDRINE
of Prussia 3
ALFRED
of Great Britain, Duke of Edinburgh 1
ALICE
ferch John 387
of Courtenay 378
of Roucy 444, 446, 448, 450, 451, 453
ALINGTON
Dorothy (Cecil) 155
Elizabeth 25
Elizabeth (Tollemache) 187
Giles, Sir 155
Juliana 187
Juliana (Noel) 187
Katherine 155
Susan 155
William, 1st Baron Alington 187
William, 2nd Baron Alington 187
William Alington, 1st Baron 187
William Alington, 2nd Baron 187

ALIX
of Dreux 380
of France 343
of Merania and Burgundy 343
ALLEN
Ellen 110
Jane 210, 332
Letitia Dorothea 25
Mary (Faircloth) 332
Thomas 332
ALLEN also ALLYN
ALLGOOD
Helen 137
d'ALLINGES
Henry, Seigneur de Coudrée 453
Marguerite (de Langin) 453
Nicolette 453
ALLISTON
Elizabeth 403
ALLYN
Abigail 396
Abigail (Warham) 396
John 205
Katherine (Deighton) Hackburne Dudley 205
Margaret (Wyatt) 396
Mary 397
Matthew 396
Thomas 396
ALLYN also ALLEN
ALMQUIST
Agnes Maria Caroline 17
ALPHONSO IX
King of Leon 303
ALPHONSO VIII
King of Castile 303
ALSOP
Anne 272
Anne (Alsop) 272
Anne (Basset) 272
Anthony 272
Dorothy (Bentley) 272
Eliza (Heires) 272
Elizabeth 272
George 272
Jane (Smith) 272
John 272
Temperance (Gilbert) 272
Thomas 272
Timothy 272
ALSTON
Dorothy (Temple) 149
Elizabeth (Turgis) Harris 149
John 149
Thomasine (Brooke) 149
William 149
ALTAMONT
John Browne, 1st Earl of 191

The Royal Descents of 500 Immigrants

Appleton, continued
Samuel 389, 459
Thomas 287, 317, 389
APPONYI
de NAGY-APPONY
Geraldine, Countess,
Queen of the
Albanians 472
Gladys Virginia
(Steuart) 472
Julius, Count 472
APSLEY
Alice 153, 317
Edward, Sir 317
Elizabeth (Elmes) 317
AQUITAINE
Eleanor of 301, 303,
343, 345, 348, 350,
352, 354, 356, 358,
360, 361, 363, 365
ARBUTHNOTT
Isabel 112
James of Arbuthnott
112
Jean (Stewart) 112
l'ARCHDEACON
Eleanor 374
Elizabeth (Talbot) 374
Warin, Sir 374
ARDEN
---- 340
ARDERNE
Agnes 402, 407
John, Sir 407
Margred (ferch
Gruffudd) 407
AREND
Auguste 4
ARGALL
Elizabeth 242
Mary (Scott) 242
Richard 242
Samuel, Sir 242
ARGYLL
Archibald Campbell,
2nd Earl of 99
Archibald Campbell,
4th Earl of 71
Archibald Campbell,
9th Earl of 31
Colin Campbell, 1st
Earl of 96, 99
Colin Campbell, 3rd
Earl of 71
George Douglas
Campbell, 8th Duke
of 22
Ian Douglas Campbell,
11th Duke of 23
John Campbell, 4th
Duke of 31
ARMAGNAC
Joanna of 197, 199
ARNOLD
Alice 257
Alicia 150
Anne (Knipe) 150

Elizabeth 394
Michael 150
d'ARPAJON
Anne Claudine Louise
104
ARRAN
James Hamilton, 1st
Earl of 53, 66, 68
James Hamilton, 2nd
Earl of 53
ARSOLI
Camillo Massimiliano
Massimo, Prince of
7
Camillo Vittorio
Emanuele Massimo,
Prince of 7
ARTHUR
Alice (Berkeley) 257
Chester Alan 332
Ellen Lewis (Herndon)
332
John 257
Margaret 257
Margaret (Butler) 257
Richard 257
ARTOIS
Blanche of 295
ARUNDEL
Eleanor 231
Elizabeth 134
Joan (Moyns) 231
John FitzAlan, 1st
Baron 295
John FitzAlan, 2nd
Baron 231
Richard FitzAlan, 10th
Earl of 227, 238,
245, 253, 255, 262,
266, 269, 274, 276,
281, 284, 285, 289
Richard FitzAlan, 9th
Earl of 233, 236,
242, 287, 295
Thomas, Sir 231
William d'Aubigny,
1st Earl of 417
William d'Aubigny,
3rd Earl of 389, 409
ARUNDELL
Anne, Hon. 136, 383
Anne (Philipson) 136
Eleanor (Grey) 136
John, Sir 136, 355
Katherine (Chidiock)
355
Margaret 355
Margaret (Howard)
136
Margaret (Willoughby)
136
Matthew, Sir 136
Thomas, 1st Baron
Arundell of Wardour
136
Thomas, Sir 136

ARUNDELL
OF WARDOUR
Thomas Arundell, 1st
Baron 136
ASFORDBY
Alice (Wolley) 213
Eleanor (Newcomen)
213
John 213
Martha (Burton) 213
William 213
ASHBURNHAM
Elizabeth (Dudley) 251
Helen 251
Thomas 251
ASHTON
Anne 441
Frances 269
Mary 245
ASKE
Anne (Sutton) 153
Eleanor (Markenfield)
153
Eleanor (Ryther) 153
Elizabeth 153
Elizabeth (Clifford)
153
Elizabeth (Dawney)
153
Helen 153
John 153
Robert 153
Robert, Sir 153
ASPALE
Margery 425
ASPINWALL
John 148, 165
John Jr. 148, 165, 245
Mary Rebecca 148,
165, 245, 457
Rebecca (Smith) 148,
165
Susan (Howland) 148,
165, 245
d'ASPRIERES
Francois de Morlhon,
Seigneur 297
d'ASTER
Antoine Adrien
Charles de Gramont,
Count 105
ASTLEY
Anne 189
Elizabeth 84, 176
Frances 172
Joan 373
Lora 438
ASTON
Edward, Sir 361
Elizabeth 128
Elizabeth (Barton) 361
Elizabeth (Delves)
361, 363
Elizabeth (Leveson)
128
Hannah (Jordan) 361

The Royal Descents of 500 Immigrants

Axson, continued
Rebecca Longstreet
(FitzRandolph) 236,
446
Samuel Edward 236,
397, 446
AYER
Adele Augusta 264,
465
Amy Gridley (Butler)
264, 465
George Manney 264,
465
AYLEN
May Somerville
(Bunny) Cooper 192
AYLESBURY
Anne (Denman) 352
Frances 352
Thomas, Sir, 1st Bt.
352
AYLMER
Alison (Fitzgerald) 216
Anne 216
Bartholomew 216, 217
Catherine 217
Christopher 217
Christopher, Sir, 1st
Bt. 217
Elizabeth 205
Ellen (Warren) 217
Gerald 217
Gerald, Sir 216
Margaret (Chevers)
216
Margaret (Plunkett)
217
AYMER I
Count of Angoulême
378
AYRE
John 451
Margery 451
Mary (Pollard) 451
AYRE also EYRE
AYSCOUGH
Anne 37
Edward, Sir 37
Elizabeth 393
Elizabeth (Wrottesley)
224
Frances (Clifford) 37
Jane 224
John 393
Margaret (Talboys)
393
Margery (Hildyard)
224
William, Sir 224
AYTON
Margaret 75
BÅÅT
(SNAKENBORG)
Helen 244
BABTHORPE
Barbara (Constable) 42
Margaret 42

William, Sir 42
BACKWELL
Mary 129
BACON
Anne 450
Anne (le Gros) 240
Edmund, Sir, 4th Bt.
155
Elizabeth 146
Elizabeth (Brooke) 240
Elizabeth (Crane) 155
Elizabeth (Duke) 241
Frances 155
Francis, 1st Viscount
St. Albans 315, 450
Jane (Cooke) 315
Jane (Ferneley) 450
Nathaniel 240, 241
Nathaniel, Sir 450
Nicholas, Sir 315
Thomas 240
de BACQUEHEM
Marie Bonne 301
BADEN
Marie Amelie
Elizabeth Caroline
of 470
BADLESMERE
Bartholomew
Badlesmere, 1st
Baron 338, 340
Bartholomew, 1st
Baron Badlesmere
338, 340
Elizabeth 227, 238,
245, 253, 255, 262,
266, 269, 274, 276,
281, 284, 285, 289
Margaret 338, 340
Margaret (de Clare)
338, 340
BAGOT
Mary 262
BAIKIE
Marjorie 28
de BAILLEUL
---- 380
BAILLIE
Alexander of Dunain
88, 109, 114
Ann Elizabeth 78, 114
Elizabeth (Forbes) 88
Elizabeth (Mackay)
114
Jean 114
Jean (Baillie) 114
Jean (Mackenzie) 88,
109, 114
John "of Balrobert"
114
Kenneth 114
Margaret 101
Mary 88, 109
William of Dunain 88
BAINBRIDGE
Phebe 72

BAINTON
Anne 249, 374
Ferdinando 249
Joan (Weare alias
Browne) 249
BAINTON
also BAYNTON
BAKER
Florence Evelyn 209
George, Sir, 3rd Bt.
41
Jane 375
Mary 385
Mary (Capen) 390,
459
Mary Isabella (Sutton)
41
Priscilla 390, 459
Thomas Jr. 390, 459
BAKEWELL
Elizabeth 285
BALDWIN
Elizabeth (Alsop) 272
Mary (----) 80
Richard 272
Sarah 272
BALDWIN II
Count of Hainault 431
BALDWIN III
Count of Hainault 431
BALDWIN IX
Count of Flanders,
King of
Constantinople 365
BALDWIN V
Count of Flanders 431
BALDWIN VI
Count of Flanders 431
BALFOUR
Barbara 28, 29
Barbara (Moodie) 28
George, of Pharay 28
Isabel 75
Janet 89
Marjorie (Baikie) 28
Patrick, of Pharay 28
BALIOL
Cecily 371
John 371
John, King of Scotland
371
BALL
Elias 119
Elizabeth (Harleston)
119
Mary 183, 243, 330
de BALSAC
Catherine 69
BALTIMORE
Benedict Leonard
Calvert, 4th Baron
9, 136
Cecil Calvert, 2nd
Baron 136, 258, 383
Charles Calvert, 3rd
Baron 136, 161

The Royal Descents of 500 Immigrants

Baltimore, continued
Charles Calvert, 5th
Baron 9
George Calvert, 1st
Baron 383
BAMFIELD
Ursula 163
BAMPFIELD
Agnes 448
Agnes (Coplestone)
448
Eleanor (Beauchamp)
448
Isabel (Cobham) 448
Joan (Gilbert) 448
John 448
Thomas 448
BANASTRE
Katherine 440
**de BANDRÉ-
DU PLESSIS**
Henriette Adolfina 412
BANISTER
Mary 146
BANKS
Katherine 169, 338
Mary 136
BANNERMAN
Margaret 73
de BAPAULME
Gilles de Beaumez,
Châtelain 380
BAR
Joan of 378
du BAR
Annibal de Grasse,
Count 292
Claude de Grasse,
Count 291
Claude de Grasse,
Seigneur 291
de BARBANCON
Yolande 103
BARBY
Agnes of 61
BARCLAY
---- 100
Ann (Ford) 48
Christian (Mollison)
48
David of Urie 48
Elizabeth Lucy 48
George 52
Jean 48, 109
John 48
Katherine (Gordon) 48
Katherine (Rescarrick)
48
Louisa Anna (Louise
Ann) Matilda
(Aufrere) 52
Priscilla (Freame) 48
Robert 48
Susanna (Willet) 48
de BARCLAY
Margaret 415

BARDOLF
Agnes (Poynings) 222,
271, 275
Cecily 222, 271, 275
Elizabeth (Damory)
222, 271, 275
John, 3rd Baron
Bardolf 222, 271,
275
John Bardolf, 3rd
Baron 222, 271, 275
William, 4th Baron
Bardolf 222, 271,
275
William Bardolf, 4th
Baron 222, 271, 275
BARGENY
John Hamilton, 1st
Baron 54
BARHAM
Charles 242
Elizabeth (Ridley) 242
Katherine (Filmer) 242
BARING
Claire Leonora 12
BARKER
Frances 246
Sarah 25
BARKHAM
Edward, Sir, 1st Bt.
287
Frances (Berney) 287
Margaret 42, 287
BARLEY
John 422
Margaret 422
Margaret (Poyntz) 422
Philippa (Bradbury)
422
BARLOW
---- 319
Arabella (Trevanion)
319
Nicola 285
William 319
BARNABY
Mary (Abington or
Habington) 334
Richard 334
Winifred 334
BARNE
Anne 237
BARNES
Elizabeth 346
BARNEWALL
Anne 216
BARON
Joan 350
BARR
Millicent 332
de BARRAS
Jeanne 343
BARRETT
Agnes (ferch Philip ap
Maredudd) 388
Anne 339

Catrin (ferch
Trahaearn ap
Morgan) 388
Cecilia 432
Edward 339
Eleanor
(l'Archdeacon) 374
Elen (ferch Owain)
388
Elizabeth (Lytton) 339
Henry 374, 388
Margaret 388
Margred (ferch Hugh
Howel) 375
Sinet (Jenet) 375
William 375, 388
BARRINGTON
Francis, Sir 37
Joan 37
Joan (Cromwell) 37
Thomas, Sir 37
Winifred (Pole) 37
BARRY
Ellice 259
BARTON
Elizabeth 361
Grace 43
BARWICK
Frances 42
de BASCHI
Anne (de Rochemore)
343
Balthazard, Seigneur
de Saint-Estève 343
Jeanne (de Barras) 343
Louis, Baron d'Aubais
343
Louis, Seigneur
d'Auzet 343
Louis, Seigneur de
Saint-Estève 343
Louise 343
Louise (de Varas) 343
Marguerite (du Faur)
343
Melchionne (de
Matheron) 343
Thadée, Seigneur de
Saint-Estève 343
di BASCHI
Berthold, Seigneur en
parti di Vitozzo 343
Marguerite (Adhémar)
343
BASIL II
Grand Prince of
Moscow 293, 413
BASIL III
Grand Prince of
Moscow 413
BASKERVILLE
Jane 303
BASSET
Anne 272
Catrin 179
Elizabeth (Meverell)
272

Basset, continued
Isabel 429
Joan 334
Katherine 419
Mary (Evans) 179
Thomas 179
William 272
BASSETT
Edward 205
Elizabeth 229
Elizabeth (Lygon) 205
Jane 205
BATH
John Bourchier, 1st
Earl of 163
BATHURST
Edward 460
Lancelot 460
Susan (Rich) 460
BATISFORD
Elizabeth 430
BATT
Alice (St. Barbe) 374
Anne (Bainton) 249,
374
Christopher 249, 374
Joan (Byley) 374
Thomas 374
BATTE
Amy (----) Butler 314
Henry 314
John 314
Katherine (Mallory)
314
Martha (Mallory) 314
Mary (----) 314
Mary (Lounds) 314
Thomas 314
William 314
de BAUDEMONT
Agnes 380
BAUGH
Anne 132
de BAUMEZ
Roberta 301
de BAVANT
Eleanor 334
BAVARIA
Isabella of 79
Jacqueline of 80, 82,
84, 85
Margaret of 194
BAXTER
Dorothy 146
Elizabeth 96
BAYLEY
Elizabeth Ann 75
Margaret (Sherburne)
330
Mary 363
Richard 330
BAYLEY
ALIAS SHERBURNE
Agnes (Stanley) 330
Richard 330
BAYLY
Sarah 184, 253

BAYNARD
Anne (Blake) 345
Anne (Hobbes) 346
Elizabeth (Barnes) 346
Elizabeth (Blackwell)
346
Henry 346
Joan (Stukeley) 345
John 346
Martha (Prickman)
346
Mary (Bennett) 346
Philip 345
Robert 345
Thomas 346
BAYNE
Anne 90
BAYNHAM
Anne 204
Margaret 363
BAYNTON
Anne (Cavendish) 248
Edward, Sir 248
Henry 248, 295
Isabel (Leigh) 248
Joan 295
Joan (Echyngham) 295
John, Sir 295
BAYNTON
also BAINTON
BEATON
Janet 53, 66, 68
BEATRIX
of Burgundy 343
of Burgundy and
Bourbon 297, 299
of Hainault 444, 446,
448, 450, 451, 453
of Hohenstaufen and
Burgundy 343
of Valkenburg 317
BEATTY
Christiana (Clinton)
143
John 143
BEAUCHAMP
Agnes 419
Catherine (de Bures)
400
Edward Seymour,
Baron 22, 25
Eleanor 110, 115, 155
Elizabeth 125, 132,
159, 184
Esther (Stourton) 400
Giles 400
Joan 227, 269, 284
Joan (Clopton) 400
Joan (FitzAlan) 227,
269, 284
John, 3rd Baron
Beauchamp of
Bletsoe 400
Margaret 400
Mary 258
Philippa 224, 291
Roger 400

Roger, 1st Baron
Beauchamp of
Bletsoe 400
Roger, 2nd Baron
Beauchamp of
Bletsoe 400
Susanna 71
Sybil (Patshull) 400
William, Baron
Abergavenny 227,
269, 284
BEAUCHAMP
OF BLETSOE
John Beauchamp, 3rd
Baron 400
Roger Beauchamp, 1st
Baron 400
Roger Beauchamp,
2nd Baron 400
de BEAUCHAMP
Alice (de Mohun) 444,
448, 451
Alice (de Toeni) 429
Beatrice 352, 361, 363
Eleanor 448
Elizabeth 444
Guy, 10th Earl of
Warwick 429
Humphrey, Sir 444,
448, 451
Ida (Longespee) 352,
361, 363
Isabel (Mauduit) 429
Jane 451
Joan 451
Joan (de Nonant) 444,
451
John, Sir 444, 451
Margaret
(Whalesburgh) 444
Maud 429
Maud (FitzJohn) 429
Robert 444, 448, 451
Sybil (Oliver) 444,
448, 451
William 352, 361,
363, 429
William, 9th Earl of
Warwick 429
BEAUCLERK
Charles George 12
Charles, 1st Duke of
St. Albans 12
Diana (de Vere) 12
Diana (Spencer) 12
Emily Charlotte
(Ogilvie) 12
Jane Elizabeth 12
Mary (Norris) 12
Sidney, Lord 12
Topham 12
BEAUFORT
Anne 110
Edmund, 1st Duke of
Somerset 110, 115,
155
Eleannor 115

Beaufort, continued
Eleanor (Beauchamp)
110, 115, 155
Henry, 2nd Duke of
Somerset 155
Henry, Cardinal
Beaufort 134, 165
Henry Beaufort,
Cardinal 134, 165
Jane 134, 165, 204
Joan 35, 40, 58, 60,
71, 73, 75-78, 99,
123, 125, 132, 136,
159, 169, 171, 176-
178, 184, 188, 189
Joan, Dowager Queen
of Scotland 71, 107,
109, 111, 112, 114
John, 1st Duke of
Somerset 400
John, Marquess of
Somerset and Dorset
107, 109, 111, 112,
114, 115, 155
Margaret 400
Margaret (Beauchamp)
St. John 400
Margaret (Holand)
107, 109, 111, 112,
114, 115, 155
de BEAUMEZ
---- 380
---- (de Bailleul) 380
Gilles, Châtelain de
Bapaulme 380
BEAUMONT
Alice (Stucley) 346
Catherine 229, 288
Constance 264
Eleanor (Sutton) 264
Henry, Sir 264
Hugh 346
Margaret 346
Mary 36
Thomas, Sir 346
Thomasine (Wise) 346
de BEAUMONT
Amicia (de Gael) 429
Ermengarde 330, 334,
336, 338, 340, 342
Hawise 387, 391, 404,
406
Isabel 421, 423, 425,
427, 429
Maud 382, 403, 419
Maud (FitzReginald)
382
Robert, 1st Earl of
Leicester 419, 421,
423, 425, 427, 429
Robert, 2nd Earl of
Leicester 429
Robert, Count of
Meulan 382, 403
BEAUPRE
Charlotte Victorine
Clémentine

Angélique de
Messey 62
de BEAUSSART
Béatrix 301
Laure (de Mauvoisin)
301
Robert, Seigneur de
Wingles 301
de BEAUVAU
Francoise 64
Isabeau (de Clermont)
64
Jacques, Seigneur du
Rivau 64
**de BEAUVOIS see
DEBEVOISE**
BECKENSHAW
Alice 206
BECKER
Elizabeth 75, 181
à BECKET
Thomas 396
BECKFORD
Bathshua (Hering) 470
Margaret (Gordon)
470
Maria (Hamilton) 470
Peter 470
Susan Euphemia 470
William 470
BECKWITH
Arthur 42
Elizabeth
(Brockenbrough)
Dickenson 42
Elizabeth (Jennings)
42, 287
Marmaduke, Sir, 3rd
Bt. 42, 287
Mary (Wyvill) 42
Roger, Sir, 1st Bt. 42,
287
BEDELL
Alice 340
BEECHER
Alice 117
BEECHING
Susanna 141
BEEKMAN
Cornelia 92
Maria 457
van BEELE
Beater 380
BÉGON
Marie Claire Thérèse
201
BEHREND
Eleonore Melitta 74
BEKE
Elizabeth 348, 356,
358, 360
Margaret 376
BELASYSE
Arabella 43
Barbara (Cholmley) 43
Grace (Barton) 43
Henry, Hon. 43

Thomas, 1st Viscount
Fauconberg 43
BELGIANS
Astrid Josephine
Charlotte Fabrizia
Elisabeth Paola
Maria, Princess of
the 65
Kings of the 291
Laurent Benoit
Baudouin Marie,
Prince of the 65
Philippe Leopold
Louis Marie, Prince
of the 65
**BELGIANS,
KING OF THE**
Albert II 65
Leopold I 195, 197
**BELGIANS,
QUEEN OF THE**
Paola (Margherita
Guiseppina Maria
Consiglia Ruffo di
Calabria) 65
BELKNAP
Elizabeth 277
BELL
Anne 204, 244, 422
Bertha Etelka (Surtees)
32
Edward 32, 422
Evangeline 32
Margaret (Barley) 422
BELLENDEN
Mary 31
BELLINGHAM
Frances (Amcotts) 224
Penelope (Pelham)
116, 225
Richard 116, 225
William 224
BELLOMONT
Richard Coote, 1st
Earl of 35, 207
BELMONT
Jordan de Grandson,
Seigneur de 453
von BELOW
Anton Georg Hugo 74
Eleonore Melitta
(Behrend) 74
Friederike Caroline
Alexandrine Emma,
Countess (von
Keyserlingk) 74
Friedrich Karl
Bogislav 74
Gustav Friedrich
Eugen 74
Karl Emil Gustav 74
Maria Karoline
Elizabeth (von der
Goltz) 74
Marie Eleonore
Dorothea 74

BENAUGES
Gaston II de Foix,
Count of 103
Gaston III de Foix,
Count of 291
BENNET
Andrew of Chesters 66
Anne 66
Archibald of Chesters
66
Barbara 66, 370
Barbara (Rutherford)
66
Dorothy
(Collingwood) 66
Isabella 12
BENNETT
Anne 141, 337
Ellen 421
Henrietta Maria
(Neale) 161
Jane 230
Joanna 442
Mary 346
Richard Jr. 161
Susannah Maria 161
BENTLEY
Dorothy 272
van BERENDRECHT
Clara 365
BERENGARIA
of Castile 303
of Leon 303
BERKELEY
Alice 159, 257
Anne 159, 204
Catherine (Heywood)
282
Catherine (Howard)
150
Eleanor (Constable)
286
Elizabeth 205, 226,
250, 253, 258, 264
Elizabeth (Burghill)
282
Elizabeth (Killigrew)
205
Elizabeth (Neville) 159
Elizabeth (Norborne)
155
Elizabeth (Reade) 205
Frances (Colepepper)
Stephens 140, 205,
432
Henry, Baron Berkeley
150
Henry, Sir 205
Henry Berkeley, Baron
150
Isabel 204
Isabel (Dennis) 205
Isabel (Mead) 82, 190,
204, 286
Isabel (Mowbray) 204,
257, 282, 286
James 82, 190

James, 6th Baron
Berkeley 204, 257,
282, 286
James Berkeley, 6th
Baron 204, 257,
282, 286
Jane 282
Joan 286
John Symmes 155
John, Sir 205
Margaret (Chettle) 282
Margaret (Dyer) 282
Margaret (Guy) 282
Margaret (Lygon) 205
Mary 46, 82, 150,
190, 206
Maurice 82, 190, 204,
286
Maurice, Sir 205
Norborne, 1st Baron
Botetourt 155
Richard 282
Richard, Sir 205
Rowland 282
Susan (Viell) 82, 190
Thomas 159, 282
Thomas, 8th Baron
Berkeley 286
Thomas Berkeley, 8th
Baron 286
William 282
William, Sir 140, 205,
432
BERNACKE
Joan (Marmion) 315
John, Sir 315
Maud 315
BERNARD
Alice (Haselwood) 144
Amelia (Offley) 144,
315
Anna (Cordray) 144,
382, 468
Anne 468
Behethland 285
Dorothy (Alwey) 144
Elizabeth (Woolhouse)
144
Francis 144
Francis, Sir, 1st Bt.
144, 315
Lucy (Higginson)
Burwell 144
Margery (Winslowe)
144
Mary (Woolhouse) 144
Richard 144, 382, 468
Sarah (----) 144
Thomas 144
William 144
de BERNARD
de SASSENAY
Marie Anne Claude 61
BERNERS
Abigail 240
John Bourchier, Baron
132, 146, 182

Margery 132, 146,
182
BERNEY
Alice (Appleton) 287
Frances 287
Henry 287
John 287
Juliana (Gawdy) 287
Margaret (Read) 287
Margery (Wentworth)
287
Thomas, Sir 287
BERRY
Anne 387
John, Duke of 197,
199
Marie of 197, 199
BERRYMAN
Elizabeth 192
BERTHA
of Aumale 455, 458,
463
BERTHIER
Maley Louise Caroline
Frédérique 19
BERWICK
Anna 431
de BESSE
Gabrielle (de Celle)
199
Gilbert, Seigneur de la
Richardie 199
Marguerite 199
BESSILES
Alice (Harcourt) 251
Elizabeth 252
William 251
BEST
Caroline (Scott) 46
Dorothy 46
Frances (Shelley) 46
George 46
James 46
BETANELLY
Helena Petrovna
(Hahn) Blavatsky
413
M.Ç. 413
de BÉTHISY
Catherine Eléonore
Eugénie 289
Eleanor (Oglethorpe)
289
Eugène Marie,
Marquis de Mézières
289
BETHOC
of Scotland 415
BETHUNE
Agnes (Anstruther) 97
Christian (Stewart) 97
John of Balfour 97
Margaret 97
BEVAN
Barbara (Aubrey) 135,
179
John 135, 179

BEVILE
Margaret 406
BEVILLE
Amy (----) Butler 182
Essex 182
John 182
Mary (Clement) 182
Mary (Saunders) 182
Robert 182
BEWICKE
Dorothy 32
BICKLEY
Francis, Sir, 3rd Bt.
383
Joseph 384
Mary (Winch) 383
Sarah (Shelton)
Gissage 384
BIDDULPH
Anne (Joliffe) 47
Augusta (Roberts) 47
John 47
Mary Anne 47
Michael 47
Penelope (Dandridge)
47
Robert 47
BIGOD
Cecilia (----) 425, 427
Hugh, 1st Earl of
Norfolk 446, 450
Hugh, 3rd Earl of
Norfolk 423, 425,
427, 429
Hugh, Sir 423
Ida (----) 345, 348,
350, 352, 354, 356,
358, 360, 361, 363,
446, 450
Isabel 429
Isabel (----) 423
Joan 423
Joan (----) 423
Joan (de Stuteville)
423
John, Sir 423
Juliana (de Vere) 446,
450
Margaret 450
Mary 446
Maud (de Felbrigg)
425, 427
Maud (Marshall) 423,
425, 427, 429
Roger, 2nd Earl of
Norfolk 345, 348,
350, 352, 354, 356,
358, 360, 361, 363,
446, 450
Roger, Sir 423, 425,
427
Simon, Sir 425, 427
BIGOD
ALIAS FELBRIGG
Alice (Thorpe) 427
Elizabeth (Scales) 427
John 425

Lucia (----) 425
Roger 425
Roger, Sir 427
Simon, Sir 427
BILL
Lydia 245
BINGHAM
Margaret (Freville)
Willoughby 334,
352
Margery 352
Richard, Sir 334, 352
BIRCHARD
Sophia 448
BIRKBECK
Elizabeth Lucy
(Barclay) 48
Emma 48
Henry 48
BIRKENHEAD
Elizabeth 348
BISBY
Phebe 335
BISCOE
Mary 374
BISHOP
Caleb 469
Jane 344
Keziah (Hibbard) 469
Lucy 469
de la BISTRATE
Isabelle Hélène 380
Jean Baptiste, Seigneur
of Laer and
Neerwinde 380
BJÖRNRAM
Carin 91
BLACKADDER
Janet 203
BLACKMAN
Jean 129
BLACKSHAW
Phebe 130
BLACKWELL
Elizabeth 346
BLACKWOOD
Caroline 11
BLADEN
Anne 152, 358
Anne (Swearingen)
152, 358
Isabella (Fairfax) 152
Nathaniel 152
William 152, 358
BLAGRAVE
Anne 403
Anne (Hungerford)
403
John 403
BLAIR
Christian 89
David of Adamton 50
John 89
Margaret 50
Margaret (Blair) 50
Margaret (Boswell) 50
Mary (Munro) 89

Sarah 50
Sarah (----) Lawson 50
William of Giffordland
50
BLAKE
Anne 345
Dorothy 260
Susan 214
BLAKENEY
Bridget 209
BLAKEWAY
Jacob 350
BLAKISTON
Barabara (Lawson)
139
Elizabeth (Bowes) 139
Elizabeth (Gerard) 139
George 139
John 139
Margaret 139, 151
Margaret (James) 139
Marmaduke 139
Nathaniel 139
Nehemiah 139
Phebe (Johnson) 139
Susan (Chambers) 139
BLANCHE
of Artois 295
la BLANCHE
Isabel 319
BLAND
Anne (Bennett) 141
Frances 208
Margaret 353
BLATCHFORD
Anne 120
BLAVATSKY
Helena Petrovna
(Hahn) 413
Madame 413
Nikifor Vassilievitch
413
BLAYNEY
Margaret (----) 115
Sarah 191
BLECHYNDEN
Alice 376
John 376
Margaret (Crispe)
Crayford 376
BLEIDT
Ann Elizabeth 50
BLENNERHASSET
Avice (Conway) 126
Catherine 126
Conway 126
Elizabeth 236
Elizabeth (Cornwallis)
236
Elizabeth (Cross) 126
Elizabeth (Harman)
126
Elizabeth (Lacy) 126
Harman 126
John 126, 236
Margaret (Agnew) 126

Bolling, continued
Sallie Spiers (White)
112, 115, 169, 339,
408
William Holcombe
112, 115, 169, 339,
408
BOLTON
Elizabeth 235
BONA
of Bohemia 103, 194,
197, 199
BONAPARTE
Charles Joseph 436
Elizabeth (Patterson)
436
Jerome, King of
Westphalia, Prince
of Montfort 436
Jerome Napoleon 436
Marie Annonciade
Caroline, Princess of
France 19
Susan May (Williams)
436
BONNER
Anthony 254
Bridget (Savage) 254
Mary 254
de BONNESON
Judith Elizabeth 93
de BONNET
de la CHABANNE
Anne 199
de BONNEVEAUX
Jean de Rovorée,
Seigneur 453
BONVILLE
Agnes 279
Alice (Dennis) 345
Catherine (Neville)
136
Cecily 136
Edith (Blewett) 279
Edmund 279
Elizabeth (Courtenay)
345
Elizabeth (FitzRoger)
345
Humphrey 279
Isabella 345
Jane (Tregion) 279
Joanna (Wynslade)
279
John 279, 345
Margaret (-----) 345
Richard 279
William, 1st Baron
Bonville 345
William, Baron
Harington and
Bonville 136
William Bonville, 1st
Baron 345
BOOTH
Anne 222
Anne (Thimbleby) 393

Audrey 338
Catherine (Mumford)
208
Eleanor 393
Elizabeth (Ayscough)
393
Ellen (Montgomery)
356
Emma Moss 208
George, Sir 356
Jane 356
John 393
Katherine (Montfort)
356
Margaret (Hopton) 338
Maud (Dutton) 356
Philip, Sir 338
William 208, 393
William, Sir 356
BOOTH-TUCKER
Emma Moss 208
Frederick St. George
de Lautour 208
BORCHGRAVE
d'ALTENA
Arnaud, Count 37
Baudouin, Count 37
de BORCHGRAVE
Alexandra D. (Villard)
37
Arnaud 37
Dorothy (Solon) 37
Eileen (Ritschel) 37
BORGIA
Cesare, Duc de
Valentinois 103
Charlotte (d'Albret)
103
Lucretia, Duchess of
Modena and Ferrara
103
BORIS
Prince of Rostow 411
BORLASE
Anne 338
Anne (Lytton) 338
John, Sir 338
de BOROUGHDON
Eleanor, Baroness
Kyme 393
Elizabeth (de
Umfreville) 393
Gilbert 393
BOROWSK
Maria of 413
von BORSSELEN
Joanna 197
Wolfart VI, Count of
Grandpré 197
BORTHWICK
Agnes 87
Catherine 70
BOSEWELL
Jane 208
BOSTOCK
Adam 407
Adam, Sir 407

Catherine (Mobberly)
407
Elizabeth (Venables)
407
George 407
Hugh 407
Isabel (Lawton) 407
Janet (Bradshaw) 407
Joan 407
Joan (Del Heath) 407
Joan (Horne) 407
Margaret 248
Margaret (Whetenhall)
407
Nicholas 407
Ralph, Sir 407
BOSTWICK
Mary 93
BOSVILE
Elizabeth 116, 136,
424
Godfrey 136
Margaret (Grevile) 136
BOSWELL
Alexander, Lord
Auchinleck 50
Anne (Cramond) 50
Anne (Hamilton) 50
David of Auchinleck
50
Elizabeth (Bruce) 50
Euphemia (Erskine) 50
Isabel (Wallace) 50
James 50
James of Auchinleck
50
John 50
Margaret 50
Margaret
(Cunningham) 50
Marion (Crawford) 50
Robert of St. Boswells
50
Sibella 50
Sibella (Sandeman) 50
BOTELER
Alice 332
Alice (Apsley) 317
Alice (Plumpton)
Sherburne 330
Anne 116, 280
Anne (Spencer) 116
Catharine (Waller) 271
Catherine (Knollys)
116
Cresset (St. John) 372
Elizabeth 331, 372
Elizabeth (Drury) 271
Elizabeth (Langham)
116
Elizabeth (Standish)
331
Elizabeth (Villiers) 271
Grizel (Roche) 271
Helen 271
Henry, Sir 271
Isabel (Harington) 331

Bowen, continued
Griffith 387, 388
Gruffudd 387
Hannah (Brewer) 387
Henry 387
John 387
Margaret (Fleming)
387, 388, 391
Philip 387
BOWERS
Anne 348
BOWES
Agnes 184
Charity 251
Elizabeth 139
Elizabeth (Clifford)
139
George, Sir 139
Muriel (Eure) 139
Ralph, Sir 139
BOWES-LYON
Claude, 13th Earl of
Strathmore and
Kinghorne 468
Claude George, 14th
Earl of Strathmore
and Kinghorne 468
Elizabeth Angela
Marguerite, Lady,
Queen Elizabeth The
Queen Mother 468
Frances Dora (Smith)
468
Nina Cecilia
(Cavendish-
Bentinck) 468
BOWLES
Joan 361
Sydney 8
BOWYER
Susanna (Woolston)
141
BOYCE
Alice 423
BOYD
Christian (Hamilton)
55, 59
Elizabeth 86
Fannie Kate (Root) vii
George Wesley vii
Hugh Blair vii
Isabel 55
Jean (Ker) 59
John vii
Margaret 53
Margaret (Campbell)
59
Marion 59
Mary Elizabeth vii
Mary Elizabeth
(Bressie) vii
Mary S. (Puryear) vii
Robert, 7th Baron
Boyd 55, 59
Robert, Hon. 59
Robert Boyd, 7th
Baron 55, 59

Thomas, 6th Baron
Boyd 59
Thomas Boyd, 6th
Baron 59
BOYLE
Jane 259
BOYLES
Mary 67
de BOYS
Alice 317
BRACHET
Marie Magdalene 201
BRACKLEY
Thomas Egerton, 1st
Viscount 263
BRADBURY
Anne (Eden) 461
Elizabeth (Whitgift)
461
Mary (Perkins) 461
Philippa 422
Sarah (Pike) 247
Thomas 461
William 461
Wymond 461
BRADDYLL
Anne (Ashton) 441
Dorothy 441
Edward 441
Emote (Pollard) 441
Jennett (Crombock)
441
Jennett (Foster) 441
John 441
Margaret (Harington)
441
Richard 441
BRADING
Elizabeth (----) 231
BRADSHAW
Alice 400
Anne 211, 363
Isabel (Kinnersley) 363
Janet 407
John 363
**BRADSHAW-
ISHERWOOD**
Christopher William
173
Francis Edward 173
Kathleen Machell
(Smith) 173
BRADSTREET
Anne 250
Anne (Dudley) 250
Anne (Wood) 250
Dudley 250
Margaret 250
Simon 250
BRADY
James Cox 38
Victoria May (Pery),
Lady 38
BRAGANZA
Catherine of 8-12
BRAITHWAITE
Anna (Lloyd) 82

Anna Lloyd 82
Isaac 82
Joseph Bevan 82
Martha (Gillett) 82
BRAMPTON
Mary 146
BRAMSHOT
Elizabeth 250
de BRANCAS
Jeanne 291
BRANCH
Catherine (Jennings)
407
Christopher 407
Christopher Jr. 407
Lionel 407
Mary 407
Mary (Addie) 407
Valentia (Sparkes) 407
William 407
BRANDENBURG
Joachim I, Elector of
61
Margaret of 61
**BRANDENBURG-
ANSPACH**
Barbara of 63
Caroline of 3
Dorothea Charlotte of
15
Frederick, Margrave
of 63
**BRANDENBURG-
SCHWEDT**
Frederick William,
Margrave of 4
Louise of 4
BRANDLING
---- 34
BRANDON
Alexander Hamilton,
10th Duke of
Hamilton, 7th Duke
of 470
Anne 262
Archibald Hamilton,
9th Duke of
Hamilton, 6th Duke
of 470
Charles, 1st Duke of
Suffolk 18, 22, 25,
27
Eleanor 18, 23, 27,
174, 266
Elizabeth (Wingfield)
262, 266
Frances 22, 25
William Alexander
Anthony Hamilton,
11th Duke of
Hamilton, 8th Duke
of 470
William, Sir 262, 266
BRANFORD
Mary 260
BRANT
Isabelle 380

Burnaby, continued
Elizabeth (Sapcotts) 171
Richard 171
Susan 171
Thomas 171
BURNELL
Margaret 403
BURNET
Alexander of Leys 107
Anna Maria (van Horne) 107
Catherine 76
Gilbert 107
Helen 107
Janet (Bruce) 107
Katherine (Gordon) 107
Margaret (Douglas) 76
Maria (Stanhope) 107
Mary (Scott) 107
Rachel (Johnston) 107
Robert 107
Thomas, Sir 107
Thomas, Sir, 1st Bt. 76
William 107
BURNETT
---- (Forbes) 76, 96
Isabel 76, 96
Robert 76, 96
BURNHAM
Alice (Eltonhead) 212, 287, 349
Mary (Lawrence) 457
Rowland 349
Thomas 457
BURR
Aaron 126
BURROUGH
Bridget (Higham) 223
Frances (Sparrow) 223
Nathaniel 223
Rebecca (Style) 223
Thomas 223
BURROUGHS
George 223
Hannah (----) 223
Mary (----) 223
Sarah (Ruck) Hathorne 223
William S. 105
BURROW
Dionis 355
BURT
Abigail 245
BURTON
Martha 213
BURWELL
Lucy (Higginson) 144
du BUS
René, Seigneur de Tizon 199
Renée 199
Sidoine alias Edmée (de Bourbon) 199

BUSH
Barbara (Pierce) 92, 211, 234, 267, 333, 362, 394
Dorothy (Walker) 92, 211, 234, 267, 333, 362, 394
Flora (Sheldon) 92, 211, 234, 267, 333, 362, 394
George Herbert Walker 92, 211, 234, 267, 333, 362, 394
Harriet Eleanor (Fay) 211, 234, 267, 333, 362, 394
James Smith 211, 234, 267, 333, 362, 394
Prescott Sheldon 92, 211, 234, 267, 333, 362, 394
Samuel Prescott 92, 211, 234, 267, 333, 362, 394
BUTLER
Almeric 451
Amory 451
Amy (----) 182, 314
Amy Gridley 264, 465
Ann (Travers) 375
Anne (Colclough) 259
Anne (de Welles) 259
Anne (Hankford) 284
Betsey (Comstock) 264, 465
Catherine (O'Reilly) 259
Courtland Philip Livingston 92
Daniel 264, 465
Dorothea 151
Edmund, Sir 259
Edmund, Sir, 2nd Bt. 259
Eleanor 259
Eleanor (de Bohun) 259
Eleanor (Eustace) 259
Eleanor (Loftus) 259
Elizabeth 227, 269
Elizabeth (Darcy) 259
Elizabeth (Elliot) 375
Elizabeth Ely (Gridley) 264, 465
Elizabeth Slade (Pierce) 92
Ellen 260
George Selden 264, 465
Grace 375
Henrietta (Fitz James) 13
Henrietta (Percy) 260
James 259
James, 1st Earl of Ormonde 259

James, 2nd Earl of Ormonde 259
James, 3rd Earl of Ormonde 259
James, 4th Earl of Ormonde 227, 269, 284
James, 9th Earl of Ormonde 259
James, Sir 259
Jane 125, 470
Jane (Boyle) 259
Joan 259
Joan (Beauchamp) 227, 269, 284
Joan (Damerie or Amory) 451
Joan (FitzGerald) 259
John 243, 375, 451
Judith (Livingston) 92
Juliana (Hyde) 259
Margaret 243, 257, 284, 442
Margaret (FitzGerald) 259
Margaret (Greeke) 243
Margaret (Sutton) 243
Mary 451
Mary Elizabeth 92
Mary (Middleton) 260
Pierce 260
Piers, 3rd Viscount Galmoye 13
Piers, 8th Earl of Ormonde 259
Richard, Sir 259
Richard, Sir, 5th Bt. 260
Sabina MacMorough (Kavanagh) 259
Samuel 451
Samuel Herrick 92
Shile (O'Carroll) 259
Thomas, 7th Earl of Ormonde 284
Thomas, Sir, 1st Bt. 259
Thomas, Sir, 3rd Bt. 259
William 243, 451
BUTLER
also BOTELER
BUTSHEAD
Winifred 244
BUTTALL
Martha 157, 306, 357
BUTTERFIELD
Anne 208
BYAM
Amelia Jane 117
Anne (Gunthorpe) 117
Dorothy (Knollys) 117
Edward 117
Edward Samuel 117
Eleanor (Prior) 117
Lydia (Thomas) 117

The Royal Descents of 500 Immigrants

CARPENTER
Alice 245
Alicia Maria 25
de CARPENTIER
Isabella (de Villers)
296
Jan 296
Josina (van Hecke)
296
Maria 296
Roelant 296
Sophia (van Culenburg
or Culemburg) 296
CARRE
Anne 180
Elizabeth 94
Margaret (Clifford)
180
Robert 180
CARRICK
Marjorie of 367, 369
Robert Bruce, Earl of
367, 369
CARRINGTON
Anne (Mayo) 257
Elizabeth Hannah 257
Emma 360
George 257
Henningham
(Codrington) 257
Jane (Mellowes) 257
Paul 257
CARROLL
Anne (Plater) 260
Charles 260
Dorothy (Blake) 260
CARROLL
also O'CARROLL
CARSTAIRS
Bethia 97
CARTER
Anne 229
Eleanor 238
Eleanor (Eltonhead)
Brocas 349
Elizabeth (Landon)
229
John 229, 349
Robert "King" 229
Sarah (Ludlow) 229,
349
Susanna 351
CARTERET
Frances (Worsley) 22
Georgiana Caroline 22
John, 1st Earl of
Granville 22
de CARTERET
Anne (Dowse) 220
Anne (Seale) 220
Elizabeth (Smith)
Lawrence 220, 386,
457
Frances 220
Francis 220
Helier 220
Peter 220

Philip 220, 386, 457
Philip, Sir 220
Rachel 220
Rachel (La Cloche)
220
Rachel (Paulet) 220
Susan 220
CARY
Margaret (Spencer)
115
Mary 115
Mary (Boleyn) 115
Thomas 115
William 115
CARYL
Anne 315
Patience 315
CASEY
Ann 38
CASIMIR IV
King of Poland 63
CASSILIS
Archibald Kennedy,
11th Earl of 87
David Kennedy, 1st
Earl of 87
Gilbert Kennedy, 2nd
Earl of 87
Gilbert Kennedy, 3rd
Earl of 87
CASSY
Agnes 398
Cecily (de Cokesey)
398
Thomas 398
CASTANOS
Aragorri Uriarte y
Olivide Maria 302
CASTELL-
REMLINGEN
Sophie Theodora of
194
Wolfgang Dietrich,
Count of 194, 197
CASTILE
Berengaria of 303
Eleanor of 210, 222,
224, 226, 229, 231,
233, 236, 238, 242,
245, 248, 250, 253,
255, 258, 259, 262,
264, 266, 268, 269,
271, 274-277, 279,
281, 284, 285, 287,
289, 291, 438
Ferdinand of, Count of
Aumale 301
Isabel of 35, 40, 45,
157, 167, 168, 179,
181, 192
CASTILE, KING OF
Alphonso VIII 303
Ferdinand III 301
CATESBY
Alice (Rudkin) 417
Anne (Hesilrig) 417
Anne (Odim) 417

Edward 417
Elizabeth 417
Elizabeth (Jekyll) 417
John 417
Kenelm 417
Mark 417
Michael 417
CATHERINE
of Braganza 8-12
of France 79
of Spain 5
of Vendôme 299
CATHERINE (II) THE
GREAT
Czarina of Russia 291,
412
CATLETT
Rebecca 253, 348
CATRIN
ferch Dafydd ap
Gethin 308
ferch Edward ap
Gruffudd 323
ferch Elisha ap Dafydd
80
ferch Hywel ap Jenkin
309
ferch Jenkin ap
Havard 179
ferch Robert ap
Gruffudd 312
ferch Trahaearn ap
Morgan 388
ferch William Dafydd
312
CAUNTON
Anna 315
CAVALERY
Frances 338
CAVE
Bridget 169
Margaret 213
Margaret (Cecil) 213
Roger 213
CAVENDISH
Anne 150, 161
Elizabeth 23
Elizabeth (Hardwick)
161, 249
Georgiana Dorothy 22,
23
Georgiana (Spencer)
22
Grace (Talbot) 161
Henry 161
Margaret (Bostock)
248
William, 5th Duke of
Devonshire 22
William, Sir 161, 248
CAVENDISH-
BENTINCK
Nina Cecilia 468
CECIL
Albinia 38
Dorothy 155
Dorothy (Neville) 155

511

The Royal Descents of 500 Immigrants

Cecil, continued
Elizabeth 276
Margaret 213
Mildred (Cooke) 315
Thomas, 1st Earl of
Exeter 155
William, 1st Baron
Burghley 155, 213,
276, 315
de CELLE
Francois, Seigneur du
Puy 199
Francoise (d'Anlezy
alias de Menetou)
199
Gabrielle 199
de CHABRIERES
Marie Anne 299
CHACE
Anne 341
de CHAHANNAI
Marie 201
de CHALENCON
Louis Melchoir
Armand de
Polignac, Marquis
105
de CHALON
Hugh, Count Palatine
of Burgundy 343
CHALONER
Frances 152
CHAMBERLAIN
Anna 371
CHAMBERLAIN
ALIAS SPICER
Amphyllis 335
CHAMBERLAYNE
Anne 233
Dorothy 44
Edmund 44
Eleanor (Colles) 44
Elizabeth (Stratton) 44
Grace (Strangways) 44
Mary (Wood) 44
Thomas 44
CHAMBERNON
Dionisia (English) 396
Henry 396
Henry, Sir 396
Isabel (----) 396
Joan (Okeston) 396
Oliver 396
Richard 396
Rose (de Tracy) 396
Wymarca (----) 396
CHAMBERNON also
CAMBERNON,
CHAMPERNOWNE
(NOUN)
CHAMBERS
Susan 139
CHAMOND
Gertrude 419
Jane (Grenville) 419
John, Sir 419
Margaret 319

Margaret (Trevener)
419
Richard 419
CHAMPAGNE
Henry I, Count of 365
Margaret of 417
Marie of 365
William of, Seigneur
de Sully 417
CHAMPERNOUN
Agnes 451
Joan 400
CHAMPERNOWNE
Eleanor (de Rohart)
396
Elizabeth 396
Joan 268
Joan (de Valletort) 396
John 396
Katherine (Daubeny)
396
Margaret (Spriggy)
396
Mary (Hamley) 396
Richard 396
Richard, Sir 396
Thomas, Sir 396
CHAMPERNOWNE
(NOUN) also
CAMBERNON,
CHAMBERNON
CHAMPION
Rachel 82
CHANDLER
Mary (Sewall) 132
CHAPLIN
Diana 40
Martha 436
CHARDIN
Julia 174
CHARLEMAGNE
Holy Roman Emperor
455, 458, 463
CHARLES
Duke of Lower
Lorraine 455, 458,
461, 463
Philip Arthur George,
of Great Britain,
Prince of Wales 468,
469
CHARLES I
Duke of Bourbon 199
Emperor of Austria 65
King of England 111,
248
CHARLES II
Grand Duke of
Mecklenburg-Strelitz
16
King of England 8-12,
79, 291
King of Navarre 103
CHARLES VI
King of France 79
CHARLES VII
King of France 64

CHARLES X
King of France 106
CHARLES XIII
King of Sweden 291
CHARLES ALBERT
King of Sardinia 5,
289
CHARLES EMANUEL
of Savoy, Prince of
Carignan 289
CHARLES
EMANUEL I
Duke of Savoy 5
CHARLES LOUIS
of Lorraine, Prince of
Lambesc, Count of
Brione 289
CHARLES
THEODORE
Prince of Salm-
Neufville 14
CHARLETON
Margaret 136
CHARLOTTE
of Bourbon-
Montpensier 18, 197
of Hanau-Lichtenberg
15
of Mecklenburg-
Schwerin 3
of Nassau-Dillenburg
18
(Louise Juliette
Grimaldi), Princess
of Monaco, Duchess
of Valentinois 471
CHARLTON
Alicia (Horde) 211
Anne 210
Anne (Mainwaring)
210
Catherine 125
Cecily 211
Emma (Harby) 125
Mary (Corbet) 210
Richard 210
Robert 125, 210
William 211
de CHARNELLS
Matilda 402
CHARROLL
---- 243
CHASE
Margaret Frances
(Towneley) 386
Richard 386
de CHASTELLUX
Charlotte 199
de CHATEAU-DU-
LOIR
Francois de Rohan,
Baron 201
CHATEAU-PORCEIN
Sybil of 461
de CHATEAUDUN
Jeanne 303

The Royal Descents of 500 Immigrants

Courtenay, continued
John, Sir 268, 382,
403
Margaret 279, 403
Margaret (de Bohun)
229, 268, 279, 288
Mary (de Vernon)
382, 403
Muriel (de Moels) 403
Peter of France, lord
of 378
Philip 268
Philip, Sir 268
Robert, Sir 382, 403
Thomas, Sir 403
COURTHOPE
Frances 283
COVENTRY
Mary 376
COVERT
Anne 251
Anne (Covert) 251
Anne (Henley) 251
Charity (Bowes) 251
Elizabeth 238, 251
John 251
Richard 251
Walter, Sir 251
COWARD
Alice (Britton) 236
Deliverance 236, 446
Hugh 236
John 236
Patience
(Throckmorton) 236
COX
Anne 123
COXE
Elizabeth 303
COYTMORE
Alice 166
Elizabeth 165
Jane (Williams) 165
Katherine (Miles) Gray
165
Rowland 165
William 165
CRABBE
Madeleine Augusta 32
**CRACROFT/
CRAYCROFT**
Anne 224
John of Hackthorne
224
John of Hackthorne
Heath 224
Martha (Amcotts) 224
Robert 224
CRADDOCK
Charlotte 128
CRADOCK
Margaret 391
CRAM
Jeanne Louise
(Campbell) Mailer,
Lady 23
John Sergeant 23

CRAMOND
Anne 50
CRANAGE
Dorothy 128
CRANE
Elizabeth 155
Frances Anita 298
Robert, Sir, 1st Bt.
155
Susan (Alington) 155
CRANMER
Agnes (Hatfield) 420
Alice 420
Alice (Sandes) 420
Edmund 420
Thomas 420
Thomas, Archbishop
of Canterbury 420
CRANSTON
Christian (Stewart) 111
James 111
John 248
John of Bold 111
Mary (Clarke) 111,
248
de CRAON
Isabel 297
CRASTER
Alice (Mitford) 152
Edmund 152
Eleanor (Forster) 152
George 152
Isabel 152
CRAUFORD
Anne (Lamont) 58
Barbara 58
William of
Auchenames 58
CRAUFORD
also CRAWFORD
CRAVEN
Christopher 130
Elizabeth (Staples) 130
Margaret (Clapham)
130
William, Sir 130
CRAWFORD
Alexander Lindsay,
2nd Earl of 100
Anna 87
Annabella 51
David Lindsay, 1st
Earl of 92, 94, 97,
100
David Lindsay, 3rd
Earl of 100
David of Kerse 50
Elizabeth 68
Elizabeth
(Cunyngham) 68
James of Crosbie 68
Jane 68
Joan (Fleming) 50
Marion 50
Patrick of Auchenames
68

CRAWFORD
also CRAUFORD
CRAYCROFT
see **CRACROFT**
CRAYFORD
Anne 376
Anne (Norton) 376
Edward 376
John 376
Margaret (Crispe) 376
Mary (Atsea) 376
William, Sir 376
CRAZE
Mary 346
CREEK
Alice (Eltonhead)
Burnham Corbin
287, 349
Henry 349
CRESSET
Joan (Wrottesley) 350
Margaret 350
Richard 350
CRESSY
Anne 280
Eleanor (Everingham)
280
Gervase 280
**du CREST and
La ROCHE
d'OLLON**
Jean de Rovorée,
Seigneur 453
CRESWICK
Elizabeth 137
CREWE
Charlotte (Lee)
Calvert, Lady 9
Christopher 9
de CREYE
Joan 456, 459
CRICHTON
Catherine (Borthwick)
70
Christian 94, 97
Elizabeth 51
James, Sir 70
Janet 73
Margaret 70
Margaret (Stewart) 70
William Crichton, 3rd
Baron 70
William, 3rd Baron
Crichton 70
de CRIOL
Ida 464
John, Sir 464
Lettice (----) 464
Margery (Pecche) 464
Nicholas, Sir 464
Rohesia (----) 464
CRIPPS
Evelyn Florence 129
CRISLI
ferch Adam Fychan
391

The Royal Descents of 500 Immigrants

CRISPE
Agnes (Queke) 376
Anne (Phillips or
  Fettiplace) 376
Avice (Denne) 376
Elizabeth 390
Henry 376
Joan (Dyer) 376
Joan (Sevenoaks) 376
John 376
Margaret 376
Matilda (Harcourt) 376
CROFT
Anne 409
Anne (Fox) 409
Margaret 416
Richard the younger
  409
de CROFT
Janet (ferch Owain)
  409
Joan 442
John, Sir 409
Margaret (Walwyn)
  409
William 409
CROKER
---- (Pascoe) 279
Agnes (Bonville) 279
Anstice (Tripp) 279
Beula Benton
  (Edmondson) 235
Elizabeth (Frazier) 235
Eyre Coote 235
Frances (Welstead)
  235
Francis 279
George 279
Harriet (Dillon) 235
Henry 235
Hugh 279
John 235
Mary (Pennefather)
  235
Richard Welstead 235
Tabitha 279
CROMARTY
George Mackenzie, 1st
  Earl of 28
George Mackenzie,
  3rd Earl of 28
John Mackenzie, 2nd
  Earl of 28
CROMBOCK
Jennett 441
CROMER
Anne 430
Catherine (Cantilupe)
  430
Elizabeth (Fiennes)
  430
Emeline 430
James, Sir 430
William 430
CROMWELL
Dorothy 247

Edward Cromwell, 3rd
  Baron 121
Edward, 3rd Baron
  Cromwell 121
Elizabeth 119
Elizabeth (Seymour)
  121
Frances 121, 353
Frances (Rugge) 121
Gregory, 1st Baron
  Cromwell 121
Gregory Cromwell, 1st
  Baron 121
Henry, 2nd Baron
  Cromwell 119, 121
Henry Cromwell, 2nd
  Baron 119, 121
Joan 37
Mary (Paulet) 119,
  121
Maud 315
Maud (Bernacke) 315
Oliver 37, 43, 247,
  353
Ralph, 2nd Baron
  Cromwell 315
Ralph Cromwell, 2nd
  Baron 315
CROPHULL
Agnes 303
John, Sir 303
Margery (de Verdun)
  303
Sybil (Delabere) 303
Thomas 303
CROSBIE
Anne 189
CROSHAW
Unity 115
CROSS
Elizabeth 126, 410,
  432
Mary 43
CROWLEY
Mary 82
CROWNE
Agnes (Mackworth)
  Watts 128
William 128
CRUMPTON
Jane (----) 350
CUDWORTH
James 270
Mary (Machell) 270
Ralph 270
CULCHETH
Anne 238
**van CULENBURG/
  CULEMBURG**
Sophia 296
CULLEN-WARD
Susan Barbara 472
CULPEPER
  see COLEPEPPER
CULVERWELL
---- 331

CUMBERLAND
Francis Clifford, 4th
  Earl of 174
Henry Clifford, 1st
  Earl of 174, 186
Henry Clifford, 2nd
  Earl of 18, 23, 27,
  174
CUMING
Alexander, Sir, 1st Bt.
  102
Alexander, Sir, 2nd
  Bt. 102
Amy (Whitehall) 102
Anne 101
Elizabeth (Swinton)
  102
**CUNNINGHAM/
  CUNYNGHAM**
Alexander of
  Craigends 68
Alexander, 5th Earl of
  Glencairn 68
Elizabeth 68, 96
Elizabeth
  (Cunyngham)
  Crawford 68
Elizabeth (Heriot) 93
Elizabeth (Livingston)
  93
Elizabeth (Napier) 68
Elizabeth (Stewart) 68
Gabriel of Craigends
  93
James of Achenyeard
  93
Janet 68
Janet (Cunyngham) 68
Janet (Gordon) 68
Jean (Hamilton) 68
Judith Elizabeth (de
  Bonneson) 93
Margaret 50
Margaret (Fleming) 93
Mary 93
Rebecca 68
Rebecca (Muirhead)
  93
Richard of
  Glengarnock 93
Robert of St.
  Christopher, B.W.I.
  93
William 93
William of Craigends
  68
William, 6th Earl of
  Glencairn 68
CUPPER
Audrey (Peto) 363
Dorothy 192, 363
John 363
CURIE
Henrietta Hedwige,
  Baroness von
  l'Esperance 61

The Royal Descents of 500 Immigrants

DANIELL
Dorothy
(Chamberlayne) 44
Robert 44
DANIELS
Arthur Noyes 62
Dolories (Dedons de
Pierrefeu) 62
DANVERS
Agnes 204
Alice 438
Dorothy 156, 403
Eleanor 156
Elizabeth (Neville) 156
John, Sir 156
DARCY
Alice 342
Arthur, Sir 176
Dowsabel (Tempest)
176
Edward, Sir 176
Eleanor (Scrope) 176
Elizabeth 259
Elizabeth (Astley) 176
Elizabeth (de Meinell)
342
Eupheme (Langton)
176
Frances 123
Isabella 176
Joan (de Greystock)
176
John 176
John, 2nd Baron
Darcy 342
John Darcy, 2nd
Baron 342
Mary (Carew) 176
Richard 176
Thomas, 1st Baron
Darcy of Darcy 176
William, Sir 176
DARCY OF DARCY
Thomas Darcy, 1st
Baron 176
DARNALL
Mary 136
Susannah Maria
(Bennett) 161
DARNLEY
Catherine 8
DARTE
Joan 346
DASHWOOD
Anne 19
DAUBENEY
Cecily 163
DAUBENY
Katherine 396
DAUNTSEY
Clemence 305, 308,
311, 321, 323, 324,
326, 328
DAVENPORT
Anna 456
Elizabeth (----) 334
Elizabeth (Fitton) 358

Henry 334
John 334
Katherine 358
Katherine (Radcliffe)
358
Margery (Mainwaring)
358
Parnell 274
Thomas 358
Winifred (Barnaby)
334
DAVID
Ellis 312
Hannah (Price) Jones
306, 312, 326
Margaret 309
of Scotland, Earl of
Huntingdon 367,
369, 371, 373, 376
Prince of North Wales
305, 308, 311, 321,
323, 324, 326, 328
DAVID I
King of Scotland 367,
369, 371, 373, 376,
429
DAVIE
Humphrey 121
John, Sir, 1st Bt. 121
Juliana (Strode) 121
Mary (White) 121
Sarah (Gibbon)
Richards 121
DAVIES
Lucy 27
Mary 10
DAVIS/DAVYS
---- 238, 377
Abigail 436
Agnes (Horton) 163
Edith (Luckett)
Robbins 397
Eleanor 57
Faith (Fulford) 163
John 163
Loyal Edward 397
Lydia (Harwood) 210
Margaret 163, 403
Mary 210
Mary (----) 163
Nancy 397
Nathaniel 163, 210
Nathaniel Jr. 210
Philip 163
Rachel 219
Sarah (Farmer) 227
Susannah (Lane) 210
DAVISON
Mary 32
DAVYE
Jane 115
DAWKIN
Alice 388
Elizabeth (Jenkin) 388,
391
Jenkin 388, 391
Margaret (Barrett) 388

William 388
DAWNEY
Anne 184
Dorothy (Neville) 184
Elizabeth 153
John, Sir 184
DAWSON
Susannah 364, 386
DAYRELL
Mary 208
DEBEVOISE/
de BEAUVOIS
Carel 365
Sophia (van
Lodensteyn) 365
DEBNAM
Ann 331
de BUTTS
Marianne (Welby) 37
Samuel 37
DEDONS
Alain, Count de
Pierrfeu 62
Aline Ann (de
Quérangal) 62
Elsa (Tudor) 62
(Louis Dolorès
Emmanuel)
Alphonse, Count de
Pierrefeu 62
Louis Joseph Léonce,
Marquis de Pierrefeu
62
Marie Simone
Léopoldine (de
Pillot) 62
DEDONS
de PIERREFEU
Dolores 62
Katharine 62
DEICWS DDU
ap Madog Goch 305
DEIGHTON
Frances 205
Jane 205
Jane (Bassett) 205
John 205
Katherine 205
Mary 35
DEINCOURT
Margaret 338, 340
DEL HEATH
Joan 407
DELABERE
Sybil 303
DE LANCEY
Susannah 217
DELANO
Catherine Robbins
(Lyman) 66, 234,
266, 394
Deborah (Church) 266
Sara 67, 148, 165,
234, 245, 266, 394,
457
Warren 266

**DOROTHEA
CHARLOTTE**
of Brandenburg-
Anspach 15
DORSET
Thomas Grey, 1st
Marquess of 136
Thomas Grey, 2nd
Marquess of 136
DOUD
Eli 273
Elivera Mathilda
(Carlson) 273
John Sheldon 273
Mamie Geneva 273
Maria (Riggs) 273
Mary Cornelia
(Sheldon) 273
Royal Houghton 273
DOUGLAS
---- (James) 57
---- (Watson) 57
Agnes (Horn) 78
Agnes (Keith) 76
Annie (Johnson) 57
Archibald, 4th Earl of
Douglas 89
Archibald, 5th Earl of
Angus 86
Archibald, Sir, of
Dornock 57
Archibald, Sir, of
Glenbervie 76, 86
Archibald Douglas,
4th Earl of 89
Barbara (Farquharson)
86
Bethiah 86
Catherine (Stewart) 53
Claire Alison 57
David, 7th Earl of
Angus 66
Egidia (Graham) 76
Eleanor 369
Eleanor (Davis) 57
Elizabeth 73, 88-91
Elizabeth (Auchinleck)
76, 86
Elizabeth (Boyd) 86
Elizabeth (Irvine) 86
Elizabeth
(Ochterloney) 86
Euphemia 78
Francis of Aberdeen
and Paisley 86
George, 1st Earl of
Angus 86, 88, 90,
91
George, 4th Earl of
Angus 86
Grizel (Forbes) 78
Isabel (Ker) 57
Isabel (Sibbald) 86
Isabella (Moncreiffe)
57
James of Jamaica 57

James, 1st Earl of
Morton 58, 73, 75,
78
James, 3rd Earl of
Morton 53
James, Sir 57
Janet 58, 75, 78, 94,
97
Janet (Crichton) 73
Jean 54, 415
Jean (Stewart) 57
Joan (Stewart) 58, 73,
75, 78
John 86
John of Inchmarlo 78
John of Leith 86
John of Tilquhillie 78
John, 2nd Earl of
Morton 73
Lucy 53
Margaret 30, 53, 66,
71, 76
Margaret (Hamilton)
54, 66
Margaret (Hay) 86
Margaret Jane
(Cannon) 57
Margaret (Stewart) 89
Mary 77
Mary (Fleming) 57
Mary (Gordon) 53
Mary (Henchman) 57
Mary (Stewart) 86, 88,
90, 91
Robert 57
Robert Langton 57
Robert of Blackmiln
86
Robert, Sir, of
Glenbervie 76
Samuel 57
Samuel of Jamaica 57
Thomas of Jamaica 57
William, 1st Earl of
Queensberry 57
William, 1st Marquess
of Douglas 53, 54
William, 2nd Earl of
Angus 86
William, 9th Earl of
Angus 76
William, Rev., of
Aboyne 86
William, Rev., of
Midmar 86
William, Sir, of
Glenbervie 86
William Douglas, 1st
Marquess of 53, 54
William Sholto, 1st
Baron Douglas of
Kirtleside 57
**DOUGLAS
OF KIRTLESIDE**
William Sholto, 1st
Baron 57

**DOUGLAS-
HAMILTON**
Mary Victoria, Lady
470
DOVER
Rohese of 251, 313,
315, 325
de DOVER
Lorette 251, 313, 315,
325
DOWDALL
Anne (Johnson) 217
Matilda Cecilia 217
Walter 217
DOWNE
Joan 336
DOWRISH
Grace 295
DOWSE
Anne 220
Elizabeth (Paulet) 220
Francis, Sir 220
DOZIER
Joan de Beauvoir (de
Havilland) Aherne
208
William 208
DRAKE
Elizabeth 271
Helen (Boteler) 271
Henry 390
Joan (Gawton) 390
John, Sir 271
Mary (Lee) 390
Robert 390
DRAYTON
Mary (Mackenzie)
Clarke, Lady 28
Thomas 28
DREUX
Alain d'Albret, Count
of 103
Alix of 380
Robert I, Count of 380
DREW
Ada 129
DREWE
Elizabeth 137
de DRIBY
Alice 210
Amy (de Gaveston)
210
John 210
de DRONAI
Aubert de Coucy,
Seigneur 296
DRUMMOND
Agnes 51, 58
Angela Mary
(Constable-Maxwell)
24
Annabella 86-91
Dorothy (Lower) 46
Henrietta Maria 46
Isabel 59
James Eric, 16th Earl
of Perth 24

The Royal Descents of 500 Immigrants

Drummond, continued
John, Sir, of
Innerpeffry 51, 55,
58, 59
Katherine 99
Margaret 48, 51, 53,
55, 58-60
Margaret (Stewart) 51,
55, 58, 59
Margaret Gwendolen
Mary, Lady 24
Maurice, Sir 46
DRURY
Anne 222
Anne (Calthorpe) 222,
271, 275
Bridget 185, 275
Elizabeth 271
Elizabeth (Sotehill)
185
Elizabeth (Stafford) 37
Frances 37
Henningham 257
Robert, Sir 222, 271,
275
William, Sir 37, 185
DRYDEN
Bridget 233, 351
Elizabeth (Cope) 233
John 233
DUCASSE
Jane 188
DUDLEY
Anne 250
Catherine (Hutton) 130
Dorothy 130
Dorothy (Sanford) 130
Dorothy (Yorke) 250,
252
Edmund 130, 250
Edmund, Sir 128, 243
Elizabeth 251
Elizabeth (Bramshot)
250
Elizabeth (Grey) 250
Elizabeth (Leighton)
250
Emma (Saunders) 250
Grace (Threlkeld) 130
John 250
John Sutton, 1st Baron
226, 250, 258, 264
Joyce (Cherleton) 243
Joyce (Tiptoft) 128
Katherine (Deighton)
Hackburne 205
Lucy 130
Mary 130
Matilda (Clifford) 128
Richard 130
Roger 250, 252
Simon 250
Susanna (Thorne) 250,
252
Thomas 130, 205,
250, 252

William Humble Eric
Ward, 3rd Earl of
12
DUFF
Anne Elizabeth
Clementina 36
Jean 77
Mary 108
DUFFELL
Judith 353
DUFFERIN and AVA
Basil Sheridan
Hamilton-Temple-
Blackwood, 4th
Marquess of 11
DUGDALE
William, Sir 161
DUKE
Elizabeth 241
DULANY
Margaret 96
DULCANTE
Morny 260
DUMARESQ
Abraham 220
Elias 220
Frances (de Carteret)
220
Jane (Payne) 220
Philip 220
Susan (de Carteret)
220
Susan (Ferry) 220
DUNBAR
---- (Stewart) 367
Agnes (McDowall)
367
Agnes (Mure) 367
Agnes of 442
Alexander of Conzie
and Kilbuyack 90,
101
Alexander of
Machermore 367
Alexander, Sir, of
Cumnock 89
Anna 88
Anne (Bayne) 90
Antoine of
Machermore 367
Archibald of Newton
and Thunderton 90
Archibald, Sir(4th Bt.
of Northfield), of
Newton and
Thunderton 90
Cuthbert of Blantyre
and Enterkine 367
David, Sir, of
Cumnock and
Blantyre 367
Dinah (Clark) 90
Edgar of 442
Elizabeth (Forbes) 90
Elizabeth (Hacket) 90
Ellen (Innes) 101

Gospatrick II, 2nd Earl
of 435, 438, 442
Gunnild of 385, 393
Isabel (Randolph) 367
James of Conzie and
Kilbuyack 101
James of Newton 90
Janet (Sutherland) 101
Jean 367
Jean (Murdoch) 367
Joan (Leslie) 89
John of Blantyre and
Enterkine 367
John of Hempriggs 90
John of Machermore
367
Juliana of 435, 438
Katherine 107
Margaret 89
Margaret (Anderson)
90
Margaret (Mackenzie)
90
Marjory 101, 102
Mary (Montgomery)
367
Patrick, Sir 367
Patrick, Sir, of
Cumnock and
Mochrum 367
Priscilla 54
Robert of Newton and
Thunderton 90
William 90
William of Hempriggs
90
DUNCAN II
King of Scotland 415,
416
DUNCH
Deborah 383
Deborah (Pilkington)
383
Harriet 46
Walter 383
DUNDAS
Anne (Murray) 107
Bethia 112
Christian 59
Elizabeth (Moore) 107
Helen (Burnet) 107
Isabel (Maule) 112
James 107
James of Doddington
112
James, Sir, of Arniston
59
John of Manour 107
Marion (Boyd) 59
Ralph of Manour 107
Thomas 107
DUNDONALD
John Cochrane, 4th
Earl of 18
DUNGAN
Frances (Latham) 111,
248, viii

The Royal Descents of 500 Immigrants

DUNGAN
also DONGAN
DUNMORE
Charles Murray, 1st
Earl of 18
John Murray, 4th Earl
of 18, 470
William Murray, 3rd
Earl of 18
DUNNE
Clare 260
DUNNE
also O'DOYNE
DUNSCOMB
Caroline Durnford 199
DUNTZFELT
Cecile Olivia 297
Christian Wilhelm 297
Marie Henriette (de
Coninck) 297
van der DUSSEN
Machteld 365
DUTTON
Eleanor 357, 360
Frances 175
John, Sir 356
Margaret (Savage) 356
Maud 356
DUYCKINCK
Maria 29
DWIGHT
Lydia 396
DYCKWOOD
alias PETERS
Martha (Treffry) 319
Thomas 319
DYDDGU
ferch Dafydd Llwyd
321
DYER
Joan 376
Margaret 282
DYKE
Constance 382
DYMOKE
Alice 213
Anne 214
Anne (Talboys) 183
Edward, Sir 183
Frances 183
Joanna (Griffith) 213
Lionel, Sir 213
Margaret 214, 272
Margaret (de Welles)
213, 214, 272
Thomas, Sir 213, 214,
272
EASLEY
Julia 50
EATON
Anne (Lloyd) Yale 321
Mabel (Harlakenden)
Haynes 424
Samuel 424
Theophilus 321

EBLES I
Count of Roucy 444,
446, 448, 450, 451,
453
ECHYNGHAM
Joan 295
Joan (FitzAlan) 295
William, Sir 295
EDDOWES
Catherine (Moulson)
238
Eleanor (Carter) 238
Elizabeth (Nevet) 238
John 238
Ralph 166, 238
Roger 238
Sarah (Kenrick) 166,
238
EDEN
Anne 461
Caroline (Calvert),
Hon. 9, 32
Catherine (Shafto) 32
Elizabeth (Heigham)
461
Henry 461
John, Sir, 2nd Bt. 32
Margaret (Lambton)
32
Mary (Davison) 32
Robert, Sir, 1st Bt. 9,
32
Robert, Sir, 3rd Bt. 32
EDENS
Ezekiel vii
Fereby (Averitt) vii
James vii
Martha Ann vii
Mary (Gammill) vii
EDGCOMBE
Anne 319
Ellen 137
EDGCUMBE
Margaret 240
Margaret (Luttrell) 240
Peter 240
EDGECUMBE/
EDGCOMB
Joan 406
EDINBURGH
Alfred of Great
Britain, Duke of 1
Marie, of 1
Philip of Greece and
Denmark, Duke of
2, 468
EDITH
of France 444, 446,
448, 450, 451, 453
of Northumberland
435, 438, 440, 442
EDMONDSON
Beula Benton 235

EDMUND
OF LANGLEY
1st Duke of York 35,
40, 45, 157, 167,
168, 179, 181, 192
EDMUND
OF WOODSTOCK
Earl of Kent 243, 280
EDNYFED
ap Llywarch Gam 465
EDUARD
Egon Peter Paul
Giovanni, Prince zu
Fürstenberg 7
EDWARD
ap John 309
ap John Wyn 309
ap Watkyn 309
Griffith 307
Jane 306, 307
Lowry (Evans) 307
Margaret 307
"The Black Prince" of
Wales 280
EDWARD I
King of England 204,
207, 210, 213, 216,
219, 222, 224, 226,
229, 231, 233, 236,
238, 240, 242-246,
248, 250, 253, 255,
257-259, 262, 264,
266, 268-272, 274-
277, 279-287, 289,
291, 352, 361, 363,
438
EDWARD III
King of England 35,
40, 45, 107, 109,
111, 112, 114, 115,
119, 123, 125, 128,
132, 134, 136, 139,
140, 142, 144, 146,
148, 150, 152, 155,
157, 159, 161, 163-
165, 167-169, 171,
172, 174, 176-186,
188-190, 192, 204,
365
EDWARD IV
King of England 32-
35, 40, 45, 140,
150, 177, 186
EDWARD VI
King of England 120
EDWARD VII
King of Great Britain
46
EDWARD
THE ELDER
King of England 455,
458, 461, 463
EDWARD GWYN
ap Hywel 404

Gerard, continued
Thomas 13, 139, 243,
255, 348
Thomas, Sir 255
William 255, 331
GERBERGA
of Germany 455, 458,
461, 463
of Lower Lorraine
455, 458, 463
GERMAN EMPEROR
Henry I the Fowler
455, 458, 461, 463
GERMANY
Emperors of 291
Gerberga of 455, 458,
461, 463
Judith of 411
**GERMANY,
EMPEROR OF**
William I 16
William II 7
de GERNON
Ranulph, 2nd Earl of
Chester 389, 398,
400, 402, 407, 409
von GERSDORFF
Augusta Theodora
(von Tschirschky
und Bögendorff) 195
Carlotta Justina 197
Heinrich August 195
von (de) GERSDORFF
Caroline (Choate) 195
Ernst Bruno 195
GERVAIS
Count of Réthel 461
GIBBES
---- (Davis) 238, 377
Ann (Murrey) 377
Basil 377
Elizabeth 238
Elizabeth (----) 377
Jane (Tournay) 376
John 377
Mary (Coventry) 376
Robert 238, 377
Robert of Barbados
376
Stephen 376
Thomas 377
GIBBINS
Hannah 264, 465
James 264, 465
Judith (Lewis) 264,
465
GIBBON
Jane 178
Sarah 121
GIBBS
Elizabeth 37
Elizabeth (Sheafe) 431
Elizabeth (Temple)
431
Gertrude (Wroughton)
431
Henry, Sir 431

Ralph, Sir 431
Robert 431
GIBSON
Alexander of Durie 73
Archibald, Baron von
Gibson 73
Elizabeth (Foulis) 73
Helen 73
Renata (Clark) 73
von GIBSON
Archibald Gibson,
Baron 73
GIBTHORPE
Katherine 393
GIDDINGS
George 456
Grace (Wardwell) 456
Jane (Lawrence) 456
Joseph 456
Joseph Jr. 456
Susanna 456
Susanna (Rindge) 456
de GIE
Charles de Rohan,
Seigneur 201
Francois de Rohan,
Seigneur 201
Pierre de Rohan,
Seigneur 201
GIFFARD
---- (Vachell) 386
Agnes (Master) 435
Agnes (Winslow) 386,
435
Alice 438
Alice (de Montfort)
438
Amy 435
Anne 386
Cassandra 258
Eleanor (Vaux) 435
Elizabeth (de
Missenden) 435
Isabel (Stretle) 435
Jane 396
Joan (Langston) 435
John 386, 435
John, Sir 435, 438
Lucy (de Morteyn)
435, 438
Margaret 423, 435
Margaret (Cobleigh)
396
Mary (Nanseglos) 435
Nicholas 435
Roger 435
Roger, Sir 396
Thomas 435
Thomas, Sir 435
William 386
GIFFORD
Anne 219
Catherine 207
Eleanor (Paulet) 219
Joan (Bruges) 219
John 219
William, Sir 219

GIGNILLIAT
Abraham 453
Jean Francois 453
Marie (de Ville) 453
Suzanne (Le Serrurier)
453
GILBERT
Horace Durham 62
Isabella 419
Joan 448
Katharine (Dedons de
Pierrefeu) 62
Temperance 272
GILL
Anna Maria 161, 255,
258, 375
Benjamin 255, 375
Mary (Mainwaring)
255, 375
Ruth Sylvia 469
GILLESPIE
Elspeth 97
GILLETT
Martha 82
GILLOIS
Yvonne Noël Marie 19
GIRLINGTON
Isabel 224
Katherine (Hildyard)
224
William 224
GISELA
of France 455, 458,
463
GISSAGE
Sarah (Shelton) 384
de GLANDEVEZ
Dauphine 343
GLEMHAM
Anne 266
Eleanor (Brandon) 266
John 266
GLENCAIRN
Alexander
Cunyngham, 5th
Earl of 68
William Cunyngham,
6th Earl of 68
GLENTWORTH
Henry Hartstonge
Pery, Viscount 38
William Cecil Pery,
1st Baron 38
GLOUCESTER
Amice of 406
Gilbert de Clare, 3rd
Earl of 210, 222,
224, 226, 231, 233,
236, 242, 248, 250,
258, 264, 271, 275,
277, 287, 291
Hugh de Audley, 1st
Earl of 224, 226,
250, 258, 264, 277,
291

Gloucester, continued
Humphrey
Plantagenet, Duke of
80, 82, 84, 85
Mabel of 387, 391,
404
Maud of 389, 398,
400, 402, 407, 409
Robert of Caen, 1st
Earl of 387, 389,
391, 396, 398, 400,
402, 404, 406, 407,
409
Thomas le Despencer,
1st Earl of 157, 167,
168, 179, 181, 192
Thomas of
Woodstock, 1st
Duke of 132, 146,
163, 182
William Fitz Robert,
2nd Earl of 387,
391, 404, 406
GLOVER
Priscilla 389, 459
GOBION
Agnes (de Merlay)
435, 438
Hugh 435, 438
Joan 435, 438
Matilda (----) 435, 438
Richard 435, 438
GODDARD
Anne (Gifford) 219
Bridget 382
Edward 219, 382
Elizabeth (Miles) 219
Elizabeth (Walrond)
219
Josiah 219
Martha 192
Mary (Kingsmill) 382
Priscilla (D'Oyley)
219
Rachel 219
Rachel (Davis) 219
Richard 219
Thomas 219
William 192, 219
GODFREY
Arabella (Churchill)
271
Charles 271
Count of Namur 461
GODMAN
Elizabeth 246
GOFFE
Frances (Whalley) 353
William 353
GOLD
Mary 441
GOLDEN HORDE
Toktai, Khan of the
413
GOLEUDDYDD
ferch Dafydd 387

**GOLITSYN/
GOLITZIN,
GALLITZIN**
Adelaide Amalia,
Countess (von
Schmettau) 414
Alexei, Prince 412,
414
Anastasia, Princess
412
Anastasia, Princess
(Prozorovsky) 414
Andrei, Prince 413,
414
Anna (----) 413
Anna (Soukine) 412
Boris, Prince 412
Demetrius Augustine,
Prince 414
Dimitri, Prince 414
Doria, Princess
(Gagarin) 414
Eudoxia (----) 413
Euphemia
(Piliemanov-
Sabourov) 414
Irina, Princess
(Khilkov) 412, 414
Ivan, Prince 413, 414
Maria, Princess 412
Maria, Princess
(Khvorostinine) 412
Michael, Prince 413
Xenia (----) 413
Youri, Prince 413
GOLOVINE
Anastasia 412
Anna, Princess
(Kholmsky) 412
Ivan 412
Maria, Princess
(Odoevsky) 412
Peter 412
von der GOLTZ
Maria Karoline
Elizabeth 74
de GONTAUT
Geneviéve 105
GONZAGA
Anna, of Nevers and
Manuta 14
GOODE
Anne (Bennett) 337
Frances (Mackarness)
337
Isabel (Penkeville) 336
Joan (Downe) 336
John 337
Richard 336, 337
GOODERE
Alice (Brent) 431
Alice (Frowick) 431
Anne 432
Henry 431
Jane (Greene) 431
Jane (Lewknor) 431
Joan (Lewknor) 431

John 431
Thomas 431
GOODHUE
Grace Anna 210, 219,
390, 459
GOODRICH
Marcus Aurelius 207
Olivia (Mary) (de
Havilland) 207
GOODRICK
Anne 214
Anne (Dymoke) 214
John 214
Lionel 214
Winifred (Sapcott) 214
GOODWIN
French Addison
(Gamble) 26
GOOKIN
Catherine 376
Daniel 376
GORBATY-SHUISKY
Alexander, Prince 412
Anastasia (Golovine)
412
Boris, Prince 412
Eudoxia, Princess 412
Ivan, Prince 411
GORDON
---- (Keir) 77
Alexander 48
Alexander of Lesmoir
107
Alexander, 12th Earl
of Sutherland 48
Alexander, 3rd Earl of
Huntly 60, 71
Alexander, 4th Duke
of Gordon 11
Alexander Gordon, 4th
Duke of 11
Annabella (Stewart)
60, 71, 73, 76, 77
Anne 31
Anne (Hamilton) 53
Catherine 11
Catherine (Burnet) 76
Catherine (Gordon) 11
Charles, 4th Earl of
Aboyne 470
Charlotte 11
Christian 90
Cosmo George, 3rd
Duke of Gordon 11
Cosmo George
Gordon, 3rd Duke
of 11
Elizabeth 60, 73, 76,
77, 88
Elizabeth (Keith) 53,
60
Elizabeth, Countess of
Sutherland 23
Geneviève (Petau) 48
George, 1st Marquess
of Huntly 53

Graham, continued
Patrick Graham, 1st
Baron 92
GRAHAME
Gloria 175
Jean 175
de GRAMONT
Anna Quintana
Albertine Ida
(Grimod) 105
Antoine Adrien
Charles, Count
d'Aster 105
Antoine Alfred
Agénor, 10th Duc
de Gramont 105
Antoine Alfred
Agénor, 11th Duc
de Gramont 105
Antoine Alfred Agénor
de Gramont, 10th
Duc 105
Antoine Alfred Agénor
de Gramont, 11th
Duc 105
Antoine Héraclius
Geneviève Agénor,
9th Duc de Gramont
105
Antoine Héraclius
Geneviève Agénor
de Gramont, 9th
Duc 105
Antoine IV, 3rd Duc
de Gramont 104
Antoine IV de
Gramont, 3rd Duc
104
Antoine Louis Marie,
8th Duc de Gramont
105, 106
Antoine Louis Marie
de Gramont, 8th
Duc 105, 106
Emma Mary
(Mackinnon) 105
Gabriel Antoine
Armand, Count de
Gramont 105
Gabriel Antoine
Armand de
Gramont, Count 105
Geneviève (de
Gontaut) 105
Just Madeleine 299
Louis de Gramont, 5th
Duc 105
Louis, 5th Duc de
Gramont 105
Louise Gabrielle Aglaé
(de Polignac) 105
Margaret (Kinnicutt)
105
Maria (Ruspoli) 105
Marie (Negroponte)
105

Marie Christine (de
Noailles) 104
Marie Louise Sophie
(de Faoucq) 105
Nancy (Ryan) 105
Sanche Armand
Gabriel 105
GRANBY
John Manners,
Marquess of 40
GRANDPRE
Wolfart VI von
Borsselen, Count of
197
de GRANDSON
Adelaide (----) 453
Barthélemy, Seigneur
de la Sarraz and
Belmont 453
Columba 453
Ebles 453
Fulk 453
Jordan, Seigneur of
Belmont 453
Petronelle (----) 453
de GRANGES
(in Valais)
Pierre de Rovorée,
Seigneur 453
GRANT
Anne Charlotte 20
Barbara 114
Elizabeth 77
Julia Boggs (Dent)
364, 386
Margaret 101
Nelly 101
Ulysses Simpson 364,
386
GRANVILLE
John Carteret, 1st Earl
of 22
de GRASSE
Angélique (de Rouxel)
292
Annibal, Count du Bar
292
Antoinette Rosalie
(Accaron) 292
Catherine (de Pien)
292
Christine (de Cibon)
292
Claire (d'Alagonia)
292
Claude, Count du Bar
291
Claude, Seigneur du
Bar 291
Francois Joseph Paul,
Count de Grasse,
Marquis de Tilly
292
Francois Joseph Paul
de Grasse, Marquis
de Tilly, Count 292

Honoré, Seigneur de
Valette 292
Jean Pierre Charles,
Seigneur de Valette
292
Jeanne (de Brancas)
291
Marguerite (de Flotte-
d'Agoult) 292
Marthe (de Foix) 291
Sylvie 292
de GRASSE de PAU
Caroline 292
**de GRASSE-
ROUVILLE**
Francois, Seigneur de
Valette 292
Véronique (de
Villeneuve-Trans)
292
GRAY
---- 33
Caroline Maria 38
Elizabeth 317
Emilie Caroline (Pery)
38
Henry 38
Katherine (Miles) 165
GRAYSON
Susannah Monroe 58
GREAT BRITAIN
Alfred of, Duke of
Edinburgh 1
Anna of 3
Anne Elizabeth Alice
Louise of, The
Princess Royal 129
Kings of 291
Sophie Dorothea of 4
**GREAT BRITAIN,
KING OF**
Edward VII 46
George I 9, 187
George II 3
George III 16, 291
George VI 468
**GREAT BRITAIN,
QUEEN OF**
Elizabeth II 2, 129,
468
Victoria 1, 16, 195,
197
GREECE
Kings of 291
Olga of 2
**GREECE and
DENMARK**
Nicholas, Prince of 2
Philip of, Duke of
Edinburgh 2, 468
GREECE, KING OF
George I 2
GREEKE
Margaret 243
GREEN
Edward 173
Elizabeth 360

The Royal Descents of 500 Immigrants

GUNTER
Gwenllian (ferch
Gwilym) 387
Jenkin 387
Margred 387
GÜNTHER XXVIII
Count of
Schwarzburg-
Blankenburg 194
GÜNTHER XL
Count of
Schwarzburg-
Blankenburg 194
GUNTHORPE
Anne 117
GUNTON
Alice 266
GURDON
Brampton 146, 317
Elizabeth 317
Muriel 146, 164
Muriel (Sedley) 146,
317
GUSTAV ADOLF
Duke of Mecklenburg-
Güstrow 15
GUSTAV I (Vasa)
King of Sweden 17
GUTHRIE
Bethia 112
Clara 20
GUY
Margaret 282
GUY XIV
Count of Laval 79
GWEN
ferch Gruffudd 324,
326
ferch Gruffudd Goch
ap Ieuan 321
ferch Ieuan Dew ap
Meurig 305
GWENHWYFAR
ferch Gronwy ap Ieuan
308, 328
ferch Ieuan 326
ferch Richard Llwyd
311
ferch Thomas 391
GWENLLIAN
ferch Einion ap Ieuan
Llwyd 305
ferch Gwilym 387
ferch Gwilym ap
Hywel Grach 391
ferch Hywel 404
ferch William ap
Gruffudd 308
GWERFUL
ferch Ieuan ab Einion
324, 326
ferch Llywelyn ap
Dafydd 305
GWILYM
ap Rhys Llwyd 387
GWINNETT
Anne (Bourne) 303

Anne (Emes) 303
Button 303
Elizabeth (Coxe) 303
Elizabeth (Laurence)
303
Elizabeth (Randle) 303
George 303
Samuel 303
GWLADYS
ferch Dafydd 391
ferch Dafydd Gam 391
ferch Llywelyn 387
GWYN
Hugh 157
Jane (Owen) 157
Sybil 157
GWYNN
Eleanor "Nell" 12
GYE
Grace (Dowrish) 295
Mary 295
Mary (Prowse) 295
Robert 295
GYLLENSVÄRD
Anna Maria 17
HABINGTON also
ABINGTON
HABSBURG-
LOTHRINGEN
Mary Jerrine (Soper) 1
Stefan 1
HACKBURNE
Katherine (Deighton)
205
Samuel 205
HACKET
Elizabeth 90
HACKSHAW
Mary 125
HADNALL
Mary 227
HAEN
Judith (Manby) 450
HAGGERSTON
Elizabeth 354
HAHN
Elena (Fadeev) 412
Helena Petrovna 413
Peter 412
HAINAULT
Baldwin II, Count of
431
Baldwin III, Count of
431
Beatrix of 444, 446,
448, 450, 451, 453
Ida of 431
John I, Count of 365
John II, Count of 365
Marie of 297, 299
Philippa of 35, 40, 45,
107, 109, 111, 112,
114, 115, 119, 123,
125, 128, 132, 134,
136, 139, 140, 142,
144, 146, 148, 150,
152, 155, 157, 159,

161, 163-165, 167-
169, 171, 172, 174,
176-186, 188-190,
192, 204, 365
Rainier IV, Count of
444, 446, 448, 450,
451, 453
HALCRO
Margaret 94
HALES
Frances 8
de HALES
Alice 204, 207, 213,
216, 219, 240, 244,
246, 257, 270, 272,
282, 283, 286
HALFIN
Diane 7
HALIBURTON
---- (Erskine) 94
Elizabeth 94
George 94
Jean 94
Jean (Clark) 94
Margaret 94
Patrick of
Muirhouselaw 94
HALICZ
Kunigunde of 293
HALIFAX
George Montagu, 1st
Earl of 33
HALL
Alice 289
Christian 403
Elizabeth 146, 253,
402
Elizabeth (Wingfield)
146, 213, 289
Francis 146, 213, 289
Jane 213
Margaret 32
Ursula (Sherington)
146, 213
HALLWARD
Adelaide Caroline
(Bloxam) 175
Charles Berners 175
Elizabeth Anne
(Morgan) 175
Emily Jane (Leslie)
175
Gloria 175
Jeannie (McDougall)
175
John 175
Mary (Lambarde) 175
Reginald Francis 175
Reginald Michael
Bloxam 175
HALSALL
Maud 188
HALSNODE
John 464
Margaret 464
Margaret (Ladd) 464
Martha (Harfleet) 464

HARBY
Emma 125
Katherine 125
Katherine
(Throckmorton) 125
Thomas 125
HARCOURT
Agnes 146, 325
Agnes (Limerick) 325
Alice 251
Anne (Norris) 325
Edith (St. Clair) 251
Ellen (la Zouche) 376
Hilaria (Hastings) 376
Isabella 128
Jane (Franceys) 251,
325
Jean IV, Sire de Rieux
and de Rochefort,
Count of 79
John 325
John, Sir 376
Margaret (Beke) 376
Margaret (Bryan) 325
Matilda 376
Maud (Grey) 251, 325
Richard, Sir 251, 376
Robert, Sir 325
Thomas, Sir 251, 325
William, Sir 376
de HARCOURT
Alice 429
HARDING
Edward Learned 472
Lucy Booker (Ramsay)
472
Mary (Learned) 472
Mary Virginia Ramsay
472
Seth 472
HARDWICK
Elizabeth, Countess of
Shrewsbury 161,
249
Elizabeth (Bakewell)
285
Elizabeth (Goushill)
Wingfield 285
Elizabeth (Leke) 161,
285
Elizabeth (Pinchbeck)
285
John 161, 285
Mary 285
Nicola (Barlow) 285
Roger 285
William, Sir 285
HARDY
Mary 134
HARFLEET
Henry 464
Marion (Brockhull)
464
Martha 464
Mary (Slaughter) 464
Thomas 464

HARINGTON
---- 348
Ada Constance Helen
129
Ada (Drew) 129
Edward Musgrave 129
Edward Templer 129
Elizabeth 262
Esther (Lens) 129
Frances 262
Helena (Gostlett) 129
Henry 129
Henry, Sir 262
Isabel 331
Isabel (English) 348,
440
James, Sir 262
Jane Anne (Thomas)
129
Joan (Dacre) 440
John 129
John, Sir 440
Katherine (Banastre)
440
Lucy (Sidney) 262
Margaret 354, 441
Margaret (de Neville)
331, 440
Margaret (Lathom)
348
Martha (Musgrave)
129
Mary (Backwell) 129
Nicholas of Huyton
348
Nicholas, Sir 348, 440
Ruth (Pilkington) 262
Sarah 35
Susanna Isabella 129
William, Sir 331, 440
HARINGTON also
HAVERINGTON
HARINGTON and
BONVILLE
Cecily Bonville,
Baroness 136
William Bonville,
Baron 136
HARLAKENDEN
Elizabeth (Bosvile)
116, 136, 424
Emlin (-----) 424
Mabel 424
Margaret (Huberd)
424
Richard 424
Roger 136, 424
HARLESTON
Affra 119
Elizabeth 119
Elizabeth (-----) 119
Elizabeth (Willis) 119
Jane (Wentworth) 119
John 119
HARLYNGRUGGE
Alice (Marmion) 461
Cecilia 461

William 461
HARMAN
Elizabeth 126
HARPERSFIELD
John 264
Joyce (Mitton) 264
HARPERSFIELD
alias MITTON
Anna (Skrimshire) 264
Edward 264
HARPUR
Isabella (Pierpont) 161
Jane 161
John, Sir 161
von HARRACH
Augusta 3
HARRI
ap Cynric 357
HARRIMAN
Pamela Beryl (Digby)
Spencer-Churchill
Hayward, Hon. 20
William Averell 20
HARRIS
Agnes 445
Anne (Ruther) 172
Arthur 172, 222
Bartholomew 445
Catherine (Esse) 419
Christopher 172
Dorothy 222
Dorothy (Waldegrave)
222
Elizabeth (Collamore)
445
Elizabeth (Turgis) 149
Frances 172, 419
Frances (Astley) 172
Francis 419
Jane 419
Jane (Harris) 419
Joan (Percy) 172
John 419
Mary 204, viii
Mary (Gedge) 172
Philippa (Grenville)
419
Sarah 387
William 172, 419
William, Sir 172
HARRISON
Anna Tuthill
(Symmes) 229, 445
Anne 43
Anne (Carter) 229
Benjamin 229, 445
Benjamin (IV) 229
Benjamin (V) 229
Caroline Lavinia
(Scott) 229, 445
Elizabeth (Bassett) 229
Elizabeth Ramsey
(Irwin) 229, 445
Frances (Whitgreaves)
132
John Scott 229, 445

Harrison, continued
Mary Scott (Lord)
Dimmick 229, 445
William Henry 229,
445
HARRY
Daniel 168
Elizabeth (Brinton)
168
Frances (----) 168
Hugh 168
John 168
Miriam 168
Sybil (----) 168
HART
Anne 177
Hannah 335
HARTLEY
Margaret 330
HARTMANN II
of Liechtenstein-
Feldsberg 197
HARTSHORN
Christian 287
HARTSTONGE
Alice 190
HARWOOD
Lydia 210
HASELDEN
Anthony 336
Beatrice 336
Elizabeth (Cheney)
336
Elizabeth (Daneys)
336
Jane (Marshall) 336
John 336
William 336
HASELRIGE
Arthur, Sir, 2nd Bt.
132
Catherine 132, 153
Dorothy (Grevile) 132
HASELRIGE also
HESILRIG
HASELWOOD
Alice 144
Alice (Gascoigne) 144
John 144
HASTINGS
Agnes (----) 417
Amicia (----) 417
Anne 148
Anne (Morley) 224
Beatrix (----) 417
Catherine 35
Catherine Maria 27
Dorothy 45
Dorothy (Port) 35
Edward, 2nd Baron
Hastings 148
Edward Hastings, 2nd
Baron 148
Elizabeth 224, 373
Elizabeth (Stanley) 27
Emeline (Heron) 417

Ferdinando, 6th Earl
of Huntingdon 27
Florence 142
Frances 36
Frances Leveson
(Fowler) 27
Francis, 2nd Earl of
Huntingdon 35
Francis, Lord Hastings
35
Francis Hastings, Lord
35
George, 4th Earl of
Huntingdon 35
George, Sir 35
Helen (Alveston) 417
Henry, 5th Earl of
Huntingdon 27
Henry, Sir 371, 373,
376
Hilaria 376
Hugh 417
Hugh, Sir 417
Isabel (de Valence)
373
Isabel (Sadington) 417
Joan (de Cantilupe)
371, 373
John, 1st Baron
Hastings 373
John, Sir 224
John Hastings, 1st
Baron 373
Katherine 35
Lora 371
Lucy (Davies) 27
Margaret 417
Margaret (Herle) 417
Mary (Hungerford)
148
Nicholas, Sir 417
Ralph, Sir 417
Sarah (Harington) 35
Seymour (Prynne) 35
Theophilus, 7th Earl
of Huntingdon 27
Thomas 417
William 417
HASWELL
Mary 129, 209
HATFIELD
Agnes 420
Agnes (Marshall) 420
Alice (Hercy) 352
Anne 209
Elizabeth 352
Henry 352
Isabel (Russell) 420
Lawrence 420
Stephen 420
HATHORNE
Sarah (Ruck) 223
HATTON
Eleanor 385
Frances 46
Martha 188

HAUGH
Atherton 211
Elizabeth (Bulkeley)
Whittingham 211
HAVERINGTON
Agnes (Cansfield) 440
Robert, Sir 440
HAVERINGTON
also HARINGTON
HAVILAND
Elizabeth (Guise) 142
Jane 142
Robert 142
de HAVILLAND
Charles Richard 207
Joan de Beauvoir 207
Lilian Augusta (Ruse)
207
Margaret Letitia
(Molesworth) 207
Olivia (Mary) 207
Walter Augustus 207
HAWES
Anne 315
Constance 335
Desire (Gorham) 335
Edmond 335
Elizabeth (Brome) 335
Jane (Porter) 335
John 335
Thomas 335
Ursula (Colles) 335
William 335
HAWKINS
Hannah 233, 394
Lois 272
HAWLEY
Agnes 350
HAWTE
Jane 123, 383
HAY
Christian 111
Eleanor 51
Elizabeth 73, 75, 78
George, 7th Earl of
Erroll 73
Isabel (Gordon) 73
Jean 60
Louisa 21
Margaret 86
Margaret (Logie) 73
Margaret (Robertson)
73
Maria 369
Mary 66
Thomas 73
William, 3rd Earl of
Erroll 73
HAYES
Chloe (Smith) 448
Ezekiel 448
Lucy Ware (Webb)
449
Rebecca (Russell) 448
Rutherford 448
Rutherford Jr. 448

The Royal Descents of 500 Immigrants

Herbert, continued
Eveline Alicia Juliana
25, 26
Henrietta Anna
(Howard) 25
Henriette Mauricette
(de Penancoët de
Kéroualle) 79
Henry, 1st Earl of
Carnarvon 25
Henry George, 2nd
Earl of Carnarvon
25
Henry John George,
3rd Earl of
Carnarvon 25
Henry William 25
Letitia Dorothea
(Allen) 25
Margaret (Cradock)
391
Maud 140, 150, 172,
174, 186
Philip, 7th Earl of
Pembroke 79
Richard of Ewyas 391
Sarah (Barker) 25
Thomas of
Abergavenny 391
William, 1st Earl of
Pembroke 391
William, Hon. 25
HERCY
Alice 352
Anne 352
Barbara 353
Elizabeth (Digby) 352
Hugh 352
Humphrey 352
Jane (Stanhope) 352
Margery (Bingham)
352
de HERDEBERG
Ela 398
HERDSON
Abigail 373
HEREFORD
Walter Devereux, 1st
Viscount 45
**HEREFORD and
ESSEX**
Humphrey de Bohun,
4th Earl of 227,
229, 233, 238, 245,
253, 255, 259, 262,
266, 268, 269, 274,
276, 279, 281, 284,
285, 288, 289
HERING
Anna Maria (Morris)
125
Bathshua 470
Bathshua (Scott) 470
Elizabeth (Cockcroft)
125, 470
Elizabeth (Hughes)
125

Julines 125, 470
Mary Helen 125
Mary (Inglis) 125
Nathaniel 125, 470
Oliver 125
HERIOT
Elizabeth 93
HERLE
Margaret 417
HERNANCE
Joan 336
HERNDON
Catherine (----) 332
Dabney 332
Edward 332
Edward Jr. 332
Elizabeth
(Stubblefield) 332
Ellen Lewis 332
Frances Elizabeth
(Hansbrough) 332
Joseph 332
Mary (Minor) 332
Mary (Waller) 332
William 332
William Lewis 332
HERON
Andrew of Bargaly
367
Andrew of
Kirrouchtrie 367
Anne (Vining) 367
Benjamin 367
Emeline 417
Isabel 417
Jean (Dunbar) 367
Margaret (Hastings)
417
Mary (Graham) 367
Mary (Howe) 367
Patrick 367
Roger, Sir 417
HERRIES
Mariot 203
Marmaduke Francis
Constable-Maxwell,
11th Baron 24
HERRING
Mary 465
HERRON
Helen 456
HERTFORD
Edward Seymour, 1st
Earl of 22, 25
Gilbert de Clare, 7th
Earl of 210, 222,
224, 226, 231, 233,
236, 242, 248, 250,
258, 264, 271, 275,
277, 287, 291
Richard de Clare, 3rd
Earl of 406
Roger de Clare, 2nd
Earl of 444, 448,
451
HERVEY
Elizabeth (Felton) 151

John, 1st Baron
Hervey of Ickworth
151
John, 1st Earl of
Bristol 151
Lepell 8
Mary 151
Mary (Lepell) 151
Susan 85
**HERVEY OF
ICKWORTH**
John Hervey, 1st
Baron 151
HESILRIG
Anne 417
Elizabeth (Brocket)
417
Elizabeth (Staunton)
417
Isabel (Heron) 417
Lucy (Entwisle) 417
Thomas 417
William 417
**HESILRIG also
HASELRIGE**
HESKETH
Helen 330
van HESSE
Margaret 43, 433
HESSE-DARMSTADT
Anna Eleanor of 187
Elizabeth of 61
Ernest Louis,
Landgrave of 15
Frederica of 16
George William,
Landgrave of 15
Louis VI, Landgrave
of 15
Louis VIII, Landgrave
of 15
**HESSE-RHEINFELS-
ROTENBERG**
Christine Henrietta of
5
**HESSE-RHEINFELS-
ROTENBURG**
Joseph, Landgrave of
14
Louise of 14
de la HESTRE
Alexandre de
Carondelet, Vicomte
301
Antoine de Carondelet,
Vicomte 301
**de la HESTRE and
du LANGUE**
Francois de
Carondelete,
Vicomte 302
Jean Louis de
Carondelete,
Vicomte 302
HETLEY
Judith 341

The Royal Descents of 500 Immigrants

HEVER
Elizabeth 464
HEVYN
Anne 334
HEWSTER
Joan 382
HEXT
Joan (Fortescue) 444
Margery 444
Thomas 444
Wilmot (Poyntz) 444
HEXTILDA
of Tynedale 415
HEYDON
Christian 346
Dorothy 123
HEYWARD
Mary 140
HEYWOOD
Catherine 282
HIBBARD
Ebenezer 469
Keziah 469
Margaret (Morgan)
469
HIBBERT
---- 264, 465
Hannah (Gibbins) 264,
465
Mary 264, 465
HICKMAN
Elizabeth 142
HIGGINSON
Lucy 144
HIGHAM
Bridget 223
Phyllis (Waldegrave)
223
Thomas 223
HIGHAM also
HEIGHAM
HILDOUIN IV
Count of Montdidier
444, 446, 448, 450,
451, 453
HILDYARD
Elizabeth (Hastings)
224
Joan (de la See) 225
Katherine 224, 225
Margery 224
Peter 225
Robert, Sir 224
HILEY
Mary 442
HILL
Anne 240
Joan 155
Mary 236, 240
Priscilla 35
Ursula 137
HILTON
---- (Brandling) 34
Anne (Yorke) 34
Elizabeth 393
Elizabeth (Kitchen) 34

Godfrey, Baron
Luttrell 393
Godfrey, Sir 393
Hannah (----) Moore
34
Hawise (Luttrell),
Baroness Luttrell
393
Henry 34
Isabel (Selby) 34
John 34
Margaret (Metcalfe) 34
Margery (----) 393
Mehitabel (Lawrence)
34
Ralph 34
Robert 34
Sarah (Clarke) 34
Sibyl (Lumley) 34
William 34
William, Sir 34
HINKLEY
Cecily 456
John 456
Margaret (Notbeam)
456
HINTON
Catherine (Palmer)
134
Elizabeth (Dilke) 134
James 134
John 134
John, Sir 134
Mary (Hardy) 134
Thomas, Sir 134
William 134
HITCHEN
Mary 331
HOAR
Bridget (Lisle) 206
Leonard 206
HOBBES
Anne 346
HODGES
Agatha (Rodney) 409
Anne (Mansell) 410
Eleanor (Rosse) 409
George 409, 410
Jane 410, 432
Thomas 409
HODGSON
Henrietta Mildred 468
Mary (Tucker) 468
Mildred (Porteus) 468
Robert 468
de HODINGTON
Agnes (Cassy) 398
Joan 398
Margery (Thurgrym)
398
Thomas 398
Walter 398
HOGE
Sarah 126
HOHENSTAUFEN
Otto of, Palatine Count
of Burgundy 343

HOHENSTAUFEN
and BURGUNDY
Beatrix of 343
HOLAND
Alice (FitzAlan) 243,
280
Constance 161
Edmund, 4th Earl of
Kent 157, 167, 168,
179, 181, 192
Eleanor 35, 40, 45,
157, 167, 168, 179,
181, 192, 243, 280
Elizabeth 345
Elizabeth (Plantagenet)
161
Joan (Plantagenet)
243, 280
John, 1st Duke of
Exeter 161
Margaret 107, 109,
111, 112, 114, 115,
155
Maud 348, 350, 356,
358, 360
Maud (la Zouche) 345,
348, 350, 356, 358,
360
Robert, 1st Baron
Holand 345, 348,
350, 356, 358, 360
Robert Holand, 1st
Baron 345, 348,
350, 356, 358, 360
Thomas, 1st Earl of
Kent 243, 280
Thomas, 2nd Earl of
Kent 243, 280
HOLBROOK
Deborah 456
HOLCROFT
John 331
Margaret 331
Margaret (Mascy) 331
HOLFORD
Dorothy 356
Jane (Booth) 356
Thomas, Sir 356
HOLLAND
Adelaide of 365
HOLLYMAN
Mary 121
HOLME
Agnes 459
Anne (Aislaby) 225
Catherine 225
John 225
Katherine (Hildyard)
225
William 225
HOLMES
Martha (Pomeroy) 406
William 406
HOLMSTEAD
Margaret 317

552

The Royal Descents of 500 Immigrants

Howard, continued
Thomas, 1st Viscount
Howard of Bindon
151
Thomas, 2nd Duke of
Norfolk 283
Thomas, 3rd Duke of
Norfolk 150, 186
Thomas, 4th Duke of
Norfolk 150
William, 1st Baron
Howard of
Effingham 283
William, Sir 283
**HOWARD OF
BINDON**
Thomas Howard, 1st
Viscount 151
**HOWARD OF
EFFINGHAM**
Francis Howard, 5th
Baron 119, 123, 283
William Howard, 1st
Baron 283
**HOWARD OF
GLOSSOP**
Edward Fitzalan-
Howard, 1st Baron
23
HOWE
Annabella (Scrope)
187
Bathsheba 373
Emanuel Scrope, 2nd
Viscount Howe 187
Emanuel Scrope
Howe, 2nd Viscount
187
George Augustus, 3rd
Viscount Howe 187
George Augustus
Howe, 3rd Viscount
187
John Grubham 187
Juliana (Alington) 187
Mary 367
Scrope Howe, 1st
Viscount 187
Scrope, 1st Viscount
Howe 187
Sophie Charlotte Marie
(von Kielmansegge)
187
HOWELL
Martha 436
Mary 214
HOWES
Joan 360
HOWIS
Frances 446
HOWLAND
Abigail (Burt) 245
Desire 335
Elizabeth (Southworth)
245
Elizabeth (Tilley) 335
John 335

Joseph 245
Lydia (Bill) 245
Martha (Cole) 245
Nathaniel 245
Nathaniel Jr. 245
Susan 148, 165, 245
HOWTH
Nicholas St.
Lawrence, 16th
Baron 216
HOYLE
Ann (Debnam) 331
Edward 331
Mary (Towneley) 331
Samuel 331
HOYT
Margaret (Bliss) 397
Margaret Jane 236,
397, 446
Nathan 397
HUBBARD
Jane 208
HUBERD
Edward 423
Elizabeth (Chauncey)
423
Jane (Southall) 423
Margaret 424
Richard 423
HUDDLESTON
Elizabeth 416
HUDSON
Anne 284
HUGFORD
Elizabeth (Fettiplace)
303
Elizabeth (Rudhall)
303
John 303
Margaret 303
Margaret (Hugford)
303
William 303
HUGH
ap Cadwaladr ap Rhys
309
**HUGH also
HUGHES or PUGH**
HUGH I
Count of Clermont
444, 446, 448, 450,
451
Count of Ponthieu
455, 458, 463
HUGH III
Count of Pontheiu
455, 458, 463
HUGH CAPET
King of France 444,
446, 448, 450, 451,
453, 455, 458, 463
HUGH KEVELIOC
3rd Earl of Chester
367, 369, 371, 373,
376, 389, 398, 400,
402, 407, 409

HUGH MAGNUS
Duke of France and
Burgundy 419, 421,
423, 425, 427, 429
HUGHES
Elizabeth 125
Ellen 306, 307, 309,
312
Grisold 174
Jane 307, 309
Mary 309, 405
**HUGHES also
HUGH or PUGH**
HULL
Elizabeth 332
Henry 345
Mary viii
Ursula 345
Ursula (Larder) 345
William 345
HUME
Bethia (Dundas) 112
Isabel 112
James 112
**HUMPHREY/
HUMPHRIES**
Alice 442
Anne 80, 116, 157,
158
Anthony 442
ap Hugh 157
ap Hywel 80
Benjamin 157
Daniel 157
Elizabeth 158
Elizabeth (Medford)
157
Elizabeth (Pelham)
116
Elizabeth (Rees) 157
Elizabeth (Thomas)
157
Goditha 157
Gwen (Jones) 307
Hannah (Wynne) 157
Jane 158
Jane (Humphrey) 158
John 116, 158, 307
Joseph 157
Lydia 157
Magdalen
(Washington) 442
Margaret (Evans) 307
Margaret (Vaughan)
157
Mary 402
Mary (Llewelyn) 157
Owen 157
Rebecca 157, 306
Robert 307
Samuel 157
Susan (Clinton), Lady
116
HUNGERFORD
Anne 129, 403
Anne (Percy) 148
Anthony, Sir 403

The Royal Descents of 500 Immigrants

James, continued
Thomas 211
William Dodge 21
JAMES I
Count of la Marche
299
King of England 14,
15, 271, 374
King of Scotland 58,
60, 71, 73, 75-78
JAMES II
King of England 8, 13,
41, 271, 291, 352
King of Scotland 48,
53, 59, 66, 68-70
JAMES IV
King of Scotland 48,
50, 51, 53, 55, 57-
60
JAMES V
King of Scotland 28,
30, 31
JAMES VI
King of Scotland 14
JANE
ferch Cadwaladr ap
Maredudd 305
ferch Humphrey ap
Hywel 80
ferch Maredudd 328
ferch Maredudd ap
Ieuan 305, 309
ferch Richard Thoma
167
JANET
ferch Owain 409
JANSSEN
Mary 9
JAQUET
Jean (Jan) Paul 296
Maria (de Carpentier)
296
JAROSLAW I
Prince of Wladimir
411
JASON
Elizabeth 225
JAY
Augusta 443
Eliza 443
JEANES
Martha 187
JEFFERSON
Jane (Randolph) 169,
338, 407
Martha (Wayles)
Skelton 169, 338,
339, 407
Mary 169, 338, 408
Mary (Branch) 407
Mary (Field) 407
Peter 169, 338, 407
Thomas 169, 338,
339, 407
Thomas Jr. 407
JEFFREYS
Charlotte (Herbert) 79

Henrietta Louisa 79
Herbert, Sir 282
Jane (Berkeley) 282
John, 2nd Baron
Jeffreys 79
John Jeffreys, 2nd
Baron 79
Susanna (----) 282
William 282
JEKYLL
Elizabeth 417
JENKIN
Alice (Herbert) 391
Elizabeth 388, 391
William 391
JENNEY
Anne (Reade) 275
Arthur 275
Arthur, Sir 275
Ela (Jernegan) 275
Francis 275
Helen (Stonard) 275
Isabel 275, 339
JENNINGS
Alice (Bright) 407
Catherine 407
Edmund 42, 287
Edmund, Sir 42, 287
Elizabeth 42, 287
Frances (Corbin) 287
Joan (Bostock) 407
Margaret (Barkham)
42, 287
Thomas 407
William 407
JERMY
Elizabeth 450
Elizabeth (Hunhall)
450
Elizabeth (Wroth) 450
Ellen (Lampett) 450
Isabel (St. Aubin) 450
Joan (Halys) 450
John 450
John, Sir 450
Margaret (Bigod) 450
Margaret (Multney)
450
Thomas, Sir 450
William, Sir 450
JERMYN
Jane 120
John 119
Mary (Tollemache)
119
Sarah (Stephens) 120
Susan 119
Thomas 120
JERNEGAN
Bridget (Drury) 275
Ela 275
Ela (Spelman) 275
George 275
John, Sir 275

JERUSALEM,
KING OF
John de Brienne,
Emperor of
Constantinople 303
JEVON
Anne 141
JEWETT
David 264, 465
Deborah (Lord) 264,
465
Elizabeth 264, 465
Joseph 264, 465
Mary (Hibbert) 264,
465
Nathan 264, 465
Sarah (Selden) 264,
465
JOACHIM I
Elector of
Brandenburg 61
JOACHIM ERNEST
Prince of Anhalt-
Zerbst 61
JOAN
ferch Evan Lloyd 84
ferch Ieuan ap Gwilym
Fychan 179
ferch Madog 387
ferch Richard ap
Twmlyn 404
of Bar 378
of Dammartin,
Countess of
Ponthieu 301
JOANNA
of Armagnac 197, 199
of France 79, 103, 201
of Navarre 103, 201
of Strathern 378
JOANNA DOROTHEA
Countess Reuss-
Ebersdorf 195
JOHN
ab Edward 309
ap Evan 306, 307
ap Gruffudd 80
ap Ieuan ab Owain 82
ap Jenkin Elliot 375
ap Maredudd 308, 328
ap Maredudd Llwyd
321
ap Rees Wynne 357
ap Roger 387
Count of Eu 417
Duke of Berry 197,
199
Duke of Burgundy 194
Gainor 306, 309
Griffith 307
Jane 306, 307, 328
Jane (Pugh or Hughes)
307, 309
Margaret 306-308
Robert 307
William 307, 309
JOHN also JONES

557

The Royal Descents of 500 Immigrants

KNIGHTON
Anne (Underhill) 456
Joan 456
Thomas 456
KNIPE
Anne 150
Anne (Wolseley) 150
Thomas 150
KNIVETON
Anne (Dethick) 378
Barbara 378
John 378
Margaret
(Montgomery) 378
KNOLLYS
Alice (Beecher) 117
Anne 115, 116
Catherine 116
Dorothy 117
Francis 117
Francis, Sir 115
Jane (Heigham) 117
Lettice 45, 116
Mary (Cary) 115
Ottilia (de Merode)
116
Richard 117
Thomas, Sir 116
KNYVETT
Anne 161
William, Sir 161
KNYVETT also
KNEVET
KOEHLER
Catherine Elisabeth
199
KOSKULL
Agders 17
Anders, Baron 17
Anna Catharina
(Stromberg) 17
Anna Maria
(Gyllensvärd) 17
Eleanora, Baroness 17
Erik 17
Maria Catharine
(Frankelin) 17
KOSTCZANKA
Anna 293
KOSTKA
Jan 293
Sophia
(Odrowazowna) 293
KUNIGUNDE
of Halicz 293
KURTWICH
Anne 33
KYME
Eleanor de
Boroughdon,
Baroness 393
Walter Talboys, Baron
393
de KYME
Lucy 393

KYNASTON
Elizabeth (Grey) 80,
82, 84, 85
Elsbeth (ferch
Maredudd ap
Hywel) 82
Humphrey 82
Jane 84
Margaret 82, 85
Mary 80, 309
Roger, Sir 80, 82, 84,
85
KYNYNMOND
Cecilia 75
LA CLOCHE
Benjamin 220
Rachel 220
Rachel (de Carteret)
220
LACY
Elizabeth 126
de LACY
---- 385, 393
LADD
Margaret 464
LADISLAUS V
King of Bohemia and
Hungary 103, 291
LADYJENSKY
Anastasia 412
Ekaterine, Princess
(Romodanovsky)
412
Ivan 412
LAER and
NEERWINDE
Jean Baptiste de la
Bistrate, Seigneur of
380
de LAFAYETTE/
de la FAYETTE
Marie Joseph Paul
Yves Roch Gilbert
Motier, Marquis 64,
104
Michel Louis
Christophe Roch
Gilbert Motier,
Marquis 64
de LAIZER
Jerôme, Seigneur de
Siougeat 199
Louise 199
Marguerite (de Besse)
199
LAKE
Anne (Stratton) 425
William 425
LAMBARDE
Grace (Parsons) 175
Mary 175
Thomas 175
LAMBERT
Count of Lens 455,
458, 463
Count of Louvain 455,
458, 463

LAMBESC
Charles Louis of
Lorraine, Prince of
289
LAMBTON
Agnes (Lumley) 32
Catherine
(Widdrington) 32
Dorothy 32
Dorothy (Bewicke) 32
Eleanor (Tempest) 32
Frances (Eure) 32
Freville 32
John 32
Katherine (Kirby) 32
Margaret 32
Margaret (Freville) 32
Margaret (Hall) 32
Ralph 32
Robert 32
Thomas 32
Thomas, Sir 32
Thomasine (Milwood)
32
William 32
LAMONT
Anne 58
Barbara (Semphill) 58
Colin, Sir, of Ineryne
58
LAMPECK
Katherine 334
LAMPETT
Ellen 450
LANCASTER
Edmund Plantagenet,
1st Earl of 295
Henry Plantagenet, 3rd
Earl of 295
Joan 137
John of Gaunt, Duke
of 107, 109, 111,
112, 114, 115, 123,
125, 132, 134, 136,
155, 159, 161, 165,
169, 171, 176-178,
184, 188, 189
Margaret 348
LANDON
Elizabeth 229
LANE
Dorothy 128, 169
Elizabeth (Vincent)
169
John Jr. 210
Katherine (Whiting)
210
Maud (Parr) 171
Ralph, Sir 128, 171
Richard 169
Susanna 210
LANGFORD
Edward 357
Eleanor (Dutton) 357
Janet 357
LANGHAM
Elizabeth 116

The Royal Descents of 500 Immigrants

de LANGIN
Guillaume 453
Isabelle (de Pontverre) 453
Jeannette (de Blonay) 453
Marguerite 453
Rodolphe 453
de LANGLE
Philippe de Noyelles, Vicomte 296
LANGSTON
Joan 435
LANGTON
Eupheme 176
Jane 446
LANNES DE MONTEBELLO
Andre Roger 294
Edith Bradford (Myles) 294
Emilie (d'Aviles) 294
George Ernest Casimir 294
Germaine (Wiener de Croisset) 294
Guy Philippe 294
Marie, Princess (Lubomirska) 294
René 294
de LANNOY
Jeanne Louise, Countess 301
LARDER
Edmund 345
Isabella (Bonville) 345
Ursula 345
LASCELLES
Elizabeth 225
de LASCELLES
Theophania 446
Tiffany 446
LATHAM
Frances 111, 248, viii
LATHOM
Margaret 348
LATIMER OF BRAYBROOKE
Thomas le Latimer, 1st Baron 371
Warin le Latimer, 2nd Baron 371
LATIMER, LE
Catherine (de la Warre) 371
Elizabeth 371
Lora (Hastings) 371
Thomas, 1st Baron Latimer of Braybrooke 371
Warin, 2nd Baron Latimer of Braybrooke 371
LATYMER
George Neville, 1st Baron 132, 184

John Neville, 4th Baron 155
Richard Neville, 2nd Baron 132, 184
LAUDER
Katherine 102
LAUNCE
Isabella (Darcy) 176
John 176
Mary 176
LAURE
of Ponthieu 301
LAURENCE
Elizabeth 303
Margaret (Hugford) 303
William 303
LAURENT
Benoit Baudouin
Marie, Prince of the Belgians 65
von der LAUSITZ
Clara Spinucci, Countess 7
Maria Christina Sabina of Saxony, Countess 7
LAVAL
Guy XIV, Count of 79
de LAVAL
Louise 79
LAWFORD
Anne (Wright) 192
Deborah (Gould) 193
Janet Turing (Bruce) 192
Margaret Sarah (Acland) 192
Mary Anne (Rowan) 193
May Somerville (Bunny) Cooper Aylen 192
Patricia (Kennedy) 192
Patricia (Seaton) 193
Peter 192
Peter (Sydney Ernest [Aylen]) 192
Samuel 192
Sydney Turing Barlow, Sir 192
Thomas Acland 192
LAWRENCE
Aimee Marie Suzanne 22
D.H. 46
Elizabeth (----) 457
Elizabeth (Bull) 456
Elizabeth (Smith) 220, 386, 457
Jane 456
Joan (Antrobus) 456
John 456
Margaret 146
Mary 457
Mary (----) 456
Mehitable 34

Susanna (----) 456
Thomas 456
William 220, 386, 457
LAWSON
Anne (Wentworth) 351
Barbara 139
Christopher 351
Elizabeth (James) 351
John 351
Mary (Savill) Porter 340
Sarah 420
Sarah (----) 50
LAWTON
Isabel 407
LEAKE
Katherine 374
LEAKE also LEEKE, LEKE
LEARNED
Edward 472
Edward Jr. 472
Mary 472
Sarah (Fuller) 472
Sarah (Pratt) 472
LEATHERBEE
Frances Anita (Crane) 298
LEDOUX
Louise Amalia 195
LEE
Agnes (Conyers) 390
Alice Hathaway 78, 114
Charles 85
Charlotte 8
Charlotte (Fitzroy) 8, 9
Charlotte, Lady 9, 136
Dorothy 128, 148
Dorothy (Browne) 148
Edmund 148
Edward Henry, 1st Earl of Lichfield 8, 9
Eleanor (----) 390
Eleanor (Wrottesley) 128
Elizabeth (Crispe) 390
Frances (Hales) 8
Geoffrey 390
George Henry, 2nd Earl of Lichfield 8
Isabella (Bunbury) 85
John 85
Joyce (Worsley) 390
Mary 313, 390
Richard 128, 390
LEEKE
Elizabeth (Savage) 238
John 238
Muriel 238
LEEKE also LEAKE, LEKE
LEETE
Anna (Payne) 336
Anne (Shute) 336

562

The Royal Descents of 500 Immigrants

Le Strange, continued
John, 4th Baron
Strange of
Blackmere 233
Maud (de Wauton)
389, 409
Richard 189
Thomas 189
Thomas, Sir 189
LE STRANGE
also
L'ESTRANGE,
STRANGE
LEUCHTENBERG
Elizabeth of 63
George, Landgrave of
63
LEVENTHORP
Anne 423
LEVERSAGE
Eleanor 358
Eleanor (Sheffield)
358
Katherine (Davenport)
358
William 358
LEVESON
Christian 124
Elizabeth 128
Frances (Sondes) 124
James 128
John, Sir 124
Margery (Wrottesley)
128
LEVESON-GOWER
Cromartie, 4th Duke
of Sutherland 12
Granville, 1st
Marquess of Stafford
23
George Granville, 1st
Duke of Sutherland
23
Louisa (Egerton) 23
Margaret Caroline 23
Millicent Fanny (St.
Clair-Erskine) 12
Rosemary Millicent 12
LEVINE
Rachel (Faucette) 68
LEWIS
Andrew 465
ap Robert 80
Eleanor (Gamage) 400
Elizabeth (Marshall)
264, 465
Elizabeth (Newlin) 80
Ellis 80
Evan Robert 305
Gwerful (ferch
Llywelyn ap
Dafydd) 305
Jane (ferch Cadwaladr
ap Maredudd) 305
Joan 134, 400
Judith 264, 465
Mary 208

Mary (----) Baldwin 80
Mary (Gamage) 400
Mary (Herring) 465
Robert 305
Susannah 92
Thomas 264, 465
William 400
LEWKNOR
Anne (Everard) 431
Barbara 284
Beatrix 432
Dorothy (Wroth) 270
Edward 270, 431
Eleanor 431
Eleanor (Camoys) 383
Elizabeth 383
Elizabeth (Carew) 431
Elizabeth (Radmylde)
431
Jane 431
Joan 431
Margaret (Copley) 270
Mary 270
Nicholas 431
Philippa (Dalyngridge)
383, 431
Roger, Sir 383, 431
Thomas, Sir 383, 431
LEWYS
ab Ieuan 465
ap Gruffudd 305
ap John Gruffudd 80
LEWYS MORGAN 404
LICHFIELD
Edward Henry Lee,
1st Earl of 8, 9
George Henry, 2nd
Earl of 8
LIECHTENSTEIN-
FELDSBERG
George Hartmann of
197
Hartmann II of 197
Judith of 197
LIECHTENSTEIN-
STEIEREGG
George VI of 197
Susanna of 197
LIGHT
Elizabeth 442
LIGON
Ann (----) vii
Elizabeth vii
Elizabeth (Anderson)
viii
Joseph vii
Mary vii
Mary (Church) vii
Mary (Harris) 204, viii
Mary (Worsham) viii
Matthew viii
Richard viii
Thomas 204, vii, viii
LIGON also LYGON
LILLIE
Abigail (Breck) 234,
394

Anna 234, 394
Hannah (Ruck) 234,
394
Hedwig Catharina,
Countess 91
John 234, 394
Theophilus 234, 394
LIMERICK
Agnes 325
Edmund Henry Pery,
1st Earl of 38
Thomas Dongan, 2nd
Earl of 216
William Hale John
Charles Pery, 3rd
Earl of 38
William Henry
Edmond de Vere
Sheaffe Pery, 4th
Earl of 38
William Henry
Tennison Pery, 2nd
Earl of 38
LINCOLN
Francis Clinton, 6th
Earl of 36
Henry Clinton, 2nd
Earl of 35, 142
LINDORES
Patrick, 1st Baron 28
LINDSAY
---- (Barclay) 100
---- (Erskine) 100
Alexander of Haltoun
100
Alexander, 2nd Earl of
Crawford 100
David 100
David, 1st Earl of
Crawford 92, 94,
97, 100
David, 3rd Earl of
Crawford 100
David, Sir, of Beaufort
and Edzell 100
Elizabeth 92, 94, 97
Elizabeth (Stewart) 92,
94, 97, 100
Isabel (Livingston) 100
Janet (Ramsay) 100
Jean (Stewart) 92, 94,
97, 100
Jerome, Sir, of
Annatland and the
Mount 100
Katherine
(Fotheringham) 100
Katherine (Stewart)
92, 94, 97, 100
Margaret 73
Margaret (Colville)
100
Marjory (----) 100
Marjory (Ogilvy) 100
Rachel 100
Susanna (----) 100

Lowe, continued
Susannah Maria
(Bennett) Darnall
161
Vincent 150, 161
LOWELL
Caroline Maureen
(Hamilton-Temple-
Blackwood) Freud
Citkowitz, Lady 11
Robert Traill Spence
IV 11
**LÖWENSTEIN-
WERTHEIM-
ROCHEFORT**
Victoria Felicitas of 14
**LÖWENSTEIN-
WERTHEIM-
ROSENBERG**
(Marie Josephine)
Sophie, Princess of
16
LOWER
Dorothy 46
Penelope (Perrott) 46
William, Sir 46
LOWER LORRAINE
Adelaide of 461
Charles, Duke of 455,
458, 461, 463
Gerberga of 455, 458,
463
Regelinde of 461
LOWNDES
Alice (----) 358
Charles 358
Christopher 358
Elizabeth (Tasker) 358
Jane (Weld) 358
John 358
Margaret (Poole) 358
Richard 358
Ruth (Rawlins) 358
Sarah (----) 358
LOWRI
ferch Dafydd 323
ferch Dafydd ap Ieuan
308
ferch Edward ap
Dafydd 312
ferch Elise 311
ferch Gruffudd Fychan
389
ferch Hywel Llwyd
309
ferch Tudur ap
Gruffudd Fychan
311
LOWTHER
Alice 416
Anne 416
Christopher, Sir 190
Dorothy (Clifford) 190
Eleanor 190
Eleanor (Fleming) 190
Eleanor (Musgrave)
190

Frances (Middleton)
190
Hugh, Sir 190, 416
John 416
John, Sir 190
John, Sir, 1st Bt. 190
Margaret (de Lucy)
416
Margaret (Strickland)
416
Margaret (Whale) 416
Mary (Fletcher) 190
Maud (----) 416
Maud (Tilloul) 416
Richard, Sir 190
Robert, Sir 416
LUBOMIRSKI
Alexander Michael,
Prince 293
Aniela Teresa
(Michowska) 293
Casimir, Prince 294
Francoise, Countess
(Zaluska) 294
Frederick, Prince 294
George Alexander,
Prince 293
George (Jerzy)
Sebastian, Prince
293
Joanna (von
Starzhausen) 293
Josef, Prince 293
Katherine Anne,
Princess (Sapieha)
293
Konstance (z Bobrku
Ligezianka) 293
Louisa Honorata
(Pociejowna) 293
Louisa (Sosnowska)
293
Marie, Princess 294
Sophia, Princess
(Ostrogska) 293
Stanislaus, Prince 293
Zeneide (Holynska)
294
LUBY
Elizabeth Pamela
Audrey 36
LUCKETT
Edith 397
LUCY
Elizabeth 32-34
de LUCY
Ada (de Morville) 416
Alan 416
Alice 416
John 416
Margaret 416
Maud 455, 458, 463
Reginald 416
Richard 416
LUDLOW
Anne 181
Edith (Windsor) 229

Elizabeth (Grey) 181
Elizabeth (Vaughan)
181
Gabriel 229, 230
George 229
Jane (Bennett) 230
Jane (Pyle) 229
John, Sir 181
Margery 402
Martha (----) 230
Mary (Cogan) 229
Phyllis (----) 229
Roger 229
Sarah 229, 349
Sarah (Hanmer) 230
Thomas 229, 230
LUDWELL
Frances (Colepepper)
Stephens Berkeley
140, 432
Philip 140, 432
LUGG
Jane (Deighton) 205
John 205
LUMLEY
---- (Gray) 33
Agnes 32
Anne (Conyers) 33
Anne (Kurtwich) 33
Anthony, Hon. 33
Eleanor (Neville) 354
Elizabeth (Plantagenet)
32-34
Felicia (Redman) 354
Frances (Jones) 33
Frances (Shelley) 33
Joan 354
John, Hon. 33
John, Sir 354
Katherine 355
Margaret (Harington)
354
Mary 33
Mary (Compton) 33
Ralph Lumley, 1st
Baron 354
Ralph, 1st Baron
Lumley 354
Richard, 1st Earl of
Scarbrough 33
Richard, 1st Viscount
Lumley 33
Richard, 5th Baron
Lumley 33
Richard Lumley, 1st
Viscount 33
Richard Lumley, 5th
Baron 33
Roger 32, 33
Sibyl 34
Thomas 32-34
Thomas, 2nd Baron
Lumley 354
Thomas Lumley, 2nd
Baron 354

LUMSDEN
Agnes 370
Jean 369
Margaret 88
LUNDEN
Hélène (Rubens) 380
Jean Baptiste 380
Jeanne Catherine 380
LUNDIE
Helen 91
LUNDIN
Christian 90
de LUNGVILLIERS
Margaret 440
LUNSFORD
Anne (Hudson) 284
Barbara (Lewknor)
284
Elizabeth (Wormeley)
Kempe 222, 284
John 284
John, Sir 284
Katherine (Fludd) 284
Katherine (Neville)
284
Mary (Sackville) 284
Thomas 284
Thomas, Sir 222, 284
de LUPE
Jean III, Seigneur de
Maravat 297
Marguerite (de
Morlhon) 297
Percide 297
de LUSIGNAN
Alice 378
Hugh X, Count of la
Marche 373, 378
LUTTRELL
Andrew, Baron
Luttrell 393
Andrew, Sir 229, 240,
288
Andrew Luttrell,
Baron 393
Anne (Aylmer) 216
Catherine 240
Catherine (Beaumont)
229, 288
Elizabeth 229, 288
Elizabeth (Courtenay)
229, 288
Godfrey Hilton, Baron
393
Hawise Luttrell,
Baroness 393
Hawise, Baroness 393
Hugh, Sir 229, 288
Joan (Talboys) 393
John, Sir 240
Margaret 216, 240
Margaret (Wyndham)
240
Mary (Ryce) 240
Thomas, Sir 216

LUXEMBURG
Philippa of 365
LYGON
Anne 253
Cecily 204, 244
Eleanor (Dennis) 204,
253
Elizabeth 205, 206
Elizabeth (Berkeley)
205, 253
Elizabeth (Pratt) 204
Frances (Dennis) 204
Henry 205, 253
Katherine 205
Margaret 205
Thomas 204
William 204, 253
LYGON also LIGON
LYKOV-OBOLENSKY
Anastasia (Romanov)
412
Boris, Prince 412
Elena, Princess 412
LYLE
Jean 96
LYMAN
Abigail (Moseley) 397
Anne Jean (Robbins)
66, 234, 394
Catherine Robbins 66,
234, 266, 394
John (III) 397
Joseph (III) 66, 234,
394
Mindwell 397
LYNDE
Elizabeth (Digby) 371
Enoch 371
Hannah (Newgate) 371
Simon 371
LYNNE
George 126
Isabel (Forrest) 126
Martha 126
Martha
(Throckmorton) 126
LYSTER
---- (O'Kelly) 188
Anne Isabella (Isdell)
188
Anthony 188
Armstrong 188
Christiana (Killkeny)
188
Deborah (Osbaldeston)
188
Elizabeth (Coddington)
188
Ellen Emily (Cooper)
188
Henry Francis
LeHunte 188
Jane (Ducasse) 188
John 188
Martha (Hatton) 188
Thomas 188
Walter 188

William John 188
William Narcissus 188
LYSTER also LISTER
LYTE
Gertrude 151
LYTE-HOWARD
Charles 151
Rebecca (Webb) 151
LYTTELTON
Alice (Thornes) 84
Anne 110
Bridget (Pakington)
110
Caroline (Bristow) 124
Christian (Temple) 124
Edward, Sir 84
Elizabeth (Coningsby)
110
Elizabeth (Talbot) 110
Gilbert, Sir 110
John 84, 110
John, Sir 110
Mary (Macartney) 124
Mary (Walter) 84
Thomas, Sir, 4th Bt.
124
William Henry, 1st
Baron Lyttelton 124
William Henry
Lyttelton, 1st Baron
124
LYTTLETON
Joan 361
**LYTTLETON also
LITTLETON**
LYTTON
Anne 338
Audrey (Booth) 338
Elizabeth 339
Frances (Cavalery)
338
Robert, Sir 338
William, Sir 338
MABEL
of Chester 389, 409
of Gloucester 387,
391, 404
MABLI
ferch Maredudd 388
MACARTNEY
Mary 124
McCANN
Helena Woolworth 19
McCLENACHAN
Martha 67
McCULLOCH
Margaret 415
MACDONALD
Florence of Morrer 71
McDONALD
Grizel 415
McDOUGALL
Jeannie 175
McDOWALL
Agnes 367

McGRUDER
Alexander 99
Margaret (Campbell)
99
McGRUDER also
MAGRUDER
MACHELL
Mary 270
Mary (Lewknor) 270
Matthew 270
McINTOSH see
MACKINTOSH
MACKARNESS
Frances 337
MACKAY
Elizabeth 114
Helen 20
MACKELLAR
Jessie Victoria 36
MACKENZIE
Agnes 109
Alexander of Coul 114
Anne (Sinclair) 28
Anne, Lady 28
Barbara (Grant) 114
Christian (Munro) 114
Colin of Kintail 114
Elizabeth (Stewart)
109, 114
George, 1st Earl of
Cromarty 28
George, 3rd Earl of
Cromarty 28
Isabel (Gordon) 28
Jean 88, 109, 114
Jean (Chisolm) 114
John, 2nd Earl of
Cromarty 28
Kenneth, Sir, 1st Bt.
114
Kenneth, Sir, of
Kintail 109, 114
Margaret 90
Mary 114
Mary (Murray) 28
Mary, Lady 28
MACKINNON
Emma Mary 105
MACKINTOSH/
McINTOSH
Agnes (Mackenzie)
109
Elizabeth 109
Elizabeth (Byfield) 109
Elizabeth (Innes) 109
Elizabeth (Mackintosh)
109
Helen (Gordon) 109
Henry 109
John Mohr 110
Lachlan 109
Lachlan of Borlum 109
Lachlan of Knocknagel
110
Lachlan of Mackintosh
109
Marjory (Fraser) 110

Mary (Baillie) 88, 109
Mary (Lockhart) 110
Mary (Reade) 109,
110
William 88
William of Borlum
109, 110
MACKWORTH
Agnes 128
Dorothy (Cranage)
128
Dorothy (Lee) 128
Richard 128
Thomas 128
McLAUGHLIN
Avice 126
Catherine
(Blennerhasset) 126
Richard 126
MACLEAN/McLEAN
Allan of Grisiboll 71
Anne (Long, Lang) 71
Anne (MacLean) 71
Anne of Kilmore 71
Archibald 71
Catherine (MacLean)
71
Catherine of
Balliphetrish 71
Charles of Borreray 71
Florence 71
Florence (MacDonald)
71
Florence (MacLean)
71
Florence (MacLeod)
71
Hannah (Stillman)
Caldwell 71
Hector of Duart 71
Hector Roy of Coll 71
Janet (Campbell) 71
John 71, 72
Lachlan of Coll 71
Margaret 72
Marion 71
Marion (MacLean) 71
Mary (Loomis) 71
Neil of Drimnacross
71
Phebe (Bainbridge) 72
Susanna (Beauchamp)
71
Susanna (Campbell) 71
MACLEOD
Florence of MacLeod
71
Katherine 415
McLEOD
Alexander 72
Margaret (MacLean)
72
Maria Anne (Agnew)
72
Neil 72

MACMURCHADA
Diarmait, King of
Leinster 421, 423,
425, 427
MACMURROUGH
Dermot, King of
Leinster 421, 423,
425, 427
McTYRE
Katherine 415
MADELEINE
of France 28, 30, 31
MADISON
Dorothea "Dolly"
(Payne) Todd 253,
348
Eleanor Rose
(Conway) 253, 348
James 253, 348
James Jr. 253, 348
MADOG
ab Elise 311, 323,
324, 326
ap Hywel Felyn 387
ap Ieuan 324
MADOG FOEL
ap Iorwerth 465
MADOG GOCH
ap Ieuan Goch 305
MAELOG
---- 391
MAGDALENA
of Schwarzburg-
Rudolstadt 194
of Waldeck 63
MAGDALENE SYBIL
of Holstein-Gottorp 15
MAGRUDER
Alexander 99
Elizabeth (----) 99
Sarah (----) 99
MAGRUDER
also McGRUDER
MAHON
Anne (Browne) 191,
209
Anne (Symes) 190,
191
Frances Catherine
(Ker) 209
George Charles 189,
190
Henry 190, 191
James 209
Jane Caroline 189
Ross 191, 209
Sarah (L'Estrange)
189, 190
Sophia Madelina
Olivia 209
MAIDMAN
Sarah 120
MAIDSTONE
Margaret 222

The Royal Descents of 500 Immigrants

Manners-Sutton,
continued
John 41
Mary Georgiana 41
MANSDOTTER
Katherine 17
MANSELL
Anne 410
MANTFIELD
Eleanor 363
MAPLATE
Bridget 130
MAR
John Erskine, 2nd Earl
of 69
de MARAVAT
Jean III de Lupé,
Seigneur 297
MARBURY
Agnes (Lenton) 233,
351
Anne 233, 234, 351
Anne (Blount) 350
Bridget (Dryden) 233,
351
Francis 233, 351
Katherine 233, 351
Katherine (Williamson)
350
Robert 350
William 233, 350, 351
MARCH
Edmund Mortimer,
3rd Earl of 35, 40,
45, 119, 128, 139,
140, 142, 144, 148,
150, 152, 164, 172,
174, 180, 183, 185,
186, 190
Roger Mortimer, 4th
Earl of 35, 40, 45
MARCHANT
Alexander, Sieur de
St. Michel 235
Dorothea (Kingsmill)
235
Elizabeth 235
La MARCHE and
VENDOME
John I, Count of 299
La MARCHE
Hugh X de Lusignan,
Count of 373, 378
James I, Count of 299
de la MARCK
Diane 64
Francoise (de Brezé)
64
Robert, Duc de
Bouillon 64
MAREDUDD
ap Henry Dwnn 388
ap Hywel ap Tudur
308, 328
ap Ieuan 305, 308,
328

ap Ieuan ap Robert
328
ap Ieuan Goch 321
MAREDUDD LLWYD
ap John 321
ap Llywelyn 321
MARGARET
ferch Ellis Morris 80
ferch John ap Lewys
80
of Austria 293
of Bavaria 194
of Blois 343
of Bourbon 297
of Brittany 103
of Burgundy 201
of Champagne 417
of Flanders 194, 365
of France 204, 207,
213, 216, 219, 240,
243, 244, 246, 257,
270, 272, 280, 282,
283, 286
of Montdidier 444,
446, 448, 450, 451
of Provence 297, 299
of Scotland 371
MARGRED
ferch Einion ap Ithel
308, 328
ferch Gronwy Llwyd
324, 326
ferch Gruffudd 323,
407
ferch Hugh Howel 375
ferch James ap Ieuan
Gwyn 404
ferch Jenkin ap Ieuan
311
ferch John ap Jenkin
387
ferch Morus 328
ferch Morus Gethin ap
Rhys 321
ferch Rhys Hen 404
ferch Thomas Gethin
308
MARIA
daughter of Toktai,
Khan of the Golden
Horde 413
of Borowsk 413
of Moscow 411, 413
of Susdal 411
of Tschernigow 411
MARIA CHRISTINA
SABINA
of Saxony, Countess
von der Lausitz 7
MARIA JOSEPHA
of Austria 7
MARIA TERESA
of Tuscany,
Archduchess of
Austria 289
MARIANNE
of the Netherlands 3

MARIE
of Anjou 64
of Berry 197, 199
of Bourbon-Soissons 5
of Brittany 296
of Champagne 365
of Edinburgh 1
of France 365
of Hainault 297, 299
of Murom 411
of Russia 1
of Saxony 289
Amelie Elizabeth
Caroline, of Baden
470
MARIE ANTOINETTE
Queen of France 91
MARIE ELIZABETH
of Saxony 15
(MARIE JOSEPHINE)
SOPHIE
Princess of
Löwenstein-
Wertheim-Rosenberg
16
MARIE SYBIL
of Reuss-Obergreiz
194
MARIE THERESE
JOSEPHE
of Lorraine-Brionne
289
MARISCHAL
George Keith, 4th Earl
73
William Keith, 2nd
Earl 73
William Keith, 3rd
Earl 73, 76
MARJORIE
of Carrick 367, 369
MARKENFIELD
Alice 164
Dorothy (Gascoigne)
164
Eleanor 153
Ninian, Sir 164
MARKHAM
Margaret 346
Mary (Widdrington)
153
Robert, Sir, 3rd Bt.
153
Ursula 153
MARLBOROUGH
George Spencer-
Churchill, 5th Duke
of 19
George Spencer-
Churchill, 6th Duke
of 19
John Churchill, 1st
Duke of 12, 13, 271
John Winston Spencer-
Churchill, 7th Duke
of 19

The Royal Descents of 500 Immigrants

MAUDUIT
Alice (de Newburgh)
429
Isabel 429
Isabel (Basset) 429
Isabel (de St. Liz) 429
Robert 429
William 429
MAUGHAM
Somerset 105
MAULE
Bethia (Guthrie) 112
Eleanor 112
Isabel 112
Isabel (Arbuthnott)
112
Robert, Sir, of
Panmure 112
William of Glaster 112
MAULEVERER
Alice (Markenfield)
164
Anne 164
Anne (Pearson) 164
Beatrice (Hutton) 164
Dorothy 164
Edmund 164
Edmund, Sir 164
Eleanor (Aldeborough)
164
James 164
Mary (Danby) 164
Robert 164
William 164
de MAULÉVRIER
Charlotte (de Valois)
64
Jacques de Brezé,
Count 64
Louis de Brezé, Count
64
MAUNDER
---- 319
de MAUROY
Radegonde 64
de MAUVOISIN
Guy IV, Seigneur de
Rosny 301
Guy V, Seigneur de
Rosny 301
Laure 301
Roberta (de Baumez)
301
MAVERICK
John 295
Mary (Gye) 295
MAWD
ferch Adam
Turberville 391
ferch Dafydd Llwyd
305, 308, 321, 328
ferch Gruffudd 391
ferch Ienaf ab Abba
311
ferch Ieuan 391
ferch Oliver ap
Thomas Pryce 82

MAXIMILIAN
Emperor of Mexico
10, 14
Prince of Salm-Salm,
Duke of
Hoogstraeten 14
MAXIMILIAN I
Holy Roman Emperor
194
**MAXIMILIAN
EGON II**
Prince zu Fürstenberg
7
MAXWELL
Jane 11
Katherine 87
Lucy (Douglas) 53
Mary 53
Robert, 4th Earl of
Nithsdale 53
MAY
Benjamin 436
Mary (Williams) 436
Susanna 436
MAYER
Eugénie 46
MAYO
Anne 257
MAZARIN(I)
Jules (Guilio),
Cardinal 105
MAZOVIA
Anna of 293
Boleslaw IV, Duke of
293
Conrad III, Duke of
293
John I, Duke of 293
Ziemowit III, Duke of
293
MEAD
Isabel 82, 190, 204,
286
MEADE
Anne 438
MEADE also MEDE
MEARS
Thomas 349
MEASE
Katherine (Eltonhead)
349
Thomas 349
MEAUTYS
Frances 315
Hercules 315
Philippa (Cooke) 315
MECKLENBURG
Henry, Duke of 3
William, Duke of 3
**MECKLENBURG-
GÜSTROW**
Christine of 15
Gustav Adolf, Duke of
15
Sophie of 15

**MECKLENBURG-
SCHWERIN**
Charlotte of 3
Paul Frederick, Grand
Duke of 3
**MECKLENBURG-
STRELITZ**
Charles II, Duke of 16
Frederica of 16
Louise of 3, 16
(Sophie) Charlotte of
16
MEDE
Catherine (Corbett)
339
Jane 339
John, Sir 339
MEDE also MEADE
MEDFORD
Elizabeth 157
van der MEER
Arend 365
Catryn (van Foreest)
365
Clara (van
Berendrecht) 365
Frank 365
Jacomina Jacob
Claesdr. (van
Ruyven) 365
Liedewey (de Wilt van
Bleyswyck) 365
Pieter 365
**van der MEER
van BERENDRECHT**
Joost 365
Machteld (van der
Dussen) 365
Sophia 365
de MEILLE
Jean de Foix, Vicomte
291
MEINELL
Nicholas de Meinell,
3rd Baron 342
de MEINELL
Alice (de Ros) 342
Elizabeth 342
Nicholas, 3rd Baron
Meinell 342
MELDRUM
Helen 108
MELLON
Ailsa 32
MELLOWES
Abraham 211
Jane 257
Martha (Bulkeley) 211
de MELUN
Anne 103
Béatrix (de Beaussart)
301
Francois, Baron
d'Antoing 103
Hippolite (de
Montmorency) 103

The Royal Descents of 500 Immigrants

de Melun, continued
Hugh, Prince d'Epinoy
103
Hugh, Seigneur
d'Antoing 301
Louise (de Foix) 103
Philippa 301
Pierre, Prince
d'Epinoy 103
Yolande (de
Barbancon) 103
de MENETOU-
COUTURE
Claude d'Anlezy,
Seigneur 199
Robert d'Anlezy,
Seigneur 199
de MENON
Elizabeth 201
Francois, Seigneur de
Turbilly 201
Madeleine (de Maillé
de la Tour-Landry)
201
Marie (de Chahannai)
201
Urbain, Seigneur de
Turbilly, Count de
Brestau 201
MENTEITH
Margaret Graham,
Countess of 96, 99,
102
MERANIA
Otto I, Duke of 343
MERANIA and
BURGUNDY
Alix of 343
MERCER
Anne (Munro) 97
Catherine 112
Christian 88, 91
Helen 276
Hugh 97
Isabel (Gordon) 97
Isabel (Smith) 97
John 97
Lilias (Row) 97
Thomas of Todlaw 97
William 97
MERE
Margaret 274
MEREDUDD
ap Hywel ap Tudur
326
MERITON see
MERRITON/
MERYTON
de MERLAY
Agnes 435, 438
Alice (de Stuteville)
435, 438
Ralph 435, 438
Roger 435, 438
MERODE
Ottilia de 116

MERRICK
Elizabeth (Trowbridge)
472
John 472
Sarah 472
MERRITON/
MERITON/
MERYTON
Anne 374
George 374
Mary (Randes) 374
de MESCHINES
Adeliza 444, 448, 451
Agnes 400
Amicia 398, 402, 407
Maud 367, 369, 371,
373, 376
METCALFE
Margaret 34
MEULAN
Robert de Beaumont,
Count of 382, 403
MEULLENT
Ida of 301
MEURIG
ap Hywel of Radur
391
MEVERELL
Elizabeth 272
Jane (Eyre) 272
Thomas 272
MEXICO,
EMPEROR OF
Maximilian 10, 14
von MEYSENBUG
Klara Elisabeth 187
de MEZIERES
Eugène Marie de
Béthisy, Marquis
289
MICHAEL
Prince of
Tschernigow, Grand
Prince of Kiev 411
MICHAEL III
Czar of Russia 412
MICHOWSKA
Aniela Teresa 293
MIDDLEMORE
Henrietta Maria
(Drummond) 46
Mary 37, 46
Robert 46
MIDDLETON
Frances 190
Henry 28, 125
Jane 374
Mary 260, 353
Mary (Bull) 260
Mary Helen (Hering)
125
Mary (Mackenzie)
Clarke Drayton
Ainslie, Lady 28
Thomas 260
MILBORNE
Anne 303

Elizabeth (Devereux)
303
Jane (Baskerville) 303
John 303
Simon, Sir 303
MILDMAY
Anne 214
Anne (Reade) 460
Frances (Rainbow)
460
John 460
Margaret (Cornish)
459
Mary 42, 460
Mary (Everard) 459
Olive (Nuttal) 460
Thomas 459, 460
Thomasine 460
Walter 459
MILES
Elizabeth 219
Katherine 165
MILHOUS
Almira Park (Burdg)
168
Edith Price (Griffith)
168
Franklin 168
Hannah 168
Joshua Vickers 168
MILICENT
of Réthel 461
MILLER
Mary 432
Thomas 433
MILLIGAN
Jane 93
MILNS
Olivia Rowlandson 22
MILWOOD
Thomasine 32
MINOR
Mary 332
MINTHORN
Hulda Randall 250
John 250
Lucinda (Sherwood)
250
Mary (Wasley) 250
Theodore 250
di MIRAFIORI and
FONTANAFREDDA
Rosa Teresa
Vercellana,
Countess 290
de MISSENDEN
Elizabeth 435
MITCHELL
Lettice 117
MITFORD
Alice 152
Barbara 123, 354
Jessica Lucy, Hon. 8
MITTON
Constance (Beaumont)
264
John 264

The Royal Descents of 500 Immigrants

Montfort, continued
Margaret (de Clinton)
356
Peter (Piers) de
Montfort, 3rd Baron
438
Robert 356
William, Sir 356
MONTFORT
also MUNFORD
de MONTFORT
Alice 438
Alice (de Audley) 438
Alice (de la Plaunche)
438
Bertrade 367, 369,
371, 373, 376, 389,
398, 400, 402, 407,
409
Jean de Sallmard,
Seigneur 299
John, 1st Baron
Montfort 438
Laure 301
Louis de Sallmard,
Seigneur 299
Peter (Piers), 3rd
Baron Montfort 438
Piers 438
MONTGOMERY
Agnes 58
Agnes (Drummond)
51, 58
Alexander, 6th Earl of
Eglinton 51
Alexander, 8th Earl of
Eglinton 51
Alexander, 9th Earl of
Eglinton 51
Anne (Livingston) 51
Elizabeth 87
Elizabeth (Baxter) 96
Elizabeth (Crichton)
51
Elizabeth
(Cunyngham) 96
Ellen 356
Euphemia 51, 470
Helen (Campbell) 96
Hugh of Brigend 96
Hugh, 1st Earl of
Eglinton 96
Hugh, 2nd Earl of
Eglinton 58
Hugh, 3rd Earl of
Eglinton 51, 58
Hugh, 7th Earl of
Eglinton 51
Isabel (Burnett) 76, 96
Jane 96
Jean 96
Jean (Lyle) 96
Jean (Montgomery) 96
Joan (Longford) 378
John of Brigend 96
Katharine (Scott) 96
Margaret 51, 96, 378

Margaret (Cochrane)
51
Margaret (Mure) 96
Mariot (Seton) 58
Mary 367
Mary (Leslie) 51
Neil, Sir, of Lainshaw
96
Nicholas, Sir 378
William 76
William of Brigend 96
de MONTIGNY
Anne 301
Antoine, Seigneur de
Noyelle 301
Charlotte (de
Nouvelles) 301
George, Seigneur de
Noyelle 301
Jeanne (de
Montmorency) 301
de MONTMORÉNCY
Anne (de Blois) 301
Anne (de Vendégies)
301
Hippolite 103
Jacques I, Seigneur
301
Jean, Baron de
Wastines 301
Jean II, Seigneur 301
Jeanne 301
Jeanne (de Fosseux)
301
Louis, Seigneur de
Fosseux 301
Marguerite (de
Wastines) 301
Ogier, Baron de
Wastines 301
Philippa (de Melun)
301
MONTPENSIER
Louis, Count of 197
MONTRÉSOR
Frances (Tucker) 129,
209
Henrietta (Fielding)
128
James Gabriel 128,
209
John 129, 209
Mary (Haswell) 129,
209
de MONTVUAGNARD
Guillauma 453
MOODIE
Barbara 28
Francis of Breckness
28
Margaret (Stewart) 28
MOODY
Deborah (Dunch),
Lady 383
Henry, Sir, 1st Bt. 383
MOOR
Abigail (Franklin) 210

Hiram D. 210
John 210
Mary (Davis) 210
Victoria Josephine
210, 219, 390, 459
MOORE
---- 226
Catherine Maria
(Long) 155
Dorothy 189
Elizabeth 107, 255
Hannah (----) 34
Henry, Sir, 1st Bt. 155
Jane 260
Jean 26
Joan 277
John, Sir 260
Mary 219
Mary (Burke) 260
Mary Elsie 5
MORAY
Amabel of 416
James Stewart, 1st
Earl of 31
James Stewart, 2nd
Earl of 31
James Stewart, 3rd
Earl of 31
James Stewart, 4th
Earl of 31
Margaret 369
Thomas Randolph, 1st
Earl of 367
William FitzDuncan,
Earl of 416
MORE
Christian (Hunt[er?])
350
Elizabeth (Smalley)
350
Ellen 350
Jane (----) Crumpton
350
Jasper 350
Katherine 350
Katherine (More) 350
Margaret (Cresset) 350
Mary 350
Richard 350
Samuel 350
Thomas 350
MOREL
Sybil 435, 438, 442
MORFUDD
ferch Gruffudd ap
Llywelyn Fychan
321
ferch Ieuan Goch 308,
328
ferch Mathew ap
Llywarch 305
MORGAN
ab Edward 404
Barbara 120
Cadwalader 312
Catherine (Robert) 307
Dorothy (Parke) 469

Morgan, continued
Edmund 134
Elizabeth Anne 175
Elizabeth (Stradling) 134
Elizabeth (Vaughan) 134
Grace 357
James 404
Jane (----) 404
Jane (Price) 312
John 405
Joseph 469
Margaret 401, 469
Margaret (Kinnicutt) 105
Mary 134
Nancy (Ryan) 105
Sarah (Evans) 405
Ted 105
Thomas 134
William 307
MORGAN LEWYS 404
MORLEY
Anne 224
Isabel (de la Pole) 224
Thomas, 5th Baron Morley 224
Thomas Morley, 5th Baron 224
de MORLHON
Francois, Seigneur d'Asprières 297
Marguerite 297
Marguerite (de Senneterre) 297
MORNINGTON
Sybil 204
MORRIS
Anna Maria 125
Eleanor (Williams) 309
Ellen 306, 309
John 309
Magdalen 55
MORRISON
Alexander, Sir, of Prestongrange 112
Bethia 100, 112
Bridget (Hussey) 142
Eleanor (Maule) 112
Elizabeth 41, 142
Richard, Sir 142
de MORTAIN
Mabel (FitzWilliam) 382, 403
Reginald, Earl of Cornwall 382, 403
de MORTEYN
Joan (de Rothwell) 435, 438
Joan (Gobion) 435, 438
John 435, 438
John, Sir 435, 438
Lucy 435, 438
MORTIMER
Anne 35, 40, 45

Edmund, 1st Baron Mortimer 303
Edmund, 3rd Earl of March 35, 40, 45, 119, 128, 139, 140, 142, 144, 148, 150, 152, 164, 172, 174, 180, 183, 185, 186, 190
Edmund Mortimer, 1st Baron 303
Eleanor (Holand) 35, 40, 45
Elizabeth 119, 128, 139, 140, 142, 144, 148, 150, 152, 164, 172, 174, 180, 183, 185, 186, 190, 246
Isabel (Howard) 246
Isolde 354
Katherine 88
Margaret (de Fienes) 303
Maud 303
Philippa (Plantagenet) 35, 40, 45, 119, 128, 139, 140, 142, 144, 148, 150, 152, 164, 172, 174, 180, 183, 185, 186, 190
Robert, Sir 246
Roger, 4th Earl of March 35, 40, 45
MORTON
Cecily (Charlton) 211
Charles 419
Elizabeth 247
Frances (Kestell) 419
James Douglas, 1st Earl of 58, 73, 75, 78
James Douglas, 3rd Earl of 53
Joan (----) 419
John Douglas, 2nd Earl of 73
Margery 211
Nicholas 419
Richard 211
Sarah Copeland 436
MORUS
ap Gruffudd ap Ieuan 323
ap John 328
de MORVILLE
Ada 416
Elena 385, 393
MORYSON
Elizabeth (Harington) 262
Francis 262
Jane (Eltonhead) 349, 354
Richard 262
Richard, Sir 262
Robert 262, 349
Winifred (----) 262

MOSCOW
Anastasia of 293
Basil II, Grand Prince of 293, 413
Basil III, Grand Prince of 413
Dimitri IV, Grand Prince of 293, 413
Ivan I, Grand Prince of 411
Ivan II, Grand Prince of 413
Maria of 411, 413
MOSELEY
Abigail 397
Abigail (Root) 397
John 397
Joseph 397
Mary 397
Mary (Newberry) 397
MOSLE
Alexander Samuel 199
Caroline Durnford (Dunscomb) 199
Charlotte Amalie (Schultze) 199
Dorothea Catharine (Rendorff) 199
Georg Rudolf 199
George 199
Marie Caroline 199
MOSTYN
Catherine 85
Elsbeth 311
MOTIER
Anastasie Louise Pauline 64
Marie Adrienne Francoise (de Noailles) 64, 104
Marie Joseph Paul Yves Roch Gilbert, Marquis de La Fayette 64, 104
Marie Louise Julie (de La Rivière) 64
Michel Louis Christophe Roch Gilbert, Marquis de La Fayette 64
MOTTROM
Anne 141, 374
Frances 120
de MOUCHY
Philippe de Noailles, Duc 104
MOULSON
Catherine 238
MOUNTJOY
William Blount, 4th Baron 137
MOUNTSTEPHEN
Joan (Christopher) 372
de MOUSTY
Paul de Carondelet, Seigneur 301

MOWBRAY
Eleanor 207, 213, 216, 219, 246, 270, 272
Elizabeth (de Segrave) 204, 207, 213, 216, 219, 240, 244, 246, 257, 270, 272, 282, 283, 286
Elizabeth (FitzAlan) 204, 240, 244, 246, 257, 282, 283, 286
Isabel 204, 257, 282, 286
John, 4th Baron Mowbray 204, 207, 213, 216, 219, 240, 244, 246, 257, 270, 272, 282, 283, 286
John Mowbray, 4th Baron 204, 207, 213, 216, 219, 240, 244, 246, 257, 270, 272, 282, 283, 286
Margaret 240, 244, 246, 283, 317
Thomas, 1st Duke of Norfolk 204, 240, 244, 246, 257, 282, 283, 286
MOYLE
Anne 231
MOYNS
Joan 231
MSCISLAWSKA
Anastasia, Princess 293
MUDIE
Janet 76
MUIRHEAD
Rebecca 93
MULGRAVE
Constantine Phipps, 1st Baron 8
MULLET
William 258
Winifred (Wolseley) 258
MULTNEY
Margaret 450
de MULTON
Alan 416
MUMFORD
Catherine 208
MUNCHENSY
Joan 373
MUNFORD
Anne (Brodnax) 361
Elizabeth (Bolling) 361
James 361
Robert 361
MUNFORD
also MONTFORT
MUNNINGS
Anne 461
MUNRO
Agnes (Munro) 89

Agnes of Durness 89
Andrew 89
Anne 97
Christian 114
Christian (Blair) 89
David of Katewell 89
Euphemia (Munro) 89
Euphemia of Pittonachy 89
George of Katewell 89
John 89
Margaret (Dunbar) 89
Mary 89
Robert, 14th Baron of Foulis 89
Sarah (Smith) Pitt 89
MUNRO
also MONROE
MURAT
Alexandre Michel Eugène Joachim Napoléon, Prince 19
Caroline Cécile Alexandrine Jeanne, Princess 19
Caroline Georgina (Fraser) 19
Joachim Joseph Napoléon, 4th Prince Murat 19
Joachim Napoléon, 5th Prince Murat 19
Joachim, 1st Prince Murat 19
Lucien Charles Joseph Napoléon, 3rd Prince Murat 19
Maley Louise Caroline Frédérique (Berthier) 19
Marie Annonciade Caroline (Bonaparte), Princess of France 19
Marie Cécile Michelle (Ney) 19
Yvonne Noële Marie (Gillois) 19
MURDOCH
Jean 367
MURE
Agnes 367
Elizabeth 96, 99, 101, 102
Margaret 96
MUROM
Marie of 411
MURRAY
Amelia 20
Amelia Sophia (Stanley) 18
Anne 18, 107
Anne (Bennet) 66
Anne Charlotte (Grant) 20

Anne (Mackenzie) Atkins, Lady 28
Barbara 67
Barbara (Bennet) 66, 370
Caroline Leonora 20
Catherine 18, 20
Catherine (Fraser) 20
Catherine (Hamilton) 11, 20
Catherine (Murray) 18
Catherine (Watts) 18
Charles, 1st Earl of Dunmore 18
Charlotte, Baroness Strange, Lady of the Isle of Man 20
Dorothy 370
Elizabeth 66, 234, 394
Emilia 20
Emilia (Murray) 20
George, Lord 20
James 66, 370
Jean (Frederick) 20
John 28, 67
John Boyles 67
John of Bowhill 66
John of Unthank 66
John, 1st Duke of Atholl 11, 20
John, 1st Marquess of Atholl 18
John, 3rd Duke of Atholl 20
John, 4th Duke of Atholl 20
John, 4th Earl of Dunmore 18, 470
Margaret 111
Margaret (Nairne) 18
Margaret (Scott) 66
Martha (McClenachan) 67
Mary 28
Mary (Boyles) 67
Susan 11
William, 2nd Baron Nairne 18
William, 3rd Earl of Dunmore 18
William, Sir, 3rd Bt. 20
MURREY
Ann 377
de MUSCEGROS
Agnes (de Ferrers) 400
Hawise 400
Robert, Sir 400
MUSGRAVE
Anne 174
Christopher, Sir, 4th Bt. 174
Christopher, Sir, 5th Bt. 174
Eleanor 190
Frances (Wharton) 174
Julia (Chardin) 174

The Royal Descents of 500 Immigrants

PALGRAVE
also PAGRAVE
PALMER
Catherine 134
Catherine (Stradling) 134
Elizabeth (Verney) 134
John 134
Thomas, Sir 134
PALMES
Andrew 227
Anne (Humphrey) 116
Edward 227
Elizabeth (----) 227
Francis, Sir 227
Jane 152
Lucy (Winthrop) 227
Margaret (Corbet) 227
Mary (Hadnall) 227
Sarah (Farmer) Davis 227
William 116
PAOLA
Queen of the Belgians 65
PARGITER
Amy 442
PARKE
Alice (Freeman) Thompson 436, 469
Dorothy 469
Dorothy (Thompson) 436, 469
Martha (Chaplin) 436
Robert 436, 469
Thomas 436, 469
PARKER
Clara 117
Ellen 177
PARR
Elizabeth 171
Elizabeth (FitzHugh) 171
Mary (Salisbury) 171
Maud 171
William, 1st Baron Parr 171
William, Sir 171
William Parr, 1st Baron 171
PARSONS
Catherine (Clifton) 175
Frances (Dutton) 175
Grace 175
John, Sir, 2nd Bt. 175
William, Sir, 3rd Bt. 175
PASCOE
---- 279
PASHLEY
Anne 236
Elizabeth 242
Elizabeth (Woodville) 242
John, Sir 242
Lowys (Gower) 242

Philippa (Sergeaux) 236, 242
Robert, Sir 236, 242
PASTON
Anne 110
Anne (Beaufort) 110
Eleanor 40
Erasmus 240
Frances 240
Mary (Wyndham) 240
William, Sir 110
PATRICK
son of Narimond 413
PATRICKSON
Bridget 130
PATRIKEEV
Eudoxia (Khovrine) 413
Irina 413
Ivan Boulgak 413
Ivan Grozdj 413
Maria (----) 413
Vassili 413
Xenia, Princess (Vsevoloje) 413
PATSHULL
Sybil 400
PATTEN
Jane 126
PATTERSON
Elizabeth 436
de PAU
Francois 292
Sylvie (de Grasse) 292
PAUL
Czar of Russia 412
PAUL FREDERICK
Grand Duke of Mecklenburg-Schwerin 3
PAUL (Karadjordjevic)
Prince Regent of Yugoslavia 2
PAULET
Alice 219
Alice (Pacy or Plesey) 219
Alice (Paulet) 219
Barbara (Hamden) 220
Constance (Poynings) 219
Eleanor 219
Eleanor (Ros) 219
Elizabeth 220
Elizabeth (Capell) 219
George 219
George, Sir 220
Hamden, Sir 220
John 219
John, Sir 219
Mary 119, 121
Mary (Moore) 219
Rachel 220
Thomas, Lord 219
William, 1st Marquess of Winchester 219

de PAULMY
Charles Yves Jacques de La Rivière, Marquis 64
Jacques de Voyer, Vicomte 64
Jean Armand de Voyer, Marquis 64
PAUNCEFORT
Joan 142
PAWLEY
Honor 398
PAYNE
Anna 336
Archibald 112, 115
Catherine 112, 115, 169, 338, 408
Dorothea "Dolly" 253, 348
Jane 220
Martha (Dandridge) 112, 115
PEARSON
Anne 164
PECCHE
Agnes (Holme) 459
Alice (FitzWalter) 456, 459, 463
Eve (----) 456, 459, 463
Gilbert 456, 459, 463, 464
Gilbert, 1st Baron Pecche 456, 459
Gilbert, 2nd Baron Pecche 456
Gilbert Pecche, 1st Baron 456, 459
Gilbert Pecche, 2nd Baron 456
Hamon 456, 459, 463
Iseult (----) 456, 459
Joan (----) 456
Joan (de Creye) 456, 459, 464
Katherine 456
Margaret 459
Margery 464
Simon, Sir 459
PEET
Abigail 272
PEETERS
Marie Louise 380
PELHAM
Catherine (Thatcher) 116
Elizabeth 33, 38, 116
Elizabeth (Bosvile) Harlakenden 116, 136, 424
Elizabeth (West), Hon. 116
Herbert 116, 136, 317, 424
Jemima (Waldegrave) 116, 317
Margaret (Vane) 123

The Royal Descents of 500 Immigrants

Phipps, continued
Lepell (Hervey) 8
William 8
PICKERING
Elizabeth 340
John 340
Lucy (Kay) 340
de PIEN
Catherine 292
PIERCE
Anna (Kendrick) 387
Barbara 92, 211, 234,
267, 333, 362, 394
Benjmain Jr. 387
Elizabeth Slade 92
Franklin 387
Jane Means (Appleton)
387
PIERPONT
George, Sir 161
Grace 40
Isabella 161
Winifred (Thwaites)
161
de PIERREFEU
Alain Dedons 62
(Louis Dolorès
Emmanuel)
Alphonse Dedons,
Count 62
Louis Joseph Léonce
Dedons, Marquis 62
PIGOT
Caroline 12
PIGOTT
Elizabeth 120
**PIJPE ALIAS
PIJPELINCKX**
Clara (de Thovion)
380
Hendrick 380
PIJPELINCKX
Jan 380
Maria 380
Maria (Typoets) 380
PIKE
Sarah 247
**PILIEMANOV-
SABOUROV**
Euphemia 414
PILKINGTON
Alice (Kingsmill) 383
Catherine 161
Deborah 383
James 383
Margaret 371
Ruth 262
de PILLOT
Anna Elizabeth (de
Sandersleben) 61
(Charles Francois)
Emmanuel
(Edwige), Marquis
de Coligny 62
Charles Ignace,
Marquis de Coligny
61

Charlotte Victorine
Clémentine
Angélique de
Messey (Beaupré)
62
Marie Anne Claude
(de Bernard de
Sassenay) 61
Marie Simone
Léopoldine 62
Thomas, Marquis de
Coligny 61
PINCHBECK
Elizabeth 285
PINNOCK
Anne 209
PINSK
Narimond, Prince of
413
PITCAIRN
David 69
Eleanor 70
Elizabeth (Dalrymple)
69
John 69
Katherine (Hamilton)
69
PITT
Sarah (Smith) 89
PITTS
Isabella (Wright) 120
de PLAINES
Philippote 299
PLANTAGENET
Anne 40, 45, 132,
146, 163, 182
Anne (Mortimer) 35,
40, 45
Antigone 80, 82, 84,
85, 181
Beatrix 296
Blanche 161
Cecily (Neville) 35, 40
Constance 157, 167,
168, 179, 181, 192
Edmund, 1st Earl of
Lancaster 295
Eleanor 295, 303
Eleanor (Cobham) 80,
82, 84, 85
Elizabeth 18, 22, 25,
27, 32-34, 140, 161,
227, 229, 233, 238,
245, 253, 255, 259,
262, 266, 268, 269,
274, 276, 279, 281,
284, 285, 288, 289
George, 1st Duke of
Clarence 35
Henry, 3rd Earl of
Lancaster 295
Humphrey, Duke of
Gloucester 80, 82,
84, 85
Isabel 45
Isabel (Marshall) 317
Isabel (Neville) 35

Joan 210, 222, 224,
226, 231, 233, 236,
242, 243, 248, 250,
258, 264, 271, 275,
277, 280, 287, 291,
305, 308, 311, 321,
323, 324, 326, 328,
389, 409
Margaret, Countess of
Salisbury 35
Margaret, Duchess of
Norfolk 204, 207,
213, 216, 219, 240,
244, 246, 257, 270,
272, 282, 283, 286
Maud (Chaworth) 295
Philippa 35, 40, 45,
119, 128, 139, 140,
142, 144, 148, 150,
152, 164, 172, 174,
180, 183, 185, 186,
190
Richard, 3rd Duke of
York 35, 40
Richard, Earl of
Cambridge 35, 40,
45
Richard, King of the
Romans 317
**von PLATEN and
HALLERMUND**
Franz Ernest, Count
187
Klara Elisabeth (von
Meysenbug) 187
Sophia Charlotte,
Countess of Leinster
and Darlington,
Countess 187
PLATER
Anne 260
de la PLAUNCHE
Alice 438
PLESEY
Alice 219
**PLEYDELL-
BOUVERIE**
Audrey Evelyn
(James) Coats Field
21
Peter 21
de PLOEUC
Marie 79
Marie (de Rieux) 79
Sébastien, Marquis de
Timeur 79
PLUMPTON
Alice 330
Christiana (----) 330
Elizabeth 185
Elizabeth (Clifford)
185
Lucy (de Ros) 330
Robert, Sir 330
William, Sir 185, 330

The Royal Descents of 500 Immigrants

RAMEYEN
Nicolas Rubens,
Seigneur of 380
RAMSAY
Elizabeth 20
Isabella 86
Janet 100
Jean 78
Lucy Booker 472
RAMSDEN
Margaret 214
RANDALL
Anne (Hynson) 141
RANDES
Mary 374
Mary (Yorke) 374
Thomas 374
RANDLE
Elizabeth 303
RANDOLPH
Dorothy (Lane) 169
Elizabeth (----) 169
Elizabeth (Ryland) 169
Henry 169
Isabel 367
Isabel (Bruce) 367
Isabel (Stewart) 367
Isham 169, 338
Jane 169, 338, 407
Jane (Rogers) 169,
338
Judith (Soane) 169
Mary (Isham) 169,
338
Richard 169
Thomas 367
Thomas, 1st Earl of
Moray 367
William 169, 338
de RAPIN
Jacob, Seigneur de
Thoyras 297
Jeanne (de Pelisson)
297
Marie Anne (Testard)
297
Paul, Seigneur de
Thoyras 297
Percide (de Lupé) 297
Pierre II, Baron de
Maivers 297
Susanne Esther 297
de RASOIR
Marie Angelique
Bernard 302
RAVENSCROFT
Anne (Stanley) 262
Eleanor (ferch Richard
ap Howell) 262
Elizabeth 263
George 262
Katherine (Grosvenor)
262
Ralph 262
Thomas 262
RAWDEN
Elizabeth (----) 357

RAWLINS
Ruth 358
RAY
Anthony 175
Gloria (Hallward)
Clements 175
Gloria (Hallward)
Clements Ray
Howard 175
Nicholas 175
RAYMOND
Anne (Warkham) 172
Frances (Harris) 172
Hannah 255
Isabella 172
Isabella (Child) 172
Margaretta (Bridges)
172
Oliver 172
Samuel 172
St. Clere 172
William 172
RAYNSFORD
Alice (Anne) 438
Alice (Danvers) 438
Anne (Meade) 438
Edward 439
Elizabeth (----) 439
George 438
Jane 363
John 438
Juliana 222
Katherine (Taverner)
438
Mary (Kirton) 439
Richard 438
Robert 439
William 438
RAYNWARD
Isabel 336
READ
Eleanor 432
Elizabeth 210
George 415
Gertrude (Ross) Till
415
Margaret 287
Sarah 112
READE
Anne 275, 460
Edward 110
Elizabeth 205, 227
Elizabeth (Cooke) 319
Elizabeth (Martiau)
183, 468
Ellen (Allen) 110
George 183, 468
Mary 109, 110, 141
Mary (Cornewall) 110
Mildred 183, 330, 468
Mildred (Windebank)
183
Robert 183
Thomas, Sir 110
REAGAN
Nancy (Davis) 397
Ronald Wilson 397

REDE
Cecilia (Harlyngrugge)
461
Joan 461
John 461
REDESDALE
Algernon Bertram
Freeman-Mitford,
1st Baron 8
David Bertram Olgilvy
Freeman-Mitford,
2nd Baron 8
REDMAN
Felicia 354
REED
Elizabeth 132
Giles 132
Katherine (Grevile)
132
REES
ap John Wynne 357
David 392
Edward 157
Elizabeth 157
Evan 392
Rebecca (Humphrey)
157
Sidney 392
REES LEWYS
ap John Gruffudd 80
REEVE
Jane 420
REGELINDE
of Lower Lorraine 461
REID
Alison 203
Janet 70
de REIGNAC
Julie Célestine
Barberin 64
RENDORFF
Dorothea Catharine
199
REPPS
Anne 450
Elizabeth (Grimstone)
450
Elizabeth (Jermy) 450
Henry 450
RESCARRICK
Katherine 48
de RESSIZ
Raymond II de
Sallmard, Vicomte
299
**de RESSIZ and
de la FAY**
Bertrand de Sallmard,
Seigneur 299
Claude I de Sallmard,
Seigneur 299
Claude II de Sallmard,
Seigneur 299

591

Rose, continued
Patrick of Lochiehills
101
Robert 101
ROSIERS, DES
Anne (de Bonnet de la
Chabanne) 199
Charles Annet,
Seigneur de
Moncelet 199
Francois, Seigneur de
Moncelet 199
Louise (de Saignes)
199
de ROSNY
Guy IV de Mauviosin,
Seigneur 301
Guy V de Mauviosin,
Seigneur 301
ROSS
Alicia (Arnold) 150
Andrew of Balbair 415
Catherine (Van Gezel)
415
Christian (Livingston)
415
David of Balbair 415
Donald of Balmachy
415
Elizabeth 57
Eupheme (----) 415
Euphemia of 92, 94,
97, 100
Euphemia, Countess of
101
George 415
George Jr. 415
George of Balmachy
415
Gertrude 415
Grizel (McDonald)
415
Hugh of Balmachy 415
Hugh of Balnagown
415
Hugh, 4th Earl of Ross
369, 415
Hugh Ross, 4th Earl of
369, 415
Janet (Tulloch) 415
Jean (Comyn) 415
Jean (Douglas) 415
Joanna 369
Joanna (Williams) 415
John 150
Katherine (Macleod)
415
Katherine (McTyre)
415
Margaret (de Barclay)
415
Margaret (Graham)
369, 415
Margaret (Innes) 415
Margaret (McCulloch)
415

Margaret (Stronach)
415
Maud (Bruce) 369
Walter of Balmachy
415
Walter of Balnagown
415
Walter of Shandwick
415
William of Balnagown
415
William of Little Allan
415
William, 2nd Earl of
Ross 415
William, 3rd Earl of
Ross 415
William, 5th Earl of
Ross 369
William Ross, 2nd
Earl of 415
William Ross, 3rd Earl
of 415
William Ross, 5th Earl
of 369
ROSSE
Eleanor 409
ROSSI
Flamina 14
ROSSLYN
Robert Francis St.
Clair-Erskine, 4th
Earl of 12
ROSTOW
Anna of 411
Boris, Prince of 411
Constantine III, Prince
of 411, 413
Vassili, Prince of 411
Wassilko, Prince of
411
**ROSTOW and
UGLITSCH**
Constantine II, Prince
of 411
ROTHES
William Leslie, 3rd
Earl of 89
de ROTHWELL
Joan 435, 438
ROTSY
Mary 142
ROUCY
Alice of 444, 446,
448, 450, 451, 453
Ebles I, Count of 444,
446, 448, 450, 451,
453
ROUMANIA
Ileana of 1
**ROUMANIA,
KING OF**
Ferdinand I 1
de ROUXEL
Angélique 292
de ROVÉRÉAZ
Claudia Antonia 453

Guigues 453
de ROVORÉE
Guigues, Seigneur de
Saint-Triphon and
des Ormonts 453
Guillauma (de
Montvuagnard) 453
Isabelle (de
Dompierre) 453
Jean, co-Seigneur de
Saint-Triphon and
des Ormonts 453
Jean, Seigneur de
Bonneveaux 453
Jean, Seigneur du
Crest and La Roche
d'Ollon 453
Marguerite (de
Greysier) 453
Marie (de Confignon)
453
Pierre, Seigneur de
Granges (in Valais)
453
ROW
Catherine 97
Elspeth (Gillespie) 97
Grizel (Ferguson) 97
John 97
Lilias 97
Margaret (Bethune) 97
ROWAN
Mary Anne 193
ROY
Elizabeth (Brooke) 47
Harry 47
ROYALL
Katherine (Banks) 169,
338
RUBENS
Constance (Helman)
380
Hélène 380
Hélène (Fourment)
380
Isabelle (Brant) 380
Jan 380
Maria (Pijpelinckx)
380
Nicolas, Seigneur of
Rameyen 380
Peter Paul 380
RUCK
Hannah 234, 394
Hannah (Hutchinson)
234, 394
John 234, 394
Sarah 223
RUDHALL
Anne (Milborne) 303
Elizabeth 303
William 303
RUDKIN
Alice 417

The Royal Descents of 500 Immigrants

RUDOLPH
Arabella (Mason) 234,
394
Lucretia 234, 395
Zebulon 234, 394
RUDYARD
Alice (----) 274
Anne (Newton) 274
Anthony 274
Thomas 274
RUFFO DI CALABRIA
Fulco Antonio
Francesco
Banjamino, Prince
65
Luisa Albertina
Cristina Giovanna
(Gazelli di Rossana)
65
Paola Margherita
Giuseppina Maria
Consiglia, (Queen
Paola of the
Belgians) 65
RUGELEY
Lettice (Knollys) 116
Mary 116
Rowland, Sir 116
RUGGE
Frances 121
RURIK I
Prince of Owrutsch,
Grand Prince of
Kiev 411
RUSE
Lilian Augusta 207
RUSPOLI
Maria 105
RUSSELL
Alice (----) 420
Archibald 55, 67
Catherine 40
Constance Charlotte
Elisa (Lennox) 11
Eleanor (de Gorges)
419
Eleanor (Oliver) 55
Elizabeth 43
George, Sir, 4th Bt. 11
Hannah (----) 107
Helen Rutherford
(Watts) 55, 67
Isabel 420
Isabel (----) 420
James 55
John 448
Marie Clotilde 11
Morris, Sir 420
Rachel 23
Ralph, Sir 420
Rebecca 448
Sarah (Trowbridge)
448
Theobald, Sir 419
RUSSIA
Czars of 291
Helen of 2

Olga of 2
RUSSIA, CZAR OF
Ivan III 413
Ivan IV the Terrible
412
Ivan VI 291
Michael III 412
Paul 412
Peter (I) the Great 412
Peter III 291
**RUSSIA,
CZARINA OF**
Catherine (II) the
Great 291, 412
RUTHER
Anne 172
RUTHERFORD
Anne 55
Barbara 66
Barbara (Abernethy)
66
Catherine 111
Catherine (Alexander)
55, 67
Eleanor (Elliot) 55, 67
Elizabeth (Cairncross)
67
Jane 55
Jean (Eliot) 66
John 55
John of Edgerston 66
John of Edgerston (and
N.Y.) 55, 67
John, Sir, of
Edgerston 67
Magdalen (Morris) 55
Marian (Riddell) 66
Robert of Edgerston
66
Sarah 336, 448
Susanna (Riddell) 67
Thomas of Edgerston
66, 67
Walter 55, 67
RUTLAND
John Manners, 1st
Duke of 40
John Manners, 2nd
Duke of 40
John Manners, 3rd
Duke of 40
John Manners, 8th
Earl of 40
Thomas Manners, 1st
Earl of 40
van RUYVEN
Jacominia Jacob
Claesdr. 365
RYAN
Nancy 105
Thelma Catherine (Pat)
168
RYCE
Mary 240
RYLAND
Elizabeth 169

RYLEY
Anne 441
RYMER
Elizabeth (Gerard)
Blakiston 139
Ralph 139
RYTHE
Elizabeth 342
RYTHER
Eleanor 153
RYVES
Alice 190
Anne (Maude) 190
Jerome 190
SACKETT
Daniel 397
Daniel Jr. 397
Mary (Weller) 397
Mehitable 397
Mehitable (Cadwell)
397
SACKVILLE
John 284
Margaret (Boleyn) 284
Mary 284
de SADE
Donatien Alphonse
Francois, Count de
Sade 79
Marquis 79
SADINGTON
Isabel 417
de SAIGNES
Jean Baptiste, Seigneur
de Grizols 199
Louise 199
Louise (de Laizer) 199
ST. ALBANS
Charles Beauclerk, 1st
Duke of 12
Francis Bacon, 1st
Viscount 315, 450
ST. AUBIN
Isabel 450
ST. BARBE
Alice 374
Joan (----) 374
Margery (Grey) 374
Richard 374
Thomas 374
ST. CLAIR
Edith 251
ST. CLAIR-ERSKINE
Blanche Adeliza
(Fitzroy) 12
Millicent Fanny 12
Robert Francis, 4th
Earl of Rosslyn 12
ST. GEORGE
Anne (Hatfield) 209
Anne (Pinnock) 209
Bridget (Blakeney) 209
Catherine (Gifford)
207
Elizabeth (Bligh) 209
Elizabeth (Blount) 207

The Royal Descents of 500 Immigrants

St. George, continued
Florence Evelyn
(Baker) 209
Frances 208
George 209
George Baker 209
George, Sir 207
Henry 209
Henry, Sir 208
Howard Bligh 209
Katherine Delano Price
(Collier) 209
Mary 207
Mary (Dayrell) 208
Richard 209
Richard, Sir 207
Richard, Sir, 1st Bt.
209
Richard Bligh, Sir,
2nd Bt. 209
Robert 209
Sarah (Persse) 209
Sophia Madelina
Olivia (Mahon) 209
de ST. HILAIRE
Maud 444, 448, 451
ST. JOHN
Agnes 403
Alice 317
Alice (Bradshaw) 400
Anne 139
Cresset 372
Elizabeth 207, 210
Elizabeth (Blount) 207
John 207
John, Sir 317, 372,
400
Margaret 400
Margaret (Beauchamp)
400
Margaret (Carew) 207
Margaret (Waldegrave)
372
Nicholas 207
Oliver, Sir 210, 400
Sarah (Bulkeley) 210
Sybil (ferch Morgan
ap Jenkin) 400
ST. LAWRENCE
Alison 216
Genet (Plunkett) 216
Nicholas, 16th Baron
Howth 216
ST. LEGER
Anne 40, 140
Anne (Plantagenet) 40
Anthony, Sir 140
Dorothy 235
Katherine 140, 205,
432
Mary 141
Mary (Heyward) 140
Mary (Scott) 140
Thomas, Sir 40
Ursula 141
Ursula (Neville) 140
Warham, Sir 140

de ST. LIZ
Isabel 429
Isabel (de Beaumont)
429
Matilda 455, 458, 463
Simon 367, 369, 371,
373, 376
Simon, Earl of
Huntingdon and
Northampton 429,
455, 458, 463
ST. MAURE
Elizabeth (Brooke) 279
Joan 279
John 279
de ST. MICHEL
Alexander Marchant,
Sieur 235
de ST. PAUL
Aymon de Blonay,
Seigneur 453
ST. POL
Guy III de Châtillon,
Count of 296
ST. QUENTIN
Lora 313
SAINT-ESTEVE
Balthazard de Baschi,
Seigneur 343
Louis de Baschi,
Seigneur 343
Thadée de Baschi,
Seigneur 343
de SAINT-NECTAIRE
Nectaire de
Senneterre, Seigneur
297
de SAINT-SEVERIN
Jeanne 201
**de SAINT-TRIPHON
and DES
ORMONTS**
Guiges de Rovorée,
Seigneur 453
Jean de Rovorée,
co-Seigneur 453
de SAINTE MELAINE
Susanne 79
SALINGER
Claire Alison
(Douglas) 57
Jerome David 57
SALISBURY
Ela, Countess of 345,
348, 350, 352, 354,
356, 358, 360, 361,
363
Elizabeth Parker Clark
151
Jane 85
Margaret Plantagenet,
Countess of 35
Mary 171
Richard Neville, 1st
Earl of 125, 136,
155, 171, 177, 188

Richard, 1st Earl of
189
William Longespee,
Earl of 345, 348,
350, 352, 354, 356,
358, 360, 361, 363
de SALLMARD
Bertrand, Seigneur de
Ressiz and de la Fay
299
Charlotte (de Sarron)
299
Claude (de Virieux)
299
Claude I, Seigneur de
Ressiz and de la Fay
299
Claude II, Seigneur de
Ressiz and de la Fay
299
Eléonore (de Guillens)
299
Francois (de Guillet)
299
Geoffrey I, Seigneur
de Ressiz de la Fay
and Montfort 299
Geoffrey II, Seigneur
de Ressiz, de la Fay
and Montfort 299
Isabeau (de Vangelet)
299
Jean, Seigneur de
Montfort 299
Jeanne Catherine (de
Bourbon) 299
Just Madeleine (de
Grammont) 299
Louis, Seigneur de
Montfort 299
Madeleine (de
Foudras) 299
Marguerite (de Tenay)
299
Marie Ann (de
Chabrières) 299
Marie Jeanne
Francoise (de
Ponchon) 299
Pauline 300
Philippe Guillaume,
Seigneur de Ressiz,
Montfort and Roche-
Pingolet 299
Raymond I, Seigneur
de Ressiz, Montfort
and Roche-Pingolet
299
Raymond II, Vicomte
de Ressiz 299
SALM-NEUFVILLE
Charles Theodore,
Prince of 14
Christina of 14
Dorothea of 14
Louis Otto, Prince of
14

SALM-SALM
Agnes Elizabeth
  Winona Leclerq Joy,
  Princess of 10, 14
Constantin, Prince of
  14
Felix Constantin
  Alexander Johann
  Nepomuk, Prince of
  10, 14
Florentin, Prince of 14
Maximilian, Duke of
  Hoogstraeten, Prince
  of 14
Nicholas Leopold,
  Prince of 14
SALTER
Catherine 85
SALTONSTALL
Elizabeth 421
Grace (Kaye) 164, 421
Judith 421
Muriel (Gurdon) 146,
  164
Richard 146, 164
Richard, Sir 164, 421
Susanna (Poyntz) 421
SALTOUN
Alexander Abernethy,
  4th Baron 107
SALTYKOV
Maria, Princess
  (Golitsyn) 412
Sergei, Count 412
Vassili, Count 412
SALWAY
Alice 277
Anne (Vaughan) 277
Richard 277
SAMPSON
George 425
Margery 425
Margery (Felbrigg)
  425
Thomas 425
SAMWELL
Amy (Giffard) 435
Richard 435
Susanna 435
SAN FAUSTINO
Carlo Bourbon del
  Monte, Prince of 7
Ranieri Bourbon del
  Monte, Prince of 7
SANCHA
of Provence 317
SANDDE
ab Elidir 465
SANDEMAN
Sibella 50
SANDERS
Anna 159
Anna (Whetenhall) 159
John 159

de SANDERSLEBEN
Anna Elizabeth,
  Countess of Coligny
  61
SANDES
Alice 420
Elizabeth 189
SANDYS
Cecily (Wilsford) 430
Edwin, Archbishop of
  York 430
George 430
Margaret 123, 430
Mercy (Colepepper)
  430
Samuel, Sir 430
SANFORD
Anne 234
Bridget (Hutchinson)
  234
Dorothy 130
John 234
Mary (Coddington)
  234
Peleg 234
SANTVOORT
Mary 457
SAPCOT(ES)
Joan 406
SAPCOTT
Winifred 214
SAPCOTTS
Elizabeth 171
SAPIEHA
Katherine Anne,
  Princess 293
SARAWAK
Charles Vyner Brooke,
  H.H. Sir, Rajah of
  47
Sylvia Leonora (Brett)
  Brooke, H.H. Hon.,
  Ranee of 47
SARDINIA
Kings of 291
SARDINIA, KING OF
Charles Albert 5, 289
Victor Amadeus II 5
Victor Emanuel II 290
SARGENT
Ellen (Makerness) 435
Hannah (----) 435
Hugh 435
Margaret (Giffard) 435
Mary (----) 435
Roger 435
Sarah (----) 435
William 435
**de la SARRAZ
and BELMONT**
Barthélemy de
  Grandson, Seigneur
  453
de SARRON
Charlotte 299
SAUNDERS
Anne 325

Emma 250
Isabel (Carew) 182
Margaret 247
Mary 182
Nicholas 182
SAVAGE
Alice 253, 348
Anne (Lygon) 253
Anne (Sheldon) 253
Anne (Stanley) 253
Anthony 253
Bridget 254
Catherine (Stanley)
  238, 253, 255, 274
Christopher 253
Christopher, Sir 253
Dulcia 348
Eleanor (Brereton)
  348, 358
Elizabeth 238
Elizabeth (Hall) 253
Elizabeth (Manners)
  41
Ellen 255
Francis 253
John, Sir 41, 238,
  253, 255, 274, 348,
  356, 358
Margaret 41, 255,
  274, 356, 358
Mary 334
Maud (Swinnerton)
  348, 356, 358
Ralph 253
Sarah 166
Sarah (Constable) 253
Walter 253
SAVILL
Mary 340
SAVILLE
Bridget 353
SAVOY
Adela of 378, 380
Charles Emanuel I,
  Duke of 5
Elizabeth of 289
Emanuel Philibert of,
  Prince of Carignan 5
Eugène, Prince of 105
Louis Victor of, Prince
  of Carignan 5
Thomas of, Prince of
  Carignan 5
Victor Amadeus I of,
  Prince of Carignan 5
Victoria Francesca,
  Madamigella di Susa
  5
SAVOY-CARIGNAN
Leopolda of 5
SAWLE
Elizabeth 319
SAXBY
Mary 248

Stafford, continued
Dorothy (Stafford) 37
Edward, 3rd Duke of
Buckingham 140,
150, 186
Eleanor (Percy) 140,
150, 186
Elizabeth 37, 150,
186, 277
Granville Leveson-
Gower, 1st
Marquess of 23
Henry, 2nd Duke of
Buckingham 140,
150, 186
Henry, Baron Stafford
37
Henry Stafford, Baron
37
Hugh, 2nd Earl of
Stafford 224, 291
Hugh Stafford, 2nd
Earl of 224, 291
Katherine 224, 226,
250, 258, 264, 291
Margaret 378
Margaret (de Audley)
224, 226, 250, 258,
264, 277, 291
Mary 140
Philippa (Beauchamp)
224, 291
Ralph, 1st Earl of
Stafford 224, 226,
250, 258, 264, 277,
291
Ralph Stafford, 1st
Earl of 224, 226,
250, 258, 264, 277,
291
Ursula (Pole) 37
William, Sir 37
STANDISH
Alexander, Sir 332
Constance (Gerard)
332
Elizabeth 331
Grace 332
Oliver 332
STANFORD
Elizabeth 236
STANHOPE
Anne 120
Bridget 128
Elizabeth 119, 187
Jane 352
Maria 107
Philip Dormer, 4th
Earl of Chesterfield
9
STANLEY
Agnes 330
Alice Caroline 189
Alice (Spencer) 23, 27
Amelia Sophia 18
Anne 253, 258, 262
Anne (Hart) 177

Anne (Hastings) 148
Catherine 238, 253,
255, 274
Charlotte (de la
Trémoille) 18
Dorothy (Tennant) 43
Edward John, 2nd
Baron Stanley of
Alderley 8
Eleanor (Neville) 177,
188
Eleanor (Sutton) 258
Elizabeth 27, 82
Elizabeth (Vere) 18
Elizabeth (Weever)
255, 262
Ferdinando, 5th Earl
of Derby 23, 27
Frances 23
George 258
George, Baron Strange
177
Henrietta Blanche 8
Henrietta Maria
(Dillon-Lee) 8
Henry 177
Henry, 4th Earl of
Derby 18, 23, 27
Henry Morton, Sir 43
James, 7th Earl of
Derby 18
James, Sir 177
Jane Caroline (Mahon)
189
Joan (Goushill) 238,
245, 253, 255, 262,
269, 274
Joan (Strange) 177
John, Sir 255, 262
Louis Crandall 189
Margaret 148, 177,
188, 245, 269
Margaret (Clifford)
18, 23, 27
Margaret (Stanley) 177
Margery 255
Thomas, 1st Baron
Stanley 238, 245,
253, 255, 262, 269,
274
Thomas, 1st Earl of
Derby 177, 188
Thomas, 2nd Earl of
Derby 148
Thomas Stanley, 1st
Baron 238, 245,
253, 255, 262, 269,
274
William, 6th Earl of
Derby 18
**STANLEY OF
ALDERLEY**
Edward John Stanley,
2nd Baron 8
STANTON
Hannah viii
Henry viii

Mary 234
Mary (Clarke) viii
Mary (Clarke)
Cranston Jones 248
Mary (Hull) viii
Robert 248, viii
STAPLES
Elizabeth 130
STAPLETON
Brian, Sir 222, 271,
275
Catherine (de la Pole)
222, 271, 275
Cecily (Bardolf) 222,
271, 275
Elizabeth 222, 271,
275
Jane 42
Katherine (Constable)
42
Miles, Sir 222, 271,
275
Robert, Sir 42
STAPLEY
Elizabeth 246
von STARHEMBERG
Anna (von Zinzendorf)
197
Conrad, Count 197
[Heinrich] Ernst
Rüdiger, Count 197
von STARZHAUSEN
Joanna 293
STAUNTON
Elizabeth 417
Margaret 334
STAVELY
Isabel 169
STEBBINS
Josephine Vail 26
STEDMAN
Mary 155
STEPHEN
King of England 365,
417
STEPHEN II
Count of Blois 417
STEPHENS
Frances (Colepepper)
140, 205, 432
Mary Gill Caldwell 49
Mary (Newdigate) 262
Samuel 140, 432
Sarah 120
William 262
STEUART
Gladys Virginia 472
Helen 55
Helen (Cockburn) 55
John Henry 472
Mary Virginia Ramsay
(Harding) 472
Robert, Sir, 1st Bt. 55
STEUART
**also STEWART,
STUART**

The Royal Descents of 500 Immigrants

von STEUBEN
  Augustin 63
  Charlotte Dorothea,
    Countess (von
    Effern) 63
  Friedrich Wilhelm
    Ludolf Gerhard
    Augustin, Baron 63
  Maria Justina
    Dorothea (von
    Jagow) 63
  Wilhelm Augustin 63
STEVENS
  Anne (Stratton) Lake
    425
  Elizabeth 181
  Jessie Anne 397
  William 425
STEWART
  ---- 107, 367
  Agnes (Keith) 31
  Agnes (of the Isles) 99
  Agnes, Countess of
    Bothwell 50, 51, 55,
    57
  Alexander, 1st Earl of
    Buchan 101
  Alexander, 6th Earl of
    Galloway 18, 470
  Alice (Cockburn) 111
  Annabella 60, 71, 73,
    76, 77
  Anne 69
  Anne (Dashwood) 19
  Anne (de la Queuille)
    69
  Anne (Gordon) 31
  Anne (Stewart) 69
  Catherine 53
  Catherine (Cochrane)
    18, 470
  Catherine (de Balsac)
    69
  Catherine (Rutherford)
    111
  Charlotte, Lady 18
  Christian 97, 111
  Christian (Erskine) 97
  Christian (Hay) 111
  David of Rosyth 97
  Eleanor (Sinclair) 109,
    112, 114
  Elizabeth 31, 48, 60,
    68, 92, 94, 97, 99,
    100, 109, 114, 203
  Elizabeth (Gordon) 60
  Elizabeth (Hamilton)
    48, 69
  Elizabeth (Stewart) 31,
    48
  Elspeth 109
  Esmé, 1st Duke of
    Lennox 69
  Francis, 1st Earl of
    Bothwell 30
  George, 8th Earl of
    Galloway 19

Harriet 470
Helen 48
Henrietta 53
Isabel 96, 99, 367
Isabel (de Ergadia)
  203
James of Traquair 111
James, 1st Earl of
  Buchan 107, 111
James, 1st Earl of
  Moray 31
James, 2nd Earl of
  Moray 31
James, 3rd Earl of
  Moray 31
James, 4th Earl of
  Moray 31
James, of Graemsay
  28
James, Sir, of Lorne
  71, 99, 107, 109,
  111, 112, 114
Jane 19
Jane (Paget) 19
Janet 60, 71, 111
Janet (Campbell) 109,
  112, 114
Janet (Kennedy) 28
Jean 28, 57, 60, 92,
  94, 97, 100, 112,
  203
Jean (Hepburn) 30
Joan 50, 51, 55, 57,
  58, 73, 75, 78, 99
Joan (Beaufort) 71,
  99, 107, 109, 111,
  112, 114
Joan (Stewart) 99
John, 1st Earl of
  Atholl 71, 109, 112,
  114
John, 2nd Baron Lorne
  99
John, 2nd Earl of
  Atholl 109, 112, 114
John, 3rd Earl of
  Lennox 48, 69
John, 4th Earl of
  Atholl 60
John, 7th Earl of
  Galloway 19
John, lord of Aubigny
  69
John, of Coldingham
  30
John, Prior of
  Coldingham 30
John, Sir, of
  Innermeath and
  Lorne 203
Katherine 92, 94, 97,
  100
Katherine (Kerr) 111
Margaret 28, 30, 48,
  51, 53, 55, 58-60,
  70, 89, 101, 102,
  470

Margaret (Douglas)
  30, 71
Margaret (Graham),
  Countess of
  Menteith 96, 99,
  102
Margaret (Home) 30,
  31
Margaret (Ogilvy)
  107, 111
Marjory 96, 99
Martha 78, 114
Mary 29, 31, 48, 53,
  66, 68, 69, 86-88,
  90, 91
Matthew, 2nd Earl of
  Lennox 48, 69
Robert, 1st Baron
  Lorne 99
Robert, 1st Duke of
  Albany 96, 99, 102
Robert, 1st Earl of
  Orkney 28
Robert, Sir, of
  Schillinglaw 111
Susan 19
William of Traquair
  111
STEWART
  also STEUART,
  STUART
STIER
  Albert Jean 380
  Henri Joseph,
    Seigneur of
    Aertselaer 380
  Isabelle Hélène (de la
    Bistrate) 380
  Marie Louise (Peeters)
    380
STILLMAN
  Hannah 71
STIRLING
  Christian 59, 94
  Christian (Stirling) 59
  George of Herbertshire
    59
  John of Herbertshire
    59
  Margaret 59
  Mary (Erskine) 59
  William, Sir, 2nd Bt.
    59
STOBO
  Patience 60
STOCKBRIDGE
  Katherine 371
STOCKETT
  Mary (Wells) 342
STOCKMAN
  Anne (Leigh) 247
  John 247
  Joseph 247
  Sarah (Pike) Bradbury
    247

607

The Royal Descents of 500 Immigrants

TEACKLE
Margaret (Nelson) 149
Thomas 149
TELLEZ D'ACOSTA
Jeanne Thérèse 201
TEMPEST
Alice 178
Anne (Carre) 180
Catherine 180
Dowsabel 176
Eleanor 32
Joan 238
Roger 180
TEMPLE
Christian 124
Christian (Leveson) 124
Dorothy 149
Dorothy (Lee) 148
Elizabeth 431
John, Sir 148
Mary 148
Mary (Knapp) 124
Peter, Sir, 2nd Bt. 124
Richard, Sir, 3rd Bt. 124
de TENAY
Marguerite 299
TENDERYNG
Joan 423
TENDRING
Alice 317
TENNANT
Charles 43
Dorothy 43
Gertrude Barbara Rich (Collier) 43
TESCHEN and GLOGAU
Margaret of 427
Przemysl I Nosak, Duke of 427
TESTARD
Marie Anne 297
THACHER
Peter 125
Theodora (Oxenbridge) 125
THATCHER
Catherine 116
THELWALL
Alice 357
Janet (Langford) 357
Simon 357
THEOBOLD V
Count of Blois 343
THIMBLEBY
Anne 393
Elizabeth (Hilton) 393
Richard 393
THOMAS
Alice 400
Anna Lloyd (Braithwaite) 82
Anne (Lloyd) 392
ap Dafydd 324
ap Dafydd Gam 391

ap Huw 392
ap Ieuan 312
ap John Wynne 357
ap Morus 323
ap Robert 312
Cadwalader 306, 392
Christian Jean (Wallace) 129
Dorothy (Carew) 135
Edgar Hastings 129
Elizabeth 135, 157
Elizabeth (King) 428
Ellen (Owen) 306, 392
Emmot 451
Gainor 168
George 428
George Hudleston 129
George, Sir, 1st Bt. 428
Hilda Margaret Rose 129
Jane Anne 129
Jane (Puleston) 168
Joan (Lewis) 134
John 134, 392
Josiah 129
Katherine (Robert) 392
Lydia 117
Mary Anne (Broadhurst) 129
Mary (Morgan) 134
of Savoy, Prince of Carignan 5
of Workington 440
Rhys 168
Richard Henry 82
Sarah (Winthrop) 428
Susanna Isabella (Harington) 129
Thomas 135
William 134
THOMAS OF BROTHERTON
Earl of Norfolk 204, 207, 213, 216, 219, 240, 244, 246, 257, 270, 272, 282, 283, 286
THOMAS OF WOODSTOCK
1st Duke of Gloucester 132, 146, 163, 182
THOMAS GETHIN
ap Hywel Llwyd 308
THOMOND
Donough O'Brien, 2nd Earl of 260
Henry O'Brien, 4th Earl of 41
Henry O'Brien, 6th Earl of 41
THOMPSON
Alice (Freeman) 436, 469
Dorothy 213, 231, 436, 469
John 355, 436, 469

Mary 436
Sarah 219
Thomasine (Ward) 355
THORNDIKE
Elizabeth (Stratton) 426
John 426
THORNE
Mary (Purefoy) 252
Susanna 250, 252
Thomas 252
THORNES
Alice 84
Elizabeth (Astley) 84
Jane (Kynaston) 84
Joan (ferch Evan Lloyd) 84
John 84
Margaret (----) 84
Richard 84
Roger 84
THORNTON
Alice (Savage) 253
Elizabeth 253, 348, 401
Francis 253
Margaret 184, 253
THOROUGHGOOD
Anne 363
THORPE
Alice 427
Isabel (Constable) 313
Margaret 313
Mary (Banks) 136
Stephen 313
de THOUARS
Claude de la Trémoille, Duc 18
Louis I de la Trémoille, Vicomte 297
de THOVION
Clara 380
de THOYRAS
Jacob de Rapin, Seigneur 297
Paul de Rapin, Seigneur 297
THRELKELD
Grace 130
THROCKMORTON
Alice (Bedell) 340
Alice (Stout) 236
Anne (Chace) 341
Bassingborne 236
Clement 125
Elizabeth 206
Elizabeth (Berkeley) 205
Elizabeth (Blennerhasset) 236
Elizabeth (Pickering) 340
Gabriel 340
George, Sir 125
Goditha 363
John 236

609

The Royal Descents of 500 Immigrants

Throckmorton,
continued
John Jr. 236
Judith (Hetley) 341
Katherine 125
Katherine (Neville)
  125
Katherine (Vaux) 125
Lionel 236
Martha 126
Mary (Hill) 236
Patience 236
Rebecca (----) 236
Robert 340, 341
Thomas, Sir 205
THURGRYM
Margery 398
THWAITES
Alice (Garneys) 161
Anne (Knyvett) 161
Christopher 161
Joan (----) 161
John 161
Margaret 313
William 161
Winifred 161
THWAITS
Isabel 280
THYNNE
Anne 151
Catherine (Howard)
  151
Dorothy 44
Frances 22
Frances (Finch) 22
Thomas, 1st Viscount
  Weymouth 22
Thomas, Sir 151
TIARKS
Ada Constance Helen
  (Harington) 129
Anne Patricia 129
Evelyn Florence
  (Cripps) 129
John Gerhard 129
John Gerhard Edward
  129
TIBETOT
John de Tibetot, 2nd
  Baron 336, 338, 340
Pain de Tibetot, 1st
  Baron 336, 338, 340
Robert de Tibetot, 3rd
  Baron 338, 340
TIBETOT
 also TIPTOFT
de TIBETOT
Ada 336
Agnes (de Ros) 336,
  338, 340
Agnes (Wrothe) 336
Elizabeth 336, 338,
  340
John, 2nd Baron
  Tibetot 336, 338,
  340

Margaret (Badlesmere)
  338, 340
Margaret (Deincourt)
  338, 340
Pain, 1st Baron Tibetot
  336, 338, 340
Pain, Sir 336
Robert, 3rd Baron
  Tibetot 338, 340
TICHBORNE
Anne (White) 342
Elizabeth (Rythe) 342
Jane 342
Joan (Wandesford) 342
John 342
Margaret (Martin) 342
Nicholas 342
TILGHMAN
Anna (Sanders) 159
Christopher 159
Elizabeth (Packham)
  159
Mary (Foxley) 159
Oswald 159
Richard 159
Susanna (Whetenhall)
  159
William 159
TILL
Gertrude (Ross) 415
Isaac 415
TILLEY
Elizabeth 335
TILLOUL
Maud 416
de TILLY
Francois Joseph Paul
  de Grasse, Count de
  Grasse, Marquis 292
TILNEY
Agnes 283
Elizabeth 146, 182
de TIMEUR
Sébastien de Plöeuc,
  Marquis 79
TINDAL also TYNDAL
TIPTOFT
John, 1st Baron Tiptoft
  243, 280
John Tiptoft, 1st Baron
  243, 280
Joyce 128, 243
Joyce (Cherleton) 243,
  280
Philippa 280
TIPTOFT
 also TIBETOT
de TIZON
René du Bus, Seigneur
  199
TOBIN
Isabella Maria 27
TODD
Dorothea "Dolly"
  (Payne) 253, 348
Sarah D. 397

de TOENI
Alice 429
Godeheut 431
Roger III 431
TOKTAI
Khan of the Golden
  Horde 413
TOLLEMACHE
Dorothy (Wentworth)
  119
Elizabeth 187
Elizabeth (Cromwell)
  119
Elizabeth (Stanhope)
  119, 187
Lionel 119
Lionel, Sir 119
Lionel, Sir, 1st Bt. 119
Lionel, Sir, 2nd Bt.
  119, 187
Mary 119
Susan 119
Susan (Jermyn) 119
TOMKYNS
Louise 207
de TONNERRE
Charles de Husson,
  Count 297
Henri de Clermont,
  Count 64
TORBOCK
Catherine (Gerard) 255
Elizabeth (Moore) 255
Margaret 255
Margery (Stanley) 255
Thomas 255
William 255
William, Sir 255
TORLONIA
Guilio, Duke of Poli
  and Guadagnolo 5
Marina 5
Marino, Prince of
  Civitella-Cesi 5
Mary Elsie (Moore) 5
Teresa (Chigi-Albani)
  5
TORREY
Anna (Davenport) 456
Deborah (Holbrook)
  456
Jane (Haviland) 142
Joseph 456
Louisa Maria 456
Samuel Davenport 456
Susan Holman
  (Waters) 456
Susanna (Giddings)
  456
William 142, 456
TORRIGLIA
Andrew IV Doria-
  Pamphili-Landi, 2nd
  Prince of 5
John Andrew V Doria-
  Pamphili-Landi, 3rd
  Prince of 5

The Royal Descents of 500 Immigrants

TOUCHET
Anne 285
Constance 157, 167, 168, 179, 192
Eleanor (Holand) 157, 167, 168, 179, 181, 192
James, 2nd Baron Audley 157, 167, 168, 179, 181, 192
Margaret 181
TOULOUSE
Louis Alexandre de Bourbon, Count of 103
de la TOUR d'AUVERGNE
Gabrielle 197
de la TOUR-LANDRY
Francois de Maillé de la Tour-Landry, Baron 201
de la TOUR-LAUBOURG
Just Charles César de Fay, Count 64
TOURNAY
Alice (Blechynden) 376
Jane 376
Thomas 376
TOWGOOD
Andriah 406
TOWNELEY
Alice (Calvert) 330
Anne (Elborough) 386
Catherine (Curson) 386
Catherine (Forster) 386
Edmund 386
Elizabeth 331
Elizabeth (Smith) Lawrence de Carteret 220, 386, 457
Frances (Andrews) 386
Francis 386
Grace 331
Helen (Hesketh) 330
Henry 330
Isabel (Sherburne) 330
Jennet (Halstead) 330
Jeremiah 386
Joanna (White) 386
John 330
Lawrence 330
Margaret Frances 386
Margaret (Hartley) 330
Mary 330, 331, 468
Nicholas 386
Richard 220, 386, 457
Sarah (Warner) 330
TOWNSHEND
Alice (Cahen d'Anvers) 37

Anne Elizabeth Clementina (Duff) 36
Audrey Dorothy Louise 37
Carolyn Elizabeth Ann, Lady 36
Charles Thornton 37
Charles Vere Ferrers, Sir 37
Charlotte (Compton), Baroness Ferrers of Chartley 36
Elizabeth Jane (Stuart) 36
Elizabeth Pamela Audrey (Luby) 36
George John Patrick Dominic, 7th Marquess Townshend 36
George John Patrick Dominic Townshend, 7th Marquess 36
George Osborne, Lord 36
George, 1st Marquess Townshend 36
George Townshend, 1st Marquess 36
Georgiana Anne (Poyntz) 36
Gladys Ethel Gwendolen Eugenie (Sutherst) 36
Jessie Victoria (MacKellar) 36
John, 4th Marquess Townshend 36
John, Lord 36
John James Dudley Stuart, 6th Marquess Townshend 36
John James Dudley Stuart Townshend, 6th Marquess 36
John Villiers Stuart, 5th Marquess Townshend 36
John Villiers Stuart Townshend, 5th Marquess 36
John Townshend, 4th Marquess 36
Louise (Graham) 37
de TRACY
---- (de Pomeroy) 396
Eve 406
Henry 406
Maud (de Braose) 406
Rose 396
William 396
William, Sir 396
TRAFFORD
Edmund, Sir 255
Margaret (Savage) 255

Margery 255
TRAILL
Barbara (Balfour) 28, 29
Isabell (Fea) 29
John 29
Mary (Gale) 29
Mary (Whipple) 29
Robert 29
William, of Kirkwall 29
William, of Westness 28, 29
TRAQUAIR
Charles Stuart, 4th Earl of 53
John Stuart, 6th Earl of 53
TRAVERS
Ann 375
TREFFRY
Elizabeth (Killigrew) 319
Emilyn (Tresithny) 319
Janet 319
John 319
Martha 319
Thomas 319
TREGARRACK
Isabel 336
TREGIAN
Mary 342
TREGION
Jane 279
TREMAYNE
Margaret 451
de la TRÉMOILLE
Antoinette 297
Catherine (d'Isle-Bouchard) 297
Charlotte 18
Claude, Duc de Thouars 18
George, Seigneur 297
Guy V, Sire 297
Louis I, Vicomte de Thouars 297
Marguerite (d'Amboise) 297
Marie (de Sully) 297
TRENOWITH
Margaret 319
TRESITHNY
Emilyn 319
TREUHAFT
Jessica Lucy (Mitford) Romilly, Hon. 8
Robert Edward 8
TREVANION
---- (Maunder) 319
Anne (Edgcombe) 319
Arabella 319
Elizabeth (----) 319
Elizabeth (Pollard) 319
Elizabeth (Sawle) 319
Hugh, Sir 319

Vaughan, continued
Margaret (Touchet)
  181
Robert 167
Roger 277
Roger, Sir 134, 179,
  181
Watkyn 179
William, Sir 179
de VAUTORT
  or VALLETORT
Joan 317
VAUX
Anne 189
Eleanor 435
Elizabeth (FitzHugh)
  125, 189
Katherine 125
Maud 336, 338, 340,
  342
Nicholas, 1st Baron
  Vaux of Harrowden
  125, 189
VAUX OF
  HARROWDEN
Nicholas Vaux, 1st
  Baron 125, 189
VEATCH
James 111
Janet (Stewart) 111
John of Peebles 111
Malcolm of Muirdeen
  111
Mary (Gakerlin) 111
VELIAMINOV
Nicholas 411
Xenia 411
VENABLES
Elizabeth 407
de VENDEGIES
Anne 301
VENDOME
Catherine of 299
de VENDOMOIS
Jeanne 299
VERCELLANA
Rosa Teresa, Countess
  di Mirafiori and
  Fontanafredda 290
VERDUN
Theobald de Verdun,
  2nd Baron 303
de VERDUN
Clemence (----) 305,
  308, 311, 321, 323,
  324, 326, 328
Clemence (Dauntsey)
  305, 308, 311, 321,
  323, 324, 326, 328
Elizabeth (de Clare)
  248
Isabel 248
Margery 303
Maud (Mortimer) 303
Nicholas 305, 308,
  311, 321, 323, 324,
  326, 328

Theobald, 2nd Baron
  Verdun 303
Theobald, Sir 248
VERE
Elizabeth 18, 285
Frances 150, 186
de VERE
Alice (de Clare) 446,
  450
Aubrey 446, 450
Diana 12
Isabel 382, 403
Joan 378
Juliana 446, 450
VERMANDOIS
Adelaide of 419, 421,
  423, 425, 427, 429
Isabel of 419, 421,
  423, 425, 427, 429
VERNEY
Anne 286
Elizabeth 134
Margaret 233
VERNON
Anne (Ludlow) 181
Anne (Talbot) 227
Dorothy 40
Eleanor 181
Elizabeth 227, 410
Henry, Sir 227
Thomas 181
de VERNON
Mary 382, 403
Maud (de Beaumont)
  382, 403
William, 5th Earl of
  Devon 382, 403
VESEY
Mary (Reade) 141
VICTOR AMADEUS I
of Savoy, Prince of
  Carignan 5
VICTOR AMADEUS II
King of Sardinia 5
of Savoy, Prince of
  Carignan 289
VICTOR EMANUEL II
King of Sardinia, 1st
  King of United Italy
  5, 290
VICTORIA
Queen of Great Britain
  1, 16, 195, 197
VICTORIA
  FELICITAS
of Löwenstein-
  Wertheim-Rochefort
  14
VICTORIA
  FRANCESCA
of Savoy, Madamigella
  di Susa 5
VIDMER
Elizabeth (Brooke)
  Roy 47
Richard 47

VIELL
Susan 82, 190
VIERECK
Edwina 4
  (Franz Georg Edwin)
  Louis (Withold) 4
George Sylvester 4
Laura 4
Laura (Viereck) 4
Margaret Edith (Hein)
  4
de la VIEUVILLE
Lucrèce Francoise 103
des VIGNOLLES
Charles, Seigneur de
  Prades 344
Charlotte 344
Gabrielle (de
  Sperandieu) 344
Jacques, Seigneur de
  Prades 343
Louise (de Baschi) 343
VILLARD
Alexandra D. 37
de VILLE-SAVOIR
Jeanne 296
de VILLE
Claudia Antonia (de
  Rovéréaz) 453
Georges 453
Marie 453
de VILLENEUVE
Anne 291
de VILLENEUVE-
  TRANS
Véronique 292
de VILLERS
Isabella 296
Jean 296
Nicole (de Noyelles)
  296
VILLIERS
Barabara 151
Barbara, Duchess of
  Cleveland 8, 9, 12
Elizabeth 271
George, 1st Duke of
  Buckingham 271
Helen 315
Susan 128
de VIMEUR
Elizabeth (de Menon)
  201
Jean Baptiste
  Donatien, Count de
  Rochambeau 91,
  201
Jeanne Thérèse (Tellez
  d'Acosta) 201
Joseph Charles I,
  Seigneur de
  Rochambeau 201
Joseph Charles II,
  Marquis de
  Rochambeau 201
Marie Claire Thérèse
  (Bégon) 201

The Royal Descents of 500 Immigrants

WILLIAM III
King of England 291
WILLIAM IV
of Orange, Stadholder
of the Netherlands 3
WILLIAM V
of Orange, Stadholder
of the Netherlands 3
**WILLIAM
THE SILENT**
Prince of Orange, 1st
Stadholder of the
Netherlands 18, 61,
63, 194
WILLIAMS
Abigail 396
Abigail (Allyn) 396
Abigail (Davis) 436
Abigail (Williams) 396
Anne 309
Benjamin 436
Catherine (----)
Edwards 324
Catherine (Griffith)
307
Dorothy (Griffith) 165
Eleanor 309
Elijah 396
Elizabeth 305, 306,
309
Ellis 308
Frances (Deighton)
205
Grace 457
Gwen 309
Jane 165
Joanna 415
John 307, 324, 396
Joseph 436
Joseph Jr. 436
Joseph (III) 436
Lydia (Dwight) 396
Margaret (John) 308
Martha (Howell) 436
Mary 436
Mary (Capen) 436
Mary (Evans) 324
Richard 205
Sarah Copeland
(Morton) 436
Sarah (Wise) 436
Stephen 436
Stephen Jr. 436
Susan May 436
Susanna (May) 436
Thomas 396
William 165
WILLIAMSON
Katherine 350
WILLING
Charles 257
Elizabeth Hannah
(Carrington) 257
WILLIS
Anne (Rich) 422
Elizabeth 119
Francis 422

WILLOUGHBY
Anne (Grey) 136
Edward 132
Eleanor 334
Elizabeth 132, 136
Henry, Sir 136
Hugh, Sir 334
Lucy 431
Margaret 136
Margaret (Freville)
334
Margaret (Neville) 132
Margery 313
WILMOT
Elizabeth 231
WILSFORD
Cecily 430
Elizabeth 248
Rose (Whetenhall) 430
Thomas 430
WILSON
Anne 465
Edith (Bolling) Galt
112, 115, 169, 339,
408
Ellen Louise (Axson)
236, 397, 447
Janet 94
(Thomas) Woodrow
112, 115, 169, 236,
339, 397, 408, 447
**de WILT
van BLEYSWYCK**
Liedewey 365
WILTSHIRE
Bridget 281
WIMBORNE
Ivor Bertie Guest, 1st
Baron 19
WINCH
Humphrey, Sir, 1st Bt.
383
Judith (Burgoyne) 383
Mary 383
Onslow 383
Rebecca (Browne) 383
WINCHESTER
Roger de Quincy, 2nd
Earl of 385, 393
William Paulet, 1st
Marquess of 219
WINCHILSEA
Heneage Finch, 3rd
Earl of 22
WINDEBANK
Frances (Dymoke) 183
Mildred 183
Thomas, Sir 183
WINDSOR
Andrews Windsor, 1st
Baron 227, 229
Andrews, 1st Baron
Windsor 227, 229
Anne 227
Edith 229
Eleanor 125

Elizabeth (Andrews)
229
Elizabeth (Blount)
227, 229
Thomas 229
WINGFIELD
---- (Kerry) 281
Anne (Touchet) 285
Anthony, Sir 285
Bridget (Wiltshire) 281
Dorothy 276
Edward Maria 281
Elizabeth 146, 213,
262, 266, 289
Elizabeth (Cecil) 276
Elizabeth (Fitz Lewis)
281, 285, 289
Elizabeth (Goushill)
262, 266, 276, 281,
285, 289
Elizabeth (Risby) 285
Elizabeth (Rokes) 276
Elizabeth (Vere) 285
Frances (Cromwell)
121
Henry 285
Henry, Sir 276
John 121
John, Sir 121, 281,
285, 289
Margery (Quarles) 276
Mary 285
Mary (----) 121
Mary (Hardwick) 285
Mary (Owen) 121
Richard 285
Richard, Sir 281
Robert 276
Robert, Sir 262, 266,
276, 281, 285, 289
Thomas 121
Thomas Maria 281
de WINGLES
Robert de Beaussart,
Seigneur 301
WINN
Endymia 250
Jacob (III) 250
Phoebe (Grout) 250
WINNINGTON
Agnes 378
WINSLOW
Abigail (Atkinson) 419
Agnes 386, 435
Anne 234, 394
Edward 234, 394, 416
Elizabeth 416
Elizabeth (Hutchinson)
234, 394
Susanna (----) White
416
WINSLOWE
Margery 144
WINSTON
Mary 448
Sarah 70

The Royal Descents of 500 Immigrants

WINTER
Elizabeth Tatham
(Dick) 199
Henry Mosle (H.M.)
West 199
Keyes 199
Marie Caroline
(Mosle) 199
WINTHROP
Catherine (Slicer) 427
Elizabeth (----) 427
Elizabeth (Reade) 227
John 222, 227, 398,
427
John Jr. 227
Joseph 427
Lucy 227
Margaret (Tyndal) 427
Margaret (Tyndal/
Tindal) 222
Mary (Forth) 227
Samuel 427
Sarah 428
Thomasine (Clopton)
222, 427
WINTON
Robert Seton, 1st Earl
of 51
WISE
Joseph 436
Mary (Thompson) 436
Sarah 436
Thomasine 346
WISEMAN
Elizabeth 116
John 116
Margaret 459
Mary (Rugeley) 116
WISHART
Elizabeth 76
Fergusia 51
WITHAM
Mary, Baroness of
Nova Scotia 214
WITTE
Sergei, Count 412
von WITTE
Ekaterina (Fadeev)
412
Julius 412
WITTER
Catherine (Van Zandt)
208
Frances (Tucker) 208
Mary (Lewis) 208
Matthew 208
Thomas 208
WITTY
Mary 401
WLADIMIR
Jaroslaw I, Prince of
411
WLADISLAW I
King of Poland 411
WODELL
Mary (Gold) 441

WODHULL
Alice 402
Alice (Wickliffe) 402
Anne (Newenham) 402
Elizabeth (Hall) 402
Fulk 402
Isabel (Trussell) 402
Joan (Etwell) 402
John 402
Lawrence 402
Margaret (----) 402
Thomas 402
**WODHULL
also WOODHULL**
**WOLFGANG
DIETRICH**
Count of Castell-
Remlingen 194, 197
**WOLHYNIEN
and GALICIA**
Roman, Prince of 411
WOLLEY
Alice 213
WOLSELEY
Anne 150, 258
Anne (Stanley) 258
Anthony 258
Cassandra (Giffard)
258
Devereux 150
Elizabeth (Zouche)
150
Ellen (Broughton) 258
Erasmus 258
John 258
Margaret (Blith) 258
Mary 258
Mary (Beauchamp)
258
Thomas, Sir 258
Walter 258
Winifred 258
WOOD
Anne 250
Eleanor (Strong) 469
Ellen 469
John 469
Katherine 464
Mary 44
WOODCOCK
Ursula 432
WOODHOUSE
Anne (Bacon) 450
Anne (Repps) 450
Henry 450
Henry, Sir 450
Judith (Manby) Haen
450
William, Sir 450
WOODHULL
Anne 171
Canning 47
Elizabeth (Parr) 171
Nicholas, Sir 171
Victoria (Claflin) 47
**WOODHULL
also WODHULL**

WOODVILLE
Anne 45
Catherine 140, 150,
186
Elizabeth 32-34, 45,
140, 150, 177, 186,
242
Jacquetta 177
WOODWARD
Frances 125
Martha 115
WOOLHOUSE
Elizabeth 144
Mary 144
WOOLSTON
Susanna 141
WOOLWORTH
Frank Winfield 19
WORCESTER
Charles Somerset, 1st
Earl of 155
Henry Somerset, 2nd
Earl of 155
WORK
Ellen (Wood) 469
Frances Eleanor
(Ellen) 469
Frank(lin H.) 469
WORKINGTON
Ada of 440
Gospatrick of 440
Thomas of 440
WORMELEY
Agatha (Eltonhead)
Kellaway 222, 231,
284, 349
Elizabeth 222, 284
Ralph 222, 284, 349
WORSHAM
Mary viii
WORSLEY
Frances 22
Frances (Thynne) 22
Isabel 248
Joyce 390
Margaret 389
Otewell, Sir 389
Robert, Sir, 4th Bt. 22
Rose (Trevor) 389
WOTTON
Margaret 136
WRAY
Albinia (Cecil) 38
Anne (Casey) 38
Christopher, Sir 38
Diana 38
Drury, Sir, 6th Bt. 38
Frances 38, 123
Frances (Drury)
Clifford 37
William, Sir 37
WREN
Christpher, Sir 120
Susan 120
WRENSHALL
Ellen Bray 364, 386

620

Bibliographical Supplement, 1993–2000

Introduction to the Bibliographical Supplement to *RD500*, 1993–2000

In the seven years since initial publication of *The Royal Descents of 500 Immigrants to the American Colonies or the United States Who Were Themselves Notable or Left Descendants Notable in American History*, a large quantity of pertinent new literature has appeared. This body of work includes two compendia by David Faris (and more, co-authored by Mr. Faris and Douglas Richardson, are planned), many articles by Richardson, Charles M. Hansen, Paul C. Reed, "Kenneth W. Kirkpatrick," John Anderson Brayton, Neil D. Thompson and others, and various additions to the *Seven Centuries: Ancestors for Twenty Generations* project by Brice McAdoo Clagett. Many *new* scholars, including Worth S. Anderson, Stewart Baldwin, Robert Battle, John C. Brandon, Thomas S. Erwin, Richard Evans, Todd A. Farmerie, Martin E. T. Hollick, Anthony Hoskins, Jack T. Hutchinson, Leslie Mahler, James R. "Jay" Mellon II, Albert M. Muth, John Plummer, John L. Scherer, Henry Sutliff III, and numerous Society members (including several former trustees or advisory council members) have kindly sent or shown me the results of detailed research, often with stated permission to use it as I see fit. Several NEHGS colleagues, including Jerome E. Anderson, David Curtis Dearborn, Henry B. Hoff, "Kirkpatrick" above, D. Brenton Simons, and Scott C. Steward, have developed new royal descents. I have perused the new 24-volume *American National Biography* (*ANB*), the new 1999 *Burke's Peerage*, and royalty volumes by Daniel Willis, formerly Brewer-Ward, and Marlene Eilers Koenig, and learned to consult the *History of Parliament* series and the Victoria County Histories much more frequently. Andrew B. W. MacEwen has kindly reviewed my Scottish section in detail, several correspondents and authors have revised some of the identifications of Welsh Quaker scholar Thomas Allen Glenn (who still, I think, deserves respect), my preparation of *Massachusetts and Maine Families in the Ancestry of Walter Goodwin Davis* occasioned a review of Davis's work in this field, and new volumes on Thomas Bradbury, Robert Abell (forthcoming from Carl Boyer, 3rd), and Dorothea (Poyntz) Owsley proved useful as well.

All of these sources together have added over 80 new *RD* immigrants to this study, eliminated a dozen, and significantly changed probably 100. In addition to these many recent discoveries, the summation of the field that I attempted in my 1993 work -- especially after the rich texture of dates, places, Parliamentary and military service, and much other biography, was added to lines for seventeenth-century immigrants of late Plantagenet descent by David Faris -- this summation and its many post-1993 updates have somewhat popularized the idea of royal ancestry among Americans. In the last seven years also, millions of potential genealogists have begun to use the Internet, databases are entered on various websites almost daily, and Don Charles Stone, David Humiston Kelley, and Marshall K. Kirk and others have brought ancient genealogy and the possibility of 50- to 100-generation pedigrees to our attention. Genealogical Publishing Company in Baltimore tells me also that *RD500* is among its most frequently requested out-of-print books.

Over the last several years, especially since early 1999, I have been preparing a second edition of *RD500* (now *RD600*, since over 635 immigrants will be included). Several months ago I gave a first draft of the manuscript to my colleague Alicia Crane Williams, the noted *Mayflower* scholar. Alicia and I will prepare copy, send it to various scholars for review, and prepare an index. As Alicia inputs further text, I shall examine a few additional sources in greater detail; these sources include *British Roots of Maryland Families* by Robert Barnes, immigrants treated in *ANB* who were born on the European continent (I have already added many therein born in England, Scotland, or Ireland), and a list prepared by long-time correspondent Joseph L. Druse of American residents treated in Daniel Willis's work on the descendants of Louis XIII of France. Because royal descent is an area of such keen interest to many of the probably over 100 million Americans who have it, because Alicia and I may take well over a year to finalize the manuscript of *RD600*, because many of the specific discoveries reported below will no doubt be welcome surprises eagerly received, and to remind readers

The Royal Descents of 500 Immigrants

that I continue to act as a "clearinghouse" for such data, I offer herewith a second printing of *RD500* with the following bibliographical supplement.

The bibliographical supplement below consists of three items: an updated version of my 1996 *NEXUS* article on *RD* changes through that date; four of my "Genealogical Thoughts" Internet columns on the subject, all composed in 2000 but somewhat rearranged and edited for this work; and a list of "Lesser Additions and Corrections to *RD500*," much expanded from such lists published in *NEXUS* in 1993 and 1996. The 1996 *NEXUS* article was due to have a second part, which in effect became the four Internet articles, so my progression through the material below, I think, is logical. I hope this supplement is widely consulted and read, I thank my many colleagues and correspondents for their invaluable contributions to it, and I again invite readers with further documentation or disproof for lines herein, or data on immigrants they wish me to consider, to write me at the New England Historic Genealogical Society, 101 Newbury St., Boston, MA 02116, (617) 536-5740, ext. 218. I can also be reached via e-mail at nehgs@nehgs.org, but please include "Royal Descents" or "*RD600*" in the subject line of your message. Happy searching herein -- the many recent requests for this compendium, now out of print for several years, have been among the most gratifying compliments of my career.

Gary Boyd Roberts
October 2000

Additions and Corrections to
The Royal Descents of 500 Immigrants (1993), Updated from *NEXUS* 13 (1996): 124–30

I.

Since the publication in October 1993 of my compendium, *The Royal Descents of 500 Immigrants to the American Colonies or the United States Who Were Themselves Notable or Left Descendants Notable in American History* (*RD500*), various new royal descents (*RDs*) have been developed; some lines therein have been further confirmed; a few have been disproved; and others have been "rearranged" -- either "improved" to descent from a later king or "downgraded" to descent from an earlier one. In all about 80 immigrants (by 2000 many more, including more than 80 not covered in *RD500*) have been affected. This article will consider those additions and corrections to *RD500* that appeared in print by late 1996, in a few cases later -- either in the 1995 edition of my *Ancestors of American Presidents* (*AAP*); in journal articles; or in major sources long available but often first brought to my attention by correspondents named below, to whom I am most grateful.

Within a year after *RD500* appeared Douglas Richardson published in the *Register* (148 [1994]: 130-40, 240-58) *RDs* for the immigrants Philip and Thomas Nelson (Jr.), brothers, of Rowley, and for Mrs. Elizabeth Haynes Cooke of Cambridge, Mass., wife of Joseph Cooke and daughter of John Haynes, governor of both Mass. and Conn., by his first wife, Mary Thornton, who probably died in England. (The second wife of Gov. Haynes, Mrs. Mabel Harlakenden Haynes Eaton, is covered in *RD500*, pp. 423-24). I outlined the Tudor descent of the former Hon. Joanna Freda Hare, wife of Supreme Court Associate Justice Stephen Gerald Breyer of Mass., and Washington, D.C., in *NEXUS* 11 (1994): 94-95; James L. Hansen contributed an *RD* for Rev. William Skepper/Skipper of Boston in *TAG* 69 (1994): 129-39; and John Anderson Brayton presented an *RD* for Christopher Calthorpe of York Co., Va. -- for whom John and I can trace only locally notable descendants (in North Carolina and Tennessee) -- in *The Virginia Genealogist* (*TVG*) 40 (1996): 67-70. Among articles stated to be forthcoming or then unpublished in *RD500*, confirmation and details concerning the descent of Mrs. Margaret Halsnode Denne of New Jersey appeared in *TAG* 68 (1993): 193-204, compiled by Col. Charles M. Hansen, who also confirmed and provided further support for the immediate five patrilineal generations behind Mrs. Anne Mauleverer Abbott, also of New Jersey, in *TAG* 69 (1994): 160-64. The monograph by David L. Greene on the brothers John, Thomas, and William Lawrence of New York City or Newtown or Flushing, Long Island, and of their sisters, Mrs. Jane Lawrence Giddings and Mrs. Mary Lawrence Burnham, both of Ipswich, Mass., appeared in *The Genealogist* 10 (1989, published 1994): 3-30. J.A. Brayton outlined a royal descent for John Fisher of Va. in *TVG* 38 (1994): 284-89, and Neil D. Thompson argued further for my identification of Col. Thomas Ligon (Lygon) of Va. (see *TVG* 22 [1978]: 253-55, 23 [1979]: 80) in *TVG* 38 (1994): 48-51. Books of interest include a second edition (1995) of J.B. Threlfall, *The Ancestry of Thomas Bradbury (1611–1695) and His Wife Mary Perkins (1615–1700) of Salisbury, Massachusetts*, plus *Massachusetts and Maine Families in the Ancestry of Walter Goodwin Davis* (3 vols., 1996), a consolidation of the latter's 16 multi-ancestor works covering his own known ancestry. In my introduction to this last I discuss the *RD*s of Samuel and Judith (Everard) Appleton, Christopher and Anne (Bainton) Batt, Thomas and Elizabeth (Marshall) Lewis, and Thomas Bressie, plus the possible line of Mrs. Thomasine Ward Thompson Buffum.

In the 1995 edition of *AAP* I included the new Skepper/Skipper descent, ancestral to Coolidge, and in covering the Lawrence line -- ancestral to Taft (via Mrs. Giddings) and probably F.D. Roosevelt (via Thomas Lawrence) -- ignored the question of the paternity of Judith of Ponthieu or Lens, niece of William the Conqueror and wife of Waltheof II, Earl of Huntingdon, Northampton, and Northumberland. Instead I outlined the descent of her mother, Adelaide of Normandy, from Robert I, King of France, d. 923 (this last change affects all lines covered in *RD500*, pp. 455-60, 463-64, including that of Mrs. Denne above). I also "improved" the likely *RD* through his father of Governor Thomas Dudley, as per a recent hypothesis developed by David Humiston Kelley and Marshall K. Kirk; and following research by NEHGS trustee Brice McAdoo Clagett "improved" the Anne/Giffard-derived *RD* of Edward Raynsford of Boston, outlining an illegitimate descent from Henry I, King of England, d. 1135 (Douglas Richardson later further "improved" the Raynsford line into a descent from Henry III, d. 1272, in *Plantagenet Ancestry of Seventeenth-Century Colonists*, 2nd ed. [*PASCC2*, 1999] and *Register* 154 [2000]: 219-26). I presented as well a newly developed likely *RD* of Theodore Roosevelt through Virginia immigrant Mrs. Diana Skipwith Dale (but Charles Martin Ward Jr. argues in *TAG* 75 [2000]: 27-29 that she was *not* the mother of likely TR ancestor Mrs. Katherine Dale Carter), but sadly had to "downgrade" the royal descent of Mrs. Elizabeth Alsop Baldwin Fowler (losing the Welles-Mowbray connection) to a line, via Dymoke, Ludlow, Marmion, and Counts of Réthel and Namur, from Louis IV, King of France, d. 954 (see *AAP*, pp. 194-97, 199-201, 207, 217-18, 222-23, 230-31, 233-34). For the more recent "upgrading" of Mrs. Baldwin (Fowler) to *another* Edward I descent, see my "Genealogical Thoughts" column #44 below. I also had to omit the earlier-given *RD* of Nixon forebear Hugh Harry of Pa., and his brother, Daniel, disproved by Neil D. Thompson in *TAG* 69 (1994): 95-97. Disproved as well, in these cases by Col. Hansen as part of his ongoing survey of claimed gentry origins for mid-Atlantic Quaker immigrants, is such ancestry for Oliver Cope of Pa. (see *TAG* 70 [1995]: 156-61) and Mrs. Margery Maude Fisher of Del. (*TAG* 72 [1997]: 244-56). Among Welsh Quaker immigrants whose *RD*s I extracted from the works of Thomas Allen Glenn (an authority some colleagues think I should disregard), Robert Lloyd and his siblings were disassociated from their alleged parents by Stewart Baldwin in *TAG* 71 (1996): 77-84, and Dr. Thomas Wynne, doubts about whose paternity were first brought to my attention by Christine Crawford-Oppenheimer, is treated by George Englert McCracken, in *The Welcome Claimants: Proved, Disproved, and Doubtful* (1970), pp. 501-72, wherein McCracken pronounces Dr. Wynne's parentage and ancestry "not yet proved." Thus all data on pages 168, 180, and 325-27 of *RD500* will be deleted from future editions. I might note also my reporting of Andrew B.W. MacEwen's doubts about the immediate ancestry of Gov. John Cranston of R.I., in *NEXUS* 11 (1994): 141.

Omitted from further consideration below are Mrs. Breyer, Gov. Dudley, Raynsford, and Mrs. Baldwin (Fowler), all covered in the above-cited *NEXUS* article, *AAP*, *PASCC2*, or "Genealogical Thoughts" column below; plus immigrants whose lines are only further confirmed, or disproved, by the articles cited above. For the Nelsons, Rev. Skepper, Mrs. Cooke, and Calthorpe, however, the following outline addenda to *RD500*, following its page numbers and format, should prove useful:

11. (from **Edward III, King of England**, d. 1377, via **7. Anne [Plantagenet]**, Duchess of Exeter and Lady St. Leger, sister of Kings Edward IV and Richard III) **Katherine Constable** = Sir Robert Stapleton (*RD500*, p. 42)

12. Philip Stapleton = Dorothy Hill

13. Dorothy Stapleton (d. 1637 in England) = Thomas Nelson of Rowley, Mass.

14. Philip Nelson of Mass. = (1) Sarah Jewett (2) Elizabeth Lowell

14. Thomas Nelson, Jr. of Mass. = (1) Anne Lambert (2) Mrs. Mary Lunt (3) Mrs. Philippa Andrews Felt Platts

6. (from **Edward III**) **Mary Clifford** = Sir Philip Wentworth (*RD500*, p. 119)

7. Elizabeth Wentworth = Sir Martin at See

8. Joan/Jane at See = Sir Piers Hildyard (*RD500*, p. 225, where they are called Peter Hildyard and Joan de la See; thus *Charles Rodes* of Va., p. 225, has an "improved" descent [from Edward III])

9. Isabel Hildyard = Ralph Legard

10. Joan Legard = Richard Skepper

11. Edward Skepper = Mary Robinson

12. Rev. William Skepper/Skipper of Boston, Mass., where he died 1640-50 = (1) ---- ---- (2) Sarah Fisher

6. (from **Edward I, King of England**, d. 1307) **Cecily Bardolf** = Sir Brian Stapleton (*RD500*, pp. 222, 271, 275)

7. Brian Stapleton = Isabel (or Elizabeth) ----

8. Elizabeth Stapleton = John Richers

9. John Richers = Elizabeth Batchcroft

10. Henry Richers = Cecily Tillys

11. Frances Richers = Edmund Cushin

12. Elizabeth Cushin = William Thornton

13. Robert Thornton = Anne Smith

14. Mary Thornton = John Haynes (ca. 1594–1653/54), colonial governor of Mass. and Conn. He = (2) Mabel Harlakenden; she = (2) Samuel Eaton (*RD500*, pp. 423-24)

15. Elizabeth Haynes of Mass. = Joseph Cooke

8. (from **Edward I**) **Elizabeth Stapleton** (dau. of **7. Sir Miles Stapleton** [and Catherine de la Pole], son of Sir Brian Stapleton and **Cecily Bardolf, 6.** above) = Sir William Calthorpe (*RD500*, pp. 222, 271, 275)

9. Edward Calthorpe = Anne Cromer

10. Edward Calthorpe = Thomasine Gaval

11. Prudence Calthorpe = Ralph Shelton

12. Grace Shelton = John Thurton

13. Maud Thurton = Christopher Calthorpe, a cousin

14. Christopher Calthorpe of Va. (d. ante 1662, possibly in N.C.) = Anne ----

II.

I now wish to cover, in format similar to the above, those "new" *RD* immigrants who have been brought to my attention by various correspondents. These latter usually developed, or at least noticed, the lines below, often mostly from printed works, but sometimes with key record or family sources as well. Again arranged, as in *RD500*, in reverse chronological order according to the death date of the most recent king in their ancestry, ten such immigrants are as follows; in each case we begin, as above, with the most recent ancestors already listed in *RD500*:

1. **Francis II, Holy Roman Emperor and Emperor of Austria**, d. 1835 = (2) Maria Theresa of the Two Sicilies

2. **Marie Louise of Austria** = (1) Napoleon I, Emperor of the French, d. 1821 (2) Adam Adalbert, Count von Neipperg

3. (by 2) **William Albert von Neipperg**, 1st Prince of Montenuovo = Juliana, Countess Batthyány-Strattman

4. **Albertine Leopoldine Wilhelmine Julia Maria von Neipperg**, Princess of Montenuovo = Zygmunt, Count Wielopolski, Marquis Gonzaga-Myszkowski

5. **Maria Malgorzata Paulina Wilhelmina Róza Leopoldyna Julia Wielopolska** of Philadelphia = Józafat, Count Plater-Zyberk. Their son, **Józafat, Count Plater-Zyberk**, married Maria Meysztowicz, and was the father of architectural educator **Elizabeth (Elzbieta) Maria Plater-Zyberk**, b. 1950, wife of Andres M. Duany.

Sources: A.C. Addington, *The Royal House of Stuart*, vol. 1 (1969), pp. 59-60, 62-63, and *Who's Who in America, 1996*, vol. 2, p. 3308 (courtesy of Francis James Dallett)

2. (from **James V, King of Scots**, d. 1542) **Robert Stewart**, 1st Earl of Orkney = Janet Kennedy (*RD500*, p. 28)

3. **Elizabeth Stewart** = James Sinclair of Murchil

4. **Agnes Sinclair** = John Mackay of Dirlot and Strathy

5. **Hugh Mackay** of Strathy = Jane Mackay of Reay

6. **John Mackay** of Strathy = Elizabeth Sinclair of Brims

7. **Hugh Mackay** of Strathy = Barbara Murray of Pennyland

8. **James Mackay**, sometime of Ga. = Ann ---- (poss. Mrs. Ann Stephens)

9. (probably illegitimate by Henrietta Sinclair of Olrig) **John Mackay** = Sarah More

10. **Sinclair Mackay** = Margaret Henderson

11. **George Mackay** (b. 1809) of Washington, D.C. = Ann Crerar

Sources: Research of F.H. Pollard, great-grandson of George and Ann (Crerar) Mackay (esp. in the baptismal register of the English Chapel in Perth and OPRs [Old Parish Registers] of Thurso); *The Scottish Genealogist* 41 (1994): 15-19, 21; Angus Mackay, *The Book of Mackay* (1906), pp. 310-12; Sir J.B. Paul, *The Scots Peerage*, 9 vols. (1904–14; hereafter *SP*), 2: 340 (Sinclair of Caithness), 6: 572-75 (Stewart of Orkney) (courtesy of F.H. Pollard; note that James Mackay of Ga. left both descendants there and the above, probably illegitimate, son in Scotland)

3. (from **James V**) **Francis Stewart**, 1st Earl of Bothwell = Margaret Douglas (*RD500*, p. 30)

4. **Elizabeth Stewart** = Hon. James Cranstoun

5. **Isabella Cranstoun** = Sir Gilbert Eliott, 1st Bt.

6. **Sir William Eliott**, 2nd Bt. = Margaret Murray

7. **Sir Gilbert Eliott**, 3rd Bt. = Eleanor Elliot, a cousin

8. **Sir John Eliott**, 4th Bt. = Mary Andrews

9. **Sir Francis Eliott**, 5th Bt. = Euphan Dickson

10. **Sir William Eliott**, 6th Bt. = Mary Russell

11. **Sir William Francis Eliott**, 7th Bt. = Theresa Boswell, daughter of Sir Alexander Boswell, 1st Bt. (and Griselle or Graca Cumming), son of James Boswell of Auchinleck, the man of letters, traveler, and biographer of Samuel Johnson (see *RD500*, p. 50), and Margaret Montgomerie

12. **Alexander Boswell Eliott** = Catherine Craigie

13. **Sir Arthur Augustus Boswell Eliott**, 9th Bt. = Lilla Burbank

14. **Beatrice Maud Boswell Eliott** of N.Y. = Frank Vincent Burton, Jr. Their daughter, Leila Eliott Burton, b. 1925, travel author, = (1) Arthur Twining Hadley II (2) Yvor Hyatt Smitter (3) William C. Musham (4) Henry Robinson Luce III, b. 1925, vice-president of Time, Inc., and publisher of *Fortune* and *Time*, son of Henry Robinson Luce, Jr., founder of Time, Inc., and Lila Hotz.

Sources: The Dowager Lady Eliott of Stobs and Sir Arthur Eliott, 11th Baronet of Stobs, *The Elliots: The Story of a Border Clan* (1974), pp. 77-95, 102-12, 116-19, and *Burke's Peerage*, 106th ed. (1999), pp. 969-71 (Eliott of Stobs); *SP* 2: 593-94, 168-72 (Cranstoun, Stewart of Bothwell), plus *Burke's Landed Gentry*, 18th ed., vol. 3 (1972; hereafter *BLG* 18:3), p. 80 (Boswell); *Who's Who of American Women* (L.E.B. Hadley) and *Who's Who in America* (H.R. Luce III) (courtesy of William Elliott)

5. (from **James II, King of Scots**, d. 1460) **William Cunyngham**, 6th Earl of Glencairn = Janet Gordon (*RD500*, p. 68)

6. **Margaret Cunyngham** = Sir Lachlan MacLean of Duart

7. **Beathag MacLean** = Hector Maclaine of Lochbuie

8. **Lachlan Maclaine** of Lochbuie = **9. Margaret MacLean**, daughter of **8. Hector MacLean** of Torloisk (and Janet MacLean), son of **7. Lachlan MacLean** of Torloisk (and Marian Campbell), son of Sir Lachlan MacLean of Duart and **Margaret Cunyngham, 6.** above

9. **Hector Maclaine** of Lochbuie = Margaret Campbell of Lochnell

10. **Mary Maclaine** = Lachlan MacLean of Kingairloch

11. **Hugh MacLean** of Kingairloch = Elizabeth McLachlan of McLachlan

12. **Hector MacLean** of Kingairloch, of Pictou, N.S. 1803–4 = Elizabeth Fraser

13. **Elizabeth McLachlan MacLean** = George McKay (Mackay)

14. **George Alexander McKay** of Mass. = Christina McMillan. Their daughter, Elizabeth Florence McKay, married Osborne Maguire and left a daughter, Edna Beatrix Maguire, wife of Harold Goodwin and mother of Shirley Elizabeth Goodwin, former NEHGS trustee and wife of Exxon director and U.S. Treasury Under-Secretary Jack Franklin Bennett (b. 1924)

Sources: Research of Shirley Goodwin Bennett, based in part on the N.S. baptismal record and Mass. VRs for G.A. McKay; *BLG* 18:3, pp. 590 (MacLean of Kingairloch, to Mrs. McKay), 583 (Maclaine of Lochbuie); J.P. MacLean, *A History of the Clan MacLean* (1889; hereafter *Clan MacLean*), pp. 91-137, 240-42, 261-63, 312-13; *SP* 4:239-43 (Cunyngham of Glencairn)

11. (from **Robert III, King of Scots**, d. 1406) **William Kennedy** of N.C. (brother of *Archibald Kennedy*, ca. 1685–1763, of N.Y., British colonial official) = Mary ---- (*RD500*, p. 87)

Sources: A Cox-Kennedy Bible (printed by John Baskett of Oxford, 1728) at the North Carolina State Archives contains the entry: "William Kennedy, son of Alexander Kennedy and Anna his wife was born at Cullzan [Culzean] Aireshire, Scotland ye 1st day of the 5th mo. 1690 and departed this life the 6th day of the 6th mo. 1749 Johnston Co." Also included are death dates for Walter, "son of William and Mary Kennedy" (1 5mo. 1750) and of Walter's wife, Sarah (Fellow) Kennedy. See also Brig. Gen. John T. Kennedy, *The Kennedy Family: A Brief Record of the Kennedy Family of Lenoir and Wayne Counties, North Carolina* (1963) (courtesy of Miriam Elliott Bertelson)

8. (from **Edward III**) **Elizabeth Gascoigne** = Sir George Talboys (*RD500*, p. 183)

9. **Elizabeth Talboys** = Sir Christopher Willoughby

10. **Anne Willoughby** = Edmund Hall, son of Francis Hall and Elizabeth Wingfield (*RD500*, p. 289)

11. **Anne Hall** = George Mackworth

12. **Sir Thomas Mackworth**, 1st Bt. = 12. **Elizabeth Hall**, daughter of 11. **Henry Hall** (and Jane Neale), son of Edmund Hall and **Anne Willoughby, 10.** above

13. **Sir Henry Mackworth**, 2nd Bt. = 13. **Mary Hopton**, daughter of 12. **Robert Hopton** (and Jane Kemeys), son of Sir Arthur Hopton and 11. **Rachel Hall**, daughter of Edmund Hall and **Anne Willoughby, 10.** above

14. **Margaret Mackworth** = (as his 2nd w.) Philip Yonge

15. **Mackworth Yonge** = Margaret Bourne

16. **Robert Yonge**, of S.C. by 1723 = (1) Mrs. Hannah Eve (2) Mrs. Elizabeth Elliott Butler D'Arques.

Sources: Research of Brice McAdoo Clagett, to appear in the forthcoming *Seven Centuries: Ancestors for Twenty Generations of John Brice de Treville Clagett and Ann Calvert Brooke Clagett* and based in part on W.B. Edgar and N.L. Bailey, eds., *Biographical Directory of the South Carolina House of Representatives*, vol. 2 (1977; hereafter *BDSCHR* 2), pp. 740-41 (Robert Yonge); Egmond, Shropshire, parish registers and Edward Yonge, *The Yonges of Caynton, Edgmond, Shropshire* (1969, hereafter *Yonges of Caynton*), pp. 98-99, 107-9, 225-29 (where Robert the immigrant is said to have "probably died young"); Thomas Blore, *The History and Antiquities of the County of Rutland* (1811), p. 128, and G.E. Cokayne, *Complete Baronetage*, vol. 1 (1900), p. 122 (Mackworth); Rev. A.R. Maddison, *Lincolnshire Pedigrees* (hereafter *Linc. Ped.*), vol. 2 (Harleian Society Publications, Visitations Series [henceforth *HSPVS*], vol. 51, 1903), pp. 442-43 (Hall), vol. 3 (*HSPVS*, vol. 52, 1904), pp. 946-47 (Talboys); Sir Egerton Brydges, ed., *Collins' Peerage of England*, 9 vols (1812; hereafter *Collins*), 6: 610 (Willoughby).

11. (from **Edward I**) **Sir George West** = Elizabeth Morton (*RD500*, p. 247)

12. **William West**, 10th Baron Delaware (de la Warr) = Elizabeth Strange

13. **Jane West** = Sir Thomas Wenman

14. **Richard Wenman**, 1st Viscount Wenman = Agnes Fermor

15. **Mary Wenman** = Sir Martin Lister

16. **Agnes Lister** = Sir William Hartopp

17. **Dorothy Hartopp** = William Yonge, son of Philip Yonge above and his 1st wife Anne Archer

18. **Francis Yonge**, chief justice of S.C. = (1) Elizabeth Fletcher; (2) Lydia ----

Sources: Research of Brice McAdoo Clagett, based in part on *TG* 10 (1989, published 1994): 55 (Yonge, by Paul C. Reed); C.A. Langley, *South Carolina Deed Abstracts, 1719-1772*, vol. 1 (1983), p. 207 (F. to R. Yonge); Kenneth Coleman and C.S. Gurr, eds., *Dictionary of Georgia Biography*, vol. 2 (1983), pp. 1102-3 (Henry Yonge, son of Francis), which cites P.K. Yonge, "The Yonge Family in America," tss. at the Univ. of Florida, Gainesville, and *Yonges of Edgmond,* pp. 98-99, 109-12, 133-45, viii-x; John Nichols, *The History and Antiquities of the County of Leicester*, vol. 2, part 1 (1795; hereafter *Nichols*), p. 267 (Hartopp); Joseph Foster, *Pedigrees of the County Families of Yorkshire*, vol. 1 (1874; hereafter *PCF Yorkshire*), Lister pedigree; *The Herald and Genealogist* 2 (1865): 521-23, and G.E. Cokayne, *The Complete Peerage*, 14 vols. (1910–59; repr. 1987; hereafter *CP*), 12, part 2: 489-90 (Wenman); 4: 158-59 (Delaware/de la Warr); W.H. Rylands, ed., *Visitations of Hampshire, 1530, 1575, and 1622–34* (*HSPVS*, vol. 64, 1913), p. 59 (West).

4. (from **Edward I**) **Elizabeth de Verdun** = Henry de Ferrers, 2nd Baron Ferrers of Groby (*RD500*, p. 248)

5. **Elizabeth de Ferrers** = David Strathbogie, 2nd Earl of Atholl

6. **Elizabeth Strathbogie** = Sir John Scrope

7. **Elizabeth Scrope** = Thomas Clarell

8. **Elizabeth Clarell** = Sir Richard Fitzwilliam
9. **Catherine Fitzwilliam** = Sir John Skipwith
10. **Sir William Skipwith** = (1) Elizabeth Tyrwhit, daughter of Sir William Tyrwhit and Anne Constable (*RD500*, p. 340) (2) Alice Dymoke (*RD500*, p. 213)
11. (maternity uncertain – probably Elizabeth Tyrwhit) **Dorothy Skipwith** = Andrew Gedney
12. **Mary Gedney** = George Ashby
13. **George Ashby** = Elizabeth Bennet
14. **John Ashby** = Elizabeth Thorowgood
15. **John Ashby** of S.C. (assemblyman 1698-1702) = Constantia Broughton

Sources: *BDSCHR* 2, pp. 41-42 (John Ashby "Jr."); H.A.M. Smith, *The Baronies of South Carolina* (1931), pp. 149-56, and *Nichols*, vol. 3, part 1 (1800), p. 298 (Ashby); *Linc. Ped.*, vol. 2 (*HSPVS*, vol. 51, 1903), p. 396 (Gedney), vol. 3 (*HSPVS*, vol. 52, 1904), pp. 889-90, 895 (Skipwith), 1019 (Tyrwhit), plus J.B. Price and Harry Hollingsworth, *The Price, Blakemore, Hamblen, Skipwith and Allied Families* (1992), pp. 21-25 (on the maternity of Sir William Skipwith's daughters esp.); *PCF Yorkshire*, vol. 1 (1874), Fitzwilliam and Clarell pedigrees; J.W. Clay, *The Extinct and Dormant Peerages of the Northern Counties of England* (1913), p. 203 (Scrope); *CP* 1: 308-9 (Scrope, Strathbogie, Ferrers) (courtesy of Bruce Harris Sinkey)

19. (from **Henry I, King of England**, d. 1135) **Lewys Morgan** = ---- ---- (*RD500*, p. 404)
20. **Evan Lewis** = ---- ----
21. **John Evans** of Radnor, Pa. = Delilah ---- (children bore the surname Jones). His brother **Edward Evans** also immigrated to Pa. but left no NDTPS. The other John Evans of Pa. (in *RD500*, p. 309), husband of Mary Hughes, was of Merion and Radnor.

Sources: T.A. Glenn, *Welsh Founders of Pennsylvania*, vol. 1 (1911; repr. 1970), pp. 131-32, 165-66, as noticed by Christos Christou,

Jr., who also noted that John Morgan of Pa. (*RD500*, p. 405) married Sarah Jones, daughter of the above John Evans and Delilah. Their son, John Morgan, Jr., married Sarah Evans, daughter of the other John Evans (of Merion and Radnor) and Mary Hughes.

15. (from **Henry I, King of France**, d. 1060) **Sir Thomas Grenville** = Isabella Gilbert (*RD500*, p. 419)

16. **Sir Roger Grenville** = Margaret Whitleigh

17. **Jane Grenville** = Edmund Specott

18. **Jane Specott** = William Snelling

19. **Thomas Snelling** = Joan Elford

20. **William Snelling** of Mass. = Margery (or Margaret) Stagg. William's brother, John Snelling, married Frances Hele (*RD500*, p. 268) and left a son, *John Snelling* (bp. 1624/5), very probably the immigrant to Mass. of that name. Scott C. Steward, former editor of *NEXUS*, is a descendant of (Dr.) William Snelling and has traced various notable descendants, including Scott's own great-great-uncle, Robert Livingston Beeckman (1866–1935), governor of R.I., 1914-20.

Sources: *Register* 52 (1898): 342-46, reprinted in *English Origins of New England Families*, 2nd ser. (1985), 3: 274-78; J.L. Vivian, *The Visitations of the County of Devon* (1895; hereafter *VD*), pp. 694 (Snelling), 706 (Specott), and *The Visitations of Cornwall* (1887), p. 191 (Grenville) (courtesy of Scott C. Steward)

I wish to note also that various correspondents, in addition to Mrs. Bennett above, have sent outlines of *RD*s for Atlantic-Canadian Scots or seventeenth-century French immigrants to Québec. Those of the former with notable descendants in the U.S. may be treated in future editions of *RD500*. *RD* immigrants to Québec are a special interest of Professor Roger Lawrence, formerly of St. Anselm College in Manchester, N.H., a co-founder of the American-Canadian Genealogical Society, whose further work on this subject is eagerly awaited.

III.

In addition to developing *RDs* for new immigrants, correspondents have also brought to my attention various "improved" or "downgraded" lines that can also be outlined as above. "Improved" descents include those for Col. Henry, Lachlan, and John Mohr Mackintosh (McIntosh) of Mass. and R.I., R.I., and Ga. respectively; the brothers Neil and Allan MacLean of Conn.; and Joseph Bickley and Mrs. Mary Butler Underwood of Va., as follows:

4. (from **Robert III**) **John Kennedy**, 2nd Baron Kennedy = Elizabeth Montgomery (*RD500*, p. 87)

5. **Janet Kennedy** = Sir Alexander Gordon of Lochinvar

6. **Janet Gordon** = Lachlan Mackintosh of Mackintosh

7. **William Mackintosh** of Mackintosh = Margaret Ogilvie of Deskford

8. **Lachlan Mackintosh** of Mackintosh = Agnes Mackenzie (*RD500*, p. 109). They were great-grandparents of *Col. Henry* (of Mass. and R.I.), and great-great-great-grandparents of *Lachlan* (of R.I.) and *John Mohr* *Mackintosh (McIntosh)* (courtesy of William Elliott, whose wife is descended from John Mohr Mackintosh/ McIntosh of Ga.)

Sources: *BLG* 18, 1 (1965): 479-80 and Alexander M. Mackintosh, *The Mackintoshes and Clan Chattan* (1903), pp. 106-92; *SP* 5: 102-4 (Gordon of Kenmure), 2:448-50, 452-60 (Kennedy of Cassillis).

5. (from **James II**) **William Cunyngham**, 6th Earl of Glencairn = Janet Gordon (see above and *RD500*, p. 68)

6. **Margaret Cunyngham** = Sir Lachlan MacLean of Duart, son of Hector MacLean of Duart and Janet Campbell (*RD500*, p. 71)

7. **Lachlan MacLean** of Torloisk = (3) Marian MacDonald of Clanranald

8. **Mary MacLean** = John Garbh MacLean of Drimnin

9. **Catherine MacLean** = Hugh (Ewen) MacLean of Balliphetrish

10. **Catherine MacLean** = Allan MacLean of Grisiboll (*RD500*, p. 71). They were parents of *Neil* and *Allan MacLean (McLean)* of Conn.

Sources: *The Scottish Genealogist* 36 (1989): 94-95 (MacLean of Balliphetrish); *Clan MacLean*, pp. 91-137, 312, 302; *SP* 4: 239-43 (Glencairn) (courtesy of Thomas Frederick Gede and Shirley Goodwin Bennett).

10. (from **Edward I**) **Elizabeth Devereux** = Sir Richard Corbet (*RD500*, p. 277)

11. **Catherine Corbet** = Robert Onslow

12. **Edward Onslow** = Anne Houghton

13. **Roger Onslow** = Margaret Poyner

14. **Richard Onslow** = Catherine Harding

15. **Cecily Onslow** = Sir Humphrey Winch

16. **Onslow Winch** = Judith Burgoyne (*RD500*, p. 383). They were great-grandparents of *Joseph Bickley* of Va.

Sources: *TG* 10 (1989, published 1994): 55 (outline of above, by Paul C. Reed); F.A. Blaydes, ed., *Visitations of Bedfordshire, 1566, 1582, and 1634* (*HSPVS*, vol. 19, 1884), p. 199 (Winch); Sir John MacLean, *Parochial and Family History of the Deanery of Trigg Manor*, vol. 3 (1879; hereafter *Trigg* 3), pp. 398-99 (Onslow); A.E.B. Corbet, *The Family of Corbet*, vol. 2 (1920), chart at end.

7. (from **Henry I, King of England**, d. 1135) **Sir Henry de Chambernon** = Dionisia English (*RD500*, p. 396)

8. **Richard de Champernowne** = Joan, possibly an illegitimate daughter of Richard (Plantagenet), King of the Romans (*RD500*, p. 317) by Joan de Vautort or Valletort

9. **Richard de Champernowne** = Elizabeth Valletort

10. **Sir Thomas Champernowne** = Eleanor de Rohart

11. **Sir Richard Champernowne** = (1) Alice Astley (2) Katherine Daubeny

12. (by 2) **John Champernowne** = Margaret Hamley

13. **Richard Champernowne** = Elizabeth Reynell

14. **Elizabeth Champernowne** = William Fortescue (matrilineal great-great-great-grandparents of *Mrs. Margaret Wyatt Allyn* of Conn.; this outline is a considerable revision of p. 396).

12. (by 1) **Joan Champernowne** = James Chudleigh (*RD500*, p. 451)

13. **James Chudleigh** = (1) ---- ---- (2) Radigond FitzWalter

14. (by 1) **John Chudleigh** = Margaret ---- (not Thomasine Kirkham), ancestors of *Mrs. Mary Butler Underwood* of Va. (these last two generations correct data on p. 451)

Sources: Research of Todd A. Farmerie, sent via the Internet and derived in part from *Devon and Cornwall Notes and Queries* 18 (1934–35): 108-12, 19 (1936-37): 26-29 (Champernowne), 12 (1922–23): 340-42, 24 (1950–51): 229-30 (Chudleigh), and *Trigg* 3, p. 427 (addendum to vol. 1, p. 531, line 14).

Several descents have also, unfortunately, been downgraded. Following J.S. Roskell, Linda Clark and Carole Rawcliffe, *The History of Parliament: The House of Commons, 1386–1421*, vol. 2 (1992), pp. 653-54, and correspondence with Dr. Clark and others, Brice McAdoo Clagett in his forthcoming *Seven Centuries: Ancestors for Twenty Generations of John Brice de Treville Clagett and Ann Calvert Brooke Clagett* offers a major revision in the royal descent of Rev. Peter Bulkeley, his two sisters and two nieces (Mrs. Elizabeth Bulkeley Whittingham Haugh, Mrs. Martha Bulkeley Mellowes, Mrs. Olive Welby Farwell and Mrs. Elizabeth St. John Whiting), all of Mass.; his great-nephew Rev. Thomas James (Jr.) (first minister of East Hampton, not Southampton, L.I.); and Henry Corbin of Va. (*RD500*, pp. 210-12). Robert Corbet (1383–1420) of Moreton Corbet, Shropshire, married *not* Margaret Malory, but Margaret ----, who later married Sir William Malory (ca. 1386–1445). Thus the "best" *RD*s for the Bulkeleys and Corbin via their shared Charlton-Mainwaring ancestry is from Henry II, King of England, d. 1189, via a Longespee-derived great-great-grandson,

The Royal Descents of 500 Immigrants

Alan la Zouche, 1st Baron Zouche of Ashby (*RD500*, pp. 345, 348, 350, 356, 358, 360) and Charltons, as per lines 30-31, 203, and 223 in F.L. Weis, W.L. Sheppard, Jr., and David Faris, *Ancestral Roots of Certain American Colonists Who Came to America Before 1700*, 7th ed. (1992; hereafter *AR7*). For Mrs. Farwell's non-Bulkeley-derived Edward I descent, and Corbin's descent from King John, see #s 44 and 51 of my "Genealogical Thoughts" column below.

Dorothy Clark, Richard Evans, Barry C. Noonan, and Neil D. Thompson all brought to my attention the fine Haslewood pedigree in Rev. Francis· Haslewood, *The Genealogy of the Family of Haslewood* (1875), pp. 3-14, and *The Genealogist* 1 (1877): 43-54, wherein Alice Haslewood, wife of Francis Bernard (ca. 1528–1602) of Abingdon, Northamptonshire -- grandmother of immigrants Col. William and Richard Bernard of Va. (the latter an ancestor of H.M. Queen Elizabeth the Queen Mother; see *RD500*, p. 468), and great-great-grandmother of Sir Francis Bernard, 1st Bt., colonial governor of N.J. and Mass. (see *RD500*, p. 144) -- is shown (pp. 8-9, 13; 48-49, 53) to be a daughter of John Haselwood and Katherine Marmion -- not Alice Gascoigne, who married John and Katherine's son Edward. Thus the "best" *RD* for the three Bernard kinsmen is from Edward I via a great-great-grandson, Hugh Stafford, 2nd Earl of Stafford (*RD500*, pp. 224, 291), Nevilles, Earls of Westmor(e)-land, Scropes, Barons Scrope of Bolton, and Bernards, as covered in Weis, Sheppard and Faris, *The Magna Charta Sureties, 1215*, 4th ed. (1991), line 46, and *AR7*, lines 8-10.

Richard Evans also brought to my attention *The Pouletts of Hinton St. George* (1976) by Colin G. Winn, from which we learn (p. 23, tabular pedigree opposite p. 120) that Rachel Paulet – wife of Sir Philip de Carteret (*RD500*, p. 220) and matrilineal great-grand-mother of Philip and Peter de Carteret, colonial governors of N.J. and N.C. respectively -- was a daughter (by Ysabel Perrin) of George Paulet, younger son not of Lord Thomas Poulett and Mary Moore, but of Sir Hugh Paulet (d. 1568) of Hinton St. George and Philippa Pollard. This last was a daughter of Sir Lewis Pollard of Girleston, Devon, and Agnes Hext, daughter of Thomas Hext and Joan Fortescue (*RD500*, p. 444); see *VD*, pp. 598 (Pollard), 484 (Hext), and *AR7*, line 246 E. Thus the "best" *RD* for the de Carteret governors becomes a line from Hugh Capet, King of France, d. 996.

The Royal Descents of 500 Immigrants

Additionally the wife of Sir Ham(p)den Paulet, great-great-great-grandfather of Philip Dumaresq of Mass., was Margaret More (P.W. Hasler, ed., *The History of Parliament: The House of Commons, 1558–1603* [1981], pp. 188-89).

IV.

In addition to new, revised or disproved *RD*s that have appeared in journal articles or in *Ancestors of American Presidents* -- and in addition to a large correspondence partly reported above -- one new compendium and several recent articles merit some discussion. The first of a projected series of *RD* studies by David Faris (*Plantagenet Ancestry of Seventeenth-Century Colonists: The Descent from the Later Plantagenet Kings of England, Henry III, Edward I, Edward II, and Edward III, of Emigrants from England and Wales to the North American Colonies Before 1701*) was published by Genealogical Publishing Company of Baltimore in June 1996. This work, with dates, places, and biographical details, superseded part of the *Ancestral Roots* series and expanded considerably on many of my outlines, pp. 115-93, 204-88, 295 especially, in *RD500*; a second edition of Dr. Faris's work, published by NEHGS, appeared in December 1999. The first edition included one "new" seventeenth-century immigrant of keen interest -- Mrs. Mary Johanna Somerset Lowther Smith of Md., wife of Col. John Lowther and Richard Smith of Calvert Co. Mary Johanna appears in *Collins* 1: 233 and Marquis of Ruvigny and Raineval, *The Plantagenet Roll of the Blood Royal: The Clarence Volume* (1905; rep. 1994), p. 28 (table XXXV); for her marriages and early Maryland progeny see H.W. Newman, *To Maryland from Overseas* (1982), p. 161, and *Maryland Genealogies: A Consolidation of Articles from The Maryland Historical Magazine*, vol. 2 (1980), pp. 374-76, 378-81. Dr. Faris also identified Matthew Kempe of Gloucester Co., Va., whom I mentioned as a possible nephew of Richard Kempe, secretary and acting governor of Va. (*RD500*, pp. 222-23) as Matthew (= ---- Heyton of Greenwich, Kent), son of Sir Robert Kempe, 1st Bt., Richard's older brother, and Jane Browne; see Thomas Wotton, *The English Baronetage*, vol. 2 (1741), pp. 285-86.

646

The Royal Descents of 500 Immigrants

In *Register* 150 (1996): 180-89, David A. Macdonald showed that George Curwen of Salem, Mass. (*RD500*, p. 416) and Matthew/ Matthias Corwin of Southold, Long Island, were brothers; he suggested, however, that the earlier Curwens of Sibbertoft, Northamptonshire, should be further studied. In *Register* 150: 315-24, F.N. Craig proposed alternative parentage (Peter de Braose and Alice ----, widow of Henry Huse), but the same paternal grandparentage (with the *RD* retained), for Sir Peter de Braose (*RD500*, p. 334), husband of Joan de Percy and ancestor of immigrants Thomas Bressie, Nathaniel Browne, Edmond Hawes, and Rev. John Davenport (this last the non-conformist clergyman, author and founder of the New Haven Colony). In *Register* 150: 327-28, moreover, Lt. Gen. Herman Nickerson, Jr., showed that Stephen Hatfield and Isabel Russell (*RD500*, p. 420) died childless. Agnes Marshall, wife of Lawrence Hatfield (now known *not* to be Stephen and Isabel's son), is identified in G.W. Marshall, ed., *Visitations of the County of Nottingham, 1569 and 1614* (HSPVS, vol. 4, 1871), p. 166, but I cannot readily trace from printed sources any alternative *RD* through her, via Binghams, Leekes, or Bruses, for the immigrants Walter Norton of Charlestown, Mass. and Henry Norton of York, Me. For a likely *RD* for Gov. William Leete of Conn. (*RD500*, pp. 336-37) via Dabridgecourt, Staverton, Burgoyne, and Shute, see #51 of my "Genealogical Thoughts" column below. As to Leete's Freville and alleged Haselden descent, Mrs. Gerald (Sarah) Polkinghorne has directed me to, among other sources, *The Victoria History of . . . Cambridgeshire and the Isle of Ely*, vol. 8 (1982), pp. 57, 221, from which we learn that Robert Freville and his wife, Beatrice Haselden (whose brother William died a minor in 1537) sold their share of a Cambridgeshire manor in 1565; since the Robert Freville who was Christopher Burgoyne's father-in-law (and Leete's matrilineal great-great-grandfather) died in 1521, and his wife Rose in 1529, the husband of Beatrice Haselden is almost certainly their grandson. Thus Beatrice is a niece-in-law, not the mother, of Burgoyne's wife Thomasine.

Among lines still being explored I wish to note especially the highly probable Welsh royal descent of Mrs. Joan Price Cleeve, wife of Portland, Maine, founder George Cleeve, deputy president of "Lygonia," published in the *Cleeve/Cleaves Clearinghouse News-*

The Royal Descents of 500 Immigrants

letter, 8: 1 (Fall 1993), 13:2 (Spring 1999) and 15:1 (Fall 2000). The author of these articles, John M. Plummer, has so far developed at least two likely English *RD*s, including one through Joan's great-grandmother, Florence Clunn, wife of Thomas Pryce, that connects to *RD500*, p. 391, generation 10. Among yet unpublished disproofs, Ken Faig, Jr., has written H.L.P. Beckwith of the NEHGS Committee on Heraldry that the 1772 PCC will of Rev. Francis Fulford of Downsford, Devon, bachelor, precludes his being the father of Mrs. Mary Lovecraft of Rochester, N.Y. (*RD500*, p. 137), whose tombstone indicates that she died 14 August 1864, aged 82. Lastly I might report being told by Paul C. Reed of (1) disproof of the parentage of John Goode of Va. (*RD500*, pp. 336-37) and (2) an alternative Machell (but not Lewknor)-derived *RD* for James Cudworth of Mass. (*RD500*, p. 270).

I am delighted that *RD500* has generated, inspired or at least provided a focus for gathering and outlining a wide variety of new scholarship and a large correspondence. I also wish to invite further contributions of *RD* studies -- for future columns, for my own files (with permission, I hope, to use at will, with acknowledgment, in future editions of *RD500*), and even for submission to major journals with considerable peer review and perhaps much editorial sharpening. Research on royal descents -- our link to the feudal and ancient world -- has never been more vibrant or productive. Often a team effort, the results of such work deserve quick and wide dissemination, an effort this essay was intended to foster.

Genealogical Thoughts of Gary Boyd Roberts, #43: New — and Deleted — Immigrants of Royal Descent

In this column and the next, I shall review progress through 15 February 2000 in my ongoing revision of *The Royal Descents of 500 Immigrants* (1993), the second edition of which I hope to publish in early or mid-2002. To date I have added 40 (by late August this figure reached 80) new immigrants and deleted 10. In the next several months I shall add, or at least investigate, another 50 or so additions, and then send the manuscript to a half-dozen or more scholars for further review. Today I wish to cover briefly the 40 new immigrants to date. The 10 who have been deleted so far are Daniel and Hugh Harry of Pa., Oliver Cope, Robert Lloyd, and Dr. Thomas Wynne of Pa., Mrs. Margery Maude Fisher of Del., Mrs. Mary Fulford Lovecraft of N.Y., and Henry and Walter Norton of Me. and Mass., as per *NEXUS* 13 below (from which the preceding article was adapted), plus John Goode of Va. on the authority of Paul C. Reed. In the next column I shall review major adjustments in the royal descents of immigrants already covered in *RD500*.

Over a dozen of the forty new immigrants were discussed in my Summer 1996 *NEXUS* column (13: 124-30), updated above. These were **Countess Plater-Zyberk (Maria M. P. W. R. L. J. Wielopolska)** of Pa.; **Hon. Mrs. Joanna Freda Hare Breyer** of Mass., wife of Supreme Court Justice Stephen Gerald Breyer; **George Mackay** of Washington, D.C.; **Mrs. Beatrice Maud Boswell Eliott Burton** of N.Y.; **Mrs. Maria Jo[h]anna Somerset Lowther Smith** of Md.; the brothers **Philip** and **Thomas Nelson, Jr.,** of Mass.; **George Alexander Mackay** of Mass.; **William Kennedy** of N.C. (brother of colonial official Archibald Kennedy of N.Y.); **Rev. William Skepper/Skipper** of Mass.; **Robert** and **Francis Yonge** of S.C.; **Mrs. Elizabeth Haynes Cooke** of Mass.; **Christopher Calthorpe** of Va.; **John Ashby** of S.C.; **Mrs. Joan Price Cleeve** of

Me.; and **William Snelling** of Mass. Mrs. M. J. S. L. Smith was noted in *NEXUS* as a newly discovered immigrant treated in the 1st edition (GPC, 1996) of *Plantagenet Ancestry of Seventeenth-Century Colonists* by David Faris. Derived from the new 2nd edition (NEHGS, 1999) are **Samuel Levis** of Pa. (two of whose sisters also immigrated there; one, **Sarah Levis**, wife of Thomas **Bradshaw**, left descendants); **Kenelm Cheseldine**, atty. gen. of Md., son-in-law of Thomas Gerard of Md. and a first cousin once removed of the Marbury sisters of R.I.; and **Thomas Booth** of Va., an ancestor of dancer Ted Shawn.

Among various 20th-century immigrant descendants of recent European kings, a great-great-granddaughter of Ferdinand II, King of the Two Sicilies (d. 1859) is **Maria Immaculata Pia, Countess von Habsburg**, of N.Y., former wife of art museum curator John Howard **Dobkin** of the Cooper-Hewitt Museum, the National Academy of Design, and Historic Hudson Valley (an immigrant I culled from reviewing a new compendium by Daniel Willis, formerly Brewer-Ward, *The Descendants of Louis XIII* [1999]). Data on advertising executive **David Mackenzie Ogilvy**, sometime of N.Y., and several other immigrants have emerged from a recent buying spree of biographies, mostly remaindered at bookshops put out of business by Internet competition. Ogilvy's mother was a first cousin of Dame Rebecca West, novelist and lover of H. G. Wells (for their son Anthony West see column #49 below); Ogilvy's father was the great-grandson of a Mackenzie baronet descended from James V, King of Scots. Noted pediatrician and educator **Josiah Ralph Patrick Wedgwood** of Seattle was a grandson of the 1st Baron Wedgwood and great-great-grandson of a brother of Mrs. Charles Robert Darwin (and great-uncle of composer Ralph Vaughan Williams). The recent Wedgwood clan, master potters of Etruria and cousins of the Cecils of Salisbury, are descended from George Plantagenet, 1st Duke of Clarence (brother of Edward IV and Richard III), and are treated in a supplement to Ruvigny's Clarence volume (published in the later Essex volume) of *The Plantagenet Roll of the Blood Royal*. **Penelope Eleanor Elphinstone-Dalrymple** of Mass., whose 2nd husband was Sandwich historian Russell **Lovell**, Jr., was the daughter of a 7th baronet and a descendant of Anne Plantagenet, sister of Edward IV and Richard III, via St. Leger,

Manners, Constable, Babthorpe, Cholmley, Strickland, Cochrane, Heron and Heron-Maxwell. **Leighton Wilson** of Ga. is one of the new immigrant discoveries of Brice McAdoo Clagett and will appear, along with twenty or more other immigrants of royal descent, in Brice's forthcoming multi-volume work covering twenty generations of his children's ancestry. Wilson's maternal grandfather, Basil Wood of Bristol (uncle of a **Leighton Wood**, auditor and solicitor-general of Va), is also treated in the Essex volume of Ruvigny's *Plantagenet Roll*.

The actor brothers **Ralph** and **Joseph Fiennes**, known respectively for *The English Patient* and *Shakespeare in Love*, are covered in the splendid new 1999 *Burke's Peerage* in a junior branch of the barons Saye and Sele. Their descent from James IV, King of Scots is through viscounts Harberton, Colleys (including a great-uncle of Wellington), and earls of Abercorn. Among several ancestors of the children of former NEHGS trustee Shirley Goodwin Bennett who have been traced by Mrs. Bennett and Paul C. Reed of Salt Lake City, is **Robert Baillie** of Ga., son-in-law of John Mohr Mackintosh of Ga., and descended via Bertrams of Nisbet, Murrays of Cardon, and Flemings of Gilmerton from the 1st earl of Wigtown, great-grandson of James IV. **Patrick Falconer** of Conn. and N.J., grandson-in-law of Gov. Theophilus Eaton of the New Haven Colony and Mrs. Anne Lloyd Yale Eaton of Conn., was the great-grandson of a Douglas of Glenbervie, descended from the earls of Angus and Robert III. A first cousin twice removed of Patrick was **Alexander Falconer** of Md., nephew of the wife of Quaker apologist Robert Barclay and husband of a Duvall kinswoman of President Truman and the Duchess of Windsor.

I first suggested the royal descent of **Mrs. Elizabeth Mansfield Wilson** of Boston, wife of Rev. John Wilson and an ancestress of President W. H. Taft, in my bibliography of early Middlesex County testators in the July 1999 *Register*. Elizabeth's siblings **John Mansfield** and **Mrs. Anne Mansfield Keayne Cole** also immigrated to Massachusetts but left no known or traceable descendants beyond immediate progeny. Research on this line was undertaken by John C. Brandon of Columbia, S.C. and a joint article by him, Robert Charles Anderson, and perhaps others will probably appear in a future issue of the *Register*. The humorist

The Royal Descents of 500 Immigrants

P. G. Wodehouse, sometime of New York, was the great-great-grandson of a 5th baronet (the head of the family is now earl of Kimberley) descended via Cottons and Howards from Surrey the poet, dukes of Norfolk and Buckingham, earls of Northumberland, Sir Henry "Hotspur" Percy, and Edward III. Wodehouse (whose *RD* was first brought to my attention by Robert Battle of Tacoma, Wash.) and Aldous Huxley (see below) are both covered in the new *American National Biography* (24 vols., 1999). Royal official **Thomas Lechmere** of Mass. (for whom the subway stop and late store chain were ultimately named) was descended via Sandys, Bulkeley, and Savage from the Somersets, earls of Worcester (later dukes of Beaufort), who were patrilineally Plantagenets through one illegitimacy and one legitimation. This line was first brought to my attention by Davida Symonds of the NEHGS advisory council. Hon. **Mrs. Cynthia Burke Roche Burden Cary** of Newport, R.I., a great-aunt of the late Diana, Princess of Wales, and matrilineal great-grandmother of the actor Oliver Platt, was a daughter of the 3rd Baron Fermoy. In addition to sharing the New England and mid-Atlantic ancestry of Princes William and Henry of Wales, Mrs. Cary was also descended from Edward III via Boothby, Curzon, Vernon, Ludlow, Vaughan or Grey, Touchet/Audley, Holand, and Constance Plantagenet, daughter of Edmund of Langley, 1st Duke of York.

 Barbara Mitford, first wife of Rev. Hawte **Wyatt** of Va., has been the subject of much study by Thomas S. Erwin of Raleigh, N.C. Her father Philip was almost certainly the son of John and Barbara (Lawson) Mitford of Seghill, Northumberland, the former descended from Widdringtons, a junior Percy line, "Hotspur" again, and Edward III. **Lydia M. Latrobe** of N.Y., wife of engineer and steamboat builder Nicholas J. **Roosevelt**, was the daughter of the architect and civil engineer Benjamin Henry Latrobe (1764–1820) and his first wife Lydia Sellon (who died in England), subject of an unpublished typescript by a former NEHGS colleague, Henry B. Hoff, that traces Lydia's descent through Speir, Castillion, St. John, Scrope, Neville, Stafford, de Audley and de Clare, to Edward I.

 I treated the ancestry of **Aldous Leonard Huxley**, of California after 1937, author of *Brave New World*, in *NEXUS* 16 (1999): 72-73. A nephew of novelist Mrs. Humphry Ward, a great-nephew of poet and literary critic Matthew Arnold, Huxley was descended via Penrose, Vinicombe, Ford, and Chudleigh from the Fortescues (later earls), Chichesters (later baronets), and Bourchiers, barons FitzWarin and earls of Bath, from Thomas of Woodstock, youngest son of Edward III. Henry Hoff has also undertaken considerable work on the ancestry of **Mrs. Abigail Brewster Burr** of Conn. (Henry is descended from Roosevelts and Latrobes, but from only a *possible*, and perhaps doubtful, younger sister of Mrs. Burr -- Sarah, wife of Jonathan Smith of Smithtown). Abigail, her possible sister Sarah, and their brother John (whose later history is unknown) were children of Rev. Nathaniel Brewster of Brookhaven, L.I. (husband secondly, almost certainly, of Sarah Ludlow) by his first wife, ---- Reymes, daughter of John and Frances (----) Reymes, granddaughter of William Reymes and Anne Evans, and great-granddaughter of William Reymes and Mary Payne, this last a daughter of Thomas Payne and Elizabeth Boleyn, first cousin of Queen Anne Boleyn. Both of Elizabeth Boleyn's parents were descendants of Edward I; her father via Bohun and Butler, her mother via Seagrave, Mowbray, Welles, and Tempest.

Thomas Danvers of Pa., husband of a Truxton and great-grandfather of NEHGS trustee Jayne S. Huntington, has been discovered by Jayne and Maryan Egan-Baker to descend from a younger branch of the Danverses of Shepshed, Leicestershire, from Cokes of Melbourne and Babingtons of Gisburne Hall (ancestors of evangelical leader Thomas Babington). Maternal ancestors of these Babingtons include Beaumonts, Suttons/Dudleys, Sancha de Ayala, and Staffords descended from Edward I. The 40th new immigrant I have added to date is **Gov. Thomas Greene** of Md., whose descent appears in line 16E of the new 5th edition of *Magna Charta Sureties* by Weis, the late W. L. Sheppard, and Beall. Greene's father was a third cousin of Margaret Sandys of Va., wife of Sir Francis Wyatt, colonial gov. of Va., brother of Rev. Hawte Wyatt named above.

Genealogical Thoughts of Gary Boyd Roberts, #44:

Some Changes in Royal Descents, 1993–2000

Last week I discussed forty new and ten deleted immigrants of royal descent -- part of my progress through mid-February 2000 on the ongoing revision, or extension to *RD600*, of *The Royal Descents of 500 Immigrants* (1993). This week I shall review some of the changes or additions to immigrants and lines I covered in 1993. Firstly among additions I should note the several hundred references to the second edition of *Plantagenet Ancestry of Seventeenth-Century Colonists* by David Faris (NEHGS, 1999), an authoritative and essential work that outlines, with known dates, places, and often parliamentary or military service, most descents from Kings Henry III, Edward I, or Edward III for all but a handful of the 150 or so 17th-century immigrants with such ancestry that I treated in 1993. For *RD600* I have also included even more near kinsmen -- usually siblings, nephews or first or second cousins of immigrants -- who also came to the colonies but left no notable descendants treated in printed sources (*NDTPS*) that I can find. Such immigrants include the sisters Lady Susan Clinton Humphrey and Lady Arbella Clinton Johnson, both of Mass., and Paul and Dannett Abney of Virginia.

Changes or additions to the first 20 pages consist largely of new husbands for actresses Catherine Oxenberg (producer Robert J. Evans and actor Casper Robert Van Dien) and Brooke Shields (tennis champion Andre Agassi), and 1996 death dates for writer Jessica Mitford, novelist Caroline Blackwood (Lady Caroline Maureen Hamilton-Temple-Blackwood Freud Citkowitz Lowell) and Pamela Harriman. Between pp. 60-115 most of my changes have been Scottish, and I have been guided in many of them by Andrew B. W. MacEwen of Stockton Springs, Maine. Douglas Robinson of N.Y., a great-grandfather of political columnists Joseph and Stewart Alsop, was descended from James IV, King of Scots, via lords Elphinstone, Fleming, and Livingston, Bruce of Airth, Innes of Edingight, Duff of Craigston, and Robinson of Gask and Clermiston. Siblings of two of Robinson's great-great-grandparents were grandparents themselves of Catherine Gordon, Mrs. John Byron, mother of George Gordon Byron, 6th Baron Byron, the poet.

In addition to "improved" Robinson, MacLean (McLean) and Mackintosh (McIntosh) descents (for these last see the preceding article, updated from *NEXUS* 13), I eliminated the section of descents from Edward III of England and his great-granddaughter Joan Beaufort, Dowager Queen of Scotland, and her second husband Sir James Stewart, "Black Knight of Lorne." For each of these lines I substituted a descent from either Robert III, King of Scots (d. 1406), or his father, Robert II (d. 1390). I also eliminated, at Andrew MacEwen's suggestion, all descents from Princess Annabella Stewart, daughter of James I and wife of George Gordon, 2nd Earl of Huntly, except through her daughter Isabel, wife of William Hay, 3rd Earl of Erroll. Eliminated firstly, then, is the line from Elizabeth Gordon, wife of William Keith, 2nd Earl Marischal, to Wernher von Braun and his wife, of Alabama (also descended from the Countess of Erroll and from Princess Annabella's sister Joan/Jean, wife of James Douglas, 1st Earl of Morton). As outlined in the preceding article, the Mackintoshes (McIntoshes) -- Henry of Mass. and R.I., Lachlan of R.I., and John Mohr of Ga. -- were descended from Robert II via lords Kennedy, Gordons of Lochinvar, and Mackintoshes of Mackintosh, Borlum, or Knocknagel. Governor John Cranston of R.I. and James Veatch of Md. were descended from Robert III via Douglas, earls of Angus, lords Hay of Yester, and Stewarts of Traquair (I also note Andrew MacEwen's doubts about the immediate ancestry of Gov. Cranston, reported in *NEXUS* 11 [1994]: 41 and *Notable Kin* 2 [1999]: 193-94). Chemist and educator John MacLean (1771–1814) of N.J. and his first cousin, Alexander McLeod (MacLeod) (1774–1833), noted Reformed Presbyterian clergyman, were descendants of Robert III via Douglas, earls of Douglas, Stewarts, earls of Atholl (and Dowager Queen Joan Beaufort), Gordons, earls of Huntly, Campbells, earls of Argyll, and MacLeans of Duart, Coll, Drimnacross, and Borreray. Thomas Gordon, Chief Justice of N.J., and his cousin, Mrs. Isabel Burnet Montgomery of N.J., were descended from Robert III via Douglas, earls of Angus, Douglas of Glenbervie, then Burnet of Leys and Gordon of Pitlurg or Forbes of Monymusk, Barnes, and Ballogie.

The Royal Descents of 500 Immigrants

Gov. William Burnet of N.Y., the brothers James and Thomas Dundas of Pa., and British commander James Abercromby (1706–1781) were descendants of Robert II, King of Scots, and his son Robert Stewart, 1st Duke of Albany, via Abernethy of Saltoun, Forbes of Pitsligo, and Gordon of Lesmoir (then Burnet of Leys, Dundas of Manour, or Abercromby of Glassaugh). Gov. Alexander Spotswood of Va. and colonial statesman James Logan of Pa. were descended from Robert II via Douglas of Nithsdale, Sinclair, earls of Orkney, Stewart, earls of Atholl, Arbuthnott of Arbuthnott, and Maule of Panmure and Glaster (then Morrison of Prestongrange and Spotswood of Dunipage, or Dundas of Doddington, Hume and Logan). Col. Kenneth Baillie of Ga., a great-great-great-grandfather of President Theodore Roosevelt, was descended from Robert II and his son, Robert Stewart, 1st Duke of Albany, via lords Campbell and Lorne, earls of Argyll, Stewart earls of Atholl, Mackenzie of Kintail and Coul and Baillie of Dunain.

Among descendants certainly of Edward III, King of England (d. 1377), the three governors Wests of Virginia; Harvard treasurer Herbert Pelham and his sister, Mrs. Penelope Pelham Bellingham of Mass., wife of Gov. Richard Bellingham; Mrs. Anne Humphrey Palmes Myles of Mass.; Mrs. Anne Boteler Copley of Md.; Wiseman Clagett, solicitor-general of N.H.; and Amelia Jane Byam of N.Y., wife of *Monitor* builder John Ericsson (1803–1889) were all descended from Sir Francis Knollys and his wife Catherine Cary, daughter of Mary Boleyn (sister of Queen Anne Boleyn and aunt of Elizabeth I), very likely by Henry VIII, not her husband William Cary. Evidence for this parentage -- and thus probably for several million American descendants of Henry VIII -- was presented by Anthony Hoskins in the March 1997 issue of *Genealogists' Magazine* (25: 9), pp. 345-52. Other changes in lines from Edward III or Edward I can be partly grouped together. In order to show fairly near American kinsmen, via de la Poles, of the Habsburg descendants of Anne of Bohemia and Emperor Ferdinand I, I added a "cross-reference outline" to Hastings-Morley and/or Kelke-Girlington descents for the Blakistons of Md. and William Asfordby of N.Y. As noted in *NEXUS* 13 (1996): 124-30, updated into the preceding article, the Bernards -- Col. William and Richard of Va., and Sir Francis, 1st Bt., gov. of N.J. and Mass. -- lose their Gascoigne line but are descended from Edward I via barons Scrope of Bolton and earls of Westmor[e]land, Stafford, Gloucester and Hertford; the Bulkeleys lose their line to Edward I through lack of a Malory descent but are descended from Henry II, King of England (d. 1189) via Grosvenor, Charlton, Knightley, la Zouche, and Ela, Stephen and William Longespee; and Philip de Carteret, gov. of N.J. and his brother Peter de Carteret, gov. of N.C., lose their descent from Edward I and William Paulet, 1st Marquess of Winchester, but via Paulets of Hinton St. George descend from Hugh Capet, King of France (d. 996) through Pollard, Hext, Fortescue, Beauchamp of Ryme, Mohun, FitzPiers, de Clare, and counts of Clermont, Montdidier, Roucy, and Hainault. Mrs. Olive Welby Farwell, a niece of Rev. Peter Bulkeley and his immigrant sisters, retains descent from Edward I, however, via Welby, Thimbleby, Tyrwhit, Talboys, Heron, Ogle, Grey, Mowbray and Segrave. And Bulkeley cousin Henry Corbin of Va. retains a descent from King John (see column #51 below) and from Amy de Gaveston (this last via Driby, Malory, Moton, Grimsby, Vincent [a line ancestral also to Henry and William Randolph of Va.], Faunt, and Corbin).

John Cra[y]croft of Md. loses his Disney-Ayscough-Hildyard-Hastings-Morley descent but retains a line from Edward I via Amcotts, an early Fulnetby-Dymoke marriage, and Welles, Mowbray and Segrave. A second Hastings-Morley line for William Farrar of Va. has been developed by Worth S. Anderson of Arlington, Va. Matthew Clarkson of N.Y. loses his descent from Edward I but retains a line from David I, King of Scots (d. 1153), and from a brother of Malcolm IV and William the Lion, via Hastings, Grey, Mitton, Grosvenor, Lodge, and Kenrick, as developed by Charles M. Hansen in *NYGBR* 127 [1996]: 193-201. John Fenwick, founder of Salem, N.J., his great-nephew John Fenwick of S.C., and a great-great-great-nephew, Ralph Eddowes of Pa., were descended from Edward III via John of Gaunt and Ferrers, Greystock, Grey, and Fenwick. The likely descent of Gov. Thomas Dudley from Edward III (and Elizabeth Woodville, Queen of Edward IV) via Grey, Bonville, Neville, and Beaufort, as developed by Marshall K. Kirk and David Humiston Kelley, has appeared in both editions of Faris's Plantagenet compendium (the 2nd edition also includes Dudley's Amy de Gaveston descent) and in my 1995 *Ancestors of American*

The Royal Descents of 500 Immigrants

Presidents. In the Sept.–Oct. 1999 issue of *NEXUS* I referred to the descent from Edward I to Sir Richard Lygon via Beauchamp of Powick, Ferrers of Chartley, Staffords, Despencers, de Audleys, and de Clares; I added a "cross-reference outline" to this same descent for Anthony Savage of Va. and Mrs. Amy Wyllys Pynchon of Mass. For a revised and perhaps lesser *RD* for James Cudworth of Mass., I await correspondence concerning Machell research by Paul C. Reed of Salt Lake City.

I am delighted to report a newly-developed descent by Albert M. Muth for Mrs. Elizabeth Alsop Baldwin Fowler of Conn. Mr. Muth noted Mrs. Fowler's mother, Temperance Gilbert, in Brig. Gen. Bulmer's edition of the 1563 visitation of Norfolk, found the marriages of Temperance and her sister "Cleer" Gilbert in the published parish records of Mickleover, co. Derby, and "Cleere" Alsop among the immigrant's sisters in the 1662–64 visitaion of Derbyshire. From these materials a descent from Edward I was readily traceable via Clere, Boleyn, Butler, earls of Ormonde, Beauchamp, barons Abergavenny, and FitzAlan and Bohun. As first noted by Paul C. Reed in *The Genealogist* 10 (1989, pub. 1994): 55, Joseph Bickley of Va. was descended via Winch and Onslow from Corbet, Devereux, Ferrers of Chartley, and Edward I. On the chart for Thomas Owsley of Va. I noted his kinship to the Marbury sisters via Cope. A last change among descendants of Edward I or Edward III was the corrected line for Hollywood writer and man of letters Christopher Isherwood (1904–1986), who loses his Percy descent but via Raymond, Harris, Astley, Denny, Champernowne, Carew, FitzAlan, Despencer and de Clare, is descended, along with his third cousin, the novelist Graham Greene, from Edward I.

I shall end this review of "corrected" lines by noting two new descendants of Henry III, King of England (d. 1272), as covered in Faris's new book and *Register* 154 (2000): 219-26. Edward Raynsford of Mass. and George Yate of Md. are descended from Plantagenets of Lancaster, barons Beaumont, Botreaux, and Hungerford, Whites of Hampshire and either Kirtons or Tichbornes.

NOTE: Since posting my last column I have also added 15 new immigrants. Colonial or early 19th-century such whose *RD*s have been developed largely by correspondents include **John William MacEwen** of Me. (great-grandson of John M[a]cGregor of

P.E.I., grandson himself of "Rob Roy"), great-grandfather of noted Scottish genealogist Andrew B. W. MacEwen; **Archibald Dunlop** of Conn. (developed by John L. Scherer in *Register* 152 [1998]: 186-96, 154 [2000]: 321-24); **Emmanuel Woolley** of R.I. (as developed for a future *Register* article by Jack T. Hutchinson); **Mrs. Audrey Divett Buller Parsons** of R.I. (forebear of Flagler and Mellon scions, developed by James Ross Mellon II); **Mrs. Jane Evans Dodge** of N.Y. (developed by Carl Boyer, 3rd in *Ancestral Lines, Third Edition* [1998] -- a very adroit linking of Bartrum and later Welsh pedigrees); **Gov. John Spencer** of Md. (developed by Henry Sutliff III) and his second wife, **Mrs. Honor Newton Seymour**; Harry Truman ancestor (AT #78) Thomas Monteith, son of **Mrs. Magdalen Dalyell Monteith** of Va., half-brother and grandson of baronets, and a descendant of Robert III three times over, via, among others, Drummonds of Riccarton and Stirlings of Keir (Thomas's parentage was brought to my attention by [Sir] Thomas [Tam] Dalyell [11th Bt.] and his wife, and this line was further developed in some detail by Andrew B. W. MacEwen); **Mrs. Elizabeth Mallory Rivers** of S.C. (via the la Zouche mother of Sir Anketil Malory, Amy de Gaveston's son-in-law, and then Cantilupe, de Braose, and Marshall, developed by Brice McAdoo Clagett); and the actor **[Ivan Simon] Cary Elwes** of Calif. (developed and brought to my attention by Robert Battle). Immigrants or sometime U.S. residents treated in the new *American National Biography* (*ANB*) (24 vols., 1999) include colonial astronomer and Newton correspondent **Arthur Storer** of Md. (brother of **Mrs. Anne Storer Truman Skinner** of Md.); the playwright **Noel Coward**, sometime of N.Y. (a line through his Veitch mother to the Stewarts of Traquair, developed largely by Coward biographer Philip Hoare); **Evelyn Ada Maude Rice Willoughby-Wade**, long of Cambridge, Mass., wife of mathematician and philosopher Alfred North Whitehead; **Primula Susan Rollo**, who died in Calif., first wife of actor David Niven (see *NEXUS* 14 [1997]: 70-71, 73); and actor **Rupert (Hector) Everett**, also of Calif., recent co-star of Madonna and Julia Roberts, who appears in the article on Vyvyan baronets in the new 1999 106th edition of *Burke's Peerage and Baronetage*. Everett's maternal grandfather was Vice Admiral Sir Hector Charles Donald MacLean, covered in the last *Burke's Peerage*, published in 1967, that included the knightage as well as peerage and baronetage. MacLean's mother was a Hope of the Linlithgow family, and the great-great-granddaughter of Lady Anne Vane, daughter of Henry Vane, 1st Earl of Darlington, and Lady Grace Fitzroy. Darlington was the great-grandson of Puritan statesman and Mass. governor Sir Henry Vane; Lady Grace was the daughter of Charles Fitzroy, 2nd Duke of Cleveland, 1st Duke of Southampton, an illegitimate son of Charles II and Barbara Villiers.

Genealogical Thoughts of Gary Boyd Roberts, #49:
Further Changes in Royal Descents, 2000

Since mid-February 2000 and columns #43-44, I have completed my review of prospective new immigrants of royal descent -- both those developed by correspondents and those I discovered myself, partly in checking the new *American National Biography* (24 vols., 1999). This column will list or summarize these most recent additions to *RD600*.

Those nearest the front of the book are **Stanislaus Albert, Prince Radziwill**, sometime of N.Y., brother-in-law of Jacqueline Kennedy Onassis and father of television producer Anthony (Stanislaus Albert, Prince) Radziwill, 1959–1999; **Curt Henry Eberhard Erdmann George, Count Haugwitz-Hardenburg-Reventlow**, also sometime of N.Y., second husband of heiress Barbara Woolworth Hutton and father-in-law of actress Jill St. John; and **Mrs. Mary Josephine "Maisie" Ward Sheed**, sometime of N.Y. once again, noted Catholic writer and social activist. Prince Radziwill was a great-great-grandson of Louise of Prussia, granddaughter and great-granddaughter of Frederick William I, King of Prussia (d. 1740). Count Haugwitz-Hardenburg-Reventlow was descended from Charles XI, King of Sweden (d. 1611). Mrs. Sheed, granddaughter of Oxford Movement leader William George Ward, was also a great-granddaughter of the 14th Duke of Norfolk. A fourth immigrant of fairly recent royal descent is **William Drake Baring-Gould** of Minneapolis, son of antiquarian Rev. Sabine Baring-Gould; father of Sherlock Holmes authority William Stuart Baring-Gould; and grandfather-in-law of one of my college roommates, St. Louis brewing scion Adolphus Busch Orthwein, Jr., now of Atlanta. W.D. Baring-Gould appears in the Essex volume of Ruvigny's *Plantagenet Roll of the Blood Royal*. Another friend, African hunter, author and Gulf Oil scion James Ross (Jay) **Mellon** II of New York City, is married to **Vivian Rüesch**, daughter of an Italian countess de la Feld, descended via Moresca Donnorso, Correale, Colonna, Ruffo, d'Avalos, Caracciolo, d'Avalos again, Gonzaga, and Este, from Ferdinand I, King of Naples (d. 1494), as well as John II, King of France (d. 1364), and Mexican conqueror Hernan Cortes, 1st Marquess of Valle de Oaxaca. Jay and Daniel MacGregor have traced this line in great detail, and their findings are confirmed by the *Libro d'Oro*, vol. 6 (1923–25), pp. 744-45, and treatments of the Moresca Donnorso, Colonna, Ruffo, d'Avalos, and Caracciolo families in vols. 6, 5, 15, and 4 of *Genealogisches Handbuch des Adels, Fürstliche Häuser* series, plus Litta on Colonna and Caracciolo, and MacGregor's *Brooke's Book: Ancestry of Brooke Shields* (privately distributed, 1988).

To my surprise, the new *American National Biography* (*ANB*) included *New Yorker* writer **Anthony West**, illegitimate son of H. G. Wells and Dame Rebecca West, the former Cicely Isabel Fairfield. The ancestry of Dame Rebecca's paternal grandmother, Arabella Rowan, is covered in vols. 5 and 6 of A. E. Casey's *O'Kief*, etc.; Arabella's own mother, Letitia Denny, was the daughter of a baronet, great-great-granddaughter of the first Earl of Coningsby, and a descendant of Edward III via Nevilles of Abergavenny. Another literary figure treated in *ANB* is novelist **Robert Louis Stevenson**, descended from Robert II, King of Scots (d. 1390), via Balfours of Pilrig and Hamiltons, sometime baronets, of Airdie. Stevenson died in Samoa but lived in both New York and California, and like the playwright Noel Coward, also in *ANB* and *RD600*, enjoyed his greatest success in America. A final new 20th-century figure is **Mrs. Kathleen Helen MacCarthy-Morrough Summersby Morgan**, the Kay Summersby who was Eisenhower's aide and confidante and later moved to New York. Her MacCarthy great-great-grandmother was Eliza Fagan, niece of the Christopher Alexander Fagan identified in recent decades as the father, illegitimately, of Hyacinthe Gabrielle Roland, wife of the 1st Marquess Wellesley, the colonial statesman and brother of Wellington, and an ancestress of H.M. Queen Elizabeth The Queen Mother. Christopher Fagan and his brother Stephen (Kay Summersby's forebear) were descended via Nangles from Sir William de Welles, Lord Deputy of Ireland, brother of the 6th Baron Welles and a descendant of Edward I.

Among eighteenth-century immigrants I have recently added **Edward Hyde**, proprietary governor of North Carolina, and father-in-law of George Clarke, lieutenant governor of New York. This second colonial governor named Edward Hyde (the first, of N.Y., was known as Lord Cornbury), also treated in *ANB*, appears in Ormerod's history of Cheshire (vol. 3, p. 11), and was descended via Brooke, Touchet, Dayrell, and Beaufort (and via Brooke, Neville, and Beaufort also) from Edward III. As noted by John Herdeg in correspondence with D. Brenton Simons, and largely confirmed by another *ANB* article, Robert Dering, first husband of **Mrs. Henrietta de Beaulieu Dering Johnston** of S.C. (the "first woman painter in America"), and maternal uncle of John Perceval, 1st Earl of Egmont, was the son of a baronet and descended via Dering, Brent, Berkeley, Neville, and Beaufort, Ashburnham, Berkeley and Neville, and Beaumont, Darcy, Greystock, Ferrers, and Beaufort, from Edward III. Lastly, R. D. Tucker's 1991 *Descendants of William Tucker of Throwleigh, Devon*, demonstrates that **Henry Tucker**, son of George Tucker of Bermuda and Frances St. George, himself immigrated to Virginia, married Elizabeth Bridger, and left descendants. This Virginia immigrant was not, then, the maternal grandfather of Thomas Witter of N.Y.; that Henry Tucker was a cousin (birth years for the two Henrys were 1649 and 1652) for whom I can at present find no readily traceable *RD*. Thus Witter unfortunately becomes the 11th immigrant from *RD500* who will be deleted from its successor.

Seventeenth-century immigrants with recently developed *RD*s include **Percival Lowell**, immigrant progenitor of the Boston Lowells and a descendant of Edward I via Percival, Yorke, Luttrell, Courtenay, and Bohun. Percival's mother was identified by Robin Bush in vol. 25 of *Search for the Passengers of the Mary and John*; the *RD* was developed by Douglas Richardson and will appear in the forthcoming *Magna Charta Ancestry* by Doug and David Faris. John Anderson Brayton has prepared an article for *The Virginia Genealogist* on the *RD* of **Daniel Dobyns** of Va., great-nephew of the poet Edmund Waller, first cousin twice removed of Parliamentary leader John Hampden, and great-great-great-grandson of Elizabeth Ferrers, granddaughter herself of Sir Henry Ferrers and Margaret Heckstall (*RD500*, p. 248), and a descendant thereby of Edward I. A second "late Plantagenet"-derived New England immigrant with probably millions of descendants is **Mrs. Rose Stoughton Otis** of N.H., whose Lewknor line (to Wests, barons de la Warr, Mowbray, and Henry III, d. 1272) was recently proved by Martin E. T. Hollick of Belmont, Calif. As originally "discovered" by Lothrop Withington, **Frances Woodward**, first wife of Rev. John Oxenbridge of Boston, and ancestress of the several Oxenbridge Thachers here, was the daughter of Ezechias/Hezekiah Woodward, a nonconformist divine whose Rudhall mother was a great-granddaughter of William Rudhall and Anne Milborne (*RD500*, p. 303), the latter a descendant of John de Brienne, d. 1237, King of Jerusalem and Emperor of Constantinople, and ancestress of "signer" Button Gwinnett of Georgia. A third New England immigrant with a large progeny and a recently developed *RD* is **Mrs. Anne Derehaugh Stratton** of Mass., mother-in-law of John Thorndike and great-granddaughter matrilineally, via Wright and Spring, of Dorothy Waldegrave, daughter of Sir William Waldegrave and Margery Wentworth (*RD500*, p. 317). This superb new Derehaugh research was undertaken by Robert Battle of Tacoma, Wash., whose article on the subject may appear in a forthcoming *Register*. **James Taylor** of Lynn, Mass.was a second cousin once removed of Thomas Bressie of New Haven; both were descendants of King John via FitzRoy, Marmion, Grey of Rotherfield, Harcourt, Peshall, Woolrich, Hopton, and Anderson, a new line also developed by Douglas Richardson for the forthcoming *Magna Charta Ancestry*. Bressie was the grandson of Edmund Bressie and Lucretia Anderson; Taylor, whose immediate forebears were traced by David Curtis Dearborn of NEHGS, was a great-grandson matrilineally of Lucretia's sister Elizabeth and Sir William Garway/Garraway. **Increase Nowell** of Mass. was the great-grandson of John Nowell and Elizabeth Kay (*RD500*, p. 331), as noted in the 1961 Stephen Bull genealogy, much expanded and partially corrected by Jerome E. Anderson of NEHGS.

As developed by Henry B. Hoff, **Jan Otten van Tuyl** of N.Y. was descended from an illegitimate daughter of Guy of Avesnes, Bishop of Utrecht, great-uncle of Philippa of Hainault (wife of Edward III of England), a great-great-great-grandson of Louis VII, King of France (d. 1180). Intervening surnames were van Amstel and van Goor. Van Tuyl and Mrs. Sophia van Lodensteyn de Beauvois/Debevoise are the only two Dutch *RD* immigrants to New Amsterdam known to have left a large progeny. **John Umfreville/ Humphreville** of New Haven, recently studied by Anthony Hoskins of Fort Lauderdale, was 9th in descent, according to a 1710 pedigree compiled by Simon Segar and one in "Philpott's Collections in the College of Arms," from Thomas de Umfreville and Joan de Roddam (*RD500*, p. 385). Also developed by Anthony Hoskins is the very likely descent of the Quaker **Thomas Brassey** of Nantwich, Cheshire and Pennsylvania from Henry I, King of England (d. 1135), via Bressey, Hassall, Mainwaring of Over Peover, Amicia de Meschines, and earls of Chester and Gloucester.

Another descendant of Henry I, via earls of Gloucester and Chester, was **Henry Sewall, Secretary of Maryland**, husband of Jane Lowe, also *RD*, who later married Charles Calvert, 3rd Baron Baltimore. Sewall (of Md.) was a nephew of both Henry Sewall of Mass. and the antiquarian Sir William Dugdale, and Brice Clagett has traced for Sewall's mother and Dugdale a descent from Mabel of Chester and Magna Charta surety William d'Aubigny, 3rd Earl of Arundel, via Swinfen, Noel, Draycott, Stafford, Bassett, and de Somery. Brice has also developed a possible *RD* for Henry Sewall of Mass., but both he and I think it contains too few generations and requires further research.

A final discovery affects several immigrants. Douglas Richardson and Henry Hoff have brought to my attention a likely *RD* for Eleanor Spinney, wife of a major immigrant *ur*-father Sir John Throckmorton, via Durvassal, de Camville, counts of Réthel and Namur, dukes of Lower Lorraine and Louis IV, King of France (d. 954). This line, partly presented in the 1930 Throckmorton genealogy and *Blackmans of Knight's Creek*, appears to be confirmed for the Réthel maternity of William de Camville by vol. 6, pp. 472-73, of the G.A. Moriarty notebooks here at NEHGS; see also *TAG* 20 (1943–44): 255-56, 21 (1944–45): 95-96 for Réthel. Among Throckmorton's descendants -- in addition to Stonington *ur*-mother and Princess of Wales ancestor Mrs. Alice Freeman Thompson Parke, Rev. William Sargent of Malden, John Throckmorton of Providence and Mrs. Elizabeth St. John Whiting of Lynn, among other New England immigrants -- is James Neale of Md., included in *RD500*, subject of an ancestor table by Brice Clagett in *Maryland Genealogical Society Bulletin* 31 (1989–90): 137-53. Another descendant via Kerrill, Dalison, Spencer (ancestors of Sir Winston Churchill and the late Princess of Wales), and Knightley, was **Jeffrey Amherst, 1st Baron Amherst**, governor of Va. 1759–68. Two other Throckmorton descendants are my final additions for this column. **Humphrey Underhill** of N.Y. and his sister **Mrs. Mary Underhill Naylor Stites**, the latter an ancestor via Ganos of billionaire Howard Robard Hughes, Jr., were great-great-grandchildren, according to the 1980 sixth volume of the Underhill genealogy, of Edward Underhill and Margaret Middlemore, granddaughter of Richard Middlemore and Margery Throckmorton, granddaughter in turn of Sir John Throckmorton and Eleanor Spinney. See also the 1901 Middlemore genealogy, plus further Middlemore research, kindly sent to Henry Hoff via e-mail, of Robert O'Connor of New Zealand.

Genealogical Thoughts of Gary Boyd Roberts, #51:

Final Changes to the Last Third of *RD600*

In this 51st column I wish to review the last changes I made to the final third of *RD600* before handing the manuscript in late August to my colleague Alicia Crane Williams for book preparation. Columns #43, #44, and #49 included, among data for this section, new immigrants and some corrections to these descents from King John of England (d. 1216) and earlier Plantagenet, Norman or Anglo-Saxon (all English), Scottish, French, or other sovereigns; I shall now cover descents of immigrants in *RD500* which I or others have altered. The first of these is a new Marmion-Bernacke-Cromwell-Fitzwilliam-Sotehill-Markenfield-Calverley line from King John to William Wentworth of N.H. and Christopher Lawson of Mass. I developed this descent independently of Wentworth research by Paul C. Reed commissioned by former NEHGS trustee Shirley Goodwin Bennett, but showed it to them in Salt Lake City. Paul has apparently reconstructed the Wentworth patrilineal line as presented in the first edition of *Magna Charta Sureties* and vol. 1 of the 1878 Wentworth genealogy. Both Paul and David Faris and Douglas Richardson have undertaken Calverley research based in part on vol. 6 of *Publications of the Thoresby Society*, and visitation or compiled pedigrees that seem to be accurate cover the Markenfields, Sotehills, and Fitzwilliams.

A second Marmion descent from King John extends through the Fitzhugh, Tunstall, Pudsey, and Grosvenor families to Henry Corbin of Virginia, whose descent from Amy de Gaveston is covered in the 2nd ed. of *Plantagenet Ancestry of Seventeenth-Century Colonists* (*PASCC2*), and whose Grosvenor, Pudsey, Tunstall and Fitzhugh ancestry is well covered in the forthcoming *Magna Carta Ancestry* (*MCA*) by David Faris and Douglas Richardson. Also outlined in *MCA* is a new line from William I the Lion, King of Scots (d. 1214) via de Ros, la Zouche, and Tyndall for Mrs. Margaret Tyndall Winthrop, fourth wife of the Massachusetts Bay Colony founder (new detail is given as well on the likely parentage of Margaret of Teschen, the "nearly royal" wife of Sir Simon de Felbrigg). In addition, *MCA* identifies Margery, wife of Godfrey Hilton, Baron Luttrell, as Margery Willoughby, daughter of Sir Hugh Willougby and Margaret Freville, based on a Nottinghamshire visitation; Margery, an ancestor of Mrs. Katherine Hamby Hutchinson of Mass., was a granddaughter of Sir Baldwin Freville (and Maud ----), 9th in descent from Henry II (d. 1189) and Countess Ida (see *RD500,* p. 352).

For child *Mayflower* passenger Richard More I had to revert to the descent, first outlined by Sir A. R. Wagner in the 1970 *Register*, from Ada of Scotland, niece of William the Lion, via Hastings, Grey, Talbot, l'Archdeacon/Archdekne, Lucy, Hopton, Corbet, and Cresset. For Harvard president Rev. Charles Chauncey and Mrs. Mabel Harlakenden Haynes Eaton of Hartford (wife of John Haynes, only colonial governor of both Mass. and Conn.), *MCA* offers an "improved" descent (based in part on vol. 1 of Baker's *Northamptonshire,* p. 123), via de Ferrers and earls of Derby, Chester, and Gloucester, from Henry I of England (d. 1135) for Sir John Bigod. And for Mrs. Anna Cordray Bernard (wife of Col. Richard Bernard and an ancestress of H. M. Queen Elizabeth the Queen Mother; see *RD500,* p. 468) and her nephews Francis and William Ironmonger,

The Royal Descents of 500 Immigrants

all of Va., Paul C. Reed in *TAG* 73 (1998): 181-93, 294-311 developed a second descent from Henry I of England, via Cordray, Seymour, Beauchamp and St. John, again to Sir Hugh Courtenay and Eleanor le Despencer. In addition to the forthcoming *Magna Carta Ancestry*, with many new Faris or Richardson discoveries, I have also long been privy to the ongoing *Ancestors for Twenty Generations* [of his children] study by Brice McAdoo Clagett. Among his most recent notes to me were corrections to two lines in the early part of *RD500*. In the descent of Henrietta Fielding, daughter of novelist Henry Fielding and wife of colonial engineer James Gabriel Montrésor, Elizabeth (Leveson) Aston was *not* the daughter of Margery (Wrottesley) Leveson, and the best line is now from Edward III via Lane, Parr, Fitzhugh, Neville, and Beaufort. Additionally, the best line for Nicholas and Henry Lowe of Md. and their aunt, Lady Jane (Lowe) (Sewall) Calvert, Baroness Baltimore, is no longer through Harpur, Pierpont, Thwaites, Knyvett (Knevet), Grey of Ruthyn, Holand, John of Gaunt and Edward III (the mistaken parentage was that of Alice [Grey] Knyvett/Knevet), but rather via Cavendish, Hardwick, Pinchbeck, and Greene to Sir Thomas Greene, 8th in descent from Edward I, ancestor of the R.I. Marbury sisters through his first wife Philippa Ferrers, and father by later wife Marina Beler of Anne (Greene) Pinchbeck.

A line on which I should appreciate reader input is that from Robert II, King of France (d. 1031), via dukes of Burgundy, counts of Ponthieu, d'Estouteville/de Stoteville, Say, and Dabridgecourt, to ---- (prob. Elizabeth) Dabridgecourt, wife of Ralph Staverton, mother of Elizabeth (Staverton) Burgoyne, great-grandmother of Thomasine (Burgoyne) Shute, and great-great-great-grandmother of Gov. William Leete of Conn. The possibility of this line was first brought to my attention by Mrs. Gerald (Sarah) Polkinghorne. *Europäische Stammtafeln* includes Estouteville and Ponthieu charts, Say and Dabridgecourt entries in *The House of Commons, 1386–1421*, vol. 4 of the *Victoria County History of Hampshire and the Isle of Wight*, and *The Topographer and Genealogist* 1 (1846), plus Charles Kerry's history of Bray (p. 62 esp.) and visitations of Hampshire and Berkshire, with discrepancies, suggest that the mother of Elizabeth (Staverton) Burgoyne was an Elizabeth Dabridgecourt, probably the daughter (on largely chronological grounds) of Thomas and Beatrice

(----) Dabridgecourt, granddaughter of Sir John and Joan (Lynde) Dabridgecourt, and great-granddaughter of Sir Nicholas Dabridgecourt and Elizabeth ----, daughter and heir of Sybil de Say. Heraldic discrepancies in Dabridgecourt coats have been brought to my attention, but I still think this line probable.

Two last notes: (1) for Louis IV of France descendant Thomas Bradbury of Mass. (*RD500*, pp. 461-62), I await a speculative descent from a much later king that will, I hope, be developed by "Kenneth W. Kirkpatrick" on the NEHGS website (*newenglandancestors.org*) or elsewhere; (2) a final deletion, unfortunately, is Christopher Tilghman of Va., probably a nephew, not grandson, of the Christopher Tilghman who married Anna Sanders, whose parents in turn may *not* be John Sanders and Anna Whetenhall (see, among other sources, Elizabeth M. Tillman, *Getting to the Roots of the Family Tree: The Story of a Saxon Family*, 3 vols. [1997], vols. 2 and 3, esp. the chart at end of vol. 3, opposite p. 1139).

Lesser Additions and Corrections to *RD500*

All major compendia, despite multiple proofreadings, contain typographical "gremlins." My work is no exception. Those that have come to my attention to date are:

pp. **vi,** 2nd paragraph, line 24, and **xxiv,** under 28: Gibbeses, not Gibbses.

p. **vi,** 2nd paragraph, line 28: Longespee, not Longspee.

p. **viii,** line 5, and **248,** generation 14, line 5: The third husband of Mary Clarke was John Stanton, not Robert.

p. **xiii,** 2nd paragraph, line 14: Averell Harriman, not Averill.

pp. **xiv,** 2nd paragraph, line 7, **xviii,** 1st paragraph, line 15: "Governor" and "Continental" should be capitalized.

p. **xviii,** line 12: 141, not 142.

p. **liii,** under 9. James I, King of England (and VI, King of Scotland) was the grandfather, not father, of Charles II and James II, Kings of England, #s 7-8.

p. **2**: Princess Elizabeth (Karadjordjevic) of Yugoslavia married (2) Neil Roxburgh Balfour and (3) Manuel Ulloa Elias (correspondence with Marlene Eilers Koenig)

p. **3**: Marianne Charlotte Katharina Stefanie, Princess Reuss-Köstritz, widow of Avery Brundage, = (2) Friedrich Karl Feldman. See *Almanach de Gotha Genealogy 1998, Volume 1* (1998), p. 208.

p. **7**: (Eduard) Egon (Peter Paul Giovanni), Prince zu Fürstenburg of N.Y., fashion designer, = (2) Lynn Marshall. See *Almanach de Gotha Genealogy 1998, Volume 1* (1998), p. 368.

p. **19**, generation 17, second line under R.R. Guest: Elizabeth Sturgis Polk, not Sturges.

pp. **21, 106, 294**, add to sources: Hubert Cuny and Nicole Dreneau, *Le Gotha Français: État Présent des Familles Ducales et Princières*

The Royal Descents of 500 Immigrants

(depuis 1940) (1989), pp. 185-86 (for Princess Caroline Murat, Mrs. R.R. Guest), pp. 93-95 (for Sanche de Gramont, known as Ted Morgan), pp. 171-73 (for Guy Philippe *Henry* Lannes de Montebello).

p. **58**, add to sources: H. B. McCall, *Some Old Families: A Contribution to the Genealogical History of Scotland* (1890), pp. 145-63 (Orr, Crauford).

p. **59**, generation 12: add "(perhaps or probably illegitimate)" before Margaret Stirling, and to sources add *NEXUS* 13 (1996): 76-78, 81-82.

p. **62**, add to sources: Michel Huberty, etc., eds., *L'Allemagne Dynastique*, vol. 2, *Anhalt-Lippe-Wurtemberg* (1979), pp. 605-9 (children of generation 8, with a chart showing the descent of Anne Aymone Sauvage de Brantes, wife of French president Valéry Guiscard d'Estaing, from the extraordinary marriage of half-siblings at generation 9).

p. **80**, generation 13: The maiden surname of the second wife of Ellis Lewis of Pa. was Beakbaine (records of the Lancaster Monthly Meeting, England, courtesy of Stewart Baldwin).

p. **86**, generation 16: Alexander Cochrane of Mass. married (2) Jane Lander (2) Elizabeth Lauder (courtesy of John Winthrop Sears).

p. **87**, generations 5-7: Cassillis, not Cassilis.

p. **99**, generation 7: Abbot, not Abbott.

p. **114**, generations 3 and 4: John Beaufort, Marquess of Somerset and Dorset (the two counties/titles were reversed); following Joan Beaufort, add "Dowager Queen of Scotland."

p. **115**, generation 8: Catherine Cary (not Mary) (courtesy of Anthony Hoskins of the Newberry Library in Chicago and Mrs. Carol J. Stirr, who both sent copies of various sources, esp. the tablet to Lady Knollys in Westminster Abbey).

p. **117**, 4th line from bottom: Wimbish, not Windish.

p. **128**, generations 11-15: Feilding, not Fielding, which begins with generation 16 (the novelist Henry Fielding).

The Royal Descents of 500 Immigrants

p. **149**, generation 17: de-bold "of S.C."

p. **161**, generation 14: After Richard Bennett, Jr., remove "governor of Va. and Md." (the governor was his father).

p. **181**, generation 8-11: Curzon, not Curson, which begins with generation 12.

pp. **189**, generation 18 and **209**, generation 21: Former Secretary of State Dean G. Acheson died in 1971, not 1991, and Mrs. Katherine D.P.C. St. George died in 1983, not 1893.

p. **195**, top two lines: Caroline Ernestine of Erbach-Schönberg, not –burg.

p. **206**, sources, lines 3-4, *TVG* 22 [not 32] and 23 [not 33]. See also *TVG* 38 (1994): 48-51, *NEXUS* 16 (1999): 156-59, 200-2, and *New England Ancestors* 1 (2000) 1: 64-66, 2:38-41, 3:42-44, 5: 68.

p. **207**, generation 13: Elizabeth St. John, not Blount.

p. **208**, generations 19-22: Henry Tucker (III) married Frances Bruere, not Brune, Henry St. George Tucker married Jane Boswell, William Thornhill Tucker married Wilhelmina Douglas de Lautour, and Frederick St. George de Lautour Booth-Tucker, whose second wife was Emma Moss Booth, married (1) Louisa Mary Bode and (3) May Ried. See R. D. Tucker, *Descendants of William Tucker of Throwleigh, Devon* (1991), pp. 196-202, 233-37.

p. **217**. Sources: under *CP*, omit the second Howth.

p. **227**, generation 13: Andrew Palmes married Elizabeth *Harrison*; see *Fosters's V of Yorkshire*, pp. 91-92.

p. **245**: An alternative Nottinghamshire origin for Edward Southworth of Leyden is suggested in *The Mayflower Quarterly* 58 (1992): 10-15.

p. **246**, generations 17, 18: omit "c."; Gov. William Shirley was born [2 Dec.] 1694.

p. **248**, generation 14: Gov. John Cranston was b. c. 1626 (not 1625), as per p. 111.

p. **255**, generation 9: The mother of 10. Jane Legh was Margaret Tyldesley, 1st wife of Peter Gerard (courtesy of Todd A. Farmerie, who cites *Ormerod* 3: 677 [Legh]).

p. **268**, generation 7: the maiden surname of Elizabeth, wife of the younger Sir Philip Courtenay, is unknown.

p. **269**, generation 11: Frances Aston, not Ashton.

p. **286**;. Sources: Add Ronny O. Bodine and Thomas W. Spalding, Jr., *The Ancestry of Dorothea Poyntz, Wife of Reverend John Owsley, Generations 1-14*, 3rd ed. (1999). The descent from Edward III via Holand, Touchet and Audley, outlined in *NEXUS* 13 (1996): 128, is rejected in *PASCC* 2: 296.

pp. **307**, #s 6-10, lines 1, 5-6, and p. **324**, generation 17: Catherine Griffith, sister of Hugh Griffith and aunt of Mrs. Jane Edward Jones, = (1) ---- Morris, (2) Alexander Edwards, and (3) John Williams (p. 324), widower of Mary Evans; Catherine seems to have left issue by her first husband only; also, the wife of William Morgan (a maternal uncle of Daniel Boone) was Elizabeth Robert, not Catherine (courtesy of Stewart Baldwin).

p. **307**, first line of sources: "Allied," not "Alled."

p. **309**, generation 21: John Evans, husband of of Mary Hughes, was of Merion and Radnor, Pa.

p. **312**, first line of sources: *TAG* 32 (1956, not 76). See also *Journal of Royal and Noble Genealogy* 1 (1995): 14-26.

pp. **330, 334, 336, 338, 340, 342**, generation 3. Lucy St. John, not FitzPiers (*MCA*, forthcoming).

p. **330**, generation 6. Christiana *Mowbray* (*AR7*, line 170). And between generations 10 and 11 add another, Robert Sherburne = Joanna Radcliffe (and renumber later generations). See T. D. Whitaker and A. W. Morant, *The History and Antiquities of the Deanery of Craven in the County of York*, 3rd ed. (1878), chart between pp. 23 and 24.

p. **331**, generation 19. Lawrence Smith of Va. married Mary Debnam, not (Hitchen?). See *TVG* 40 (1996): 5-6.

The Royal Descents of 500 Immigrants

p. **332**, generation 18, line 7, after *AP&P*, pp. 248-50, add *TVG* 37 (1993): 228-29.

p. **353**, generation 17: Edward Whalley. Insert marriage marks between "Conn." and "(1)."

p. **356**, generations 10 and 11: The wife of Sir William Mortfort was Margaret *Pecche* (*CP* 10: 344, note b) and the wife of Robert Montfort may be Mary Stapleton (John Fetherston, *Visitation of Warwick, 1619* [*HSPVS*, vol. 12, 1877], p. 56, a Montfort pedigree known, however, to contain errors) (courtesy of Clyde A. Bridger).

p. **366**, first line of sources: after *NYGBR* 66 (1935): 376-83 add "122 (1991): 161; *Genealogisches Bijdragen Leiden en Omgeving* 7 (1992): 476-79 (Ilpendam) and *Gens Nostra* 45 (1990) 10/11: 370-72, 380-81, 423-24, 434, 437, 440, 443 (generations 2-16);"

p. **378**, generation 16: Barbara Kniveton was a daughter certainly of [gen.] 14 or 15, probably 15 (not "16 or 17, probably 17").

p. **384**, first line of sources: add *TAG* 73 (1998): 181-93, 294-311 (Cordray, Ironmonger).

p. **400**, generation 13: Edith Stourton, not Esther. For a revised descent for her husband, Sir John Beauchamp, I will follow *TG* 6 (1985): 149, 13 (1999): 255, sources cited therein, and the forthcoming *MCA*.

p. **404**, generation 9: Sir Rhys Hen ap Gruffudd did not marry Isabel Stackpole (her husband was his son, Sir Rhys Ieuan), and thus the mother of 10. Margaret ferch Rhys Hen must be Joan Somerville (courtesy of Todd A. Farmerie, who cites *The Topographer and Genealogist* 1 [1846]: 533-35 and Historical Manuscript Commission, Rutland, 4: 28).

p. **405**: John Morgan of Pa. = Sarah Jones, daughter of John Evans of Radnor, Pa., ARD, SETH, and Delilah ----.

p. **430**, generations 13, 16, and 14, 17. The mother of Elizabeth Fiennes was *not* Emmeline Cromer and thus Elizabeth's husband, William Cromer, was not a cousin (forthcoming *MCA*, courtesy of Douglas Richardson).

p. **434**, line 5: *HSPVS*, vol. 42, not 62.

p. **450**, generation 20, lines 1-2, generations 21-22, and first line of sources: Sir Nicholas Bacon, Lord Keeper, not Sir Nathaniel; and Henry Woodhouse, not of Va., governor of Bermuda. The Virginia immigrant Henry Woodhouse was a son of this last by Judith (Manby?) Haen, and himself married (1) Mary (Sothren?) and (2) Mary ----. The *AP&P* reference should be to pp. 699-701.

p. **460**, second line of sources: after "Pecche article in CP" add *TG* 10 (1989, published 1994): 3-5, 23-24.

p. **463**, generation 5, line 9: Enguerrand I, Count of Ponthieu, not Pontieu.

p. **464**, generation 19: The wife of William Brockhull is unknown (*TAG* 68 [1993]: 202).

p. **469**; generation 34: Lady Diana Frances Spencer, later H.R.H. The Princess of Wales and Diana, Princess of Wales (1961–1997).